WORLD HISTORY IN BRIEF

Major Patterns of Change and Continuity

FOURTH EDITION

PETER N. STEARNS
George Mason University

Longman

New York   San Francisco   Boston
London   Toronto   Sydney   Tokyo   Singapore   Madrid
Mexico City   Munich   Paris   Cape Town   Hong Kong   Montreal

Cover Image: The Madaba Mosaic in present day Jordan dates from the sixth century and measures 50 by 18 feet. This mosaic depicts much of the eastern part of the Empire including Israel, Jordan, Saudi Arabia, and portions of Egypt. AKG Berlin/Jean-Louis Nou.

Publisher: Priscilla McGeehon
Acquisitions Editor: Erika Gutierrez
Executive Marketing Manager: Sue Westmoreland
Supplements Editor: Kelly Villella
Media Supplements Editor: J. Patrick McCarthy
Production Manager: Mark Naccarelli
Project Coordination, Text Design, and Electronic Page Makeup: Nesbitt Graphics, Inc.
Cover Design Manager: Nancy Danahy
Cover Designer: Keithley & Associates, Inc.
Art Studio: Mapping Specialists Limited
Photo Researcher: Photosearch, Inc.
Manufacturing Buyer: Al Dorsey
Printer and Binder: The Maple-Vail Book Manufacturing Group
Cover Printer: Phoenix Color Corps.

Library of Congress Cataloging-in-Publication Data
Stearns, Peter N.
    World history in brief : major patterns of change and continuity / Peter N. Stearns.—4th ed.
        p. cm.
    Includes bibliographical references and index.
    ISBN 0-321-07694-X
    1. World history. I. Title.

D21.3 .S77 2002
909—dc21   2001038045

Please visit our website at http://www.ablongman.com

ISBN 0-321-07694-X

    2 3 4 5 6 7 8 9 10—MA—04 03 02 01

BRIEF CONTENTS

iii

DETAILED CONTENTS

Part IV   A New World Economy, 1450–1750   257

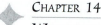

LIST OF MAPS

PREFACE

World history courses are steadily gaining ground at the college level for several reasons. Global issues dominate our newspapers, television screens, and computer monitors daily. Americans must gain a perspective on the dynamics of these issues and understand the diverse societies around the globe that help shape them and our future. History—even history that might seem rather remote—explains how the world became what it is now, including why global influences loom larger than ever before. Global issues are at work even within the United States, since it is increasingly a nation of people of different heritages from all around the world. Finally, world history raises some classic issues of historical interpretation, allowing its students to sharpen their understanding of how to interpret change and historical causation and providing a rich field for comparative analysis. Some educators still prefer to concentrate on Western civilization, arguing that it lies at our origins and, sometimes, that it is measurably superior. Although Western heritage must be included in any study of world history, it is increasingly clear that a purely Western interpretation cannot describe the world as we need to know it.

APPROACH

World History in Brief, now entering its fourth edition, has always had two goals. The first is to present a truly global approach to world history. This is accomplished through the focus on forces that cut across individual societies, through a balanced treatment of major societies themselves, and through invitations to comparisons on a global sale. The second goal is brevity and manageability. It is no secret that many world history texts are large and demand a major commitment from instructors and students. *World History in Brief* offers an alternative. Its length is compatible with a serious treatment of the major issues in world history, but it is concise enough to set aside time for careful analysis and to use with other types of materials beyond the textbook.

World history demands a commitment to a global rather than a Western-centered approach. *World History in Brief* shows how different civilizations have encountered the various forces of life—for example, population growth, economic changes, and international currents in diplomacy and art—over the centuries. Western civilization is included as one of the major world societies, but East Asian, Indian, Middle Eastern, East European, African, and Latin American civilizations are all subjects of study in order to achieve a genuine worldwide perspective. World history also demands a balance between the examination of individual societies, within which the lives of most people are played out, and attention to the larger interactions across regional boundaries. These global interactions include trade, cultural contact, migrations, and disease. *World History in Brief* presents the major civilizations through a narrative overview combined with emphasis on regional and global political, cultural, social, and economic characteristics and trends. A grasp of these characteristics, in turn, facilitates comparisons and assessments of change.

World History in Brief is also designed to inspire additional readings and analytical exercises. World history teaching must follow the precedent of other survey history courses in reducing the emphasis on coverage and sheer memorization in favor of materials that provide facts which can be used to build larger understandings. Overwhelming detail, therefore, is not the chief goal of this book. Instead, *World History in Brief* presents enough data to facilitate comparison and assessment of changes and to highlight major developments in the world's history. Students can readily refer to large reference works if they wish to follow up on themes of special interest with greater factual detail. For this purpose, a list of suggested readings and websites follows each chapter.

PERIODIZATION

Chronological divisions—the basic periods of world history—reflect successive stages of international contact, from relative isolation to regional integration to the formation of global systems. This periodization is not conveniently tidy for the whole of world history, but it captures the leading dynamics of change at the global level. *World History in Brief* focuses on six major periods. The first involves the early features of human development, particularly the emergence of agriculture and civilization as a form of organization. The second examines the great classical societies from 1000 B.C.E. to 500 C.E. and their relationships with surrounding regions. The third, the postclassical period, from 500 to 1450 C.E., highlights the emergence of new contacts in trade and culture, the spread of world religions, and the development of civilizations in new as well established centers. The early modern period, from 1450–1750 C.E., treats the new world role of Europe, but also the diverse and often quite independent developments in many other societies. The fifth period emphasizes the age of European industrialization and imperialism in the "long" nineteenth century and again the opportunity for varied reactions. The emergence of a new period in world history in the twentieth century draws the text to a close. In all these periods, major themes are carefully defined, as a springboard for assessing the interactions of individual societies with more global forces and as a basis for both comparison and discussions of change and continuity over time.

THEMES

Using the global focus plus international periodization, students can follow the themes of change and continuity across time and comparative analysis. For example, we can track and compare the juxtaposition of the traditions and novel forces that have shaped the modern world; the response of China or Latin America to the issues of the modern state; or the conditions of women in developing and industrial economies. How different societies respond to common issues and contacts, and how these issues and contacts change over time: This is the framework for examining world history. By focusing on these problems of comparison and assessment of change, the text uses the leading patterns of world history to provide experience in analysis that will apply to other historical studies beyond a survey.

FEATURES

World History in Brief is the most accessible world history text available in the market. Its brevity allows instructors and students flexibility about what additional readings will be included in their study of world history. The text focuses only on substansive topics so students understand major themes and developments in world history rather than memorizing an array of unconnected facts. The text is organized chronologically by civilizations allowing for easy and orderly understanding by students. A number of features distinguish *World History in Brief,* and they have been carefully constructed over four editions.

- Chapter openers called *Focal Points* frame each chapter by raising key questions and thereby setting learning goals.
- *History Debates,* included in almost every chapter, offer students a brief synopsis (usually two paragraphs long) of some topic over which historical debate currently rages. Topics include "Is Latin America Western?", "Why did slavery end when it did?", "What is western civilization?", etc. Students are given an opportunity to see that the discipline of world history is focused on actively debating the past.

NEW TO THIS EDITION

- An increased number of *World Profiles* (formerly *Biographical Portraits*) provide additional emphasis on the human component of world history through biographies. These profiles explore the history of an individual and how his or her story illuminates aspects of his or her society or a particular cultural interaction.
- *Understanding Cultures* sections help students explore specific cultural issues in world history, such as the role of cultures in causing historical changes, the nature of cultural contact, the unique cultural features of particular societies, the interaction of social and economic forces.
- *Suggested Websites* at the end of each chapter encourage students to further explore a particular topic, period, or historical figure.
- A comprehensive, full-color *Timeline,* free in every new copy of the text, gives students a chronological context in which to contemplate their knowledge and compare important political and diplomatic, social and economic, and cultural and technological events that have occurred across the globe.

- A *Companion Website* provides students and professors with a wealth of resources, including a syllabus manager, student practice tests, Web activities, chapter links, and a glossary. Also on the website are additional analytical highlights under the heading *Challenges*. These are ideal for organizing further classroom analysis and discussion.
- A *Study-Wizard CD-ROM* helps students learn the major facts and concepts of world history through drill and practice exercises and diagnostic feedback. Students receive an individual, self-paced review of text material using multiple-choice, short-answer, true-false questions, and detailed feedback. Free when bundled.

The text has been updated, of course, to include developments and shifts since the late 1990s. This complements the text's long-standing emphasis on helping students see the connections between past patterns in world history and the world we live in today and will inhabit tomorrow.

I must add a personal note. World history has been a late love for me. I was trained in Western history, with an education that encouraged, although it did not require (the fault was mine), a largely Western focus. I increasingly chafed against my ignorance not of current world events but of the perspective, the historical understanding, that would give such events meaning. Belatedly schooled in world history, I have found continued reading and teaching in the field an endless source of fascination, a perpetual window for contemplating the varieties of and similarities in the human condition. I can only wish the same pleasure for many others, colleagues and students alike.

SUPPLEMENTS

The following supplements are available for use in conjunction with *World History in Brief*.

FOR QUALIFIED ADOPTERS

Instructor's Manual/Test Bank. Written by Peter Stearns, this tool provides guidance in using the textbook, and suggestions for structuring the syllabus for a world history course complete with assignment ideas; chapter summaries; multiple-choice, short-answer, and essay questions; and map exercises.

TestGen Computerized Testing System. An easy-to-customize test-generation software package that presents a wealth of multiple-choice, true-false, short-answer, and essay questions. Allows users to add, delete, and print test items.

Discovering World History Through Maps and Views, Second Edition, by Gerald Danzer, University of Illinois, Chicago, winner of the AHA's James Harvey Robinson Award for his work in the development of map transparencies. The second edition of this set of 100 four-color transparencies is completely updated and revised to include the newest reference maps and most useful source materials. These transparencies are bound with introductory materials in a three-ring binder with an introduction on teaching history with maps and detailed commentary on each transparency. The collection includes source and reference maps, views and photos, urban plans, building diagrams, and works of art.

World History Atlas Transparencies. These overhead transparencies are correlated to the *Longman World History Atlas,* listed below.

Guide to Advanced Media and Internet Resources for World History by Richard M. Rothaus of St. Cloud University. This pamphlet provides a comprehensive review of CD-ROM, software, and Internet resources for world civilization, including a list of the primary sources, syllabi, articles, and discussion groups available online.

Longman-Penguin USA Value Packages in World History. Twenty classic titles from Penguin USA are available at a significant discount when bundled with any Longman world history textbooks.

Companion Website (www.ablongman.com/stearns). Instructors can take advantage of the online course companion that supports this text. The instructor section of the website includes the Instructor's Manual, a list of instructor links, downloadable images from the text, and Syllabus Builder, our comprehensive course management system.

Longman World History: Primary Sources and Case Studies (www.longmanworldhistory.com). An online source "book" to be used in a world history survey course. The core of the Website is its large database of thought-provoking primary sources, case studies, maps and images carefully chosen and edited by scholars and teachers of world history. The contents and organization of the site encourage students to analyze the themes, issues, and complexities of world history in a meaningful, exciting, *and* informative way.

FOR THE STUDENT

New! StudyWizard Computerized Tutorial. This interactive program features multiple-choice, true-false, and short-answer questions. It also contains a glossary and gives users immediate test scores and answer explanations. Free when bundled.

Longman World History Atlas. This four-color atlas contains 56 historical maps designed especially for the world history course. Free when bundled.

World History Map Workbook: Volume I (to 1600) and Volume II (from 1600), both prepared by Glee Wilson of Kent State University. Each volume includes over 40 maps accompanied by more than 120 pages of exercises. Each volume is designed to teach the location of various countries and their relationship to one another. Also included are numerous exercises aimed at enhancing students' critical thinking capabilities.

Documents in World History: Volume I (The Great Traditions: From Ancient Times to 1500) and Volume II (The Modern Centuries: From 1500 to the Present), both edited by Peter Stearns of George Mason University. A collection of primary source documents that illustrates the human characteristics of key civilizations during major stages of world history.

Timelink: World History Computerized Atlas by William Hamblin of Brigham Young University. A highly graphic, Hyper-based computerized atlas and historical geography tutorial for the Macintosh.

Mapping Civilizations: Student Activities. A free student workbook compiled by Gerald Danzer, University of Illinois, Chicago. Features numerous map skill exercises written to enhance students' basic geographical literacy. The exercises provide ample opportunities for interpreting maps and analyzing cartographic materials as historical documents. Free when bundled.

Companion Website (www.ablongman.com/stearns). This online course companion provides a wealth of resources for students using *World History in Brief*. Students can access chapter summaries, practice test questions, a guide to doing research on the Internet, and over 400 annotated Web links with critical thinking questions.

Longman World History: Primary Sources and Case Studies (www.longmanworldhistory.com). A fully functional online source "book" to be used in a world history survey course. The core of the website is its large database of thought-provoking primary sources, case studies, maps and images carefully chosen and edited by scholars and teachers of world history. The contents and organization of the site encourage students to analyze the themes, issues, and complexities of world history in a meaningful, exciting, *and* informative way.

ACKNOWLEDGMENTS

Many people helped shape this book. I am grateful to Barry Beyer, Donald Schwartz, William McNeill, Andrew Barnes, Donald Sutton, Erick Langer, Jayashiri Rangan, Paul Adams, Merry Wiesner-Hanks, and Michael Adas, who aided my understanding of world history in various ways. Comments by Steven Gosch and Donald Sutton, and editorial assistance by Clio Stearns, greatly aided in the preparation of this revised edition. Other colleagues who have furthered my education in world history include Ross Dunn, Judith Zinsser, Richard Bulliet, Jerry Bentley, and Stuart Schwartz. I also thank the various readers of earlier drafts of this manuscript, whose comments and encouragement improved the end result: Jay P. Anglin; Richard D. Lewis; Kirk Willis; Arden Bucholz; Richard Gere; Robert Roeder; Stephen Englehart; Marc Gilbert; John Voll; Erwin Grieshaber; Yong-ho Choe; V. Dixon Morris; Elton L. Daniel; Thomas Knapp; Edward Homze; Albert Mann; J. Malcom Thompson; Peter Freeman; Patrick Smith; David McComb; Charles Evans; Jerry Bentley; John Powell; B. B. Wellmon; Penelope Ann Adair; Linda Alkana; Samuel Brunk; Alexander S. Dawson; Lydia Garner; Surendra Gupta; Craig Hendricks; Susan Hult; Christina Michelmore; Lynn Moore; Joseph Norton; Elsa Nystrom; Diane Pearson; Louis Roper; and Robert H. Welborn.

My gratitude extends also to Erika Gutierrez and J. Patrick McCarthy whose editorial assistance has been vital. Sincere thanks to Karen Callas and Cordelia Stearns for help with the manuscript. I have been taught and stimulated as well by my students in world history courses at George Mason University. And thanks, finally, to my family, who have put up with my excited babble about distant places for some time now.

PETER N. STEARNS

About the Author

Peter N. Stearns is Provost and Professor of History at George Mason University. He received his Ph.D. from Harvard University, and, before moving to George Mason University, he taught at Rutgers University, the University of Chicago, and Carnegie Mellon where he won the Robert Doherty Educational Leadership Award and the Elliott Dunlap Smith Teaching Award. He teaches world history and has for the past 15 years. He currently serves as chair of the Advanced Placement World History Committee and also founded and is the editor of the *Journal of Social History*.

Peter Stearns has written a number of books on topics in world history. In addition to textbooks and readers, his books include studies of gender and consumerism in a world history context. Other books address modern social and cultural history, and include studies on gender, old age, work, dieting, and emotion. His most recent book in this area is *Battleground of Desire: The Struggle for Self-Control in Modern America*.

PART I

The Rise of Agriculture and Agricultural Civilizations

INTRODUCTION: A SMALL WORLD?

The idea that the world is becoming smaller is, like much folk wisdom, only partly true. For several hundred years, but particularly during the past century, worldwide transportation and communication facilities have become steadily more elaborate and rapid. It was less than 500 years ago that a ship first sailed around the entire world, a dangerous and uncertain journey that took many months. Now, political leaders, business people, and even wealthy tourists can routinely travel across half the world in less than a day. Telephone and radio communications have for several decades provided worldwide linkages, and, thanks to satellites, even global television hookups have become routine. As a result, for the first time in world history, events of widespread interest can be simultaneously experienced by hundreds of millions of people in all parts of the globe. World Cup soccer finals and recent Olympic Games have drawn audiences of over a billion people.

The smallness of our world involves more than speedy international contact; it also involves the nature and extent of that contact. Our century is the first to experience world wars, as well as the fear of surprise attacks by enemies 6000 miles away. International negotiations and diplomatic contacts are not so novel, but the impact of events in distant parts of the globe has obviously increased. As an example, we can consider the conflicts between Christians and Muslims in unfamiliar parts of the Balkans that prompted several interventions by American troops in the late 1990s. Worldwide economic contacts have increased at least as fast as those in the military and diplomatic fields. Production surges in China or Mexico vitally affect Americans as consumers and workers; shifts in the oil prices levied by Middle Eastern nations influence the driving habits of Americans and Europeans. Cultural linkages have also proliferated, as witness the existence of international sporting events and the widespread audience for French films or American television. Only in the twentieth century has a traveler been able to journey to cities on every inhabited continent and

1

find buildings that look just like those at home. Indeed, U.S. hotel and restaurant chains now literally span the earth.

To some observers, our smaller world is also an increasingly homogeneous world. Certain people lament the widespread adoption of various customs that seem to reduce valuable and interesting human diversity. Thus, purists in France deplore the practice of modern French supermarkets in imitating American packaging of cheese, just as many in Japan or Egypt deplore the decline of traditional costumes in favor of more Western-style dress. Probably more people, or at least more Americans, rejoice that our life-style has been adopted by other societies. Many Americans, comfortable in their own ways, are pleased to see familiar products and styles in other countries. Others, firm believers in the importance of international harmony, are eager to minimize the strangeness of foreign lands.

Despite new and important international linkages, our world is also marked by fundamental, often agonizing, divisions and diversities. Japan, in 1984, ordered a government inquiry into the use of chopsticks among schoolchildren. Their use had been declining because of a growing eagerness to eat quickly. Surely, to many American eyes, this might seem to represent a quaint, if harmless, concern for distinctive traditions. But such concerns are not altogether different from those of Muslim leaders, many of whom from the late 1970s to the present have thundered against Western influences, ranging from styles of women's dress to the idea that economic development rather than religion should be society's foremost priority. Varied reactions to Western influence reflect serious global divisions. And there are the direct conflicts over identity that rage in various parts of the world.

Correspondingly, certain systematic *separations* shape our world as much as linkages. As Russia experiments with democracy, China resolutely combines political authoritarianism with economic innovations. Stark divisions separate societies that have industrialized, and in which a minority of people are directly engaged in food production, from the larger number of nations in which full industrialization remains a distant dream. Cultural divisions also remain strong. India is the leading producer of films in the contemporary world, but these films, steeped in traditional Indian themes and values, rarely find non-Indian audiences. The United States, although able to export some films and television shows widely, also enjoys certain sports, notably football, that have only modest appeal to other cultures. Japan, in copying televised American quiz shows, imposes shame on losing contestants in a fashion that would seem bizarre to the West. Changes in the role of women in the workplace and their growing assertiveness and independence, commonplace factors in Western societies, find limited echoes in the Muslim world or even in Japan.

The point is clear: The smallness of the world, as represented by the new and sometimes beneficial exchanges among diverse peoples, exists alongside deep divisions. International contacts do not necessarily bring harmony or friendship. Any interpretation of the contemporary world must take into account this complex tension, involving the undeniable existence of certain patterns that have worldwide influence but the equally undeniable existence of divergencies and conflicts that stubbornly persist. Policymakers face this conflict in applying their beliefs to the wider world: Should U.S. policy be based on assumptions that most of the world will become increasingly like us, or should it build on assumptions of permanent political and cultural differences? U.S. policy in recent decades has, in fact, oscillated between both approaches, in part because each approach—the vision of expanding contact and imitation, and the vision of deep-seated, possibly growing differentiation—has much to commend it.

The same tension must inform any study of how the world became what it is today—that is, any effort to convey the basic dynamics of world history. Both international influences and major diversities are rooted in the past. Humankind has always been united in some respects. The human species displays certain common responses, and as a result, all human societies share certain basic features. Moreover, there have always been some links among different human societies in various parts of the world, although admittedly such linkages have only recently become complex and rapid. Cultural diffusion—the process by which an idea or technique devised in one society spreads to another—describes the way plowing equipment first invented in China ultimately was adopted in Europe, or the way a numbering system conceived in India reached the Middle East and then Europe many centuries ago. The same basic process of cultural diffusion, now speeded up, indicates how the Japanese copied and then improved upon American assembly-line production during the 1970s and 1980s. There have always been, in other words, some common themes in world history, affecting many peoples and establishing a common dynamic for developments in many parts of the world in a given set of centuries. However, there also have always been important differences among the world's peoples, as even prehistoric societies differed markedly in how they viewed death, how they treated the elderly and children, or the kind of government they established.

There are two ways to make the study of these complexities relatively manageable. The evolution of worldwide processes—that is, developments that ultimately shaped much of the world's population—can be understood by dividing the past into coherent periods of world history, from the prehistoric age to the development of agriculture to the spread of the great religions and on to more recent stages. The leading diversities of human society for at least the past 3000 years can be conveyed by concentrating on the development of particularly extensive and durable civilizations, whose impact runs from their own origins to the present time. These civilizations, while not embracing the entire human species even today, have come to include most people, and they are, fortunately, not infinite in number. Five early traditions—in the Middle East (Mesopotamia and Persia), the Mediterranean (the Middle Eastern coast, North Africa, and Southern Europe), India, China, and Central America—ultimately were replaced by seven major patterns of government, society, and culture. Exploring the nature of these patterns in the world's seven regions—East Asia; India and Southeast Asia; the Middle East; Eastern Europe; sub-Saharan Africa; Western Europe and North America; and Latin America—and then assessing their interaction with the larger processes of world history provide the key to understanding the essential features of human society past and present.

Think of a pattern as follows: Each civilization deals with some common issues, such as how to organize a state, how to define a family, how to integrate technology and whether or not to encourage technological change, how to explain and present the natural universe, and how to define social inequality. The distinctive ways that each civilization handles these issues follows from geographical differences plus early cultural and historical experience. The goal in comparing the major civilizations involves understanding these different approaches to common social issues. But civilizations were never entirely isolated, and ultimately they all had to decide what to do about growing international trade, migrations, spreading diseases, and missionary religions. They also had to decide how to respond to examples and influences from other societies. Responses to these common forces sometimes drew civilizations together, but they also often reflected very diverse adjustments. The puzzle of world history—its pieces composed of distinct civilizations, contacts, and ongoing change—is not hard to outline but it is undeniably challenging.

Not long ago, many Americans believed that world history consisted of the rise of their own Western civilization and its interaction with the rest of the globe. Not long ago, many Chinese believed that world history involved little more than the fascinating story of the evolution of the only civilization that mattered—their own. These were attractive visions, adequate for many purposes; they certainly offered simpler explanations than a focus on the interaction and differentiation of several vibrant civilizations. But just as many people today see that the world is growing "smaller," in the same way, many also observe that it is growing more complex. A study of world history can and should respond to this complexity.

SUGGESTED READINGS

Important explorations of world history that provide greater detail or a somewhat different vantage point from this study include: W. McNeill, *Rise of the West: A History of the Human Community* (1970) and *A History of the Human Community* (1996); J. M. Roberts, *The Pelican History of the World* (1984); Peter N. Stearns, Michael Adas, and Stuart B. Schwartz, *World Civilizations: The Global Experience* (2000); Richard Bulliet et al., *The Earth and Its Peoples* (1997); Jerry Bentley, *Traditions and Encounters: A Global Perspective on the Past* (2000). Also useful for background on the geographic distribution of the world's people is G. Murdock, *Ethnographic Atlas* (1967).

From Human Prehistory to the Early Civilizations

FOCAL POINTS *Examining the long early stages of human history involves several key issues, centering mainly around agriculture and the definition of a civilization: Why did agriculture develop and how did it change the potential of human societies? What are the debates about defining "civilization" as a form of human society, and why are they significant? Why did most early civilizations center in river valleys? What did these early civilizations have in common, and how did they differ? Is the early story of the human species, particularly once agriculture and then civilization became increasingly common, a story of increasing progress, or is some other interpretive model more accurate?*

GETTING STARTED IS ALWAYS HARD

The human species has accomplished a great deal in a relatively short period of time. There are significant disagreements over how long an essentially human species, as distinct from other primates, has existed. However, a figure of 2 or 2.5 million years seems acceptable. This is approximately 1/4000 of the time the earth has existed. That is, if one thinks of the whole history of the earth to date as a 24-hour day, the human species began at about 5 minutes until midnight. Human beings have existed for less than 5 percent of the time mammals of any sort have lived. Yet in this brief span of time—by earth-history standards—humankind has spread to every landmass (with the exception of the polar regions) and, for better or worse, has taken control of the destinies of countless other species.

To be sure, human beings have some drawbacks as a species, compared to other existing models. They are unusually aggressive against their own kind: While some of the great apes, notably chimpanzees, engage in periodic wars, these conflicts can hardly rival human violence. Human babies are dependent for a long period, which requires some special family or child-care arrangements and often has limited the activities of many adult women. Certain ailments, such as back problems resulting from an upright stature, also burden the species. And, insofar as we know, the human species is alone in its awareness of the inevitability of death—a knowledge that imparts some unique fears and tensions.

Distinctive features of the human species account for considerable achievement as well. Like other primates, but unlike most other mammals, people can manipulate objects fairly readily because of the grip provided by an opposable thumb on each hand. Compared to other primates, human beings have a relatively high and regular sexual drive, which aids reproduction; being omnivores, they are not dependent exclusively on plants or animals for food, which helps explain why they can live in so many different climates and settings; the unusual variety of their facial expressions aids communication and enhances social life. The distinctive human brain and a facility for elaborate speech are even more important: Much of human history depends on the knowledge, inventions, and social contracts that resulted from these assets. Features of this sort explain why many human cultures, including the Western culture that many Americans share, promote a firm separation between human and animal, seeing in our own species a power and rationality, and possibly a spark of the divine, that "lower" creatures lack.

Although the rise of humankind has been impressively rapid, however, its early stages can also be viewed as painfully long and slow. Most of the 2 million plus years during which our species has existed are described by the term *Paleolithic,* or *Old Stone Age.* Throughout this long time span, which runs until about 14,000 years ago, human beings learned only simple tool use, mainly through employing suitably shaped rocks and sticks for hunting and warfare. Fire was tamed about 750,000 years ago. The nature of the species also gradually changed during the Paleolithic, with emphasis on more erect stature and growing brain capacity. Archeological evidence also indicates some increases in average size. A less apelike species, whose larger brain and erect stance allowed better tool use, emerged between 500,000 and 750,000 years ago; it is called, appropriately enough, *Homo erectus.* Several species of *Homo erectus* developed and spread in Africa, to Asia and Europe, reaching a population size of perhaps 1.5 million 100,000 years ago.

Considerable evidence suggests that more advanced types of humans killed off or displaced many competitors over time, which explains why there is only one basic human type throughout the world today, rather than a number of rather similar human species, as among monkeys and apes. The newest human breed, *Homo sapiens sapiens,* of which all humans in the world today are descendants, originated about 120,000 years ago, also in Africa. The success of this subspecies means that there have been no major changes in the basic human physique or brain size since its advent.

Even after the appearance of *Homo sapiens sapiens,* human life faced important constraints. People who hunted food and gathered nuts and berries could not support large numbers or elaborate societies. Most hunting groups were small, and they had to roam widely for food. Two people required at least one square mile for survival. Population growth was slow, partly because women breast-fed infants for several years to limit their own fertility. On the other hand, people did not have to work very hard—hunting took about seven hours every three days on average. Women, who gathered fruits and vegetables, worked harder but there was significant equality between the sexes based on common economic contributions.

Paleolithic people gradually improved their tool use, beginning with the crude shaping of stone and wooden implements. Speech developed with *Homo erectus* 100,000 years ago, allowing more group cooperation and the transmission of technical knowledge. By the later Paleolithic period, people had developed rituals to lessen the fear of death and created cave paintings to express a sense of nature's beauty and power. Goddesses often played a prominent role in the religious pantheon. Thus, the human species came to develop cultures—that is, systems of belief that helped explain the environment and set up rules for various kinds of social behavior. The development of speech provided rich language and symbols for the transmission of culture and its growing sophistication. At the same time, different groups of humans, in different locations, developed quite varied belief systems and corresponding languages.

The greatest achievement of Paleolithic people was the sheer spread of the human species over much of the earth's surface. The species originated in eastern Africa; most of the earliest types of human remains come from this region, in the present-day countries of Tanzania, Kenya, and Uganda. But gradual migration, doubtless caused by the need to find scarce food, steadily pushed the human reach to other areas. Key discoveries, notably fire and the use of animal skins for clothing—both of which enabled people to live in colder climates—facilitated the spread of Paleolithic groups. The first people moved out of Africa about 750,000 years ago. Human remains (Peking man, Java man) have been found in China and Southeast Asia dating from 600,000 and 350,000 years ago, respectively. Humans inhabited Britain 250,000 years ago. They first crossed to Australia 60,000 years ago, followed by another group 20,000 years later; these combined to form the continent's aboriginal population. Dates of the migration from Asia to the Americas are under debate. Most scholars believe that humans crossed what was then a land bridge from Siberia to Alaska about 17,000 years ago and quickly began to spread out, reaching the tip of the South American continent possibly within a mere thousand years. But some recent carbon-dating of Native American artifacts suggests an earlier arrival date. Settlers from China reached Taiwan, the Philippines, and Indonesia 4500 to 3500 years ago.

In addition, soon after this time—roughly 14,000 years ago—the last great ice age ended, which did wonders for living conditions over much of the Northern Hemisphere. Human development began to accelerate. A new term, *Mesolithic,* or *Middle Stone Age,* designates a span of several thousand years, from about 12,000 to 8000 B.C.E.,* in which human ability to fashion stone tools and other implements improved greatly. People learned to sharpen and shape stone, to make better weapons and cutting edges. Animal bones were used to make needles and other precise tools. From the Mesolithic also date the increased numbers of log rafts and dugouts, which improved fishing, and the manufacture of pots and baskets for food storage. Mesolithic people domesticated more animals, such as cows, which again improved food supply. Population growth accelerated, which also resulted in more conflicts and wars. Skeletons from this period show frequent bone breaks and skull fractures caused by weapons.

In time, better tool use, somewhat more elaborate social organization, and still more population pressure led people in many parts of the world to the final Stone

---

*In Christian societies, historical dating divides between years "before the birth of Christ" (B.C.) and after (A.D., *anno Domini,* or "year of our Lord"). This system came into wide acceptance in Europe in the eighteenth century, as formal historical consciousness increased (although ironically, 1 A.D. is a few years late for Jesus' actual birth). China, Islam, Judaism, and many other societies use different dating systems, referring to their own history. This text, like many recent world history materials, uses the Christian chronology (one has to choose some system) but changes the terms to B.C.E. ("before the common era") and C.E. ("of the common era") as a gesture to less Christian-centric labeling.

Human Development: Geographical and Physical Determinants

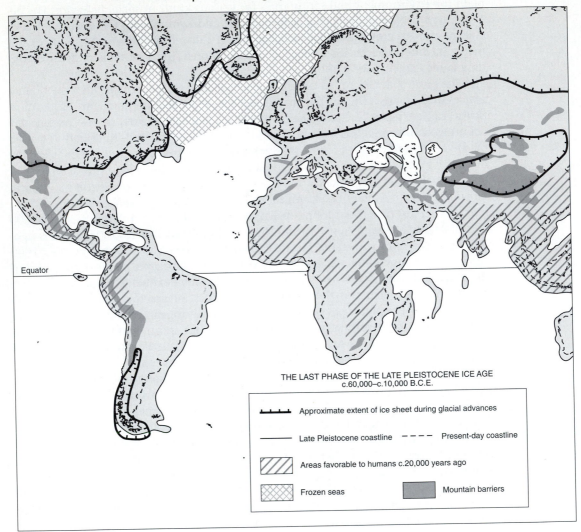

THE LAST PHASE OF THE LATE PLEISTOCENE ICE AGE
c.60,000–c.10,000 B.C.E.

⊢━┴━┴━ Approximate extent of ice sheet during glacial advances	
——— Late Pleistocene coastline	– – – Present-day coastline
▨ Areas favorable to humans c.20,000 years ago	
▦ Frozen seas	▓ Mountain barriers

Equator

Age—the *Neolithic,* or *New Stone Age.* And from Neolithic people, in turn, came several more dramatic developments that changed the nature of human existence—the invention of agriculture, the creation of cities, and other foreshadowings of civilization, which ended the Stone Age altogether throughout much of the world.

THE NEOLITHIC REVOLUTION

Human achievements during the various ages of stone are both fascinating and fundamental, and some points are hotly debated. Our knowledge of Stone Age society is of course limited, although archeologists have been creative in their interpretations of tool remains and other evidence, such as cave paintings and burial sites, that Stone Age people produced in various parts of the world. What people accomplished during this long period of prehistory remains essential to human life today; our ability to make and manipulate tools thus depends directly on what our Stone Age ancestors learned about physical matter.

However, it was the invention of agriculture that most clearly moved the human species toward more elaborate social and cultural patterns of the sort that people today would find recognizable. With agriculture, human beings were able to settle in one spot and focus on particular economic, political, and religious goals and activities. Agriculture also spawned a great increase in the sheer number of people in the world—from about 6 to 8 million across the earth's surface during early Neolithic times, to about 100 million some 3000 years later.

The initial development of agriculture—that is, the deliberate planting of grains for later harvest—was probably triggered by two results of the ice age's end. First, population increases, stemming from improved climate, prompted people to search for new and more reliable sources of food. Second, the end of the ice age saw the retreat of certain big game animals, such as mastodons. Human hunters had to turn to smaller game, such as deer and wild boar, in many forested areas. Hunting's overall yield declined. Here was the basis for new interest in other sources of food. There is evidence that by 9000 B.C.E., in certain parts of the world, people were becoming increasingly dependent on regular harvests of wild grains, berries, and nuts. This undoubtedly set the stage for the deliberate planting of seeds (probably accidental to begin with) and the improvement of key grains through the selection of seeds from the best plants.

As farming evolved, new animals were also domesticated. Particularly in the Middle East and parts of Asia, by 9000 B.C.E. pigs, sheep, goats, and cattle were being raised. Farmers used these animals for meat and skins and soon discovered dairying as well. These results not only contributed to the development of agriculture, they also served as the basis for nomadic herding societies.

Farming was initially developed in the Middle East, in an arc of territory running from present-day Turkey to Iraq and Israel. This was a very fertile area, more fertile in those days than at present. Grains such as barley and wild wheat were abundant. At the same time, this area was not heavily forested, and animals were in short supply, presenting a challenge to hunters. In the Middle East, the development of agriculture may have begun as early as 10,000 B.C.E., and it gained ground rapidly after 8000 B.C.E. Gradually during the Neolithic centuries, knowledge of agriculture spread to other centers, including parts of India, North Africa, and Europe. Agriculture, including rice cultivation, soon developed independently in China. Thus, within a few thousand years agriculture had spread to the parts of the world that would produce the first human civilizations. We will see that agriculture spread later to much of Africa south of the Mediterranean coast, reaching West Africa by 2000 B.C.E., although here too there were additional developments with an emphasis on local grains and also root crops such as yams. Agriculture had to be invented separately in the Americas, based on corn cultivation, where it was also a slightly later development (about 5000 B.C.E).

Many scholars have termed the development of agriculture a "Neolithic revolution." The term is obviously misleading in one sense: Agriculture was no sudden

TIMELINE: Prehistoric Landmarks

BEGINNINGS **About 4 million years ago**	Beginnings of separation between humanlike apes (hominids) and other apes.
PALEOLITHIC AGE **About 2–2.5 million years ago** **750,000–1 million years ago**	More humanlike species, larger brain size; initially in eastern Africa. Further development of the species into *Homo erectus*, a tool-using human; upright stance, close to modern human brain size. Growth of infant brain and head size, leading to more complicated child care; more division of labor between males as hunters and females as seed gatherers, child caretakers.
600,000–700,000 years ago	Spread of species, although in small numbers, across Asia, Europe, and Africa; signs of fire use (in China); improved human hunting abilities; more big game, less vegetarian.
200,000 years ago	Development of Neanderthal species across Europe and Asia; burial rituals and monuments, suggesting knowledge of death.
120,000 years ago	Arrival of *Homo sapiens sapiens*; displacement of Neanderthals and other species across Asia and Europe from initial center in Africa.
20,000 B.C.E.	Worst ice age.
15,000 B.C.E.	Passage of people to the Americas, via land link from Asia.
MESOLITHIC AGE **12,000–8,000 B.C.E.**	Great improvements in stone tools; use of bone; development of some ships; domestication of some animals.
10,000 B.C.E.	End of ice age.
NEOLITHIC AGE **8000–5000 B.C.E.**	Further improvements in tool making; first development of agriculture; great expansion in human population.
BRONZE AGE **4000 B.C.E.** **3500 B.C.E.** **1500 B.C.E.**	Early use of bronze and copper tools. First civilization, in Middle East; end of "prehistoric" ages of humankind. Early use of iron tools and weapons.

transformation, even in the Middle East where the new system had its roots. Learning the new agricultural methods was difficult, and many peoples long combined a bit of agriculture with considerable reliance on the older systems of hunting and gathering. A "revolution" that took over a thousand years, and then several thousand more to spread to key population centers in Asia, Europe, and Africa, is hardly dramatic by modern standards.

The concept of revolution is, however, appropriate in demonstrating the magnitude of change involved. Early agriculture could support far more people per square mile than hunting ever could; it also allowed people to settle more permanently in one area. The system was nonetheless not easy. Agriculture required more regular work, at least of men, than hunting did. Hunting groups today, such as the pygmies of the Kalihari Desert in southwest Africa, work an average of 2.5 hours a day, alternating long, intense hunts with periods of idleness. Settled agriculture concentrated populations and encouraged the spread of disease. As much as agriculture was demanding, it was also rewarding: Agriculture supported larger populations, and with better food supplies and a more settled existence, agricultural peoples could afford to build houses and villages. Animals provided not only hides but also wool for more varied clothing.

We know next to nothing of the debates that must have raged when people were first confronted with agriculture, but it is not hard to imagine that many would have found the new life too complicated, too difficult, or too unexciting. Most evidence suggests that gathering and hunting peoples resisted agriculture as long as they could. Gradually, of course, agriculture did gain ground. Its success was hard to deny. And as farmers cleared new land from forests, they automatically drove out or converted many hunters. Disease played a role: Settled agricultural societies suffered from more contagious diseases because of denser population concentrations. Hunting and gathering peoples lacked resistance and often died when agriculturists who had developed immunity to these diseases carried them into their areas.

Not all the peoples of the world came to embrace the slowly spreading wave of agriculture, at least not until very recently. Important small societies in southern Africa, Australia, the islands of Southeast Asia, and even northern Japan were isolated for so long that news of this economic system simply did not reach them. The white-skinned hunting tribes of northern Japan disappeared only about a hundred years ago. Northern Europeans and southern Africans converted to agriculture earlier, about 2000 years ago, but well after the Neolithic revolution had transformed other parts of their continents. Agriculture was initiated in the Americas as early as 5000 B.C.E. and developed vigorously in Central America and the northern part of South America. However, most Indian tribes in North America continued a hunting and gathering existence, sometimes combined with limited agriculture, until recent centuries. Finally, the peoples of the vast plains of central Asia long resisted a complete conversion to agriculture, in part because of a harsh climate; herding, rather than grain-growing, became the basic socioeconomic system of this part of the world. And from this area would come waves of tough, nomadic invaders whose role in linking major civilizations was a vital force in world history until a few centuries ago.

Development possibilities among people who became agriculturists were more obvious than those among smaller populations who resisted or simply did not know of the system: Agriculture set the basis for more rapid change in human societies. Greater wealth and larger populations freed some people for other specializations, from which new ideas or techniques might spring. Agriculture itself depended on control over nature that could be facilitated by newly developed techniques and objects. For example, during the Neolithic period itself, the needs of farming people for storage facilities, for grains and seeds, promoted the development of basket-making and pottery. The first potter's wheel came into existence around 6000 B.C.E., and this, in turn, encouraged faster and higher-quality pottery production. Agricultural needs also encouraged certain kinds of science, supporting the human inclination to learn more about weather or flooding.

Much of what we think of as human history involves the doings of agricultural societies—societies, that is, in which most people are farmers and in which the production of food is the central economic activity. Nonagricultural groups, like the nomadic herders in Central Asia, made their own mark, but their greatest influence usually occurred in interactions with agricultural peoples. Many societies remain largely agricultural still today. The huge time span we have thus far considered, including the Neolithic revolution itself, is all technically "prehistorical"— involved with human patterns before the invention of writing allowed the kinds of records-keeping historians prefer. In fact, since we now know how to use surviving tools and burial sites as records, the prehistoric–historic distinction means less than it once did. The preagricultural–agricultural distinction is more central. Fairly soon after the development of agriculture—although not, admittedly, right away— significant human change began to occur in decades and centuries, rather than in the sizable blocks of time, several thousand years or more, that describe preagricultural peoples.

Indeed, one basic change took place fairly soon after the introduction of agriculture, and, again, societies in the Middle East served as its birthplace. The discovery of metal tools dates back to about 4000 B.C.E. Copper was the first metal with which people learned how to work, although the more resilient metal, bronze, soon entered the picture. In fact, the next basic age of human existence was the Bronze Age. By about 3000 B.C.E., metalworking had become so commonplace in the Middle East that the use of stone tools dissipated, and the long stone ages were over at last—although, of course, an essentially Neolithic technology persisted in many parts of the world, even among some agricultural peoples.

Metalworking was extremely useful to agricultural or herding societies. Metal hoes and other tools allowed farmers to work the ground more efficiently. Metal weapons were obviously superior to those made from stone and wood. Agricultural peoples had the resources to free up a small number of individuals as toolmakers, who would specialize in this activity and exchange their products with farmers for food. Specialization of this sort did not, however, guarantee rapid rates of invention; indeed, many specialized artisans seemed very conservative, eager to preserve methods that had been inherited. But, specialization did improve the conditions or climate for discovery, and the invention of metalworking was a key result. Like agriculture, knowledge of metals gradually fanned out to other parts of Asia and to Africa and Europe.

Gradually, the knowledge of metal tools created further change, for not only farmers but also manufacturing artisans benefited from better tools. Woodworking, for example, became steadily more elaborate as metal replaced stone, bone, and fire in the cutting and connecting of wood. We are, of course, still living in the metal ages today, although we rely primarily on iron—whose working was introduced around 1500 B.C.E. by herding peoples who invaded the Middle East—rather than copper and bronze.

CIVILIZATION

Agriculture encouraged the formation of larger as well as more stable human communities than had existed before Neolithic times. A few Mesolithic groups had formed villages, particularly where opportunities for fishing were good, as around some of the lakes in Switzerland. However, most hunting peoples moved in relatively small groups, or tribes, each containing anywhere from 40 to 60 individuals, and they could not settle in a single spot without the game running out. With agriculture, these constraints changed. To be sure, some agricultural peoples did move around. A system called *slash and burn* agriculture existed in a few parts of the world, including portions of the American South, until about 150 years ago. Here, people would burn off trees in an area, farm intensively for a few years until the soil was depleted, and then move on. Herding peoples also moved in tribal bands, with strong kinship ties. But, most agricultural peoples did not have new lands close by to which they could move after a short time. And, there were advantages to staying put: Houses could be built to last, wells built to bring up water, and other "expensive" improvements afforded because they would serve many generations. In the Middle East, China, and parts of Africa and India, a key incentive to stability was the need for irrigation devices to channel river water to the fields. This same need helps explain why agriculture generated communities and not a series of isolated farms. Small groups simply could not regulate a river's flow or build and maintain irrigation ditches and sluices. Irrigation and defense encouraged villages—groupings of several hundred people—as the characteristic pattern of residence in almost all agricultural societies from Neolithic days until our own century.

One Neolithic village, Çatal Hüyük in southern Turkey, has been elaborately studied by archeologists. It was founded about 7000 B.C.E. and was unusually large, covering about 32 acres. Houses were made of mud bricks set in timber frameworks, crowded together, with few windows. People seem to have spent a good bit of time on their rooftops in order to experience daylight and make social contacts—many broken bones attest to frequent falls. Some houses were lavishly decorated, mainly with hunting scenes. Religious images, both of powerful male hunters and "mother goddesses" devoted to agricultural fertility, were common, and some people in the village seem to have had special religious responsibilities. The village produced almost all the goods it consumed. Some trade was conducted with hunting peoples who lived in the hills surrounding the village, but apparently, it was initiated more to keep the peace than to produce economic gain. By 5500 B.C.E., important production activities developed in the village, including those of skilled toolmakers and jewelers. With time also came links with other communities. Large villages like Çatal Hüyük ruled over smaller communities. This meant that some families began to specialize in politics, and military forces were organized. Some villages became small cities, ruled by kings who were typically given divine status.

Çatal Hüyük. Superimposed bulls' heads, which symbolized a god, were used for worship in this village.

By 3000 B.C.E., Çatal Hüyük had become part of a civilization. Although many of the characteristics of civilization had existed by 6000 or 5000 B.C.E. in this Middle Eastern region, the origins of civilization, strictly speaking, approximately date to only 3500 B.C.E. The first civilization arose in the Middle East along the banks of the Tigris and Euphrates rivers. Another center of civilization started soon thereafter in northeast Africa (Egypt), and a third by around 2500 B.C.E. along the banks of the Indus River in northwestern India. These three early centers of civilization had some interaction. The fourth and fifth early civilization centers, a bit later and considerably more separate, arose in China and Central America.

Unlike an agricultural society, which can be rather precisely defined, civilization is a more subjective construct. Some scholars prefer to define civilizations only as societies with enough economic surplus to form divisions of labor and a social hierarchy involving significant inequalities. This is a very inclusive definition and under it most agricultural societies and even some groups like North American Indians who combined farming with hunting would be drawn in. Others, however, press the concepts of civilization further, arguing, for example, that a chief difference between civilizations and other societies (whether hunting or agricultural) involves the emergence of formal political organizations, or states, as opposed to dependence on family or tribal ties. Most civilizations produce political units capable of ruling large regions and some, of course, characteristically produce huge kingdoms or empires.

The word *civilization* itself comes from the Latin term for *city,* and in truth most civilizations do depend on the existence of significant cities. In agricultural civilizations, most people do not live in cities. But, cities are crucial because they amass wealth and power, they allow the rapid exchange of ideas among relatively large numbers of people, thereby encouraging intellectual thought and artistic expression, and they promote specialization in manufacturing and trade.

Most civilizations developed writing, starting with the emergence of cuneiform (writing based on wedgelike characters; see p. 19) in the Middle East around 3500 B.C.E. Societies that employ writing can organize more elaborate political structures because of their ability to send messages and keep records. They can tax more efficiently and make contracts and treaties. Societies with writing also generate a more explicit intellectual climate because of their ability to record data and build on past, written wisdom. (One of the early written records from the Middle East is a recipe for making beer—a science of a sort.) Some experts argue that the very fact of becoming literate changes the way people think, encouraging them to consider the world as a place that can be understood by organized human inquiry, or "rationally," and less by a host of spiritual beliefs. In all agricultural civilizations—that is, in all human history until less than 200 years ago—only a minority of people were literate, and usually that was a small minority. Nonetheless, the existence of writing did make a difference in such societies.

Since civilizations employ writing and are by definition unusually well organized, it is not surprising that almost all recorded history is about what has happened to civilized societies. We simply know the most about such societies, and we often are particularly impressed by what they produce in the way of great art or powerful rulers. It is also true that civilizations tend to be far more populous than noncivilized societies. Therefore, the history of civilization generally covers the history of most people.

But, the history of civilization does not include everybody. No hunting or nomadic peoples could generate a civilization—they lacked the stability and resources, and, with the exception of a limited number of signs and symbols, they never developed writing, unless it came from the outside. Furthermore, some agricultural peoples did not develop a full civilization, *if* our definition of civilization goes beyond the simple acquisition of economic surplus to formal states, cities, and writing. Portions of West Africa, fully agricultural and capable of impressive art, have long lacked writing, major cities, or more than loose regional government.

People in civilizations, particularly during the long centuries when they were surrounded by noncivilized peoples, characteristically looked down on any society lacking in civilization. The ancient Greeks coined the word "barbarian" to describe such cases—indeed, they were prone to regard all non-Greeks as barbarians. As a result of labels like this, it is easy to think of much human history as divided between civilizations and primitive nomads.

Such a distinction is incorrect, however, and it does not follow from the real historical meaning of civilization. In the first place, like agriculture, civilization brings losses as well as gains. As Çatal Hüyük moved toward civilization, distinctions based on social class and wealth increased. Civilizations often have firmer class or caste divisions, including slavery, than do "simpler" societies. They also often promote greater separation between the rulers and ruled, monarchs and subjects. Frequently, they are quite warlike, and there is greater inequality between men and women than in "noncivilized" societies. With civilization, more fully patriarchal structures emerged. In cities, male superiority was even clearer than in agriculture, as men did most of the manufacturing and assumed political and religious leadership, thus relegating women to subordinate roles. "Civilization," then, is not a synonym for "good."

By the same token, noncivilized societies may be exceptionally well regulated and have interesting, important cultures. Many noncivilized societies, in fact, have more regulations—in part, because they depend on rules transmitted by word of mouth—than civilized societies. Some of the societies most eager to repress anger and aggression in human dealings, such as Zuni Indians in the American Southwest, are noncivilized. Although some noncivilized societies treat old people cruelly, others display more respect and veneration toward elders than most civilizations do. In other words, noncivilized societies are not all alike. They are not characteristically populated with cannibals and warmongers, but rather are often shocked by the do-ings of civilized peoples. For example, American Indians were appalled at the insis-tence of European settlers on spanking their children, a behavior they regarded as vi-cious and unnecessary. A fascinating, although probably unanswerable, question involves determining whether or not the civilization form has left more or less good in its wake.

The development of civilization continued the process of technological change and political organization, of increasingly elaborate artistic and intellectual forms. It is in this context that the term has real meaning and in which it legitimately com-mands the attention of most historians.

Civilizations also increased human impact on the environment. For example, the first center of copper production in Europe, along the Danube valley, led to such de-forestation that the fuel supply was destroyed, and the industry collapsed after about 3000 B.C.E. The extensive agriculture needed to support Indus river cities opened the land to erosion and flooding because of overuse of the soil and removal of trees.

Having started in 3500 B.C.E., civilization developed in its four initial centers—the Middle East, Egypt, northwestern India, and northern China—over the following 2500 years. These areas covered only a tiny portion of the inhabited parts of the world, although they were the most densely populated. Such early civilizations, all clustered in key river valleys, were in a way pilot tests of the new form of social or-ganization. Only after about 1000 B.C.E. did a more consistent process of develop-ment and spread of civilization begin—and with it, came the main threads of world history. However, the great civilizations unquestionably built on the achievements of the river valley pioneers, and so some understanding of this contribution to the list of early human accomplishments is essential.

TIGRIS-EUPHRATES CIVILIZATION

The most noteworthy achievements of the earliest civilizations were early versions of organizational and cultural forms that most of us now take for granted—writing it-self, formal codes of law, city planning and architecture, and institutions for trade, including the use of money. Once developed, most of these building blocks of hu-man organization did not have to be reinvented, although in some cases they spread only slowly to other parts of the world.

It is not surprising then, given its lead in agriculture, metalworking, and village structure, that the Middle East generated the first example of human civilization. Indeed, the first civilization, founded in the valley of the Tigris and Euphrates rivers in a part of the Middle East long called Mesopotamia, forms one of only a few cases of a civilization developed absolutely from scratch—and with no examples from any place else to imitate. (Chinese civilization and civilization in Central America also developed independently.) By 4000 B.C.E., the farmers of Mesopotamia were familiar with bronze and copper and had already invented the wheel for transportation. They had a well-established pottery industry and interesting artistic forms. Farming in this area, because of the need for irrigation, required considerable coordination among communities, and this in turn served as the basis for complex political structures.

By about 3500 B.C.E., a people who had recently invaded this region, the Sumerians, developed a cuneiform alphabet, the first known case of human writing. Their alphabet at first used different pictures to represent various objects but soon shifted to the use of geometric shapes to symbolize spoken sounds. The early Sumerian alphabet may have had as many as 2000 such symbols, but this number was later reduced to about 300. Even so, writing and reading remained complex skills, which only a few had time to master. Scribes wrote on clay tablets, using styluses shaped quite like the modern ballpoint pen.

Sumerian art developed steadily, as statues and painted frescoes were used to adorn the temples of the gods. Statues of the gods also decorated individual homes. Sumerian science aided a complex agricultural society, as people sought to learn more about the movement of the sun and stars—thus founding the science of astronomy—and improved their mathematical knowledge. (Astronomy defined the calendar and provided the astrological forecasts widely used in politics and religion.) The Sumerians employed a system of numbers based on units of 10, 60, and 360 that we still use in calculating circles and hours. In other words, Sumerians and their successors in Mesopotamia created patterns of observation and abstract thought about nature that a number of civilizations, including our own, still rely on, and they also introduced specific systems, such as charts of major constellations, that have been current at least among educated people for 5000 years, not only in the Middle East but, by later imitation, in India and Europe as well.

Sumerians developed complex religious rituals. Each city had a patron god and erected impressive shrines to please and honor this and other deities. Massive towers, called ziggurats, formed the first monumental architecture in this civilization. Professional priests operated these temples and conducted the rituals within. Sumerians believed in many powerful gods, for the nature on which their agriculture depended often seemed swift and unpredictable. Prayers and offerings to prevent floods as well as to protect good health were a vital part of Sumerian life. Sumerian ideas about the divine force in natural objects—in rivers, trees, and mountains—were common among early agricultural peoples; a religion of this sort, which sees gods in many aspects of nature, is known as *polytheism*. More specifically, Sumerian religious notions, notably their ideas about the gods' creation of the earth from water and about the divine punishment of humans through floods, later influenced the writers of the Old Testament and thus continue to play a role in Jewish, Christian, and Muslim cultures. Sumerian religious ideas, which had a decidedly gloomy cast, also included a belief in an afterlife of punishment—an original version of the concept of hell.

Afro-Eurasia: The Growth of Civilization to 200 C.E.

The Growth of Civilization to 200 C.E.

- Iron Age Sites
- Civilized areas in Third Millennium B.C.E.
- Civilized areas in Second Millennium B.C.E.
- Civilization 1000 B.C.E.–200 C.E.

PACIFIC OCEAN

INDIAN OCEAN

ATLANTIC OCEAN

GOBI DESERT

Lung-Shan
Choukoutien
Anyang
Yang-Shoa
Ordos
Chi-Chia
Nyangu
Hoa-Binh
Kota-Tampan

Silk Route First millennium B.C.E.

TIEN SHAN

HIMALAYAS

THAR DESERT

Amri
Quetta
Kulli

Sea Routes
First millennium B.C.E.

Anau

CASPIAN SEA

Bakun

Al-Ubaid
Eridu

ARABIAN DESERT

Gagarino

BLACK SEA

Jericho

Naqada

Kiev

Troy
Mersin

Cnossos
Badari
Kharga Oasis

Merimde

La Tène
Hallstadt
Villanova

MEDITERRANEAN SEA

Gafsa
ATLAS MOUNTAINS

SAHARA DESERT

Irkutsk

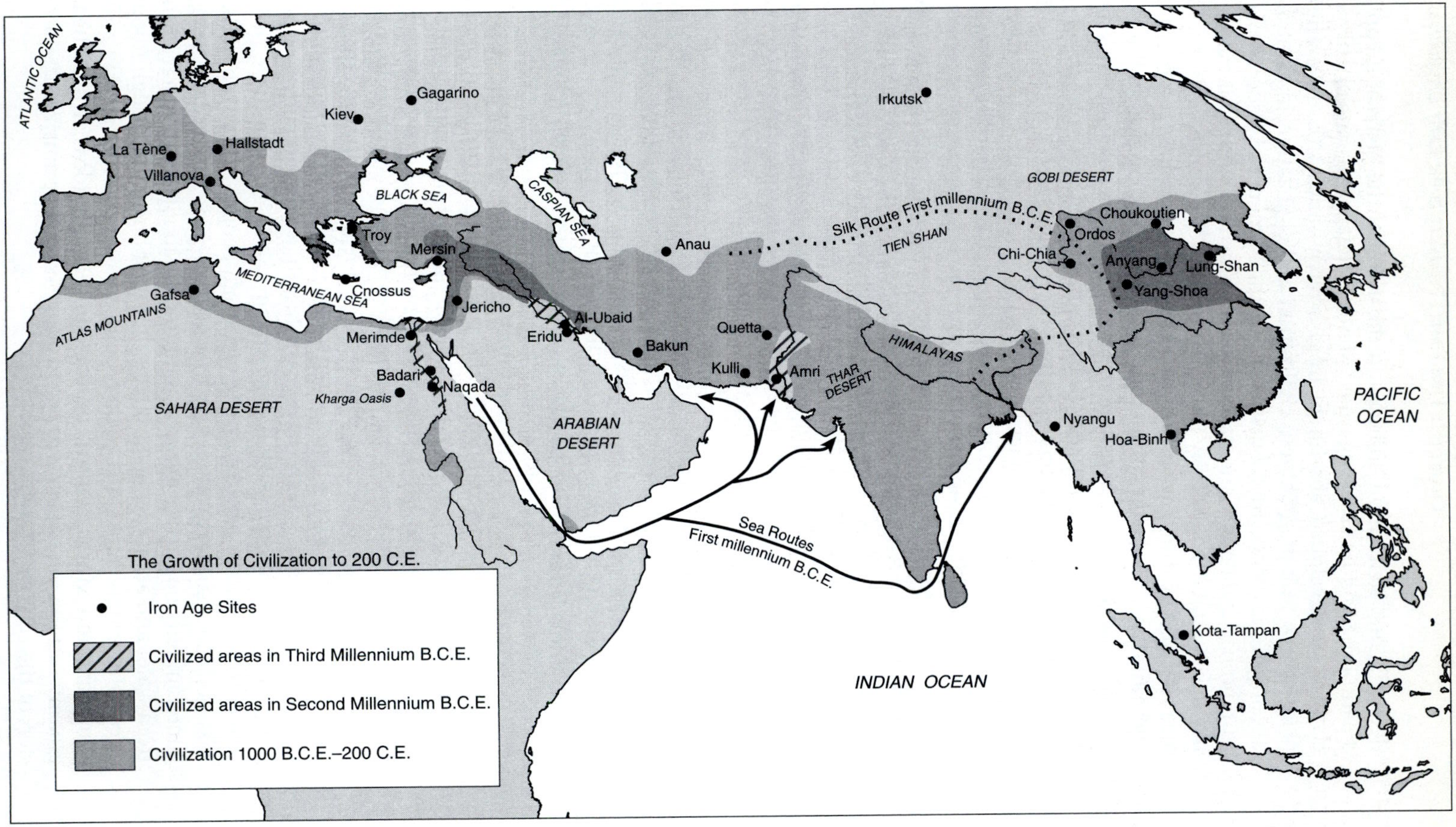

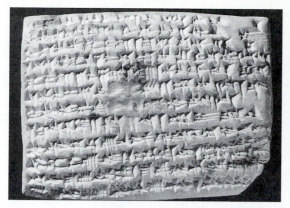 

Cuneiform and Chinese lettering. *Left*: Cuneiform tablet from the Middle East. *Right*: A Shang dynasty oracle bone with ideographs.

Sumerian political structures stressed tightly organized city-states, ruled by a king who claimed divine authority. The Sumerian state had carefully defined boundaries, unlike the less formal territories of precivilized villages in the region. Here is a key early example of how civilization and a more formal political structure came together. The government helped regulate religion and enforce its duties; it also provided a court system in the interests of justice. Kings were originally military leaders during times of war, and the function of defense and war, including leadership of a trained army, remained vital in Sumerian politics. Kings and the noble class, along with the priesthood, controlled considerable land, which was worked by slaves. Thus began a tradition of slavery that would long mark Middle Eastern societies. Warfare remained vital to ensure supplies of slaves taken as prisoners during combat. At the same time, slavery was a variable state of existence, and many slaves were able to earn money and even buy their freedom.

The Sumerians added to their region's agricultural prosperity not only by using wheeled carts but also by learning about fertilizers and by adopting silver as a means of exchange for buying and selling—an early form of money. However, the region was also hard to defend and proved a constant temptation to outside invaders from Sumerian times to the present. The Sumerians themselves fell to a people called the Akkadians, who continued much of Sumerian culture. Another period of decline was followed by conquest by the Babylonians, who extended their own empire and thus helped bring civilization to other parts of the Middle East. It was under Babylonian rule that the king Hammurabi introduced the most famous early code of law, boasting of his purpose:

> to promote the welfare of the people, me Hammurabi, the devout, god-fearing prince, to cause justice to prevail in the land, to destroy the wicked and the evil, that the strong might not oppress the weak.

Hammurabi's code established rules of procedure for courts of law and regulated property rights and the duties of family members, setting harsh punishments for crimes.

HISTORY DEBATE

Why Women's Status Deteriorated

Despite stereotypical images of cavemen dragging women off by the hair, it is quite clear that hunting and gathering societies did not subordinate women systematically. Women's economic contributions were reflected in a religious culture that often stressed the principle of female creativity. This situation changed as agriculture became established, and the resulting trend occurred everywhere that farming spread. (Interestingly, nonagricultural societies, like the herding peoples in Central Asia, continued to give women a greater voice, which led to some important cultural clashes when these societies encountered agricultural civilizations.)

The historical signs of women's changing status abound. Men did the heaviest agricultural work; Middle Eastern art by 3000 B.C.E. depicted men as always responsible for plowing. Because men's relative economic importance grew, male children were favored and men assumed primary rights of property ownership. Although religions long continued to feature gods and goddesses, emphasis on a primary male creator, like Marduk in the Middle East or Zeus in Greece, increased. Goddesses became more peripheral. The Jewish religion, emphasizing a single god, elevated this principle of a masculine divinity still further. Laws and social habits often followed suit. By 2000 B.C.E., many Middle Eastern women were veiled in the belief that this would help to ensure their sexual fidelity.

The question, of course, is why women's status deteriorated. The study of women's history in many contemporary settings and new debates about women's rights today open the question of the sexual inequality of the past to analysis; the answers no longer seem self-evident. Current explanations refer to several factors, and it is unlikely that such a basic shift in a society's structure resulted from one development alone. Agricultural societies, needing to defend themselves from attack and in their not infrequent territorial conquests, organized more formal military forces, which gave new emphasis to male power. The human birthrate also increased, as agricultural societies found uses for more labor and also needed to compensate for higher disease and mortality rates: This meant that women spent more of their lives bearing and caring for children. In addition, men may have sought greater power to compensate for the decline of the hunt. In the upper classes, at least, the establishment of agricultural property made inheritance more important: Men wanted to know which children were theirs and so tried to regulate women's sexual behavior. We do not know exactly how these various developments worked together. In this sense, the debate is still lively. However, the result of these societal changes is clear. And in most agricultural societies, women's inferiority tended to increase with time, as success prompted more male groups to demonstrate their status by lording over women.

For many centuries during and after the heyday of Babylon, peace and civilization in the Middle East were troubled by the invasions of hunting and herding groups. Indo-European peoples pressed in from the north, starting about 2100 B.C.E. In the Middle East itself, invasions by Semitic peoples from the south were more important, and Semitic peoples and languages increasingly dominated the region. The new arrivals adopted the culture of the conquered peoples as their own so the key features of the civilization persisted. But, large political units declined in favor of smaller city-states or regional kingdoms, particularly during the centuries of greatest turmoil, between 1200 and 900 B.C.E. Thereafter, new invaders, first the Assyrians and then the Persians, created large new empires in the Middle East.

EGYPTIAN CIVILIZATION

A second center of civilization sprang up in northern Africa, along the Nile River. Egyptian civilization, formed by 3000 B.C.E., benefited from the trade and technological influence of Mesopotamia, but it produced a quite different society and culture. Less open to invasion, Egypt retained a unified state throughout most of its history. The king, or pharaoh, possessed immense power. The Egyptian economy was more fully government-directed than its Mesopotamian counterpart, which had a more independent business class. Government control may have been necessary because of the complexity of coordinating irrigation along the Nile. It nonetheless resulted in godlike status for the pharaohs, who built splendid tombs for themselves—the pyramids—from 2700 B.C.E. onward. During periods of weak rule and occasional invasions, Egyptian society suffered a decline, but revivals kept the framework of Egyptian civilization intact until after 1000 B.C.E. At key points, Egyptian influence spread up the Nile to the area now known as the Sudan, with an impact on the later development of African culture. The kingdom of Kush interacted with Egypt and invaded it at some point.

Neither Egyptian science nor the Egyptian alphabet was as elaborate as its Mesopotamian equal, although mathematics was more advanced in this civilization. Egyptian art was exceptionally lively; cheerful and colorful pictures decorated not only the tombs—where the belief in an afterlife made people want to be surrounded by objects of beauty—but also palaces and furnishings. Egyptian architectural forms were also quite influential, not only in Egypt but in other parts of the Mediterranean as well. Egyptian mathematics produced the idea of a day divided into 24 hours, and here too Egypt influenced the development of later Mediterranean cultures.

INDIAN AND CHINESE RIVER VALLEY CIVILIZATIONS

River valley civilizations developed in two other centers. A prosperous urban civilization emerged along the Indus River by 2500 B.C.E., supporting several large cities, including Harappa, whose houses even had running water. Indus River peoples had trading contacts with Mesopotamia, but they developed their own distinctive alphabet and artistic forms. Invasions by Indo-Europeans, however, resulted in such complete destruction of this culture that we know little about its nature or its subsequent

Ancient Egypt and Mesopotamia

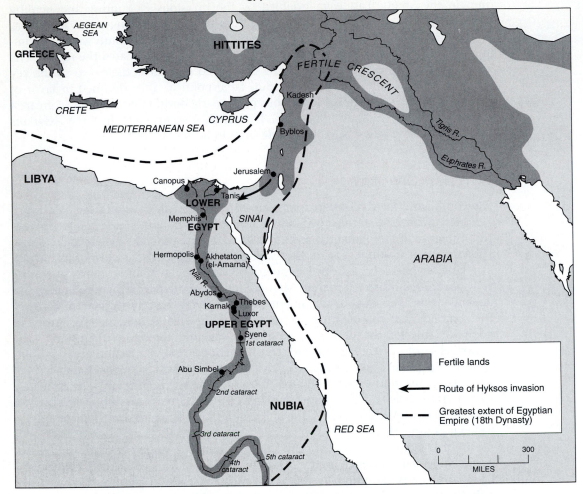

influence on India. Harappan writing, for example, has yet to be deciphered. It remains true that civilization never had to be fully reinvented in India. The Indo-European invaders combined their religious and political ideas with those that had taken root in the early cities. In recent times, Indians' pride in their early civilized history has become an important part of their national identity.

Civilization along the Hwang He (Yellow River) in China developed in considerable isolation, although some overland trading contact with India and the Middle East did develop. Hwang He civilization was the subject of much later Chinese legend, which praised the godlike kings of early civilization, starting with the mythic ancestor of the Chinese, P'an Ku. The Chinese had an unusually elaborate concept of their remote origins, and they began early to record a part-fact, part-fiction history of their early kings. What is clear is the following: First, the existence of an organized

UNDERSTANDING CULTURES

Uses and Varieties

A society's culture involves its basic beliefs and values, and the styles it uses to express these values. All societies, whether civilizations or not, have cultures. Cultures profoundly shape the way people behave. For example, a recent study showed that when a French person becomes jealous, he or she gets angry. In a similar situation, a Dutch person grows sad, whereas the typical American consults with others to determine if he or she seems to be acting strangely. All responses involve the same emotion, but different cultures inspire vastly different reactions. Another recent study showed that Americans and Jamaicans try hard to conceal jealousy, whereas the Chinese feel that jealousy can be usefully expressed.

Human beings rely heavily on cultures because, as a species, we have relatively few instincts. We have to learn a lot, which explains why people can adapt to so many more environments than most complex animals, but also why beliefs and values play such a significant role in our lives.

Cultures obviously vary from one place to the next. Sometimes, they respond to different geographical environments. Always, they reflect different past traditions, although we do not always fully understand why the traditions differed initially. Sumerian culture, for example, was much gloomier than Egyptian, with more of a focus on punishments after death and on the tragic potential of human life. Egyptians were more optimistic, their art more colorful and cheerful. Was this because the Nile River provided more predictable prosperity? Did Egypt's orderly government and freedom from frequent invasion encourage more orderly thinking, or was it the other way around? Whatever the case, Sumerian pessimism ultimately had greater influence. It was the story of a Sumerian flood that ultimately entered the Jewish Bible as a sign of divine punishment. Cultural differences can have surprisingly durable results.

state that carefully regulated irrigation in the fertile but flood-prone river valley. Second, by about 2000 B.C.E. the Chinese had produced an advanced technology and developed an elaborate intellectual life. They had learned how to ride horses and were skilled in pottery; they used bronze well and by 1000 B.C.E. had introduced iron, which they soon learned to work with coal. Their writing progressed from knotted ropes to scratches of lines on bone to the invention of ideographic symbols. Science, particularly astronomy, arose early. Chinese art emphasized delicate designs, and the Chinese claim an early interest in music. Because of limits on building materials in the region, the Chinese did not construct many massive monuments, choosing to live in simple houses built of mud. By about 1500 B.C.E., a line of kings called the

Statuette of a mother goddess from Harappa, Indus River.

Shang ruled over the Hwang He valley, and these rulers did construct some impressive tombs and palaces. Invasions disrupted the Shang dynasty and caused a temporary decline in civilization. However, there was less of a break between the river valley society and the later, fuller development of civilization in China than occurred in other centers.

THE HERITAGE OF THE RIVER VALLEY CIVILIZATIONS

Many accomplishments of the river valley civilizations had a lasting impact. Monuments such as the Egyptian pyramids have long been regarded as one of the wonders of the world. Other achievements, although more prosaic, are fundamental to world history even today: the invention of the wheel, the taming of the horse, the creation of usable alphabets and writing implements, the production of key mathematical concepts such as square roots, the development of well-organized monarchies and bureaucracies, and the invention of functional calendars and other divisions of time.

Early Chinese art. An elaborate clay vase, imitating bronze, from the Shang dynasty. (Freer Gallery of Art, The Smithsonian Institute, Washington, DC, Early Chinese Art, 39.42)

These basic achievements, along with the awe that the early civilizations continue to inspire, are vital legacies to the whole of human history. Almost all the major alphabets in the world today are derived from the writing forms pioneered in the river valleys, apart from the even more durable concept of writing itself. Almost all later civilizations, then, built on the massive foundations first constructed in the river valleys.

Despite these accomplishments, most of the river valley civilizations were in decline by 1000 B.C.E. The civilizations had flourished for as many as 2500 years, although of course with periodic disruptions and revivals. But, particularly in India, the new waves of invasion did produce something of a break in the history of civilization, a dividing line between the river valley pioneers and later cultures.

And, this break raises one final question: Besides the vital achievements—the fascinating monuments and the indispensable advances in technology, science, and

HISTORY DEBATE

Agriculture as Progress?

The rise of agriculture used to be presented in strongly progressive terms, which is a common way, in many modern cultures, to think about history. With agriculture, technology improved, specialization became more possible, and so on. People became capable of sustaining larger populations, and with agricultural surpluses they generated more complex institutions and grander monuments. Could these measurements be disputed?

The answer is yes. Many recent historians, perhaps a bit more pessimistic about progress generally, have pointed out agriculture's drawbacks. With agriculture, more people could be born, but diseases also spread far more widely. In addition, people had to work harder. Environmental deterioration escalated, although not of course to modern levels. We have seen that the first center of copper production in Europe, along the Danube valley, led to extensive deforestation, such that the fuel supply was destroyed and the industry collapsed. Extensive agriculture needed to support Indus river cities opened the land to erosion and flooding because of the overuse of the soil and removal of trees. Again, the result was economic deterioration and a decline in civilization even before new invasions occurred. On another front, social inequality, and particularly inequality between men and women, increased with agriculture, in ways which even today have not been fully repaired. It is easy to regard agriculture as responsible for a deterioration in the human experience—even though it led to significant population growth. One critic has suggested, not entirely facetiously, that the only reason agriculture caught on was because it allowed fermented grain and so periodic inebriation.

Is there an alternative to interpreting agriculture as either progress or decline? Are there other examples of major technological change that raise similar issues about the quality of key results?

art—What legacies did the river valley civilizations impart for later ages? The question is particularly important for the Middle East and Egypt. In India, we must frankly admit much ignorance about possible links between Indus River accomplishments and what came later; in China, there is a definite connection between the first civilization and subsequent forms. Indeed, the new dynasty in China, the Zhou, took over from the Shang about 1000 B.C.E., ruling a loose coalition of regional lords; recorded Chinese history flowed smoothly at this point. But, what was the legacy of Mesopotamia and Egypt for later civilizations in or near their centers?

Europeans, even North Americans, are sometimes prone to claim these cultures as the "origins" of the Western civilization in which we live. These claims should not be taken too literally. It is not altogether clear that either Egypt or Mesopotamia contributed much to later political traditions, although the Roman Empire emulated the concept of a godlike king, as evidenced in the trappings of the office, and the existence of strong city-state governments in the Middle East itself continued to be significant. Ideas about slavery may also have been passed on from these early civilizations. Specific scientific achievements are vital, but scholars argue over how much of a connection exists between Mesopotamian and Egyptian science and later Greek thinking, aside from certain techniques of measuring time or charting the stars. Some historians of philosophy have asserted a basic division between a Mesopotamian and Chinese understanding of nature, which they claim affected later civilizations around the Mediterranean in contrast to China. Mesopotamians were prone to stress a gap between humankind and nature, whereas Chinese thinking developed along ideas of basic harmony. It is possible, then, that some fundamental thinking helped shape later outlooks, but the continuities here are not easy to assess. Mesopotamian art and Egyptian architecture had a more measurable influence on Greek styles, and through these, in turn, later European and Muslim cultures. The Greeks thus learned much about temple building from the Egyptians, whose culture had influenced island civilizations, such as Crete, which then affected later Greek styles.

There was a final connection between early and later civilizations in the form of regional cultures that sprang up under the influence of Mesopotamia and Egypt, along the eastern shores of the Mediterranean mainly after 1200 B.C.E. Although the great empires from Sumer through Babylon were disrupted and the Egyptian state finally declined, civilization in the Middle East had spread widely enough to encourage a set of smaller cultures capable of surviving and even flourishing after the great empires became weak. These cultures produced important innovations that would affect later civilizations in the Middle East and throughout the Mediterranean. They also created a diverse array of regional identities that would continue to mark the Middle East even as other forces, like the Roman Empire or the later religion of Islam, took center stage. Several of these small cultures proved immensely durable, and in their complexity and capacity to survive, they would influence other parts of the world as well.

A people called the Phoenicians, for example, devised a greatly simplified alphabet with 22 letters around 1300 B.C.E.; this alphabet, in turn, became the predecessor of Greek and Latin alphabets. The Phoenicians also improved the Egyptian numbering system and, as great traders, set up colony cities in North Africa and on the coasts of Europe. Another regional group, the Lydians, first introduced coined money.

The most influential of the smaller Middle Eastern groups, however, were the Jews, who gave the world the first clearly developed monotheistic religion. We have seen that early religions, both before and after the beginnings of civilization, were polytheistic, claiming that many gods and goddesses worked to control nature and human destiny. The Jews, a Semitic people influenced by Babylonian civilization, settled near the Mediterranean around 1200 B.C.E. The Jewish state was small and relatively weak, retaining independence only when other parts of the Middle East were in political turmoil. What was distinctive about this culture was its firm belief that a single God, Jehovah, guided the destinies of the Jewish people. Priests and prophets defined and emphasized this belief, and their history of God's guidance of the Jews formed the basis for the Hebrew Bible. The Jewish religion and moral code persisted even as the Jewish state suffered domination by a series of foreign rulers, from 772 B.C.E. until the Romans seized the state outright in 63 B.C.E. Jewish monotheism has sustained a distinctive Jewish culture to our own day; it would also serve as a key basis for the development of both Christianity and Islam as major world religions.

Because Judaism stressed God's special compact with the chosen Jewish people, there was no premium placed on converting non-Jews. This belief helps explain the durability of the Jewish faith itself; it also kept the Jewish people in a minority position in the Middle East as a whole. However, the elaboration of monotheism had a wide, if not immediate, significance. In Jewish hands, the concept of God became less humanlike, more abstract. This represented a basic change in not only religion but also humankind's overall outlook. Jehovah had not only a power but also a rationality far different from what the traditional gods of the Middle East or Egypt possessed. These gods were whimsical and capricious; Jehovah was orderly and just, and individuals would know what to expect if they obeyed God's rules. God was also linked to ethical conduct, to proper moral behavior. Religion for the Jews was a way of life, not merely a set of rituals and ceremonies. The full impact of this religious transformation on Middle Eastern civilization would be realized only later, when Jewish beliefs were embraced by other, proselytizing faiths. However, the basic concept of monotheistic religion was one of the legacies of the end of the first great civilization period to the new cultures that would soon arise.

CONCLUSION: THE FIRST CIVILIZATIONS

Overall, then, the river valley civilizations, flourishing for many centuries, created a basic set of tools, intellectual concepts such as writing and mathematics, and political forms that would persist and spread to other parts of Europe, Asia, and Africa. Invasion in India, and invasion and political decline in Egypt, marked a fairly firm break between river valley institutions and those that would later develop. Hwang He civilization, in contrast, flowed more fully into the more extensive Chinese civilization that would follow. The Middle East, where civilization had first been born, provided the most complex heritage of all. Here too there was a break between the initial series of riverine empires and the civilizations of Greece and Persia that would later dominate the region. However, the development of smaller cultures provided a bridge between the river valley period and later Middle Eastern society, producing vital new inventions and ideas. The smaller cultures also generated a deeply entrenched network of regional or minority values and institutions that would continue to make the Middle East a complex, vibrant, and sometimes troubled part of the world.

One final result of the first, long period of human civilization is certainly clear: a pattern of division among the world's peoples. The diffusion of *Homo sapiens sapiens* set the initial stage. Small groups of people spread to almost every corner of the world but maintained little contact with each other thereafter. Separate languages and cultures developed widely. The rise of agriculture stimulated new links, and the

Timeline: River Valley Civilizations (All dates = B.C.E., or Before the Common Era)

Mesopotamia	Coast Cultures	Egypt	Indus River	Hwang Ho
3500–2600 Sumerian kingdom, development of cuneiform writing.		**3200–2780** Unification of regional kingdoms under one pharaoh.	**3000–1300** Indus River cities.	
2600–2420 Akkadian invasions and empire.		**2100–1788** Expansion to Sudan, Palestine.		
2050–1750 Kingdom of Babylon.				
2000 Writing of the *Gilgamesh*, world's first-known heroic epic.				**2000? ff.** Hsia dynasty, heroic myths of golden age.
1700 Hammurabi and his code.				
1500 Spread of use of iron.				**1500–1000** Shang dynasty, use of iron.
	1400–774 Rise of Phoenician cities, colonies; 1300, alphabet.		**1300 ff.** Aryan (Indo-European) invasions.	
1200–900 Particularly intense invasions.	**1225–1200** Moses: spread of Jewish tribes in Israel.			
	1150–130 Writing of books of Old Testament.	**1090 ff.** Decline of pharaohs, loss of territory.		**1000** Zhou dynasty.
933–605 Assyrian Empire.	**933–722** Kingdom of Israel.	**800** Kushites rule Egypt.		

spread of farming and new technologies began to cut into local isolation. Trade soon entered the picture: Although most commerce centered within a region, linking a city to its hinterland, a few routes traveled greater distances. By 1000 B.C.E., Phoenicians traded with Britain for metals (they bought lead to make bronze), while Chinese silk was reaching Egypt. Here we have one of the basic themes of world history: steadily proliferating contacts against a background of often fierce local identity.

The rise of civilization further reduced local autonomy, as kings and priests tried to spread trade contacts and cultural forms and warred to gain new territory. Civilization itself was an integrating force at a larger regional level, although, as we have seen in the Middle East, smaller identities persisted. However, individual civilizations had only sporadic contacts with each other. They, and their leading institutions and cultural forms, developed separately. Thus, four distinct centers of civilization developed (five, if the emerging Olmec culture in Mexico, discussed in Chapter 12, is included), each with widely varied patterns, from style of writing to beliefs about nature. The early civilizations shared important features, including cities, trade, and writing, that helped them meet the common basic definition of civilization in the first place. They also frequently developed some mutual relationships, although the Hwang He culture in China is one example of a civilization that flourished in relative isolation. Egypt and Mesopotamia, in particular, had recurrent contacts through trade and war. But, the values or belief systems of each civilization, and their manifestation in political and business styles, were not so easily disseminated. Even relatively close neighbors, such as Egypt and Mesopotamia, developed radically different political attitudes, beliefs about death, and artistic styles. Civilization and considerable diversity thus co-existed hand in hand.

SUGGESTED WEBSITES

On early human life forms, up to *Homo sapiens sapiens,* see *http://www.iinet.net.au/~chawkins/heaven.htm;* for a virtual tour of Egyptian cities, see *http://www.ancientegypt.co.uk/menu.html;* on the Gilgamesh epic, see *http://www.wsu.edu/~dee/MESO/GILG.HTM;* on the evolution of Hindu epics and beliefs, see *http://campus.northpark.edu/history/WebChron/India/India.html.*

SUGGESTED READINGS

Two collections of sources offer some materials on early China and India: W. T. De Bary, Jr., et al., eds., *Sources of Chinese Tradition* (1960) and W. T. De Bary, Jr., et al., eds., *Sources of Indian Tradition* (1958). On prehistory, see Robert J. Wenke, *Patterns in Prehistory* (1984); Brian Fagan, *The Journey from Eden: The Peopling of Our World* (1990); Richard Adams, *Prehistoric Mesoamerica (1991);* and Chris Scarre, ed., *Smithsonian Timelines of the Ancient World* (1994). On early civilizations, see C. L. Redman, *The Rise of Civilization: From Early Farmers to Urban Society in the Ancient Near East* (1988); H. Crawford, *Sumer and the Sumerians* (1991); J. Bright, *A History of Israel* (1981); and A. Nibbi, *Ancient Egypt and Some Eastern Neighbors* (1981). On India and China, see G. O. Possehl, ed., *Harappan Civilization: A Contemporary Perspective* (1982); V. & R. Allchin, *The Rise of Civilization in India and Pakistan* (1982); Ping-ti Ho, *Cradle of the East: An Inquiry into the Indigenous Origins of Techniques and Ideas of Neolithic and Early History in China* (1975); Wolfram Eberhard, *History of China* (1977 ed.);

and K. C. Wu, *The Chinese Heritage* (1982). On the crucial issue of gender, see M. Ehrenberg, *Women in Prehistory* (1989) and G. Robins, *Women in Ancient Egypt* (1993). On other key topics, refer to Richard Gabriel, *The Culture of War: Invention and Early Development* (1991); and Paul Bairach, *Cities and Economic Development: From the Dawn of History to the Present* (1988). For a challenging statement on the legacy of African and Middle Eastern societies to later Greece, read Martin Bernal, *Black Athena*: *The Africanistic Roots of Classical Civilization* (1987). On the environment, see I. G. Simmons, *Environmental History* (1993). On patterns of contact, see Luce Boulnois, *The Silk Road* (1966); Philip D. Curtin, *Cross-Cultural Trade in World History* (1984); Xinru Liu, *Ancient India and Ancient China: Trade and Religious Exchanges* (1988); and Shereen Ratnagar, *Encounter: The Westerly Trade of the Harappan Civilization* (1981). The science and technology of the ancient world are discussed in Richard Bulliet, *The Camel and the Wheel* (1975); George Ifrah, *From One to Zero: A Universal History of Numbers* (1985); and Edgardo Marcorini, ed., *The History of Science and Technology: A Narrative Chronology* (1988).

The Classical Period, 1000 B.C.E.–500 C.E.

INTRODUCTION: NEW ISSUES FOR EXPANDING SOCIETIES

Having quickly reviewed the hundreds of thousands of years of human prehistory and the 3000 years of developments in the river valley civilizations, we now slow down our discussion considerably. In the remainder of this book, we deal with the most recent 3000 years of human experience, from roughly 1000 years before the common era (B.C.E.) until the present. There are several reasons for this radical change of pace. Available knowledge is one. Civilizations over the past 3000 years have produced far more records than their predecessors. We not only know more about events such as wars and rebellions, but we also have a fuller sense of how ordinary people in these societies thought about daily issues such as health and family. More important is the fact that civilizations created after 1000 B.C.E. have direct links to civilizations which exist today. Chinese civilization, indeed, flows quite coherently from the middle of the Zhou dynasty (500 B.C.E.) to the present, with surges and declines and significant changes but with equally important connections to preceding events. Even in Western society, where there have been far more shattering disruptions than in China, we can look back to Greek and Roman civilizations and find philosophies and political institutions directly related to contemporary ideas and forms.

The period in the history of civilization after the decline of the river valley cultures is known as *classical;* it runs from about 1000 B.C.E. until the fifth century C.E. In three parts of the world—China, India, and the Mediterranean area (which extends from the Middle East to southern Europe and North Africa)—new or renewed civilizations arose that proved very durable. These civilizations did not touch all the world's peoples, although they spread well beyond the boundaries of the river valleys. It is important to remember that the history of classical civilization does not reflect the whole of world history during this period, because it does not include northern Europeans, central Asians, most Africans below the Sahara, and of course all American Indians. Historical developments in these regions were significant, but they followed more diverse patterns.

Also during the classical period, new empires arose around the Tigris-Euphrates valley, resuming the developments of those started by the Sumerians and Babylonians. First the Assyrians and then the Persians established large empires that at times extended through the Middle East and even into Europe and India. These empires boasted not only great power but also important new religious ideas and artistic styles that influenced both Greek and Indian cultures later on.

The three classical civilizations of China, India, and the Mediterranean left the most substantial legacies, however, and they also included the largest population concentrations in the world at that time. Moreover, all three classical civilizations set in motion institutions and values that would continue to shape these key parts of the world long after the classical period was over. Some of the continuing diversity of our world is the result of distinctions created during the classical period. Examples include the intense political centralization of the Chinese in contrast to the greater regionalism of Indian political life, or the emotional restraint the Chinese and Japa-

Centers of Classical Civilizations, First Century C.E.

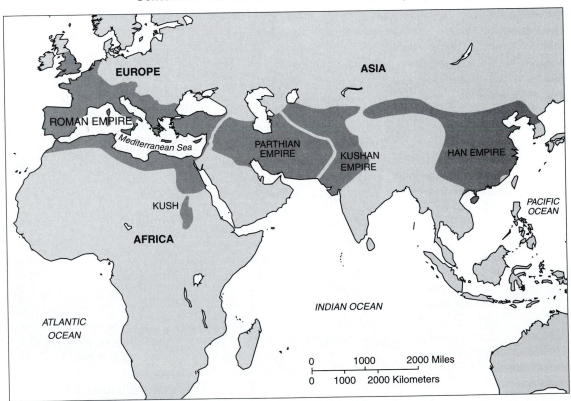

nese were taught to exhibit compared with the greater display of feeling allowed many Mediterranean peoples.

All three classical civilizations built on the achievements of the river valley societies. In the Mediterranean, Greeks benefited from the influence of the earlier Minoan civilization, which had been centered on the Greek islands and partially derived from the greater Egyptian culture. Here, and still more obviously in India and China, classical peoples relied on the technologies developed in the river valley societies; they also utilized earlier artistic styles and possibly some more abstract ideas. And, of course, they adapted earlier writing systems and mathematical concepts.

However, the classical civilizations were not, in the final analysis, simple continuations of the earlier societies from which they derived. Use of iron weapons, first by invading peoples, gave governments a new military edge. Classical civilizations also created larger political structures, capable of controlling more territory. They shifted their geographical base: The center of Indian development moved from the Indus to the Ganges River; China expanded to include the rice-growing Yangtze River (Chiang Jiang) as well as the Hwang He. All the classical civilizations improved on earlier technologies for agriculture, manufacturing, and urban life. They established more elaborate philosophical and religious systems and expanded scientific and mathematical knowledge. The sophistication of these achievements helps account for the enduring influence of classical civilizations today, not only in the regions where they flourished but also in other areas of the world to which their heritage ultimately spread.

Expansion and integration dominated the outcomes of classical civilizations, even though each created a distinctive specific culture. Each classical civilization spread beyond a regional center to embrace a growing diversity of people and a growing amount of territory. This, in turn, created the challenge of building institutions and beliefs that could integrate these peoples, without necessarily homogenizing them. Integration included politics, so it was no accident that massive empires grew, at least toward the end of the classical era, within each center. Integration also included growing internal trade. And it also came to involve cultural systems deliberately designed to draw people together in common beliefs. The problem of integrating new territories, and the processes that resulted, led to the fundamental characteristics of the classical period.

Expansion resulted from massive population growth and encouraged the further development of the classical civilizations. In the final centuries before the common era, China's population tripled, to 60 million. At 14 B.C.E., the Roman Empire had a population of about 54 million people and India about 50 million. Expansion included the migration of farming populations from the regional center to escape crowding and deliberate commercial efforts to seek new sources of food supply—the factor behind Greek colonies scattered around the Mediterranean. It also included explicit military expansion, particularly by the great empires of China, India, Greece, and Rome, which often resulted in significant resettlement efforts. Military conquest by these three civilizations was backed by well-organized political units and often the advantage in weaponry that iron-based technology provided.

In the Mediterranean, expansion was actually aided by the various diseases settlers brought to the new lands: It reduced local populations and hence the pressure

TIMELINE: Classical Civilizations

China	India	Mediterranean (Greece and Rome)
		1700 B.C.E. Indo-European invasions.
	1500–1000 B.C.E. Recovery from Aryan invasions, Vedic Age, formative period.	**1400 B.C.E.** Kingdom of Mycenae.
	1000–600 B.C.E. Epic Age, beginnings of early Hinduism, *Upanishads*.	**800 B.C.E.** Rise of Greek city-states and economy; Homeric epics, *Iliad* and *Odyssey*; beginnings of Rome.
1029–258 B.C.E. Zhou dynasty.	**c. 563–483 B.C.E.** Gautama Buddha.	**509–450 B.C.E.** Beginnings of Roman republic; Twelve Tables of Law.
700 B.C.E. Zhou decline.		**500–449 B.C.E.** Greek defeat of Persia; spread of Athenian Empire.
c. 500 B.C.E. Lao-zi and Daoism.		**470–430 B.C.E.** Athens at height; Pericles, Phidias, Sophocles, Socrates, etc.
551–478 B.C.E. Confucius.		
c. 500 B.C.E. Editing of the Five Classics.		**431–404 B.C.E.** Peloponnesian Wars.
	322–184 B.C.E. Maurya dynasty.	**330 B.C.E. ff.** Macedonian Empire, Alexander the Great.
221–202 B.C.E. Qin dynasty, Great Wall.		**330–100 B.C.E.** Hellenistic period.
202 B.C.E.–220 C.E. Han dynasty.		**264–146 B.C.E.** Rome's Punic Wars.
140–87 B.C.E. Rule of Wu Ti; increased bureaucracy, examinations, spread of Confucianism.	**30 B.C.E.–220 C.E.** Kushan rule, Hindu beliefs develop.	**133 B.C.E.** Decline of Roman republic.
c. 100 B.C.E. Invention of paper.		**27 B.C.E.** Augustus Caesar, rise of Roman Empire.
220–589 C.E. Nomadic invasions, disorder, considerable spread of Buddhism.		**180 C.E.** Death of Marcus Aurelius, beginning of empire's decline.
	320–535 C.E. Gupta dynasty.	**313 C.E.** Constantine adopts Christianity.
		476 C.E. Fall of Rome.

The World According to Ptolemy, About 150 C.E.

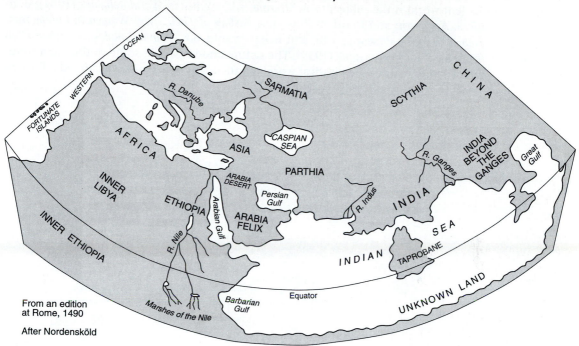

From an edition
at Rome, 1490

After Nordensköld

or need to deal with local diversities. Expansion in China and India meant embracing large local populations, already resistant to the contagions of agricultural society. This resulted in greater attention to social, cultural, and political institutions. Both China and India, though in very different ways, worked harder on the process of integration than Greece and Rome. Everywhere, however, the need to innovate in response to expansion, to draw peoples and territories into manageable interaction, determined many of the key characteristics of this period of world history.

Each classical civilization operated separately for the most part. Trade brought silk from China to the Middle East and the Roman Empire, but while such luxuries were welcomed, no economy was deeply affected by international commerce. There was important cultural exchange between Greece and India, but India's adaptation of Greek artistic style and the Mediterranean's adoption of Indian religious concepts were unusual occurrences. For the most part, developments within each expanding civilization, more than contacts between them, marked this phase of world history.

SUGGESTED READINGS

There are several useful treatments of cross-cultural themes and topics in antiquity. See, for example, Richard A. Gabriel, *War in the Ancient World* (1992); W. H. McNeill, *Plagues and People* (1977); Irving Rouse, *Migrations in Prehistory* (1986); and Chester G.

Starr, *The Influence of Sea-power on Ancient History* (1989). The role of women in the ancient world is the subject of A. Sharma, ed., *Women in World Religions* (1987); Bonnie S. Anderson and Judith P. Zinsser, *A History of Their Own: Women in Europe from Prehistory to the Present* (1988); and Bella Vivante, ed., *Women's Roles in Ancient Civilizations: A Reference Guide* (1999). The nature and impact of some of the most influential individuals of the classical world are the focus of S. N. Eisenstadt, ed., *The Origins and Diversity of the Axial Age* (1986).

Classical Civilization: China

2

FOCAL POINTS

The emergence of a classical civilization in China involved the spread of Chinese institutions and values over a large area. These institutions and values also changed dramatically over time. Conditions around 500 B.C.E. were much different from those of 100 C.E., and comparing these two points within the classical period helps us determine basic trends that occurred. How did Chinese leaders alter their government to successfully rule over an expanded territory? How did they change the ways in which they expressed their values? What were the most distinctive features of Chinese society by the end of the classical period, as a result of shifts in institutions and values? Which of the classical achievements were most likely to endure into later periods? How did China position itself in relation to the rest of the world?

INTRODUCTION

China generated the first of the great classical societies. The region remained rather isolated. This limited its ability to learn from other cultures, but also spared it frequent invasion and encouraged an intense, and distinctive, Chinese identity. The decline of the Shang dynasty did not result in as much internal chaos as did invasions of parts of the Middle East and particularly India. Hence, the Chinese could build more strongly on Hwang He precedents. Particularly important was a general, if somewhat vague, world view developed by Hwang He thinkers and accepted as a standard approach in later Chinese thinking. This intellectual heritage stressed the basic harmony of nature: Every feature is balanced by an opposite, every *yin* by a *yang*. Thus for hot there is cold, for male, female. According to this philosophy, an individual should seek a way, called *Dao,* to relate to this harmony, avoiding excess and appreciating the balance of opposites. Individuals and human institutions existed within this world of balanced nature, not, as in later Mediterranean philosophy, on the outside. Chinese traditions about balance, Dao, and yin/yang were intrinsic to diverse philosophies and religions established in the classical period itself, and they provided some unity among various schools of thought in China.

Despite important cultural continuity, classical China did not simply maintain earlier traditions. The formative centuries of classical Chinese history were witness to a great many changes, as the religious and particularly the political habits of the Shang kingdom were substantially modified as part of building the world's largest classical empire. As a result of these new centuries of development, resulting in much diversity but often painful conflict, the Chinese emerged with an unusually well-integrated system in which government, philosophy, economic incentives, the family, and the individual were intended to blend into a harmonious whole.

PATTERNS IN CLASSICAL CHINA

Of all the societies in the world today, it is China that has maintained the clearest links to its classical past—a past that has been a source of pride but also the cause of some problems of adaptation. Already in the period of classical Chinese history, a pattern was set in motion that lasted until the early part of the twentieth century. A family of kings, called a "dynasty," would start its rule of China with great vigor, developing strong political institutions and encouraging an active economy. Subsequently, the dynasty grew weaker and tax revenues declined, while social divisions increased in the larger society. Internal rebellions and sometimes invasions from the outside hastened the dynasty's decline. As the ruling dynasty declined, another dynasty emerged, usually from the family of a successful general, invader, or peasant rebel, and the pattern would start anew. Small wonder that many Chinese conceive of history in terms of cycles, in contrast to the Western tendency to think of steady progress from past to present.

Three dynastic cycles cover the many centuries of classical China: the Zhou, the Qin, and the Han. The Zhou dynasty lasted from 1029 to 258 B.C.E. Although lengthy, this dynasty flourished, in fact, only until about 700 B.C.E.; it was then beset by a decline in the political infrastructure and frequent invasions by nomadic peoples from border regions. Even during its strong centuries, the Zhou did not establish a powerful government, ruling instead through alliances with regional princes and noble families. The dynasty initially came into China from the north, displacing its predecessor, the Shang rulers. The alliance systems the Zhou used as the basis for their rule were standard in agricultural kingdoms. (We will see similar forms later emerge in Japan, India, Europe, and Africa.) Rulers lacked the means to control their territories directly and so gave large regional estates to members of their families and other supporters, hoping that their loyalties would remain intact. The supporters, in exchange for land, were supposed to provide the central government with troops and tax revenues. This was China's feudal period, with rulers depending on a network of loyalties and obligations to and from their landlord-vassals. Such a system was, of course, vulnerable to regional disloyalties, and the ultimate decline of the Zhou dynasty occurred when regional landowning aristocrats solidified their own power base and disregarded the central government.

The Zhou did, however, contribute in several ways to the development of Chinese politics and culture in their active early centuries. First, they extended the territory of China by taking over the Yangtze River valley. This stretch of territory, from the Hwang He to the Yangtze, became China's core—often called the "Middle Kingdom." It provided rich agricultural lands plus the benefits of two different agricultures—wheat-growing in the north, rice-growing in the south—a diversity that encouraged population growth. The territorial expansion obviously complicated the problems of central rule, for communication and transport from the capital to the outlying regions were difficult. This is why the Zhou relied so heavily on the loyalty of regional supporters.

Despite these circumstances, the Zhou did actually heighten the focus on the central government itself. Zhou rulers claimed direct links to the Shang rulers. They also asserted that heaven had transferred its mandate to rule China to the Zhou emperors. This political concept of a mandate from heaven remained a key justification for Chinese imperial rule from the Zhou onward. Known as Sons of Heaven, the emperors lived in a world of awe-inspiring pomp and ceremony.

The Zhou worked to provide greater cultural unity in their empire. They discouraged some of the primitive religious practices of the Hwang He civilization, banning human sacrifice and urging more restrained ceremonies to worship the gods. They also promoted linguistic unity, beginning the process by which a standard spoken language, ultimately called Mandarin Chinese, would prevail over the entire Middle Kingdom. This resulted in the largest single group of people speaking the same language in the world at this time. Regional dialects and languages remained, but educated officials began to rely on the single Mandarin form. Oral epics and stories in Chinese, many gradually recorded in written form, aided in the development of a common cultural currency.

Increasing cultural unity helps explain why, when the Zhou empire began to fail, scholars were able to use philosophical ideas to lessen the impact of growing political confusion. Indeed, the political crisis spurred efforts to define and articulate Chinese culture. During the late sixth and early fifth centuries B.C.E., the philosopher known in the West as Confucius (see p. 48) wrote an elaborate statement on political ethics, providing the core of China's distinctive philosophical heritage. Other writers and religious leaders participated in this great period of cultural creativity, which later reemerged as a set of central beliefs throughout the Middle Kingdom.

Cultural innovation did not, however, reverse the prolonged and painful Zhou downfall. Regional rulers formed independent armies, ultimately reducing the emperors to little more than figureheads. Between 402 and 201 B.C.E., a period known aptly enough as the Era of the Warring States, the Zhou system disintegrated.

At this point, China might have gone the way of civilizations such as India, where centralized government was more the exception than the rule. But, a new dynasty arose to reverse the process of political decay. One regional ruler deposed the last Zhou emperor and within 35 years made himself sole ruler of China. He took the title Qin Shih Huangdi, or First Emperor. The dynastic name, Qin, conferred on the whole country its name of China. Shih Huangdi was a brutal ruler, but effective given the circumstances of internal disorder. He understood that China's problem lay in the regional power of the aristocrats, and like many later centralizers in world history, he worked vigorously to undo this force. He ordered nobles to leave their regions and appear at his court, assuming control of their feudal estates. China was organized into large provinces ruled by bureaucrats appointed by the emperor; and Shih Huangdi was careful to select his officials from nonaristocratic groups, so that they would owe their power to him and not dare to develop their own independent bases. Under Shih Huangdi's rule, powerful armies crushed regional resistance.

The First Emperor followed up on centralization by extending Chinese territory to the south, reaching present-day Hong Kong on the South China Sea and even influencing northern Vietnam. In the north, to guard against barbarian invasions, Shih Huangdi built a Great Wall, extending over 3000 miles, wide enough for chariots to move along its crest. This wall, probably the largest construction project in human history, was built by forced labor, conscripted by the central bureaucracy from among the peasantry.

The Qin dynasty was responsible for a number of innovations in Chinese politics and culture. To determine the empire's resources, Shih Huangdi ordered a national census, which provided data for the calculation of tax revenues and labor service. The government standardized coinage, weights, and measures through the entire realm. Even the length of axles on carts was regulated to promote coherent road planning. The government also made Chinese written script uniform, completing the process of creating a single basic language in which all educated Chinese could communicate. The government furthered agriculture, sponsoring new irrigation projects, and promoted manufacturing, particularly that of silk cloth. The activist government also attacked formal culture, burning many books. Thinking, according to Shih Huangdi, was likely to be subversive to his autocratic rule.

Although it created many durable features of Chinese government, the Qin dynasty was short-lived. Shih Huangdi's attacks on intellectuals, and particularly the high taxes needed to support military expansion and the construction of the Great Wall, made him fiercely unpopular. One opponent described the First Emperor as a monster who "had the heart of a tiger and a wolf. He killed men as though he

China's Great Wall at Nanken. Over 6000 kilometers long, the Great Wall of China was built during the Qin dynasty and has often been repaired.

thought he could never finish, he punished men as though he were afraid he would never get around to them all." On the emperor's death, in 210 B.C.E., massive revolts organized by aggrieved peasants broke out. One peasant leader defeated other opponents and in 202 B.C.E. established the third dynasty of classical China, the Han.

And it was the Han dynasty, which lasted over 400 years, to 220 C.E., that rounded out China's basic political and intellectual structure. Han rulers retained the centralized administration of the Qin, but sought to reduce the brutal repression of that period. Like many dynasties during the first flush of power, early Han rulers expanded Chinese territory, pushing into Korea, Indochina, and central Asia. This expansion gave rise to direct contact with India and also allowed the Chinese to develop contact with the Parthian empire in the Middle East, through which trade with the Roman Empire around the Mediterranean was conducted. The most famous Han ruler, Wu Ti (140–87 B.C.E.), enforced peace throughout much of the continent of Asia, rather like the peace the Roman Empire would bring to the Mediterranean region a hundred years later, but embracing even more territory and a far larger population. Peace brought great prosperity to China itself. A Han historian conveys the self-satisfied, confident tone of the dynasty:

> The nation had met with no major disturbances so that, except in times of flood or drought, every person was well supplied and every family had enough to get along on.

China Under Emperor Wu, About 100 B.C.E.

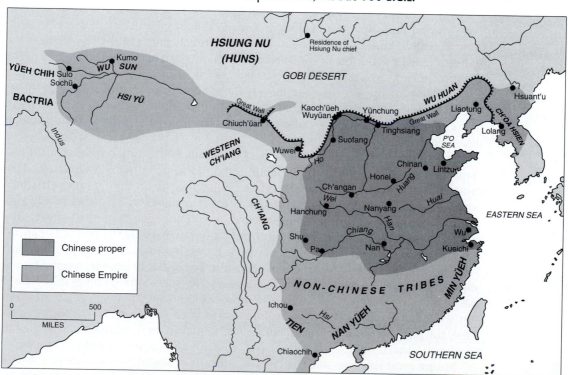

The granaries in the cities and the countryside were full and the government treasures were running over with wealth. In the capital the strings of cash had stacked up by the hundreds of millions until . . . they could no longer be counted. In the central granary of the government, new grain was heaped on top of the old until the building was full and the grain overflowed and piled up outside, where it spoiled and became unfit to eat. . . . Even the keepers of the community gates ate fine grain and meat.

Under the Han dynasty, the workings of the state bureaucracy also improved and the government was linked to formal training that emphasized the values of Confucian philosophy. Reversing the Qin dynasty's policies, Wu Ti urged support for Confucianism, seeing it as a vital supplement to formal measures on the government's part; shrines were established to promote the worship of the ancient philosopher as a god.

The quality of Han rule declined after about two centuries. Central control weakened, and invasions from central Asia, spearheaded by a nomadic people called the Huns, who had long threatened China's northern borders, overturned the dynasty entirely. Between 220 and 589 C.E., China was in a state of chaos. Order and stability were finally restored, but by then the classical or formative period of Chinese civilization had ended. Well before the Han collapse, however, China had established distinctive political structures and cultural values of unusual clarity, capable, as it turned out, of surviving even three centuries of renewed confusion.

POLITICAL INSTITUTIONS

The Qin and Han dynasties of classical China established a distinctive, and remarkably successful, kind of government. The Qin stressed central authority, whereas the Han expanded the powers of the bureaucracy. More than any other factor, it was the structure of this government that explained how such a vast territory could be effectively ruled—for the Chinese empire was indeed the largest political system in the classical world. This structure would change after the classical period, particularly in terms of streamlining and expanding bureaucratic systems and procedures, but it never required fundamental overhaul.

The political framework that emerged as a result of the long centuries of China's classical period had several key elements. Strong local units never disappeared. Like most successful agricultural societies, China relied heavily on tightly knit patriarchal families. Individual families were linked to other relatives in extended family networks that included brothers, uncles, and any living grandparents. Among the wealthy landowning groups, family authority was enhanced by the practice of ancestor worship, which joined family members through rituals devoted to important forebears who had passed into the spirit world. For ordinary people, among whom ancestor worship was less common, village authority surmounted family rule. Village leaders helped farming families regulate property and coordinate planting and harvest work. During the Zhou dynasty, and also in later periods when dynasties weakened, the regional power of great landlords also played an important role at the village level. Landed nobles provided courts of justice and organized military troops.

Strong local rule was not the most significant or distinctive feature of Chinese government under the Qin and Han dynasties, however. Shih Huangdi not only attacked local rulers, he also provided a single law code for the whole empire and established a uniform tax system. He appointed governors to each district of his domain, who exercised military and legal powers in the name of the emperor. They, in turn, named officials responsible for smaller regions. Here indeed was a classic model of centralized government that other societies would replicate in later times: The establishment of centralized codes and appointment of officials directly by a central authority, rather than reliance on arrangements with numerous existing local governments. The effectiveness of a central government was further enhanced by the delegation of special areas and decisions to the emperor's ministers. Some dealt with matters of finance, others with justice, others with military affairs, and so on.

Able rulers of the Han dynasty resumed the attack on local warrior-landlords. In addition, they realized the importance of creating a large, highly skilled bureaucracy, one capable of carrying out the duties of a complex state. By the end of the Han period, China had about 130,000 bureaucrats, representing 0.2 percent of the population. The emperor Wu Ti established examinations for his bureaucrats—the first example of civil service tests of the sort that many governments have instituted in modern times. These examinations covered classics of Chinese literature as well as law, suggesting a model of the scholar-bureaucrat that would later become an important element of China's political tradition. Wu Ti also established a school to train men of exceptional talent and ability for the national examinations. Although most bureaucrats were drawn from the landed upper classes, who alone had the time to learn the complex system of Chinese characters, individuals from lower ranks of society were occasionally recruited under this system. China's bureaucracy thus provided a slight check on complete upper-class rule. It also tended to limit the exercise of arbitrary power by the emperor himself. Trained and experienced bureaucrats, confident in their own traditions, could often control the whims of a single ruler, even one who, in the Chinese tradition, regarded himself as divinely appointed—the "Son of Heaven." It was no accident then that the Chinese bureaucracy lasted from the Han period until the twentieth century, outliving the empire itself.

Small wonder that from the classical period at least until modern times, and possibly still today, the Chinese were the most tightly governed people in any large society in the world. When it worked well—and it is important to recall that the system periodically broke down—Chinese politics represented a remarkable integration of all levels of authority. The edicts of an all-powerful emperor were administered by trained scholar-bureaucrats, widely respected for their learning and, often, their noble birth. Individual families also emphasized this strong principle of authority, with the father in charge, presumably carrying on the wishes of a long line of ancestors to which the family paid reverence. The Chinese were capable of periodic rebellions, and gangs of criminals more regularly came to disrupt the social scene—indeed, frequently harsh punishments reflected the need of the government to eradicate such deviant forces. Nevertheless, whether within the family or the central state, most Chinese in ordinary times believed in the importance of respect for those in power.

Government traditions established during the classical period included an impressive list of state functions. Like all organized states, the Chinese government operated military and judicial systems. Military activity fluctuated, as China did not depend on steady expansion. Although classical China produced some enduring examples of the art of war, the state was not highly militaristic by the Han period.

Judicial matters—crime and legal disputes—commanded more attention by local government authorities.

The government also sponsored much intellectual life, organizing research in astronomy and the maintenance of historical records. Under the Han rulers, the government played a major role in promoting Confucian philosophy as an official statement of Chinese values and in encouraging the worship of Confucius himself. The government developed a durable sense of mission as the primary keeper of Chinese beliefs.

The imperial government was also active in the economy. It directly organized the production of iron and salt. Its standardization of currency, weights, and measures facilitated trade throughout the vast empire. The government additionally sponsored public works, including complex irrigation and canal systems. Han rulers even tried to regulate agricultural supplies by storing grain and rice in good times to control price increases—and potential popular unrest—when harvests were bad.

China's ambitious rulers in no sense directed the daily lives of their subjects; the technology of an agricultural society did not permit this. Even under the Han, it took over a month for a directive from the capital city to reach the outlying districts of the empire—an obvious limit on imperial authority. A revealing Chinese proverb held that "heaven is high, and the emperor is far away." However, the power of the Chinese state did extend considerably. Its system of courts was backed by a strict code of law; torture and execution were widely employed to supplement the preaching of obedience and civic virtue. The central government taxed its subjects and also required some annual labor on the part of every male peasant—this was the source of the incredible physical work involved in building canals, roads, and palaces. No other government had the organization and staff to reach ordinary people so directly until virtually modern times, except in much smaller political units such as city-states. The power of the government and the authority it commanded in the eyes of most ordinary Chinese people help explain why its structure survived decline, invasion, and even rebellion for so many centuries. Invaders like the Huns might topple a dynasty, but they could not devise a better system to run the country, and so the system and its bureaucratic administrators normally endured.

RELIGION AND CULTURE

The Chinese way of viewing the world, as this belief system developed during the classical period, was closely linked to a distinct political structure. Upper-class cultural values emphasized a good life on earth and the virtues of obedience to the state, more than speculations about God and the mysteries of heaven. At the same time, the Chinese tolerated and often combined various specific beliefs, so long as they did not contradict basic political loyalties.

Rulers in the Zhou dynasty maintained belief in a god or gods, but little attention was given to the nature of a deity. Rather, Chinese leaders stressed the importance of a harmonious earthly life, which would maintain proper balance between earth and heaven. Harmony included carefully constructed rituals to unify society and prevent individual excess. Among the upper classes, people were trained in elaborate exercises and military skills such as archery. Commonly, ceremonies venerating ancestors and even marking special meals were conducted. The use of chopsticks began at the end of the Zhou dynasty; it encouraged a code of politeness at meals. Soon after this, tea was introduced, although the most elaborate tea-drinking rituals developed later on.

Even before these specific ceremonies arose, however, the basic definition of a carefully ordered existence was given more formal philosophical backing. Amid the long collapse of the Zhou dynasty, many thinkers and religious prophets began to challenge Chinese traditions. From this ferment came a restatement of the traditions that ultimately reduced intellectual conflict and established a long-lasting tone for Chinese cultural and social life.

Confucius, or K'ung Fu-tse, (which means Kung the philosopher), lived from roughly 551 to 478 B.C.E. His life was devoted to teaching, and he traveled through many parts of China preaching his ideas of political virtue and good government. Confucius was not a religious leader; he believed in a divine order but refused to speculate about it. Chinese civilization was unusual, in the classical period and well beyond, in that its dominant values were secular rather than religious.

Confucius saw himself as a spokesman for Chinese tradition and for what he believed were the great days of the Chinese state before the Zhou declined. He maintained that if people could be taught to emphasize personal virtue, which included a reverence for tradition, a solid political life would naturally result. The Confucian list of virtues stressed respect for one's social superiors—including fathers and husbands as leaders of the family. However, this emphasis on a proper hierarchy was balanced by an insistence that society's leaders behave modestly and without excess, shunning abusive power and treating courteously those people who were in their charge. According to Confucius, moderation in behavior, veneration of custom and ritual, and a love of wisdom should characterize the leaders of society at all levels. And with virtuous leaders, a sound political life would inevitably follow: "In an age of good government, men in high stations give preference to men of ability and give opportunity to those who are below them, and lesser people labor vigorously at their husbandry to serve their superiors."

Confucianism was primarily a system of ethics—do unto others as your status and theirs dictate—and a plea for loyalty to the community. It confirmed the distaste that many educated Chinese had developed for religious mysteries, as well as their delight in learning and good manners. Confucian doctrine, carefully recorded in a book called the *Analects,* was revived under the Han emperors who saw the usefulness of Confucian emphasis on political virtue and social order. Confucian learning was also incorporated, along with traditional literary works, into the training of aspiring bureaucrats.

The problems Confucius set out to rectify, notably political disorder, were approached through an emphasis on individual virtuous behavior, both by the ruler and the ruled. "When the ruler does right, all men will imitate his self-control. What the ruler does, the people will follow." According to Confucius, only a man who demonstrated proper family virtues, including respect for parents and compassion for children and other inferiors, should be considered for political service. "When

World Profiles

Confucius, or K'ung Fu-tse (c. 551–479 B.C.E.)

Confucius was the single most important thinker in Chinese history. He was responsible for developing an orderly political and social philosophy as the Zhou dynasty became more unstable. He believed that an emphasis on personal virtue would preserve Chinese tradition and restore what he regarded as the great days of the Chinese state. He spent much of his life traveling to many parts of China preaching his ideas of personal virtue, which included respect for one's social superiors and a reverence for tradition. Tempering this emphasis on hierarchy, Confucius maintained that society's leaders must also exhibit personal virtue through moderation in behavior, veneration of custom and ritual, and a love of wisdom. The eighteenth-century Chinese nobleman who painted the image shown here depicts the philosopher with the costume and headdress of his own scholar-gentry class. What does the portrait suggest about the characteristics later generations attributed to Confucius?

Stone rubbing taken from a painting of Confucius by an eighteenth-century Chinese nobleman.

the ruler excels as a father, a son, and a brother, then the people imitate him." Confucius thus built into his own system the links among many levels of authority that came to characterize larger Chinese politics at their best. His system also emphasized personal restraint and the careful socialization of children.

For subordinates, Confucius largely recommended obedience and respect; people should know their place, even under bad rulers. However, he urged a political system that would not base rank simply on birth, but would make education accessible to all talented and intelligent members of society. The primary emphasis still rested nonetheless on the obligations and desirable characteristics of the ruling class. According to Confucius, force alone cannot permanently conquer unrest, but kindness toward the people and protection of their vital interests will. Rulers should also be humble and sincere, for people will grow rebellious under hypocrisy or arrogance. Nor should rulers be greedy; Confucius warned against a profit motive in leadership, stressing that true happiness rested in doing good for all, not individual gain. Confucius projected the ideal of a gentleman, best described by his benevolence and self-control, a man always courteous and eager for service and anxious to learn.

During the Qin and early Han periods, an alternate system of political thought, called "Legalism," sprang up in China. Legalist writers prided themselves on their pragmatism. They disdained Confucian virtues in favor of an authoritarian state that ruled by force. Human nature for the Legalists was evil and required restraint and discipline. In a proper state, the army would control and the people would labor; the idea of pleasures in educated discourse or courtesy was dismissed as frivolity. Although Legalism never captured the widespread approval that Confucianism did, it too entered the political traditions of China, where a Confucian veneer was often combined with strong-arm tactics.

Confucianists did not explicitly seek popular loyalty. Like many early civilizations, China did not produce a single system of beliefs, as different groups embraced different values, with the same individual even turning to contrasting systems depending on his or her mood. Confucianism had some obvious limits in its appeal to the masses and indeed to many educated Chinese. Its reluctance to explore the mysteries of life or nature deprived it of a spiritual side. The creed was most easily accepted by the upper classes, who had the time and resources to pursue an education and participate in ceremony. However, elements of Confucianism, including a taste for ritual, self-control, and polite manners, did spread beyond the upper classes. But, most peasants needed more than civic virtue to understand and survive their harsh life, where in constant toil they eked out only a precarious and meager existence. During most of the classical period, polytheistic beliefs, focusing on the spirits of nature, persisted among much of the peasant class. Many peasants strove to attract the blessing of conciliatory spirits by creating statues and emblems, and household decorations honoring the spirits, by holding parades and family ceremonies for the same purpose. A belief in the symbolic power of dragons stemmed from one such popular religion, which combined fear of these creatures with a more playful sense of their activities in its courtship of the divine forces of nature. Gradually, ongoing rites among the ordinary masses integrated the Confucian values urged by the upper classes.

Classical China also produced a more religious philosophy—Daoism—which arose at roughly the same time as Confucianism, during the waning centuries of the Zhou dynasty. Daoism first appealed to many in the upper classes, who had an interest in a more elaborate spirituality. Daoism embraced traditional Chinese beliefs in nature's harmony and added a sense of nature's mystery. As a spiritual alternative to Confucianism, Daoism produced a durable division in China's religious and philosophical culture. This new religion, vital for Chinese civilization although never widely exported, was furthered by Lao-zi, who probably lived during the fifth century B.C.E. Lao-zi (often called Lao-tsu in popular Daoist texts) stressed that nature contains a divine impulse which directs all life. True human understanding comes in withdrawing from the world and contemplating this life force. Dao, which means *the way of nature,* refers to this same basic, indescribable force:

There is a thing confusedly formed,
Born before heaven and earth.
Silent and void
It stands alone and does not change,
Goes round and does not weary.
It is capable of being the mother of the world.
I know not its name,
So I style it "the way."

Along with secret rituals, Daoism promoted its own set of ethics. Daoist harmony with nature best resulted through humility and frugal living. According to this movement, political activity and learning were irrelevant to a good life, and general conditions in the world were of little importance.

Daoism, which would join with a strong Buddhist influence from India during the chaos that followed the collapse of the Han dynasty, guaranteed that China's people would not be united by a single religious or philosophical system. Individuals did come to embrace some elements from both Daoism and Confucianism, and indeed many emperors favored Daoism. They accepted its spread with little anxiety, partly because some of them found solace in Daoist belief but also because the religion, with its otherworldly emphasis, posed no real political threat. Confucian scholars disagreed vigorously with Daoist thinking, particularly its emphasis on mysteries and magic, but they saw little reason to challenge its influence. As Daoism became an increasingly formal religion, from the later Han dynasty onward, it provided many Chinese with a host of ceremonies designed to promote harmony with the mysterious life force. Finally, the Chinese government from the Han dynasty onward was able to persuade Daoist priests to include expressions of loyalty to the emperor in their temple services. This heightened Daoism's political compatibility with Confucianism.

Confucianism and Daoism were not the only intellectual products of China's classical period, but they were the most important. Confucianism blended easily with the high value of literature and art among the upper classes. In literature, a set of Five Classics, written during the early part of the Zhou dynasty and then edited during the time of Confucius, provided an important tradition. They were used, among other things, as a basis for civil service examinations. The works provided in the Five Classics included some historical treatises, speeches, and other political materials, a discussion of etiquette and ceremonies; in the Classic of Songs, over 300 poems dealing with love, joy, politics, and family life appeared. The Chinese literary tradition developed on the basis of mastering these early works, plus Confucian writing; each generation of writers found new meanings in the classical literature, which allowed them to express new ideas within a familiar framework. Several thinkers during the Han dynasty elaborated Confucian philosophy. In literature, poetry commanded particular attention because the Chinese language featured melodic speech and variant pronunciations of the same basic sound, a characteristic that promoted an outpouring of poetry. From the classical period onward, the ability to learn and recite poetry became the mark of an educated Chinese. Finally, the literary tradition established in classical China reinforced the Confucian emphasis on human life, although the subjects included romance and sorrow as well as political values.

This elaborate bronze vase dates from the late Zhou dynasty (c. 300 B.C.E.). It might be compared with the simpler, more primitive Chinese designs depicted earlier from the Shang dynasty. (Freer Gallery of Art, The Smithsonian Institute, Washington, DC, Early Chinese Art, 15.103.)

Chinese art during the classical period was largely decorative, stressing careful detail and craftsmanship. Artistic styles often reflected the precision and geometric qualities of the many symbols of Chinese writing. Calligraphy itself became an important art form. In addition, Chinese artists painted, worked in bronze and pottery, carved jade and ivory, and wove silk screens. Classical China did not produce monumental buildings, aside from the awe-inspiring Great Wall and some imperial palaces and tombs, in part because of the absence of a single religion; indeed, the entire tone of upper-class Confucianism was such that it discouraged the notion of temples soaring to the heavens.

In science, finally, important practical work was encouraged, rather than imaginative theorizing. Chinese astronomers had developed an accurate calendar by 444 B.C.E., based on a year of 365.5 days. Later astronomers calculated the movement of the planets Saturn and Jupiter and observed sunspots—more than 1500 years before comparable knowledge developed in Europe. The purpose of Chinese astronomy was to make celestial phenomena predictable, as part of the wider interest in ensuring har-

Horse figure from Han dynasty, second century C.E. The Chinese developed new horse breeds as they expanded into central Asia. This statue celebrates the improvement over the early, short-legged horses that were known to the Chinese.

mony between heaven and earth. Chinese scientists steadily improved their instrumentation, inventing a kind of seismograph to register earthquakes during the Han dynasty. The Chinese were also active in medical research, developing precise anatomical knowledge and studying principles of hygiene that could promote longer life.

Chinese mathematics also stressed the practical. Daoism encouraged some exploration of the orderly processes of nature, but far more research focused on how things actually worked. For example, Chinese scholars studied the mathematics of music in ways that led to advances in acoustics. This focus for science and mathematics contrasted notably with the more abstract definition of science developed in classical Greece.

ECONOMY AND SOCIETY

Although the most distinctive features of classical China centered on politics and culture, developments in the economy, social structure, and family life also shaped Chinese civilization and continued to have impact on the empire's history for a significant period of time.

As in many agricultural societies, considerable gaps developed between China's upper class, which controlled large landed estates, and the masses, farmer-peasants who produced little more than what was needed for their own subsistence. The difficulty of becoming literate symbolized these gaps, for landlords enjoyed not only wealth but also a culture denied to most common people. Prior to the Zhou dynasty, slave-holding may have been common in China, but by the time of the Zhou the main social division existed between the landowning gentry—about 2 percent of the total population—and peasants, who provided dues and service to these lords while also controlling some of their own land. The Chinese peasantry depended on intensive cooperation, particularly in the southern rice region; in this group, property was characteristically owned and regulated by the village or the extended family, rather than by individuals. Beneath the peasantry, Chinese social structure included a group of "mean" people who performed rough transport and other unskilled jobs and suffered from the lowest possible status. In general, social status was passed from one generation to the next through inheritance, although unusually talented individuals from a peasant background might be given access to an education and rise within the bureaucracy.

Officially then and to a large extent in fact, classical China consisted of three main social groups. The landowning aristocracy plus the educated bureaucrats, or Mandarins, formed the top group. Next came the laboring masses, peasants and also urban artisans who manufactured goods. These people, far poorer than the top group and also condemned to a life of hard manual labor, sometimes worked directly on large estates but in other cases had some economic independence. Finally, came the mean people, the general category we already identified as applying to those without meaningful skills. Interestingly, performing artists were ranked in this group, despite the fact that the upper classes enjoyed plays and other entertainments provided by this group. Mean people were punished for crime more harshly than other groups and were required to wear identifying green scarves. Household slaves also existed within this class structure, but their number was relatively few and China did not depend on slaves for actual production.

Trade became increasingly important during the Zhou and particularly the Han dynasties. Much trade focused on luxury items for the upper class, produced by skilled artisans in the cities—silks, jewelry, leather goods, and furniture. There was also food exchange between the wheat- and rice-growing regions. Copper coins began to circulate, which facilitated trade, with merchants even sponsoring commercial visits to India. Although significant, trade and its attendant merchant class did not become the focal points of Chinese society, and the Confucian emphasis on learning and political service led to considerable scorn for lives devoted to money-making. The gap between the real importance and wealth of merchants and their officially low prestige was an enduring legacy in Confucian China.

If trade fit somewhat uncomfortably into the dominant view of society, there was no question about the importance of technological advance. Here, the Chinese excelled. Agricultural implements improved steadily. Ox-drawn plows were introduced around 300 B.C.E., which greatly increased productivity. Under the Han, a new collar was invented for draft animals, allowing them to pull plows or wagons without choking—this was a major improvement that became available to other parts of the world only many

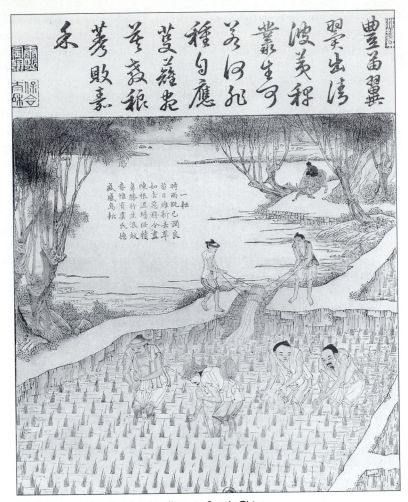

Peasants transplanting rice seedlings in South China.

centuries later. Chinese iron mining was also well advanced, as pulleys and winding gear were devised to bring material to the surface. Iron tools and other implements such as lamps were widely used. Production methods in textiles and pottery were also highly developed by world standards. Under the Han, the first water-powered mills were introduced, allowing further gains in manufacturing. Finally, during the Han, paper was invented, which was a major boon to a system of government that emphasized the bureaucracy. In sum, classical China reached far higher levels of technical expertise than Europe or western Asia in the same period, a lead that it would long maintain.

The relatively advanced technology of classical China did not however steer Chinese society away from its primary reliance on agriculture. Farming technology itself helped increase the size of the population in the countryside; with better tools and seeds, smaller amounts of land could support more families. But, China's solid agricultural base, backed by some trade in foodstuffs among key regions, did permit the

World Profiles

Pan Chao (c. 48–117 C.E.)

Pan Chao, now known as China's most famous woman scholar, was long esteemed as an advisor on female humility and an example of chaste widowhood. Her life and ideas illustrate the complexities of a patriarchal society in action, and also the several sides of Confucianism.

Pan Chao was the daughter of a leading scholar, with two able brothers, one a historian, the other a general. She received a good education. Pan Chao married and had a son, but was widowed at an early age. Living with her historian-brother, she collaborated with him on a history of the Han dynasty. When her brother died, the emperor insisted she complete the history, and she seems to have been responsible for some of its most original sections. She also tutored women at the imperial court, in literature, history, mathematics, and astronomy, and exerted considerable influence when one of her students became Empress, serving as regent for a time. Pan Chao wrote widely, although most of her works have been lost over the centuries. Her most famous effort was "Lessons for Women," reprinted and actively circulated in China through the nineteenth century. In this work, Pan Chao urged humility and domestic skills, a point of view that seemed at odds with although not in complete contrast to her own life. Young girls, for example, were urged to sleep at the foot of a brother's bed, so they would begin to learn their proper station. Accepting a Confucian family hierarchy, Pan Chao also insisted that men had specific obligations to women, particularly to provide an appropriate education—and she emphasized that this aspect of their reciprocal relationship was

not being met. Still, the dominant tone of "Lessons for Women" was subservient. Her work raises obvious questions: Why would an educated, self-sufficient woman condone the notion of women's inferiority to men? How can the contradiction between Pan Chao's life and her public views be explained?

This woodcut of the Pan Chao appeared in 1690, obviously long after her death. The drawing is a sign of her ongoing importance as an advisor on gender. Since it reflects no knowledge of what the famous author actually looked like, the drawing should be interpreted in terms of what symbolic qualities of hers artists had decided to emphasize.

expansion of cities and of manufacturing. Nonagricultural goods were mainly produced by artisans, working in small shops or in their homes. Even though only a minority of the work force was involved in such tasks that used manual methods for the most part, the output of tools, porcelain, and textiles increased considerably, aided in this case as well by the interest in improving techniques.

In all major social groups, tight family organization helped solidify economic and social views as well as political life. The structure of the Chinese family resembled that of families in other agricultural civilizations in emphasizing the importance of unity and the power of husbands and fathers. Within this context, however, the Chinese stressed authority to unusual extremes. Confucius said, "There are no wrongdoing parents"—and in practice, parents could punish disobedient children freely. Law courts did not prosecute parents who injured or even killed a disobedient son, but they would severely punish a child who scolded or attacked a parent. In most families, the emphasis on obedience to parents, and a corresponding emphasis on wives' obedience to husbands, did not produce great friction. Chinese popular culture stressed strict control of one's emotions, and the family was seen as the center of such an orderly, serene hierarchy. Indeed, the family served as a great training ground for the principles of authority and restraint that applied to the larger social and political world. Women, although subordinate, had their own clearly defined roles and could sometimes gain power through their sons and as mothers-in-law of younger women brought into the household. The mother of a famous Confucian philosopher, Mencius, continually claimed how humble she was, but during the course of his life she managed to exert considerable influence over him. There was even a clear hierarchical order for children, with boys superior to girls and the oldest son having the most enviable position of all. Chinese rules of inheritance, from the humblest peasant to the emperor himself, followed strict primogeniture, which meant that the oldest male child would inherit property and position alike.

CONCLUSION: HOW CHINESE CIVILIZATION FIT TOGETHER

Classical Chinese technology, religion, philosophy, and political structure evolved with very little outside contact. Although important trade routes did lead to India and the Middle East, most Chinese saw the world in terms of a large island of civilization surrounded by barbarian peoples with nothing to offer save the periodic threat of invasion. Proud of their culture and of its durability, the Chinese had neither the need nor the desire to learn from other societies. Nor, except to protect their central territory by exercising some control over the mountainous or desert regions that surrounded the Middle Kingdom, did Chinese leaders have any particular desire to teach the rest of the world. A missionary spirit was foreign to Chinese culture and politics. Of course, China displayed some patterns that were similar to those of the other agricultural civilizations, but it also did occasionally embrace the concepts of these cultures. Indeed, the spread of Buddhism from India, during and after the Han decline, was a notable instance of a cultural diffusion that altered China's religious map and also its artistic styles. Nevertheless, the theme of unusual isolation, developed during the formative period of Chinese civilization, was to prove persistent in later world history—in fact, it has not entirely disappeared to this day.

Chinese civilization was also noteworthy for the relative harmony among its various major features. We have, in this chapter, examined the pattern of leading historical events in classical China and then the systems of government, belief, economy, and social structure. All these facets were closely meshed. Although the centralized government, with its elaborate functions and far-reaching bureaucracy, gave the clearest unity and focus to Chinese society, it did not do so alone. Confucianism provided a vital supplement, making the bureaucracy more than a collection of people with similar political objectives, but rather a trained corps with some common ideals. In appreciation of distinctive artistic styles, poetry, and the literary tradition added to this common culture. Cohesive government and related beliefs about human ideals and aesthetics were linked, in turn, to the economy. Political stability over a large and fertile land aided economic growth, and the government took a direct role in encouraging both agriculture and industry. A strong economy, in turn, provided the government with vital tax revenues. Economic interests were also related to the pragmatic Chinese view of science, whose aim was to determine how nature worked. Finally, social relationships reinforced all these systems. The vision of a stable hierarchy and tight family structures meshed with the strong impulse toward orderly politics and helped instill the virtues of obedience and respect that were important to the larger political system.

Not surprisingly, given the close links among the various facets of their civilization, the Chinese tended to think of their society as a whole. They did not distinguish clearly between private and public sectors of activity. They did not see government and society as two separate entities. In other words, these Western concepts that we have used to define classical China and to facilitate comparisons with other societies do not really fit the Chinese view of their own world. Confucius himself, in seeing government as basically a vast extension of family relationships, similarly suggested that the pieces of the Chinese puzzle were intimately joined.

A grasp of Chinese civilization as a whole, however, should not distract us from recognizing some endemic tensions and disparities. The division in belief systems, between Confucianism and Daoism, modifies the perception of an ultimately tidy classical China. Confucianists and Daoists tolerated each other. Sometimes, their beliefs coincided in such a way that a single individual who behaved politically as a Confucianist, explored deeper mysteries through Daoist rituals. However, between both groups there was considerable hostility and mutual disdain, as many Confucianists found Daoists superstitious and over-excited. Daoism did not inherently disrupt the political unity of Chinese culture, but at times the religion did inspire attacks on established politics in the name of a mysterious divine will.

Tension in Chinese society showed in the way Confucian beliefs were combined with strict policing. Chinese officials did believe in fundamental human goodness and the importance of ceremony and mutual respect. However, they also believed in the force of stern punishment, not only against criminals but also as warnings to the larger, potentially restless population. People arrested were presumed guilty and often subjected to torture before trial. The Chinese, in fact, early discovered the usefulness of alternating torture with benevolence, to make accused individuals confess. In the late Han period, a thief who refused to confess even under severe torture was then freed from chains, bathed, and fed, "so as to bring him in a happy mood"—whereupon he usually confessed and named his whole gang. In sum, both Confucianism and the Chinese penal system supported tight control, and the combination of the two was typically effective; however, they involved quite different approaches and quite different moral assumptions.

All of this suggests that classical China, like any vigorous, successful society, embraced a diversity of features that could not be fully united by any single formula. Elites and masses were divided by both economic interests and culture. Some shared the same values, particularly as Confucianism spread, and upper-class concern for careful etiquette and the general welfare of the population mitigated the tension. But, such calm was a precarious balance, and when overpopulation or some other factor tipped the scale, recurrent and often violent protest could be the result.

Despite any divisions, the symbiosis among the various institutions and activities of many people in classical China does deserve strong emphasis. It helps account for the durability of Chinese values. Even in times of political turmoil, families would transfer beliefs and political ideals by the ways in which they instructed their children. The overall wholeness of Chinese society also helps account for its relative immunity to outside influence and for its creativity despite considerable isolation.

Chinese wholeness, finally, provides an interesting contrast to the other great Asian civilization that developed in the classical period. India, as fully dynamic as China in many ways, produced different emphases, but also a more disparate society in which links among politics and beliefs and economic life were less well defined. Many would argue that this contrast between the two Asian giants persists to our own time.

SUGGESTED WEBSITES

On Daoism, see *http://www.his.com/~merkin/DaoBrief.html*; for a virtual tour of the Great Wall, see *http://www.chinavista.com/travel/greatwall/greatwall.html*.

SUGGESTED READINGS

Several sources offer original materials on classical Chinese thought and politics: John Fairbank, ed., *Chinese Thought and Institutions* (1973); Wing-stit Chan, *A Source Book in Chinese Philosophy* (1963); and P. Ebrey, *Chinese Civilization and Society: A Sourcebook* (1981). Two excellent general surveys for this period and later ones are John Fairbank and Albert Craig, *East Asia: Tradition and Transformation* (1993); E. O. Reischauer and John Fairbank, *A History of East Asian Civilization, Vol. I: East Asia, The Great Tradition* (1961); see also Arthur Cotterell, *The First Emperor of China* (1981). Briefer but useful are M. J. Coye and J. Livingston, eds., *China, Yesterday and Today* (1975); Wolfram Eberhard, *A History of China* (1977); and X. Z. Liu, *Ancient India and Ancient China* (1988). See also D. Twitchett and M. Loewe, eds.,

The Cambridge History of China, Vol. I (1986). On more specialized topics, see E. Balazs, *Chinese Civilization and Bureaucracy* (1964); J. Needham, *Science and Civilization in China*, 4 vols. (1970); Richard J. Smith, *Traditional Chinese Culture: An Interpretive Introduction* (1978); Benjamin Schwartz, *The World of Thought in Ancient China* (1983); Michael Loewe, *Everyday Life in Early Imperial China* (1968); Cho-yun Hsu and K. M. Linduff, *Western Chou Civilization* (1988); Michele Pirazzoli-t'Sersteven, *The Han Civilization of China* (1982); R. Wilke and M. Wolf, *Women in Chinese Society* (1975); and Bella Vivante, ed., *Women's Roles in Ancient Civilizations: A Reference Guide* (1999).

Classical Civilization: India

FOCAL POINTS

The emergence of a second classical civilization, in India, raises many of the same issues as its Chinese counterpart: How did Indian society have to change to encompass a much larger territory? Indian answers to the problems of integrating a large region involved a distinctive value system, emphasizing two related religious traditions and a seemingly rigid, but clearly functional, social structure. Despite great social inequality, India provided cultural links between the masses of ordinary people and the elite groups: How did this system work? Indian political structures fluctuated more than those in classical China: Was there an Indian political tradition? Did Indian society cohere well—that is, did all the parts come together in a reasonably harmonious way? How did successful commercial activity and a bustling merchant class coexist with a strong religious emphasis and the rigid social castes?

INTRODUCTION

The classical period of Indian history includes a number of contrasts to that of China—and many of these contrasts have proved enduring. Whereas the focus in classical China was on politics and related philosophical values, the emphasis in classical India shifted to religion and social structure; a political culture existed, but it was less cohesive and central than its Chinese counterpart. Less familiar but scarcely less important were distinctions that arose in India's scientific tradition and the tenor of the economy and family life. Here, too, the classical period generated impulses that are still felt in India today—and that continue to distinguish India from other major civilizations in the world.

India's distinctiveness was considerable, but a comparison must not be one-sided. India was an agricultural society, and this dictated many similarities with China. Most people were peasant farmers, with their major focus on food production for their own family's survival. The clustering of peasants in villages, to provide mutual aid and protection, gave a strong localist flavor to many aspects of life in China and India alike. In addition, agriculture influenced family life, with male ownership of property creating a strongly patriarchal flavor, and women held as inferiors and often treated as possessions. As agricultural civilizations, both China and India produced important cities and engendered significant trade, which added to social and economic complexity and also created the basis for most formal intellectual life, including schools and academies.

THE FRAMEWORK FOR INDIAN HISTORY: GEOGRAPHY AND A FORMATIVE PERIOD

Important reasons for India's distinctive paths lie in geography and early historical experience. India was much closer to the orbit of other civilizations than China. Trading contacts with China, developed late in the classical period, had little impact—interestingly, China was more affected. But, India was frequently open to influences from the Middle East and even the Mediterranean world. Persian empires spilled over into India at several points, bringing new artistic styles and political concepts. Briefly, Alexander the Great invaded India, and while he did not establish a durable empire, he did allow important Indian contacts with Hellenistic culture. Periodic influences from the Middle East continued after the classical age, forcing India to react and adapt in ways that China, more isolated, largely avoided.

In addition to links with other cultures, India's topography shaped a number of vital features of its civilization. The vast Indian subcontinent is partially separated from the rest of Asia, and particularly from East Asia, by northern mountain ranges, notably the Himalayas. Important passes through the mountains, especially in the northwest, linked India to other civilizations in the Middle East; although it lacked the isolation of China's Middle Kingdom, the subcontinent was somewhat set apart within Asia. At the same time, divisions within the subcontinent made full political unity difficult: India was thus marked by greater diversity than China's Middle Kingdom. The most important agricultural regions are those along the two great rivers, the Indus and the Ganges. However, India also has mountainous northern regions, where a herding economy took root, and a southern coastal rim, separated by mountains and the Deccan plateau, where an active trading and seafaring economy arose. India's separate regions help explain not only economic diversity but also the racial and language differences that, from early times, have marked the subcontinent's populations.

Much of India is semitropical in climate. In the river valley plains, heat can rise to 120°F during the early summer. Summer also brings torrential monsoon rains, crucial for farming. But, the monsoons vary from year to year, sometimes bringing too little rain or coming too late and causing famine-producing drought, or sometimes bringing catastrophic floods. Certain features of Indian civilization may have resulted from a need to come to terms with a climate that could produce abundance one year and grim starvation the next. In a year with favorable monsoons, Indian farmers were able to plant and harvest two crops and could thus support a sizable population.

Indian civilization was shaped not only by its physical environment but also by a formative period, lasting several centuries, between the destruction of the Indus River civilization and the revival of full civilization elsewhere on the subcontinent. During this formative period, called the Vedic and Epic ages, the Aryan (Indo-European) migrants—hunting and herding peoples orginally from Central Asia—gradually came to terms with agriculture, but had their own impact on the culture and social structure of their new home. Also during the Vedic Age, from about 1500 to 1000 B.C.E., Indian agriculture extended from the Indus River valley to the more fertile Ganges valley, as the Aryans used iron tools to clear away the dense vegetation.

Most of what we know about this preclassical period in Indian history comes from literary epics developed by the Aryans, initially passed on orally. They were later written down in Sanskrit, which became the first literary language of the new culture. The initial part of this formative period, the Vedic Age, takes its name from the Sanskrit word *Veda,* or "knowledge." The first epic, the *Rig-Veda,* consists of 1028 hymns dedicated to the Aryan gods and composed by various priests. New stories, developed during the Epic Age between 1000 and 600 B.C.E., include the *Mahab-harata,* India's greatest epic poem, and the *Ramayana,* both of which deal with real and mythical battles; these epics reflect a more settled agricultural society and better-organized political units than the *Rig-Veda.* The Epic Age also saw the creation of the *Upanishads,* epic poems with a more mystical religious flavor.

Aryan ideas and social and family forms also became increasingly influential. As the Aryans settled down to agriculture, they encouraged tight levels of village organization that came to be characteristic of Indian society and politics. Village chiefs, initially drawn from the leadership of one of the Aryan tribes, helped organize village defenses and also to regulate property relationships among families. Family structure itself emphasized patriarchal controls, and extended family relationships among grandparents, parents, and children were close.

The characteristic Indian caste system also began to take shape during the Vedic and Epic ages, as a means of establishing relationships between the Aryan conquerors and the indigenous people, whom the Aryans regarded as inferior. Aryan social classifications partly enforced divisions familiar in agricultural societies. Thus, a warrior or governing class, the Kshatriyas, and the priestly caste, or Brahmins, stood at the top of the social pyramid, followed by Vaisyas, the traders and farmers, and Sudras, or common laborers. Many of the Sudras worked on the estates of large landowners. A fifth group gradually evolved, the *untouchables,* who were confined to a few jobs, such as transporting the bodies of the dead or hauling refuse. It was widely believed that touching these people would defile anyone from a superior caste. Initially, the warrior group ranked highest, but during the Epic Age the Brahmins replaced them, signaling the importance of religious links in Indian life. Thus, a law book stated, "When a Brahmin springs to light he is born above the world, the chief of all creatures, assigned to guard the treasury of duties, religious and civil." Gradually, the five social groups became hereditary, with marriage between castes forbidden and punishable by death; the basic castes divided into smaller subgroups, called Jati, each with distinctive occupations and each tied to its social station by birth.

The *Rig-Veda,* the first Aryan epic, attributed the rise of the caste system to the gods:

When they divided the original Man
into how many parts did they divide him?
What was his mouth, what were his arms,
what were his thighs and his feet called?
The brahmin was his mouth, of his
arms was made the warrior.
His thighs became the vaisya, of
his feet the sudra was born.

CHAPTER 3: *Classical Civilization: India*

The Aryans brought to India a religion of many gods and goddesses, who regulated natural forces and possessed human qualities. Thus, Indra, the god of thunder, was also the god of strength. Gods presided over fire, the sun, death, and so on. This system bore some resemblances to the gods and goddesses of Greek myth or Scandinavian mythology, for the very good reason that they were derived from a common Indo-European oral heritage. However, India was to give this common tradition an important twist, ultimately constructing a vigorous, complex religion that, apart from the Indo-European polytheistic faiths, endures to this day. During the epic periods, the Aryans offered hymns and sacrifices to the gods. Certain animals were regarded as particularly sacred, embodying the divine spirit. Gradually, this religion became more elaborate. The epic poems reflect an idea of life after death and a religious approach to the world of nature. Nature was seen as informed not only by specific gods but also by a more basic divine force. These ideas, expressed in the mystical *Upanishads,* added greatly to the spiritual power of this early religion and served as the basis for later Hindu beliefs. By the end of the Epic Age, the dominant Indian belief system included a variety of convictions. Many people continued to emphasize rituals and sacrifices to the gods of nature; specific beliefs, as in the sacredness of monkeys and cattle, illustrated this ritualistic approach. The Brahmin priestly caste specified and enforced prayers, ceremonies, and rituals. However, the religion also produced a more mystical strand through its belief in a unifying divine force and the desirability of seeking union with this force. Toward the end of the Epic period one religious leader, Gautama Buddha, built on this mysticism to create what became Buddhism, another major world religion.

PATTERNS IN CLASSICAL INDIA

By 600 B.C.E., India had passed through its formative phase. Regional political units grew in size, cities and trade expanded, and the development of the Sanskrit language, although dominated by the priestly Brahmin caste, furthered an elaborate literary culture. A full, classical civilization could now build on the social and cultural themes first launched during the Vedic and Epic ages.

Indian development during the classical era and beyond did not take on the convenient structure of rising and falling dynasties characteristic of Chinese history. Political eras were even less clear than in classical Greece. The rhythm of Indian history was irregular and often consisted of landmark invasions that poured in through the mountain passes of the subcontinent's northwestern border.

Toward the end of the Epic Age and until the fourth century B.C.E., the Indian plains were divided among powerful regional states. Sixteen major states existed by 600 B.C.E. in the plains of northern India, some of them monarchies, others republics dominated by assemblies of priests and warriors. Warfare was not uncommon. One regional state, Magadha, established dominance over a considerable empire. In 327 B.C.E., Alexander the Great, having conquered Greece and much of the Middle East, pushed into northwestern India, establishing a small border state called Bactria.

Political reactions to this incursion produced the next major step in Indian political history, in 322 B.C.E., when a young soldier named Chandragupta seized power along the Ganges River. He became the first of the Maurya dynasty of Indian rulers, who in turn were the first rulers to unify much of the entire subcontinent. Borrowing from Persian political models and the example of Alexander the Great, Chandragupta and his successors maintained large armies, with thousands of chariots and elephant-borne troops. The Mauryan rulers also developed a substantial bureaucracy, even sponsoring a postal service.

Chandragupta's style of government was highly autocratic, relying on the ruler's personal and military power. This style would surface periodically in Indian history, just as it did in the Middle East, a region with which India had important contacts. A Greek ambassador from one of the Hellenistic kingdoms described Chandragupta's life:

> Attendance on the king's person is the duty of women, who indeed are bought from their fathers. Outside the gates [of the palace] stand the bodyguards and the rest of the soldiers. . . . Nor does the king sleep during the day, and at night he is forced at various hours to change his bed because of those plotting against him. Of his nonmilitary departures [from the palace] one is to the courts, in which he passed the day hearing cases to the end. . . . [When he leaves to hunt,] he is thickly surrounded by a circle of women, and on the outside by spear-carrying bodyguards. The road is fenced off with ropes, and to anyone who passes within the ropes as far as the women, death is the penalty.

Such drastic precautions paid off. Chandragupta finally designated his rule to a son and became a religious ascetic, dying peacefully at an advanced age.

Column to Ashoka, third century B.C.E.

Chandragupta's grandson, Ashoka (269–232 B.C.E.), was an even greater figure in India's history. First serving as a governor of two provinces, Ashoka enjoyed a lavish lifestyle, with frequent horseback riding and feasting. However, he also engaged in a study of nature and was strongly influenced by the intense spiritualism not only of the Brahmin religion but also of Buddhism. Ashoka extended Mauryan conquests, gaining control of all but the southern tip of India through fierce fighting. His methods were bloodthirsty; in taking over one coastal area, Ashoka himself admitted that "one hundred and fifty thousand were killed (or maimed) and many times that number later died." But, Ashoka could also be compassionate. He ultimately converted to Buddhism, seeing in the belief in *dharma,* or the law of moral consequences, a kind of ethical guide that might unite and discipline the diverse people under his rule. Ashoka vigorously propagated Buddhism throughout India, while also honoring Hinduism, sponsoring shrines for its worshippers. Ashoka even sent Buddhist missionaries to the Hellenistic kingdoms in the Middle East, and also to Sri Lanka to the south. The "new" Ashoka urged humane behavior on the part of his officials and insisted that they oversee the moral welfare of his empire. Like Chandragupta, Ashoka also worked to improve trade and communication, sponsoring an extensive road network dotted with wells and rest stops for travelers. Stability and the sheer expansion of the empire's territory encouraged growing commerce.

The Mauryan dynasty did not, however, succeed in establishing durable roots, and Ashoka's particular style of government did not have much later impact, although a strong Buddhist current persisted in India for some time. After Ashoka, the empire began to fall apart, and regional kingdoms surfaced once again. New invaders, the Kushans, pushed into central India from the northwest. The greatest Kushan king, Kanishka, converted to Buddhism but actually hurt this religion's popularity in India by associating it with foreign rule.

The collapse of the Kushan state, by 220 C.E., ushered in another hundred years of political instability. Then a new line of kings, the Guptas, established a large empire, beginning in 320 C.E. The Guptas produced no individual rulers as influential as the two great Mauryan rulers, but they had perhaps greater impact. One Gupta emperor proclaimed his virtues in an inscription on a ceremonial stone pillar:

> His far-reaching fame, deep-rooted in peace, emanated from the restoration of the sovereignty of many fallen royal families. . . . He, who had no equal in power in the world, eclipsed the fame of the other kings by the radiance of his versatile virtues, adorned by innumerable good actions.

Bombast aside, Gupta rulers often preferred to negotiate with local princes and intermarry with their families, which expanded influence without constant fighting. Two centuries of Gupta rule gave classical India its greatest period of political stability, although the Guptas did not administer as large a territory as the Mauryan kings had. The Gupta empire was overturned in 535 C.E. by a new invasion of nomadic warriors, the Huns.

Classical India thus alternated between widespread empires and a network of smaller kingdoms. Periods of regional rule did not necessarily suggest great instabil-

India, 400 C.E.

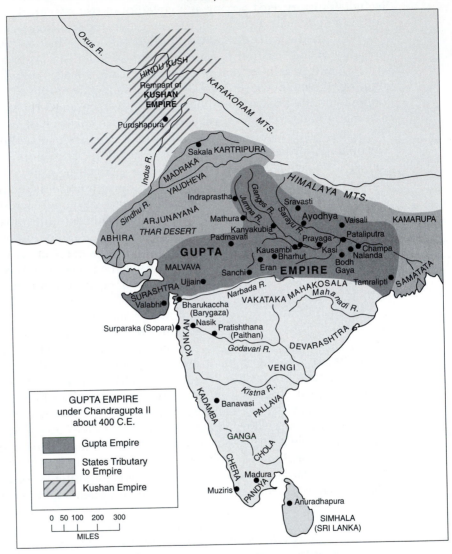

ity, and both economic and cultural life advanced in these periods as well as under the Mauryas and Guptas.

POLITICAL INSTITUTIONS

Classical India did not develop the solid political traditions and institutions of Chinese civilization, or the high level of political interest that would characterize classical Greece and Rome. The most persistent political features of India, in the classical period and beyond, involved regionalism, plus considerable diversity in political forms. Autocratic kings and emperors dotted the history of classical India, but there were also aristocratic assemblies in some regional states with the power to consult and decide on major issues.

As a result of India's diversity and regionalism, even some of the great empires had a rather shaky base. Early Mauryan rulers depended heavily on the power of their large armies, and, as we have seen, often feared betrayal and attack. Early rulers in the Gupta dynasty used various devices to consolidate support. They claimed that they had been appointed by the gods to rule, and they favored the Hindu religion over Buddhism because the Hindus believed in such gods. The Guptas managed to create a demanding taxation system, seeking up to a sixth of all agricultural produce. However, they did not create an extensive bureaucracy, rather allowing local rulers whom they had defeated to maintain regional control so long as they deferred to Gupta dominance. The Guptas stationed a personal representative at each ruler's court to ensure loyalty. A final sign of the great empire's loose structure, was the fact that no single language was imposed. The Guptas promoted Sanskrit, which became the language of educated people, but this made no dent in the diversity of popular, regional languages.

The Guptas did spread uniform law codes. Like the Mauryan rulers, they sponsored some general services, such as road building. They also served as patrons of much cultural activity, including university life as well as art and literature. These achievements were more than enough to qualify the Gupta period as a golden age in Indian history.

The fact remains, however, that the political culture of India was not very elaborate. There was little formal political theory and few institutions or values other than regionalism that carried through from one period to the next. Chandragupta's chief minister, Kautilya, wrote an important treatise on politics, but it was devoted to telling rulers what methods would work to maintain power—somewhat like the Legalists in China. Thinking of this sort encouraged efficient authority, but it did not spread political values or a sense of the importance of political service very widely, in contrast to Confucianism in China and also to the intense interest in political ethics in Greece and Rome. Ashoka saw in Buddhism a kind of ethic for good behavior, as well as a spiritual beacon, but Buddhist leaders in the long run were not greatly interested in affairs of state. Indeed, Indian religion generally did not stress the importance of politics, even for religious purposes, but rather the preeminence of holy men and priests as sources of authority.

The limitations on the political traditions developed during this period of Indian history can be explained partly by the importance of local units of government—the tightly organized villages—and particularly by the essentially political qualities of social relationships under the caste system. Caste rules, interpreted by priests, regulated many social relationships and work roles. To a great extent, the caste system and religious encouragement in the faithful performance of caste duties did for Indian life what more conventional government structures did in many other cultures, in promoting public order.

India's caste system became steadily more complex after the Epic Age, as the five initial castes subdivided until ultimately almost 300 castes or Jati subcastes were defined. Hereditary principles grew ever stronger, so that it became virtually impossible to rise above the caste in which a person was born or to marry someone from a higher caste. It was possible to fall to a lower caste by marrying outside one's caste or

HISTORY DEBATE

Interpreting Civilization, Round Two

World historians have frequently debated the validity of the concept of civilization. We saw in Chapter 1 that civilizations differ from other societies but that the boundary lines are fuzzy; and also that societies that were not civilizations might be interesting and, in some cases, important historically. In dealing with the classical period, the initial definition of civilization is extended. The term still designates societies that have cities, organized governments, and, usually, writing. However, now it also designates some degree of coherence and distinctiveness within a given region—hence, Chinese civilization is different from Indian civilization.

Coherence, however, is not always easy to define. Except for Mesopotamia after Sumer, the river valley civilizations are not too problematic. Egypt, for example, usually had a single government and religion. By the classical centuries, however, civilizations covered large areas and embraced much diversity. South China differed from the north, even under the same government; there was much ethnic and linguistic tension. India, never entirely united by a single government (except briefly under foreign rule, well after the classical period) and with widely varied castes, is an even tougher case. Here, no single religion ever fully dominated, although Brahmanism and then Hinduism were the most characteristic. Even modern-day India does not control the whole subcontinent, in large part because of religious divisions. Here, the idea of a coherent, distinct civilization denotes predominant values (including the important overlap between Hinduism and Buddhism) and social structures, not full unity or identity. Treating major civilizations as tendencies that include important internal divisions and tensions, as entities that must be defined rather than assumed, helps capture the reality of how people have acted and continue to act in world history. Examining a classical civilization like India or China even helps frame the other major themes of world history, including the degree of openness to outside influences. Here too, however, some world historians differ, seeing common human impulses and global forces as the whole story, with civilizations merely an invention of scholars unable to shake off the arrogant claims of particular societies like China or, more recently, Western Europe. Here, it is important to establish one's own position as to how useful or misleading the concept of civilization is, while recognizing the main alternatives.

One other complication: The basic features of a given civilization do not stand still, nor do its boundaries. The transitions from river valley to classical civilizations illustrate this kind of passage. Each major period of world history requires a renewed definition, still with the basic goal of testing coherence and a certain degree of distinctiveness. India can still be labeled a civilization today: How do its characteristics and territory compare with those of its classical counterpart?

by taking on work deemed inappropriate for one's caste. Upward mobility could occur within castes, as individuals might gain greater wealth through success in the economic activities appropriate to the caste. The fact that Brahmins replaced warriors as the top caste also indicates some flexibility. And rulers, like the Mauryans, might spring from the merchant caste, although most princes were warrior-born. It is important not to characterize the caste system in an oversimplified way, for it did offer some flexibilities. Nevertheless, the system did give India the most rigid overall framework for a social structure of any of the classical civilizations.

In its origins, the caste system provided a way for India's various races, the conquerors and the conquered, to live together without perpetual conflict and without full integration of cultures and values. Quite different kinds of people could live side by side in village or city, separated by caste. In an odd way, castes promoted tolerance, and this was useful, given India's varied peoples and beliefs. The caste system also meant that extensive outright slavery was avoided. The lowest, untouchable caste was scorned, confined to poverty and degrading work, but its members were not directly owned by others.

The political consequences of the caste system derived from the detailed rules for each caste. These rules governed marriages and permissible jobs, but also social habits such as eating and drinking. For example, a person could not eat or drink with a lower-caste individual or perform any service for that person. This kind of regulation of behavior made detailed political administration less necessary. Indeed, no state could command full loyalty from subjects, for their first loyalty was to caste.

More of the qualities of Indian civilization rested on widely shared cultural values than was the case in China. Religion, and particularly the evolving Hindu religion as it gained ground on Buddhism under the Guptas, was the clearest cultural cement of this society, cutting across political and language barriers and across the castes. Hinduism itself embraced considerable variety, and it gave rise to important religious dissent. Nor did it ever displace important minority religions. However, Hinduism has shown a remarkable capacity to survive and is the major system of belief in India even today. It also promotes other features in Indian culture. Thus, contemporary Indian children are encouraged to indulge their imaginations longer than Western children, are confronted less sharply with outside reality. Some observers argue that even Indian adults, on average, are less interested in general, agreed upon truths than in individually satisfying versions. A mind set of this sort goes back to the religious patterns created over 2000 years ago in classical India, where Hinduism encouraged imaginative links with a higher, divine reality. It is this kind of tradition that illustrates how classical India, although not the source of enduring political institutions beyond the local level, produced a civilization that would retain clear continuity and cultural cohesiveness from this point onward—even through centuries in which political control escaped Indian hands almost completely.

RELIGION AND CULTURE

Hinduism, the religion of India's majority, developed gradually over a period of many centuries. Its origins lie in the Vedic and Epic ages, as the Aryan religion gained greater sophistication, with concerns about an overarching divinity supplementing the rituals and polytheistic beliefs supervised by the Brahmin caste of priests. The *Rig-Veda* expressed the growing interest in a higher divine principle in its Creation Hymn:

> Then even nothingness was not, nor existence. There was no air then, nor the heavens beyond it. Who covered it? Where was it? In whose keeping. . . ? The gods themselves are later than creation, so who knows truly whence it has arisen?

Unlike all the other world religions, Hinduism had no single founder, no central holy figure from whom the basic religious beliefs stemmed. This fact helps explain why the religion unfolded so gradually, sometimes in reaction to competing religions such as Buddhism or Islam. Moreover, Hinduism pursued a number of religious approaches, from the strictly ritualistic and ceremonial approach many Brahmins preferred, to the high-soaring mysticism that sought to unite individual humans with an all-embracing divine principle. Unlike Western religions or Daoism (which it resembled in part), Hinduism could also encourage political and economic goals (called Artha) and worldly pleasures (called Karma)—and important textbooks of the time spelled out these pursuits. Part of Hinduism's success, indeed, was the result of its fluidity, its ability to adapt to the different needs of various groups and to change with circumstance. With a belief that there are many suitable paths of worship, Hinduism was also characteristically tolerant, coexisting with several offshoot religions that garnered minority acceptance in India.

Under Brahmin leadership, Indian ideas about the gods gradually became more elaborate (initially, the religion was simply called Brahminism). Original gods of nature were altered to represent more abstract concepts. Thus, Varuna changed from a god of the sky to the guardian of ideas of right and wrong. The great poems of the Epic Age increasingly emphasized the importance of gentle and generous behavior, and the validity of a life devoted to concentration on the Supreme Spirit. The *Upanishads*, particularly, stressed the shallowness of worldly concerns—riches and even health were not the main point of human existence—in favor of contemplation of the divine spirit. It was in the *Upanishads* that the Hindu idea of a divine force informing the whole universe, of which each individual creature's soul is thought to be part, first surfaced clearly, in passages such as the following:

> *"Fetch me a fruit of the banyan tree."*
> *"Here is one, sir."*
> *"Break it."*
> *"I have broken it, sir."*
> *"What do you see?"*
> *"Very tiny seeds, sir."*
> *"Break one."*
> *"I have broken it, sir."*
> *"What do you see now?"*
> *"Nothing, sir."*
> *"My son, . . . what you do not perceive is the essence, and in that essence the mighty banyan tree exists. Believe me, my son, in that essence is the self of all that is. That is the True, that is the Self. . . ."*

Brahmin (early Hindu) painting from an epic story: Krishna playing the flute under the sacred tree.

However, the *Upanishads* did more than advance the idea of a mystical contact with a divine essence. They also attacked the conventional Brahmin view of what religion should be, a set of proper ceremonies that would lead to good things in this life or rewards after death. And from the Epic Age onward, Hinduism embraced this clear tension between a religion of rituals, with fixed ceremonies and rules of conduct, and the religion of mystical holy men, seeking communion with the divine soul.

The mystics, often called gurus as they gathered disciples around them, and the Brahmin priests agreed on certain doctrines, as Hinduism became an increasingly formal religion by the first centuries of the common era. The basic holy essence, called *Brahma*, formed part of everything in this world. Every living creature participates in this divine principle. The spirit of Brahma enters several gods or forms of gods, including Vishnu, the preserver, and Siva, the destroyer, who could be worshipped or placated as expressions of the holy essence. The world of our senses is far less important than the world of the divine soul, and a proper life is one devoted to seeking union with this soul. However, this quest may take many lifetimes, and Hindus stressed the principle of reincarnation, in which souls do not die when bodies do but pass into other beings, either human or animal. Where the soul goes, whether it rises to a higher-caste person or falls perhaps to an animal, depends on how good a life the person has led. Ultimately, after many good lives, the soul reaches full union with the soul of Brahma, and worldly suffering ceases.

Hinduism provided several channels for the good life. For the holy men, there was the meditation and self-discipline of yoga, which means "union," allowing the mind to be freed to concentrate on the divine spirit. For others, there were the rituals and rules of the Brahmins. These included proper ceremonies in the cremation of bodies at death, appropriate prayers, and obedience to injunctions such as treating cows as sacred animals and refraining from the consumption of beef. Many Hindus also continued the idea of lesser gods represented in the spirits of nature, or purely local divinities, which could be seen as expressions of Siva or Vishnu. Worship to these divinities could aid the process of reincarnation to a higher state. Thus, many ordinary Hindus placed a lot of importance on prayers, sacrifices, and gifts to the gods that would bring them through reincarnation into a higher caste.

Hinduism also provided a basic, if complex, ethic that helped supply some unity amid the various forms of worship. The epic poems, richly symbolic, formed the key texts. They illustrated a central emphasis on the moral law of *dharma* as a guide to living in this world and simultaneously pursuing higher, spiritual goals. The concept of *dharma* directed attention to the moral consequences of action and at the same time the need to act. Each person must meet the obligations of life, serving the family, producing a livelihood and even earning money, and serving in the army when the need arises. These actions cannot damage, certainly cannot destroy, the eternal divine essence that underlies all creation. In the *Bhagavad Gita,* a classic sacred hymn, a warrior is sent to do battle against his own relatives. Fearful of killing them, he is advised by a god that he must carry out his duties. He will not really be killing his victims because their divine spirit will live on. This ethic urged that honorable behavior, even pleasure seeking, is compatible with spirituality and can lead to a final release from the life cycle and to unity with the divine essence. The Hindu ethic explains how devout Hindus could also be aggressive merchants or eager warriors. In encouraging honorable action, it could legitimize government and the caste system as providing the frameworks in which the duties of the world might be carried out, without distracting from the ultimate spiritual goals common to all people.

The ethical concept of *dharma* was far less detailed and prescriptive than the ethical codes associated with most other world religions, including Christianity and Islam. *Dharma* stresses inner study and meditation, building from the divine essence within each creature, rather than adherence to a fixed set of moral rules.

The spread of Hinduism through India and, at least briefly, to some other parts of Asia had many sources. The religion accommodated extreme spirituality. It also provided satisfying rules of conduct for ordinary life, including rituals and a firm emphasis on the distinction between good and evil behavior. The religion allowed many people to retain older beliefs and ceremonies, derived from a more purely polytheistic religion. It reinforced the caste system, giving people in lower castes hope for a better time in lives to come and giving upper-caste people, including the Brahmins, the satisfaction that if they behaved well, they might be rewarded by communion with the divine soul. Even though Hindu beliefs took shape only gradually and contained many ambiguities, the religion was sustained by a strong caste of priests and through the efforts of individual gurus and mystics.

Indian relief: Buddha renouncing the world.

At times, however, the tensions within Hinduism broke down for some individuals, producing rebellions against the dominant religion. One such rebellion, which occurred right after the Epic Age, led to a new religion closely related to Hinduism. Around 563 B.C.E., an Indian prince, Gautama, was born who came to question the fairness of earthly life in which so much poverty and misery abounded. Gautama, later called "Buddha" or "enlightened one," lived as a Hindu mystic, fasting and torturing his body. After six years, he felt that he had found truth, then spent his life traveling and gathering disciples to spread his ideas. Buddha accepted many Hindu beliefs, but he protested the Brahmin emphasis on ceremonies. In a related sense, he downplayed the polytheistic element in Hinduism by focusing on the supreme divinity over separate, lesser gods. Buddha believed in rewards after life, seeing the ultimate goal as destruction of the self and union with the divine essence, a state that he called "nirvana." Individuals could regulate their lives and aspirations toward this goal, without elaborate ceremonies. Great stress was placed on self-control: "Let a man overcome anger by love, let him overcome evil by good, let him overcome the greedy by liberality, the liar by the truth." A holy life could be achieved through individual effort from any level of society. Here, Buddhism attacked not only the priests but also the caste system; this was another sign of the complexity of Indian social life in practice.

Buddhism spread and retained coherence through the example and teachings of groups of holy men, organized in monasteries but preaching throughout the world. Buddhism attracted many followers in India itself, and its growth was greatly spurred by the conversion of the Mauryan emperor Ashoka. Increasingly, Buddha himself was seen as divine. Prayer and contemplation at Buddhist holy places and works of charity and piety gave substance to the idea of a holy life on earth. Ironically, however, Buddhism did not witness a permanent following in India. Brahmin opposition was strong, and it was ultimately aided by the influence of the Gupta emperors. Furthermore, Hinduism showed its adaptability by emphasizing its mystical side, thus retaining the loyalties of many Indians. Buddhism's greatest successes, aided by the missionary encouragement of Ashoka and later the Kushan emperors, came in other parts of Southeast Asia, including the island of Sri Lanka, off the south coast of India, and in China, Korea, and Japan. Still, pockets of Buddhists remained in India, particularly in the northeast. They were joined by other dissident groups who rejected aspects of Hinduism. Thus, Hinduism, although dominant, had to come to terms with the existence of other religions early on.

If Hinduism, along with the caste system, formed the most distinctive and durable products of the classical period of Indian history, they were certainly not the only ones. Even aside from dissident religions, Indian culture during this period was vibrant and diverse, and religion encompassed only part of its interests. Hinduism itself encouraged many wider pursuits.

Indian thinkers wrote actively about various aspects of human life. Although political theory was sparse, a great deal of legal writing occurred. The theme of love was important also. A manual of the "laws of love," the *Kama-sutra,* written in the fourth century C.E., is an unusually elaborate and expressive discussion of the sexual experience.

Indian literature, taking many themes from the great epic poems and their tales of military adventure, stressed lively story lines. The epics themselves were recorded in final written form during the Gupta period, and other story collections, like the *Panchatantra,* which includes Sinbad the Sailor, Jack the Giant Killer, and the Seven League boots, produced adventurous yarns now known all over the world. Classical stories were often secular, but they sometimes included the gods and also shared with Hinduism an emphasis on imagination and excitement. Indian drama flourished also, again particularly under the Guptas, and stressed themes of romantic adventure in which lovers separated and then reunited after many perils. This literary tradition created a cultural framework that still survives in India. Even contemporary Indian movies reflect the tradition of swashbuckling romance and heroic action.

Classical India also produced important work in science and mathematics. The Guptas supported a vast university center—one of the world's first—in the town of Nalanda that attracted students from other parts of Asia as well as Indian Brahmins. Nalanda had over a hundred lecture halls, three large libraries, an astronomical observatory, and even a model dairy. Its curriculum included religion, philosophy, medicine, architecture, and agriculture.

At the research level, Indian scientists, borrowing a bit from Greek learning after the conquests of Alexander the Great, made important strides in astronomy and medicine. The great astronomer Aryabhatta calculated the length of the solar year and improved mathematical measurements. Indian astronomers understood and calculated the daily rotation of the earth on its axis, predicted and explained eclipses, and developed a theory of gravity, and through telescopic observation they identified seven planets. Medical research was hampered by religious prohibitions on dissection, but Indian surgeons nevertheless made advances in bone setting and plastic surgery. Inoculation against smallpox was introduced, using cowpox serum. Indian hospitals stressed cleanliness, including sterilization of wounds, while leading doctors promoted high ethical standards. As was the case with Indian discoveries in astronomy, many medical findings reached the Western world only in modern times.

Indian mathematics produced still more important discoveries. The Indian numbering system is the one we use today, although we call it Arabic because Europeans imported it secondhand from the Arabs. Indians invented the concept of zero, and through it they were able to develop the decimal system. Indian advances in numbering rank with writing itself as key human inventions. Indian mathematicians also developed the concept of negative numbers, calculated square roots and a table of sines, and computed the value of pi more accurately than the Greeks did.

Brahmin (early Hindu) sculpture: The god Siva Natarajah as the lord of dance.

Finally, classical India produced lively art, although much of it perished under later invasions. Ashoka sponsored many spherical shrines to Buddha, called "stupas," and statues honoring Buddha were also common. Under the Guptas, sculpture and painting moved away from realistic portrayals of the human form toward more stylized representation. Indian painters, working on the walls of buildings and caves, filled their work with forms of people and animals, captured in lively color. Indian art showed a keen appreciation of nature, and some of it also suggested several of the erotic themes expressed in works like the *Kama-sutra*. This was an art that could pay homage to religious values, particularly during the period in which Buddhism briefly spread, but could also celebrate the joys of life.

There was, clearly, no full unity to this cultural outpouring. Religion, legalism, abstract mathematics, and a sensual and adventurous art and literature coexisted. The result, however, was a somewhat distinctive overall tone, different from the more rational approaches of the West or the Chinese concentration on political ethics. In various cultural expressions, Indians developed an interest in spontaneity and imagination, whether in fleshly pleasures or a mystical union with the divine essence.

UNDERSTANDING CULTURES

Comparing Systems of Belief

One of the key challenges in dealing with cultures in world history involves comparison. China and India during the classical period obviously developed very different cultural emphases. The contrast between Confucianism and Hinduism was sharp. Confucianists emphasized goals in this world and the primary quest for order; Hinduism focused on otherworldliness, and encouraged spiritual intuition and imagination. Differences spilled into art, with India's sensuality and Chinese emphasis on more restrained, balanced portrayals of nature.

These differences, however, should not be exaggerated. Both civilizations produced diversity. Chinese Daoists used language more similar to that of Hindus and Buddhists. Indian scientists, although more mathematically inclined than the Chinese, worked on some similar problems in astronomy and medicine.

Further, both civilizations used culture to help hold diverse populations together. Confucianism and Hinduism alike, although in very different ways, provided justifications for social inequality. According to Confucianism, inferiors should accept their lot, knowing that the upper classes will treat them responsibly and that orderliness is vital. According to Hinduism, inferiors should accept their lot, knowing that performing one's caste duty in this life would lead to spiritual advances in a subsequent existence. Contrast, in other words, must not monopolize a cultural comparison. Sometimes, the functions of cultures are far more similar than their specific forms.

ECONOMY AND SOCIETY

The caste system described many key features of Indian social and economic life, as it assigned people to occupations and regulated marriages. Low-caste individuals had few legal rights, and servants were often abused by their masters, who were restrained only by the ethical promptings of religion toward kindly treatment. A Brahmin who killed a servant for misbehavior faced a penalty no more severe than if he had killed an animal. This extreme level of abuse was uncommon, but the caste system did unquestionably make its mark on daily life as well as on the formal structure of society. The majority of Indians living in peasant villages had less frequent contact with people of higher social castes, and village leaders were charged with trying to protect peasants from too much interference by landlords and rulers.

Family life also emphasized the theme of hierarchy and tight organization, as it evolved from the Vedic and Epic ages. The dominance of husbands and fathers remained strong. One Indian code of law recommended that a wife worship her husband as a god. Indeed, the rights of women became increasingly limited as Indian civilization took clearer shape. Although the great epics stressed the control of husband and father, they also recognized women's independent contributions. As agriculture became better organized and improved technology reduced (without eliminating) women's economic contributions, the stress on male authority expanded. This is a common pattern in agricultural societies, as a sphere of action women enjoyed in hunting cultures was gradually circumscribed. Hindu thinkers debated whether a woman could advance spiritually without first being reincarnated as a man, and there was no consensus. The limits imposed on women were reflected in laws and literary references. A system of arranged marriage evolved in which parents contracted unions for children, particularly daughters, at quite early ages, to spouses they had never even met. The goal of these arrangements was to ensure solid economic links, with child brides contributing dowries of land or domestic animals to the ultimate family estates, but the result of such arrangements was that young people, especially girls, were drawn into a new family structure in which they had no voice.

However, the rigidities of family life and male dominance over women were often greater in theory than they usually turned out to be in practice. The emphasis on loving relations and sexual pleasure in Indian culture modified family life, since husband and wife were supposed to provide mutual emotional support as a marriage developed. The Mahabharata epic called a man's wife his truest friend: "Even a man in the grip of rage will not be harsh to a woman, remembering that on her depend the joys of love, happiness, and virtue." Small children were often pampered. "With their teeth half shown in causeless laughter, their efforts at talking so sweetly uncertain, when children ask to sit on his lap, a man is blessed." Families thus served an important and explicit emotional function as well as a role in supporting the structure of society and its institutions. They also, as in all agricultural societies, formed economic units. Children, after early years of indulgence, were expected to work hard. Adults were obligated to assist older relatives. The purpose of arranged marriages was to promote a family's economic well-being, and almost everyone lived in a family setting.

The Indian version of the patriarchal family was thus subtly different from that in China, although women were officially just as subordinate and later trends—as in many patriarchal societies over time—would bring new burdens. But, Indian culture often featured clever and strong-willed women and goddesses, and this contributed to women's status as wives and mothers. Stories also celebrated women's emotions and beauty.

The economy of India in the classical period became extremely vigorous, certainly rivaling China in technological sophistication and probably briefly surpassing China in the prosperity of its upper classes. In manufacturing, Indians invented new uses for chemistry, and their steel was the best in the world. Indian capacity in iron-making outdistanced European levels until a few centuries ago. Indian techniques in textiles were also advanced, as the subcontinent became the first to manufacture cotton cloth, calico, and cashmere. Most manufacturing was done by artisans who formed guilds and sold their goods from shops.

Indian emphasis on trade and merchant activity was far greater than in China, and indeed greater than that of the classical Mediterranean world. Indian merchants enjoyed relatively high caste status and the flexibility of the Hindu ethic. And, they traveled widely, not only over the subcontinent but, by sea, to the Middle East and East Asia. The seafaring peoples along the southern coast, usually outside the large empires of northern India, were particularly active. These southern Indians, the Tamils, traded cotton and silks, dyes, drugs, gold, and ivory, often earning great fortunes. From the Middle East and the Roman Empire, they brought back pottery, wine, metals, some slaves, and above all gold. Their trade with Southeast Asia was even more active, as Indian merchants transported not only sophisticated manufactured goods but also the trappings of India's active culture to places like Malaysia and the larger islands of Indonesia. In addition, caravan trade developed with China.

The Indian economy remained firmly agricultural at its base. The wealth of the upper classes and the splendor of cities like Nalanda were confined to a small group, as most people lived near the margins of subsistence. But India was justly known by the time of the Guptas for its wealth as well as for its religion and intellectual life—always understanding that wealth was relative in the classical world and very unevenly divided. A Chinese Buddhist on a pilgrimage to India wrote:

> The people are many and happy. They do not have to register their households with the police. There is no death penalty. Religious sects have houses of charity where rooms, couches, beds, food, and drink are supplied to travelers.

INDIAN INFLUENCE

Classical India, from the Mauryan period onward, had a considerable influence on other parts of the world. In many ways, the Indian Ocean, dominated at this point by Indian merchants and missionaries, was the most active linkage point among cultures, although admittedly, the Mediterranean, which channeled contact from the Middle East to North Africa and Europe, was a close second. Indian dominance of the waters of southern Asia, and the impressive creativity of Indian civilization itself, carried goods and influence well beyond the subcontinent's borders. No previous civilization had developed in Southeast Asia to compete with Indian influence. And while India did not attempt political domination, dealing instead with the regional kingdoms of Burma, Thailand, parts of Indonesia, and Vietnam, Indian travelers or settlers did bring to these locales a persuasive way of life. Many Indian merchants married into local royal families. Indian-style temples were constructed and other forms of Indian art traveled widely. Buddhism spread from India to many parts of Southeast Asia, and Hinduism converted many upper-class people, particularly in several of the Indonesian kingdoms. India thus serves as an early example of a major civilization expanding its influence well beyond its own regions.

Indian influence had affected China, through Buddhism and art, by the end of the classical period. Earlier, Buddhist emissaries to the Middle East stimulated new ethical thinking that informed Greek and Roman groups like the Stoics and through them aspects of Christianity later on.

Within India itself, the classical period, starting a bit late after the Aryan invasions, lasted somewhat longer than that of China or Rome. Even when the period ended with the fall of the Guptas, an identifiable civilization remained in India, building on several key factors first established in the classical period: the religion, to be sure, but also the artistic and literary tradition and the complex social and family network. The ability of this civilization to survive, even under long periods of foreign domination, was testimony to the meaning and variety it offered to many Indians themselves.

CONCLUSION: CHINA AND INDIA

The thrusts of classical civilization in China and India reveal the diversity generated during the classical age. The restraint of Chinese art and poetry contrasted with the more dynamic sensual styles of India. India ultimately settled on a primary religion, though with important minority expressions, that embodied diverse impulses within it. China opted for separate religious and philosophical systems that would serve different needs. China's political structures and values found little echo in India, whereas the Indian caste system involved a social rigidity considerably greater than that of China. India's cultural emphasis was, on balance, considerably more other-worldly than that of China, despite the impact of Daoism. Quite obviously, classical India and classical China created vastly different cultures. Even in science, where there was similar interest in pragmatic discoveries about how the world works, the Chinese placed greater stress on purely practical findings, whereas the Indians ventured further into the mathematical arena.

Beyond the realm of formal culture and the institutions of government, India and China may seem more similar. As agricultural societies, both civilizations relied on a large peasant class, organized in close-knit villages with much mutual cooperation. Cities and merchant activity, although vital, played a secondary role. Political power rested primarily with those who controlled the land, through ownership of large estates and the ability to tax the peasant class. On a more personal level, the power of husbands and fathers in the family—the basic fact of patriarchy—encompassed Indian and Chinese families alike.

However, Indian and Chinese societies differed in more than their religion, philosophy, art, and politics. Ordinary people had cultures along with elites. Hindu peasants saw their world differently from their Chinese counterparts. They placed less emphasis on personal emotional restraint and detailed etiquette; they expected different emotional interactions with family members. Indian peasants were less constrained than were the Chinese by recurrent efforts by large landlords to gain control of their land. Although there were wealthy landlords in India, the system of village control of most land was more firmly entrenched than in China. Indian merchants played a greater role than their Chinese counterparts. There was more sea trade, more commercial vitality. Revealingly, India's expanding cultural influence was due to merchant activity above all else, whereas Chinese expansion involved government initiatives in gaining new territory and sending proud emissaries to satellite states. These differences were less dramatic, certainly less easy to document, than those generated by elite thinkers and politicians, but they contributed to the shape of a civilization and to its particular vitality, its areas of stability and instability.

Because each classical civilization developed its own unique style, in social relationships as well as in formal politics and intellectual life, exchanges between two societies like China and India involved specific borrowings, not wholesale imitation. India and China, the two giants of classical Asia, remain subjects of comparison to our own time, because they have continued to build distinctively on their particular traditions, established before 500 C.E. These characteristics, in turn, differed from those of yet another center of civilization, the societies that sprang up on the shores of the Mediterranean during this same classical age.

SUGGESTED WEBSITES

On the Guptas, see *http://www.meadev.gov.in/culture/history/history3.htm*. India's first great emperor, Chandragupta Maurya, is discussed at *http://www.itihaas.com/ancient/chandra.html*.

SUGGESTED READINGS

Two useful sources for Indian religion and philosophy are Franklin Edgerton, tr. and ed., *The Bhagavad Gita, Translated and Interpreted* (1944) and S. Radhakrishnan and Charles Moore, eds., *A Source Book in Indian Philosophy* (1957). There are fewer provocative surveys of Indian history than available about China, but at least four competent efforts exist: Romila Thaper, *A History of India,* Vol. 1 (1966); P. Spear, *India* (1981); Stanley Wolpert, *A New History of India* (1994); and D. D. Kosambi, *Ancient India, A History of Its Culture and Civilization* (1965). See also Rhoads Murphy, *A History of Asia* (1992). On more specialized topics, see J. W. Sedlar, *India and the Greek World* (1952); H. Scharff, *That State in Indian Tradition* (1988); T. Hopkins, *The Hindu Religious Tradition* (1971); Jeannine Auboyer, *Daily Life in Ancient India* (1961); A. L. Basham, *A Cultural History of India* (1975); and Trevor Ling, *The Buddha* (1973).

Classical Civilization in the Mediterranean: Greece and Rome

The Mediterranean, as the third center of classical civilization, must be characterized and then compared with China and India. What were the main institutions and values of classical Greece? What did the Hellenistic period and then Roman society add to the patterns of this particular classical civilization? What features did the classical Mediterranean share with India and China, and what were the most important differences? There are particular challenges in analyzing Greece and Rome: Amid a variety of political forms, including democracy in parts of Greece, what were the most characteristic government structures? What was the political and economic impact of widespread slavery? Why, compared to India and China, did Rome prove especially vulnerable to deterioration after the heyday of its empire?

INTRODUCTION

The classical civilizations that sprang up on the shores of the Mediterranean Sea from about 800 B.C.E. until the fall of the Roman Empire in 476 C.E. rivaled their counterparts in India and China in richness and impact. Centered first in the peninsula of Greece, then in Rome's burgeoning provinces, the new Mediterranean culture did not embrace all of the civilized lands of the ancient Middle East. Greece rebuffed the advance of the mighty Persian Empire and established some colonies on the eastern shore of the Mediterranean, in what is now Turkey, but it only briefly conquered more than a fraction of the civilized Middle East. Rome came closer to conquering surrounding peoples, but even its empire had to contend with strong kingdoms to the east. Nevertheless, Greece and Rome do not merely constitute a westward push of civilization from its earlier bases in the Middle East and along the Nile—although this is a part of their story. They also represent the formation of new institutions and values that would reverberate in the later history of the Middle East and Europe alike.

For most Americans, and not only those who are descendants of European immigrants, classical Mediterranean culture constitutes "our own" classical past, or at least a goodly part of it. The framers of the American Constitution were extremely conscious of Greek and Roman precedents. Designers of public buildings in the United States, from the early days of the American republic to the present, have dutifully copied Greek and Roman models, as in the Lincoln Memorial and most state capitols. Plato and Aristotle continue to be thought of as the founders of our philosophical tradition, and skillful teachers still rely on some imitation of the Socratic method. Our sense of debt to Greece and Rome may inspire us to find in their history special meaning or links to our own world; the Western educational experience has long included elaborate explorations of the Greco-Roman past as part of the standard academic education. But from the standpoint of world history, greater balance is obviously necessary. Greco-Roman history is one of the three major classical civilizations, more dynamic than its Chinese and Indian counterparts in some respects but noticeably less successful in others. The challenge is to discern the leading features of Greek and Roman civilization and to next compare them with those of their counterparts elsewhere. We can then clearly recognize the connections and our own debt without adhering to the notion that the Mediterranean world somehow dominated the classical period.

Classical Mediterranean civilization is complicated by the fact that it passed through two centers during its centuries of vigor, as Greek political institutions rose and then declined and the legions of Rome assumed leadership. Roman interests were not identical to those of Greece, although the Romans carefully preserved most Greek achievements. Rome mastered engineering, Greece specialized in scientific thought. Rome created a mighty empire, whereas the Greek city-states proved rather inept in forming an empire. It is possible, certainly, to see more than a change in emphases from Greece to Rome, and to talk about separate civilizations instead of a single basic pattern. And it is true that Greek influence was always stronger than Roman in the eastern Mediterranean, whereas Western Europe would encounter a fuller Greco-Roman mixture, with Roman influence predominating in language and law. However, Greek and Roman societies shared many political ideas; they had a common religion and artistic styles; they developed similar economic structures. Certainly, their classical heritage would be used by successive civilizations without fine distinctions drawn between what was Greek and what was Roman.

THE PERSIAN TRADITION

As a vibrant classical civilization developed in the Mediterranean, a second center flourished in the Middle East, inheriting many of the achievements of the earlier Mesopotamian society. By 550 B.C.E., Cyrus the Great established a massive Persian Empire across the northern Middle East and into northwestern India. Although tolerant of local customs, the Persians advanced iron technology, developed a new religion—Zoroastrianism—and a lively artistic style. While the Persians had only limited influence on the Mediterranean coast and were ultimately toppled by the Greek-educated conqueror Alexander the Great, Persian language and culture survived in the northeastern portion of the Middle East, periodically affecting developments elsewhere in the region even into the twentieth century. A separate empire in the area, the Sassanid, emerged again during Rome's imperial centuries.

PATTERNS OF GREEK AND ROMAN HISTORY

Greece.   Even as Persia developed, a new civilization took shape to the west, building on a number of earlier precedents. The river valley civilizations of the Middle East and Africa had spread to some of the islands near the Greek peninsula, although less to the peninsula itself. The island of Crete, in particular, showed the results of Egyptian influence by 2000 B.C.E., and from this the Greeks were later able to develop a taste for monumental architecture. The Greeks themselves were an Indo-European people, like the Aryan conquerors of India, who took over the peninsula by 1700 B.C.E. An early kingdom in southern Greece, strongly influenced by Crete, developed by 1400 B.C.E. around the city of Mycenae. This was the kingdom later memorialized in Homer's epics about the Trojan War. Mycenae was then toppled by a subsequent wave of Indo-European invaders, whose incursions destroyed civilization on the peninsula until about 800 B.C.E.

The rapid rise of civilization in Greece between 800 and 600 B.C.E. was based on the creation of strong city-states, rather than a single political unit. Each city-state had its own government, typically either a tyranny of one ruler or an aristocratic council. The city-state served Greece well, for the peninsula was so divided by mountains that a unified government would have been difficult to establish. Trade developed rapidly under city-state sponsorship, and common cultural forms, including a rich written language with letters derived from the Phoenician alphabet, spread throughout the peninsula. The Greek city-states also joined in regular celebrations such as the athletic competitions of the Olympic games. Sparta and Athens came to be the two leading city-states: The first represented a strong military aristocracy dominating a slave population; the other was a more diverse commercial state, also including the extensive use of slaves, justly proud of its artistic and intellectual leadership. Between 500 and 449 B.C.E., the two states cooperated, along with smaller states, to defeat a huge Persian invasion. It was during and immediately after this period that Greek and particularly Athenian culture reached its highest point. Also during this period several city-states, and again particularly Athens, developed more colonies in the eastern Mediterranean and southern Italy, as Greek culture fanned out to create a larger zone of civilization.

It was during the fifth century B.C.E. that the most famous Greek political figure, Pericles, dominated Athenian politics. Pericles was an aristocrat, but he was part of a democratic political structure in which each citizen could participate in city-state assemblies to select officials and pass laws. Pericles ruled not through official position, but by wise influence and negotiation. He helped restrain some of the more aggressive views of the Athenian democrats, who urged even further expansion of the empire to garner more wealth and build the economy. Ultimately, however, Pericles' guidance could not prevent the tragic war between Athens and Sparta, which would deplete both sides.

Political decline soon set in, as Athens and Sparta vied for control of Greece during the bitter Peloponnesian Wars (431–404 B.C.E.). Ambitious kings from Macedonia, in the northern part of the peninsula, soon conquered the cities. Philip of Macedonia won the crucial battle in 338 B.C.E., and then his son Alexander extended the Macedonian Empire through the Middle East, across Persia to the border of India, and southward through Egypt. Alexander the Great's empire was short-lived, for its creator died at the age of 33 after a mere 13 years of breathtaking conquests. However, successor regional kingdoms continued to rule much of the eastern Mediterranean for several centuries. Under their aegis, Greek art and culture merged with other Middle Eastern forms during a period called "Hellenistic," the name derived because of the influence of the Hellenes, as the Greeks were known. Although there

Alexander the Great and the Hellenistic World

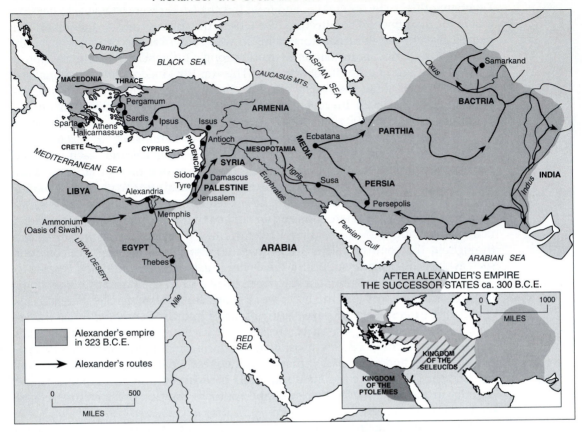

was little political activity under the autocratic Hellenistic kings, trade flourished and important scientific centers were established in such cities as Alexandria in Egypt. In sum, the Hellenistic period saw the consolidation of Greek civilization even after the political decline of the peninsula itself, as well as some important new cultural developments.

Rome.   The rise of Rome formed the final phase of classical Mediterranean civilization, for by the first century B.C.E. Rome had subjugated Greece and the Hellenistic kingdoms alike. The Roman state began humbly enough, as a local monarchy in central Italy around 800 B.C.E. Roman aristocrats succeeded in driving out the monarchy around 509 B.C.E. and established more elaborate political institutions for their city-state. The new Roman republic gradually extended its influence over the rest of the Italian peninsula, among other things conquering the Greek colonies in the south. Thus, the Romans early acquired a strong military orientation, although initially they may have been driven simply by a desire to protect their own territory from possible rivals. Roman conquest spread more widely during the three Punic Wars, from 264 to 146 B.C.E., during which Rome fought the armies of the Phoenician city of Carthage, situated on the northern coast of Africa. These wars included a bloody defeat of the invading forces of the brilliant Carthaginian general Hannibal, whose troops were accompanied by pack-laden elephants. The war was so bitter that the Romans in a final act of destruction spread salt around Carthage to prevent agriculture from surviving there. Following the final destruction of Carthage, the Romans proceeded to seize the entire western Mediterranean along with Greece and Egypt.

The politics of the Roman republic itself grew increasingly unstable, however, as victorious generals sought even greater power while the poor of the city rebelled. Civil wars between two generals led to a victory by Julius Caesar, in 45 B.C.E., and the effective end of the traditional institutions of the Roman state. Caesar's grand-nephew, ultimately called Augustus Caesar, seized power in 27 B.C.E., following another period of rivalry after Julius Caesar's assassination, and established the basic structures of the Roman Empire. For 200 years, through the reign of the emperor Marcus Aurelius in 180 C.E., the empire maintained great vigor, bringing peace and prosperity to virtually the entire Mediterranean world, from Spain and North Africa in the west to the eastern shores of the great sea. The emperors also moved northward, conquering France and southern Britain and pushing into Germany. Here was a major, if somewhat tenuous, extension of the sway of Mediterranean civilization to Western Europe.

Then the empire suffered a slow but decisive fall, which lasted over 250 years, until invading peoples from the north finally overturned the government in Rome in 476 C.E. The decline manifested itself in terms of both economic deterioration and population loss: Trade levels and the birthrate both fell. Government also became generally less effective, although some strong later emperors, particularly Diocletian and Constantine, attempted to reverse the tide. It was the emperor Constantine who, in 313, adopted the then somewhat obscure religion called Christianity in an attempt to unite the empire in new ways. However, particularly in the western half of the empire, most effective government became local, as the imperial administration could no longer guarantee order or even provide a system of justice. The Roman armies depended increasingly on non-Roman recruits, whose loyalty was suspect. And then, in this deepening mire, the invasion of nomadic peoples from the north marked the end of the classical period of Mediterranean civilization—a civilization that, like its counterparts in Gupta India and Han China during the same approximate period, could no longer defend itself.

To conclude: The new Mediterranean civilization built on earlier cultures along the eastern Mediterranean and within the Greek islands, taking firm shape with the rise of the Greek city-states after 800 B.C.E. These states began as monarchies but then evolved into more complex and diverse political forms. They also developed a more varied commercial economy, moving away from a purely grain-growing agriculture; this spurred the formation of a number of colonial outposts around the eastern Mediterranean and in Italy. The decline of the city-states ushered in the Macedonian conquest and the formation of a wider Hellenistic culture that established deep roots in the Middle East and Egypt. Then Rome, initially a minor regional state distinguished by political virtue and stability, embarked on its great conquests, which would bring it control of the Mediterranean with important extensions into western

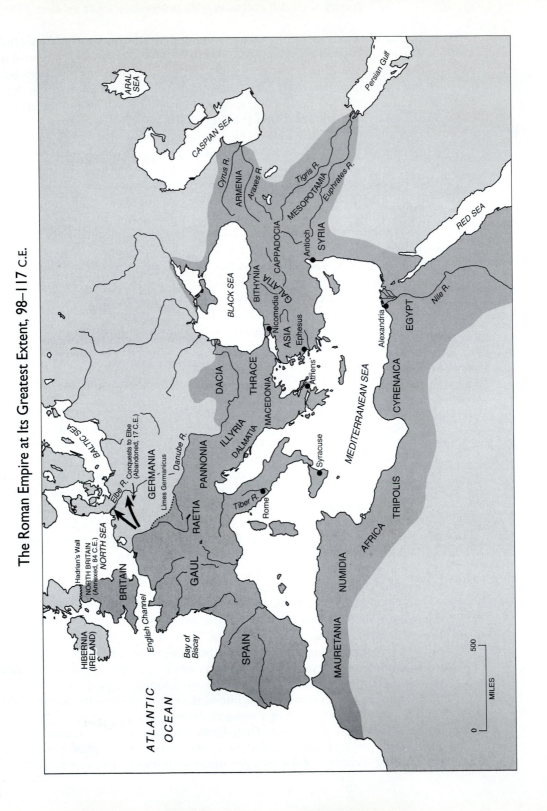

The Roman Empire at Its Greatest Extent, 98–117 C.E.

and southeastern Europe plus the whole of North Africa. Rome's expansion ultimately overwhelmed its own republic, but the successor empire developed important political institutions of its own and resulted in two centuries of peace and glory.

GREEK AND ROMAN POLITICAL INSTITUTIONS

Politics were very important in classical Mediterranean civilization, from the Greek city-states through the early part of the Roman Empire. Indeed, our word *politics* comes from the Greek word for city-state, *polis,* which correctly suggests that intense political interests were part of life in a city-state in both Greece and Rome. The "good life" for an upper-class Athenian or Roman included active participation in politics and frequent discussions about the affairs of state. The local character of Mediterranean politics, whereby the typical city-state governed a surrounding territory of several hundred square miles, contributed to this intense preoccupation with politics. Citizens felt that the state was theirs, that they had certain rights and obligations without which their government could not survive. In the Greek city-states and also under the Roman republic, citizens actively participated in the military, which further contributed to this sense of political interest and responsibility. Under the Roman Empire, of course, political concerns were restricted by the sheer power of the emperor and his officers. Even then, however, local city-states retained considerable autonomy in Italy, Greece, and the eastern Mediterranean—the empire did not try to administer most local regions in great detail. And, the minority of people throughout the empire who were Roman citizens were intensely proud of this privilege.

Strong political ideals and interests created some similarities between Greco-Roman society and the Confucian values of classical China, although the concept of active citizenship was distinctive in the Mediterranean cultures. However, Greece and Rome did not develop a single or cohesive set of political institutions to rival China's divinely sanctioned emperor or its elaborate bureaucracy. So in addition to political intensity and localism as characteristics of Mediterranean civilization, we must note great diversity in political forms. Here the comparison extends to India, where various political forms—including participation in governing councils—ran strong. Later societies, in reflecting on classical Mediterranean civilization, did select from a number of political precedents. Monarchy was not a preferred form; the Roman republic and most Greek city-states had abolished early monarchies as part of their prehistory. Rule by individual strongmen was more common, and our word *tyranny* comes from this experience in classical Greece. Many tyrants were effective rulers, particularly in promoting public works and protecting the common people against the abuses of the aristocracy. Some of the Roman generals who seized power in the later days of the republic had similar characteristics, as did the Hellenistic kings who succeeded Alexander in ruling regions of his empire.

Greece.   Democracy (the word is derived from the Greek *demos,* "the people") was another important political alternative in classical Mediterranean society. The Athenian city-state traveled furthest in this direction, before and during the Peloponnesian

Wars, after earlier experiences with aristocratic rule and with several tyrants. In fifth-century Athens, the major decisions of state were made by general assemblies in which all citizens could participate—although usually only a minority attended. This was direct democracy, not rule through elected representatives. The assembly met every ten days. Executive officers, including judges, were chosen for brief terms to control their power, and they were subject to review by the assembly. Furthermore, they were chosen by lot, not elected—on the principle that any citizen could and should be able to serve. To be sure, only a minority of the Athenian population were active citizens. Women had no rights of political participation. And half of all adult males were not citizens at all, being slaves or foreigners. This, then, was not exactly the kind of democracy we envision today. But, it did elicit widespread popular partic-ipation and devotion, and certainly embodied principles that we would recognize as truly democratic. The Athenian leader Pericles, who led Athens during its decades of greatest glory between the final defeat of the Persians and the agony of war with Sparta, described the system this way:

> The administration is in the hands of the many and not of the few. But while the law se-cures equal justice to all alike in their private disputes, the claim of excellence is also rec-ognized; and when a citizen is in any way distinguished he is preferred to the public ser-vice, not as a matter of privilege but as the reward of merit. Neither is poverty a bar, but a man may benefit his country whatever be the obscurity of his condition.

During the Peloponnesian Wars, Athens even demonstrated some of the potential drawbacks of democracy. Lower-class citizens, eager for government jobs and the spoils of war, often encouraged reckless military actions that weakened the state in its central dispute with Sparta.

Neither tyranny nor democracy, however, was the most characteristic political form in the classical Mediterranean world. The most widely preferred political frame-work centered on the existence of aristocratic assemblies, whose deliberations estab-lished guidelines for state policy and served as a check on executive power. Thus, Sparta was governed by a singularly militaristic aristocracy, intent on retaining power over a large slave population. Other Greek city-states, although less bent on disci-plining their elites for rigorous military service, also featured aristocratic assemblies. Even Athens during much of its democratic phase found leadership in many aristo-crats, including Pericles himself. The word *aristocracy,* which comes from Greek terms meaning "rule of the best," suggests where many Greeks—particularly, of course, aris-tocrats themselves—thought real political virtue lay.

Rome.   The constitution of the Roman republic, until the final decades of dissen-sion in the first century b.c.e., which led to the establishment of the empire, tried to reconcile the various elements suggested by the Greek political experience, with pri-mary reliance on the principle of aristocracy. All Roman citizens in the republic could gather in periodic assemblies, the function of which was not to pass basic laws but rather to elect various magistrates, some of whom were specifically entrusted with the task of representing the interests of the common people. The most impor-tant legislative body was the Senate, composed mainly of aristocrats, whose members held virtually all executive offices in the Roman state. Two consuls shared primary executive power, but in times of crisis the Senate could choose a dictator to hold emergency authority until the crisis had passed. In the Roman Senate, as in the aristocratic assemblies of the Greek city-states, the ideal of public service, featuring eloquent public speaking and arguments that sought to identify the general good, came closest to realization.

The diversity of Greek and Roman political forms, as well as the importance ascribed to political participation, helped generate a significant body of political theory in classical Mediterranean civilization. True to the aristocratic tradition, much of this theory dealt with appropriate political ethics, the duties of citizens, the importance of incorruptible service, and key political skills such as oratory. Roman writers like Cicero, himself an active senator, expounded eloquently on these subjects. Some of this political writing resembled Confucianism, although there was less emphasis on hierarchy and obedience or bureaucratic virtues, and more on participation in deliberative bodies that would make laws and judge the actions of executive officers. Classical Mediterranean writers also paid great attention to the structure of the state itself, debating the virtues and vices of the various political forms. This kind of theory both expressed the political interests and diversity of the Mediterranean world and served as a key heritage to later societies.

The Roman Empire was a different sort of political system from the earlier city-states, although it preserved some older institutions, such as the Senate, which became a rather meaningless forum for debates. Of necessity, the empire developed organizational capacities on a far larger scale than the city-states; it is important to remember, however, that considerable local autonomy prevailed in many regions. Only in rare cases, such as the forced dissolution of the independent Jewish state in 63 C.E. after a major local rebellion, did the Romans take over distant areas completely. Careful organization was particularly evident in the vast hierarchy of the Roman army, whose officers wielded great political power even over the emperors themselves.

In addition to considerable tolerance for local customs and religions, plus strong military organization, the Romans emphasized carefully crafted laws as the one factor that would hold their vast territories together. Greek and Roman republican leaders had already developed an understanding of the importance of codified, equitable law. Aristocratic leaders in eighth-century Athens, for example, sponsored clear legal codes designed to balance the defense of private property with the protection of poor citizens, including access to courts of law administered by fellow citizens. The early Roman republic introduced its first code of law, the Twelve Tables, by 450 B.C.E. These early Roman laws were intended, among other things, to restrain the upper classes from arbitrary action and to subject them, as well as ordinary people, to some common legal principles. The Roman Empire carried these legal interests still further, in the belief that law should evolve to meet changing conditions without, however, fluctuating wildly. The idea of Roman law was that rules, objectively judged, rather than personal whim should govern social relationships; thus, the law steadily took over matters of judgment earlier reserved for fathers of families or for landlords. Roman law also promoted the importance of common-sense fairness. In one case cited in the law texts of the empire, a slave was being shaved by a barber in a public

World Profiles

Julius Caesar (100–44 B.C.E.)

Julius Caesar was, along with his grand-nephew Augustus, the leading figure in transforming the Roman republic into an imperial form of government ruled by one dictator. Caesar had become a minor political official by the age of forty. Then, however, he began to attain greater power, serving as governor of southern Gaul and northern Italy, from where he went on to conquer most of the territory now covered by France, Belgium, part of The Netherlands, and part of Germany. Opening these territories to classical Mediterranean civilization was his greatest and most lasting achievement. But, his personal goals turned to ruling Rome itself, where he defied republican tradition in favor of open dictatorship. He was killed by conservative members of the Senate for this ambition. His death did not save the republic—the kind of government he planned, including wider citizenship for the empire, came about 14 years later. The statue pictured here conveys an image of Caesar that became popular long after his death: calm, soldierly, statesmanlike. Why was Caesar so idealized, not only in Rome but in later European history?

No representations of Julius Caesar survive from his lifetime. This statue was made 100 years after his death.

square; two men were playing ball nearby, and one accidentally hit the barber with the ball, causing him to cut the slave's throat. Who was responsible for the tragedy: the barber, catcher, or pitcher? According to Roman law, the slave—for anyone so foolish as to be shaved in a public place was asking for trouble and bore the responsibility himself.

Roman law codes spread widely through the empire, and with them came the notion of law as the regulator of social life. Many non-Romans were given the right of citizenship—although most ordinary people outside Rome itself preferred to maintain their local allegiances. With citizenship, however, came full access to Rome-appointed judges and uniform laws. Imperial law codes also regulated property rights and commerce, thus creating some economic unity in the vast empire. The idea of fair and reasoned law, to which officers of the state should themselves be subject, was a key political achievement of the Roman Empire, comparable in importance, although quite different in nature, to the Chinese elaboration of a complex bureaucratic structure.

The Greeks and Romans were less innovative in the functions they ascribed to government than in the political forms and theories they developed. Most governments concentrated on maintaining systems of law courts and military forces. Athens and, more durably and successfully, Rome placed great premium on the importance of military conquest. Mediterranean governments regulated some branches of commerce, particularly in the interest of securing vital supplies of grain. Rome, indeed, undertook vast public works in the form of roads and harbors to facilitate military transport as well as commerce. And the Roman state, especially under the Empire, built countless stadiums and public baths to entertain and distract its subjects. The city of Rome itself, which at its peak contained over a million inhabitants, provided cheap food as well as gladiator contests and other entertainment for the masses—the famous "bread and circuses" that were designed to prevent popular disorder. Colonies of Romans elsewhere were also given theaters and stadiums. This provided solace in otherwise strange lands like England or Palestine. Governments also supported an official religion, sponsoring public ceremonies to honor the gods and goddesses; civic religious festivals were important events that both expressed and encouraged widespread loyalty to the state. However, there was little attempt to impose this religion on everyone, and other religious practices were tolerated so long as they did not conflict with loyalty to the state. Even the later Roman emperors, who advanced the idea that the emperor himself was a god as a means of strengthening authority, were normally tolerant of other religions. They only attacked Christianity, and then irregularly, because of the Christians' refusal to place the state first in their devotion.

Localism and fervent political interests, including a sense of intense loyalty to the state; a diversity of political systems together with the preference for aristocratic rule; the importance of law and the development of an unusually elaborate and uniform set of legal principles—these were the chief political legacies of the classical Mediterranean world. The sheer accomplishment of the Roman Empire itself, which united a region never before or since brought together, still stands as one of the great political monuments of world history. This was a distinctive political mix. Although there was attention to careful legal procedures, no clear definition of individuals' rights existed. Indeed, the emphasis on duties to the state could lead, as in Sparta, to an essentially totalitarian framework in which the state controlled even the raising of children. Nor, until the peaceful centuries of the early Roman Empire, was it an entirely successful political structure, as wars and instability were common. Nonetheless, there can be no question of the richness of this political culture or of its central importance to the Greeks and Romans themselves.

RELIGION AND CULTURE

The Greeks and Romans did not create a significant, world-class religion; in this, they differed from India and to some extent from China. Christianity, which was to become one of the major world religions, did of course arise during the Roman Empire. It owed some of its rapid geographical spread to the ease of movement within the huge Roman Empire. However, Christianity was not really a product of Greek or Roman culture, although it would ultimately be influenced by this culture. It took on serious historical importance only as the Roman Empire began its decline. The characteristic Greco-Roman religion was a much more primitive affair, derived from a belief in the spirits of nature elevated into a complex set of gods and goddesses who were seen as regulating human life. Greeks and Romans had different names for their pantheon, but the objects of worship were essentially the same: A creator or father god, Zeus or Jupiter, presided over an unruly assemblage of gods and goddesses whose functions ranged from regulating the daily passage of the sun (Apollo) or the oceans (Neptune) to inspiring war (Mars) or human love and beauty (Venus). Specific gods were the patrons of other human activities such as metalworking, the hunt, even literature and history. Regular ceremonies to the gods had real political importance, and many individuals sought the gods' aid in foretelling the future or in ensuring a good harvest or good health.

In addition to its political functions, Greco-Roman religion had certain other features. It tended to be rather human, of-this-world in its approach. The doings of the gods made for good story-telling; they read like soap operas on a superhuman scale. Thus, the classical Mediterranean religion early engendered an important literary tradition, as was also the case in India. (Indeed, Greco-Roman and Indian religious lore reflected the common heritage of Indo-European invaders.) The gods were often used to illustrate human passions and foibles, thus serving as symbols of a serious inquiry into human nature. Unlike the Indians, however, the Greeks and Romans became interested in their gods more in terms of what they could do for and reveal about humankind on this earth, than the principles that could elevate people toward higher planes of spirituality.

This dominant religion also had a number of limitations. Its lack of spiritual passion failed to satisfy many ordinary workers and peasants, particularly in times of political chaos or economic distress. "Mystery" religions, often imported from the Middle East, periodically swept through Greece and Rome, providing secret rituals and fellowship and a greater sense of contact with unfathomable divine powers. Even more than in China, a considerable division arose between upper-class and popular belief.

The gods and goddesses of Greco-Roman religion left many upper-class people dissatisfied also. They provided stories about how the world came to be, but little basis for a systematic inquiry into nature or human society. And while the dominant religion promoted political loyalty, it did not provide a basis for ethical thought either. Hence, many thinkers, both in Greece and Rome, sought a separate model for ethical behavior. Greek and Roman moral philosophy, as issued by philosophers like Aristotle and Cicero, typically stressed the importance of moderation and balance in human behavior as opposed to the instability of much political life and the excesses

Greek sculpture: the god Zeus. Compare this work to the more sensual Hindu religious art illustrated on pages 73 and 75.

of the gods themselves. Other ethical systems were devised, particularly during the Hellenistic period. Thus, Stoics emphasized an inner moral independence, to be cultivated by strict discipline of the body and by personal bravery. These ethical systems, established largely apart from religious considerations, were major contributions in their own right; they would also be blended with later religious thought, under Christianity.

The idea of a philosophy separate from the official religion, although not necessarily hostile to it, informed classical Mediterranean political theory, which made little reference to religious principles. It also considerably emphasized the powers of human thought. In Athens, Socrates (born in 469 B.C.E.) encouraged his pupils to question conventional wisdom, on the grounds that the chief human duty was "the improvement of the soul." Socrates himself ran afoul of the Athenian government, which thought that he was undermining political loyalty; given the choice of suicide or exile, Socrates chose the former. However, the Socratic principle of rational inquiry by means of skeptical questioning became a recurrent strand in classical Greek thinking and in its heritage to later societies. Socrates' great pupil Plato accentuated the positive somewhat more strongly by suggesting that human reason could approach an understanding of the three perfect forms—the absolutely True, Good, and Beautiful—which he believed characterized nature. Thus, a philosophical tradition arose in Greece, although in very diverse individual expressions, which tended to deemphasize the importance of human spirituality in favor of a celebration of the human ability to think. The result bore some similarities to Chinese Confucianism, although with greater emphasis on skeptical questioning and abstract speculations about the basic nature of humanity and the universe.

Greek interest in rationality carried over an inquiry into the underlying order of physical nature. The Greeks were not outstanding empirical scientists. Relatively few new scientific findings emanated from Athens, or later from Rome, although philosophers like Aristotle did collect large amounts of biological data. The Greek interest lay in speculations about nature's order, and many non-Westerners believe that this tradition continues to inform what they see as an excessive Western passion for seeking basic rationality in the universe. In practice, the Greek concern translated into a host of theories, some of which were wrong, about the motions of the planets and the organization of the elemental principles of earth, fire, air, and water, and into a considerable interest in mathematics as a means of rendering nature's patterns comprehensible. Greek and later Hellenistic work in geometry was particularly impressive, featuring among other achievements the basic theorems of Pythagoras. Scientists during the Hellenistic period made some important empirical contributions, especially in studies of anatomy; medical treatises by Galen were not improved on, in the Western world, for many centuries. The mathematician Euclid produced what was long the world's most widely used compendium of geometry. Less fortunately, the Hellenistic astronomer Ptolemy produced an elaborate theory of the sun's motion around a stationary earth. This new Hellenistic theory contradicted much earlier Middle Eastern astronomy, which had recognized the earth's rotation; nonetheless, it was Ptolemy's theory that was long taken as fixed wisdom in Western thought.

Roman intellectuals, actively examining ethical and political theory, had nothing to add to Greek and Hellenistic science. They did help to preserve this tradition in the form of textbooks that were administered to upper-class schoolchildren. The Roman genius was more practical than the Greek and included engineering achievements such as the great roads and aqueducts that carried water to cities large and small. Roman ability to construct elaborate arches so that buildings could carry great structural weight was unsurpassed anywhere in the world. These feats, too, would leave their mark, as Rome's huge edifices long served as a reminder of ancient glories. But ultimately, it was the Greek and Hellenistic impulse to extend human reason to nature's principles that would result in the most impressive legacy.

In classical Mediterranean civilization itself, however, science and mathematics loomed far less large than art and literature in conveying key cultural values. The official religion inspired themes for artistic expression and the justification for temples, statues, and plays devoted to the glories of the gods. Nonetheless, the human-centered qualities of the Greeks and Romans also registered, as artists emphasized the

Greek pottery. Depicting Greek soldiers (hoplites) fighting amid their chariots, this piece dates from sixth-century Athens.

beauty of realistic portrayals of the human form and poets and playwrights used the gods as foils for inquiries into the human condition.

All the arts received some attention in classical Mediterranean civilization. Performances of music and dance were vital parts of religious festivals, but their precise styles have unfortunately not been preserved. Far more durable was the Greek interest in drama, for plays, more than poetry, took a central role in this culture. Greek dramatists produced both comedy and tragedy, indeed making a formal division between the two approaches that is still part of the Western tradition, as in the labeling of current television shows as either form. On the whole, in contrast to Indian writers, the Greeks placed the greatest emphasis on tragedy. Their belief in human reason and balance also involved a sense that these virtues were precarious, so a person could easily become ensnared in situations of powerful emotion and uncontrollable consequences. The Athenian dramatist Sophocles, for example, so insightfully portrayed the psychological flaws of his hero Oedipus that modern psychology long used the term *Oedipus complex* to refer to a potentially unhealthy relationship between a man and his mother.

Greek literature contained a strong epic tradition as well, starting with the beautifully crafted tales of the *Iliad* and *Odyssey,* attributed to the poet Homer, who lived in the eighth century B.C.E. Roman authors, particularly the poet Virgil, also worked in the epic form, seeking to link Roman history and mythology with the Greek forerunner. Roman writers made significant contributions to poetry and to definitions of the poetic form that would long be used in Western literature. The overall Roman literary contribution was less impressive than the Greek, but it was substantial enough both to provide important examples of how poetry should be written and to furnish abundant illustrations of the literary richness of the Latin language.

In the visual arts, the emphasis of classical Mediterranean civilization was sculpture and architecture. Greek artists also excelled in ceramic work, whereas Roman painters produced realistic (and sometimes pornographic) decorations for the homes of the wealthy. In Athens' brilliant fifth century—the age of Pericles, Socrates, Sophocles, and so many other intensely creative figures—sculptors like Phidias developed unprecedented skill rendering simultaneously realistic yet beautiful images of the human form, from lovely goddesses to muscled warriors and athletes. Roman sculptors, less innovative, continued this heroic-realistic tradition. They molded scenes of Roman conquests on triumphal columns and captured the power but also the human qualities of Augustus Caesar and his successors on busts and full-figure statues alike.

Greek architecture, from the eighth century B.C.E. onward, emphasized monumental construction, square or rectangular in shape, with columned porticos. The Greeks devised three embellishments for the tops of columns supporting their massive buildings, each more ornate than the next: the Doric, the Ionic, and the Corinthian. The Greeks, in short, invented what Westerners and others in the world today still regard as "classical" architecture, although the Greeks themselves were influenced by Egyptian models in their preferences. Greece, and later Italy, provided abundant stone for ambitious temples, markets, and other public buildings. Many of these same structures were filled with products of the sculptors' workshops. They were brightly painted, although over the centuries the paint would fade so that later imitators came to think of the classical style as involving unadorned (some might say drab) stone. Roman architects adopted the Greek themes quite readily. Their engineering skill allowed them to construct buildings of even greater size, as well as new forms such as the free-standing stadium. Under the empire, the Romans learned how to add domes to rectangular buildings, which resulted in some welcome architectural diversity. At the same time, the empire's taste for massive, heavily adorned

A great temple to Theseus, the legendary founder of Athens. This temple is an example of Doric architecture, the earliest Greek column style, in Athens during the fifth century B.C.E.

UNDERSTANDING CULTURES

When Two Belief Systems Meet

One of the most interesting developments in world history involves points at which two quite different cultures encounter each other. Contact may result from trade, missionary activity, migration, or conquest. And, its ramifications can be just as varied: The two cultures may detest each other, or one might try (or be forced) to copy the other. However, the most common result, even when one culture is promoted by force, is a certain blending. This blending is called syncretism.

When Alexander's conquests established a Hellenistic state for many decades in northwestern India, cultural contact ran high. Indians learned some additional mathematics from Greeks in the royal bureaucracy. They also admired Greek artistic styles. For some time, Buddhas in statues and other art forms were shown wearing Mediterranean-type hairdos and togas. Despite such displays, the Indians involved were not Hellenized: They maintained their own religion, for example, and their belief that art should serve this religion. Here was an early case of syncretism.

The impact on the Mediterranean was less clear. Indians grew more aware of the Middle East and sent Buddhist missionaries to the region. No major conversions resulted, but Buddhist ethical ideas may have influenced some Greek ethical systems and, through them, Christianity—it is simply not possible to be sure. Some obvious Indian development, such as their superior numbering system, were ignored. Cultural borrowing is, among other things, oddly unpredictable.

monuments and public buildings, while a clear demonstration of Rome's sense of power and achievement, moved increasingly away from the simple lines of the early Greek temples.

Classical Mediterranean art and architecture were intimately linked with the society that produced them. There is a temptation, because of the formal role of classical styles in later societies, including our own, to attribute a stiffness to Greek and Roman art that was not present in the original. Greek and Roman structures were built to be used. Temples and marketplaces and the public baths that so delighted the Roman upper classes were part of daily urban life. Classical art was also flexible, according to need. Villas or small palaces—built for the Roman upper classes and typically constructed around an open courtyard—had a light, even simple quality rather different from that of temple architecture. Classical dramas were not merely examples of high art, performed in front of a cultural elite. Indeed, Athens lives in the memory of many humanists today as much because of the large audiences that trooped to performances of plays by authors like Sophocles, as for the creativity of the writers and philosophers themselves. Literally thousands of people gathered in the large hillside theaters of Athens and other cities for the performance of new plays and for associated music and poetry competitions. Popular taste in Rome, to be sure, seemed less elevated. Republican Rome was not an important cultural center, and many Roman leaders indeed feared the more emotional qualities of Greek art. The Roman Empire is known more for monumental athletic performances—chariot races and gladiators—than for high-quality popular theater. However, the fact remains that, even in Rome, elements of classical art—the great monuments if nothing more—were part of daily urban life and the pursuit of pleasure.

ECONOMY AND SOCIETY IN THE MEDITERRANEAN

Politics and formal culture in Greece and Rome were mainly affairs of the cities—which means that they were of intense concern only to a minority of the population. Most Greeks and Romans were farmers, tied to the soil and often to local rituals and festivals that were rather different from urban forms. Many Greek farmers, for example, annually gathered for a spring passion play to celebrate the recovery of the goddess of fertility from the lower world, an event that was seen as a vital preparation for planting and that also suggested the possibility of an afterlife—a prospect important to many people who endured a life of hard labor and poverty. A substantial population of free farmers, who owned their own land, flourished in the early days of the Greek city-states and later around Rome. However, there was a constant tendency, most pronounced in Rome, for large landlords to squeeze these farmers, forcing them to become tenants or laborers or to join the swelling crowds of the urban lower class. Tensions between tyrants and aristocrats or democrats and aristocrats in Athens often revolved around free farmers' attempts to preserve their independence and shake off the heavy debts they had incurred. The Roman republic declined in part because too many farmers became dependent on the protection of large landlords, even when they did not work their estates outright, and so no longer could vote freely.

Farming in Greece and in much of Italy was complicated by the fact that soil conditions were not ideal for grain growing, and yet grain was the staple of life. First in Greece, then in central Italy, farmers were increasingly tempted to shift to the production of olives and grapes, which were used primarily for cooking and wine making. These products were well suited to the soil conditions, but they required an unusually extensive conversion of agriculture to a market basis. That is, farmers who produced grapes and olives had to buy some of the food they needed, and they had to sell most of their own product in order to do this. Furthermore, planting olive trees or grape vines required substantial capital, for they would not bear fruit for at least five years after planting. This was one reason why so many farmers went into debt. It was also one of the reasons that large landlords gained increasing advantage over independent farmers, for they could enter into market production on a much larger scale if only because of their greater access to capital.

The rise of commercial agriculture in Greece and then around Rome was one of the prime forces leading to efforts to establish an empire. Greek city-states, with Athens usually in the lead, developed colonies in the Middle East and then in Sicily mainly to gain access to grain production; for this, they traded not only olive oil and wine but also manufactured products and silver. Rome pushed south, in part, to acquire the Sicilian grain fields and later used much of North Africa as its granary. Indeed, the Romans encouraged such heavy cultivation in North Africa that they pro-

The Colosseum in Rome. In the ancient imperial city of Rome, the Colosseum was a triumph of Roman monumental architecture and a center for sports and ceremonies.

moted a soil depletion which helps account for the region's reduced agricultural fertility in later centuries.

The importance of commercial farming obviously dictated extensive concern with trade. Private merchants operated most of the ships that carried agricultural products and other goods. Greek city-states and ultimately the Roman state supervised the grain trade, promoting public works and storage facilities and carefully regulating the vital supplies. Other kinds of trade were vital also. Luxury products from the shops of urban artists or craftsworkers played a major role in the lifestyle of the upper classes. There was some trade also beyond the borders of Mediterranean civilization itself, for goods from India and China. In this trade, interestingly, the Mediterranean peoples found themselves at some disadvantage, for their manufactured products were less sophisticated than those of eastern Asia; thus, they typically exported animal skins, precious metals, and even exotic African animals for Asian zoos in return for the spices and artistic products of the east.

HISTORY DEBATE

Mediterranean Civilization and "Western" Civilization

The impulse to regard Greece and Rome as the origins of what is now called Western civilization runs very deep. Rome's glory and the power of Greek culture obviously impressed thinkers and statesmen in Western Europe, who looked back to these times for inspiration. This was a key theme in European history after the classical period. From Western Europe, fascination with the classical Mediterranean world would later spread to North America.

All the classical civilizations left strong imprints on later developments. At the same time, these imprints require careful assessment, because none of the civilizations remained static. The nature and impact of the legacy must be weighed against innovations. This general analytical requirement is doubly important when considering classical Mediterranean culture, for the simple reason that, after Rome, Mediterranean civilization split apart. Some common features remained, including cultural aspects like a strong emphasis on the defense of personal honor plus social-economic institutions like relatively large villages. However, no Mediterranean civilization continued to exist as a whole.

Some historians argue that regarding Greece and Rome as the origins of Western civilization is completely off the mark. Greece, particularly, was proud of its own uniqueness, and when it sought to expand, it looked to the lands of the Middle East, not the West; Rome also ended up placing special value on its eastern holdings. Not surprisingly, Greek-Roman heritage lived on more directly in southeastern Europe than in the West. Certainly, the West does not have sole claims to Mediterranean heritage.

Nonetheless, selective Greek-Roman values and institutions did affect Western Europe, either immediately or in later revivals. So, the debate continues about positioning the classical Mediterranean civilization in light of later developments.

The issue involves both the facts and judgment. What were the most important surviving characteristics of the classical Mediterranean? Were they taken out of context, as they helped shape later civilizations? Take democracy, for example: To what extent did Mediterranean democracy "cause" later democracy in the West? (And, if it was responsible for causing this democracy, why did the process take so long?) Your evaluation may focus on cultural and political achievements, but it must also address the social and economic framework of this third major classical civilization.

For all the importance of trade, merchants enjoyed a somewhat ambiguous status in classical Mediterranean civilization. Leading Athenian merchants were usually foreigners, mostly from the trading peoples of the Middle East—the descendants of Lydians and Phoenicians. Merchants had a somewhat higher status in Rome, clearly forming the second most prestigious social class under the landed patricians, but here, too, the aristocracy frequently disputed the merchants' rights. Overall, merchants fared better in the Mediterranean than in China, in terms of official recognition, but worse than in India; classical Mediterranean society certainly did not set in motion a culture that distinctly valued capitalist money-making.

Slavery was another key ingredient of the classical economy. Philosophers such as Aristotle produced elaborate justifications for the necessity of slavery in a proper society. Athenians used slaves as household servants and also as workers in their vital silver mines, which provided the manpower for Athens' empire and commercial operations alike. Sparta used slaves extensively for agricultural work. Slavery spread steadily in Rome from the final centuries of the republic. Since most slaves came from conquered territories, the need for slaves was another key element in military expansion. Here was a theme visible in earlier civilizations in the eastern Mediterranean, and within later societies in this region as well, which helps explain the greater importance of military forces and expansion in these areas than in India or China. Roman slaves performed household tasks—including the tutoring of upper-class children, for which cultured Greek slaves were highly valued. They also worked the mines, for precious metals and for iron; as in Greece, slave labor in the mines was particularly brutal, and few slaves survived more than a few years of such an existence. Roman estate owners used large numbers of slaves for agricultural work, along with paid laborers and tenant farmers. This practice was another source of the steady pressure placed upon free farmers who could not easily compete with unpaid forced labor.

Partly because of slavery, partly because of the overall orientation of upper-class culture, neither Greece nor Rome was especially interested in technological innovations applicable to agriculture or manufacturing. The Greeks made important advances in shipbuilding and navigation, which were vital for their trading economy. Romans, less adept on the water, developed their skill in engineering to provide greater urban amenities and good roads for the swift and easy movement of troops. But, a technology designed to improve the production of food or manufactured goods did not figure largely in this civilization, which mainly relied on the earlier achievements of previous Mediterranean societies. Abundant slave labor probably discouraged concern for more efficient production methods. So did a sense that the true goals of humankind were artistic and political. One Hellenistic scholar, for example, refused to write a handbook on engineering because "the work of an engineer and everything that ministers to the needs of life is ignoble and vulgar." As a consequence of this outlook, Mediterranean society lagged behind both India and China in production technology, which was one reason for its resulting unfavorable balance of trade with eastern Asia.

Both Greek and Roman society emphasized the importance of a tight family structure, with a husband and father firmly in control. Women had vital economic functions, particularly in farming and artisan families. In the upper classes, especially in Rome, women often commanded great influence and power within a household. But in law and culture, women were held inferior. Families burdened with too many children sometimes put female infants to death because of their low status and their potential drain on the family economy. Pericles stated common beliefs about women when he noted, "For a woman not to show more weakness than is natural to her sex is a great glory, and not to be talked about for good or for evil among men." Early Roman law stipulated that "the husband is the judge of his wife. If she commits a fault, he punishes her; if she has drunk wine, he condemns her; if she has been guilty of adultery, he kills her." (Later, however, such customs were held in check by family courts composed of members of both families.) Here was a case where Roman legal ideas modified traditional family controls. If divorced because of adultery, a Roman woman lost a third of her property and had to wear a special garment that set her apart like a prostitute. On the other hand, the oppression of women was probably less severe in this civilization than in China. Many Greek and Roman women were active in business and controlled a portion, even if only the minority, of all urban property.

Because of the divisions within classical Mediterranean society, no easy generalizations about culture or achievement can be made. An eighteenth-century English historian called the high point of the Roman Empire, before 180 C.E., the period in human history "during which the condition of the human race was most happy or prosperous." This is doubtful, given the technological accomplishments of China and India. And certainly, many slaves, women, and ordinary farmers in the Mediterranean world itself might have disagreed with this viewpoint. Few farmers, for example, actively participated in the political structures or cultural opportunities that were the most obvious mark of this civilization. Many continued to work largely as their ancestors had done, with quite similar tools and in very similar poverty, untouched by the doings of the great or the bustle of the cities except when wars engulfed their lands.

We are tempted, of course, exclusively to remember the urban achievements, for they exerted the greatest influence on later ages that recalled the glories of Greece and Rome. The distinctive features of classical Mediterranean social and family structures had a less enduring impact, although ideas about slavery or women were revived in subsequent periods. However, the relatively unchanging face of ordinary life had an important influence as well, as many farmers and artisans long maintained the habits and outlook they developed during the great days of the Greek and Roman empires, and because their separation from much of the official culture posed both a challenge and opportunity for new cultural movements such as Christianity.

CONCLUSION: TOWARD THE FALL OF ROME

Classical Mediterranean society had one final impact on world history through its rather fragmentary collapse. Unlike China, classical civilization in the Mediterranean region was not simply disrupted, only to revive. Unlike India, there was no central religion, derived from the civilization itself, to serve as link between the classical period and what followed. Furthermore, the fall of Rome was not uniform; in essence, Rome fell more in some parts of the Mediterranean than it did in others. The result, among other things, was that no single civilization ultimately rose to claim the mantle of Greece and Rome. At the same time, there was no across-the-board maintenance of the classical Mediterranean institutions and values in any of the civilizations that later claimed a relationship to the Greek and Roman past. Greece and Rome would live on, in more than idle memory, but their heritage was unquestionably more complex and more selective than proved to be the case for India or China.

SUGGESTED WEBSITES

For websites on Alexander, see *http://www.mediatime.net/*alex; on Greek religion, see *http://www.greekciv.pdx.edu/religion/relig.htm;* for a virtual tour of ancient Rome, see *http://library.thinkquest.org/11402/homeforum.html;* on Roman women, see *http://library.thinkquest.org/11402/women in rome.html.*

SUGGESTED READINGS

There are a number of excellent sources on classical Greece and Rome, even aside from translations of the leading thinkers and writers. See M. Crawford, ed., *Sources for Ancient History* (1983); C. Fornara, *Translated Documents of Greece and Rome* (1977); N. Lewis, *Greek Historical Documents: The Fifth Century* B.C. (1971); M. Crawford, *The Roman Republic* (1982); P. Green, *Alexander to Actium: The Historical Evolution of the Hellenistic Ages* (1990); and M. M. Austin, *The Hellenistic World from Alexander to the Roman Conquest* (1981). Useful surveys on ancient Greece include K. Dover, *The Greeks* (1981), and F. J. Frost, *Greek Society* (1980). Important specialized works include M. Crawford and D. Whitehead, *Archaic and Classical Greece* (1983); Cyril Robinson, *Everyday Life in Ancient Greece* (1987); W. Burkert, *Greek Religions* (1985); G. E. R. Lloyd, *The Revolutions of Wisdom: Studies in the Claims and Practices of Ancient Greek Science* (1987); Sarah Pomeroy, *Goddesses, Whores, Wives, and Slaves: Women in Classical Antiquity* (1975); A. R. Burn, *Persia and the Greeks* (1962); and Moses Finley, *Slavery in the Ancient World* (1972). On Rome, K. Christ, *The Romans: An Introduction to Their History and Civilization* (1984) is eminently readable and provocative. See also M. Crawford, *The Roman Republic* (1978); L. P. Wilkinson, *The Roman Experience* (1974); B. Cunliffe, *Rome and the Empire* (1978); Cyril Robinson, *Everyday Life in Ancient Greece* (1987); J. Boardman et al., *Oxford History of the Classical World* (1986); and R. Saller, *The Roman Empire* (1987).

On early history, see H. H. Schulhard, *A History of the Roman World, 753–146* B.C. (1961). For social aspects, good sources include R. MacMuleen, *Roman Social Relations, 50* B.C.–A.D. *284* (1981); P. Garnsey and R. Saller, *The Roman Empire: Economy, Society and Culture* (1987); K. Hopkins, *Conquerors and Slaves, Slaves and Masters in the Roman Empire* (1987); K. R. Bradley and W. Philips, Jr., *Slavery from Roman Times to the Early Transatlantic Trade* (1985); Peter Gamsey and R. Saller, *The Roman Empire: Economy, Society, and Culture* (1987); and Y. Garlan, *War in the Ancient World* (1975).

A useful reference on women's history in the classical period, and in later Western history, is R. Bridenthal and C. Koonz, eds., *Becoming Visible: Women in European History* (1977); see also M. Lefkowitz and M. Faut, *Women and Life in Greece and Rome* (1992). The rise and spread of Christianity are treated in two outstanding studies, R. MacMullen, *Christianizing the Roman Empire* (1984), and Peter Brown, *The World of Late Antiquity*, A.D. *150–750* (1971). (Brown has also written a number of more specialized studies on early Christianity in the West.)

The Classical Period: Directions, Diversities, and Declines by 500 C.E.

FOCAL POINTS

The decline of the great empires of the classical period raises obvious questions about its causes. What were the chief strengths of the classical civilizations at their height, and how can once dynamic societies deteriorate? Are there some general explanations, or must one examine each case separately to determine the reasons? Why did some regions in the classical world change more fully than others? The process of decline also generated some new forces in world history. Why did major religions gain new impetus? Did they have any features in common? Decline and change, finally, must be summed up: What were the major differences between the map of civilization of 500 C.E. and that of 200 C.E. when the classical world had just begun to crumble?

INTRODUCTION

The basic themes of the three great classical civilizations involved expansion and integration. From localized beginnings in northern China, the Ganges region, or the Aegean Sea, commercial, political, and cultural outreach pushed civilization through the Middle Kingdom and beyond, through the Indian subcontinent, and into the western Mediterranean. The growth set in motion deliberate but also implicit attempts to pull the new civilizations together in more than name. Correspondingly, the most telling comparisons among the three classical civilizations—identifying similarities as well as differences—involve this same process of integration and some of the problems it encountered.

Throughout the classical world, integration and expansion faltered between 200 and 500 C.E. Decline, even collapse, began to afflict civilization first in China, then in the Mediterranean, and finally in India. These developments signaled the end of the classical era and ushered in important new themes in world history that would define the next major period. The response of major religions to political decline formed a leading direction for world history to come.

Classical civilizations (including Persia) had never embraced the bulk of the territory around the globe, although they did include the majority of the world's population. Developments outside the classical orbit had rhythms of their own during the classical period, and they would gain new prominence as the great civilizations themselves faltered. This describes the third historical theme—along with basic comparisons and the process of decline and attendant religious responses—that must be addressed in moving from the classical period to world history's next phase.

EXPANSION AND INTEGRATION

The heritage of the classical civilizations involves a host of new ideas, styles, technologies, and institutions. Many of these arose as part of the broad process of adjusting to the expansion of civilization. Thus, it was not entirely accidental that in scarcely more than a century, between about 550 and 400 B.C.E., seminal thinkers arose in all three civilizations—Confucius and Lao-zi, Buddha, and Socrates. The thinkers had no contact with each other, and their specific ideas varied widely. However, all three were inspired by the common need to articulate central values in their respective societies, as part of a larger process of generating a shared culture on the basis of which their expanding societies might operate.

China, India, and the Mediterranean set about the tasks of uniting their expanding civilizations in different ways. China emphasized greater centralization, particularly in politics, generating a political culture to match. India and the Mediterranean remained more localized and diverse. India, however, used key religious values, and particularly the spread of Hinduism, to cement its civilization even across political boundaries. Mediterranean cultural achievements spread widely also, but involved less of the population—one reason why the region proved more vulnerable to fragmentation after its political unity collapsed under Rome.

Integration involved two basic issues, the most obvious of which was territorial. China had to reign in its new southern regions, and the government devoted considerable attention to settling some northerners in the south, promoting a common language for the elite, and other techniques. The southward spread of the caste system and ultimately Hinduism in India addressed territorial issues. Rome combined considerable local autonomy and tolerance with common laws, the expansion of citizenship to elites across the empire, and a tight commercial network that created interdependencies between grain-growing regions and the olive-and-grape regions.

The second challenge to integration was social. All three classical civilizations fostered great inequalities between men and women and between upper and lower classes. The nature of the inequalities varied, from Mediterranean slavery to the Indian caste system to the Confucian sense of hierarchy; these differences were significant. Nevertheless, the assumption of inequality as normal was common to all three societies. Most leading thinkers—Buddha was an exception—did not oppose inequalities, writing openly of the need for deference and even (in the case of the Mediterranean) for slavery.

All the classical civilizations made some efforts to maintain a basic social cohesion while acknowledging inequality. None took the modern, Western-inspired route of arguing for opportunities of upward mobility. Confucianism stressed mutual respect between upper and lower classes, along with special deference on the part of the lower social orders. Shared values about family and self-restraint provided some further links across the social hierarchy. Mediterranean aristocrats treated some locals as clients, offering them protection; they also supported civic rituals intended to foster loyalty. India offered a religion that was shared by all social classes and gave the hope of future incarnation to the lower castes. None of these approaches consistently united the society. Lower-class risings, even slave rebellions, were part of the classical experience as well. On balance, however, some techniques may have worked better than others. Again, as the Roman Empire fell, many elements of the lower classes quickly turned their attention to other interests. This suggests that here, too, the integration of Mediterranean society was slightly more tenuous than that of the classical civilizations of Asia.

BEYOND THE CLASSICAL CIVILIZATIONS

Although the development of the three great civilizations is the central thread in world history during the classical period, significant changes also occurred in other parts of the world. On the borders of the major civilizations, as in northeastern Africa, Japan, and northern Europe, these changes bore some relationship to the classical world, although they were partly autonomous. Elsewhere, most notably in the Americas, new cultures evolved in an entirely independent way. In all cases, changes during the classical period set the stage for more important links in world history later on. Southeast Asia gained access to civilization during the classical period mainly through its contacts with India. Regional kingdoms had already been established, and agricultural economies were familiar on the principal islands of Indonesia as well as on the mainland. Participation in wider trade patterns developed through the efforts of Indian merchants. Hindu and particularly Buddhist religion and art also spread from India. Here was a case of the outright expansion of civilization without the creation of a fully distinctive or unified culture.

A similar case of expansion from an established civilization affected parts of sub-Saharan Africa; indeed, in this case the interaction had begun well before the rise of Greece and Rome. By the year 1000 B.C.E., the independent kingdom of Kush was flourishing along the upper Nile. It possessed a form of writing derived from Egyptian hieroglyphics (and which has not yet been fully deciphered) and mastered the use of iron. Briefly, around 750 B.C.E., armies from Kush conquered Egypt itself. Major cities were built. The Kushites seem to have established a strong monarchy, with elaborate ceremonies illustrating a belief that the king was divine. The kingdom of Kush was defeated by a rival kingdom called Axum by about 300 B.C.E.; Axum ultimately fell to another regional kingdom, Ethiopia. Axum and Ethiopia had active contacts with the eastern Mediterranean world until after the fall of Rome. They traded with this region for several centuries. The activities of Jewish merchants brought some conversions to Judaism, and a small minority of Ethiopians have remained Jewish to the present day. Greek-speaking merchants also had considerable influence, and it was through them that Christianity was brought to Ethiopia by the fourth century C.E. The Ethiopian Christian Church was, however, cut off from mainstream Christianity thereafter, flourishing in isolation to modern times. And Ethiopia could boast, into the late twentieth century when it was abolished, of having the oldest continuous monarchy anywhere in the world.

It is not clear how much influence, if any, the kingdoms of the upper Nile had on the later history of sub-Saharan Africa. Knowledge of ironworking certainly

Kush and Axum, Successive Dynasties

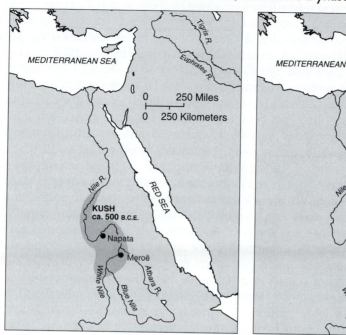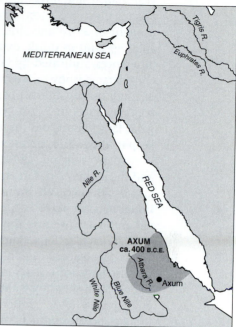

spread, facilitating the expansion of agriculture in other parts of the continent. Patterns of strong, ceremonial kingship—sometimes called divine kingship—would surface in other parts of Africa later, but whether this occurred through some contact with the Kushite tradition or independently is not known. Knowledge of Kushite writing did not spread, which suggests that the impact of this first case of civilization below the Sahara was somewhat limited.

For most of Africa below the Sahara, but north of the great tropical jungles, the major development up to 500 C.E. was the further extension of agriculture itself. Well-organized villages arose, often very similar in form and structure to those that still exist. Farming took earliest root on the southern fringes of the Sahara, which was less arid than it is today. Toward the end of the classical era, important regional kingdoms were forming in western Africa, leading to the first great state in the region—Ghana. Because of the barriers of dense vegetation and the impact of African diseases on domesticated animals, agriculture spread only slowly southward. However, the creation of a strong agricultural economy did prepare the way for the next, more long-lasting and influential wave of African kingdoms, far to the west of the Nile. New crops, including root crops and plantains introduced through trade with Southeast Asia about 100 C.E., helped African farmers push into new areas.

Advances in agriculture and manufacturing also occurred in other parts of the world besides sub-Saharan Africa. In northern Europe and Japan, there was no question, as yet, of elaborate contacts with the great civilizations, no counterpart to the influences that affected parts of Southeast Asia and the upper Nile valley. Japan, by the year 200 C.E., had established extensive agriculture. The population of the islands had been formed mainly by migrations from the peninsula of Korea, over a 200,000-year span. These migrations had ceased by the year 200. In Japan, a regional political organization based on tribal chiefs evolved; each tribal group had its own god, thought of as an ancestor. A Chinese visitor in 297 described the Japanese as law-abiding, fond of drink, expert at agriculture and fishing; they observed strict social differences, indicated by tattoos or other body markings. Japan had also developed considerable ironworking; interestingly, the Japanese seem to have skipped the stage of using bronze and copper tools, moving directly from stone tools to iron. Finally, regional states in Japan became increasingly sophisticated, each controlling somewhat larger territories. In 400 C.E., one such state brought in scribes from Korea to keep records—this represented the introduction of writing in the islands.

Japan's religion, called Shintoism, provided for the worship of political rulers and the spirits of nature, including the all-important god of rice. Many local shrines and rituals revolved around Shinto beliefs, which became unified into a single national religion by 700 C.E. However, this was a simple religion, rather different in ritual and doctrine from the great world religions and philosophies developing in the classical civilizations. Something like national politics arose only around 400 C.E., when one regional ruler began to win the loyalty and trust of other local leaders; this was the basis for Japan's imperial house, with the emperor worshipped as a religious figure. Such growing political sophistication and national cultural unity were just emerging by 600 C.E., however. And, it was at this point that Japan was ready for more elaborate contacts with China—a process that would move Japan squarely into the orbit of major civilizations.

Much of northern Europe lagged behind Japan's pace. Teutonic or Celtic peoples in what is today Germany, England, and Scandinavia, and Slavic peoples in much of Eastern Europe, were loosely organized into regional kingdoms. Some, in Germany and England, had succumbed to the advances of the distant Roman Empire, but after Rome's decline the patterns of regional politics resumed. There was no written language, except in cases where Latin had been imported. Agriculture, often still combined with hunting, was rather primitive. Scandinavians were developing increasing skill as sailors, which would lead them into wider trade and pillage in the centuries after 600 C.E. Religious beliefs featured a host of gods and rituals designed to placate the forces of nature. This region would change, particularly through the spread of the religious and intellectual influences of Christianity. However, these shifts still lay in the future, and even conversions to Christianity did not bring northern and eastern Europe into the orbit of a single civilization. Until about 1000 C.E., northern Europe remained one of the most backward areas in the world.

Yet another portion of the world was developing civilization by 600 C.E.—indeed, its progress was greater than that of much of Europe and Africa. In Central America, an Indian group called the Olmecs developed and spread an early form of civilization from about 800 until 400 B.C.E. The Olmecs seem to have lacked writing, but they produced massive, pyramid-shaped religious monuments.

The first American civilization was based on many centuries of advancing agriculture, expanding from the early cultivation of corn. Initially, in the wild state, corn ears were scarcely larger than strawberries, but patient breeding gradually converted this grain into a staple food crop. In the Andes areas of South America, root crops were also grown, particularly the potato. The development of American agriculture was limited by the few domesticated animals available—turkeys, dogs, and guinea pigs in Central America. Nevertheless, Olmec culture displayed many impressive achievements. It explored artistic forms in precious stones such as jade. Religious statues and icons blended human images with those of animals. Scientific research produced accurate and impressive calendars. Olmec culture, in its religious and artistic emphases, powerfully influenced later Indian civilizations in Central America. The Olmecs themselves disappeared without a clear trace around 400 B.C.E., but their successors soon developed a hieroglyphic alphabet and built the first great city—Teotihuacan—in the Americas, as a center for trade and worship. This culture, in turn, suffered setbacks from migrations and regional wars, but from its base developed a still fuller American civilization, starting with the Mayans, from about 400 C.E. onward.

In essence, the Olmecs and their successors had provided for the Central American region the equivalent of the river valley civilizations in Asia and the Middle East, although many centuries later. A similar early civilization arose in the Andes region in present-day Peru and Bolivia, where careful agriculture allowed the construction of elaborate cities and religious monuments. This culture would lead, later, to the civilization of the Incas. The two centers of early civilization in the Americas developed in total isolation from developments elsewhere in the world. As a result, they lacked certain advantages that come from the ability to copy and react to other societies, including such basic technologies as the wheel or the capacity to work iron. However, the early American Indian cultures were considerably ahead of most of those in Europe during the same period. And, they demonstrate the common, although not invariable, tendency of humans to move from the establishment of agriculture to the creation of the more elaborate trappings of a civilized society.

Another case of isolated development featured the migration of agricultural peoples to new island territories in the Pacific. Polynesian peoples had reached islands such as Fiji and Samoa by 1000 B.C.E. Further explorations in giant outrigger canoes led to the first settlement of island complexes such as Hawaii by 400 C.E., where the new settlers adapted local plants, brought in new animals (notably pigs), and imported a highly stratified caste system under powerful local kings.

Agriculture, in sum, expanded into new areas during the classical period; early civilizations, or early civilizations contacts, were also forming. These developments were not central to world history during the classical period itself, but they folded into the larger human experience thereafter.

The herding peoples of central Asia also contributed to world history, particularly toward the end of the classical period. Some nomadic groups gained new contacts with established civilizations, like China, which brought changes in political organization as well as some new goals for conquest. Central Asian herders played a vital role in trade routes between east Asia and the Middle East, transporting goods like silk across long distances. Other herding groups produced important technological innovations, such as the stirrup, which allowed mounted horsemen to aim weapons better. The herding groups thus enjoyed an important history of their own and also provided important contacts among the civilizations that they bordered. Finally, perhaps because of internal population pressure as well as new appetites and opportunities, herding groups invaded the major civilizations directly, helping to bring the classical period as a whole to an end.

DECLINE IN CHINA AND INDIA

Between 200 and 600 C.E., all three classical civilizations collapsed entirely or in part. During this four-century span, all suffered from outside invasions, the result of growing incursions by groups from central Asia. This renewed wave of nomadic expansion was not as sweeping as the earlier Indo-European growth, which had spread over India and much of the Mediterranean region many centuries before, but it severely tested the civilized regimes. Rome, of course, fell directly to Germanic invaders, who fought on partly because they were, in turn, harassed by the fierce Asiatic Huns. The Huns themselves swept once across Italy, invading the city of Rome amid great destruction. It was another Hun group from central Asia who overthrew the Guptas in India, and similar nomadic tribes had earlier toppled the Chinese Han dynasty. The central Asian nomads were certainly encouraged by a growing realization of the weakness of the classical regimes. For Han China as well as the later Roman Empire suffered from serious internal problems long before the invaders dealt the final blows. And, the Guptas in India had not permanently resolved that area's tendency to dissolve into political fragmentation.

By about 100 C.E., the Han dynasty in China began to enter a serious decline. Confucian intellectual activity gradually became less creative. Politically, the central government's control diminished, bureaucrats became more corrupt, and local landlords took up much of the slack, ruling their neighborhoods according to their own wishes. The free peasants, long heavily taxed, were burdened with new taxes and demands of service by these same landlords. Many lost their farms and became day laborers on the large estates. Some had to sell their children into service. Social unrest increased, producing a great revolutionary effort led by Daoists in 184 C.E. Daoism now gained new appeal, shifting toward a popular religion and adding healing practices and magic to earlier philosophical beliefs. The Daoist leaders, called the Yellow Turbans, promised a golden age that was to be brought about by divine magic. The Yellow Turbans attacked the weakness of the emperor but also the self-indulgence of the current bureaucracy. As many as 30,000 students demonstrated against the decline of government morality. However, their protests failed, and Chinese population growth and prosperity both spiraled further downward. The imperial court was mired in intrigue and civil war.

This dramatic decline paralleled the slightly later collapse of Rome, as we shall see. It obviously explained China's inability to push back invasions from borderland nomads, who finally overthrew the Han dynasty outright. As in Rome, growing political ineffectiveness formed part of the decline. Another important factor was the spread of devastating new epidemics, which may have killed up to half of the population. These combined blows not only toppled the Han, but led to almost three centuries of chaos—an unusually long span of unrest in Chinese history. Regional rulers and weak dynasties rose and fell during this period. Even China's cultural unity was threatened as the wave of Buddhism spread—one of the only cases in which China imported a major idea from outside its borders until the twentieth century. Northern China, particularly, seemed near collapse.

Nonetheless, China did revive itself near the end of the sixth century. Strong native rulers in the north drove out the nomadic invaders. The Sui dynasty briefly ruled, and then in 618 C.E. it was followed by the T'ang, who sponsored one of the most glorious periods in Chinese history. Confucianism and the bureaucratic system were revived, and indeed the bureaucratic tradition became more elaborate. The period of chaos left its mark somewhat in the continued presence of a Buddhist minority and new styles in art and literature. But, unlike the case of Rome, there was no permanent disruption.

The structures of classical China were simply too strong to be overturned. The bureaucracy declined in scope and quality, but it did not disappear during the troubled centuries. Confucian values and styles of life remained current among the upper class. Many of the nomadic invaders, seeing that they had nothing better to offer by way of government or culture, simply tried to assimilate the Chinese traditions. China thus had to recover from a serious setback, but it did not have to reinvent its civilization.

The decline of classical civilization in India was less drastic than the collapse of Han China. The ability of the Gupta emperors to control local princes was declining by the fifth century. Invasions by nomadic peoples, probably Hun tribes similar to those who were pressing into Europe, affected some northern portions of India as early as 500 C.E. During the next century, the invaders penetrated much deeper, destroying the Gupta empire in central India. Many of the invaders were integrated into the warrior caste of India, forming a new ruling group of regional princes. For several centuries, no native ruler attempted to build a large Indian state. The regional princes, collectively called "Rajput," controlled the small states and emphasized military prowess. Few political events of more than local significance occurred.

Within this framework, Indian culture continued to evolve. Buddhism declined further in India proper. Hindu beliefs gained ground, among other things converting the Hun princes, who had originally worshipped gods of battle and had no sympathy for the Buddhist principles of calm and contemplation. Within Hinduism, the worship of a mother goddess, Devi, spread widely, encouraging a new popular emotionalism in religious ritual. Indian economic prosperity also continued at high levels.

Although Indian civilization substantially maintained its position, another threat was to come, after 600 C.E., from the new Middle Eastern religion of Islam. Arab armies, fighting under the banners of their god Allah, reached India's porous northwestern frontier during the seventh century, and while there was initially little outright conquest on the subcontinent, Islam did win some converts in the northwest. Hindu leaders reacted to the arrival of this new faith by strengthening their emphasis on religious devotion, at the expense of some other intellectual interests. Hinduism also underwent further popularization; Hindu texts were written in vernacular languages such as Hindi, and use of the old classical language, Sanskrit, declined. These reactions were largely successful in preventing more than a minority of Indians from abandoning Hinduism, but they distracted from further achievements in science and mathematics. Islam also hit hard at India's international economic position and affected its larger impact throughout Asia. Arab traders soon wrested control of the Indian Ocean from Tamil merchants, and India, though still prosperous and productive, saw its commercial dynamism reduced. In politics, regionalism continued to prevail. Clearly, the glory days of the Guptas were long past, although classical traditions survived particularly in Hinduism and the caste system.

DECLINE AND FALL IN ROME

The Roman Empire exhibited a great many symptoms of decay after about 180 C.E. There was statistical evidence in the declining population in addition to growing difficulties in recruiting effective armies. There were also political manifestations in the greater brutality and arbitrariness of many Roman emperors—victims, according to one commentator at the time, of "lustful and cruel habits." Tax collection became increasingly difficult, as residents of the empire fell on hard times. The governor of Egypt complained that "the once numerous inhabitants of the aforesaid villages have now been reduced to a few, because some have fled in poverty and others have died . . . and for this reason we are in danger owing to impoverishment of having to abandon the tax-collectorship."

Above all, there were human symptoms. Inscriptions on Roman tombstones increasingly ended with the slogan, "I was not, I was, I am not, I have no more desires," suggesting a pervasive despondency over the futility of this life and despair at the absence of an afterlife.

The decline of Rome was more disruptive than the collapse of the classical dynasties in Asia. For this reason, and because memories of the collapse of this great empire became part of the Western tradition, the process of deterioration deserves particular attention. Every so often, Americans or Western Europeans concerned about changes in their own society wonder if there might be lessons in Rome's fall that apply to the uncertain future of Western civilization today.

We have seen that the quality of political and economic life in the Roman Empire began to shift after about 180 C.E. Political confusion produced a series of weak emperors and many disputes over succession to the throne. Intervention by the army in the selection of emperors complicated political life and contributed to the deterioration of rule from the top. More important in initiating the process of decline was a series of plagues that swept over the empire. As in China, the plagues' source was growing international trade, which brought diseases endemic in southern Asia to new areas like the Mediterranean, where no resistance had been established even to contagions such as the measles. The resulting diseases decimated the population. The population of Rome decreased from a million people to 250,000. Economic life worsened in consequence. Recruitment of troops became more difficult, so the empire was increasingly reduced to hiring Germanic soldiers to guard its frontiers. The need to pay troops added to the demands on the state's budget, just as declining production cut into tax revenues.

Here, perhaps, is the key to the process of decline: a set of general problems, triggered by a cycle of plagues that could not be prevented, resulting in a rather mechanistic spiral that steadily worsened. However, there is another side to Rome's downfall, although whether as a cause or result of the initial difficulties is hard to say. Rome's upper classes became steadily more pleasure-seeking, turning away from the political devotion and economic vigor that had characterized the republic and early empire. Cultural life decayed. Aside from some truly creative Christian writers—the fathers of Western theology—there was very little sparkle to the art or literature of the later empire. Many Roman scholars contented themselves with writing textbooks that rather mechanically summarized earlier achievements in science, mathematics, and literary style. Writing textbooks is not, of course, proof of absolute intellectual incompetence—at least, not in all cases—but the point was that new knowledge or artistic styles were not being generated, and even the levels of previous accomplishment began to slip. The later Romans wrote textbooks about rhetoric instead of displaying rhetorical talent in actual political life; they wrote simple compendiums, for example, about animals or geometry, that barely captured the essentials of what earlier intellectuals had known, and often added superstitious beliefs that previous generations would have scorned. This cultural decline, finally, was not clearly due to disease or economic collapse, for it began in some ways before these larger problems surfaced. Something was happening to the Roman elite, perhaps because of the deadening effect of authoritarian political rule, perhaps because of a new interest in luxuries and sensual indulgence. Revealingly, the upper classes no longer produced many offspring, for bearing and raising children seemed incompatible with a life of pleasure-seeking.

Rome's fall, in other words, can be blamed on large, impersonal forces that would have been hard for any society to control or a moral and political decay that reflected growing corruption among society's leaders. Probably elements of both were involved. Thus, the plagues would have weakened even a vigorous society but they would not necessarily have produced an irreversible downward spiral had not the morale of the ruling classes already been sapped by an unproductive lifestyle and superficial values.

Regardless of precise causes, the course of Roman decay is quite clear. As the quality of imperial rule declined, as life became more dangerous and economic survival more precarious, many farmers clustered around the protection of large landlords, surrendering full control over their plots of land in the hope of military and judicial protection. The decentralization of political and economic authority, which was greatest in the western, or European, portions of the empire, foreshadowed the manorial system of Europe in the Middle Ages. The system of estates gave great political power to landlords and did provide some local stability. But, in the long run, it weakened the power of the emperor and also tended to move the economy away from the elaborate and successful trade patterns of Mediterranean civilization in its heyday. Many estates tried to be self-sufficient. Trade and production declined further as a result, and cities shrank in size. The empire was locked in a vicious circle, in which responses to the initial deterioration merely lessened the chances of recovery.

Some later emperors tried vigorously to reverse the tide. Diocletian, who ruled from 284 to 305 C.E., tightened up the administration of the empire and tried to improve tax collection. Regulation of the dwindling economy increased. Diocletian also attempted to direct political loyalties to his own person, exerting pressure to worship the emperor as god. This was what prompted him to persecute Christians with particular viciousness, for they would not give Caesar preference over their God. The emperor Constantine, who ruled from 312 to 337 C.E., experimented with other methods of control. He set up a second capital city, Constantinople, to regulate the eastern half of the empire more efficiently. He tried to use the religious force of Christianity to unify the empire spiritually, extending its toleration and adopting it as his own faith. These measures were not without result. The eastern empire, ruled

Mosaic in a Roman villa: the pleasures of the hunt.

from Constantinople (now the Turkish city of Istanbul), remained an effective political and economic unit. Christianity spread under his official sponsorship, although there were some new problems linked to its success.

None of these measures, however, revived the empire as a whole. Division merely made the weakness of the western half worse. Attempts to regulate the economy reduced economic initiative and lowered production; ultimately, tax revenues declined once again. The army deteriorated further. And, when the Germanic invasions began in earnest in the 400s, there was scant basis to resist. Many peasants, burdened by the social and economic pressures of the decaying empire, actually welcomed the barbarians. A priest noted that "in all districts taken over by the Germans, there is one desire among all the Romans, that they should never again find it necessary to pass under Roman jurisdiction." German kingdoms were established in many parts of the empire by 425 C.E., and the last Roman emperor in the west was displaced in 476 C.E. The Germanic invaders numbered at most 5 percent of the population of the empire, but so great was the earlier Roman decline that this small, poorly organized force was able to put an end to one of the world's great political structures.

The collapse of Rome echoed mightily through the later history of Europe and the Middle East. Rome's fall split the unity of the Mediterranean lands that had been so arduously won through Hellenistic culture and then by the Roman Empire itself. This was one sign that the end of the Roman Empire was a more serious affair than the displacement of the last classical dynasties in India and China. For Greece and Rome had not produced the shared political culture and bureaucratic traditions of China that could allow revival after a period of chaos. Nor had Mediterranean civilization, for all its vitality, generated a common religion that appealed deeply enough, or satisfied enough needs, to maintain unity amid political fragmentation, as in India. Such religions would reach the Mediterranean world as Rome fell, but they came too late to save the empire and produced a deep rift in this world—between Christian and Muslim—that has not been healed to this day.

However, Rome's collapse, although profound, was uneven. In effect, the fall of Rome divided the Mediterranean world into three zones, which formed the starting points of three distinct civilizations that would develop in later centuries.

In the eastern part of the empire, centered now on Constantinople, the empire in a sense did not fall. Civilization was more deeply entrenched here than in some of the Western European portions of the empire, and there were fewer pressures from invaders. Emperors continued to rule Greece and other parts of southeast Europe, plus the northern Middle East. This eastern empire—later to be known as the Byzantine Empire—was a product of late imperial Rome, rather than a balanced result of the entire span of classical Mediterranean civilization. Thus, although its language was Greek, it maintained the authoritarian tone of the late Roman rulers. But, the empire itself was vibrant, artistically creative, and active in trade. Briefly, especially under the emperor Justinian (who ruled from 527 to 565 C.E.), the eastern emperors tried to recapture the whole heritage of Rome. However, Justinian was unable to maintain a hold in Italy and even lost the provinces of North Africa. He did issue one of the most famous compilations of Roman law, in the code that bore his name. But, his was the last effort to restore Mediterranean unity.

The Byzantine Empire did not control the whole of the northern Middle East, even in its greatest days. During the late Hellenistic periods and into the early centuries of the Roman Empire, a Parthian empire had flourished, centered in the Tigris-Euphrates region but spreading into northwestern India and to the borders of Rome's holdings along the Mediterranean. Parthian conquerors had taken over this portion of Alexander the Great's empire. They produced little culture of their own, being content to rely on Persian styles, but they long maintained an effective military and bureaucratic apparatus. Then, around 227 C.E., a Persian rebellion displaced the Parthians and created a new Sassanid empire that more directly revived the glories of the earlier Persian empire. Persian religious ideas, including the religion of Zoroastrianism, revived, although there was some conversion to Christianity as well. Persian styles in art and manufacturing experienced a brilliant resurgence. Both the Parthian and the Sassanid empires served as bridges between the Mediterranean and the East, transmitting goods and some artistic and literary styles between the Greek-speaking world and India and China. As the Roman Empire weakened, the Sassanids joined

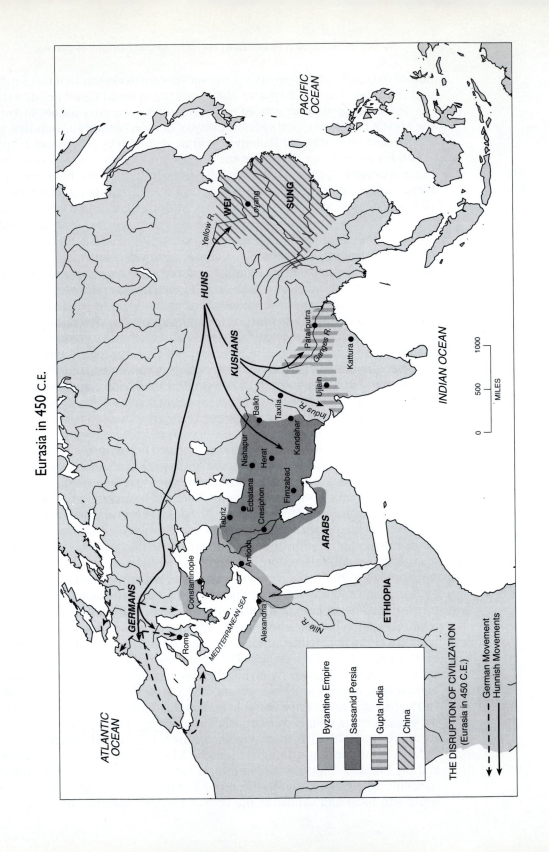

Eurasia in 450 C.E.

PACIFIC OCEAN

WEI

Loyang

SUNG

Yellow R.

HUNS

KUSHANS

Pataliputra

Ganges R.

Kattura

Ujjain

Indus R.

Balkh

Taxila

INDIAN OCEAN

Nishapur

Herat

Kandahar

1000

Ecbatana

Firozabad

500

Ctesiphon

MILES

Tabriz

0

Antioch

ARABS

Constantinople

GERMANS

ETHIOPIA

Rome

Alexandria

MEDITERRANEAN SEA

Nile R.

ATLANTIC OCEAN

THE DISRUPTION OF CIVILIZATION
(Eurasia in 450 C.E.)

Byzantine Empire

Sassanid Persia

Gupta India

China

German Movement

Hunnish Movements

the attack, at times pushing into parts of southeastern Europe. Ultimately, however, the Byzantine Empire managed to create a stable frontier. The Sassanid empire preserved the important strain of Persian culture in the eastern part of the Middle East, and this continued to influence this region as well as India. The Sassanids themselves, however, were finally overthrown by the surge of Arab conquest that followed the rise of Islam, in the seventh century C.E.

Rome's fall, then, did not disrupt the northern Middle East—the original cradle of civilization—as much as might have been expected. Persian rule simply continued in one part of the region, until the Arab onslaught, which itself did not destroy Persian culture. Byzantium maintained many of the traditions of the later Roman Empire, plus Christianity, in the western part of the Middle East and in Greece and other parts of southeastern Europe.

The second zone that devolved from Rome's fall consisted of North Africa and the southeastern shores of the Mediterranean. Here, a number of regional kingdoms briefly succeeded the empire. And while Christianity spread into the area—indeed, one of the greatest Christian theologians, Augustine, was a bishop in North Africa—its appearance was not so uniformly triumphant as in the Byzantine Empire or Western Europe. Furthermore, separate beliefs and doctrines soon split North African Christianity from the larger branches, producing most notably the Coptic Church in Egypt, which still survives as a Christian minority in that country. Soon this region would be filled with the still newer doctrines of Islam and a new Arab empire.

Finally, there was the western part of the empire—Italy, Spain, and points north. Here is where Rome's fall not only shattered unities but also reduced the level of civilization itself. Crude, regional Germanic kingdoms developed in parts of Italy, France, and elsewhere. Cities shrank still further, and especially outside Italy, trade almost disappeared. The only clearly vital forces in this region emanated not from Roman traditions but from the spread of Christianity. Even Christianity could not sustain a sophisticated culture of literature or art, however. In the mire of Rome's collapse, this part of the world forgot for several centuries what it had previously known.

In this western domain, what we call the fall of Rome was scarcely noted at the time, for decay had been progressing for so many decades that the failure to name a new emperor meant little. There was some comprehension of loss, some realization that the present could not rival the past. Thus, Christian scholars were soon apologizing for their inability to write well or to understand some of the doctrines of the earlier theologians like Augustine. This sense of inferiority to classical achievements would long mark the culture of this western zone, even as times improved.

THE NEW RELIGIOUS MAP

The end of the classical period is not simply the story of decay and collapse. This same period, from 200 to 600 C.E., saw the effective rise of many of the world's major religions. The devastating plagues caused new interest in belief systems that could provide solace amid rising death rates. From Spain to China, growing political instability clearly prompted many people to seek solace in joys of the spirit, and while the

The Germanic Migrations, Fourth to Sixth Centuries

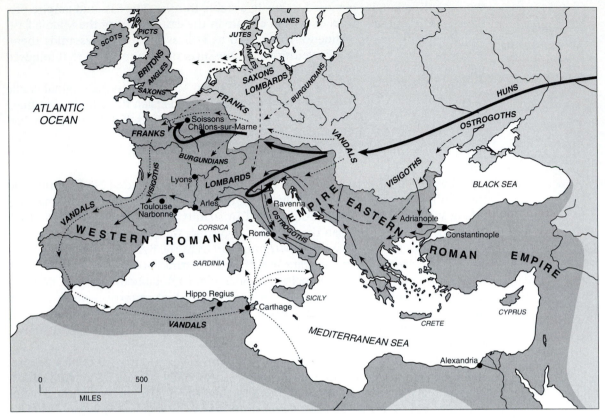

religious surge was not entirely new, the resulting changes in the religious map of Europe and Asia and the nature and intensity of religious interests were significant new forces. Christianity, born two centuries before Rome's collapse began, became a widespread religion throughout the Mediterranean region as the empire's political strength weakened. Buddhism, although launched still earlier, saw its surge into eastern Asia furthered by the growing problems of classical China. Thus, two major faiths, different in many ways but similar in their emphasis on spiritual life and the importance of divine power, reshaped major portions of Europe and Asia precisely as the structures of the classical period declined or disappeared. Finally, shortly after 600 C.E., an entirely new religion, Islam, surfaced and became the most dynamic force in world history during the next several centuries. In sum, the religious map of the world, although by no means completed by 500 C.E., was beginning to take on dramatic new contours. And, this means that while civilization in many ways declined, it was also being altered, taking new directions as well as losing some older strengths. Never before had single religions spread so widely, crossing so many cultural and political boundaries.

The newly expanding religions shared some general features. Christianity, Buddhism, and Hinduism (as well as Islam later on) all emphasized intense devotion and

HISTORY DEBATE

What Caused Decline and Fall

Determining what causes major developments is never easy. Unlike laboratory science, repeated experiments, to narrow down the causes of a phenomenon, are not possible. It remains important to discuss causes, as part of understanding what happened, and some plausible analysis is possible. However, debate is a vital part of the process.

In the case of the classical decline, particularly for Rome, debate has raged on and off for centuries. Even at the time, people wondered if perhaps the spread of Christianity was sapping Roman virtues and weakening the state (this is not a common explanation today). Other attempts to provide an appealing framework have included arguments that new patterns of sunspots reduced agricultural productivity (again, not widely believed now).

Current debates focus on inevitability and on external pressures vs. internal decay. One of the great world historians of the twentieth century, Arnold Toynbee, argued that civilizations inevitably undergo a life cycle in which prosperous middle age is followed by collapse. Loss of creativity, growing luxury, bureaucratic routine, attacks from outside provide a law of history, in which great empires finally shatter. Toynbee used Rome as one of his prime examples, and many historians concur with the approach. More recently, another well-known historian, David Kennedy, offered a slightly different interpretation: Many societies, like Rome, over-expand, and end up reducing their internal strength by trying to support impossibly wide frontiers.

On the other hand, some historians disagree with such sweeping explanations. Rome, after all, did not decline across the board—part of Eastern Rome survived quite well. It is important, in this counterargument, to look for more specific factors, on a case-by-case basis.

The internal-external quarrel runs like this. Many historians have long pointed to moral collapse as a key component of Rome's fall (and the argument can be applied to China and India too). Lower classes were sapped by bread and circuses, upper classes became greedy and pleasure-seeking, and the result was an inability to sustain vigorous institutions. There is evidence supporting this viewpoint, to be sure. But is the explanation necessary? The pressure of outside invasion plus, even more important, new evidence about the widespread impact of epidemic disease (particularly in Rome and China) may make the moral factors less salient. Some moral confusion may have resulted from growing death rates, rather than the other way around. The debate continues.

piety, stressing the importance of spiritual concerns beyond the daily cares of earthly life. All three offered the hope of a better existence after this life had ended, and each one responded to new political instability and to the growing poverty of people in various parts of the civilized world.

The spread of the major religions meant that hundreds of thousands of people, in Asia, Europe, and Africa, underwent a conversion process as the classical period drew to a close. Radically changing beliefs is an unusual human experience, symptomatic in this case of the new pressures on established political structures and on ordinary life. At the same time, many people blended new beliefs with the old, in a process called syncretism. This meant that the religions changed too, sometimes taking on the features of individual civilizations even while maintaining larger religious claims.

Despite these important common features, the major religions were themselves very different. Hinduism, as we have seen, retained its belief in reincarnation and its combination of spiritual interest in union with the divine essence and extensive rituals and ceremonies. The religion did experience greater popular appeal after the fall of the Guptas, associated with the expanded use of popular languages and with the worship of the mother goddess Devi.

BUDDHISM

Buddhism was altered more substantially, as it traveled mainly beyond India's borders, becoming only a small minority faith in India itself. The chief agents of Buddhist expansion and leadership were monks, for Buddhism tended to divide the faithful among a minority who abandoned earthly life in favor of spiritual dedication and the larger number who continued to work in the world while doing the best they could to meet their spiritual obligations. Some centuries after Buddha's death, a doctrine of *bodhisattvas* developed, which held that some people could attain nirvana through their own meditation while choosing to remain in the world as saints and to aid others by prayer and example. Buddhism increasingly shifted from an original emphasis on ethics to become a more emotional cult stressing the possibility of popular salvation. The role of the bodhisattvas, in broadening the prospects of salvation for ordinary people by leading them in prayer and advising on spiritual matters, was crucial in this transformation.

Buddhism evolved further as the religion spread seriously to China after the fall of the Han dynasty, when the idea of a celestial afterlife proved almost irresistible. Monasteries in India and the Himalaya Mountains continued to serve as spiritual centers for Chinese Buddhism, but the religion developed strong roots in East Asia directly, spreading through China and from there to Korea and Japan. The East Asian form of Buddhism, called Mahayana, or the Greater Vehicle, retained basic Buddhist beliefs. However, the emphasis on Buddha himself as god and savior increased in the Mahayana version. Statues devoted to Buddha as god countered the earlier Buddhist hostility to religious images. And, the religion improved its organization, with priests, temples, creeds, and rituals. Buddhist holy men, or bodhisattvas, remained important. Their souls after death resided in a kind of superheaven, where they could receive prayers and aid people. Intense spirituality continued to inform Buddhist faith as well. But, prayers and rituals could now help ordinary people to become

Spread of Buddhism: a Buddhist grotto in China. (The Granger Collection)

holy. Buddha himself became a god to whom one could appeal for solace, "the great physician for a sick and impure world." East Asian Buddhism also spurred new artistic interests in China and, later, in Japan, including the pagoda style of temple design and the statues devoted to Buddha himself.

Buddhism had a fascinating impact on women in China, largely among families who converted. On the face of things, Buddhism should have disrupted China's firm belief in patriarchal power, because Buddhists believed that women, like men, had souls. Indeed, some individual women in China captured great attention because of their spiritual accomplishments. But, Chinese culture generated changes in Buddhism within the empire. Buddhist phrases like "husband supports wife" were changed to "husband controls his wife," whereas "the wife comforts the husband"— another Buddhist phrase from India—became "the wife reveres her husband." Here was a vital case of cultural blending, or syncretism. Finally, many men valued pious Buddhist wives, because they might benefit the family's salvation and because Buddhist activity would keep their wives busy, calm, and out of mischief. Buddhism was perhaps appealing to Chinese women because it led to a more meaningful life, but it did not really challenge patriarchy. A biography of one Buddhist wife put it this way: "At times of crisis she could be tranquil and satisfied with her fate, not letting outside things agitate her mind."

Buddhism was not popular with all Chinese. Confucian leaders, particularly, found in Buddhist beliefs in an afterlife a diversion from appropriate political interests. They disliked the notion of such intense spirituality and also found ideas of the holy life incompatible with proper family obligations. More important, Buddhism was seen as a threat that might distract ordinary people from loyalty to the emperor. When imperial dynasties revived in China, they showed some interest in Buddhist piety for a time, but ultimately they attacked the Buddhist faith, driving out many missionaries. Buddhism remained a minority current in China, and many villages worshipped in Buddhist shrines. Thus, China's religious composition became increasingly complex, but without overturning earlier cultural directions. Daoism reacted to Buddhism as well, by improving its organization and emphasizing practical benefits obtainable through magic. It was at this point that Daoism developed a clear hold on many peasants, incorporating many of their beliefs in the process. Buddhism had a greater lasting influence in the religious experience of other parts of East Asia, notably Japan, Korea, and Vietnam, than in China itself. And, of course, Buddhism had also spread to significant parts of Southeast Asia, where it remained somewhat truer to earlier Buddhist concepts of individual meditation and ethics.

In the world today, some 255 million people count themselves as Buddhists. Most live in the areas of East and Southeast Asia, where the religion had taken root by 500 C.E. Buddhism did not, by itself, dominate any whole civilization; rather, it lived alongside other faiths. However, it provided major additions to Asia's religious map and an important response to changing conditions in the troubled centuries after the classical period had ended.

CHRISTIANITY

Christianity moved westward, from its original center in the Middle East, as Buddhism was spreading east from India. Although initially less significant than Buddhism in terms of the number of converts, Christianity would ultimately prove to be one of the two largest faiths worldwide. And, it would play a direct role in the formation of two postclassical civilizations, those of Eastern and Western Europe. Despite important similarities to Buddhism in its emphasis on salvation and the guidance of saints, Christianity differed in crucial ways. It came to place more emphasis on church organization and structure, copying from the example of the Roman Empire itself. Even more than Buddhism, it placed a premium on missionary activity and widespread conversions. More, perhaps, than any other major religion, Christianity stressed the exclusive nature of its truth and was intolerant of competing beliefs. Such fierce confidence was not the least of the reasons for the new religion's success.

Christianity began in reaction to rigidities that had developed in the Jewish priesthood during the two centuries before the birth of Jesus Christ. A host of reform movements sprang up, some of them preaching the coming of a Messiah, or savior, who would bring about a Last Judgment on humankind. Many of these movements also stressed the possibility of life after death for the virtuous, which was a new element in Judaism. Jesus of Nazareth, believed by Christians to be the son of God sent to earth to redeem human sin, crystallized this radical reform movement. Combining extraordinary gentleness of spirit and great charisma, Jesus preached widely in Israel and gathered a group of loyal disciples around him. Initially, there seems to have been no intent on his or his followers' part to found a new religion. After Jesus' crucifixion, the disciples expected his imminent return and with it the end of the world.

Only gradually, when the Second Coming did not transpire, did the disciples begin to fan out and, through their preaching, attract growing numbers of supporters in various parts of the Roman Empire.

The message of Jesus and his disciples seemed clear: There was a single God who loved humankind despite earthly sin. A virtuous life was one dedicated to the worship of God and fellowship among other believers; worldly concerns were secondary, and a life of poverty might be most conducive to holiness. God sent Jesus (called "Christ" from the Greek word for *God's annointed*) to preach his holy word and through his sacrifice to prepare his followers for the widespread possibility of an afterlife and heavenly communion with God. Belief, good works, and the discipline of fleshly concerns would lead to heaven; rituals, such as commemorating Christ's Last Supper with wine and bread, would promote the same goal.

Christianity's message spread at an opportune time. The official religion of the Greeks and Romans had long seemed rather sterile, particularly to many of the poor. The Christian emphasis on the beauty of a simple life and the spiritual equality of all people, plus the fervor of the early Christians and the satisfying rituals they created, captured growing attention. The great reach of the Roman Empire made it relatively easy for Christian missionaries to travel widely in Europe and the Middle East, to spread the new word, although as we have seen, they also reached beyond, to Persia, Axum, and Ethiopia. Then when conditions began to deteriorate in the empire, the solace this otherworldly religion provided resulted in its even wider appeal. Early Christian leaders made several important adjustments to maximize their conversions. Under the guidance of Paul, not one of the original disciples but an early convert, Christians began to see themselves as part of a new religion, rather than part of a Jewish reform movement, and they welcomed non-Jews. Paul also encouraged more formal organization within the new church, with local groups selecting elders to govern them; soon, a single leader, or bishop, was appointed for each city. This structure paralleled the provincial government of the empire. Finally, Christian doctrine became increasingly organized, as the writings of several disciples and others were collected into what became known as the New Testament of the Christian Bible.

During the first three centuries after Christ, the new religion competed among a number of eastern mystical religions. It also faced, as we have seen, periodic persecution from the normally tolerant imperial government. Even so, by the time Constantine converted to Christianity and accepted it as the one true legitimate faith, perhaps 10 percent of the empire's population had accepted the new religion. Constantine's conversion brought new troubles to Christianity, particularly some interference by the state in matters of doctrine. However, it became much easier to spread Christianity with official favor, and the continued deterioration of the empire added to the impetus to join this amazingly successful new church. In the eastern Mediterranean, where imperial rule remained strong from its center in Constantinople, state control of the church became a way of life. But in the West, where conditions were far more chaotic, bishops had a freer hand. A centralized church organization under the leadership of the bishop of Rome, called "Pope" from the word *papa*, or father, gave the Western Church unusual strength and independence.

By the time Rome collapsed, Christianity had thus demonstrated immense spiritual power and developed a solid organization, although one that differed from East

Early Christian art: Figure of Christ on the door of a Roman church.

to West. The new church faced a number of controversies over doctrine but managed to promote certain standard beliefs as against several heresies. A key tenet involved a complex doctrine of the Trinity, which held that the one God had three persons—the Father, the Son (Christ), and the Holy Ghost. Experience in fighting heresies promoted Christian interest in defending a single belief and strengthened its intolerance for any competing doctrine or faith. Early Christianity also produced an important formal theology, through formative writers such as Augustine. This theology incorporated many elements of classical philosophy with Christian belief and aided the church in its attempts to gain respectability among intellectuals. Theologians like Augustine grappled with such problems as freedom of the will: If God is all-powerful, can mere human beings have free will? And if not, how can human beings be justly punished for sin? By working out these issues in elaborate doctrine, the early theologians, or church fathers, provided an important role for formal, rational thought in a religion that continued to emphasize the primary importance of faith. Finally, Christianity was willing to accommodate some earlier polytheistic traditions among the common people. The celebration of Christ's birth was thus moved to coincide with winter solstice, a classic example of syncretism, which allowed the new faith to benefit from the power of selective older rituals.

Like all successful religions, Christianity combined a number of appeals. It offered blind devotion to an all-powerful God. One church father, denying the validity of human thought, simply stated, "I believe because it is absurd." However, Christianity also developed its own complex intellectual system. Mystical holy men and women flourished under Christian banners, particularly in the Middle East. In the West, soon after the empire's collapse, this impulse was partially disciplined through the institution of monasticism, first developed in Italy under Benedict, who started a monastery among Italian peasants whom he lured away from the worship of the sun god Apollo. The Benedictine Rule, which soon spread to many other monasteries and convents, urged a disciplined life, with prayer and spiritual fulfillment alternating with hard work in agriculture and study. Thus, Christianity attempted to encourage but also to discipline intense piety, and to avoid a complete gulf between the lives of saintly men and women and the spiritual concerns of ordinary people. Christianity's success and organizational strength obviously appealed to political leaders. But, the new religion never became the creature of the upper classes alone. Its popular message of salvation and satisfying rituals continued to draw the poor, more than most of the great classical belief systems; in this regard, it was somewhat like Hinduism in India. Christianity also provided some religious unity among different social groups. It even held special appeal for women. Christianity did not create equality among men and women, but it did preach the equal importance of male and female souls. And, it encouraged men and women to worship together, unlike many other faiths.

Christianity promoted a new culture among its followers. The rituals, the otherworldly emphasis, the interest in spiritual equality—these central themes were far different from those of classical Mediterranean civilizations. Christianity modified classical beliefs in the central importance of the state and of political loyalties. Although Christians accepted the state, they did not put it first. Christianity also worked against other classical institutions, such as slavery, in the name of brotherhood (although later Christians would accept slavery in other contexts). Christianity may have fostered greater respectability for disciplined work than had been the case in the Mediterranean civilization, where an aristocratic ethic dominated. Western monasteries, for example, set forth rigid work routines for monks. Certainly, Christianity sought some changes in classical culture beyond its central religious message, including greater emphasis on sexual restraint. But Christianity preserved important classical values as well, in addition to an interest in solid organization and some of the themes of classical philosophy. Church buildings retained Roman architectural styles, although often with greater simplicity if only because of the poverty of the later empire and subsequent states. Latin remained the language of the church in the West, Greek the language of most Christians in the eastern Mediterranean. Through the patient librarianship of monks, monasticism played an immensely valuable role in preserving classical as well as Christian learning.

When the Roman Empire fell, Christian history was still in its infancy. The Western Church would soon spread its missionary zeal to northern Europe, and the Eastern Church would reach into the Slavic lands of the Balkans and Russia. By then, Christianity was already established as a significant world religion—one of the few ever generated. A world religion is defined as a faith of unusual durability and drawing power, one whose complexity wins the devotion of many different kinds of people. Major world religions, like Christianity and Buddhism, do indeed show some ability to cut across different cultures, to win converts in a wide geographic area and amid considerable diversity.

Islam

One final world religion remained. Islam, launched early in the seventh century, would initially surpass Christianity as a world faith and has remained Christianity's most tenacious rival. With Islam, the roster of world religions was essentially completed. Changes would follow, but no totally new religion of major significance arose—unless one counts some of the secular faiths, like communism, that appeared in the last century. The centuries after Christianity's rise, the spread of Buddhism, and the inception of Islam would see the conversion of most of the civilized world to one or another of the great faiths, producing a religious map that, in Europe and Asia and even parts of Africa, would not alter greatly until our own time. Table 5.1 shows the distribution of religions in the world today.

The spread of major religions—Hinduism in India, Buddhism in East and Southeast Asia, a more popular Daoism in China, Christianity in Europe and parts of the Mediterranean world, and ultimately Islam—was a vital result of the changes in classical civilizations brought on by attack and decay. Despite the important diversity among these great religions, which included fierce hatreds, particularly between Christian and Muslim, their overall development suggests the way important currents could run through the civilized world, crossing political and cultural borders—thanks in part to the integrations and contacts built by the classical civilizations.

TABLE 5.1 ✦ Religions and Their Distribution in the World Today*

Religion	Distribution (million)
Christianity	995
Roman Catholic	580
Protestant	340
Eastern Orthodox	75
Islam	600
Hinduism	480
Buddhism	255
Confucianism	155
Shintoism	57
Daoism	31
Judaism	14

*Figures for several religions have been reduced, over the past 50 years, by the impact of Communism in Eastern Europe and parts of Asia.

Common difficulties, including invading forces that journeyed from central Asia and contagious epidemics that knew no boundaries, help explain parallel changes in separate civilizations. Trade and travel also provided common bonds. Chinese travelers learned of Buddhism through trading expeditions to India, whereas Ethiopians learned about Christianity from Middle Eastern traders. The new religions spurred a greater interest in spiritual matters and resulted in a greater tendency to focus on a single basic divinity instead of a multitude of gods. Polytheistic beliefs and practices continued to flourish as part of popular Hinduism and popular Daoism, and they were not entirely displaced among ordinary people who converted to Christianity, Buddhism, or Islam. But the new religious surge reduced the hold of literal animism in much of Asia and Europe, and this too was an important development across boundaries.

CONCLUSION: THE WORLD AROUND 500 C.E.

Developments in many parts of the world by 500 C.E. produced three major themes for world history in subsequent centuries. First, and particularly in the centers of classical civilization, there was a response to the collapse of classical forms. Societies in China, India, and around the Mediterranean faced the task of reviving or reworking their key institutions and values after internal decline and external invasion. Second, in these areas but also in other parts of Africa, Europe, and Asia, was the need to react to the new religious map that was taking shape, to integrate new religious institutions and values into established civilizations or, as in northern Europe, to use them as the basis for a civilization that had previously been lacking. Finally, increased skill in agriculture and the creation of early civilizations or new contacts—like the Japanese import of writing—prepared parts of Europe, Africa, Asia, and the Americas for new developments in the centuries to come. The centers of classical civilization would still hold a dominant position in world history after 500 C.E., but their monopoly would be increasingly challenged by the spread of civilization to other areas.

SUGGESTED WEBSITES

On Kushite civilization, see *http://library.thinkquest.org/22845/kush/meroitic royal.shtml;* on Benedict, the early Christian monk, and his monastic rule, see *http://www.worth.org.uk/guides/m6.htm.*

SUGGESTED READINGS

The fall of the Roman Empire has generated rich and interesting debate. For recent interpretations and discussion of earlier views, see A. H. M. Jones, *The Decline of the Ancient World* (1966); J. Vogt, *The Decline of Rome* (1965); and F. W. Walbank, *The Awful Revolution— The Decline of the Roman Empire in the West* (1960). On India and China in decline, worthwhile sources include R. Thaper, *History of India,* Vol. 1 (1966); R. C. Majumdar, ed., *The Classical Age* (1966); Raymond Dawson, *Imperial China* (1972); J. A. Harrison, *The Chinese Empire* (1972); and Twitchett and Fairbanks, eds., *The Cambridge History of China,* Vol. 3, Part 1 (1979). On Africa, see K. Shillington, *History of Africa* (1989); Graham Connal, *African*

Civilizations: Precolonial Cities and States in Tropical Africa, an Archeological Perspective (1987). On the role of disease, W. McNeill, *Plagues and Peoples* (1977) is useful. For the rise or spread of new religions, consult Geoffrey Parinder, ed., *World Religions* (1971); Jamail Ragi al Farugi, ed., *Historical Atlas of the Religions of the World* (1974); and Lewis M. Hopke, *Religions of the World* (1983). Important recent works on the world religions include N. C. Chandhuri, *Hinduism, a Religion to Live By* (1979); S. Renko, *Pagan Rome and the Early Christians* (1986); M. Hengel, *Acts and the History of Earliest Christianity* (1986); A. Sharma, ed., *Women in World Religions* (1987); D. Carmody, *Women and World Religions* (1985); G. Clark, *Women in Late Antiquity: Pagan and Christian* (1993); and B. Witherington, *Women in the Earliest Churches* (1988). The causes of the rise and fall of civilizations are addressed in Jared Diamond, *Guns, Germs and Steel: The Fate of Human Societies* (1997); Christopher Chase-Dunn and Thomas D. Hall, *Rise and Demise: Comparing World-Systems* (1997); H. M. Jones, *The Decline of the Ancient World* (1966); Joseph A. Tainter, *The Collapse of Complex Societies* (1988); and Norman Yoffee and George L. Cowgill, *The Collapse of Ancient States and Civilizations* (1991).

centers in both Eastern and Western Europe, and the rise of African merchant routes along the eastern coast and overland through the Sahara all contributed as well. With growing trade and periodic military encounters, other kinds of exchanges occurred across civilizations. Technology spread. Thus, Muslim troops fighting on China's western border in the ninth century came to learn of paper, developed earlier in China. Paper production in the Middle East resulted, and as Western Europeans made contact with this region through trade and religious wars, they learned of the new product as well. The first European paper-making plant was established in Italy in the thirteenth century. Technological dissemination of this sort was hardly speedy, but it did occur at a more rapid pace than with previous innovations. Cultural exchange was another vital source of contact. Religious ideas spread from India to China and then to Japan, Korea, and Indochina; they spread from the Middle East to Africa and many parts of Asia. This was part of the great missionary wave. But, other kinds of ideas spread as well. Arabs gained knowledge of Indian mathematics, especially the number system. Later in the period, Western Europeans began to learn Arab mathematics, including the same number system, and they also took an interest in Arab philosophy.

Defining the world network is not easy; there are no clear statistics, no succinct or simple analyses by farsighted contemporary observers. The exchange of technologies, such as papermaking, is one useful preliminary indication. Another measurement directly compares the world network of about 1300 C.E. with the more limited contacts of the classical era. Affluent Romans under the empire had bought small amounts of silk cloth manufactured in and transported from China, but the Romans had only vague ideas about where the silk came from, and they had scant influence over its delivery. International trade was limited, and it passed through a variety of groups as it moved from region to region. In contrast, wealthy Westerners in 1300 bought silks and other goods from Asia in larger quantities and with a fair idea of their origins. They also could identify key agents of international trade, notably Arab merchants. Furthermore, Western leaders were beginning to wish they could control the source of the trade, and they began to learn the improved mapmaking pioneered by the Arabs, plus navigational techniques and weapons devised by the Chinese. The world network was tightening. World trade continued to involve luxury products for the most part, but the volume was higher, the geographic range more extensive, and the impact on the economies of many civilizations greater.

A handful of world travelers began to emerge from the twelfth century onward. Several Muslims journeyed to Europe, Africa, and south Asia, reporting on what they saw. A smaller number of Europeans ventured in similar directions, whereas an unusually large number of Chinese travelled under Mongol rule. This development reflected the new connections in most of the civilized world, and the resulting journals and news accounts spread some international knowledge to wider groups.

Civilizations still defined key differences in institutions and values; new contacts did not destroy separate cultures and political institutions. Most people were still far removed from any direct contact with international trade. Increasingly, however, many civilizations operated in a genuinely international framework within which the world network of commercial, technological, and cultural exchanges clearly affected their operations. The development of the world network distinguished the postclassical era and all subsequent ages, including our own, from the earlier periods in which regional isolation predominated.

The Middle East	India and Southeast Asia	Western Europe	The Americas
	200 ff. Spread of Indian influence in Southeast Asia.		
	500s Hun invasions; beginning of the Rajput (princedoms) period.	**500–800** "Dark Ages," missionary work in northern Europe.	
570–632 Muhammed and the foundation of Islam.		**732** Franks defeat Muslims in France.	**Seventh century** End of Olmec culture; rise of Mayans in Central America.
622 Muhammed's flight to Medina (Hejira).	**700 ff.** Spread of Hinduism in southern India.	**800–814** Charlemagne's empire.	**900** Movement north by Mayans; intermingling with Toltecs.
632–634 Abu Bekr, first caliph.		**962** Germanic kings revive "Roman" empire.	**1100 ff.** Rise of Incas.
632–738 Islamic expansion beyond Arabia.		**1018 ff.** Beginning of Christian reconquest of Spain.	
711 Invasion of Spain.	**711** Arab raids begin.	**1066** Norman conquest of England; strong feudal monarchy.	
661–750 Umayyad caliphate.		**1073–1085** Reform papacy of Gregory VII.	
750–1258 Abbasid caliphate.		**1096 ff.** Crusades.	
788–809 Harun al-Rashid caliph.		**1194 ff.** French Gothic cathedrals.	
813–833 Capital transferred to Baghdad.	**1192 ff.** Muslim invasions, leading to Delhi sultanate.	**1200–1274** Thomas Aquinas and flowering of scholasticism.	
906 ff. Decline of caliphate, growing Turkish influence.		**1215** Magna Carta.	**1200 ff.** Mayan decline.
1095 ff. Attacks by Western crusaders.	**1253** Formation of Thai state (Siam).	**1265** English parliament.	
		1303 Seizure of papacy by French King.	**1350 ff.** Formation of Aztec empire.
1200 ff. Rise of the Sufi movement.		**1338–1453** Hundred Years' War.	**1400** Height of Incan empire.
1258 Mongol conquest of Baghdad, fall of Abbasid caliphate.	**1338 ff.** Decline of Delhi sultanate.	**1479** Formation of single Spanish monarchy.	**1493** Beginnings of Spanish government in the Americas (second voyage of Columbus).

Sub-Saharan Africa	East Asia	Byzantium and Eastern Europe
	589–618 Sui dynasty. **600 ff.** Increasing Japanese contact with China. **618–907** Tang dynasty. **800s** Flowering of Japanese feudalism.	**527–569** Justinian emperor. **718** Defeat of Arab attack on Constantinople. **855** According to legend, Rurik king of Kievan Russia. **864** Beginning of missionary work of brothers Cyril and Methodius in Slavic lands.
c. 800–1200 Empire of Ghana at its height. **800 ff.** Bantu migrations. **1210–1400** Empire of Mali. **1312–1337** King Mansa Musa. **1300** Height of Zimbabwe. **1500–1591** Kingdom of Songhai.	**841–846** Persecution of Buddhists, China. **907–960** Disputes over China by rival dynasties. **960–1279** Sung dynasty. **1120–1200** Philosopher Chu Hsi. **1161** Use of explosives in war. ***Twelfth century (or before)*** Invention of magnetic compass. **1185–1333** Kamakura shogunate, Japan. **1206** Temujin named Chingghis Khan of Mongols; Mongol invasions of China. **1271–1295** Marco Polo to China. **1279** Toppling of Sung dynasty by Kubilai Khan and Mongols. **1281** Failure of second Mongol invasion of Japan; "divine wind" typhoon. **1368** Mongols driven from China by Ming dynasty. **1405–1433** Chinese expeditions.	**980–1015** Conversion of Vladimir I of Russia to Christianity. **1054** Schism between Eastern and Western Christianity. **1100 ff.** Byzantine decline; growing Turkish attack. **1203–1204** Capture of Constantinople by fourth crusade. **1236** Capture of Russia by Mongols (Tatars). **1453** Turkish capture of Constantinople; end of Byzantine Empire. **1480** Expulsion of Tatars from Russia.

FRAGMENTATION VERSUS INTERACTION

The postclassical period embraced important tensions between fragmentation, as the effect of so many separate civilizations, and interaction, as evidenced in so many new contacts and cultural parallelisms. It was revealing that empires, as political forms, became less common in this period than during the classical age, for many postclassical civilizations were not open to this kind of political integration or relied on religious ties instead.

The tension between fragmentation and interaction was modified by the fact that the spread of civilization mostly extended from established bases. New civilizations, in other words, remained in contact with old centers, and this provided some real coherence even as the number of major civilizations grew. Lines of contact extended between the eastern Mediterranean and northeastern Europe, including Russia; between China and Korea, Vietnam, and Japan; between the Arab Middle East and North Africa, and important parts of sub-Saharan Africa; and between various parts of the Mediterranean world and the rising civilization of Western Europe.

The tension between separate civilizations, some of them new, and global contacts was further mediated by novel patterns of imitation. Although many centers of civilization worked to define their own identity, such development was actually accelerated by their attempts to copy the established centers. Thus, imitating did not erase one's identity; rather, it contributed to separate cultures or civilizations. It also enhanced connections and hence the development of an international network. Trade, ideas, even diseases spread more widely through these contacts.

Older centers included China, India, the Middle East, and (in southeastern Europe and present-day Turkey) the Byzantine Empire. These areas had the largest cities—Constantinople, Baghdad, Zhangan, and Hangzhou. Clustered around them were the newer centers—the imitators.

Japan, much of Southeast Asia, northern Europe, and parts of sub-Saharan Africa defined their civilizations while also copying key features of one of the more established centers. These areas participated in the world network, although their level of participation changed over time (as with the West's growing involvement from the twelfth century onward). Societies in this second zone usually participated in international exchange at some disadvantage, being the recipients of more influence than they, in fact, generated. But, even these activities showed how the expansion of civilizations and development of global contacts could coexist.

There was a third zone of civilizations where important developments occurred with no link whatsoever to the world network; isolation prevailed. Neither technological exchange nor missionary religions touched this zone. Civilizations in the Americas and Polynesian societies best illustrate this third zone. Important developments occurred but within separate frameworks and with only a few accidental parallels to patterns elsewhere. Here, the expansion of civilization stands alone. But, the lack of contact, ironically, demonstrates the importance of the world network elsewhere, simply through what turned out to be missing.

The Rise of Islam: Civilization in the Middle East

FOCAL POINTS

Arab expansion into areas previously dominated by other peoples and the concomitant emergence of Islam brought great changes to the Middle East and North Africa (and beyond). When studying Islam itself, we must ask: How does it compare to the other world religions? Why was it both a stabilizing and revolutionary force in the Middle East and elsewhere? When studying the Middle East and North Africa, we need to examine the questions: What caused the dynamism of the Arabs and Islam? How much was due to the nature of this newest world religion, and how much resulted from other factors? What were the new political and social structures that accompanied the rise of Islam? Amid great change, were there also continuities from previous civilizations, like the Persian and the classical Mediterranean? How can these be integrated into the overall characterization of the postclassical civilization of the Middle East? Finally, why did the vigor of Arab society begin to lag somewhat by the thirteenth century?

THE BEGINNINGS OF ISLAM

We begin with what became the center of the postclassical world: the Islamic Middle East and North Africa. Military conquests and a new empire, called caliphate, were one key ingredient. More important were an explosion of trade activity and the new religion of Islam. "There is no God but Allah, and Muhammed is his prophet." This prophet, an Arab born in the city of Mecca, intended to perfect a religion that would focus on the power of a single god more clearly than any other religion—and by many measures he succeeded. The new faith of Islam sought to place its believers under the tutelage of an all-powerful divinity. Common Islamic names still reflect this orientation; many names include the Arabic word *Abd*, meaning "slave," to indicate subjugation to God. The religion's name, Islam, means "submission to the will of God." Islam quickly became the fastest-growing religion in the world, maintaining this pace throughout the postclassical period.

Islam was born among the Arab people and served to carry their influence over much of the Middle East. This Semitic people had long existed on the southern fringes of Middle Eastern civilization, from their center in and around the Arabian desert. They had considerable experience in trade because of their proximity to the main routes between the Mediterranean and the wealth of India. They had undertaken agriculture, although some (called Bedouins) remained nomadic herders with a

137

tribal organization under their warrior chiefs, or sheiks. The Arabs had developed writing and a literature. They had also produced great works of art. Their religion was polytheistic, with priests organizing prayers and sacrifices to the various gods.

The rise of Islam and the Arabs supported major changes in Middle Eastern civilization from the sixth century onward. A vital new religion spread over this region and beyond, although minorities of Christians and Jews remained. While Islam ultimately pushed beyond the Arabs, it initially served as a vehicle for Arab assertion against states like Persia and Christian Byzantium that had long dominated the region. Arabs brought a new language as well, although again, pockets of other languages were still current. However, there was important continuity. Muhammed, Islam's founder, viewed himself as a prophet who spoke in God's voice and not the founder of a new religion. He deliberately built on other religions in the Middle East, notably Judaism and Christianity. Furthermore, older traditions survived in other respects. Middle Eastern culture, although altered by Islam, retained some of the traditions of Hellenistic philosophy and science. Arab merchants extended Middle Eastern commercial patterns, but they built on the trading practices that had already made the Middle East a vital commercial link between the Mediterranean and Asia. The Middle East, in sum, displayed new powers with the rise of Islam and the Arabs, but it relied heavily on the earlier achievements of civilization in the region.

The Arabs' burst into larger Middle Eastern history started with the life of Muhammed, who around 570 C.E. was born of poor parents in Mecca, a trading city that already had some religious significance for the Arabs. First a camel driver, then a businessman happily married to a wealthy woman, Muhammed increasingly turned his thoughts to religious subjects. He was fascinated by the Christian and Jewish faiths, both of which had many followers in Mecca, but he sought a purer statement of God's divinity—one uncluttered, for example, by complex doctrines such as the Christian Trinity—and a statement that was uniquely Arab. Writing what he thought were God's words, he argued that Allah, previously a rather vague Arab divinity, was the one true God and that Jewish and Christian leaders had merely been earlier prophets of Allah's truth. In Muhammed's view, the Jewish Old Testament and the work of Jesus, seen as a preacher but not as divine, provided a basis for the true religion. A series of ecstatic revelations convinced Muhammed that he had been called upon to organize this religion. He began attracting converts, whom he called Muslims ("surrendered to God").

Chased from Mecca by authorities who feared that he was organizing insurrection against them, Muhammed fled in 622 to Medina, whose citizens looked to him for religious and political leadership. His flight to Medina, called the Hejira, is regarded as the year 1 in the Islamic calendar. In Medina, Muhammed built a mosque for Muslim worship and led the city's government in a war with Mecca. Medina won, and many Arab tribesmen began to then negotiate peace with Muhammed. In one such negotiation, Mecca yielded to Islam but retained its status as the chief holy place. Muhammed, who had first ordered his followers to pray in the direction of Jerusalem, now told the supplicants to face toward Mecca. His decision was eased by the fact that most Jews, whom he had hoped to convert, rejected the new faith.

Muhammed died in 632. The revelations he received from Allah, via the intermediary of the archangel Gabriel, formed the Muslim holy book, called the Quran or

World Profiles

Muhammed (570–632 C.E.)

Muhammed is a fascinating historical figure. He was born into a poor family but later served as camel driver to a wealthy widow, whom he eventually married. No official portrait exists, but he was described as a handsome man with piercing black eyes and a full beard. Not an active businessman, Muhammed spent 15 years happily married and, in the eyes of local merchants, he was regarded as somewhat indolent. Despite a lack of formal learning, he contemplated religious matters, experiencing a conversion that brought him an immediate understanding of Allah, a rather shadowy divinity in Arab tradition, as sole God. Future visions impelled Muhammed to convert others to his faith. These efforts culminated in the conversion of most of the Arabian peninsula by his death in 632. With their conversion to Islam, the Arabs swept through Syria, Persia, Armenia, across North Africa, and into Spain over the next 120 years. What would Middle Eastern, indeed world, history have been like had Muhammed not existed?

Islam's disapproval of representational art limited attempts to depict Muhammed even in an idealized fashion. But, this miniature, in the Persian artistic tradition, shows the prophet building a mosque in Medina with his disciples.

Koran. To loyal Muslims from this time onward, the Quran has stood as the direct word of God, brooking no contradiction. It is God's "full and complete" statement of a perfect religion, including the "pillars of faith," or basic religious obligations. After his death, Muhammed's disciples also began to assemble the Hadith, based on the prophet's sayings and other rules and regulations for the Islamic community.

Muhammed's death thus did not disrupt the religious message he had developed. As one of his disciples said, "Whoso worshippeth Muhammed, let him know that Muhammed is dead. But whoso worshippeth God, let him know that God liveth and dieth not." However, the new religion, and the political organization Muhammed had formed in Medina, needed new leadership. One of Muhammed's closest followers, Abu Bakr, was selected as caliph, or successor. Abu Bakr restructured his regional state and what was still a regional religion into a war machine, using small but brilliantly generaled armies to vanquish a series of rebellions against the rule of the Muslim states. The Arab people became firmly converted as a result.

Conversion seemed to galvanize the Arabs into several generations of conquest. Religion and a desire for material gain, through conquest, made for a powerful mixture. Muhammed had encouraged military effort in the name of Islam, claiming that anyone killed in a jihad, or holy war in defense of the faith, would automatically attain an afterlife in heaven. This religious motive contributed to the economic desire of a poor people to gain access to the wealth of their neighbors. The Arab armies were not particularly large, nor did they benefit from advanced weaponry. They were ably led, however, by the generals who served under Abu Bakr and several subsequent caliphs. And, they profited from the weakness of their neighbors, who had been ineffectually ruled from Constantinople since the fall of Rome. Egypt and North Africa lacked strong governments. To the north, the Byzantine Empire and the Persians had exhausted each other by repeated wars. As a result, there was territory ripe for the plucking.

PATTERNS OF ISLAMIC HISTORY

During the decades following Muhammed's death and the creation of a government by his successors, called the caliphate, swift expansion grew. The speed and extent of Arab victories rivaled the earlier sweep of Alexander the Great. Islamic forces first turned northward to the heart of the Middle East. In 635, they defeated a larger Byzantine army and conquered Syria and Palestine. The Muslims also defeated the Persians after a three-day battle during which Arab poets chanted war songs and pious Muslims recited the Quran. This victory pushed the borders of the Islamic caliphate north to the Caucasus mountains and east to the frontiers of India. The Arabs also turned west, attacking Egypt and establishing a new capital on the Nile. Then, later in the seventh century, the Arabs invaded the rest of North Africa, conquering or assimilating the native Berber peoples. Berber opposition, at first fierce, eased as the people converted to Islam and gradually accepted the Arab language. Finally, aided by Berber troops, the Muslims invaded Spain in 711, defeating a weak Germanic kingdom there. Only beyond the Pyrenees were the Muslims stopped— Frankish leader Charles Martel defeated their forces in 732—although it was, in fact, the strain on Muslim troops and supplies, not Frankish power, that turned the tide. Most of Europe thus remained outside the Islamic orbit, although Spain and parts of southern Italy were Muslim-ruled for several centuries. The Muslims also failed to conquer Byzantium and began to encounter new resistance in northwestern India. These various setbacks ended the period of Arab conquest by the second quarter of the eighth century.

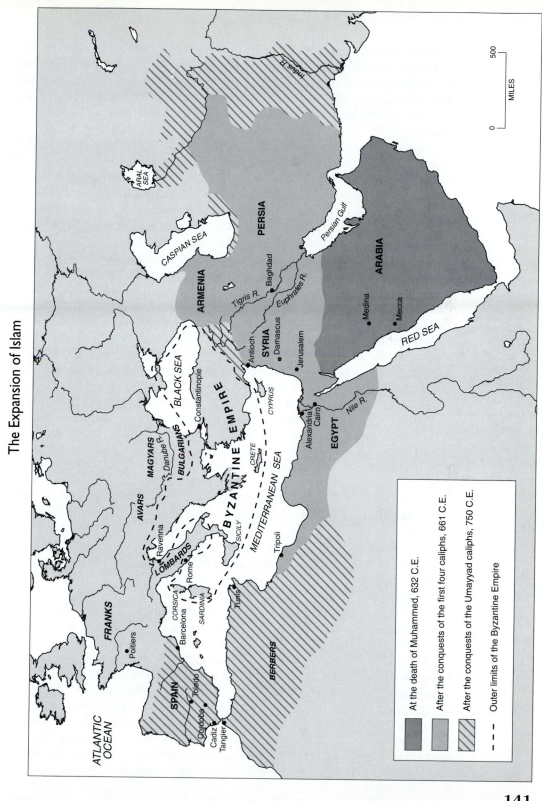

The Expansion of Islam

Legend:
- At the death of Muhammed, 632 C.E.
- After the conquests of the first four caliphs, 661 C.E.
- After the conquests of the Umayyad caliphs, 750 C.E.
- Outer limits of the Byzantine Empire

500 / 0 MILES

ATLANTIC OCEAN

FRANKS

Poitiers

SPAIN
Toledo
Cordoba
Cadiz
Tangier

Barcelona

CORSICA
SARDINIA

Rome
LOMBARDS
Ravenna

AVARS
MAGYARS
BULGARIANS

Danube R.

BLACK SEA

Constantinople

BYZANTINE EMPIRE

SICILY
CRETE
CYPRUS

MEDITERRANEAN SEA

Tunis

Tripoli

BERBERS

ARAL SEA

CASPIAN SEA

ARMENIA

PERSIA

Indus R.

Persian Gulf

ARABIA

Medina
Mecca

RED SEA

Tigris R.
Baghdad
Euphrates R.

Antioch
SYRIA
Damascus
Jerusalem

Alexandria
Cairo
EGYPT

Nile R.

141

Nevertheless, even as it settled into a period of consolidation after the conquests, the Islamic caliphate ruled a larger territory and more people than the Romans had. The orders of the caliph were obeyed from Spain to the western borders of India and China. Organizing this huge area was no small matter. The second caliph, Umar, who spearheaded early Arab conquests, began the process of forming a larger government apparatus.

One source of control was the leadership of the Arab military itself. As leaders fanned out in conquest, they acquired considerable wealth and became something of a local ruling class. Islamic belief, holding that all land belonged to Allah, justified their seizure of property, but in fact most Arabs were content to leave the land in the hands of the original owners, collecting a tax instead. This tax became the main financial support for not only the new Arab ruling class, but also the government of the caliphate.

The Islamic conquerors were also tolerant of other religions. They believed that Judaism and Christianity were kindred faiths, just not aware or accepting of the complete truth. This policy of tolerance facilitated Islamic rule, resembling earlier Roman policies. However, Islam did win many new converts because of the purity of its doctrine and admiration for Arab success in conquest. Most converts, such as the North African Berbers, learned Arabic, for Islamic leaders were reluctant to see the Quran translated into other languages. Thus, a process of conversion to not only Islam, but also a larger common culture began throughout much of the Middle East and North Africa. This process, too, consolidated Arab rule.

The actual government of the caliphate was not strikingly original. Under Umar, the caliph claimed great authority, down to the amount of pension each soldier was to receive. However, the assertions of authority were not backed up with solid power. Many caliphs were assassinated; others proved to lack political talents. A recurrent difficulty was the lack of agreement, in Arab custom, over procedures for succession to the throne after a ruler died. Umar established an election process, but it was soon ignored in favor of heredity. Throughout the history of Middle Eastern civilization in the postclassical period, assassinations and plots frequently disrupted political tranquility.

One dynasty did establish power over the caliphate for about a century (661–750). This dynasty, under the Umayyad family, transferred the caliph's government to Damascus, Syria, where greater prosperity allowed a more luxurious court. But, another family, the Abbasids, seized power in 750, although a few regions including Spain remained in Umayyad hands. The Abbasid dynasty moved the capital still further east, to Baghdad. It also began the use of professional soldiers and slaves for troops, a sign that the military zeal of the Arabs was beginning to falter. This policy, like that of Rome before it, was risky in the long run. The use of mercenary troops from a central Asian people called the Turks proved particularly questionable, as Turkish influence in the Middle East gradually began to increase.

But for several centuries, Abbasid power remained solid, despite some important rebellions and even though the dynasty itself was often severely troubled by plots and counterplots. The Abbasids continued the process of broadening Islam's base in the Middle East beyond the Arab peoples alone. Abbasid rulers held that all Muslims, Arabs or not, were equal in the sight of God and roughly equal in law as well. Further, any Muslim who spoke Arabic was regarded as Arab—a move that solidified the hold of the Arab language over most of the Middle East and North Africa. Only in Persia did conversion to Islam not bring acceptance of Arabic; Persia, now Iran, remains one of the only non-Arab-speaking parts of the region even today.

The Abbasids not only extended Islam and the Arab language as unifying elements in their vast empire, they also served as sponsors of art and literature. The greatest flowering of Islamic creativity took place under their auspices, with Baghdad as its center.

Politically, however, Abbasid rule began to decline before the year 1000, although the dynasty officially lasted until 1258. A number of internal revolts rocked the royal family. The hold of mercenary troops and Turkish advisors became increasingly important. As more non-Arab people converted to Islam, the special tax revenues levied on nonbelievers declined—an ironic effect of Muslim success. Several key provinces broke away, including Egypt and Spain. European troops reconquered southern Italy (in 1061) and began to push back the Muslim rulers of Spain. The weakness of the Abbasid government allowed Christian crusaders in the eleventh and twelfth centuries to conquer parts of the Holy Land, establishing the short-lived kingdom of Jerusalem. More ominous still, Turkish nomads, already converted to Islam, began to move in from central Asia, causing Abbasid power to further erode.

The long and painful decline of the Abbasids did not, initially, signal a decline in the larger Islamic-Arab culture. Creative works in art, literature, and theology survived into the thirteenth century. Gradually, however, political difficulties had a severe impact. Islam still reigned. Indeed, political chaos served to extend its hold on the common people, particularly those in the countryside, some of whom had been only superficially touched by the new religion previously. But, religious devotion increasingly monopolized Arab culture, to the detriment of other outlets. After 1200, a new movement, called Sufism, took hold; it expanded Islam's spiritual power while narrowing other interests in the name of piety. The Sufi leaders were holy men who experienced mystical visions of God. They gathered followers and inspired them by their holiness, using highly emotional rituals, including elaborate dances. The spread of the Sufi movement signaled important changes in Middle Eastern civilization, especially in Arab culture, even as it deepened the hold of Islam in the countryside and inspired missionary movements in other parts of the world.

The decline of the Abbasids did not signify a permanent disruption of the Middle East. A few areas were lost. The last Muslims were driven from Spain in 1492, but Christianity had won back most of this country beforehand. The northwestern tip of North Africa, the kingdom of Morocco, although firmly Islamic, became independent. But, the rise of Turkish military power soon brought new and in some ways more effective government to most of the Islamic Middle East. What the Abbasid decline did result in, however, was a prolonged political eclipse of the Arab world. The caliphate itself was toppled by a brutal invasion of Mongol troops in 1258. From that point until after World War II, most Arabs were governed by others. Initially, the rulers were Turks and Muslims, but even they looked down on their Arab subjects because of their political and military fall from power.

The story of Arab civilization is thus one of swift rise and extension and equally swift, though incomplete, decline. Despite these sudden changes, the civilization that was partially redefined by the Islamic religion and Arab leaders produced durable institutions and values in the Middle East. Other regions were affected as well. By 1300, Islam was spreading to parts of Africa south of the Sahara, to India, and to Southeast Asia. Here, the agents of diffusion were not military conquerors, but traders who brought religion and a sophisticated lifestyle along with their wares and fervent missionaries, including those inspired by the new Sufi movement. Military conquest played little role in Islam's surge beyond the borders of the Middle East. But, Islam's entry into other civilizations, while creating some similarities to Middle Eastern society, is, in part, a separate story to be taken up in later chapters. Before 1300, the greatest impact of Islam lay in reshaping Middle Eastern civilization itself.

ISLAMIC POLITICAL INSTITUTIONS

Muhammed and his immediate followers generated significant political ideals. In their view, shaped in part by Muhammed's own experience in running the city of Medina, a perfect state should be governed by a religious leader—there was no differentiation between secular aims and religious goals. The state and its leader should put the faith first and serve as agents of Allah.

This was an important vision, and one that would endure in the new Middle Eastern civilization. Political movements even during the twentieth century would return to the notion that state and religion are one. In practice, however, the ideal did not prove entirely feasible. Umayyad and Abbasid rulers did not always keep the interest of the faith foremost, particularly as their taste for luxury and for cultural patronage increased. But, Islam did not formulate clear principles to guide a state that fell short of the ideal. Should Muslims obey any government, regardless of quality? Muhammed had declared this for the sake of emphasizing attention to religion. Or, should Muslims try to work toward a government more attuned to Islamic ideals? These are questions still debated in Islam.

Officially, of course, the caliphs continued a tradition of combining political rule with the enforcement of religious law. Many Abbasid caliphs were indeed personally pious, which aided their popularity. However, their governments, in fact, became increasingly rigid and depended heavily on the whims of an individual ruler. A number of caliphs were cruel and arbitrary, often ordering the execution of not only potential rivals for the throne but also chief ministers. A leading Abbasid caliph, the pious Harun al-Rashid, provided an important period of peace and stability for much of the Middle East, but a study of his regime also reveals the use of arbitrary power. He is reported to have ordered the execution of his favorite minister on sudden impulse. Then, overcome with remorse, he put the executioner to death because he could not bear to look on the man who had slain his favorite. Many caliphs impressed their subjects as much with their luxury—traveling in public surrounded by an escort of parasol carriers, flag bearers, and musicians—as by their religious fervor or political acumen. Harun al-Rashid won a great reputation by frequent acts of generosity, including his support to writers. An Arab admirer wrote: "No Caliph had been so profusely liberal to poets, lawyers, and divines, though as the years advanced he wept over his extravagance among his other sins."

The Caliphate at Its Greatest Extent, About 750 C.E.

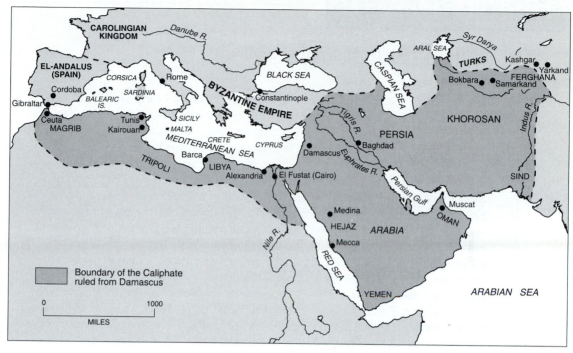

The caliphate could provide effective rule. Harun was an able soldier, conquering rebellions and maintaining the upper hand in warfare with the Byzantine Empire. The absence of a strong titled aristocracy, with claims on political power, facilitated central administration. However, the Abbasid caliphs did suffer for their reliance on slaves and foreigners as chief bureaucrats. Many bureaucratic positions became virtually hereditary, unless their occupants were unseated by assassination. Thus, it was small wonder that the Abbasid dynasty lost effective control of its own government and that important new groups, particularly the Turks, established regional administrations of their own.

In fact, the caliphate, especially under the later Abbasids, became increasingly remote, not even very actively commanding its provincial bureaucracy. Local administrators, although appointed by the central court, had substantial autonomy, so long as they returned satisfactory tax revenues to the caliph in Baghdad. Reliance on mercenary troops and slave soldiers reduced the need to recruit directly from the Arab population. The caliph's growing use of Turkish, Persian, and even Christian advisors, although designed to limit the power of upper-class Arabs, underscored the remoteness of the government from most people. To be sure, all governments in agricultural societies, even in China, were remote by modern standards: They had little contact with most peoples' day-to-day lives. But the caliphate, and the lack of political ideals in Islam that would help organize an "imperfect" or not simply religious state, intensified this remoteness. And, this fact almost certainly explains the caliphate's rather swift decline.

HISTORY DEBATE

Political Implications of Islam

Historians find various messages in the political ideals and early experience of Islam. There is no question that the religiously preferred political form differed from that in Christian Western Europe, where a separate church institution reduced the theoretical importance of the state. In asking for a state that pursued religious goals first and foremost, Islam set a high standard. The ensuing debate involves what Islam should encourage if the standard is not met. Muhammed specifically urged obedience to the state no matter what, for the goals of a religious person transcended political problems. Many historians argue that this stance, plus the development of a separate system of religious law and increasing popular piety, produced a political passiveness among Muslims. This, it is argued, accounts for the frequent authoritarian governments in the Middle East, the common use of non-Muslims in the bureaucracy, and (some contend, by extension) the difficulties for modern democracy to take root. However, other leading historians try to show that Islam suggested two paths, not one. Passivity might be replaced by an eager desire to make the state better, to bring it closer to the religious ideal—and this, in a modern context, could even generate support for the goal of democratic political participation, so that the true Muslim voice can be heard.

Comparison with Christianity usefully supplements the debate, for despite their mutual hostility Christianity and Islam shared a host of features. Christianity could support active political movements against a state regarded as evil. And, some forms of Christianity promoted the idea of participation in church governance. But, Christianity also urged obedience, and in the Catholic Church, it established a model of authority, not participation; zealous Christians could ignore political life. Thus, the complexity of Islam is not unique, and attempts to use the religion to explain current political practices may be risky or overly simplistic. All the world religions generated complex political impulses, and Islam needs to be assessed within this framework.

However, the limitations of the government established by the caliphate were not the whole story of Islamic politics. Islamic political ideals were far more closely realized in the religiously run legal system that spread throughout the Middle East. Islam did not establish an elaborate, centralized organization outside the state. But, local religious leaders, schooled in Islamic law, did more than lead prayers. Building on the Quran and the Hadith, Islamic leaders gradually developed an elaborate body of law known as the *Sharia,* or "straight path." This law regulated many aspects of social behavior, including family relations, economic contacts, and outright crimes. It was interpreted and extended by groups of Islamic scholars and religious leaders known as the *ulema*. The ulema, which initially arose spontaneously and was then encouraged by the caliphate, consisted of local experts in Islamic law and doctrine—and Islam was a highly legalistic religion, generating a wide array of rules of conduct. The ulema were knowledgeable about the Quran and skilled in interpreting the deeds of the prophet Muhammed and other precedents so they might be able to determine God's will in any matter of conduct. The result, after generations of expertise following Muhammed's death, was an elaborate system of rules and laws, built by the learned men of Islam and regarded as sacred and unchangeable. This was no generalized code of behavior to be captured in a few, powerful commandments, but a very detailed set of laws.

By the time of the Abbasids, Islamic experts existed in every town and marketplace, passing judgment on all matters of conscience brought before them. A good deal of the work of government was handled by village authorities—called imams—and the regional ulema. Much of what we Westerners think of as falling within the realm of laws and courts remained, in Middle Eastern civilization, in the hands of these religious officials. And here, surely, is a partial reflection of Muhammed's belief that state and faith were one and the same—there was no need for two court systems, for the ulema alone could carry out God's will for the community by enforcing the Sharia.

Dome of the Rock. Built by Muhammed's second successor, Caliph Omar, this was the first Islamic building constructed in Jerusalem after the conquest of Palestine. Note the geometrical design, which follows Muslim rules on art.

Religious minorities, particularly Jews and Christians, were of course not covered by the Sharia and they were shown considerable tolerance in the decision to allow them to run their own community affairs. This was the final ingredient in the political system developed by the Arab dynasties, and one which helps explain their success in maintaining authority over a wide region amid the fluctuations of the caliphate.

ISLAM AND MIDDLE EASTERN CULTURE

Not surprisingly, the Islamic religion formed the core of the new culture of Middle Eastern civilization, but although the Arabic word for religion means "way of life," it was not the only ingredient during several centuries of remarkable artistic creativity. It was Islam, however, that survived most successfully among the various elements of the new Middle Eastern civilization at its height. Islam also helped organize various other cultural features or movements, particularly in the visual arts.

As in politics, the intellectual impact of the Islamic religion was an emphasis on Allah's great power and the pervasive legalism. The power of Allah and the clarity of Islam as a perfect religion rested on five "pillars of Islam," as stipulated in the Quran. Observance of these five basic obligations was central to religious life, for Islam offered no special avenues to divine grace or sacraments: Obedience was central. The first pillar was faith itself; there was no God but Allah, and Muhammed was his final prophet. The second pillar required all Muslims to pray at five different times of the day, facing in the direction of Mecca. The prayers did not have to occur in a mosque, except for the midday prayer on Friday, the holy day. Callers from the mosque's tower, or minaret, issued the five daily calls to prayer, with the faithful observing wherever they might be. The third pillar was the fast of Ramadan, the month in which God revealed himself to Muhammed. In this month, Muslims were not supposed to eat or drink during daylight hours. The fourth pillar involved charity. Islam held that all faithful Muslims were brothers, but they were not equally wealthy. It was therefore essential that charity be extended to the Muslim poor. Finally, as the fifth pillar, the faithful were required if possible to make at least one pilgrimage to the Holy City of Mecca during a lifetime—the *hadj*. The pilgrimage reminded all Muslims of their essential unity, and it also involved a number of rituals in Mecca itself.

The five pillars of Islam spelled out the central observances of a good Muslim life. They formed a bridge between lowly humans and the all-powerful Allah, otherwise awe-inspiring in his omnipotence.

However, the emphasis on legalistic observance extended beyond the five pillars to a host of other regulations that were not required for a holy life, but were enjoined for proper social relations and even personal hygiene. Muhammed and other Islamic leaders were interested in disciplining certain traditional habits of the Arabs. Thus, the religion forbade alcoholic drink, for Arabs had earlier acquired a reputation for excess in this regard. Several rules related directly to health; prohibitions against eating pork, for example, followed from the diseased state of hogs in the Middle East. Sexual behavior was also strictly regulated; women, particularly, were enjoined to re-

This photograph of ritual purification in a Moroccan mosque shows the characteristic geometrical design of Islamic religious buildings.

main pure before marriage and faithful to their husbands within marriage. Thus, Islam, rather like Christianity but unlike many of the religions of South Asia, displayed much sensual restraint. The tendency to see in Islam an elaborate legal code, beyond the five pillars, was reinforced by Islamic support for harsh earthly punishments for misbehavior, although careful rules of evidence and a belief in mercy set important limits. Thus, the Quran on theft:

> Male or female, cut off his or her hands: a punishment by way of example, from God, for their crime; and God is Exalted in Power. But if the thief repent after his crime, and amend his conduct, God turneth to him in forgiveness; for God is Oft-forgiving. Most Merciful.

On a larger scale, belief in a day of judgment—"when the World on High is unveiled; when the Blazing Fire is kindled to fierce heat; and when the Garden is brought near;—Then shall each soul know what it has put forward"—and belief in life after death were central to Islamic teaching. The Muslim heaven featured boundless delight of mind, body, and soul. In contrast, the Muslim hell was full of the darkest pain and torture, surpassing most Christians' visions of Satan's torments.

Islam was not a constant, although its basic principles persisted. As the Sufi movement arose, from 1200 onward, mystical leaders, called dervishes, played a growing role in inspiring the faithful. Their activities bore some resemblance to those of monks in Christianity, but there was no general discipline of the Benedictine sort.

Spiritual and emotional example gave new force to Islam. It also helped inspire missionary activity.

The religious fervor Islam could generate, plus the local quality of much of the religious organization, guaranteed that religious divisions would occur. The most serious rift in Islam took place as a result of fights over the succession to the early caliphate in the seventh century. Supporters of Muhammed's son-in-law, Ali, bitterly resented the rise of the Umayyad dynasty. This group, the Shi'ite Muslims, continued to revere the memory of Ali and lament the martyrdom of his son Huseyn. They also believed that they were truer to Islamic law than the majority group, called the Sunni. Shi'ites continued to expect additional prophecies. And, they formed a clearer religious structure than the majority group, identifying religious leaders, such as the ayatollahs in Persia, who could direct the faithful and select and instruct local religious officials. The Shi'ite minority gained particular strength in the north, in the present-day countries of Iran and Iraq, but elements of Shi'ite culture may be found in many parts of the region. Their special religious fervor remains an important factor in Middle Eastern life in the early twenty-first century. The Shi'ite-Sunni split frequently encouraged political disunity in the Middle East, including periodic assassinations and other acts of terrorism. This penchant, too, would continue into modern times.

Islam did not encourage a wide-ranging theology as did Christianity. There were fewer discussions about the nature of God or problems of free will. Islamic theology was mainly confined to the search for truths in the Quran and to the study of the traditions of Muhammed and his early followers. Simply keeping track of the various traditions and laws of the Sharia was no easy task. By the time of the Abbasid dynasty, Muslim scholars found it necessary to collect the traditions that had developed. One scholar spent 16 years touring the Middle East gathering 600,000 customs and beliefs, which he reduced to 7275 regarded as authentic religious truths. This code is now considered a part of Islamic faith. It helped promote the Islamic emphasis on charity and the importance of God's rules for humankind, one of the important attractions of Islamic faith. But, the task of interpreting the traditions of Islam remained a challenging assignment. Strict Muslims believed that no other intellectual enterprise was valid, for faith alone was all that Allah required.

Nevertheless, a wider philosophy persisted in Middle Eastern civilization, inspired in part by knowledge of older Greek and Persian learning still available in the region. By the ninth century, a host of scholars were busy translating Greek and Persian sources into Arabic. Huge libraries were erected in cities like Baghdad. This bustling cultural life was aided by the introduction of paper from China, which made book production more extensive and cheaper.

Greek tradition, of course, contradicted the strictest Islamic belief system, for it held that people could understand a great deal through the use of reason. Arab philosophers grappled with this schism for several centuries, and many urged a rationalistic approach without breaking with Islam. A similar disparity would arise later in the Christian West, in part because of the Arab precedent. By the 1100s, many Arab philosophers were trying to build a rationalistic framework for all knowledge, mixing religious truth, science, mathematics, and rational speculation. This work both preserved and extended the Hellenistic heritage.

As in philosophy, the fine arts were strongly influenced by Islamic rules—but not entirely constrained by them. Muhammed, eager to develop the purest possible focus on Allah, forbade idols, and later the ulema extended prohibitions against all representation of human or animal forms. The goal was to purge Muslims of any impulse to worship lesser images. As a result, most Islamic art centered on the nonrepresentational. Only a few artists, particularly those in Persia, continued to create sculpture or painting involving human or animal figures. Muslim artists instead placed distinctive geometric designs and the flowing patterns of Arab script on pottery, metalware, textiles, and leather and on buildings' tile and stucco. Mosques, which are the Muslim houses of prayer, and palaces were especially covered with glazed tile and stucco relief in intricate designs. This powerful artistic style spread beyond the Middle East to influence art in Spain and Portugal, even after the expulsion of the Muslims, and in India. In the Middle East itself, concern for rich decorative images on buildings and in the form of a host of artifacts remained central to the arts.

Middle Eastern architects learned much from the earlier classical styles of the Mediterranean. Palaces often reflected a Roman influence, with an open courtyard and fountain surrounded by separate rooms. For mosques, Muslim architects created a distinctive kind of tower, the minaret, from which the faithful would be called to prayer at the appointed hours. Most mosques were domed buildings, preceded by a hall of columns with distinctive, horseshoe-shaped arches. These innovations in arches and towers helped inspire the Gothic style that later emerged in Western Europe. Both Muslims and Christians sought structures that would direct the eye toward heaven.

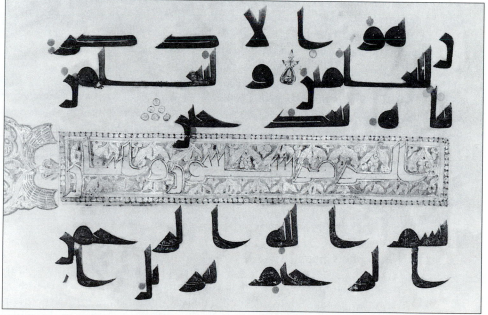

Arab caligraphy: A leaf from the Quran, dating from the eighth or ninth century, illustrates the Kufic form of Arabic calligraphy. (Freer Gallery of Art, The Smithsonian Institute, Washington, DC, 30.60)

World Profiles

Omar Khayyam, (c. eleventh–twelfth centuries)

The vitality of Islamic intellectual life shows in the career of the Persian Omar Khayyam, the type of person who in Western culture might be known as a "Renaissance man." Omar's early life is obscure; his last name means "tentmaker," which may suggest his father's occupation. He obtained an extensive education and came to the attention of the Turkish sultan then ruling the region (despite the continuance of the Abbasid caliphate). The sultan sponsored his scientific work. Omar became a royal astonomer and helped reform the Islamic calendar. His books on algebra were particularly notable, as he classified equations of the first degree. He is best known in the world at large for his poems called the *Rubaiyat*, which were translated into English during the ninteenth century. These poems feature complex, multiple rhymes in the first, second, and fourth lines. Their subject matter emphasized the pleasures of this life. Omar was at times humble toward Allah, at other times defiant; he was also very critical of Islamic extremists, like the Sufis, who nonetheless adapted his work. The main theme of the *Rubaiyat* was the beauty of earthly existence; God created man as he is, so he will not punish; a person should enjoy the only life he can be sure of. How does Omar Khayyam fit the main themes of Middle Eastern culture during the postclassical period?

This representation of Omar Khayyam is based on an English painting by H. M. Burton. It reflects a later Western interpretation of the great poet and scientist and his setting. Omar Khayyam is shown working out a calendar, surrounded by samples of his philosophic aphorisms and astronomical work.

Music also received considerable attention. Muhammed and his followers frowned on the frivolity of music, which was not part of Islamic prayer services. However, most people in the Middle East did not take this particular prohibition too seriously. As one writer put it, "Wine is as the body, music as the soul, and joy is their offspring." Musicians, and particularly singers, gained in respect. The singer Tways, who lived from 632 to 710, was the originator of the high-pitched, nasal singing style popular in the Arab world. He introduced new rhythms and was the first to sing with accompaniment—a tambourine. Other instruments commonly used were the lute and guitar. Arab rhythm and instrumentation influenced Spanish musical styles, which in turn influenced the styles later developed in Latin America.

Middle Eastern literature emphasized poetry above all. Most cultivated Arabs and Persians have rated poetry as the highest achievement of their civilization after Islam itself. Arab poetry predated Muhammed. But, as the Arabs came into contact with other peoples in the Middle East, their literary efforts became more polished. Abbasid caliphs patronized scores of poets, and the knowledge of poetry and ability to express oneself in verse became the mark of a cultivated person—as in Confucian China.

Poets wrote on many themes, most of them nonreligious, as in Omar Khayyam's *Rubaiyat*. A black ex-slave in Baghdad gained great popularity with poems that poked fun at the traditional Arab emphasis on heroism. Many Persian poets, writing in Arabic, used sensual themes, praising the joys of hunting and drinking, but also expressing some religious sentiments.

Overall, Arabic poetry showed a growing concern for polished manners and a life of refinement, characteristic of an aristocracy that was becoming more devoted to culture and the good life than to military prowess. The poetry also revealed an unusual interest in pure style, as poets strove for perfection in each individual line and, by Western literary standards, seemed more preoccupied with their stylistic devices than content. Frequent changes of subject, word associations, and images were the hallmarks of this poetry, which focused on both nature and human experience. Thus, one poet praised the lion-mouthed fountain at an Arab palace in Grenada, Spain (a palace that still exists). His description served as a trigger for all sorts of word associations:

> *And lions people this official wood*
> *encompass the pools with thunder*
> *and profuse over aureate-banded*
> *bodies their skulls gush glass. . . .*
>
> *Sun is tinder to the stirred*
> *colors, is light to long tongues,*
> *is a hand to unsheathe the lunging*
> *blades that shiver out in a splash.*

However, Arab poetry could also be terse and humorous, as in this verse, "The Radish":

> *The radish is a good*
> *And doubtless wholesome food,*
> *But proves, to vex the eater,*
> *A powerful repeater.*
> *This only fault I find:*
> *What should be left behind*
> *Comes issuing instead*
> *Right from the eater's head.*

Science, including history and geography, provided the final outlet for the high culture of the Middle East. A scientific interest followed, of course, from the rationalistic concerns of the leading philosophers and from the Hellenistic heritage. Arabs found a practical application for it in the study of medicine, astronomy, and geography. Medicine could cure. Knowledge of the stars, it was believed, might help predict the future—hence, interest in astrology ran high. And, geography served the direct needs of Arab trade. Abbasid caliphs supported considerable scientific study in all these areas, in addition to the translation of earlier Greek and Persian scholarship.

Arab astronomers made no major advances, in part because they relied heavily on the theories of the Hellenistic astronomer Ptolemy and his claim that the earth was the center of the universe. However, observatories checked the accuracy of various Greek measurements, and scientists acquired more precise knowledge of eclipses and the length of the solar year. Arab scientists, aware that the earth was a sphere, also calculated the planet's circumference. In medicine, a host of empirical observations were recorded. Doctors in Baghdad chose the location for the central hospital by carefully studying environmental conditions. Although in medical science, too, there were no new general theories, the idea of contagion was strongly suggested as a practical finding. As one doctor wrote: "The result of my long experience is that if a person comes into contact with a patient, he is immediately attacked by the disease with the same symptoms." In a similar pragmatic spirit, doctors described the symptoms of a variety of common diseases and the properties of hundreds of therapeutic drugs. Finally, some advances were made in the study of chemical elements, and Greek and Indian discoveries in chemistry and physics were assimilated within this body of knowledge. Without question, Arab science predominated in the world by 1200, with only Chinese scholarship a near rival.

Arab scholars also showed some interest in mathematics, taking over the Indian numbering system. Particular advances were made in algebra, which is an Arab-derived word. The text written by the greatest Arab mathematician, al-Khwarismi, was translated and used in European universities until the sixteenth century. It established new territory in algebraic multiplication and division and in equations of the second degree.

Because of their extensive travels, Arab merchants and missionaries produced more abundant geographical knowledge than the world had ever known—or was to know again until the age of European exploration began in the fifteenth century. In history, the North African Ibn-Khaldun, writing in the fourteenth century and building on a long tradition of narrative accounts of the past, achieved an understanding of the dynamics of social behavior that has had few rivals before or since.

Overall, Arab scientists were not as adept at formulating general theories as they were at recording careful observation and preserving the learning of their own scholars and scholars of the past. Nonetheless, they contributed to a flourishing intellectual life, in which not only scholars but also aristocrats and other wealthy urbanites gained an extensive education that combined the Muslim faith with a healthy enjoyment of secular culture. In this spirit, an unusually large elite became literate and a series of major universities were founded, as in Egypt in the tenth century and in Baghdad in 1065. Schools and universities taught religion, poetry, philosophy, the sciences, and history—a fair sampling of the cultural knowledge Middle Eastern civilization had created.

ECONOMY AND SOCIETY IN THE MIDDLE EAST

A lively economy was a vital part of the new Middle Eastern civilization, and it built on earlier traditions of agriculture and trade. Economic activity served as a key element in the spread of Islam to Africa and Southeast Asia. It also set the stage for the bustling cities, the educated elite, and the luxurious court life of the caliphate.

Agriculture, long established in this area, remained highly productive. The Abbasid caliphate drained swamps, extended systems of irrigation, and otherwise supported agricultural development. Wheat, barley, and rice were the main crops, whereas dates and olives constituted important secondary goods. A free peasant class did most of the farming, and under the early Abbasids the conditions of the peasants improved somewhat. Most peasants remained poor, however, and they owed heavy taxes to the state and local landlords. The Abbasid caliphate provided more equitable treatment by assessing a percentage of the crops produced, rather than a fixed fee, as taxes, so that peasants would not suffer unduly when harvests were bad.

The Islamic empire had substantial mineral holdings, including iron and precious metals. Some large private mining operations arose; one, in the tenth century, employed 10,000 miners.

Manufacturing was extensive and, like agriculture, won encouragement from the state. Textile production, including carpets and other luxury items, gained ground steadily. Persian rugs, of course, became particularly famous. City centers were crowded with artisans who manufactured in and sold from their own homes. The bustle of a Middle Eastern marketplace, or bazaar, reflected the abundant production of craft goods and vigorous trade.

There were, however, few significant technological improvements in Middle Eastern agriculture or manufacturing. The Arabs did import papermaking from China. The manufacture of fine iron products, particularly of swords, made Damascus famous. But, careful organization and vigorous activity, not innovation in techniques, served as the hallmarks for this economy.

Commerce, nevertheless, flourished, and a strong merchant spirit was a central feature of this renewed civilization. To be sure, governments often seemed to consider merchants mainly as subjects for taxation and did little to encourage transportation or trade. However, a large merchant class evolved, both for the local trade at bazaars and for international operations. Most overseas trade centered on luxury products, but some basic goods, such as timber from India and slaves from Africa and Europe, were also involved. Merchants brought silks, spices, and tin from India, China, and Southeast Asia, for use at home and for sale to Europe and Africa. One source lists the goods brought from China: perfumes, silks, crockery, paper, ink, peacocks, swift horses, saddles, felt, cinnamon, and rhubarb; from the Byzantine Empire: gold and silver, drugs, slave girls, engineers, marble workers, locks, and trinkets; and from India: tigers, panthers, elephants, skins, rubies, sandalwood, ebony, and coconuts.

Islamic sailors were quite at home in all the Asian waters from the eighth century onward, aided by good mapmaking. By sailing into the Black and Caspian seas, Muslims traded with Russians and Scandinavians. Thousands of Muslim coins have been found in Sweden, brought back from this trade; indeed, the first Swedish coins copied Muslim models. Active trade developed with Africa. Overland expeditions imported gold, salt, and slaves. Slave marches were brutal affairs, with many thousands perishing. Islamic ships also traded with ports further down the East African coast. Trade with Western Europe was less active, because the Europeans had few goods of interest to the more sophisticated Middle East. However, there was some exchange, often undertaken by Jewish entrepreneurs, through which the Middle East obtained cloth, furs, and slaves. Here, technology did play a role. Arab ships improved, with new designs for ocean-going transportation. Mapmaking and navigational instruments changed as well.

Far-flung trade led to improvements in banking. Some Baghdad banks had branch offices in other cities. It was thus possible, for example, to draw a check in Baghdad and cash it in Morocco.

Islamic culture gave merchants considerable esteem—more than in any other civilization at that time. The Islamic religion did not see profit-making as a contradiction of spirituality or honor, so long as active charity ensued. Muhammed, with merchant experience of his own, proclaimed merchants to be models of a virtuous life: "On the day of judgment, the honest, truthful Islamic merchant will take rank with the martyrs of the faith" and "Merchants are the couriers of the world and the trusted servants of God upon earth." One caliph supposedly said: "There is no place where I would be more gladly overtaken by death than in the marketplace, buying and selling for my family." Manuals were written to encourage good commercial and investment practices.

The commercial zeal of Islam, along with the religion itself, made the new Middle Eastern civilization the most significant force in the world for many centuries. Although India, Southeast Asia, and East Africa were most closely affected, more remote parts of Europe and Africa also experienced the impact of this unusual dynamism. Economic life solidified important values in the Middle East itself and brought luxury and wealth to the upper classes. The attractiveness of the urban marketplaces, as evidenced in the vital role that trade came to play in city life, survives to the present day. Even more than artistic achievement, trade expressed the central spirit of the Middle East.

Socially, Middle Eastern civilization displayed many of the features expected in a prosperous agricultural region. A landlord class flourished, as had long been the case in the Mediterranean world. Arab conquerors, some of them even former merchants, assumed the landlord role in many areas. Urban artisans, as well as the merchants, were numerous and well organized. Although some peasants worked entirely for landlords, we have seen that, in the most prosperous centuries before the Abbasid decline, a significant free peasant class existed.

The social order was complicated by three factors. First, the mixture of racial groups and minority religions added to the region's social diversity. Even among Muslims, tensions often surfaced between Arabs and non-Arabs. Second, Islam maintained a strong egalitarian theme. Muslims believed that all people were basically equal under God. Such a doctrine did make some adherents uncomfortable with existing social inequality, and it spurred some lower-class elements to revolt in the name of religion itself. But, Muhammed had not intended to preach social equality. His insistence on the importance of charity acknowledged, in fact, that there would always be the rich and the poor in this life. However, the spiritual equality that Muhammed avowed sometimes added bitterness and confusion to the society shaped by Islam.

The third complicating factor in the civilization of the Middle East was the substantial presence of slavery. Islamic civilization during this period depended more heavily on slave labor than did any of the other major civilizations except Central America. In India, slavery had been largely displaced by the caste system, whereas in East Asia and Europe slavery, although it did exist, was not extensive and confined primarily to occasional household service. The existence of slavery was, to be sure, less important in the Islamic Middle East than it had been under the Roman Empire. Agriculture, for example, did not rely on slave labor. But, slaves provided domestic service, manual labor for many of the mines and sailing vessels, and above all, troops for military operations. As we have seen, the Abbasids also used elite slaves as soldiers and bureaucrats. Furthermore, Islam developed an extensive slave trade. Initially, most slaves in the Middle East had been taken in conquest, as had been the case in most other slave-holding societies. However, the need for slaves did not cease when Arab conquests stopped, and the active trading impulse of the Arabs provided a clear alternative. Slaves formed the most sought-after goods in sub-Saharan Africa and parts of Europe. Their use, particularly in the armies of the caliphate, made them virtually indispensable. And, some slave-holding was to survive in the Middle East until quite recent times.

In principle, slaves could not be Muslim; their being so would contradict the spiritual equality of all believers. But, slaves who converted to Islam were not promised their liberty—although the freeing of slaves was considered a pious act that could win rewards in heaven.

Slave uprisings were rare, but they did occur. Black slaves revolted between 869 and 889. Inspired by a leader aware of Islamic values, the slaves claimed that "God would save them" and "make them masters of slaves and wealth and dwellings." Their leader was executed, his head brought to Baghdad on a pole as a warning against similar uprisings. This was, to be sure, an unusual rising. Slaves used for other functions, including palace service and the army, were better positioned to exert pressure. Periodic revolts involved military troops who were legally slaves.

Peasant revolts also occurred in the name of greater equality. Some of these had racial overtones, with non-Arab Muslims protesting Arab control. One of the goals of the rebellions was the sharing of property; the peasants argued that social equality should match religious equality. A poet thus captured the spirit of peasant rebellions in the tenth century:

By God, I shall not pray to God while I am bankrupt . . .
Why should I pray—where are my wealth, my mansion
And where are my horses, trappings, golden belts?
Were I to pray, when I do not own
An inch of earth, then I would be a hypocrite.

Peasant uprisings were always vanquished, but they cropped up recurrently.

Families served as a basic institution for the upper class, merchants, and peasants alike. Family discipline was tight, although often tempered by affection. One caliph described how he wanted a tutor to treat his son:

Be not strict to the point of stiffening his faculties nor lenient to the point of making him enjoy idleness. Treat him as much as thou canst through kindness and gentleness. Fail not to resort to force and severity should he not respond.

The position of women was particularly noteworthy in the Muslim family. Muhammed carefully stated the spiritual importance of women, noting that they had souls just the same as men. And, he introduced some rules designed to protect women. For example, he granted women the right to divorce men and not simply the reverse. He tried to prevent the killing of female babies, a common practice in many agricultural societies where women were regarded as less useful than men and female infanticide was a means of population control. Despite Muhammed's attention to certain conditions of women, Islam helped maintain the pronounced inferiority of females within the Islamic family. Women worshipped separately, and the Hadith characterized them as particularly likely to become sinners. As in Christianity, spiritual equality warred with disdain in its views of women.

One sign of the subjugation of women, of course, was polygamy. A woman could take but one spouse, whereas a man could have up to four wives. In fact, only the very wealthy could contemplate more than one wife, so polygamy was never widely practiced. Other rules were more important. A man could divorce his wife far more easily than the other way around. A woman typically married early, at the age of 13 or 14, according to an arrangement made by her father. Once she was married, the duty of a wife was "the service of the husband, care of the children, and the management of the household." In public life, the segregation of the sexes increased steadily, for as in many advanced agricultural societies, inequalities increased over time. By the tenth century, women rarely left their household compound. In the eleventh century, a caliph decreed that women had to wear a veil when mixing with men and in all public places, extending the pre-Muslim Arab and Middle Eastern custom.

In this segregated situation, Muslim women established intricate social contacts with each other, particularly among other women in the same extended household. Furthermore, the severest limitations on women were not always strictly imposed. Especially in peasant households, where women's work was vital, the total seclusion and veiling of women were often ignored. Nevertheless, a strict differentiation between men and women, in the family and beyond, developed during this formative period and persisted as a basic feature of Middle Eastern civilization.

DECLINE

After about the year 1200, Middle Eastern civilization began to display a number of symptoms of decline. We have seen that, at the top, the Abbasid caliphate was already in a compromised position, losing control over its provinces and about to topple completely. However, disintegration ran even deeper than this. At the same time, the decline of Arab civilization was never complete—not like the fall of Rome. What was occurring involved a loss of vitality and diversity, and political problems were only one symptom.

By 1300, a shift in intellectual life was noteworthy. Increasingly, religious leaders gained the upper hand over poets, philosophers, and scientists. The earlier tension among diverse cultural elements yielded to the predominance of the faith. The new piety associated with the rising Sufi movement was both the cause and result of this development. In literature, an emphasis on secular themes, such as the joys of feasting and hunting, gave way to more strictly religious ideas. Persian poets, writing now in their own language instead of Arabic, led the way. Religious poetry, and not poetry in general, became part of the education of upper-class children. In philosophy, the rationalistic current encountered new attack. In Islamic Spain, the philosopher Ibn-Rushd (known as Averroës in Europe) espoused Greek rationalism, but his efforts were largely ignored in the Middle East. European scholars were, in fact, more heavily influenced by his teachings. In the Middle East proper, a more typical philosopher now claimed to use Aristotle's logic to show that it was impossible to discover religious truth by human reason—in a book revealingly, if not subtly, titled *The Destruction of Philosophy.*

The Sufi movement itself was a reaction to both the secularism and corruption of the declining caliphate and the formalism of Islam itself. The movement emphasized individual contact with God, and at first it surfaced in purely personal formulations. Sufi groups began to form in the twelfth and thirteenth centuries, often among outlying peoples like the Turks. They reflected an interesting cultural syncretism, borrowing several features from the Christian monastic movement and others from Buddhism. Some Sufi groups stressed works of charity, but others practiced auto-hypnotism that could allow people to swallow burning embers or pass knives through their bodies; these groups also featured impassioned dances. Sufism contradicted traditional Islam in emphasizing saints or holy men, but in so doing, it provided an outlet for a vital religious impulse. It not only furthered the Islamic missionary effort but also increased the piety of ordinary people.

Increasingly, then, Middle Eastern scholarship focused on religion and the Islamic legal tradition. Some interest in science remained, although it too began to fade. In its place, many Sufi scholars wrote excitingly of their mystical contacts with God and the stages of their religious transformation. This narrowing of Middle Eastern cultural life had less impact on the arts. Artisans' production continued to flourish in many centers, maintaining the Middle East's distinctive commitment to richly decorated rugs, leather goods, and other wares.

Changes in society and the economy were still more subtle, but in many ways at least as ominous as the shifts in politics and intellectual life. As the authority of the caliphate declined, landlords seized greater power over the peasantry. From about 1100 onward, peasants increasingly lost their freedom, becoming serfs on large estates. This loss was not the peasants' alone, for agricultural productivity suffered as a result. Landlords turned to draining whatever profit they could from their estates, rather than trying to develop a more vital agriculture; peasants had little incentive and no means to do better, as they were tied to the land and obligatory labor and production output for the landlords. With this gradual social deterioration came fewer tax revenues for the state and less of a basis for flourishing trade. Indeed, Arab traders began to lose ground. Few Arab coins have been found in Europe dating from later than 1100; European merchants were beginning to control their own turf and soon began to challenge the Arabs in other parts of the Mediterranean. Arab commerce remained active in the Indian Ocean, but the time fast approached when it would face new competition there as well.

By 1400, the most serious decline of the Middle East was still in the future. The creation of a new empire, under the Ottoman Turks, would indeed restore great political and military vitality to the region for another several centuries. Economic and cultural changes were harder to reverse. There was one further irony: Most leaders in the area were unaware of their eroding base of power. Faith in Islam and a recollection of the past glories of the civilization precluded a full understanding of their civilization's decline. In particular, those in authority failed to recognize the region's growing decline in relation to Western Europe. Europe had been so long a backwater, compared to the splendors of Islamic civilization at its height, that only a severe jolt could produce a realization of the shifting balance between the two societies. This jolt, unquestionably, was still well in the future; it would come only at the end of the 1700s.

CONCLUSION: NEW CULTURE IN THE MIDDLE EAST

The main point is clear: Between 600 and 1400, a significant new culture arose in the Middle East. It was unquestionably the most dynamic in the world during most of the period. Important ingredients of this culture remained dominant in the region even after 1400, for this was a durable new society. By 1400, the peak of the civilization's vigor was beginning to pass. Yet the region's role in a complex set of international relationships continued, for Middle Eastern society changed its shape during the postclassical period. It also galvanized a new set of contacts that ran from China in the east to Spain in the west.

SUGGESTED WEBSITES

On Muhammed and Islam, see *http://library.think.quest.org/17/137/main/history/key/points.html*, and *http://www.erols.com/zenithco/abubakr.html*; on Islamic art, see *http://islamicart.com*; on scientific and intellectual life under the Abbasids, refer to *http://users.erols.com/zenithco/index.html*.

SUGGESTED READINGS

B. Lewis, *The Arabs in History* (1966), offers a brief and provocative survey. A splendid interpretation is M. Hodgson, *The Venture of Islam* (1975). On the development of Islam, see T. Andrae, *Mohammed: The Man and His Faith* (1970), and W. M. Watt, *What Is Islam?* (1968). Good sources for other topics include G. E. Von Grunebaum, *Medieval Islam* (1961); Roman Ghirshman, *Iran from the Earliest Times to the Islamic Conquest* (1961); and Seyyed H. Nasr, *Science and Civilization in Islam* (1968). Ira M. Lapidus' *A History of Islamic Societies* (1988) is a masterful survey. See also M. M. Ahsan, *Social Life Under the Abbasids* (1979); Bernard Lewis, *Race and Slavery in the Middle East* (1990); Lois Beck and Nikki Keddi, eds., *Women in the Muslim World* (1978); F. Mermiss, *The Veil and the Male Elite: A Feminist Interpretation of Women's Rights in Islam* (1992); and L. Ahmed, *Women and Gender in Islam* (1992). Two useful source collections are Eric Schroeder, *Muhammed's People* (1955), with Arabic poetry, and W. M. Watt, tr., *The Faith and Practice of Al-Ghazali* (1953). The Quran has also been widely translated.

India and Southeast Asia Under the Impact of Islam

The postclassical period was less dramatic in India than the Middle East. There was more continuity from the past. What major features of classical India persisted in this new period? Why were they so durable? There was, however, important change, as India participated in the larger themes of this period of world history. Islam became a minority force on the subcontinent. Why would some Indians be attracted to this new religion? Why, in contrast, did most Indians continue to embrace Hinduism (and how did Hinduism change in response to Islam)? How did India participate in the emerging world network? What relationship did the spread of civilization in Southeast Asia have to India and to the Arabs and Islam?

INTRODUCTION

The impact of Islam extended to many areas besides the Middle East and North Africa. Some military activity, plus trade and missionary outreach, installed Islam in Central Asia, as far as western China. Sub-Saharan Africa was another important case, where trade and missionary endeavor were largely responsible for Islamic success; we turn to the African experience in the next chapter. This chapter deals with two other areas of Islamic impact: India and Southeast Asia. Islam provided a key new ingredient in these regions, along with growing levels of world trade. The results persist to the present day.

The force of Islam and growing involvement in the world network did not result in the exact replication of Middle Eastern patterns in these other locations. Africa and Southeast Asia, for instance, retained distinctive characteristics. The real challenge is for us to understand how change combined with the patterns of still-separate civilizations during the postclassical period.

Such a combination is even more central to the experience of postclassical India, where Islam provided a new political force and a new religious minority, but in a civilization already well-established. Key features of classical India, including the Hinduism of the majority, the caste system, high levels of trade, and regional politics, all continued. This was a period of persistence combined with modification. Hinduism adjusted somewhat, in order to remain a vital force in the face of Islamic competition. Indian traders adjusted also to the growing dominance of Arab commerce in the Indian Ocean. Significant trade and manufacturing survived, and India was a key participant in the world network.

Developments in Southeast Asia partially paralleled those on the Indian subcontinent. This was no accident, for Indian trade and culture left a strong mark on several parts of this extensive region as Indian influence radiated before the arrival of Islam. Hinduism receded in Indonesia, but the Buddhist influence that had spread out from India established deep roots in Burma and Thailand and on the island of Sri Lanka. Like India, Southeast Asia operated under decentralized or regional governments—there was no great national empire. Like India, Southeast Asia participated actively in Indian Ocean trade, producing spices and other goods for a wide market.

The dynamic impact of Islam began to be felt from the seventh century onward. Neither India nor Southeast Asia completely fell under Islam's sway, although a minority of Indians converted and several areas in Southeast Asia became fervently Muslim—indeed, the largest single Islamic nation in the world today, Indonesia, began its conversion process during this period. The elaboration of a new and rather complex religious map in India and Southeast Asia was a major development in the centuries between 600 and 1400. Through Islamic contacts and growing trade links, parts of Southeast Asia were drawn more fully into the mainstream of world history than ever before, another specific illustration of civilization's general spread during the centuries after the classical age. Thus, this period holds a significant place in southern Asian history.

THE DEVELOPMENT OF INDIAN CULTURE

Even during the classical age, India had never functioned as a single political unit. Unity came closest during the Maurya dynasty, but even then it was incomplete. After the Hun invasions, regional political units characteristically prevailed for many centuries. In northern India, a few vigorous states were formed. One military leader in the north, Harsha, conquered a number of states early in the seventh century. A Buddhist, Harsha through his conquests helped extend this religion to Tibet. However, although Harsha himself was an able administrator, he was unable to extend his bureaucracy throughout the empire, and after his death regional units resurfaced. In general, northern India was dotted with small states ruled from capital cities by princes, called Rajput when they came from the dominant military caste. The princes maintained few paid officials, rewarding their administrators with land grants instead. This system produced limited governments with few functions. Frequent wars pitted these feeble states against each other, for in conquest the princes sought new lands with which to reward new followers. Here is one of many cases in world history in which a weak government promoted attempts at conquest, for only through successful fighting could armies be maintained and their loyalties ensured.

The political situation in southern India was somewhat different. This area had not been a center of Indian culture previously. During the classical age, most attention, and the most vigorous political forms, focused on the great river valleys of the north. After about 600 C.E., however, stronger kingdoms arose in southern India, particularly among Tamil-speaking peoples. Less subject to invasion than northern India, this region also maintained more active trading contracts with other societies, especially parts of Southeast Asia. Trade, and the merchant wealth it produced, provided the financial basis for the new southern kingdoms. Here, too, regional units prevailed; there was no single southern Indian state. Few of the governments developed tightly centralized systems even within their own boundaries, and local autonomy for landlords and peasant villages remained considerable. A few kingdoms had regional assemblies of landlords, merchants, and even artisans to provide advice; assemblies took place also at the village level. Taxes, which in theory ranged from one-tenth to one-sixth of all agricultural produce, in fact provided only a limited income. Hence, southern kingdoms were also likely to engage in warfare to secure the means to support their armies and administrators. Some of the southern states also maintained navies and occasionally fought with states of Southeast Asia, such as the empire that developed on several islands in present-day Indonesia.

Ironically, during the very period when regional politics predominated, greater cultural unity emerged than ever before. Even more than in West European society, religion and the state were largely separate in India—which helps account for frequent violence and cruelty on the part of Indian governments despite the concept of dharma. As in the West, however, cultural unity, based on religion, spread even amid divided, sometimes chaotic, politics. Buddhism, already a fading religion in India, was virtually eliminated after the seventh century. In the north, Hun invaders disliked the contemplative emphasis of Buddhism, preferring the more varied approach provided by Hinduism. Hinduism also spread to the south with increasing force, after some earlier interest in Buddhism within this region. In addition, the caste system gained acceptance in the south; many of the new regional kings saw it as a good means of organizing society and providing greater stability. With the caste system came greater influence from the Brahmin or priestly caste, which further encouraged Hinduism. Hindu leaders controlled a flourishing educational system. Schools and colleges were attached to the Hindu temples. Some minority religions, including Buddhism, still survived in India, but before the Muslim challenge the influence of Hinduism became increasingly pervasive.

Hinduism also tended to reach out, more clearly than before, to the ordinary Indian. Although Sanskrit remained the literary language of the Brahmins, a substantial literature—not all of it religious—also arose in more popular languages such as Hindi and Tamil. This ensured that India would not be unified linguistically, but it increased the service of Hinduism as a cultural bond across linguistic and political boundaries. Various Hindu thinkers worked within the basic tradition of the Vedas. The philosopher Shankara argued that the world is an illusion, or maya, which obstructs pure perception. He established a number of centers to promote his teachings. Another philosopher, Ramanuja, emphasized devotion rather than pure intellect as the path to God. Writing in the eleventh century, he inspired devotional groups all over the subcontinent.

Religion guided important artistic activity. A number of temples were constructed, with painted walls depicting religious stories and legends. Around the temples clustered not only schools but also centers for dance and music, and a host of stores and banks. Ornate designs and statues adorned many temple complexes.

This eighth-century temple pavilion at Ellora, dedicated to Siva, was constructed from living rock.

Along with the religion-centered culture, characteristic economic and social forms predominated throughout the subcontinent, supported of course by the pervasive caste system. Urban society, although open only to a minority of the whole population, continued to flourish during this period of Indian history. Merchants enjoyed respectable social status, in contrast to China and early Christian Europe. Indian merchants participated in the exchange of goods with Southeast Asia and also caravan trade with China and the Middle East. Indian cities harbored artisans and small shopkeepers. Some artisans were of a low caste. Leatherworkers, for example, because they handled the skins of dead animals, were members of the untouchable caste, even though their products were essential. Artisans like carpenters and brickmakers enjoyed higher status.

Throughout most of India, the caste system solidified into the form that was to persist into our own century. The four major groups, Brahmins, warriors, peasants, and untouchables, had subdivided, in part according to precise occupation, so that over 3000 castes and Jati subcastes had come into existence. Each caste had a governing body to enforce caste rules and make sure no caste member was "polluted" by inappropriate contact with other caste members. Caste organization also provided some mutual assistance to its members. As before, in many ways this system replaced government in regulating relations among Indians.

For those at the bottom of the caste system—the untouchables—life in some ways differed little from that of menial slaves or serfs in other societies. For them, there was perhaps a more varied routine and a greater sense of belonging to a partly separate society, but a similar vulnerability to great poverty and harsh treatment by superiors existed. Overall, however, the caste system produced a distinctive society, by differentiating social rules and contacts for all groups and so providing a clear identity at all social levels. Even aside from the sheer number of castes, the system was complex. A class system coexisted within castes, so that in some cases people who were Brahmins could be found not serving as priests but as peasants tilling the soil. Inherited status protected their caste membership but did not prevent confusing occupational differentiation and mobility within a caste.

Family ties continued to serve as a focal point for Indians of all castes. Considerable loving attention was lavished on children, particularly boys. Literacy was fairly widespread in wealthier groups, so that even the children of prosperous farming families could often read and write. Increasingly, Indian parents arranged marriages for their children at an early age, in part to ensure that girls would be virgins on their wedding night. Thus, most girls were legally married before they reached puberty, often to men they had never seen. The actual wedding, however, was delayed until after puberty, when the wife could start a family of her own. Despite the arranged marriage practice, it was assumed that husbands and wives could learn to love each other. Hindu law recommended that couples forgo sex for the first three nights after their marriage so they could get to know each other and form an emotional bond before a physical union was attempted. As wives, women were expected to obey their husbands and were usually confined to household activities. Within the warrior caste, a practice called *sati* developed in these centuries, whereby wives were expected to throw themselves on the funeral pyre of their husbands, confirming in death that the two could have no life apart. This practice was never widespread, and some argue that it developed to protect widows against rape or imprisonment by invaders. It nevertheless symbolized the principles of Indian law: "A woman is never fit for independence."

In practice, however, many Indian women developed a strong role in the family based on their household authority. One Indian poem showed the power of a vigorous wife:

> But when she has him [her husband] in her clutches, it's all housework and errands. Fetch a knife to cut this gourd. Get me some fresh fruit. We want wood to boil the greens, and for a fire in the evening. Now paint my feet. Come and massage my back.

THE MUSLIM CHALLENGE IN INDIA

The weakness of Indian political structures after the Hun invasions left the subcontinent a tempting target for subsequent attack. Arab forces approached northwestern India during their great military campaigns following Muhammed's death. Arab armies pushed into the Indus valley. There was no durable conquest at this point. However, conversions to Islam took place in the northwestern region, which, because of its proximity to the Islamic Middle East, was to be the center of Islam in India proper. This first threat helped convince Hindu leaders that they needed to de-

A temple sculpture dating from the eleventh century in central India. The sensual aspect of Indian art is evident here.

velop clearer popular ties in their own religion, thus encouraging some of the cultural changes that affected India more generally.

A second wave of Islamic invasion occurred toward the end of the tenth century. Again, the path lay through the valleys of northwestern India. But, the Muslim armies this time were composed of Turks, not Arabs. While some Turks had been moving from their original home in central Asia into the Middle East itself, influencing the caliphate and, as we will see, also attacking the Byzantine Empire, others remained in the East, although they too had converted to Islam from their earlier animist beliefs. A Turkish kingdom in present-day Afghanistan provided the starting point for the invasions into India. A Turkish chieftain named Sabuktigin, a devout Muslim, raided as far as the Ganges valley, attacking many Hindu shrines and statues because they represented false gods.

Once again, invasion did not lead to conquest. But then, in 1192, a new line of Turkish kings in Afghanistan mounted an attack, this time with plans to annex the conquered territory rather than simply raiding it. Turkish forces seized the city of Delhi, in the Ganges valley, and extended their control throughout most of northern India. Again, Hindu shrines and statues were destroyed, and Buddhist centers were also demolished. A Turkish general established a new regional kingdom, called the Delhi sultanate, that produced additional territory in central and southern India. This

Islamic kingdom represented a deliberate imposition of minority rule over the Hindu majority. Most administrators were brought in from the Middle East. Mosques were constructed in many places, changing the face of Indian architecture. Ultimately, a new language developed, combining Persian with Turkish and Hindi. This language, called Urdu, was favored by Indian converts to Islam and now serves as the official tongue of Pakistan, one of the two present-day Islamic nations on the subcontinent.

UNDERSTANDING CULTURES

Comparison and Contact

The results of encounter between different cultures constitute one of the leading topics in world history, and the issues apply to all time periods, not just the modern centuries. Differences between Middle Eastern and Indian traditions could easily apply to the treatment of women. Veiling of women in the Middle East contrasted with customs of greater public freedom and a greater emphasis on female sensuality in India. Muslims often commented on these aspects of India, even after the postclassical period. One Arab observer in 1595 noted that Indian women often dealt with political officials and "chief public transactions fall to the lot of women." Islam did not, in other words, immediately transform gender relations in India. Even women who converted to Islam did not adopt all the gender habits characteristic of the Middle East, and of course the majority of Indians, male and female, remained Hindu. Strong contact between cultures does not necessarily produce blending.

Over time, however, Islamic example had more effects in India, even on many Hindus. Islam was a conquering force in many parts of India, and this might have influenced even Hindus to believe that some aspects of this culture should be copied. Furthermore, both Hinduism and Islam were strongly patriarchal, although in different specific ways. It was not surprising then that many Indians, despite their rejection of Islam, welcomed its support of an officially patriarchal system.

Thus by the last postclassical period, and beyond, contact had more effects. Indian Muslim women began to adopt the veil, and gradually their patterns of working alongside men in agricultural tasks were also limited. (But, Indian women, including Muslims, persisted in wearing colorful dress, in contrast to the dark tones of women's clothing in the Middle East.) Even among Hindus, at least in the upper castes, customs of greater isolation gained ground. In the system called purdah, women were not permitted to leave their own sections of the home except under careful male supervision. Purdah persisted into the twentieth century, when it was attacked by Indian nationalists eager for women's support. The challenge here is obvious: to realize that over time, initial differences can be eroded by the example of another culture. The results often have a profound impact on even very personal aspects of life.

Under the encouragement of the Delhi sultanate, Islam gained a solid hold on northwestern India—where Pakistan is now located. Here, Islam had the appeal of a conquering force. It also won Indian converts from the lower castes, for Islamic belief had no place for the caste system. Elsewhere in India, though, Hinduism largely prevailed. Most Indians viewed the Delhi sultans as merely another outside force that could be largely endured. Isolated by the regulations of the separate castes, Indians could ignore foreign rule more readily than other people. Furthermore, Hinduism had deep roots that were not easily shaken.

Hindus objected to Islam on many grounds. Its rituals conflicted with Hindu practice. Muslims shunned pork, which Hindus often enjoyed, whereas Muslims saw no reason to avoid beef. Hindus also saw no virtue in abstaining from alcohol or avoiding religious music or statues created to honor the gods. Turkish attacks on Hindu religious centers obviously added to the clash between the two religions. Finally, Hindus disagreed with the Muslim practice of veiling and secluding women.

The Delhi sultanate did not consistently attack the Hindu faith, although the destruction of leading Hindu shrines during their invasions could not be reversed. (One result was that present-day India has few remaining examples of earlier Hindu monumental architecture.) Islamic rulers, while not viewing Hinduism as embodying as much of the true faith as Christianity or Judaism, did see some religious validity in Hindu spirituality. Hence, the Muslim impulse of religious tolerance was given some sway. Increasing Hindu emphasis on popular devotion to key Hindu gods encouraged intense religious piety among the masses of Hindu faithful, which helped solidify the religion among about 70 percent of the subcontinent's population.

The Delhi sultanate itself encountered the characteristic problems of any regime seeking control over India, for smaller political units soon reemerged. Southern kingdoms arose by the 1330s, confining the sultanate once more to the north. A new Turkish raid in 1398 weakened the sultanate in the north, and by 1400 India was again politically divided, with the Delhi sultanate merely a regional kingdom.

The first waves of Islamic invasions thus had brought no permanent political change to India. They had created a new religious minority, of great importance to India's future. Moreover, they had tightened the hold of Hinduism on the majority and actually stimulated a growing piety among the general population.

SOUTHEAST ASIA

Even before the end of India's classical age, civilization in Southeast Asia had developed under considerable stimulus from the subcontinent. Hindu traders brought Indian artistic as well as religious forms to several centers in the islands of Indonesia. Buddhism had already begun to spread overland, to other parts of Southeast Asia. Furthermore, the Southeast Asian form of Buddhism, with its emphasis on personal devotion and meditation, remained truer to the Buddhist ideal than the Buddhist variants adopted in China and Japan. However, Southeast Asia was not purely and simply an extension of Indian culture. Hinduism did not gain a durable hold in the region. Nor did the caste system develop, because among other factors, Buddhists were always hostile to this Brahmin-devised structure.

Indian influences did penetrate more widely in Southeast Asia between about 650 and 1250, nonetheless. Buddhist missionaries and Indian (particularly Tamil) merchants played a leading role in this movement. Indian emissaries in many places encountered new peoples moving into the region from the north. Their relations with most of these peoples were peaceful, but there were some important wars between southern Indian kingdoms and local states on the Malay Peninsula and the islands of the Indian Ocean.

Buddhism spread to Vietnam, although in other respects Chinese influences predominated. Further west, tribes of Thai people pushed southward in the eighth century, establishing the Buddhist kingdom of Thailand. Another people, the Burmese, set up a kingdom in the ninth century. Yet another people, the Khmers, established a Cambodian empire in 782, which long served as the largest political unit on the Southeast Asian mainland. This empire, again largely Buddhist, began to decline around 1200.

On the main Indonesian islands of Borneo, Sumatra, and Java, another empire took shape, the Srivijaya. At its height, this empire also controlled the southern part of the Malay Peninsula. The empire was weakened in the eleventh century by attacks from a leading kingdom in southern India. During the thirteenth century, traders from China began to exert influence in the region as well, crippling the power of the local merchant group. By the fourteenth century, local kingdoms constituted most of the civilized portions of Indonesia.

Thus, diverse and largely regional kingdoms became characteristic of Southeast Asia during the centuries of civilization's expansion. In contrast to India, there was never even a brief tradition of political unity. Cultural unity was somewhat greater,

The great temple at Angkor-Wat, in Cambodia.

although it was affected by competing influences from India and China. Indian artistic forms helped inspire a number of great temples, particularly in Cambodia and Indonesia. Indian literature and legends spread widely. Southeast Asian monarchs, greatly attracted to Indian culture, passed it along to their subjects.

Buddhism was the clearest winner in this process of cultural diffusion. Buddhist emphasis on direct contact with ordinary people, its strong missionary impulse, and its intense focus on religious devotion and ethical behavior gave it a clear edge over Hinduism in Southeast Asia. Many Southeast Asians made pilgrimages to Buddhist centers in India and on the island of Sri Lanka, which further confirmed the religion's influence. Many rulers, inspired by Buddhist promptings toward an ethical life as preparation for nirvana, offered humane government to their subjects.

Indian influence also surfaced in the area of economics. Indian merchants encouraged the considerable production of spices and other goods for a wider market, which brought Southeast Asia firmly into contact with the central routes of world trade. From this point onward, Southeast Asian goods would play a vital role in world trade.

Then, by about 1300, a third influence added new complexity to the Southeast Asian mix. By this point, Arab traders had gained increasing dominance in Southeast Asian trade, displacing many Indian merchants. Southeast Asian spices and teas were brought to the Middle East and even Europe in Arab vessels. This merchant influence was particularly strong in the Indonesian islands, as well as in the southern part of the Philippine islands and on the Malay Peninsula. The reduction of Indian independence, during the Delhi sultanate, added to the possibility of growing Islamic activity in this region. Then the new missionary spirit that arose in the Middle East with the Sufi movement sent another vigorous signal to Southeast Asia. Increasing numbers of Malays, Indonesians, and Filipinos converted to Islam. By 1400, Buddhism had been almost entirely eliminated in these places, while Hinduism was displaced except on a few islands, such as Bali, where it continues to be practiced.

By this point, the diverse religious map of Southeast Asia had become established fact. Hinduism was a minor strand, but Buddhism held great importance in most of the regional kingdoms of the mainland. On the islands, however, as on the Malay Peninsula, Islam was becoming dominant. Written forms were similarly diverse. Writing for many of the Southeast Asian languages derived from scripts used in India, including Sanskrit. However, Malay writing developed under Arabic influence, whereas in Vietnam writing derived from Chinese ideographs. In essence, many features of Southeast Asian culture were derivative, but came from no one center, despite the special importance of Indian influences.

CONCLUSION: ISLAM IN SOUTHERN ASIA

The driving forces in southern Asia—both India and Southeast Asia—in the centuries after 600 were the surging military, commercial, and missionary power of Islam and the remarkable vitality of Indian civilization—its religious vigor most obviously but also its trading success. Overall, Indian dominance declined during the latter part of the period. Muslim rule over parts of India helped turn trade in the Indian Ocean increasingly over to Muslim hands. In India, under the Delhi sultanate, an important gap arose between the values of the ruling Muslim elite and the basic culture of the masses. The result of varied influences in Southeast Asia was a checkerboard of cultural patterns combined with growing involvement in international trade.

SUGGESTED WEBSITES

On Muslim mysticism in India (the poet Kabir),
see *http://goto.bilkent.edu.tr/gunes/KabirPoems.htm;* on the spread of Islam in south and southeast Asia, see *http://users.erols.com/ zenithco/indiamus.htm;* and on Sufism, see *http://www.geocities.com/Athens/5738/intro.htm.*

SUGGESTED READINGS

For Indian history in this period, see Romila Thapar, *A History of India* (1966) and M. Habib and K. A. Nizami, eds., *Comprehensive History of India,* Vol. V (1967). Good sources on vital new developments are A. Embree, ed., *Muslim Civilization in India* (1964); S. M. Ikram, *Muslim Civilization in India* (1964); and Aziz Ahmad, *Studies in Islamic Culture in the Indian Environment* (1964). India's wider influence is examined in H. B. Q. Wales, *The Indianization of China and Southeast Asia* (1967). For the important but often neglected southern kingdoms in India, consult K. A. Nilakanta Sustri, *A History of South India from Prehistoric Times to the Fall of Vijuganagan,* 3rd ed. (1966). An excellent summary on Southeast Asia is D. G. E. Hall, *A History of Southeast Asia* (1981). Other useful works are John F. Cady, *Southeast Asia: Its Historical Development* (1964); H. B. Q. Wales, *The Making of Greater India: A Study in Southeast Asian Culture Change* (1950); and J. C. van Leur, *Indonesian Trade and Society* (1943). On Indian Ocean trade patterns, see J. L. Abu-Lughod, *Before European Hegemeny: The World System* A.D. *1250–1350* (1988).

Africa and Islam

8

FOCAL POINTS

During the postclassical period, Africa participated actively in the expansion of civilization and in new contacts with the developing world network. Why were key parts of Africa important trading partners for societies elsewhere? Why was Islam attractive to many Africans, but what were the limits to its impact south of the Sahara? Is it possible, despite great variety, to speak of some basic characteristics of African civilization as it took shape in the postclassical period?

SUB-SAHARAN AFRICA AND THE WORLD NETWORK

Islam's sweep across North Africa effectively joined this region to the Middle East in a single, if sometimes politically fragmented, civilization. Below the Sahara desert, Islam also gained important influence, although as in southern Asia, it competed with other beliefs. Sub-Saharan Africa remained an area of independent civilization, even as it participated in the radiation of religion, commerce, and politics from Islam. A distinct set of African identities persisted. At the same time, portions of sub-Saharan Africa borrowed more than India from Islam, importing not only religion but also Arabic writing. Parts of the African economy were more closely tied to the Arab world than was true in India, as Africans sent gold, raw materials, and slaves in return for horses and some luxury craft items. Africa, in this sense, imitated the more established centers of civilization, as did Russia, Japan, and Western Europe during this same postclassical period.

Because of its diverse sources and the vast territory involved, sub-Saharan African history, before the modern centuries, is not easy to grasp. Since most African societies did not develop writing, the historical record is sparse, gleaned from accounts of non-African travelers (notably the Muslims), archeological remains, and the fantastic stories and family histories that many African peoples transmitted by word of mouth. Technology, although benefiting from the extensive use of iron—introduced below the Sahara by 1000 B.C.E.—lagged behind Asian standards. Animal diseases, including the dreaded tse-tse fly, limited livestock and animal transportation.

Although political organization allowed monarchies in many parts of Africa—emerging at about the same time and in some of the same ways that monarchies arose in Western Europe—there were more African societies without formal politics beyond villages and tribes than was the case in Asia and Europe.

Furthermore, African societies were diverse. The continent, even below the Sahara, is vast. It includes huge deserts—like the southern Sahara and, in the south, the Kalihari; extensive mountains in the east; grasslands below the Sahara and again in the south; and the dense tropical jungle in the center. Large African empires developed but none ever embraced more than a fraction of the sub-Saharan region. Fragmentation produced considerable diversity. No religion has ever swept over the whole of sub-Saharan Africa, nor has any language provided unified communication.

However, diversity was not absolute. Although there are over 1000 languages in use in sub-Saharan Africa, they derive from no more than four or five basic tongues, which means that many of the languages are closely related to one another. While political unity was never achieved, there were some recurring political trends in many parts of the continent. Although a single religion never flourished, a strong polytheistic leaning resulted in some basic common ground where the African religious experience was concerned. Similarities of this sort, while they cannot be pressed too far, allow for some discussion of certain tendencies in African civilization—tendencies that reached fuller expression when civilization itself began to spread widely, although not universally, from about the year 600 C.E.

The impetus for this spreading civilization was twofold. First, familiar enough from the example of other early civilizations, was the sheer passage of time. Civilization had flourished in the northeast for over a millennium. Agriculture had been well entrenched in the northern and western regions of sub-Saharan Africa even longer. It had not, by 500 C.E., reached into or through the equatorial jungles, where small hunting and gathering groups persisted. Thus, the southern part of the continent, ultimately a fertile agricultural region, remained untouched. But in the north and west, long centuries of agriculture had provided a solid economic base. Iron-working was also well established. Village organization was tightly knit, and the local communities, along with firm ties among kinship or extended family groups, provided a durable political base for further cultural achievements. In some African societies, the stable local units and tight links among family members sufficed to ensure order. Family or lineage bonds were a distinctive feature, and Africans devoted great attention to memorizing elaborate family trees so that relatives could be identified even in fairly distant regions. In many kinship groups, or clans, certain vocations were inherited, like the work of traders, peasants, political officials, even slaves. The importance of clans explains the often unstructured quality of African government.

Finally, religion, although varying widely in specific local forms, gave Africans an explanation of the workings of nature, including rites and beliefs to deal with illness and natural disasters, and also a firm sense of their own identity. Each clan had its own sacred animal that expressed a divine spirit and could not be killed by clan members. Because most African religions included both the worship of spirits in nature and a veneration of ancestors, they served a social as well as mystical function.

In sum, the first context for expanding civilization in Africa was the solid foundation formed by an agricultural economy many centuries old and a supportive religious and political culture. Stronger kingdoms, like Ghana in West Africa, began to emerge as early as 300 C.E. on these bases.

The second stimulus for the spread of civilization resulted from trading contacts that developed between the seventh and the tenth centuries. New levels of international exchange established two principal channels. On Africa's east coast, Islamic sailors from southern Arabia set up urban centers. Trade to and from these centers, across the Indian Ocean, became extensive. Ivory and gold, plus some slaves, were exported to the Middle East, India, and even China, in return for manufactured products including Chinese porcelain. Although this commerce remained largely in non-African hands, the Arab traders settled in the east African cities, intermarried extensively, and provided the foundation for a number of city-states and local kingdoms. They even developed a language, Swahili, that combined Arab and African features to promote wider communication. East African cities did not have extensive contacts with the interior, which limited their impact in Africa, but they were also a noteworthy development.

More significant was the second trade channel, across the Sahara from Muslim North Africa. Here, caravans traveled, by camel and by foot, on arduous journeys. Although the domestication of camels occurred earlier, widespread African use of camels began about 200 C.E. and revolutionized trading opportunities. By 700, Muslim traders were seeking gold, ivory, salt, and some slaves from sub-Saharan Africa. They also traded for the cola nut, a stimulant not mentioned in the Quran and therefore permitted to the faithful. The wealth that resulted permitted the development of thriving African cities. Timbuktu, in the southern Sahara, was the greatest center, boasting a large military force, a huge treasury, and—in the words of an early European visitor—"many magistrates, learned doctors, and men of religion." Here was a stimulus to growing trade, the manufacture of cloth and precious metals, and new social and political patterns in a wide stretch of Africa below the Sahara. African merchants expanded their operations through many parts of West Africa. Social divisions began to form, between rich and poor, between soldiers, artisans, and farmers, some of which cut across traditional kinship lines.

Africa was thus part of the Islamic orbit and a growing participant in international trade. It was also one of the first societies to imitate other civilizations, using its trade contacts and selective borrowings from Islam to accelerate aspects of its historical development. The postclassical period saw distinctive characteristics persist in Africa, but also the increasing influence of larger world trends.

THE GREAT KINGDOMS

Not surprisingly, the first great African kingdoms—not counting the states in the upper Nile—arose in the region of the southern Sahara and the grasslands below. This area is called the Sudan, from the Arab word for black; in these centuries, however, it stretched all along the southern Sahara rather than the upper Nile nation that is now called the Sudan. The Sudanese kingdoms exacted some tribute from merchants, which provided considerable wealth without the extensive taxation of the peasant class.

Ghana was the earliest of a series of Sudanic kingdoms. Its origins extended to the classical period, but its clearer development from about 800 related to the growth of cross-Saharan trade and the expansion of salt and gold mining in the region. The kingdom, built around several cities that have since vanished, served as a crossroads between North Africa and the gold and ivory producers of the grassland and forest areas to the south. Kings of Ghana imposed taxes on the trade that crossed their region. According to one Arab writer, "All pieces of gold that are found in this empire belong to the king." This monopoly carefully protected against the unauthorized production of gold that might flood the market and supplemented the direct tax (also to be paid in gold) levied on every donkey or camel bearing salt. With these resources, the Ghanese king sustained a lavish court, offering banquets to thousands of guests and surrounding himself with luxurious trappings. Ceremony and ritual helped the king express his power; so did the related belief that the king was in some sense divine, descended from and protected by the gods. The features of divine kingship, as it has been called, became common in African political organization during this period and beyond.

Ghana developed a complex relationship with the Islamic world. Its kings hired Arabs to keep records, which helped them develop the bureaucracy necessary for the expansion of the state. Trade with Islamic North Africa was needed not only for tax revenues, but also as a source for horses, on which military activities, notably the cavalry, depended (local horse breeding was limited by the presence of the tse-tse fly). The cavalry allowed the state to expand into the plains of the Sudan, to exact tribute and acquire slaves. However, these contacts with Islam and a growing dependence on trade also made Ghana vulnerable to nomadic raiders and invasions from states to the north. The kingdom's wealth inevitably drew attention from North Africa, while local Islamic residents may have invited the presence of fellow Muslims. The kingdom of Ghana, always loosely organized through alliances between king and local leaders, lacked the ability to survive this situation. Although its wealth was great, Ghana's defense depended on arrangements with local military groups, rather than professional soldiers. And, the kingdom maintained only a rudimentary bureaucracy, understandably focused on tax collection. Weakened by military raids from outside its borders, the kingdom collapsed around 1200.

A number of other kingdoms had already formed in the Sudan region, some of them organized with councils as well as kings. Copper production and textiles flourished in several of these kingdoms, a few of which endured into the nineteenth century. A number of African trading companies developed, sometimes organized along hereditary lines so that their administration remained within the same extended family across generations. Some of these companies, too, survived into present times. Thriving market centers assumed a major place in the life of West Africa, in portions of contemporary nations such as Nigeria.

The clearest successor state to Ghana, however, emerged during the thirteenth century. Its regional basis was slightly different from that of Ghana, and its political organization was better developed. It too, however, relied on cavalry, trade, and contact with Islam. The kingdom of Mali was established under the leadership of an able general named Sundiata, who defeated a number of smaller states and ruled for about a quarter century until his death in 1260. Sundiata's state rested on the wealth derived from trade with North Africa, and also on the unusual fertility of the Gambia river valley, where rice and several other crops thrived. Sundiata and his successors were regarded as divine monarchs, similar to the situation in Ghana, where a ruler's religious authority and magical power were emphasized. They also formed alliances with a variety of local leaders. But, Sundiata converted to Islam, partly as a gesture of goodwill toward his North African trading partners. Although he did not force Islam on his subjects, he and his successors employed Islamic bureaucrats and popularized the use of Arabic script. As a religion of the elite, Islam provided a sense of coherence and also skills in law and writing that allowed the development of a more extensive bureaucracy and legal system than had prevailed in Ghana.

The rulers of Mali also accrued great wealth. One successor to Sundiata, Mansa Musa, making a pilgrimage to Mecca in 1334–35, dazzled Egyptians and other Arabs with the gold and ornaments of his entourage. His staff loaded 90 camels with gold dust, each load weighing 300 pounds, to provide spending money for the trip. Several thousand subjects accompanied Mansa Musa on the pilgrimage. He himself offered substantial gifts to people he met along the way and to the holy cities of Mecca and Medina. Not surprisingly, his reputation spread widely. (Also not surprisingly, he ran out of gold and had to borrow in Egypt; the size of the loan, quickly repaid, threw Egyptian banks into some confusion.) A French map, some decades later, recalled Mansa Musa's name, adding provocatively that "so abundant is the gold that is found in his land that he is the richest and most noble king of all the area." But, Mansa Musa was more than a big-spending pilgrim. He organized a pool of many Muslim scholars, from as far away as Egypt, in his capital city; his government engaged in diplomacy, including the exchange of ambassadors, with other North African countries and possibly other even more distant nations.

Mali became one of the great nations of the Islamic world, extending from the Atlantic deep into the interior of the Sudan. Mali emperors promoted active trade and also patronized Islamic learning; Timbuktu became a major center of Islamic scholarship, where books, it was said, were valued above gold. Laws were strictly enforced, and the empire enjoyed a long period of peace and prosperity. The great trading families extended their commercial skills. An Arab visitor noted, "Neither the man who travels nor he who stays at home has anything to fear from robbers or men of violence."

Mali began to decline, however, by about 1400. Its place was taken by a third great Sudanese kingdom, Songhai, which flourished from the late fifteenth century to 1591. Songhai, although somewhat smaller than Mali, continued the development of a civil service to supplement the personal authority of the king. This state, too, was Islamic, though again, most of the inhabitants remained true to their polytheistic traditions, and in the freedom granted women, especially in public, and in other respects, it greatly offended Islamic purists. Rather than depending on alliances with local lords, the kings of Songhai built armies that owed loyalty only to them; some of their soldiers were slaves, the personal possessions of the monarchy. Many new territories were gained by conquest. The kingdom of Songhai collapsed only as a result of new attacks from North Africa, notably from the kingdom of Morocco, and internal rebellion. With its downfall, the great period of the Sudanic kingdoms came to an end, although in fact a variety of new kingdoms formed in subsequent centuries until, in the nineteenth century, the full onslaught of European imperialism interrupted this internal political development.

Timbuktu as sketched above by the French artist, René Caillié, in 1828. Often conquered and destroyed, at this point the city was only a remnant of its greatness under the Empire of Mali.

Partly through the example of the Sudanic kingdoms, by the fourteenth century a number of other states formed in northern and western sub-Saharan Africa. Most were monarchies, with kings claiming the authority and trappings of divine right. Characteristically, such divine claims were balanced by rather weak control over most subjects and by councils of local leaders and townspeople that provided, although informally, something of the same pattern of government existing in the early parliamentary institutions of medieval Europe during the same period. The kingdoms that spread into the forested areas of West Africa, in parts of present-day Nigeria and other states, also benefited from the trading and craft skills of the Sudanic peoples. Particularly in the loosely organized kingdom of Benin, an important artistic tradition developed in woodcarving and metal sculpture, featuring powerful portrayals of divine spirits and human forms alike.

By about 1400, then, much of northern and central Africa south of the Sahara was organized into regional kingdoms, with an especially potent imperial tradition in the Sudan. Most states were not tightly organized. Some were Muslim in leadership, others strictly polytheistic. Boundaries among states were not firmly set, in part because bureaucracies were too small to enforce them, in part because political rule still depended heavily on personal loyalties and alliances. And there were areas, including many active trading centers and artistic cultures, organized on a purely local basis in addition to the city-states of East Africa. The forested regions of West Africa contrasted with the large states of the Sudan, in part because their geography prevented the travel and operation of the cavalry. Clearly, however, agriculture and advances in crafts, manufacturing, and trade were spreading ever more widely into the tropical forests themselves, and with this came a tendency toward more formal and effective political administration.

One further development was noteworthy from about the ninth century onward. Agricultural peoples, members of the Bantu language group, began to journey through the dense tropical forests toward the south, a process of migration that would extend over several centuries—not really ending until the nineteenth century—and that would bring agricultural society to southern Africa. Bantu languages had common origins; the word itself meant "many people." Migration from western Africa was probably triggered by the movement southward of Saharan farmers as their economy and political organization in the Sudan improved. New crops, such as the plantain, which was introduced around 100 C.E., and the growing use of iron fueled the further migration of the Bantus. The Bantus, at first mainly herders and fishers, spread into present-day Congo and fanned out to the east and south. They acquired iron tools and began to cultivate new crops. As early as 860 C.E., some Bantu

Bust of a king from Benin, West Africa, center of some of the most imaginative African art. Gold braided hair and necklace show the man's royal status.

HISTORY DEBATE

Handles for African History

Until fairly recently, most Westerners viewed Africa as a land of considerable mystery and backwardness, the "dark continent," and assumed that most of it had little history until the arrival of Europeans. Important research and scholarly work on African history has proved this imperialistic attitude wrong. More recently, some scholars have blasted what they see as consistent efforts to belittle the African past, arguing that the continent's great achievements, beginning with ancient Egypt, need far more emphasis and that Western criteria for measuring a society's success are distorted and narrow.

In between some of these debates, a number of historians seek explanations for some general features of African civilization in the postclassical period and beyond. Comparison can help. One scholar has noted how similar African and West-European societies were around 1200. Both imitated more advanced centers in the Mediterranean. Both had fairly loose political organizations, although African kingdoms were larger than their European counterparts; tribal loyalties were important in both regions. Both saw the rapid advance of trade and merchants. Of course, differences exist, particularly in the degree of impact world religions have had and in the extent of writing, but the similarities are revealing. Two hundred years later, the comparison changes shape: Europe was beginning to explore more widely, whereas Africa maintained established patterns to a greater extent. Africa had never emphasized ocean-going activity, in part because (particularly on the Atlantic coast) it did not have a rich network of navigable rivers. Its relations with Islam were smooth, in contrast to Christian Europe where a dependence on Islam for trade was viewed negatively. Unlike Europe, Africa gained little from new knowledge of Asian technologies. This represents a complex mix of factors, reflecting some African "limitations" by European standards, but also an absence of some of the problems that beset postclassical Europe. Does a society largely content with its substantial achievements—as African leaders were by 1400—require special explanation?

farmers had reached territory in what is now the nation of South Africa. Bantus also spread into the rich agricultural plateaus of eastern Africa, in present-day Kenya and Uganda. This was a gradual migration, spurred by recurring land shortages. Until 1500, many of the Bantu settlements were short-lived, as farming problems or conflicts with local hunting groups forced periodic movement. As a result, not many large political units developed until a later point. A few kingdoms arose, often with Bantu overlords ruling a subject local people; two such kingdoms, Ruanda and Burundi, survived into the twentieth century.

One great empire flourished for a time in Zimbabwe. This was a gold-producing region, with links to the trading cities of East Africa. Powerful kings built a huge stone-walled city, the ruins of which fascinated archeologists in later ages. The sheer size of the stone monuments of Zimbabwe rivals the buildings of ancient Egypt and the Mayans. Concepts of divine kingship prevailed in this great state, which at its height around 1300 ruled a vast territory in southeastern Africa. Zimbabwe declined, as mysteriously as it rose, after about 1400. Although unique in its monument-building capacity, it serves as additional evidence of the spread, however uneven, of new political organization across much of Africa.

FEATURES OF AFRICAN CIVILIZATION

African civilization, as it had developed by the fifteenth century, was characterized by obvious diversity and disunity, on the one hand, and common general themes, on the other. In politics, the tendency to embrace a divine monarch, but to temper this form of government with some kind of advisory councils, set a clear—although again far from uniform—political pattern. Africans in many regions were acquiring skills in the art of state-building. In the Sudanic kingdoms, increasingly sophisticated forms of organization were devised, and, on the whole, African political development shows a progression much like that of Western Europe during the Middle Ages.

Africans were also creating a significant commercial tradition, particularly, of course, on the east coast and in the Sudan. There were no institutional innovations, such as banking networks, but the family-based trading companies had genuine cohesion. Land-owning lords emerged in many parts of Africa, and in some cases one tribal group was controlled by an upper class from another tribe; this was true in some areas settled by the Bantu. In general, however, African farmers were freer than their counterparts in Western Europe during most of the Middle Ages; there was no manorial system to dispute peasants' control of property. At the same time, slavery was practiced in a number of areas. Many slaves were taken in the frequent wars that occurred during early African history. Some families, however, were enslaved on a hereditary basis. Slaves were used for a variety of tasks, ranging from personal service to mining and soldiering.

The African economy was bounded by limitations on technology. Despite the displays of great wealth in some states, there was less wealth overall than in the civilizations of Asia, and populations were smaller as a result. African farmers established irrigation systems and developed considerable knowledge of a variety of crops. Mining techniques improved steadily, as Africans discovered ways to sink deeper shafts and refine gold more efficiently. By the fifteenth century, West African miners had produced a total of perhaps 5500 tons of gold, and they would produce as much again during the next four centuries. Copper and ironworking also had developed extensively, although overall, by 1400, manufacturing technology (as opposed to artistic creativity) was lagging behind Eurasian standards, in part because Africans imported fewer technologies from Asia.

African society characteristically featured tight family structures. The links among extended kin, even in different villages, formed one of the key bonds of

African society even when political structures, in a more formal sense, were weak. African families, moreover, devoted considerable time to children. Mothers typically carried infants while at work, in contrast to the Western tendency to separate mother and child as early as possible. Women were officially inferior in the African family, and some African groups controlled women's behavior rigorously. In general, however, women had considerable status in not only the family, but also public functions such as operating shops in the open market. Their diverse roles in agriculture and commerce stood in contrast to their place in most Asian societies.

Women's public freedom and colorful costumes, as we have seen, contrasted with the Islamic traditions of North Africa and the Middle East. The famous fourteenth-century Arab traveler, Ibn Battuta, an admirer of African wealth, political power, and piety, was nonetheless shocked by what he saw among women. "With regard to their women, they are not modest in the presence of men, they do not veil themselves in spite of their perseverance in the prayers. . . . The women there have friends and companions among men." Here was another case where contact and even imitation did not erase regional traditions. Although Africans participated in the spread of Islam, and such involvements resulted in real change, they did so in their own way.

By 1400, religious divisions were important in sub-Saharan Africa. Ethiopia maintained its Christianity. Islam had spread to various parts of the Sudan and to the port cities on the Indian ocean. Islam was not yet a mass religion in Africa, but its hold over a substantial portion of the north and west was already established.

Most Africans, even in the sub-Saharan Islamic states, remained polytheists. As in many other agricultural societies, Africans relied heavily on magical explanations of natural occurrences that they could not otherwise explain. African polytheism was elaborate and comprehensive in its scope, which helps account for its durability even when competing against monotheistic religions like Islam. It involved belief in a supreme being, who was responsible for creating the universe and a corresponding set of beliefs, and subsidiary gods and spirits, good and evil, who actually managed daily affairs like crops and wars. These lesser gods, who had the greatest influence on people's lives, received the most attention. Religious rituals, organized by medicine men, played an important role in treating illness. At the same time, Africans had a certain sense of skepticism; too much religious fervor was regarded with suspicion. A Nigerian proverb held that when a person displayed excessive religious belief, "people can tell him the wood he is made of"—that is, they can remind him that he is only mortal.

Religion played a significant role in directing African artistic achievements. Work in wood, ivory, and terra-cotta had advanced steadily by 1400, particularly in West Africa. Many masks and statues had religious significance and were used in dances of worship and other ceremonies. African art emphasized strong, stark portrayals, without intricate detail. Artists had an important place in urban society, along with most other artisans. In certain areas, such as the Bantu regions, African art displayed a particular interest in the circle, rather than in other shapes, as the basic geometric unit for art and architecture. Many homes and great temples—in Zimbabwe, for instance—were built in a circular form. Even today, many African children readily draw perfect circles, in contrast to the great reliance on squares and angles characteristic of European and Asian education.

African development was proceeding actively by 1400. New kingdoms would endure for many centuries, as would artistic, religious, and family traditions. European contacts would alter the face of some regions in Africa increasingly after about 1500, but without the overwhelming disruption of an entire society that occurred in the Americas. Among other things, Africans had maintained sufficient ties with other cultures to develop adequate immunity to some of the great diseases of Europe and Asia; hence, the population was not decimated through plagues, as happened among the native peoples of the Americas. The arrival of Europeans by the late fifteenth century thus represents a partial break in African history. However, European explorers and settlers would interact with a highly developed African society, and for many centuries basic trends established during the formative period of civilization south of the Sahara continued.

SUGGESTED WEBSITES

On Zimbabwe, see
http://www.mc.maricopa.edu/academic/cult_sci/anthro/lost_tribes/zimbabwe/ intro.html.

SUGGESTED READINGS

On sub-Saharan Africa, several source collections are interesting reading: G. S. P. Freeman-Greenville, *The East African Coast: Select Documents from the First to the Earlier Nineteenth Century* (1962); D. T. Niane, *Sundiata, an Epic of Old Mali* (1986); and H. A. R. Gibb, *The Travels of Ibn Batuta,* 2 vols. (1962). Surveys include Philip Curtin et al., *African History from Earliest Times to Independence* (1995); B. Davidson, *Africa in History* (1974); J. D. Fage, *Africa Discovers Her Past* (1970); Richard Olaniyan, *African History and Culture* (1982); R. S. Smith, *Warfare and Diplomacy in Pre-Colonial West Africa* (1969); J. D. Fage, *A History of West Africa* (1969); N. Leutzion and Hopkins, eds., *Ancient Ghana* (1981); Anne Hilton, *The Kingdom of the Kongo* (1985); David Birmingham and Phyllis Martin, *History of Central Africa,* 2 vols. (1983); Derek Nurse and Thomas Spear, *The Swahili: Reconstructing the History and Language of an African Society* (1985); and J. Middleton, *The World of the Swahili and African Mercantile Civilization* (1992). On women, refer to N. Hafkin and E. Bay, *Women in Africa* (1976), and H. Loth, *Women in Ancient Africa* (1992). See also A. H. M. Jones and Elizabeth Monroe, *A History of Ethiopia* (1955), and two studies by one of the pioneers in using new sources to reexamine early African history, J. Vansina, *The Children of Woot: A History of the Kuba People* (1978), and *Art History in Africa* (1984). On trade patterns, see Richard W. Bulliet, *The Camel and the Wheel* (1975).

9

East European Civilization: Byzantium and Russia

FOCAL POINTS

Important civilizations expanded in Europe during the postclassical period. Eastern Europe initially led the way. The existence of a successor empire to Rome, in the northeastern Mediterranean, served as a beacon to emerging kingdoms in Eastern Europe, particularly among many Slavic groups. Why and in what ways did Eastern Europe separate itself from Western Europe? What regions were affected by both societies? What were the similarities and differences between the Byzantine empire and its Roman predecessor? What aspects of this empire were other peoples, like the Kievan Russians, able to imitate? Why did Eastern Europe, including Byzantium, seem to falter in the last centuries of the postclassical period?

EASTERN EUROPE AS A CIVILIZATION

The rise of Islam in the Middle East was matched in importance by the spread of religion and trade, through Islamic auspices, to central, southern, and southeastern Asia and to Africa. We now turn to Europe, where the Islamic movement also played a role, but without significant religious conversion. Europe operated on the fringes of the Islamic world. Much of its trade passed through Muslim hands, and there was much imitation. Western Europe, particularly, can be compared to Africa in its attempts to imitate Islam. But, European societies were predominantly Christian, often warring with the Muslims. As a result, contact with the growing international trade network also occurred on somewhat different bases—with Europeans often anxious about their inferiority to Arab merchants.

Europe thus illustrates not only the expansion of civilization, but also the impact of Islam and the world network and the role of explicit imitation. However, European developments in the postclassical period also had distinctive features of their own. Furthermore, even within Europe, two somewhat different Christian patterns emerged, one looking to Byzantium, the other to the Roman Church. We begin with Eastern Europe, where disruption after the fall of the Roman Empire had been comparatively modest.

Two major Christian zones arose in Europe during the postclassical centuries. Each represented a distinctive version of that faith, symbolized by the formal split between the Eastern Orthodox and Western Catholic churches in the eleventh century. Similar beliefs, some shared memories of classical Greece and Rome, and their geographical position as neighbors produced some common features in East and West European civilizations. On the whole, however, the two societies took different forms, and the centuries after 500 saw these differences develop and then solidify.

Indeed, Byzantium had much the same kind of outreach that India and China demonstrated during the postclassical period, as it helped shape other parts of Eastern Europe in establishing basic cultural and political patterns. Byzantium itself, at its height, approximated the economic and political sophistication of the Asian civilizations, as evidenced by its great capital city, Constantinople. Like its purely Asian counterparts, Bynzatium built on classical foundations while responding to new religious fervor. East European civilization, initially centered in the Byzantine Empire, had the closest contacts with the traditions of the classical Mediterranean world. As a result, for many centuries this East European civilization greatly surpassed the West in political sophistication, culture, and economic vitality. Like its neighbor to the west, however, it had one important feature: a strong desire to expand, particularly through the Christian religion itself. Blocked from expansion to the east and south by the rise of the Islamic empire, the Byzantine emperors and church patriarchs turned their eyes to the northern peoples. As in Western Europe, where Italian-based popes sponsored conversion drives to the Germanic and Celtic peoples, effective lines ran south–north during the postclassical period. By 1400, two Europes existed, with few contacts and limited similarities.

PATTERNS OF EAST EUROPEAN HISTORY: A SECOND AND THIRD "ROME"

THE BYZANTINE PHASE

The development of the Byzantine Empire may be traced back to the fourth century C.E. It was at this point that the Roman Empire established its eastern capital in Constantinople, which quickly became the most vigorous center of the otherwise fading empire. The emperor Constantine ordered the construction of many elegant buildings, including Christian churches, in his new city, which was built on the foundations of a previously modest town called Byzantium. Soon, separate eastern emperors ruled from this city, even before the western portion of the empire fell to Germanic invaders. Constantinople was responsible for the Balkan peninsula, the northern Middle East, the Mediterranean coast, and North Africa. Although for several centuries Latin served as the court language of the Eastern empire, Greek was the common tongue and, after the emperor Justinian, became the official language as well. Indeed, in the eyes of Easterners, Latin became an inferior, barbaric means of communication. Knowledge of Greek enabled the people of the Eastern empire to freely read the philosophical and literary classics of ancient Athens and the Hellenistic culture.

As the Eastern empire took shape, Christianity also began its split between East and West. In the West, the Roman pope controlled basic church organization. But,

World Profiles

The Emperor Justinian (527–565 C.E.)

The Emperor Justinian attempted to revive the Roman Empire; he achieved considerable although short-term success. He also served, somewhat unintentionally, as a founding figure in the Byzantine Empire that would long survive. Justinian and his generals briefly succeeded in regaining Roman territories in Western Europe and North Africa. The law code compiled during his reign assembled and reconciled the laws and legal precedents of the later Roman Empire, thus preserving and clarifying Roman law for all of Europe. Justinian also oversaw the construction of Saint Sophia, the great church of Constantinople that influenced Byzantine and Islamic architecture for centuries. Despite his desire, in part, to restore Roman culture, it is interesting to note the revealing differences between his image in art and the more traditional portrayal of the Roman Caesars (see Chapter 4). In the mosaic shown here, Justinian's costume, and the surrounding group of church and court officials, indicate the unity of the Byzantine state and the Orthodox Church, as the emperor is portrayed as both king and priest. How does this depiction compare with the Roman political tradition?

This mosaic of Justinian is from San Vitale in Ravenna, Italy. Ravenna was one of the many cities Justinian recaptured in Western Europe, a city that also served at times as the capital of the Western empire.

there was no comparable leader in the Eastern church. The patriarch, or bishop, of Constantinople held top prestige, but there were three other patriarchs in the East, none of whom had political control over the church. For several centuries, the Eastern church in principle acknowledged the authority of the pope, but in practice papal directives had no hold over the Byzantine church. Rather, the Eastern emperors regulated church organization, creating a pattern of state control over church structure far different from the tradition that developed in the West, where the church insisted, although not always successfully, on its independence. Disputes over doctrine, including such issues as the recipe used to make bread for the eucharist, the sacramental celebration of Christ's sacrifice in the mass, further divided the two churches. Even the two churches' monastic movements differed, following separate rules.

The early history of the Eastern empire, which came to be known as Byzantine after the capital city's name, was marked by the constant threat of invasion. The Eastern emperors vanquished Sassanid Persian and Germanic attacks. Early emperors developed a solid military base, recruiting local soldiers in addition to hiring some mercenaries. Upper-class Greeks, recapturing their lapsed military tradition, provided a series of able generals. The Emperor Justinian tried, of course, to regain Roman territories in Western Europe and North Africa, but despite brief successes his effort left the Eastern empire exhausted and financially drained. Justinian's monumental law code, assembling and reconciling the law and legal precedents of the later Roman Empire, was of vital service in preserving and clarifying Roman law for both Eastern and Western Europe. However, Justinian's ideas on territorial expansion were less fortunate. He himself was a somber personality, autocratic by nature, and prone to grandiose conceptions. A contemporary historian named Procopius, no friend of the emperor, described him as "at once villainous and amenable; as people say colloquially, a moron. He was never truthful with anyone, but always guileful in what he said and did, yet easily hoodwinked by any who wanted to deceive him." The emperor was also heavily influenced by his wife, Theodora, of humble origin but willful and eager for power. Justinian, urged on by Theodora, did contend successfully with massive popular unrest at one point by putting 30,000 rebels to death.

Later emperors were eager to consolidate the Eastern territories alone, recognizing that grander visions were unrealistic. The Persians were defeated early in the seventh century, and the newer threat, from the Arabs, was also averted, although not without the loss of most of the Mediterranean portions of the empire south of Constantinople. Arab armies besieged the capital city, but they were repelled in part through the use of a flammable weapon called "Greek fire," a mixture of petroleum, quicklime, and sulfur. Greek fire was shot through long copper tubes and could, among other things, burn enemy ships. The result of these battles was an empire about half the size of the previous eastern half of Rome, united around its Greek and Balkan populations. Once more, carefully organized military recruitment served the embattled empire well since strong army officers were often able to control weak emperors. After a final invasion attempt, in 718 C.E., the Arabs never seriously threatened Constantinople again.

Soon after this, the Byzantine Empire began to seek new territories and cultural allies in the vast stretches of Eastern Europe. The attractions of Hellenistic culture remained strong. Many regional rulers in southeastern Europe, such as the kings of Bulgaria, admired its accomplishments and often were educated at Constantinople.

The Byzantine Empire and Its Decline

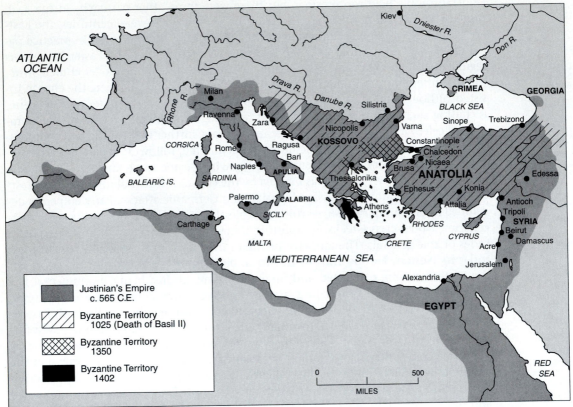

They were not easy neighbors, however, sometimes seeking territory at the empire's expense and, during the many disputes over legitimate ascendancy to the Byzantine throne, occasionally claiming imperial rule directly. A Bulgarian king in the tenth century took the title of Tsar, a Slavic version of the word "caesar." However, diplomacy, intermarriage, and, above all, war eroded regional kingdoms such as Bulgaria. In the eleventh century, the Byzantine emperor Basil II, known appropriately enough as Bulgaroktonos, or slayer of the Bulgarians, used the empire's wealth to bribe many Bulgarian nobles and generals. He defeated the Bulgarian army in 1014 and blinded as many as 15,000 captive soldiers—the sight of whom later brought on the Bulgarian king's death. Thus, Bulgaria became part of the empire, its aristocracy settling in Constantinople and merging with the leading Greek families.

Even more important than Byzantine expansion into the Balkans—into all or part of the present-day countries of Bulgaria, Yugoslavia, Romania, and Hungary—was the extension of Eastern, or Orthodox, Christianity to these regions and beyond. A major missionary effort was mounted to convert the Slavic and other peoples in the Balkans and points north to Eastern, or Orthodox, Christianity. In 864, the government sent the missionaries Cyril and Methodius to the territory that is now the

Use of "Greek fire" by a ninth-century Byzantine fleet against an invader. (The Granger Collection)

Czech Republic and Slovakia. The conversion attempt failed in this region, where Roman Catholic missionaries were more successful. But, the Byzantine missionaries did pull back into the Balkans and southern Russia, where their ability to speak the Slavic language greatly aided their efforts. They devised a written script for this language, derived from Greek letters; to this day, the Slavic alphabet is known as Cyrillic.

The Byzantine Empire entered a particularly stable period during the ninth and tenth centuries under a family dynasty from Macedonia. This dynasty managed to avoid the quarrels over succession that had beset earlier ruling families. The result was growing prosperity as well as solid political rule. The luxury of the court and its buildings steadily increased. Elaborate ceremonies and rich imperial processions created a magnificence designed to dazzle the empire's subjects. The Macedonian dynasty also extended the empire's territories in central Asia and the Balkans. Substantial trade with Asia developed, along with a thriving production of silk. Constantinople, in the northeastern corner of the Mediterranean and at the entrance to the Black Sea, was an ideal location for trade, both east to west and south to north. The empire became the hub of a new trade northward, through Russia to Scandinavia. Not only silks but also other luxury products such as gold and jewelry gave the empire a favorable trading position with less sophisticated lands. Briefly, at the end of the tenth century, the Byzantine emperor may have been the most powerful single monarch on earth, with a capital city whose rich buildings and abundant popular entertainments awed visitors from Western Europe.

It was at the end of this vigorous period that Byzantium broke fully with Western Catholicism. There had been no serious contact between the two branches of Christianity for several centuries, but neither side had cared to make a definitive statement on this fact. In 1054, however, an ambitious patriarch in Constantinople raised a host of old disputes, including the quarrel over what kind of bread to use for mass. He also attacked the Roman Catholic practice of insisting on celibacy for its priests; Eastern Orthodox priests could marry. Delegations of the two churches discussed the disputes, but this led only to renewed bitterness. The Roman pope finally excommunicated the patriarch and his followers; the patriarch, in turn, excommunicated all Roman Catholics. Thus, the split between the Roman Catholic Church and Eastern Orthodoxy, which came to include several Orthodox churches—the Greek, the Russian, and the Serbian, among others—became formal; it has endured to this day. The schism was not, despite the drama, a sudden or total break. But, there was growing estrangement between the two branches of Christianity.

Shortly thereafter, the Byzantine Empire itself entered a long period of decline. Turkish invaders began to attack the eastern borders, having already gained increasing influence in the Islamic caliphate. In the later eleventh century, Turkish troops seized almost all the Asiatic provinces of the empire, thus cutting off the most prosperous sources of tax revenue as well as the territories that had supplied most of the empire's food. The empire eked by for another four centuries, but its doom was virtually sealed. At one point, a force of crusaders from Italy and other West European territories even captured Constantinople, on the pretext that they were seeking reconquest of the Holy Land. This fourth crusade, in 1204, destroyed three-quarters of the city and also furthered a process by which Western, particularly Italian, merchants came to dominate trade with the Middle East, enforcing the economic decline of Byzantium. Then a new group of Turks, the Ottomans, invaded, closing in on Constantinople by the early fifteenth century. The Turks finally laid siege to the city in 1453, using the largest cannon ever constructed up until that point. Byzantine ef-

Saint Sophia, the great church in Constantinople built under Justinian. It was converted to a mosque by the Turks after their successful conquest. At that point, the minarets were added.

forts to obtain help from Western Europe failed, because the Western and Eastern churches could not agree on religious terms. The city fell, becoming the capital of a new Ottoman Empire. The great cathedral built by Justinian, St. Sophia, was converted to a magnificent Islamic mosque. As the Turks took control of the final remnants of the empire in the Balkans, in the eight years after 1453, the long history of Byzantium finally closed.

Elements of its heritage, however, lived on. If Byzantium achieved nothing else, its contribution to forming a new civilization among many of the Slavic peoples of Eastern Europe would alone justify its place in history. With the decline and fall of the Byzantine Empire, the focus of East European civilization passed northward, particularly to Russia.

THE EARLY RUSSIAN PHASE: KIEVAN RUS

Slavic peoples had moved into the sweeping plains of Russia and Eastern Europe during the time of the Roman Empire. They were already familiar with the use of iron, and they extended agriculture in the rich soils of what is now western Russia. Their political organization long rested in family tribes and villages; they maintained a polytheistic religion with gods for the sun, thunder, wind, and fire. Gradually, some loose regional kingdoms formed among the Slavs.

During the sixth and seventh centuries, traders from Scandinavia began to journey to the Slavic lands, moving along the great rivers of western Russia, particularly the Dnieper. Through this route they were able to reach the Byzantine Empire, and a flourishing trade developed between Scandinavia and Constantinople. The Scandinavian traders, who were militarily superior to the Slavs, gradually established some governments along their trade route. A monarchy emerged, and according to legend, Rurik, a native of Denmark, became the first king of Russia, ascending to the throne around 855. This kingdom soon established its center in the city of Kiev, which remained the capital of Russia until the twelfth century. Kievan Rus centered in what is now the Ukraine, but its contacts affected Russia proper as well. It was the Scandinavian traders, indeed, who coined the term *Russia*—possibly from a Greek word for "red," referring to the hair color of many of the northern people. The Scandinavians gradually mingled with the larger Slavic population.

Contacts between Kievan Russia and Byzantium extended steadily. Russia became one of the several societies during the period who freely imitated Byzantine civilization. Kiev, because of its central location, became a prosperous trading center, channeling goods, from the Muslim lands as well as from Byzantium, that had first passed through Constantinople. Many Russians visited Constantinople. These exchanges led to a growing knowledge of Christianity. King Vladimir I (980–1015) finally took the step of converting to Christianity, not only in his own name, but in that of all his people. Vladimir was eager to avoid the influence of Roman Catholicism, because he feared papal control as being competitive with his own power; he was also influenced by his neighbor, the king of Poland, who had recently converted to Catholicism. In addition, Russian awe at the splendor of religious services in Constantinople may have played a role. Once converted, Vladimir proceeded to organize mass baptisms for his subjects, forcing conversions by military pressure when necessary. Remnants of the old religion were incorporated into Russian Orthodoxy, as when gods of nature were made into Christian saints.

An early Russian chronicle described the conversion of Vladimir and his subjects to Christianity as follows:

> For at this time the Russes were ignorant pagans. The devil rejoiced thereat, for he did not know that his ruin was approaching. He was so eager to destroy the Christian people, yet he was expelled by the true cross even from these very lands. . . . Vladimir was visited by Bulgars of the Mohammedan faith. . . . [He] listened to them for he was fond of women and indulgence, regarding which he heard with pleasure. But . . . abstinence from pork and wine were disagreeable to him. "Drinking," said he, "is the joy of the Russes. We cannot exist without that pleasure." [Russian envoys sent to Constantinople] were astonished [by the beauty of the churches and the chanting], and in their wonder praised the Greek ceremonial. . . .
>
> [Later, Vladimir was suffering from blindness; a Byzantine bishop baptized him] and as the bishop laid his hand upon him, he straightway recovered his sight. Upon experiencing this miraculous cure, Vladimir glorified God, saying, "I have now perceived the one true God." When his followers beheld this miracle, many of them were also baptized. . . . Thereafter Vladimir sent heralds throughout the whole city to proclaim that if any inhabitant, rich or poor, did not betake himself to the river [for mass baptism] he would risk the Prince's displeasure. When the people heard these words, they wept for joy and exclaimed in their enthusiasm, "If this were not good, the Prince and his nobles would not have accepted it." . . . There was joy in heaven and upon earth to behold so many souls saved. But the devil groaned, lamenting, "Woe is me. How am I driven out hence . . . my reign in these regions is at an end."

By this point, Kievan Russia was the largest state in Europe, although it remained loosely organized. Rurik's descendants tried to avoid damaging fights over succession to the throne. The Russian kings were able to issue a formal law code, borrowed in part from Byzantium; this code among other things reduced the severity of traditional punishments in Russia and replaced personal vendettas with state-run courts.

The Kievan kingdom began to decline from about 1100 onward. Rival princes established their own regional governments. Invaders from Asia whittled away at Russian territory. The eclipse of Byzantium reduced Russia's wealth, for the kingdom had always depended heavily on the greater prosperity and sophisticated manufacturing of its southern neighbor. A new kingdom was briefly established around a city near present-day Moscow, but by 1200, Russia was weak and disunited. The final blow, in this stage of Russian history, came in 1236, when a large force of Mongols from central Asia moved through Russia, hoping to add not only this country but also the whole of Europe to their growing empire. The Mongols, or Tatars as they are called in Russian history, easily captured the major Russian cities and moved into other parts of Eastern Europe, including Poland, ending their invasions only because of political difficulties in their own homeland. For over two centuries, Russia would remain under Tatar control, although regional differences increased as both the Baltic

Pre-Russian art in the Ukraine. Scythian warriors on a silver vessel, from the fourth century B.C.E.

peoples and Ukrainians began to emancipate themselves from Mongol-dominated Russia proper.

EAST EUROPEAN POLITICAL INSTITUTIONS

The postclassical period was a formative one for what proved to be a durable East European civilization, particularly in Russia. Even the era of Mongol rule did not displace basic characteristics established in Russia in part through Byzantine influence, including, of course, Orthodox Christianity. Obviously, much was yet to happen in the development of East European civilization, as Russia came into its own again in the late 1400s. Furthermore, as in other cases of cultural diffusion during the postclassical period, the great influence Byzantium exerted on Russia did not result in complete assimilation. Nevertheless, especially in politics and culture, some customs and traditions dating from Byzantine and early Russian history still echo in East European civilization to the present day.

The Byzantine and early Russian political system emphasized authoritarian rule under an emperor or king. A key ingredient of this authoritarianism involved the state's control over the Orthodox churches. Unlike the West, where the church remained partly separate from the state, and unlike the Muslim lands, where the ulema maintained separate religious institutions, East European rulers expected to be able to regulate church organization and even intervene in doctrinal disputes. This did not lessen the intense piety of Orthodox Christianity, but it unquestionably enhanced the power of the state.

In Byzantium, that power was also exemplified by the elaborate ceremonies and luxury of the imperial court itself. The functions of government were also extensive. As a state almost constantly at war, the Byzantine Empire naturally stressed strong military organization and recruitment. It also attended to economic affairs. The state directly operated an immense silk factory and was active in regulating trade. An elaborate bureaucracy supported the various state functions. Its efficiency was sometimes questionable, as complex deals had to be struck to conduct new policies or even to make simple arrangements. In the English language, the term *byzantine* came to suggest a pattern of bargaining and bribing rather than straightforward procedures.

The early Russian monarchy, ruling over a less prosperous area, could not rival Byzantine splendor or the functions that the imperial government maintained. Yet Russian rulers, too, were attracted to luxurious ceremonies and to the idea, if not yet the reality, that the state should have widespread duties and a sweeping range of activity. The Russian bureaucracy remained small, as regional rulers owing allegiance to the king performed most administrative duties, but some features of Byzantine bureaucratic procedures would surface in Russia later on.

Russian authoritarianism was more directly enhanced by the Byzantine example through a sense of special mission. Byzantine rulers understandably claimed their imperial mantle as the heritage of the great Roman Empire. Early Russian kings acknowledged this, calling the Byzantine ruler tsar, or caesar. But when Byzantium fell, and when the Russian monarchy extricated itself from Tatar rule after 1450, Russian rulers took on the title tsar for themselves and claimed a new sense of imperial mission.

EAST EUROPEAN RELIGION AND CULTURE

The dominant feature of East European culture, in this early period, was of course Orthodox Christianity—the Greek Orthodox Church established under the patriarch of Constantinople and the Russian and other Slavic Orthodox churches formed as a result of missionary efforts and state-led conversions.

Organizationally, the Orthodox churches, under some direction by the state, established bishoprics and they assigned priests to conduct worship and maintain the faith. Many early Russian bishops were appointed by the patriarch in Constantinople, but the Russian church acquired increasing independence. Leading bishops were characteristically appointed by the king or a regional prince, one of the chief mechanisms of state control even though the bishops would then maintain considerable powers through appointments and the administration of church property and church law in their own right.

Orthodox Christianity conveyed a vivid sense of the power of God. A large number of saints, holy men and women whom the church recognized for their religious example, also commanded the attention of the faithful, becoming objects of prayer and veneration. Orthodox Christianity emphasized the importance of ritual. Churches were usually ornate, filled with the pungent smell of incense. Pictures of religious figures, including the saints, that were called icons helped direct religious

Interior of Saint Sophia, in the domed style characteristic of Eastern Orthodox churches and cathedrals. Calligraphy and other details show the church's conversion to a mosque.

devotion. Some Orthodox leaders attacked the use of icons, fearing that they would become religious objects in and of themselves, but their creation and use persisted.

In addition to ritual and the adoration of holy figures, Orthodox religion stressed Christian morality and charity toward the poor and unfortunate. Rulers as well as ordinary people were encouraged to behave ethically. Traditional practices, such as polygamy among the early Russians, gradually yielded to the Christian family ethic, which held that a man should take only one wife. Almsgiving to the poor and aid to institutions that comforted the sick received great emphasis, in Kiev as well as in Constantinople. Good works of this sort were seen as a vital component of faith and worship. The strong tradition of personal almsgiving as a means of gaining God's grace would actually delay the development of more formal charitable and welfare organizations in imperial Russia.

Orthodox Christianity did not encourage an elaborate theology—that is, an intricate examination of the nature of God and the universe. Even in Byzantium, despite the accessibility of Greek philosophical texts, no extensive tradition of rational speculation or scientific inquiry developed. The importance of faith and good works seemed to preclude this kind of activity. Certainly in Russia, which remained intellectually more backward than its Byzantine exemplar, most religious writing continued to be strictly devotional, full of praises to the saints and invocations of the power of God. Disasters, according to Russian writers, came as just expressions of the wrath of God against the wickedness of humanity; success in war involved the aid of God and the saints, in the name jointly of Russia and the Orthodox faith. Beliefs of this sort were common in Western Europe as well as in the Eastern European zone, but the absence of other kinds of philosophical and scientific inquiry proved to be a distinctively Eastern trait.

The special cultural attributes of Eastern Orthodoxy showed clearly in the monastic movement, both in the Byzantine Empire and Kievan Russia. Monasteries received large grants of property from charitable donors. Some monks, to be sure, maintained an existence as hermits, an Eastern tradition of mortification of the flesh that was not so widely adopted in the West. But, most monks lived in congregations, under rules established by St. Basil of Cappadocia in the fourth century. Orthodox monks lived their lives performing useful works, presiding over hospitals, orphanages, and homes for the aged and administering extensive charity to the poor. But, unlike Western monks, they did not devote much attention to intellectual activities, seeing a life of zealous faith and good works as sufficient service to God.

The spread of Christianity to Russia and the development of the Cyrillic alphabet facilitated the creation of Russian literature. A strong tradition of oral history existed already, although many sagas would not be recorded until later. Early Russian literature consisted primarily of chronicles by members of the clergy, who sought to record the histories of their region and what they perceived as God's work in the world. The first of these narratives dates from the twelfth century. Some secular poetry also described wars and the activities of the princes.

Byzantine art and architecture, brought to Russia along with Christianity, established a rich decorative tradition. Orthodox churches were typically built in the form of a cross, surmounted by a dome. Many early Russian churches were wooden and have not survived, but some stone buildings were also constructed. For decoration, the Byzantines and early Russians used elaborate mosaics, depicting religious figures and scenes from the lives of the saints. Some paintings were created, particularly in the form of frescoes (wall paintings), and there were abundant icons, usually picturing the heads of saints. Following the Byzantine example, a Russian tradition of icon painting arose in Kiev, along with some fine work in illuminated manuscripts; this technique featured attention to detail and miniature figures.

Music also played a vital role in Russian culture, and Russian kings and princes maintained court musicians. In Orthodox religious services, chants helped move the spirits of the faithful.

Along with the religiously oriented art and literature, a vigorous popular oral tradition continued, combining music, street entertainments, and some theater. The Russian church constantly tried to suppress these forms, because they contained pre-Christian elements, but it was not entirely successful in this regard.

Overall, this formative period in East European civilization saw the development of a powerful religious sentiment. Religion and art alike developed quite separately from the forms of West European culture during the same time period. Cultural distance would long supplement geographical distance in keeping East European religious and intellectual life on its own wavelength. During much of the period from 500 to 1400, the fact that Byzantium so clearly outshone the West in art and some branches of literature only enhanced East European indifference to available Western models. Then, the long period of Tatar rule, while it did great harm to levels of cultural life in Russia itself, added to the differentiation of East and West in Europe, for the West was spared this kind of invasion and control.

EAST EUROPEAN ECONOMY AND SOCIETY

During most of the postclassical centuries, Eastern Europe was well ahead of the West in technology and commerce; even Russia and the Balkans dominated iron manufacturing and other key processes. However, from about the twelfth century onward, the balance began to shift—as Western European dominance over Constantinople in the Mediterranean amply signified. After centuries of Mongol rule, Russia would emerge as distinctly inferior to the West in terms of levels of manufacturing and commercial skills. Thus, the leading economic achievements of this period did not create a significant legacy for East European society later on.

There were, however, some features worthy of note in the economy and social patterns of Eastern Europe at this point. In both the Byzantine Empire and Russia, a large free peasantry was the dominant social class. This contrasted with the serfdom of many West European peasants and contributed to the productive agriculture of Eastern Europe. Both Byzantium and Russia tolerated some slavery, a practice that was considerably rarer in the West at this time. Widespread slavery would persist in Russia through the seventeenth century, although the Orthodox Church tried to curtail it.

An important aristocracy developed in Eastern Europe as well. Aristocrats in Russia, called *boyars*, had less political power than their counterparts in Western Europe, except when kings were weak, the nobility exerted some authority. Along with the church, aristocrats controlled considerable land, and their hold over the land would only increase in later centuries, thus reducing the holdings of the free peasantry. Unlike the feudal pattern of Western Europe (or Japan), aristocrats did not join together in bonds of mutual loyalty.

Socially and economically, as in other ways, Eastern Europe developed according to its own dynamic; it was not simply a distant echo of Western European civilization. Even when Eastern European social trends later shifted, this characteristic would on the whole remain.

CONCLUSION: EAST EUROPEAN CIVILIZATION IN ECLIPSE

The period that had seen an early East European civilization rise and extend its borders ended with that same civilization in apparent disarray. The collapse of the Byzantine bastion and Tatar control of Russia might well have destroyed the civilization outright. It is certainly true that the active south–north trade that had linked the various centers of Eastern Europe never reoccurred. Even within Russia, commerce fell off and the levels of manufacturing deteriorated. Cultural activity withered as well. Some chronicles continued to be written, but literacy declined; many priests did not know how to read. In this respect as well as in economics, Eastern Europe would emerge after 1400 with a great deal of catching up to do.

Although Byzantine society was never restored, the decline of East European civilization overall proved only temporary. In Russia, key political traditions, major social groups including the boyar aristocracy, and religious and artistic traditions emerged virtually unscathed. In this sense, Tatar domination, although frightening to Russians, was fairly superficial in its effects. There were also some benefits, such as the introduction of a postal system and paper money. In defining a new area of civilization, and in preparing for a period of greater vigor in the future, the formative centuries of East European society played an important role.

One final point requires clarification, as it relates to both the formative East European centuries and more recent developments. Eastern European civilization initially developed within the context of large empires: first the Byzantine, then the Russian. However, the civilization, both before 1400 and since, also spilled over to other parts of Eastern Europe that never formed durable empires. Orthodox Christianity and a Cyrillic rather than Latin alphabet thus spread to Bulgaria and Serbia as well as to Russia. Yet other East European territories, such as Poland and Bohemia (now Czechoslovakia), had more contacts with the West than the East. Although Slavic, these countries used a Latin alphabet and largely adopted Roman Catholicism. Their regional kingdoms, at points quite extensive, long existed as a sometimes uncomfortable buffer between Russia and the monarchies of Western Europe. In other words, the boundary between Western and Eastern European civilizations was somewhat fluid, and it has shifted at different points over the centuries. The existence of a "border region" between Russia and the West was itself an important product of the spread of civilization northward in Europe from distinct Eastern and Western bases during the postclassical period.

SUGGESTED WEBSITE

On the Byzantine empress Theodora, see
http:/campus.northpark.edu/history/Webchron/EastEurope/Theodora.html.

SUGGESTED READINGS

For studies on the Byzantine Empire, see J. Hussey, *The Byzantine World* (1982); A. A. Vasiliev, *History of the Byzantine Empire* (1968); S. Runciman, *Byzantine Civilization* (1956); Norman Baynes and H. St. L. B. Moss, eds., *Byzantium* (1961); G. Every, *The Byzantine Patriarchate, 451–1204* (1978); D. M. Nicol, *Church and Society in the Last Centuries of Byzantium* (1979); E. Kitzinger, *Byzantine Art in the Making* (1977); and H. J. Magoulia, *Byzantine Christianity: Emperor, Church and the West* (1982). On Byzantine influence in Eastern Europe, D. Obolensky, *The Byzantine Commonwealth: Eastern Europe, 500–1453* (1971), is an excellent analysis. See also S. Runciman, *A History of the First Bulgarian Empire* (1930). On Russian history, the best survey is Nicholas Riasanovsky, *A History of Russia,* 5th ed. (1993); it also includes a good bibliography. See also J. H. Billington, *The Icon and the Axe: An Interpretive History of Russian Culture* (1966).

10

Western Civilization: The Middle Ages

Levels of political, economic, and cultural activity were rather low in Western Europe at the beginning of the postclassical era. Gradually, however, a stronger society emerged due to many factors. It recaptured selected features of the Greco-Roman past; actively imitated patterns in Islam and Byzantium and adopted Asian technologies; and developed its own innovations in Europe itself, like the elaboration of feudal politics. Seeing how a more complex society developed, and how the three themes of a revived tradition, imitation, and innovation commingled, will help us identify the major features of this expanding area of civilization. In what respects did Western Europe remain at a disadvantage in relationship to the leading centers of civilization in Asia and North Africa? In what sense did some of the institutions of postclassical Europe decline by about 1300, and why was this compatible with new initiatives in Europe's relationship with the wider world?

COMBINING THE OLD, THE NEW, AND THE BORROWED

In contrast to Eastern Europe, civilization declined markedly in Western Europe after Rome's fall. The deterioration of political forms, trade, city life, and intellectual endeavor reduced the achievements of classical Mediterranean civilization to only a faint memory. Between 700 and 1400 C.E., however, Western Europe revived, creating new institutions and styles to accompany the selective adoption of earlier Roman and Greek traditions. During most of this period, the area remained backward by standards of the great civilizations of the world. But, with the advantage of hindsight, we see that Western civilization was not only taking shape, it was also beginning to develop growing dynamism, particularly from the eleventh century onward.

Like other societies on the borders of the former classical world—Japan, Russia, the Sudanic kingdoms, and Southeast Asia—Western Europe borrowed actively during the postclassical period, although in ways that preserved a distinctive identity. There was no single source for imitation in this case, however, as West Europeans looked to Islam and Byzantium as well as the earlier traditions of Greece and Rome for guidance. The availability of several models may have been an advantage. Certainly, it helped open West Europeans to the importance of maintaining international contacts, even as they experienced fierce rivalries with many neighboring civilizations. In certain respects, however, Western Europe resembled other borrowing societies, not only in its eagerness to imitate but also in its relatively loose political framework and the limitations (compared to the most advanced centers) on urban and manufacturing forms.

The postclassical period in Western Europe thus saw the establishment of a largely new civilization and its extension northward. During much of the time, the leading centers of activity were in France, the Low Countries, Germany, and England—areas at best peripheral to civilization in Roman days. Spain lay in Muslim hands; Italy, although the center of the Catholic Church and usually active in trade, was somewhat outside the Western mainstream in other respects. The usual label for this era of Western history is *medieval,* or the *Middle Ages.* The term is, in some sense, misleading; it suggests a way station between classical times and the more modern versions of Western civilization that would take shape only after 1300 or 1400. Rather than being "in between" two grander eras, the Middle Ages, in fact, witnessed the development of a largely new civilization and its presence in parts of Europe that had previously been isolated. But, it is true that some of the institutions and values developed in the Middle Ages were unique to the period. Thus, in viewing these centuries as formative for a new Western civilization, we must also distinguish between important but peculiar features of medieval life, on the one hand, and, on the other, significant customs and traditions created by medieval people that would shape Western society even in later periods of development.

EARLY PATTERNS IN WESTERN CIVILIZATION

From 500 to almost 1000, major events in Western Europe were few and far between. Effective political organization was largely local, although Germanic kings ruled some territories such as a portion of present-day France. Most people lived on self-sufficient agricultural estates called "manors." They received some protection from their landlords, including the administration of justice, and in return they were obligated to turn over part of the goods they produced and to remain on the land. The manorial system had originated in the later Roman Empire; it was strengthened by the decline of trade and the lack of larger political structures.

Landlords themselves formed some alliances. Greater lords provided protection and aid to lesser lords, called "vassals"; vassals, in turn, owed their lords military service, some goods or payments, and advice. This system formed the beginnings of the European version of feudalism. However, early feudalism did not prevent a great deal of disorder. Many local wars occurred. In addition, Western Europe was often raided by Viking pirates from Scandinavia and other groups. Because of the disarray, poverty, and general educational decline from the late Roman Empire onward, few cultural developments of any note took place. The scattered intellectuals who existed, all members of the clergy, were busy trying to preserve and understand older Christian and classical learning.

During these centuries, the Catholic Church provided the only extensive example of solid organization. Roman popes built a careful hierarchy through their control over local bishops. The popes did not always appoint the bishops, for monarchs and local lords often claimed this right, but they did nonetheless issue directives and receive important information. The popes also regulated doctrine, successfully undermining several heresies that threatened a unified Christian faith. Moreover, they sponsored extensive missionary activity. Papal missionaries converted the English and Irish to Christianity. They brought the religion to northern and eastern Germany, beyond the borders of the previous Roman Empire, and ultimately, by the tenth century, to Scandinavia. They were active, of course, in the border regions of Eastern Europe, sometimes competing directly with Orthodox missionaries. The solid structure of the church, which gave it a vital organizational edge over what secular government there was in the West, and the spread of Christianity constituted significant developments in the history of the West. Christian values increasingly became the essential cement of the newly developed civilization that covered virtually the whole of Western Europe.

One significant political development occurred during these difficult centuries, sometimes called the Dark Ages. The royal house of a Germanic people, the Franks, grew in strength during the eighth century. A new family, the Carolingians, assumed the monarchy of these people, which was based in northern France, Belgium, and western Germany. One founder of the Carolingian line—Charles Martel, or Charles the Hammer—was responsible for defeating the Muslims in the Battle of Tours in 732. This defeat helped confine the Muslims to Spain and, along with the Byzantine defeat of the Arabs during the same period, preserved Europe for Christianity.

A later ruler in this same royal line, Charles the Great, known as Charlemagne, established a substantial empire in France, the Low Countries, and Germany around the year 800. Briefly, it looked as if a new Roman Empire might revive in the West, and indeed the term Holy Roman Empire ("Holy" denoted that it was firmly Christian) was later used by Charlemagne's successors in Germany. Charlemagne helped to restore some church-based education in Western Europe, and the level of intellectual activity began a slow recovery, in part due to these efforts. When Charlemagne died in 814, however, his empire did not survive him. Rather, it was split into three geographic sectors—the outlines of modern France, Germany, and a middle strip consisting of the Low Countries, Switzerland, and northern Italy. Several of Charlemagne's successors, with nicknames like "the Bald" or "the Fat," were not models of political dynamism even in their regional kingdoms.

From this point onward, the essential political history of Western Europe consisted of the gradual emergence of national monarchies. This was to be a civilization with strong cultural unity, initially centered in Catholic Christianity, but with pronounced political division.

The royal houses of several lands gained new power soon after Charlemagne's empire split. At first, the emperors who reigned over Germany and northern Italy were in the strongest position. It was they who claimed the title Holy Roman Emperor, beginning around the twelfth century. By this time, however, their rule had become increasingly shallow, precisely because they relied too much on their imperial claims and did not build a solid monarchy from regional foundations. The future lay elsewhere, with the rise of monarchies in individual states—states that ultimately would become nations.

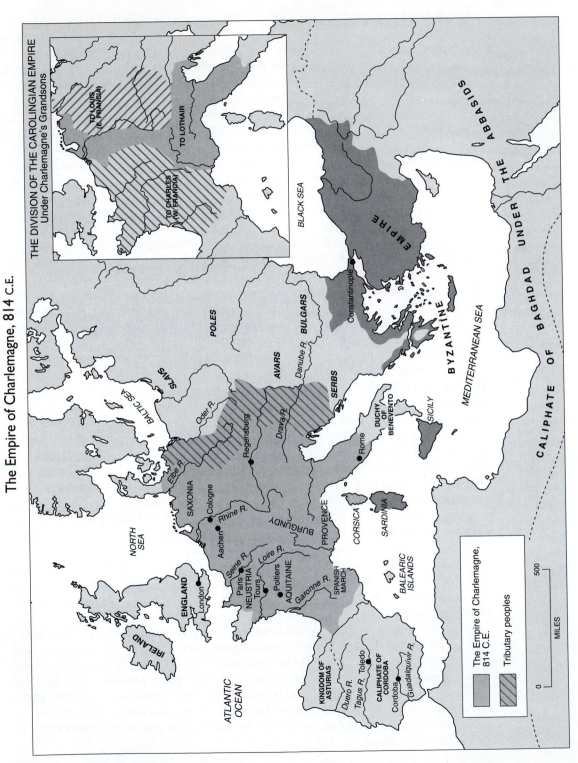

The Empire of Charlemagne, 814 C.E.

THE DIVISION OF THE CAROLINGIAN EMPIRE
Under Charlemagne's Grandsons

TO LOUIS
(E. FRANCIA)

TO LOTHAIR

TO CHARLES
(W. FRANCIA)

BLACK SEA

ATLANTIC
OCEAN

IRELAND

ENGLAND
London

NORTH
SEA

SLAVS

BALTIC SEA

POLES

Elbe R.

Oder R.

SAXONIA
Cologne
Rhine R.
Aachen
Seine R.
Paris
NEUSTRIA
Tours
Poitiers
AQUITAINE
Garonne R.
Loire R.
BURGUNDY
PROVENCE
SPANISH
MARCH

AVARS
Regensburg
Drava R.

Danube R.

BULGARS

SERBS

Constantinople

BYZANTINE
EMPIRE

Rome
DUCHY
OF
BENEVENTO

CORSICA

SARDINIA

SICILY

MEDITERRANEAN SEA

BALEARIC
ISLANDS

CALIPHATE OF BAGHDAD UNDER THE ABBASIDS

KINGDOM OF
ASTURIAS
Duero R.
Tagus R. Toledo
CALIPHATE OF
CORDOBA
Cordoba
Guadalquivir R.

The Empire of Charlemagne,
814 C.E.

Tributary peoples

MILES
0   500

From the 900s onward, the kings of France began to assume growing authority. They amassed territory, around their base in Paris, directly under their control; they formed feudal alliances with great lords in other parts of France, creating what is called a feudal monarchy. Regional monarchies began to form in Spain as Christian lords were able to push back the Muslims, from 1018 onward, but a national royal house was formed only in the fifteenth century with the marriage of Ferdinand and Isabella. In England, an invasion from the French province of Normandy occurred in 1066. The Duke of Normandy, who was of Viking descent, had already built a strong feudal domain in northwestern France, and he now extended this system to England. William the Conqueror and his successors thus tied the great lords of England to the royal court by bonds of feudal loyalty, giving them estates in return for their military service.

The development of stronger feudal units and some powerful monarchies increased the orderliness of European life, starting in the tenth century. Invasions by the Vikings ceased; both trade and intellectual pursuits began to revive rapidly. The growth in the West European population reflected the new stability and encouraged improvements in agriculture and commerce. City life perked up gradually, as metropolitan areas became the centers for economic and cultural activity. Medieval Europe blossomed, and the centuries between 1000 and 1300 form the high point of this early version of Western civilization. It was during this period that the West began to show its muscle beyond its borders, as a series of Crusades set out, from 1096 until the early fourteenth century, to reconquer and defend the Holy Land from the Muslims. The Crusades had only limited success in achieving their explicit goal, as a Kingdom of Jerusalem was established for about two centuries; even this success did not demonstrate real Western superiority against Muslim civilization, for the West remained backward. But as an expression of a combination of religious zeal—the Crusades were initiated by the pope—and growing commercial and military vigor on the part of the knights and merchants who organized the largest efforts, the Crusades unquestionably showed the distinctive spirit of the Western Middle Ages at their height. They also helped open the West to new cultural and economic influences from the Middle East, a major spur to further change.

As medieval society developed, the Catholic Church went through several periods of decline and renewal. At times, church officials and the leading monastic groups became preoccupied with their holdings in land and their political interests. Reform-minded popes, such as Gregory VII (1073–1085), sought to purify the church more generally. They began to insist that all priests remain unmarried, to separate the priesthood from the ordinary world of the flesh. Gregory also endeavored to free the church from any vestige of state control. He quarreled vigorously with the Holy Roman Emperor, Henry IV, over the practice of state appointment, or investiture, of bishops in Germany. Ultimately, by excommunicating the emperor from the church, Gregory won his point. Gregory and several later popes made clear their beliefs that the church was to be not only free from state interference, but also superior to the state in its function as the direct communicator of God's word. These claims were not entirely accurate, as governments influenced religious affairs still, but they were not altogether untrue. It was this sort of affirmation, indeed, that enabled the church to inspire kings and warriors to fight in the Crusades and also to war against several heresies that arose during the same centuries.

Even in the centuries of its greatest strength, the church was by no means the only institution of importance during the High Middle Ages. As feudal monarchs extended their power, particularly in France and England, they became increasingly involved in the administration of justice and, through taxation, in the economic affairs of their subjects. Growing military strength made it possible for the royal families to assert their power against the claims of the church. Early in the fourteenth century, the French king actually imprisoned the pope in a dispute over taxation rights. Finally, the raising of armies by the national monarchs led to the beginning of a long series of wars in Europe. The chief rivals were the kings of France and England. The English throne claimed large sections of French territory, from the days when they also had been dukes of Normandy; French kings steadily pressed against these territories. This rivalry evolved during the fourteenth and fifteenth centuries into a long, intermittent struggle called the Hundred Years' War, in which France ultimately triumphed. From this point onward, no century was to pass without major warfare among the leading nations of Western Europe.

MEDIEVAL POLITICAL INSTITUTIONS

The characteristic political structure of the High Middle Ages, and the one of greatest importance for the later history of Western civilization, was the feudal monarchy. This was not, of course, the only political form in existence. Territories like Germany and Italy remained more loosely organized, despite the grandiose claims of the Holy Roman Emperors. Feudal monarchy itself was a gradual development, not a carefully planned institution. It reflected a balance between the principles of feudalism pure and simple and the growing claims of the leading royal families. The result was an effective but distinctly limited government.

The monarchies of France, England, and ultimately Spain acquired several key functions during and after the eleventh century, in addition to a general if vague recognition that kings and queens deserved some special loyalty. Medieval royal families, from the tenth and eleventh centuries onward, used the lands under their direct control to pay for armies and a small central bureaucracy. Often, they chose urban business or professional people to serve in this bureaucracy, partly because such people had expertise in financial matters and partly because, unlike the aristocracy, they would owe allegiance to the crown alone. French and English monarchs began to introduce bureaucratic specialties, so that some of their ministers would handle justice, others finance, still others military matters. They found ways to send centrally appointed emissaries to the provinces, to supervise tax collection and the administration of justice. In England, from the Norman Conquest onward, kings appointed local sheriffs to oversee the administration of justice. None of these activities gave the monarchs extensive contacts with ordinary subjects; for most people, effective governments were still local. But once the principle of central control was established, a steady growth of state-sponsored rule followed. By the end of the Middle Ages, monarchs were gaining the right to tax their subjects directly. And, they were beginning to recruit professional armies, instead of relying solely on an aristocratic cavalry, whose loyalties depended on feudal bonds or alliances. Several medieval kings also

HISTORY DEBATE

Western Civilization

For some time, Americans have talked about "Western civilization." The concept of the West was actively used in the Cold War with the Soviet Union, yet it is hard to define. We have seen that the classical Mediterranean did not directly identify a "Western" civilization, and this classical heritage was used most selectively by postclassical Western Europe. Further, the consistent absence of political unity in Western Europe complicates any definition of common structures.

West Europeans could not have identified Western civilization in the postclassical period, but they would have recognized the concept of Christendom, along with some difference between their version of this religion and that of Eastern Europe. The first definition of this civilization was primarily religious, although artistic forms associated with religion also figured in this definition. Regional cultures varied, of course, and there was no linguistic unity, but cultural developments in one area—for example, the creation of universities, which started in Italy—surfaced elsewhere fairly quickly. Supplementing culture were some reasonably common social structures—like manors and guilds—and trade patterns that increasingly joined northern and much of southern Europe. The resulting civilization was by no means as coherent as Chinese civilization; many of its members detested each other, like the English and French who were often in conflict and sometimes engaged in "name-calling" (the English were "les goddams," because they swore so much, and the French were "frogs" because of what they ate). Until very recently, Europeans thought in terms of distinctive national histories, not European ones. But, it is possible to define some common features that differed from those of neighboring civilizations. Even as the civilization began to change, late in the postclassical period, it preserved some common directions. Debate continues about the balance between the Western and more purely national features.

gained a solid reputation as law givers, which allowed the gradual centralization of legal codes and court systems. Rediscovery of Roman law, in countries like France, encouraged this centralization effort.

However, feudal monarchy was a delicately balanced institution, of which the central government formed only one of the key ingredients. The power of the church served to check royal ambitions. As we have seen, the church could often win in a clash with the state by excommunicating rulers and thus threatening to turn the loyalties of the population against them. Although the church entered a period of decline at the end of the Middle Ages, the principle was rather clearly established, as part of feudal monarchy, that there were areas of belief and morality that were not open to manipulation by the state.

The second limitation on the royal families came from the traditions of feudalism, and from the landed aristocracy as a powerful class. Aristocrats tended to resist too much monarchical control in the West. And, they had the strength to make their objections heard, for these aristocrats, even when they were vassals of the king, had their own economic base and their own military force—sometimes, in the case of certain powerful nobles, an army greater than that of the king. The growth of the monarchy reduced aristocratic power, but this led to new limits on kings. In 1215, an unpopular English king, John, faced opposition to his taxation measures from an alliance of nobles, townspeople, and church officials. Defeated in battle, John was forced to sign the Great Charter, or Magna Carta, which confirmed basically feudal rights against monarchical claims. John promised to observe restraint in his dealings with the nobles and the church. The few references to the general rights of the English people against the state that were included in the Magna Carta largely served to show where the feudal concept of mutual limits and obligations between rulers and the ruled could later lead.

This same feudal balance led, late in the thirteenth century, to the creation of parliaments, as bodies representing not individual voters but privileged groups such as the nobles and the church. The first full English parliament convened in 1265, with the House of Lords representing the nobles and the church hierarchy and the Commons made up of elected representatives from wealthy citizens of the towns. The parliament institutionalized the feudal principle that monarchs should consult with their vassals. In particular, parliaments gained the right to rule on any proposed changes in taxation; through this power, they could also advise the crown on other policy issues. While the parliamentary tradition became strongest in England, similar institutions arose in France, Spain, and several of the regional governments in Germany. Other countries, as we have seen, used councils in government. However, it was Western feudalism alone that led to the more formal institutions of parliament.

Medieval government was not modern government. People had rights according to the estate into which they were born; there was no general concept of citizenship. Thus, parliaments represented only a minority, and even this minority only in terms of three or four estates (nobles, clergy, urban merchants, sometimes wealthy peasants), not some generalized group of voters. But by creating a concept of limited government and some hint of representative institutions, Western feudal monarchy produced the beginnings of a distinctive political tradition. This tradition differed from the political results of Japanese feudalism discussed in the next chapter, which emphasized group loyalty more than checks on a central power. Nonetheless, remnants of medieval traditions, embodied in institutions like parliaments and ideas like the separation between God's authority and state power, would define a basic thread in the Western political process even in the later twentieth century.

One other feature of medieval politics deserves note: its unusual focus on war. Although feudal monarchies created increasing internal order within individual countries, the idea of the state as an institution for warfare remained strong. Given the failure to develop any lasting political unity in Europe, this penchant ensured recurrent conflict within Western civilization. It is true that during the Middle Ages warfare continued to be a fairly limited activity. The basic military force was composed of the landed nobility, who alone could afford horses, weapons, and armor and the training needed for skill in battle. However, this interest in war sparked attention in improved weaponry. During the Hundred Years' War, states learned to use archery and, particularly, the longbow, which opened the way to larger armies and began to limit the effectiveness of the aristocratic cavalry. At about the same time, the introduction of gunpowder stimulated still more portentous developments, as Europeans by the fourteenth century improved cannons so they could project fire-power over considerable distances. Now, not only cavalry but also the fortified castles of the aristocracy became increasingly vulnerable. Warfare thus stimulated techno-logical advances in Western society, which ultimately enhanced the power of the state and increased the means available for destruction. The inclination to rely on the battlefield to settle disputes also proved a durable part of the Western political tradition. It contrasted particularly with the lower level of interest of civilizations like China in matters of military goals and technologies.

MEDIEVAL RELIGION AND CULTURE

As in Eastern Europe and Islam during these centuries, religion was the focal point of medieval cultural life. But, Western Christianity spawned a number of cultural ten-sions and increasingly diverse intellectual and artistic movements, so that a substan-tial array of interests describes the philosophy and literature of the High Middle Ages.

During the centuries before about 1000, a small number of theologians contin-ued the efforts of preserving and interpreting past wisdom, particularly the writings of church fathers like Augustine, as well as some non-Christian Latin authors. During Charlemagne's time, a favorite practice was to gather quotations from ancient writers around key subjects. Efforts of this sort showed little creativity, but they gradually produced a fuller understanding of past thought and improvements in Latin writing style and in organizing philosophical materials. Interest in the classical principles of rhetoric and, particularly, logic reflected the concern for coherent organization; Aris-totle, known to the Middle Ages as *the* Philosopher, was valued because of his clear exposition of rational thought.

From 1000 onward, a series of outstanding clerics advanced the logical exposi-tion of philosophy and theology to new levels. They stressed the importance of ab-solute faith in God's word, but they believed that human reason could move mankind toward an understanding of some aspects of religion and the natural order as well. Thus, according to several theologians, it was possible to prove the existence of God, to use logic to help explain the Trinity, and to develop certain moral princi-ples. A concomitant interest in collecting Roman law and codifying church law (called "canon law") also promoted the use of careful logical exposition. Fascination with logic led some intellectuals to a certain zeal in pointing out inconsistencies in past wisdom, even in the writings of church fathers. In the twelfth century, Peter Abelard, in Paris, wrote a treatise called *Yes and No,* in which he highlighted a num-ber of logical contradictions in established doctrine.

This logical-rationalist current in Western philosophy was hardly unopposed. Quite apart from the fact that most ordinary Christians knew nothing of these de-bates, seeing their religion as a matter of beliefs not to be questioned, appointed sacraments, and comforting rituals that would remove sin and promote salvation, many church leaders emphasized the role of faith alone. A powerful monk, St. Bernard of Clairvaux, challenged Abelard and had him condemned. Bernard was an intellectual of a different sort, who stressed the importance of a mystical union with God, which was attainable even on this earth in brief moments of blissful enlightenment, rather than rationalist endeavor.

However, the thirst to assimilate rational philosophy with Christian faith was a dominant medieval theme. By the twelfth century, the zeal for knowledge produced several distinctive results. First, a number of universities were founded in Italy and France, then in England and Germany. Some specialized in law or medicine, but the most prestigious centers, like those in Paris and Oxford, emphasized philosophy and theology. Degrees granted to aspiring scholars, ranging from the bachelor's to the doctorate, originated the system still in use today in Western universities. These schools were under church control, but already they produced great intellectual diversity as well as a serious quest for knowledge. Another key development was the translation of newly discovered texts from Greek and Arabic philosophy and science. Translators in Spain and Constantinople could barely keep up with the growing Western demand to discover everything there was to know. It was in culture that Western Europe ranked as one of the great imitative societies of the postclassical period.

With much fuller knowledge of Aristotelian and Hellenistic science, plus the work of Arab rationalists like Ibn-Rushd (Averroës), Western philosopher-theologians in the thirteenth century proceeded to the final great synthesis of medieval learning. The leading figure was Thomas Aquinas, an Italian-born monk who taught at the University of Paris. Aquinas maintained the basic belief that faith came first, but he greatly expanded the role of reason. Through reason alone, humans could know much of the natural order, moral law, and the nature of God. Thomas had complete confidence that all essential knowledge could be coherently organized, and he produced a number of treatises, called *Summas*, that disposed, through careful logic, of all possible objections to truth as revealed by reason and faith alike. Here was a masterful demonstration of medieval confidence in the fundamental orderliness of not only learning but also God's creation. Essentially, this work restated in Christian terms Greek efforts to seek a rationality in nature that would correspond to the rational capacities of the human mind.

Medieval philosophy did not encourage a great deal of new scientific work. The emphasis on mastering past learning and organizing it logically led to perhaps an overemphasis on previous discoveries, rather than much new empirical research. However, toward the end of the thirteenth century, a current of practical science developed. At Oxford, members of the clergy like Roger Bacon performed experimental work with optics, pursuing research earlier done by Muslim scholars. An important by-product of this interest was the invention of eyeglasses, an indispensable aid to many Western (and other) scholars ever since. During the fourteenth and fifteenth centuries, experimentalists also advanced knowledge in chemistry and astronomy. This early work set the stage for the flourishing of Western science later on.

Like most philosophy, medieval art and architecture were intended to serve the glory of God. Western painters used religious subjects almost exclusively. Painting mainly on wooden panels, artists in most parts of Western Europe depicted Christ's birth and suffering and the lives of the saints using stiff, stylized figures. By the four-

Adoration of the Magi: twelfth-century French enamel. (The Granger Collection)

teenth and fifteenth centuries, artists improved their ability to render natural scenes realistically and portrayed a host of images of medieval daily life as backdrops to their religious subjects. Designs and scenes in stained glass windows for churches were another important form of artistic expression.

Medieval architecture initially followed Roman models, particularly in church building, by utilizing rectangular (Romanesque) style, sometimes surmounted by domes. During the eleventh century, however, a new style termed Gothic took hold, which was far more original (although it benefited from the knowledge of Muslim arches). Gothic architects, taking advantage of growing engineering expertise, built soaring church spires and massive, arched windows. Although their work focused on the creation of large churches and great cathedrals, some Gothic architects did create civic buildings and palaces, using the same design motifs. The Gothic was one of the three main architectural styles ever developed in Western culture (the others being the earlier classical and the later modern). Music for church use also flourished during the Middle Ages.

Medieval literature reflected strong religious interests. Most Latin writing dealt with points of philosophy, law, or political theory. There was little concern with style for its own sake. But alongside writing in Latin came the development of a growing literature in the spoken languages, or vernaculars, of Western Europe. A number of

Gothic architecture and religious statues: entrance to Chartres cathedral in France.

oral sagas were written down, dealing with the deeds of great knights and mythic figures from the past. From this tradition evolved the first known writing in early English, *Beowulf,* and in French, the *Song of Roland.* Late in the Middle Ages, a number of writers created adventure stories, comic tales, and poetry in the vernacular tongues, such as Chaucer's *Canterbury Tales.* Much of this work, and also a number of plays written for performance in the growing cities, reflected a tension between Christian values and a desire to portray the harshness of life on this earth. Chaucer's narrative in its colorful language thus shows a willingness to poke fun at the hypocrisy of many Christians, as well as an ability to capture some of the tragedies of human existence. In France, a long poem called the *Story of the Rose* wove together various kinds of sexual imagery, while the poet Villon wrote, in largely secular terms, of the terror and poignancy of death. Finally, again in vernacular language, a series of courtly poets (troubadours), based primarily in southern France, wrote hymns to the love that could flourish between men and women. Although such verses stressed platonic devotion, rather than sexual love, and paid homage to courtly ceremonies and polite behavior, the troubadours' concern with love was the first sign of the new value this emotional experience had taken on in the Western tradition.

Medieval intellectual and artistic life, in sum, created a host of important themes. Religion served as the centerpiece, but it did not curtail a growing range of interests from science to romantic poetry. Medieval culture was a rich intellectual achievement in its own right. It also set in motion a series of developments—in rationalist philosophy, science, artistic representations of nature, and vernacular literature—that would serve as building blocks for later Western thought and art.

ECONOMY AND SOCIETY

Medieval thinkers liked to picture their society in rather simple terms, not unlike the metaphors of classical India. Borrowing from classical Greek and Roman concepts, John of Salisbury, an English churchman, likened society to the human body. Peasants were the feet, without which society could not function. Knightly warriors were the hands, to defend. Priests provided heart and soul, the king the head. Each part was essential, but each fit into a clear hierarchy in which subordinates were properly ruled by their superiors.

In fact, medieval society was far more complicated, and it evolved toward ever-greater complexity. In the early Middle Ages, and to some extent throughout the period, the key social relationship, as far as most people were concerned, was that between landlord and serf. Just as feudal relationships described contacts among the landlords, so manorialism described contacts between those who ruled the landed estates and those who performed the manual labor of farming. There were a few free farmers in the early Middle Ages, but most peasants were serfs, clustered in villages on the lords' estates. From the lords, the peasant-serfs received some military and judicial protection, and some aid, where possible, during periods of poor harvest. To the lords, they owed a portion of their harvests and considerable work service. Serfs were not free to leave their land, but they were not outright slaves, because in normal circumstances they could not be evicted from their land. Most land was, in this sense, jointly owned, with both the serf and lord having some control over it—although the lords and church owned some estates outright, which they worked mainly through the serfs' labor.

This agricultural society was quite primitive. Tools were simple. Peasants had to leave a third or more of their land fallow each year, to replenish the soil. Most estates produced mainly for their own subsistence, and there was little market activity.

By the ninth and tenth centuries, partly because of the restoration of order, the agricultural economy began to improve. New techniques developed through contacts with Eastern Europe and Asia. A heavier plow was devised, the moldboard, which made it much easier to till the heavy soils of Europe. The horse collar, first invented in Asia but now finally introduced in the West, allowed for the use of horses as well as oxen to pull plows and carts. Advances of this sort increased agricultural productivity and promoted a steady growth of population, which lasted until the fourteenth century. This rising population, in turn, encouraged the settlement of new lands in various parts of Europe, as forests were cleared and swamps drained. To attract farmers to the new lands, the conditions of serfdom were relaxed. There was great variety in this process; in many parts of Western Europe, a strict manorial system lasted well beyond the Middle Ages. However, by the twelfth and thirteenth centuries, many peasants retained very few obligations to their lords, often little more than rent (which also reflected the fact that many peasants were now able to directly

Peasants and lords work near a fictional late-medieval castle in the Loire valley of France. (Illuminated manuscript from the *Très Riches Heures du duc de Berry*.)

sell part of their produce to the market). Some peasants owned their land outright and could sell it if they wished. Compared to East European and most Asian civilizations by 1400, the European peasantry was unusually free, and although its agricultural techniques were not as advanced as those in some areas, such as East Asia, there had nonetheless been considerable improvement in this regard.

Shifts in agriculture promoted and reflected changes in commerce. With rising agricultural productivity, from about 1000 onward, a minority of people were able to concentrate on other economic activities. In parts of Italy, the Low Countries, England, and northern Germany, about 20 percent of the population could now be supported away from the farms. This meant new possibilities for trade and for the expansion of cities. New commercial opportunities, in turn, inspired some peasants and landlords to turn more fully to the market, rather than concentrate on subsistence agriculture. The use of money spread steadily, to the dismay of many Christian moralists and many ordinary people who preferred the more direct, personal methods of traditional society.

Rising trade took a number of forms. There were exchanges between Western Europe and other parts of the known world. Western Europe became an active part of the world network, which allowed cultural borrowings from Byzantium and Islam and stimulated commerce as well. Wealthy Europeans developed a taste for some of the spices and luxury goods of Asia; the Crusades played a role in bringing these products to wider attention. A Mediterranean trade redeveloped, mainly in the hands of Italian merchants dealing with Arab traders, in which European cloth and some other products were exchanged for the higher-quality goods of the East. Commerce within Europe involved exchanges of timber and grain from the north for cloth and metal products manufactured in Italy and the Low Countries. England, at first an exporter of raw wool, developed some manufactured goods for exchange by the later Middle Ages. Huge fairs, in northern France and the Low Countries, brought together merchants from various parts of Europe. Commercial alliances developed. Cities in northern Germany and southern Scandinavia united in the Hanseatic League to encourage trade. Banking facilities spread, particularly through the efforts of the Italians. It thus became possible to organize commercial transactions throughout much of Western Europe. Bankers, including a number of Jewish businessmen, were valued for their service in lending money to monarchs and to the papacy. The growth of trade and banking in the Middle Ages served as the genesis of capitalism in Western civilization. The greater Italian and German bankers, the long-distance merchants of the Hanseatic cities, were clearly capitalistic in their willingness to invest considerable sums of money in trading ventures with the expectation of substantial profit.

This was not, by world standards, a totally unprecedented merchant spirit. European traders were still less venturesome and less wealthy than some of their Muslim counterparts. Nor was Western society any more tolerant of merchants than Muslim or Indian societies. But, Western commercial endeavors were clearly gaining in dynamism. Because Western governments were weak, with few economic functions, merchants had a freer hand than in many other civilizations. Many of the growing cities, in particular, were ruled by commercial leagues. Monarchs liked to encourage the cities as a counterbalance to the power of the landed aristocracy, and in the later

Middle Ages and beyond, traders and kings were typically allied. But aside from taxing merchants and using them as sources of loans, royal governments did not interfere extensively with trading activities. Merchants even developed their own codes of commercial law, administered by city courts. Thus, the rising merchant class, although not unusual in strength or its adventurous spirit, was staking out an unusually powerful and independent role in European society. Christian concerns about profit-making began to decline.

However, capitalism was not yet typical of the Western economy. Most peasants and landlords had not become enmeshed in a market system. In the cities, the dominant economic ethic stressed group protection, not unlimited profit seeking. The characteristic institution was not the international trading firm, but the merchant or artisan guild. These organizations, new in Western Europe but similar to guilds in various parts of Asia, stressed security and mutual control. Merchant guilds thus sought to ensure all members a share in any endeavor. If a ship docked with a cargo of wool, the clothiers' guild of the city insisted that all members participate in the purchase of that commodity, so no one member would monopolize the ensuing profits. Artisan guilds were composed of the people in the cities who actually made cloth, bread, jewelry, or furniture. These guilds tried to limit membership, so that all members would be assured of work. They regulated apprenticeships to guarantee good training, but also to make sure that no member would employ too many apprentices and thus garner undue wealth. They discouraged new methods, again because security and general equality, not maximum individual profit, was the goal. Guilds also tried to guarantee good workmanship, so that consumers would not have to worry about shoddy quality on the part of some unscrupulous profit seeker. Guilds played an important political and social role in the cities, ensuring their members of recognized status and, often, a voice in city government. Their statutes were, in turn, upheld by municipal law and often backed by the royal government as well.

Despite the traditionalism and security-mindedness of the guilds, manufacturing as well as commercial methods did improve in medieval Europe. Western Europe was not yet as advanced as Asia in ironmaking or textile manufacture, but it was beginning to catch up. In a few areas such as clockmaking—which reflected both sophisticated technology and an interest in precise time—and heavy metallurgical casting for monumental church bells, European artisans, had in fact, forged a world lead. Furthermore, some manufacturing spilled beyond the bounds of guild control. Particularly in the Low Countries and parts of Italy, groups of workers were employed by capitalists to produce for a wide market, while working with simple equipment in their homes.

The plain fact was that, by the later Middle Ages, Western Europe's economy and society embraced a number of contradictory groups and principles. Commercial and capitalist elements coexisted alongside the slower pace of economic life in the countryside and even the dominant group protectionism of most urban guilds. Most people remained peasants, but a minority had escaped to the cities, where they found more excitement, although also increased danger and higher rates of disease. A few prosperous capitalists flourished, but most people operated according to quite different economic values. At the same time, the conditions of serfdom were easing for many in rural life. This was not, in sum, either a static society or an early model of a modern commercial society. It simply had its own flavor and its own tensions—the fruit of several centuries of economic and social change.

WOMEN AND FAMILY LIFE

The increasing complexity of medieval social and economic life may have had one final effect that is familiar from patterns in other agricultural societies: setting new limits on the conditions of women. Women's work remained, of course, vital in most families. Christian emphasis on the equality of all souls and the practical importance of monastic groups organized for women, offering some an alternative to marriage, continued to lend distinctive features to women's lives in Western society. The popular veneration of Mary and other female religious figures gave women real cultural prestige, counterbalancing the Biblical emphasis on Eve as the source of human sin. In some respects, women in the West had higher status than their sisters under Islam: they were less segregated at religious services (although they could not lead them) and less confined to the household. Still, women's effective voice in the family may have declined during the Middle Ages. Urban women often played important roles in local commerce and even operated some craft guilds, but they found themselves increasingly constrained by male-dominated organizations. By the late Middle Ages, a literature arose that stressed women's subordinate role to men, listing supplemental household tasks and extolling docile behaviors as women's distinct destiny. Patriarchal structures seemed to be taking deeper root.

TENSIONS IN THE LATER MIDDLE AGES

Medieval society reached its apogee in the twelfth and thirteenth centuries. Beginning about 1300 and continuing for about 150 years, it exhibited a number of symptoms of stagnation and decline. This was not a collapse of Western civilization or even a deterioration of the long-term sort that began to affect Muslim civilization during the same period. Rather, Western Europe encountered a number of short-term difficulties. These, in turn, prompted the society to shed part of its medieval skin, snakelike, only to emerge with renewed dynamism in somewhat different garb toward the middle of the fifteenth century.

Item. By the early 1300s, medieval population had clearly surpassed the limits of the existing economy to sustain. Growing food crises caused widespread starvation through severe periodic famines. Then massive plague, sweeping through city and countryside alike, took its deadly toll. The Black Death, the bubonic plague of the late fourteenth century, alone killed over a quarter of the population. Population loss of this sort both reflected and caused economic dislocation.

Item.   During the fourteenth century, the ruling class of medieval society, the land-owning aristocracy, began to show signs of confusion about its function. It had long staked its claim to power on its control of much of the land and also on its military prowess. However, its skill in warfare was now open to question. The growth of professional armies and particularly the new weaponry of crossbow and cannon made traditional fighting methods increasingly irrelevant. The aristocracy did not, as a result, simply disappear. Rather, the nobility chose to emphasize a rich ceremonial lifestyle, featuring tournaments in which military expertise could be employed in competitive games. The spread of courtly love poems signaled another new focus, an interest in a more refined culture. The idea of chivalry—carefully controlled, polite behavior, especially toward women—gained ground. This was a potentially fruitful development in indicating increased cultivation among the upper class. We have seen similar transformations in considering earlier changes in the Chinese and Muslim aristocracy. But at the time of transition in the West, some of the elaborate ceremonies of chivalry seemed rather shallow, even a bit silly—a sign that medieval values were losing hold without being replaced by a new set of beliefs.

Item.   The balance between church and state, which had characterized medieval life, began to shift decisively after 1300. For several decades, French kings controlled the papacy, which they relocated from Rome to a town in France; then rival claimants to the papacy confused the issue further. Ultimately, a single pope was returned to Rome, but the church was clearly weakened. Moreover, the church began to lose some of its grip over Western religious life. Church leaders were so preoccupied with their political quarrels that they tended to neglect the spiritual side of their faith. Religion did not decline as a result. Indeed, signs of intense popular piety blossomed, along with the formation of new religious groups. But, devotion became partially separate from the institution of the church. One result, again starting in the fourteenth century, was a series of popular heresies, with leaders in places like England and Bohemia preaching against the hierarchical structure of the church in favor of a more direct experience of God.

Item.   The medieval intellectual and even artistic movements started to falter. After the work of Aquinas, later rationalists engaged in petty debates over such topics as how many angels could dance on the head of a pin. Church officials became less tolerant of intellectual pursuit, as they even declared some of Aquinas's writings heretical. In art, a growing interest in realistic portrayals of nature suggested the beginnings of a shift away from medieval artistic standards. Some medieval artistic styles became trite; Gothic design, for example, soon exhibited great detail, in a style called flamboyant Gothic—a symptom of waning creativity.

Item.   Social unrest increased in the fourteenth and fifteenth centuries, spurred in part by the new economic problems and also popular religious heresies. Many peasants and townspeople joined in egalitarian protests against the control of guild masters or landlords. Sometimes, they spoke out for greater equality. As an English rioter put it, "When Adam delved and Eve span, Who was then a gentleman?" In the Italian city of Florence, a democratic government was briefly installed after an artisan revolt in 1378. These revolts had little lasting success, although they did set in motion a new current of protest that would, in certain respects, last for several centuries. Peasants were beginning to seek greater freedom from what was left of serfdom, and lower-level artisans wondered if the guild system was working equitably. At times, these groups revolted in a violent manner. One English observer wrote of peasant attacks on manorial lords and records:

> These myschevous people thus assembled without capitayne or armoure, robbed, brent and slewe all gentylmen that they coude lay handes one, and forced and ravysshed ladyes and dawmosels and dyd such shameful dedes that no hymayne creature ought to think on any such. . . .

Again, elements of this protest tradition would last well beyond the period of medieval decline and ultimately help reshape political and social relationships in the West. At the time, popular uprisings served as one final indication that the medieval version of a social and economic structure was losing its validity.

CONCLUSION: AFTER THE MEDIEVAL, WHAT?

Thus, by about 1400, Western Europe was in many ways ready for substantial change. The basic dynamism of the region, generated during the postclassical centuries, was hardly affected. From the perspective of world history, the problems generated by a waning Middle Ages were scarcely perceptible. Western civilization, on the rise although still somewhat backward, continued its growth, embarking on an age of exploration and discovery literally around the world during the fifteenth century. However, changes in key medieval structures, ranging from artistic styles to the position of the church, meant that the West, which was to gain world prominence as it journeyed across the Atlantic and Indian oceans, was a partly new society. A genuine medieval heritage would combine with other impulses to give rise to traditions that still endure today.

SUGGESTED WEBSITES

On the Magna Carta, see *http://www.nara.gov/exhall/charters/magnacarta/magmain.html*; on Charlemagne, see *http://www.humnet.ucla.edu/santiago/histchrl.html*; on Bernard of Clairvaux, see *http://www.stbernardkeene.com/patron.html*; on William the Conqueror, see *http://www.knight.org/advent/cathen/15642c.htm*; on serfdom in Western Europe, see *http://www.fordham.edu/halsall/source/manumission.html*; on Thomas Aquinas and scholastic learning, see *http://www.aquinasonline.com*.

SUGGESTED READINGS

B. Tierney, *The Middle Ages* (1978), provides useful source material. For unusual insight into medieval society, also with considerable source material, see the highly readable E. Leroy-Ladurie, *Montaillou: The Promised Land of Error* (1979). A fine survey of medieval history is J. R. Strayer, *Western Europe in the Middle Ages* (1982); see also H. Trevor-Roper, *The Rise of Christian Europe* (1965), and Roberto S. Lopez, *The Commercial Revolutions of the Middle Ages* (1976). Excellent studies on more specialized topics include J. R. Strayer, *On the Medieval Origins of the Modern State* (1972); C. Brooke, *The 12th Century Renaissance* (1970); H. Rashdall, *The Universities of Europe in the Middle Ages* (1936); H. Berman, *Law and Revolution: The Formation of the Western Legal Tradition* (1983); R. Bridenthal and C. Koonz, *Becoming Visible: Women in European History* (1977); and N. Pevsner, *An Outline of European Architecture* (1963).

On the medieval economy, consult J. Gimpel, *The Medieval Machine: The Industrial Revolution of the Middle Ages* (1977), and David Landes, *Revolution in Time: Clocks and the Making of the Modern World* (1985). Social history has dominated much recent research on the period; see P. Ariès and G. Duby, eds., *A History of Private Life,* Vol. 2 (1984), and Barbara Hanawalt, *The Ties That Bound: Peasant Families in Medieval England* (1986), for important findings in this area. David Herlihy, *Medieval Households* (1985), is a vital contribution, as is J. Chapelot and R. Fossier, *The Village and House in the Middle Ages* (1985). J. Kirshner and S. F. Wemple, eds., *Women of the Medieval World* (1985), is a good collection. On tensions in popular religion, see C. Bynum, *Jesus as Mother: Studies in the Spirituality of the High Middle Ages* (1982), and L. Little, *Religious Poverty and the Profit Economy in Medieval Europe* (1978).

The Spread of East Asian Civilization

11

FOCAL POINTS

China in the postclassical period was affected by some of the same basic trends as the other civilizations of Asia and Africa, but in different ways. How did China respond to the rise of Islam, the spread of world religions, and the developing world network? How did it participate in the expansion of civilization within eastern Asia, and what were the results of Chinese guidance for societies such as Japan? Did an "East Asian civilization" emerge, or should the great differences between China and its near neighbors be emphasized? Continuity in China itself was strong, as cultural forms and institutions were revived after the disruption of the late classical period. In what ways did China change? Did any of these changes represent fundamental breaks with previous patterns, or did they merely advance prior trends?

INTRODUCTION

This chapter turns to a second set of connections within the world network, radiating from China. This was a decidedly smaller orbit than the one Islam had generated. It affected East Asia primarily, southeast Asia to an extent. And, it was linked, through trade and some technology exchange, to the rest of Asia and, through this, to Europe and Africa. Developments in East Asia were crucial in their own right. Japan, for example, formed some of its key characteristics during this period. Furthermore, some specific innovations, for instance, advances in technology, would soon have worldwide importance. The massive changes in religious affiliations and trading patterns that erupted throughout the Middle East and southern Asia after 600 C.E. had little impact on China and its East Asian neighbors. The Chinese encountered Arab soldiers on their western borders briefly and had more interaction with Turkish converts to Islam; at times, western China included an Islamic minority. And trade in Chinese goods, toward points west, passed increasingly into Arab hands. However, these developments were really peripheral to Chinese history in the period. The Chinese did, after the year 500, react to the one serious outside influence that had reached deeply into their population: the Buddhist religion. Apart from this interchange, however, the Chinese proceeded, as they long had done, as if there was little to learn from beyond their borders.

Nonetheless, the postclassical centuries formed a vigorous and important period in Chinese history and in China's relations with other parts of East Asia. China itself introduced innovations in bureaucracy, art, foreign policy, and technology. Indeed, during this period the Chinese were responsible for more fundamental improvements in technology than any other civilization.

Any student of world history, after mastering some of the basic patterns of individual civilizations, is tempted to look for larger themes or lessons. Do civilizations, for example, follow some general law of rise and fall? There certainly seems to be a common scenario in which a culture starts to grow with unusual vigor—like the Arabs in the seventh century—and then, some centuries later, begins to wane. But, one should not make too much of such a rise-and-fall pattern. For while some civilizations decline or stagnate, others go through temporary periods of readjustment only to emerge again with equal or even greater strength. China clearly illustrates this latter process and may still be exemplifying it in our own day as the nation revives after more than a century of partial eclipse.

Furthermore, China radiated a vigorous regional influence, serving as a model to many other societies in East Asia. Vietnam, Korea, and Japan did not become smaller versions of China; each had distinctive features that would long differentiate it from its giant neighbor. But, important elements of Chinese society were exported, making it possible to see a larger East Asian zone of civilization taking shape. The spread of civilization in East Asia on the basis of a significant Chinese example indeed forms one of the key illustrations of the general phenomenon of civilization's extension and the new process of borrowing during the postclassical centuries between 600 and 1400 C.E.

The period opens, neatly enough, soon after the year 500, with the renewal of the sequence of dynasties ruling China, which ended the long period of disruption following the collapse of the Han dynasty. Around 500 also, Japan began to import techniques from China, including writing, becoming a clear domain of East Asian civilization—although during this entire period, it played a far less commanding part than China itself.

The era did not end quite so smoothly, which reflects the fact that East Asian patterns remained somewhat separate from those in other parts of the Eurasian world. In 1278, Mongol invaders toppled the reigning Chinese dynasty; the invaders were expelled 90 years later. These decades serve as something of a transition in Chinese history. During the 1330s, Japan entered a new period of political instability. Thus, there was some sense of change, in Japan and China alike although for different reasons, during the fourteenth and early fifteenth centuries.

POLITICAL AND CULTURAL DEVELOPMENTS IN CHINA

Since Chinese civilization was not new, even reformulated during the centuries after 500, there is no need to dwell on its most familiar features. Following China's recovery from the nomadic invasions, during the sixth century, the dynastic cycle resumed and served to express and organize much of the nation's political structure. The first postclassical dynasty, the Sui, formed in 589 and was short-lived, although it reestablished a centralized state and repaired the Great Wall. The Sui dynasty also undertook a series of new conquests, pressing into Vietnam and the island of Taiwan and also extending westward, into Turkish lands of central Asia. A period of popular unrest against high taxes brought an end to the Sui ruling family, however, and the T'ang dynasty emerged in its place. The reign of this dynasty, along with the earlier Han, is regarded as one of the two golden eras of Chinese history.

The T'ang dynasty continued the policy of expansion. Its conquest of Turkish areas in central Asia helped push the Turks westward, thus setting in motion their advance toward the Middle East. The T'ang regime also formed protectorates over Tibet, Vietnam, and Korea, which helped spread Chinese institutions without directly annexing these areas to the empire. Japan paid tribute to the T'ang. In effect, the Chinese now controlled the entire world as they knew it.

Under rulers like the Empress Wu (690–705), one of the few women to reign over China, the T'ang reestablished the power of the central government. Like earlier dynasties, notably the Qin and Han, the T'ang government reduced the power of independent landlords. Their taxing power was abolished, in favor of direct payment by peasants to the state. The government required the free peasants to submit to military training, which greatly increased the power of the state and its role in individual lives. Finally, the government established comprehensive, accurate censuses of people and property, as the means for imposing fair but also reliable taxation. A growing bureaucracy accompanied these new measures, and the civil service examinations, based on political knowledge but also Chinese philosophy and literature, were revived. As before, this examination system provided relatively able bureaucrats, although drawn mainly from the upper classes, and also promoted cultural unity within the empire. Indeed, the bureaucratic system was greatly elaborated under the T'ang. Examinations became stricter, and education counted far more than birthright as the aristocratic role faded in favor of a scholar-bureaucrat ideal. Bureaucrats even amassed the authority to correct the emperor by citing relevant Confucian wisdom or historical examples.

The T'ang dynasty resumed the tradition of extensive government functions, regulating trade, building roads and canals, and organizing justice and defense. A new agency, the Board of Censors, was created to supervise the bureaucracy and guard against misconduct.

The T'ang program ultimately included a vigorous attack on Buddhism as a potentially subversive element. Although early T'ang emperors had favored Buddhism, the religion was finally officially rejected, as alien and subversive. Thousands of shrines and monasteries were destroyed. Buddhism remained an important minority religion in China, but its period of growth was forcibly brought to a halt. The T'ang, even more than their Han predecessors, clearly felt that they had both the right and the duty to regulate the beliefs of their subjects in the interests of political loyalty.

The dynastic decline of the T'ang began in the late 700s. Government became less effective. Earlier population growth, the result of T'ang prosperity, had increased poverty; there was not enough land to go around. T'ang policy of direct taxation on peasants drove the latter to seek landlord protection and spurred a series of major popular protests. The T'ang were finally displaced by civil war, in the year 906. However, this time chaos did not last long, for the traditions of centralized rule were too

World Profiles

T'ai-Tsung (626–649 C.E.)

The Tang emperor T'ai-Tsung was a brilliant general and an astute administrator. He set the stage for one of China's major dynasties by restoring the imperialist bureaucratic system of the Han and increasing the emphasis on education. He was a tolerant and cosmopolitan emperor as well, unperturbed by the continued spread of Buddhism. Finally, T'ai-Tsung masterminded Chinese military gains in Vietnam, Tibet, Mongolia, and Korea, where Chinese influence combined with continued political autonomy. Through his immense personal abilities, T'ai-Tsung was responsible for the revival and dissemination of basic trends in Chinese political history. How does his role as an individual compare to that of his near-contemporary in the Middle East—Muhammed?

This image of Tang emperor T'ai-Tsung was created by a Sung dynasty court painter several centuries after the emperor's death. (Collection of National Palace Museum, Taipei)

powerful to lapse. The dynasty might fade, but the bureaucratic state was virtually indestructible. A new dynasty, the Sung, came into power in 960. Again, it broke the power of local military leaders, encouraging them to enter civilian life. The Sung dynasty did not regain all the territory the T'ang had held; indeed, northern China, along the Hwang River, remained in the hands of nomadic invaders, including some Mongol groups. The founder of the Sung dynasty, a northern general named Chao K'uang-yin, realized that he could not take on all enemies simultaneously, and so he was willing to allow the continued presence of the nomadic warriors in the north. But, he developed an excellent strategy for assuming control of the prosperous southern states, and he extended his influence into Indochina. Despite sporadic warfare, the Sung dynasty was prosperous, with abundant tax revenues and a tight central administration. Population growth and the expansion of cities followed from improved agricultural productivity and advances in the output of coal and iron. The use of commodities like tea, previously an upper-class luxury, spread more widely. Trade within China increased, and, although mainly in the hands of foreign merchants, exports to India and the Middle East grew as well. Sung taxation relieved the peasantry by focusing on merchants instead, and peasant revolts subsided for centuries.

Nonetheless, the Sung, too, soon began to fade, in part because they never definitively resolved the problem of nomadic warriors in the north. Although the economy remained prosperous, administrative inefficiency reduced tax revenues. One Sung emperor tried to introduce reforms to relieve the hard-pressed peasantry, but he was undermined by the powerful, conservative bureaucracy. Invasions by nomadic peoples, particularly the Mongols, became harder to contain. Finally by 1278, under brilliant new generalship, the Mongols conquered the entire Sung empire.

The Political Divisions of China

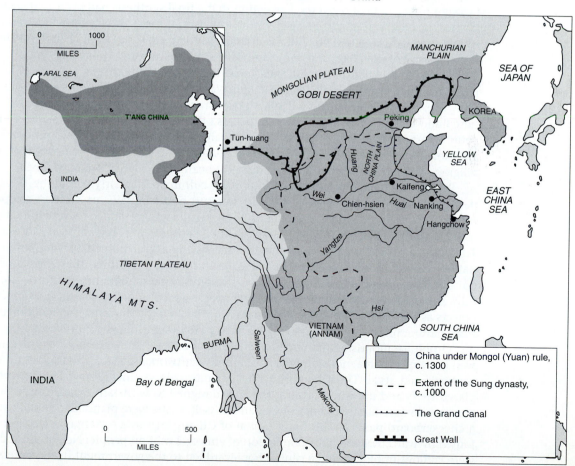

During the Sui, Tang, and Sung dynasties, Chinese culture enjoyed a brilliant period. Confucianism remained the dominant philosophy. The challenge of Buddhism led Confucian thinkers to expand their range of philosophical concerns. The philosopher Chu Hsi (1120–1200) played a major role in drawing together some Buddhist themes and orthodox Confucianism, to discuss the nature of the universe and its basic patterns as well as the more familiar issues of ethics and political loyalty. Chu Hsi emphasized family rule, under the benevolence of the father, and the state as a family system applied to the whole empire. He demonstrated how Confucian traditions could be confirmed but also taken in new directions. Giving Confucianism a scope it previously lacked, he also opened a dialogue on basic philosophical issues that had been monopolized earlier by Buddhist thinkers and urged meditation. Such was Chu Hsi's creativity that his own work became part of the Chinese classics, read and relied on for centuries along with the Confucian *Analects* and the Five Classics. And it was true that, while confirming basic features of the Confucian ethic, with emphasis on moral teaching and self-restraint, Chu Hsi had added depth to the Chinese philosophical tradition, extending it to areas that Buddhist beliefs, urging meditative union with some basic essence, had opened to new consideration. However, Chu Hsi's success had some drawbacks. Its breathtaking range, from philosophy through history, encouraged the perception that a final synthesis had been achieved; further speculation was discouraged. In the long run, this promoted a growing sterility in Chinese intellectual life, but the accomplishments of Chu Hsi himself illustrate the creativity of the T'ang and Sung periods of Chinese history.

Daoism and Buddhism continued to be important popular religions. The Chinese introduced several variants of the Mahayana Buddhist faith. The most famous, known as Zen, its later Japanese name, stressed meditation and spiritual growth. Chinese Buddhism continued, however, to be less otherworldly than its Southeast Asian counterpart. Chinese Buddhists stressed the value of hard work and a love of nature, and not simply contemplation. For its part, Daoism continued its development as a religion, integrating popular beliefs in magical healing as it spread more widely.

The incorporation of Buddhism in popular culture, particularly before the T'ang persecutions, led to new developments in literature and especially art. Chinese sculptors copied some Indian styles of statuary. The pagoda was introduced as a new architectural form and spread from China to other parts of Asia, including Japan and Thailand. Buddhist artists painted religious scenes and also acquired a new interest in nature. Even after Buddhism declined as a cultural force in China, the reliance on natural subjects remained. Chinese artists stressed simple statements of nature, carefully arranged and with muted colors. An emperor issued a guide to painters: "Depict objects as they exist. Simplicity and nobility of line is to be the aim." A small object from nature, like a spray of bamboo, was held to represent the whole universe.

Other arts flourished under the T'ang and the Sung, and many artists became well known by name, not simply as anonymous craftworkers. Pottery took on a more sophisticated style. The emperors built elaborate palaces, including pagodas with glazed roofs and upturned eaves at the end, designed to withstand windstorms. Urban architecture became something of an art itself. Cities were planned rationally, in a checkerboard pattern. The T'ang capital of Ch'ang-an was a rectangular city, contained by walls, which held a population of almost 2 million people. Neighborhoods were laid out in blocks, and a central boulevard led to the government headquarters.

"Trees Against a Flat Vista" (detail) by Kuo Hsi. (The Metropolitan Museum of Art, New York. Gift of John M. Crawford, Jr., in honor of Douglas Dillon, 1981, 1981.276)

In sum, Chinese art combined growing sophistication in technology and orderly planning with a love of nature inspired by Daoist and Buddhist thought. Chinese art showed the diversity of a civilization that, although traditionalist, remained creative.

In literature, the traditional pursuits of compiling the classics and writing histories combined with new styles. In poetry a new, five-syllable meter, called the *shih,* became increasingly popular. Both Daoist and Confucian poets flourished. Li Po (701–762) was a Daoist who wrote of his love of wine; legend has it that he drowned while reaching out in drunken ecstasy for the reflection of the moon in the water. The popularity of poetry as an art for educated gentlemen led to the composition of hundreds of thousands of poems during this period, with themes ranging from Confucian morality to the beauties of nature. Many verses had a slightly melancholy ring, like these lines from the Sung poet Meng Chiae:

> *Man's life is like morning dew,*
> *A flame eating up the oil night by night.*
> *Why should I strain my ears*
> *Listening to the squeaks of this autumn insect?*
> *Better lay aside the book*
> *And drink my cup of jade-white wine.*

During the Sung period, finally, more urban literary forms appeared, particularly through the rise of popular romantic stories and an active theater.

Chinese science retained its vitality. The government sponsored mapmaking and astronomical observation. Chemistry advanced, and biologists accumulated new information on the pharmaceutical uses of plants and minerals. Texts were written on forensic medicine; in fact, the Chinese were the first to develop a science on crime detection. Hosts of encyclopedias summed up available scientific knowledge ranging from mathematics to the principles of magnetism. As before, the Chinese did not emphasize sweeping scientific theories, but rather placed value on precise and practical observations. Their scientists knew a great deal about the actual working of the physical universe, and their grasp increased steadily through research and compilation.

Science, in this Chinese tradition, was linked closely to technology, and here the mastery of this civilization remained unmatched. Experiments led to new procedures in insect control. Engineers developed the first suspension bridges, the first locks on canals, the first gear systems to be applied to the milling of grain. The invention of the magnetic compass served as a great aid to navigation. The abacus came into use in calculating commercial transactions. Even the invention of the simple wheelbarrow, not known in other societies for many centuries, was a great boost to agriculture and construction. Porcelain manufacture arose under the T'ang, creating a new artistic and production specialty.

The most significant inventions of the T'ang–Sung period were explosive powder and the printing press. Explosive powder, first used for fireworks, was applied to weaponry by the Sung dynasty, which developed land mines, hand grenades, and other projectiles. Printing (first introduced in Korea) resulted from the desire to circulate authentic versions of important books like the Buddhist sutras. By the seventh century, the Chinese could rub paper over inked, carved stone, in a primitive form of the block press. Woodblocks were soon in use. By the middle of the tenth century, every classic was in print, and books of all types became common under the Sung. Paper currency and playing cards were other resulting uses of print. The technology of printing, like explosive powder, would spread to the West by the fifteenth century, via central Asia and the Middle East.

ECONOMY AND SOCIETY IN CHINA

Chinese politics and culture depended on a flourishing economy, and many of the new inventions directly spurred agricultural production and manufacturing. The state continued to encourage economic development, particularly by extending the transportation network. The Chinese genius for practical organization led to standardized measurements for grain, silk, and other goods, an innovation that facilitated both taxation and commerce.

In the vigorous periods of the T'ang and Sung dynasties, China became the most prosperous agricultural society in the world. As a result of prosperity, the empire's population tripled, passing the 100 million mark even in the restricted territory of the Sung dynasty.

Chinese agriculture benefited from the introduction of quick-growing strains of rice and an increasing use of fertilizers. Production of commercial crops like tea and cotton expanded. In the manufacturing sector, such enterprises as food processing, ceramic making, shipbuilding, and papermaking all improved in technique. A major iron and steel industry developed, with coal heated to make coke, which was then used to fire blast furnaces for iron smelting. Iron was used mainly for weapons, but also for farming and construction tools.

Landscape by Yen Tz'u-Yu (1180–1230 C.E.). Characteristic of restrained, evocative nature painting in China.

An expanding commerce followed from the growth of agriculture and manufacturing. China underwent something of a commercial revolution between 700 and 1200. Marketplaces and shops cropped up throughout the cities, and commercial cities, rather than urban areas serving primarily as political centers, came into being for the first time. (Canal building encouraged trade, particularly between the rice-growing regions and the north.) Private merchants proliferated, and merchant associations, called *hang*, coordinated their efforts and aided in banking and long-distance transactions. The use of money spread rapidly, with paper currency making its debut in 811.

Foreign trade flourished, although overseas operations remained mainly in the hands of Muslim merchants who exported Chinese goods as far as East Africa. Koreans dominated China's trade with Japan. But under the Sung, Chinese merchants took a more active role in ocean-going trade. Overall, China was the most commercial society in the world by 1300, with the most highly developed manufacturing sector. Clear evidence of China's economic power lay in its ability to export finished manufactured goods and import mainly cheaper raw materials, including horses, leather, and precious stones.

Despite all its accomplishments, China did not break the basic mold of an agricultural economy. Some scholars have speculated that it could have done so in this period by parlaying its extensive natural resources, excellent technology, and sheer wealth into an industrial revolution. The advancement of Chinese society was restricted by at least three factors. Population growth often outstripped available resources, making it difficult for the economy to keep up, much less to evolve into radically new forms. Periods of stability encouraged population increases, which put pressure on the available land, making subsistence, not change, the main goal. The government bureaucracy remained conservative, eager for abundant tax revenues but not interested in pioneering commercial ventures. Government taxation and regulation, indeed, often interfered with economic growth. Finally, Chinese society retained its adherence to values that stressed the importance of scholarship and bureaucratic achievement. Merchants, for all their gains, were still frowned upon, and many traders used their wealth not to establish the basis for further economic gains but to seek entry into the educated, bureaucratic, land-owning elite. So, China did not alter its course and, indeed, by the later Sung period the pace of economic growth began to slow. By 1500, China would no longer lead the world in economic advances.

Economic change, relatedly, did not produce corresponding social change. Cities did spring up, and an important urban culture developed. Urban entertainments, including houses of prostitution, and theaters and gambling establishments, proliferated for a wealthy minority. But, the landlord-bureaucratic class continued to command peak prestige. Many in this group, in fact, resided in the growing cities and scorned the backwardness of rural ways. Upper-class society increasingly turned away from military pursuits, devoting itself instead to a life of ceremony and cultivated amusements.

The masses of people in China did not find the rhythms of their life greatly interrupted, even when new crops and tools were introduced. Village life did not change significantly for most peasants. The growth of cities did create a burgeoning class of urban poor, who were aided, inadequately, by private and government charity efforts.

The position of women deteriorated somewhat during the T'ang and Sung periods, ironically as a result of rising prosperity. Chinese family life had long been strictly patriarchal. In upper-class life, women had fewer functions than they had maintained before, particularly in the cities. As a result, they were increasingly treated as mere ornaments. Officials and some merchants often took more than one wife. The upper class introduced the custom of binding women's feet. While still young, girls had their feet tightly wrapped until the arch was broken and the toes bent under. The practice resulted in permanent crippling, but produced small, delicate feet and a shuffling walk that were considered to be the marks of great beauty. The custom of footbinding gradually spread to the masses mainly between 1500 and 1900, except in a few parts of South China, and it persisted among wealthier groups into the twentieth century.

Developments in Chinese society, although significant, displayed on the whole less vitality than parallel alterations in economic and cultural life. Basic values did not shift, and stability was cherished. To most Chinese, or at least to the civilization's

"Going Up the River at the Spring Festival": Life in the city of Kaifeng. This painting illustrates China's development of a larger urban culture.

leaders, it seemed that a satisfying balance had been achieved, in which prosperity and cultivated diversions were compatible with continuities in political and intellectual life. Increasingly, China's upper class began to think in terms of protecting this rich tradition from outside forces. The 90 years of Mongol rule enhanced the perception that the world outside China was a hostile, dangerous, but inferior place, from which China would do well to isolate itself. This adherence to tradition and suspicion of outside forces persisted into modern times, providing the Chinese with great and understandable pride in their own culture but compromising their ability to respond to changes in other parts of the world.

CIVILIZATION IN KOREA, VIETNAM, AND JAPAN

China's power and prestige during the T'ang and Sung dynasties guided the spread of civilization to other parts of East Asia. Korea and Vietnam adapted Chinese ideographs to their local languages, resulting in the first writing in these languages. Chinese artistic styles, the bureaucratic examination system, and Confucian learning were assimilated in these areas as well, along with the Buddhist religion as it had passed through China. Chinese influence in Korea peaked between the seventh and ninth centuries, during which time Korean rulers imitated Chinese city planning, imported Confucianism, and copied Chinese artistic styles. The Korean economy was less advanced than China's, however, and depended on virtual slave labor for work in the mines to produce raw materials for export. The aristocracy oppressed the Korean masses, although Buddhism was shared across class lines. A social revolt in the fourteenth century resulted in a new dynasty, the Yi, who ruled until the twentieth century, and quickly restored aristocratic rule. Chinese influence in Vietnam also affected the upper classes more than the common people, whose culture, including the enjoyment of cockfights, was more like that of other parts of Southeast Asia. Vietnamese rulers, after periods of Chinese occupation, realized they needed to emulate Chinese strengths simply to protect their region, and Chinese bureaucracy and agricultural technology were widely imitated. After the fall of the T'ang dynasty in China, Vietnamese rulers gained their independence and began a process of expansion southward. Unlike Korea, political unity was rare, and internal warfare frequently consumed Vietnamese energies.

Japan was the third geographic area to enter the Chinese orbit. Even more than Korea and Vietnam, however, Japan remained distinct in important respects as well, in part because, as an island network, it was never conquered by the Chinese. Thus, the Japanese produced a unique variant of East Asian civilization, akin to Chinese but sufficiently different as to make Japan, ultimately, a major separate force in the world.

As Japan became aware of Chinese achievements, by about the year 400, it developed the habit of selective borrowing—a practice the Chinese had never seen fit to adopt. The custom would remain in Japan's collective memory, promoting, much later, a response to Western influences that bore some resemblance to Japan's acceptance of Chinese ways. In the centuries after the year 500, the Japanese proved willing to learn from a superior culture—the Chinese—while retaining a vigorous sense of their own traditions. Particularly in social and political structure, however, the Japanese ultimately did not imitate the Chinese model.

Before Chinese influences happened upon the scene, the Japanese had already developed strong regional political units; the Shinto religion, which worshipped the spirits of nature in local shrines and regarded the emperor as divine; and a prosperous agriculture based on the cultivation of rice. The fragmentation of politics was fostered by the mountains that divide the major islands of Japan, making communication difficult. Shintoism provided a simple, satisfying ritual in which priests led ceremonies and offerings to the gods. The religion also emphasized rituals of cleanliness and discouraged popular festivals featuring games and drinking. Shintoism, like the regional political pattern, would long survive influences from the outside, indeed coexisting with them; thus, Japanese Confucianists, Buddhists, and, more recently, dynamic business leaders combine newer values with older Shinto practices.

Japan began copying China in earnest around the year 600. Students and envoys traveled to China and were impressed with the economic and political achievements there. In 604, the Japanese ruler, Prince Shotoku, issued a constitution establishing a centralized government and bureaucracy and urging reverence for Buddhism and Confucian virtues. Chinese-style architecture and urban planning were introduced, along with Chinese ideographs. Regular exchanges with China, organized by the Japanese government, brought back increasing knowledge, as well as the artistic products of the neighboring giant. Under Chinese influence, a new calendar was adopted. A significant result of Japan's assimilation of Chinese culture was that the position of Japanese women deteriorated. Japanese families had long been tightly knit, but with important public and workplace roles for women. Confucian values led to women's being considered inferior, and although the Japanese never went as far as their Chinese mentors, they did confine women's authority to household and child-rearing alone. In the arts, too, Japan mirrored its neighbor. Chinese dance and musical forms were introduced to court ceremonies and remain the basis for traditional Japanese culture in these areas even today.

As noted, however, complete imitation did not take place, in part because the Japanese economy remained more backward and less commercial than the Chinese model. The centralized bureaucracy did not succeed in displacing local land-owning aristocrats. And, it was in politics, particularly, that the Chinese model soon began to pall. The Japanese aristocracy became sufficiently comfortable with other aspects of Chinese culture that it did not hesitate to part company in terms of political style. In any event, the decline of the T'ang dynasty made the Chinese model less attractive for a time. The short-lived Japanese experiment with centralized government soon faded. The emperor remained, but chiefly as a religious figure, rather than an effective political ruler. Real government lay in the hands of regional military leaders.

Japanese rule was, by the year 800, a full-blown feudal system, quite similar to that which would develop, separately, in Western Europe during roughly the same period. Powerful regional aristocrats grouped local landowners under their banners, providing protection and courts of law in return for economic aid and military service. The result was a pyramid, with the peasant masses at the bottom of this power structure. The great lords, called *daimyo,* or "great names," used their revenues to hire professional soldiers, called *samurai.* This feudal system was, obviously, a step backward from centralized rule. It brought frequent periods of warfare to the islands and a considerably greater emphasis on military virtues than prevailed in China. Major wars occurred between 1051 and 1088, and again in the following centuries. Nonetheless, the feudal system blended with Confucian values learned from China. Samurai soldiers had a powerful code of honor and bravery and were expected to commit ritual suicide if they dishonored this code. At the same time, the samurai valued literary accomplishments, such as the writing of poetry, and important ceremonies, such as the tea ceremony. In this respect, Japanese feudal lords were different from their rougher-hewn European counterparts. Other distinctions existed between Eastern and Western feudalism. Because Confucianism encouraged the Japanese lords to believe that good government required absolute loyalty, Japanese feudalism did not give way to institutions designed to check the power of the greater lords, like the parliaments that would arise from European feudalism. According to the Japanese, admirable personal conduct, the loyalty of the lesser lords, and the mutual devotion of the daimyo to their servants would produce proper government. Japanese feudalism involved tight group cohesion, whereas the western European version was characterized by a greater sense of contrast between individuals. These differences between Japanese and Western society, translated today into business organizations, are a key example of how successful features of a civilization survive and adapt.

Japanese feudalism was used to build a somewhat stronger government structure after 1185. A single aristocratic family, the Minamoto, gained military dominance over the whole of Japan, establishing a central office called the shogunate. Each shogun served officially as chief officer to the emperor, but in fact the shogun was the real ruler of the country and commanded the fidelity of the regional lords. Faithful generals were rewarded with estates scattered throughout the country, which helped convert feudal loyalties into effective national politics. The new shogunate took its name from its capital city of Kamakura. Under the Kamakura shogunate, which lasted until 1333, Japan experienced greater peace than ever before. The new government was strong enough, among other things, to resist two attempts by Mongol invaders from China to conquer their country. In the second invasion effort, the Mongols massed the largest overseas expedition the world had ever known, with 140,000 men. However, a typhoon destroyed the fleet, and this "divine wind" would be long remembered by the Japanese, who believed that their country was uniquely blessed by the gods.

Japanese politics, as it had developed by the end of the Kamakura period, provided a unique mix of Chinese and local ingredients. Confucian loyalty and ceremony blended with military skills, including elaborate exercises in horsemanship, archery, and fencing, and with intense devotion to one's lord. The bureaucratic element of Chinese culture played little role as yet. The feudal code, imposing mutual bonds between leaders and followers, served instead as the principal political link. Even today, the feudal heritage of Japan manifests itself in the close connection between government, business managers, and workers. The Kamakura shoguns translated the dominant sense of group loyalty into a series of committees to oversee their administration. The tradition of collective rule, rather than individual or purely bureaucratic control, also maintains a strong hold on Japanese society; it is, in part, responsible for the unusual skill of the Japanese in group leadership and for the economic surge of their nation in contemporary time.

"Scroll with Depictions of the Night Attack on the Sanjo Palace" *(Sanjo-den youchi no emaki)* Illustrated scrolls on the events of the Heiji Era, Japan, second half of the thirteenth century, Kamakura period. Handscroll; ink and colors on paper (41.3 × 699.7). (Courtesy Museum of Fine Arts, Boston/Fenollosa-Weld Collection)

CULTURE, SOCIETY, AND ECONOMY IN JAPAN

The Japanese economy developed steadily under the feudal system and the Kamakura shogunate. Even periods of internal warfare did not permanently retard economic growth. Farming became increasingly productive. The aristocracy was conscious of the importance of good agricultural administration, and village leaders instilled the same goals among ordinary peasants. Japanese agriculture, supported by careful systems of irrigation for the rice crop, sustained a far larger population than most areas of comparable size elsewhere in the world.

Commercial ties spread among the islands. By the twelfth century, trading cities dotted the nation; manufacturing increased, with a focus on metallurgy, paper, and pottery as well as textiles. Japan still depended on China for most luxury products, including silks, but it offered some manufactured goods in exchange. Moreover, trade and manufacturing produced a growing group of townspeople and merchants. Japanese society was, like Chinese society, originally centered on divisions between aristocratic landlords and peasants, and of course the feudal system tended to reinforce this heirarchy. A small number of slaves also existed, confined to menial occupations. The rise of an aggressive merchant group, skilled in seafaring and navigation through the use of instruments invented in China, jostled the foundations of an agricultural society. Japan did not officially value the merchant middle class highly, but it never developed the intense prejudice against money-making characteristic of Chinese elites.

The Japanese borrowed more heavily from China in culture than in politics or social structure. A Japanese system of writing developed, after an initial attempt to use Chinese characters to express the quite different spoken language of Japan; the new system was still based on Chinese ideographs. As in China, poetry was the preferred literary form, although some novels and adventure stories were also produced during the Kamakura period. A collection of some 4500 poems appeared around the year 700. Japanese poetry emphasized form, particularly short poems written in a careful sequence of syllables. For example, the *tanka* form required 31 syllables written in 5 lines, in a 5–7–5–7–7 syllable sequence. Japanese poetry often involved the use of words with multiple meanings. The phrase *Senkata naku* means "there is nothing to be done," with the word *naku* making the sentence negative, but the same word also means "to cry," allowing a poet to suggest futility and sorrow in the same phrase. As in China, then, although with different specific forms, Japanese poetry stressed elegance, technical virtuosity, and a pervasive melancholy.

Thus, one poet expressed his sorrow over the death of his wife:

> *Suddenly there came a messenger*
> *Who told me she was dead—*
> *Was gone like a yellow leaf of autumn,*
> *Dead as the day dies with the setting sun,*
> *Lost as the bright moon is lost behind the clouds,*
> *Alas, she is no more, whose soul*
> *Was bent to mine like bending seaweed.*

As in China, finally, the growth of cities added new literary interests to the Japanese repertoire, particularly through the development of theater. The *No*-plays, dramatic poems enacted by dancers, became an especially popular and symbolic form, alternating ritualistic gestures and slapstick comedy.

Japanese literature was, even apart from specific differences in form, no mere imitation of Chinese styles. A delight in war stories provided a distinctive element. But, the strong similarities between Japanese and Chinese literary styles brought complexity to Japanese life. The warlords and samurai differed greatly from their Chinese counterparts in political relationships and military ardor, but they shared an interest in appreciating and even writing poetry and drama.

Japanese art derived much from China as well. Buddhist temples, often using the pagoda form, were sometimes built by Chinese architects. Buddhist statuary developed widely. Many Buddhist painters and sculptors created both frightening images to ward off hell and temple decorations representing spiritual joys. Japanese painters featured landscape scenes as well as religious subjects, using bold strokes to capture mountains, waterfalls, and forests. Gardening and flower arrangement, or *ikebana*, became an important art form in Japan as well as in China. Emphasis was placed on small, carefully constructed courtyard gardens, often with one or two artificial hills and a pond with an island and bridge.

Japanese culture during this period did not involve elaborate philosophical speculations or significant scientific work. In this respect, Japan simply omitted some important aspects of Chinese intellectual life. Confucian ethics, as well as a sense of ceremony, did spread widely. Many Japanese combined Buddhism with Shintoism, seeing Shintoism as a set of comforting rituals and Buddhist ceremonies as an avenue to salvation. Buddhist scholars provided detailed descriptions of the horrors of hell and the bliss of paradise; adherents of the Buddhist faith ranged from the emperor down to many common people, whose religious fervor tended to strengthen in times of political strife. This religious mix was considerably different from that in China and included not only a greater Buddhist element, but also an emphasis on popular congregations and the doctrines of salvation that made Japanese Buddhism increasingly distinctive.

Japanese society was still in the process of development when the Kamakura shogunate fell in 1333, bringing on a new period of internal warfare. Further developments in Japanese culture would evolve only in later centuries. Yet, the Japanese had already created a distinctive variant of East Asian civilization, combining Chinese forms with local religious, political, and social traditions. The result was a society with more contradictory ingredients than in China—which may have been a source of creativity in the long run.

The rising Japanese did not do what many other newly civilized people have done in history: embark on an effort of conquest. During the sixteenth century, they did try to capture Korea, but failed. Logically, the Japanese, increasingly skilled in seafaring, might have moved toward the Philippines, or even North America. But at this point, the Japanese orbit was so firmly set by China that expansion in other directions made little sense. Like the Chinese, the Japanese considered real civilization to exist in their world, and they were not tempted to stray widely from its path. And while Japanese trade on the sea did expand, it was not yet a match for Muslim fleets or for the navies from Christian Europe that would follow later.

CONCLUSION: EAST ASIAN SELF-CONFIDENCE

The Japanese, like the Chinese, concentrated mainly on their own development. They even came to believe in their own peculiar destiny. When China was overrun by the Mongols, Japan found itself—by its own standards—the only real civilization it knew about. Thus, the Japanese became accustomed to thinking in terms of their own superiority. This confidence would remain part of Japanese culture, characterizing the Japanese even during the past century as they have freely imitated Western society. It would also serve, ironically, to limit Japanese influence in the wider world for many centuries, for the Japanese, like the Chinese, were accustomed to the isolation of their civilization and not eager to participate in exchanges with other cultures. And so, East Asian civilization entered the next period of world history in many ways the best developed of any of the major world cultures, but among the least eager to investigate what was happening outside its own orbit. Thus, without intending to, the civilization would leave the door open for expansionary forces from other areas, regions in many ways less developed than East Asia itself.

SUGGESTED WEBSITES

On footbinding, see *http://acc6.its.brooklyn.cuny.edu/~phalsall/images.html* (scroll to "customs"); on Japanese military technology and the samurai code, see *http://victorian.fortunecity.com/duchamp/410/main.html.*

SUGGESTED READINGS

Several studies deal with special features of Chinese history during this period (but see also the general surveys mentioned in Chapter 2): Arthur Wright and Denis Twitchett, eds., *Perspectives on the T'ang* (1973); Mark Elvin, *The Pattern of the Chinese Past* (1973); Jacques Gernet, *Daily Life in China on the Eve of the Mongol Invasion, 1250–1276* (1962); J. T. C. Liu, *Reform in Sung China: Wang An-shih (1021–1086) and His New Policies* (1959); E. Zurcher, *The Buddhist Conquest of China,* 2 vols. (1959); H. D. Martin, *The Rise of Ghinghis Khan and His Conquest of North China* (1950); and J. Dardess, *Conquerors and Confucians: Aspects of Political Change in Late Yuan China* (1973). On Korea, see William Henthorn, *History of Korea* (1971). On Vietnam, see Alexander Woodside, *Vietnam and the Chinese Model* (1971). On Japan, G. Sansom, *A History of Japan to 1334* (1958), provides an excellent survey. Fine specialized studies include P. Duus, *Feudalism in Japan* (1969); G. Sansom, *Japan: A Short Cultural History,* rev. ed. (1943); J. W. Hall, *Government and Local Power in Japan: 500–1700: A Study Based in Bizen Province* (1966); J. W. Hall, *Japan from Prehistory to Modern Times* (1970); H. Paul Varley, *Japanese Culture: A Short History* (1973); and J. M. Kitagawa, *Religion in Japanese History* (1966).

Centers of Civilization in the Americas

12

Civilizations in the Americas became much more elaborate than their predecessors during the postclassical period and spread over wider areas of the Andes and Central America. What new systems and institutions accompanied this spread of civilization? How does the process compare with the earlier development of river valley civilizations in Asia and North Africa? Unlike the other centers of the postclassical world, American civilizations developed entirely outside the world network. How did they compensate for the absence of borrowing? What potential weaknesses resulted from isolation?

SOCIETIES OUTSIDE THE WORLD NETWORK

A final expression of the spread of civilization between 500 and 1400 C.E. involves two centers in the Western Hemisphere: Central America and the Andes region. Civilization was not, of course, brand new to either of these areas. The Olmecs and others had already established a basis for solid political organization, an elaborate religion whose followers worshipped at massive monuments, and extensive agriculture and trade.

The centers of civilization in the Americas had no link with the international network taking shape in Asia, Africa, and Europe. At most, they serve, by negative example, to highlight how important the network was. The Americas formed a separate system in the history of world civilizations, although the two major American centers of civilization had no regular contact even with each other. For this reason, as well as the lack of domesticated animals, American Indian civilizations, though impressive in many ways, lagged behind other societies in the level of technology available. While groups in the Andes used the llama for carrying light cargo, Central Americans had no animals for transport, and there were no animals usable for plowing anywhere. Furthermore, American Indian civilizations did not utilize the wheel, save for children's toys. Ironworking was not practiced. Nevertheless, the civilizations developed a complex agriculture, capable of sustaining large populations. The leading Aztec city was far bigger than European cities of the time and would awe the first Spanish invaders.

In many respects, the flourishing of impressive civilizations in the Americas resembled a somewhat earlier stage in civilization's rise elsewhere. There are more similarities to the growth of civilization in Egypt and Mesopotamia than classical China or the Islamic Middle East and North Africa. The resulting differences in religion and technology levels between the Americas and the European-Asian axis guaranteed significant conflict in later encounters, when the Americas were drawn into worldwide contacts for the first time.

THE AMERICAS

MAYANS AND AZTECS

The disappearance of the first agricultural societies in Central America, those of the Olmecs and their immediate successors, is shrouded in considerable mystery. Direct traces of these civilizations, except for the monumental ruins that still remain, vanished by the seventh century. Probably one factor in their decline involved invasion by peoples farther north, in the valley that runs through present-day central Mexico. Several of these peoples, in turn, were able to build on the earlier civilizations, creating still more elaborate cultures of their own. The most important of these societies were the Mayans, who established their initial civilization by about 100 C.E. and emerged as the dominant group in the middle region of Central America by the year 600. From this point, Mayan history divided into three stages: the first phase of particular creativity, from 600 to about 900, centered in the northern portion of present-day Guatemala; then a decline and move northward to the Yucatán peninsula in Mexico, where the Mayans intermingled with other American Indian groups from the north, notably the Toltecs; and then the definitive collapse of this mixed culture, from about 1200 onward, and culminating in the virtual destruction of formal Mayan society, including its written language, in the Spanish conquest of the sixteenth century.

Mayan civilization sprang from a tropical rain forest, in areas of great fertility that required immense efforts to maintain. The difficulty of preserving agricultural land from animals, insects, and lush vegetation helps explain the intensity of Mayan polytheistic religion, bent on placating a host of savage gods. Central American civilization practiced blood-letting, with Mayans believing it alone kept the universe going. Body piercing was common.

It was religion that gave the clearest structure to Mayan society. Huge temples and pyramids were erected to honor the gods. The Mayans did not construct cities in the usual sense, where a variety of activities could take place; they instead built enormous ceremonial complexes, such as Chichén Itzá. Here, priests conducted rituals to honor the gods. Religious festivals in these centers stimulated intense involvement among ordinary men and women, who produced richly decorated costumes and performed elaborate dances. Games were conducted in the religious centers as well, again to honor the gods. In one game, played in a rectangular courtyard, opposing teams tried to throw a ball through a small circular hoop attached to the side wall; the team that lost was killed as a sacrifice—although it is important to note that scoring was so difficult that most games ended in a tie. Political organization, too, seems to have been dominated by the priestly caste, who organized secret societies to preserve their aura of power and mystery.

The Americas Before the Spanish Conquest

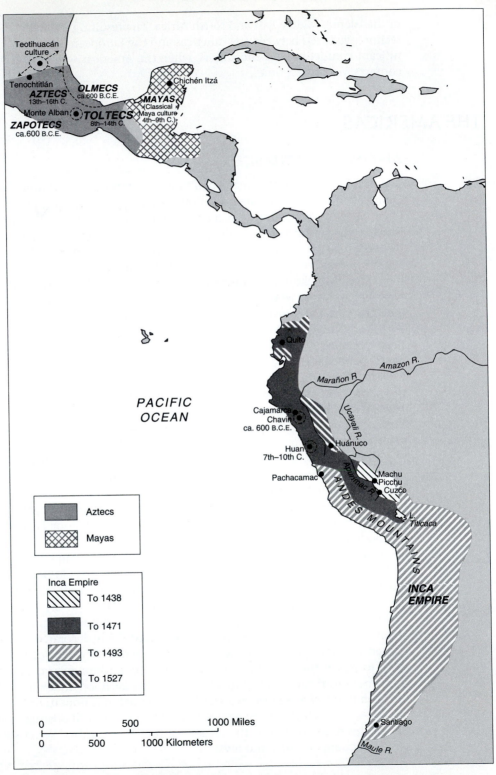

Teotihuacán culture

Tenochtitlán

AZTECS
13th–16th C.

OLMECS
ca. 600 B.C.E.

Monte Alban

TOLTECS
8th–14th C.

ZAPOTECS
ca. 600 B.C.E.

Chichén Itzá

MAYAS
(Classical Maya culture 4th–9th C.)

PACIFIC OCEAN

Quito

Amazon R.

Marañon R.

Cajamarca

Chavin
ca. 600 B.C.E.

Ucayali R.

Huánuco

Huari
7th–10th C.

Pachacamac

Apurimac R.

Machu Picchu

Cuzco

ANDES MOUNTAINS

L. Titicaca

INCA EMPIRE

Santiago

Maule R.

	Aztecs
	Mayas

Inca Empire

	To 1438
	To 1471
	To 1493
	To 1527

0	500	1000 Miles
0	500	1000 Kilometers

Mayan ruins: Temple of Inscriptions, Palenque, Mexico. Priests ruled the tops of these pyramids, which contained rooms for secret meetings and places to lead prayer and sacrifice.

Science was also oriented toward the service of religion. Along with the massive monuments the Mayans constructed, the development of a detailed calendar, based on careful astronomical studies made from observatories in the religious centers, rates as their highest achievement. More than any other people at this point, the Mayans had an extraordinary sense of time. The calendar was used particularly to regulate the cycle of religious celebrations and coordinate them with the cycle of the agricultural year. However, the Mayans also used their calendar to calculate back by hundreds of thousands of years, perhaps realizing that time had no beginning. Associated with calendar development came unusually accurate measurements of the length of the year (which Mayans figured out to within two hours) and sophisticated mathematics; the Mayans were one of only three civilizations to independently devise the concept of zero.

Religion, finally, dominated art. The great pyramids, normally uninhabited except for priests, were designed to impress observers with the remoteness of the gods and the power of those who climbed the steps to commune with them. Statues portrayed gods, often in semianimal form with emphasis on the feline grace and ferocity of the jaguar; other statues, particularly in female form, celebrated more benign deities of fertility. Finally, the Mayans developed a hieroglyphic writing, which they used for decorating temples, composing books, and establishing markers for the passage of time.

Several features of Mayan civilization remain unknown. The jungle now claims many religious centers. Few books have survived, for the Spanish tried zealously to destroy all traces of Mayan culture in their thirst to Christianize the heathen. Somewhat more extensive evidence of the Mayan-Toltec culture exists on the Yucatán peninsula than for classical Mayan achievements. Through the Toltecs, the Mayans added to their religion some human sacrifice, chiefly involving prisoners of war. Secular rulers seem to have gained increasing prominence. Invasions by other Indian groups proved to be a growing problem; in the thirteenth century, the great center of Chichén Itzá was sacked by invaders. The Mayans then constructed another capital defended by five miles of walls. This too was conquered, apparently by an uprising of Mayan peasants, in about 1460. By this point, Mayan civilization was virtually extinguished, although the last Mayan stronghold surrendered to the Spanish only in 1699.

Because of technological limitations, particularly the absence of extensive ironworking and the lack of a usable wheel, but also because of the failure to develop arches as a means of support for their buildings, Mayan culture depended on immense human labor. At the same time, the extensive religious activity, especially in the ceremonial complexes, required a great deal of human effort. Perhaps it was for this reason that the Mayans proved so vulnerable to invasion and that their art and political skills deteriorated relatively quickly after the high point of the civilization—in some contrast to the more complex ebb and flow of most civilizations in Asia and the Mediterranean. A related explanation of the dramatic declines of American civilizations like the Mayan emphasizes the problems of maintaining adequate agriculture. With no metal tools and few fertilizers, it was hard to maintain the land, keep weeds at bay, and expand acreage. Periods of Mayan decline remain hard to interpret. A recent theory suggests that Mayan political structure may have permitted families to simply move away when the ruling class became too oppressive.

Aztec civilization developed separately. Around 1350, the Aztecs entered the central valley of Mexico from the north, overthrowing the Toltecs and then extending

Aztec and Mayan Civilizations

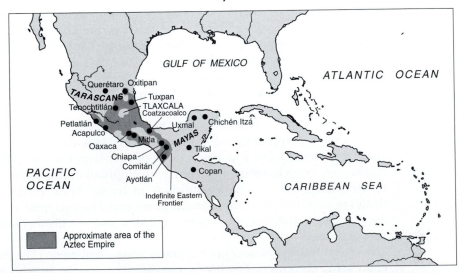

an empire into other parts of Central America. Their capital was a new city constructed on the marshes around Lake Texcoco, where they built an elaborate network of bridges and causeways to support their great center, called Tenochtitlán. The Aztec empire was a military establishment, controlled by a warrior people who allowed subordinate groups, including the Mayans, to run their own regions so long as they paid regular, high tribute in the form of gold and slaves. Aztec religion, featuring gods of war as well as gods of nature, blended fairly readily with the religions already current in the region, and the Aztecs devoted considerable attention to works of art and pyramidal monuments in honor of the gods.

The Aztec empire displayed great magnificence. Tenochtitlán, which was to serve as forerunner to the Spanish capital Mexico City, contained about 100,000 inhabitants and featured ornate palaces, statuary, and temples. The most intensive agriculture in the world developed to support a population of perhaps 20 million. Extensive regional trade included vibrant markets, though the Aztecs also used merchants as spies. Culturally, Aztecs relied on the earlier stylistic achievements of the Mayans and Toltecs. More important, they depended on extensive slave labor and, as noted, exacted tributes to maintain their luxury. Thus, although their wealth and engineering accomplishments awed the first Spanish settlers, who claimed that their cities surpassed the glories of Rome or Constantinople, they failed to create any basis other than force for their political regime. Government was centralized, under a king who claimed divine authority, and the level of violence was high.

To glorify their gods, the Aztecs extended earlier practices of human sacrifice, killing no less than 20,000 people at the dedication of one of the great pyramids. The Aztecs believed that the gods themselves had been sacrificed in order to create the sun, which needed human blood as food, and their worship reenacted this drama. As a result, not only the economy but also the religion required a steady flow of victims, mainly drawn from persistent warfare. This was a tense and brutal period in Central American history, and an inherently fragile one, for the subjects of Aztec rule had no reason to revere their masters. In fact, many Indian groups initially welcomed the arrival of the Spanish explorers as liberators from their harsh tyranny. Ironically, the Aztecs themselves would be hampered in their response to Spanish incursions, not only by their inferior weaponry—for they lacked guns or iron weapons of any sort—but also by their own uncertainty about the future of their rule. Their empire, built on the greater creativity of earlier civilizations in the region, proved to have scant impact beyond its own time.

THE INCA EMPIRE

A second and quite separate center of American Indian civilization developed, during the centuries of Mayan and Aztec ascendancy, in the Andes mountains of present-day Peru and Bolivia. Here, building on the earlier culture that had extended carefully terraced agriculture in the region and constructed substantial monuments to the gods, an Incan empire arose from the twelfth century onward.

Indian civilization in Central America, particularly before the final Aztec period, in certain features resembled the earlier river valley civilization of Mesopotamia. The emphasis on regional states, the creativity in science, the interest in art and active trade in luxury goods, even the pessimistic tone of the religion—all offer vague

"Lady of the Serpent Skirt": carving of the Aztec goddess Coatlicue. Coatlicue was also mother of the war god and goddess of the earth and death.

echoes of Sumeria and its successors. In contrast, the Inca empire reflects, again in very general terms, the styles of ancient Egypt, especially in its focus on the sun god and the establishment of a highly centralized state led by a ruler regarded as divine.

The Incas, centered initially in a small area in what is now Peru, began expanding their authority over other civilized peoples in the regions, learning more elaborate political and artistic forms as they went. By the late 1400s, their empire extended from Ecuador to central Chile, constituting the largest governmental unit ever created up until that time in the Americas. The empire included a network of roads over 10,000 miles of mountain terrain. On these roads, runners regularly carried messages, both carefully memorized oral communications—for the Incas never developed writing—and records coded by knots in colored ropes (a system called "quipu"). The Inca people themselves served as a ruling caste in their empire. They were led by a man called Sapa Inca, or "only Inca." This ruler governed despotically, regulating marriage and movement and officially controlling all produce. The government, in other words, monitored the labor force closely. Exchanges, carried by llama transport, provided food for craft workers and cloth for the farmers: There was no trade in the sense of a money economy, and local self-sufficiency was emphasized. Copper tools were manufactured, and gold and silver were used for luxurious ornamentation in the royal palaces. The government regulated the education of local elites among the conquered peoples to ensure their allegiance. Protest was dealt with by military force, followed by the resettlement of disaffected peoples to reduce the potential for further trouble.

The Inca system, far less brutal than that of the Aztecs, was extremely tolerant of local beliefs and religion, although the Incas themselves worshipped a sun deity from whom the royal family was presumably descended. Like the ancient Egyptians, the Incas mummified their dead to preserve them for an afterlife.

By the 1400s, the Incas had probably overextended their territory. Without writing, their record-keeping ability was limited, which meant substantial dependence on local leadership. Conquered peoples were not always content and technology lagged, which further limited the economic and political links that could be sustained. Thus, the Inca empire was already receding somewhat even before the Spanish conquest, and in any event the methods and weapons of war the Incas had developed were no match for the guns of the Spaniards.

AMERICAN INDIAN CIVILIZATION: A CONTINUING HERITAGE

There were few traces of the high cultures of the Mayans and Incas left for later civilization in the Americas, because of their own internal limitations but above all else because of conquest by Europeans, beginning in the sixteenth century. Tragically, the Europeans brought with them not only greater firepower but also a host of diseases for which the original Americans had not developed immunity, so 80 percent of the Indian population was stricken without the benefit of available treatment. The civilizations that did arise in the Americas after European conquest owed little to previous Indian patterns at the level of formal religion or politics. Had the Europeans not come, with their superior technology, civilization might well have spread or diversified. Even as the Incas began to decline, new centers of advanced culture began to develop in places like present-day Colombia. And in North America, although many Indian groups followed a hunting and gathering economy combined with seasonal farming, settled agriculture had spread not only to the Southwest, from the more advanced centers in Mexico, but also along the Atlantic coast. Pueblo Indians reflected Central American civilization, whereas slash-and-burn farming enhanced Indian societies in the Mississippi and New England regions. Loose political alliances had formed among certain peoples, such as the five Iroquois tribes around the eastern Great Lakes, which might ultimately have developed into a tighter form of administration. This future was undone, however, by European control and the spread of certain diseases.

However, in two important respects, the history of American Indian civilizations did reverberate in later periods, even aside from the fact that surviving Indian groups in both North and South America preserved an important sense of language and heritage. First, the crops so laboriously developed in centuries of agriculture, particularly in Central America and the Andes, were a vital contribution to the nutrition of peoples worldwide when they were disseminated by European traders. European settlers in the Americas, as well as Africans, Asians, and Europeans, found their diets and thus their lives substantially altered by corn, squash, and the potato, whose cultivation had been developed by the Incas and Mayans and their ancestors. The spread of important new foods from the Americas from the sixteenth and seventeenth centuries onward was a major new factor in world history.

Second, beneath the surface, where Indian civilizations had taken deepest root, significant traces of Indian society remained long after official European conquest. Thus in Central America and the Andes, Indians long preserved elements of older religious beliefs, even under a facade of Christianity. Communal festivals as well as some secret rituals allowed traditional dances, games, and other recreations to survive. More important still, many American Indian groups preserved certain artistic patterns in their geometrically designed pottery and jewelry and their brightly colored clothing that would be characteristic of the new civilization formed by a merger between Spanish and Indian heritages. Finally, Indians in these areas maintained distinctive local customs and economic and political styles into the twentieth century. The very appearance of Indian villages, notably in Central America, resembled that of traditional communities, with a Christian church and perhaps an official govern-

UNDERSTANDING CULTURES

The Question of Legacies

Interpreting what survives from one culture for later periods is one of the central tasks of historical interpretation. Ultimately, it helps us connect present to past, by seeing what beliefs and values we entertain as a result of legacies from the past.

Cultural heritage from great periods of civilization includes such things as major religions or venerated literary and artistic models. It also includes ways to approach science. We have traced and will continue to trace connections of this sort in dealing with China, India, Islam, and the classical Mediterranean.

Heritage from the American Indian civilizations that flourished during the postclassical period is much harder to assess. When the Spanish arrived, from the early sixteenth century onward, they resolutely attacked Mayan, Aztec, and Inca high culture in favor of Christianity. Even Mayan writings were largely destroyed, so it is only now that scholars are regaining the ability to decipher remnants of the Mayan alphabet.

Nonetheless, it is difficult, in fact, to uproot a culture entirely. Popular beliefs and rituals are harder to dislodge than a more formal intellectual life, for popular systems do not depend mainly on writing. Spanish conquerors, furthermore, had to tolerate some popular holdovers as part of persuading ordinary people to also accept the trappings of Christianity. Thus, Mayan colors and designs were used to decorate Christian statues. Elements of polytheism and traditional celebrations were combined with Christianity, from Central America to the Andes. The Indian component of Latin American culture would remain a serious factor even as European and African elements were introduced following the postclassical period.

ment building merely supplementing earlier housing patterns and a characteristic market square.

Many villages also preserved a communal system of agriculture that had supported the larger American Indian civilization. In the Andes, villagers frequently held land in common, rather than through individual ownership, and stressed the production of most goods essential to village life. Elaborate market systems and a profit-making motive would long remain foreign to this village tradition. Important segments of the Indian population thus long resisted fully embracing the habits and institutions of the conquering Europeans. This fact encouraged a distinctive, sometimes uncomfortable kind of fusion between European and Indian ways, beneath the levels of official government and religion, toward forming a Latin American culture that would be neither purely Indian nor purely European in nature. The surviving traditions also ensured future conflicts, when as in recent decades, customary economic values encountered much more direct challenges than initial Spanish conquest and administration had compelled. It is overly simplistic to claim that popular culture in the areas of Latin America where Indian populations remained largest—notably, those areas that had previously been civilized and so possessed a vigorous agricultural base—merely combined European and Indian customs to produce a new culure. Such a statement ignores the fact that the governing institutions of American Indian civilization really were destroyed; therefore, there were great differences in the bargaining power of the conqueror and the conquered. But, important popular forms did persist alongside new or imported patterns brought by the Spaniards and their heirs, and they continue to influence the lives of Latin Americans in Mexico, Peru, and other countries of these regions even in the present day.

THE ISSUE OF ISOLATION

The achievements of the American civilizations were impressive by any standard, but particularly when viewed within the context of unusually stark isolation from any other civilized areas. All societies in Asia, Africa, Europe, even China had benefited from ideas and techniques they borrowed from others, and as we have seen in previous chapters, the importance of borrowing increased during the postclassical period for several areas of new civilization. The Americas had no part in this or in the shared disease pool that resulted from international contacts.

Several other major areas sponsored important new developments in isolation during the postclassical centuries. Polynesian contacts with Hawaii became more extensive, and the settlement of New Zealand began. Polynesians adapted an essentially Neolithic technology in their new settings, utilizing local resources for foods while importing certain animals. As in Central America, a rigid social structure helped compensate for technological limitations; it included an important priestly caste and was geared for frequent warfare. Polynesian society was able to maintain its isolated development until the eighteenth century, when European contacts brought many of the same results, in terms of conquest and disease, that the Americas had earlier experienced. Here, too, isolation became a historical issue—and a very grave one—when it was ended.

SUGGESTED WEBSITES

On the Web, Toltec and Aztec civilization is explored at *http://www.stockton.edu/~gilmorew/consorti/1gcenso.htm*. The Incas are examined at *http://www.sscf.ucsb.edu/~ogburn/inca/inca.htm*.

SUGGESTED READINGS

On Indian civilization in the Americas, see Ignacio Bernard, *Mexico Before Cortez: Art, History, Legend* (1975); M. D. Coe, *Mexico* (1984); Frances Berdan, *The Aztecs of Central Mexico: An Imperial Society* (1982); M. P. Weaver, *The Aztec, Maya and Their Predecessors* (1981)—this is particularly up-to-date on archeological findings; and Eric R. Wolf, ed., *The Valley of Mexico: Studies in Pre-Hispanic Ecology and Society* (1976). Inga Clendinnen, *The Aztecs* (1991), is splendid.

On the Incas, consult J. A. Mason, *The Ancient Civilizations of Peru* (1973); Richard W. Keatinge, ed., *Peruvian Prehistory* (1988); Alfred Metraux, *The History of the Incas* (1970); John Murra, *The Economic Organization of the Inca State* (1980); Irene Silverblatt, *Moon, Sun, and Witches: Gender Ideologies and Class in Inca and Colonial Peru* (1987); and John V. Murra, Nathan Wachtel, and Jacques Revel, eds., *Anthropological History of Andean Politics* (1986). For more general coverage, see Geoffrey W. Conrad and Arthur A. Demerest, *Religion and Empire: The Dynamics of Aztec and Inca Expansionism* (1984); on North as well as South America, see Alvin M. Josephy, Jr., *The Indian Heritage of America* (1968).

The Mongol Interlude and the End of the Postclassical Period

13

FOCAL POINTS *Mongol conquests ranged from East Asia to Eastern Europe during the thirteenth and fourteenth centuries. Why were such wide-ranging conquests possible? Why was this relatively short period so crucial in establishing new international contacts? Aside from the Mongols themselves, what societies gained the most from the Mongol period, and what societies gained the least?*

CIVILIZATIONS RISE OR RECEDE

In this chapter, we move back to the world network, and to huge changes that were occurring in the centuries between 1250 and 1450. These changes involved the decline of Arab leadership and the rise of new frameworks for global interactions in Afro-Eurasia. Contacts increased. Both East Asia and Western Europe became more involved. Africa, partly because it worked through the Middle East as an intermediary, was less affected. The end result was a different world balance, by 1450, from that prevailing two centuries before. As part of this shift, key technologies had also changed, establishing the groundwork for further developments in the future.

Not surprisingly, trends among major societies varied greatly as the postclassical period drew to a close. Peasants in Western Europe gained some new freedom from serfdom as their counterparts in the Middle East encountered new landlord demands. Russia began to lose vitality, even before the Mongol invasions, as Japan and Western Europe in some respects gained further momentum. A few general trends remained firm, at least in much of Asia, Africa, and Europe. Many aristocracies shifted from warlike emphasis to greater cultural sophistication. Conditions for women deteriorated as agricultural economies yielded larger surpluses, permitting families to treat women as mere ornaments. The great world religions continued to gain ground, as with Islam in Southeast Asia. There is no question, however, that societies in the postclassical world remained widely separated, following quite different patterns—some of which, like the formation of regional kingdoms in Africa, persisted easily into the next period of world history.

Nevertheless, because the international network had intensified during the postclassical period, several developments caused more general changes that brought the period itself to a close while setting the stage for the initial dynamics of the period that was to come. To be sure, the isolated civilizations were not affected, and even Africa was less touched than Asia and Europe.

247

The first development was quite simply the decline of Arab political strength and the narrowing of Middle Eastern culture and economy. The Arabs had played such a leadership role in forming the international network that their problems inevitably reverberated beyond their borders. African trading, although still vigorous, was constrained by the shifts in the society with which African merchants most closely interacted. Western Europe, although heartened by Arab decline, grew anxious as more vigorous invaders into the Middle East (the Turks) began to establish a new Muslim empire. Turkish success in capturing Constantinople in 1453 and assuming control of Byzantine holdings in the Balkans as well as much of the Arab Middle East revealed a major new configuration in this region. It also provoked reactions, particularly on the part of the nervous Europeans, who redoubled their efforts to find trade routes that would allow them to bypass the Muslim heartland.

Arab decline and Turkish invasion were furthered by an even greater event—the Mongol conquests in Asia and Eastern Europe.

MONGOL EMPIRES

These conquests, the last of their kind in which nomadic warriors overturned the governments of agricultural societies, contributed to important changes in East Asia, southern Asia, the Middle East, and Russia. Even more, they enhanced the international network, facilitating new exchanges and whetting appetites for greater international involvements.

Mongol herders had been pressing at the northern frontiers of China for some time. They were superb equestrians and archers, using an iron stirrup that allowed them to fire their bows while riding; peasant foot soldiers could not compete with such military prowess. Organized in family clans by leaders who advanced because of their military abilities, they formed a tightly knit fighting unit, highly trained and able to ride in close formation. Europeans called this fighting force a "horde." The Mongol cavalry ultimately included between 50,000 and 70,000 horsemen, all adept at avoiding head-on clashes with larger forces and skilled at organizing ambushes and cutting off supply routes.

The great Mongol conqueror, Chinggis (or Genghis) Khan, was born about 1147. His first task was to unify the tribal groups of Mongols themselves; his name, which meant "universal ruler," was adopted at the end of this process, in 1206. Chinggis was a superb general and also an able administrator who used Turkish writing or script to facilitate his bureaucracy. Chinggis Khan invaded China early in the thirteenth century; he also conquered a Turkish kingdom in south central Asia. Each conquest fed Mongol wealth and increased the size of the armies. Successors to Chinggis Khan swept through the Middle East, toppling the Abbasid caliphate. The Mongols' impact on the eastern Islamic lands, including the terror they generated, long reverberated. They also seized all of Russia and pressed into the smaller kingdoms of Eastern Europe. They might have continued farther west, but they were called back by a domestic political crisis. Mongol forces completed the conquest of China, unseating the Sung dynasty in 1279. From the Chinese base, the greatest Mongol emperor, Chinggis Khan's grandson Kubilai Khan, organized invasions into Southeast Asia and India. He also attempted seaborn attacks on Indonesia and Japan, although these ended in failure. Despite these setbacks, by 1300 the Mongols ruled or influenced most of the Eurasian civilized world.

The Mongol period produced fascinating interactions between personalities and history. Various Mongol rulers converted to Buddhism or Islam. Kubilai Khan himself ruled China in grand style. Of necessity, he preserved the Chinese bureaucratic system, but used foreigners—Turks and other Muslims and even a handful of Europeans—as his chief ministers because he distrusted the Chinese Mandarins, who were assigned to lower bureaucratic ranks. Repressive laws that prevented the Chinese from assembling or traveling by night, of course, bred resentment. But for some decades, Kubilai Khan ruled as few Chinese dynasts had ever done before him, operating a splendid court that was completely open to foreign visitors. Among these, in turn, were members of an Italian family—Marco Polo and his father and uncle—who had traveled across Asia to serve at the Great Khan's court. Encouraged by the Khan's friendly curiosity, Marco Polo was able to learn a great deal about China. Some items he could not understand, given his European background, including the use of coal to smelt iron. However, his travel account was widely read; at first regarded as fantasy, it contributed greatly to acquainting Europeans with the East.

But, the Mongol empire was short-lived. China withdrew from Mongol control later in the fourteenth century, and the main Mongol legacy in China was an enhanced distaste for foreigners, for the Mongols had been bitterly resented as barbarians. Mongol impact in the Middle East was also short-lived, for the Turks increasingly held power in this region. Direct Mongol influence in India was also slight, although a later Mongol-Turkish force, pressing into India early in the 1500s, established another great Muslim empire in much of the subcontinent. Only in Russia did Mongol control leave an enduring legacy, perhaps setting back economic and cultural levels but also stimulating an intense desire, on the part of the Russians, to imitate Mongol conquests. Russia gained full freedom from Mongol domination in 1480 and began a pattern of expansion of great importance in world history.

The Mongols' impact on world history, however brief, was significant in several respects. First, the vast stretch of territory under Mongol control made possible the interchange of knowledge and products among the various civilizations of Europe and Asia. In particular, Chinese discoveries—gunpowder, paper money, printing, porcelain, medical techniques, even playing cards—began to make their way westward. Mongol-facilitated diffusion was of special benefit to Western Europe, previously backward, and helps explain this region's subsequent rise, as Asian technology was combined with a territorially ambitious, aggressive spirit. The Mongol presence was also significant in keeping Western Europe, albeit accidentally, out of the hands of foreign powers. For a century (and more than that in Russia), most major civilizations in Europe and Asia were preoccupied with invasion, the threat of invasion, or foreign control. Western society enjoyed the fruits of new contacts with Asia without the attendant hardships and distractions. This, too, helps us understand why Western nations displayed such surprising vigor on the world scene by the late fifteenth century.

The Mongols also affected the conduct of war. They helped teach both the Turks and Europeans the effective use of explosive powder. By the early fifteenth century, both groups were utilizing the cannon in warfare, to great effect.

New international contacts also promoted new contagions, an unhappy byproduct of the increased level of Eurasian commerce by the end of the postclassical

World Profiles

Chabi Khan

Chabi, wife of the great Mongol emperor Kubilai Khan (who ruled from 1260 to 1294), was an important historical personage in her own right. Obviously, in patriarchal societies, women most commonly gained access to power (even on a very local level) through the positions of their husbands. Chabi advised Kubilai actively, guiding counterstrategies against his ambitious brothers and promoting Buddhist interests in the highest government circles. Chabi also urged tolerance for the defeated Chinese rulers, arguing that leniency would best reconcile the Chinese to Mongol rule; she influenced her husband to abandon a plan to turn farmland near the capital into pastures for the Mongol's horses. At the same time, Chabi and other Mongol women resisted integration with Chinese customs concerning women, from Confucian doctrines to footbinding. They moved freely in public, hunted on horseback both with their husbands and in parties of their own. These women had no enduring impact on Chinese gender patterns, however. Does this suggest some distinctive limitations on the historical role of even great women in the postclassical era? Or, do great people in general have limited power to change the directions of a society?

Chabi, wife of Kubilai Khan, the thirteenth-century Mongol ruler of China. (The Granger Collection)

period. Bubonic plague broke out in western China early in the fourteenth century. Carried probably by fleas on pack animals, it reached the Middle East by the mid–fourteenth century, hitting North African ports by the 1360s. From there, it spread quickly to Italian ports and then to the rest of Western Europe. The overall result was one of the most deadly world epidemics in all of human history, with mortality rates over 25 percent in parts of the Middle East and Europe. Only the plagues of the late classical period and the later European-borne diseases in the Americas and Pacific island areas rival this international plague in known consequences.

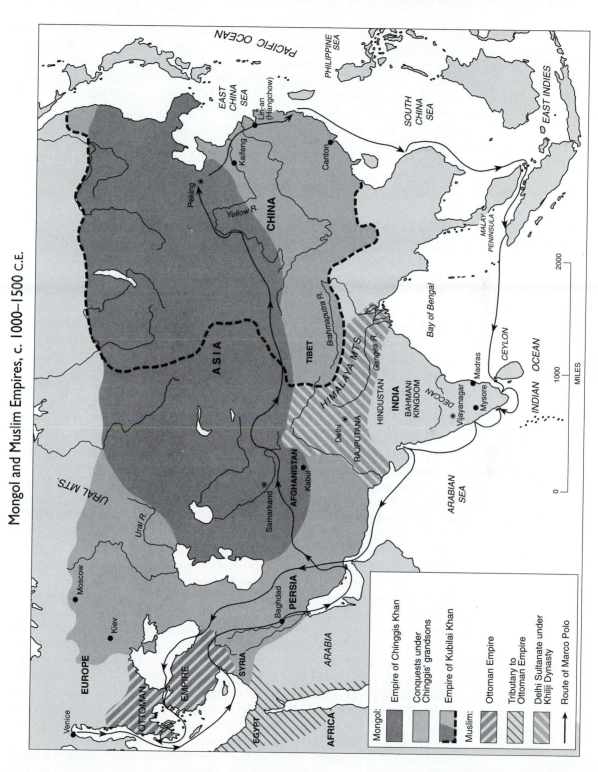

Mongol and Muslim Empires, c. 1000–1500 C.E.

Mongol:
- Empire of Chinggis Khan
- Conquests under Chinggis' grandsons
- Empire of Kubilai Khan

Muslim:
- Ottoman Empire
- Tributary to Ottoman Empire
- Delhi Sultanate under Khilji Dynasty
- → Route of Marco Polo

PACIFIC OCEAN

PHILIPPINE SEA

EAST CHINA SEA

Lin-an (Hangchow)

Kaifeng

Canton

SOUTH CHINA SEA

EAST INDIES

Peking

Yellow R.

CHINA

MALAY PENINSULA

ASIA

TIBET

Brahmaputra R.

HIMALAYA MTS.

Ganges R.

Bay of Bengal

CEYLON

INDIAN OCEAN

HINDUSTAN

INDIA

BAHMANI KINGDOM

DECCAN

Madras

Vijayanagar

Mysore

Delhi

RAJPUTANA

AFGHANISTAN

Kabul

Samarkand

ARABIAN SEA

URAL MTS.

Ural R.

Moscow

Kiev

Baghdad

PERSIA

ARABIA

EUROPE

OTTOMAN EMPIRE

SYRIA

EGYPT

AFRICA

Venice

2000

1000

0

MILES

The Mongol period was finite, of course. By the fourteenth century, China had expelled the great Khans, and soon after Russia would do the same. With the revival of separate civilizations, some barriers to international exchange were restored. European contacts with China, for example, were reduced for some time. Nevertheless, the knowledge of new techniques, products, and trade routes could not be reversed. The international network was poised for further definition.

At the same time, the decline of the Arabs and then the Mongols left a certain vacuum of power within the international network. Who would now sponsor the most important commercial exchanges? It was testimony to the solidity and significance of the international network that this was a question which had to be answered.

CHINA AND THE WEST AS NEW WORLD POWERS

The revived Chinese empire, under its new Ming dynasty, provided the first response. The Ming dynasty turned out to be a period of unusual stability in Chinese history, but it began with an unaccustomed display of expansionist behavior. It was as if a release from Mongol control awakened a desire to push outward—as happened later, with more durable results, in Russia. The first Ming emperor rather naturally expanded China's land boundaries by pushing the Mongols to the north. The Ming also reestablished influence over neighboring governments, as in the earlier T'ang period, winning tribute from states in Korea, Vietnam, and Tibet. What was more unusual was a new policy, adopted in the early 1400s, of mounting huge, state-sponsored trading expeditions to southern Asia. A first fleet, under a Muslim Chinese admiral, Chang Ho, sailed in 1405 to India, with 62 ships carrying 28,000 men. Later voyages reached the Middle East and the eastern coast of Africa, bringing chinaware and copper coins in exchange for local goods. Chinese shipping at its height consisted of 2700 coast guard vessels, 400 armed naval ships, and at least as many long-distance ships. Nine great "treasure ships" were the biggest in the world, capable of carrying a year's supply of grain and equipped with tubs to grow garden vegetables. Ships of this sort, the most sophisticated in the world at the time in their size and provisions and also in the improved compasses they used for navigation, explored not only the Indian Ocean but also the Persian Gulf and Red Sea, establishing regular trade with all parts of southern Asia and the Middle East.

There is no question that, had the Chinese thrust continued, the course of world history would have been immeasurably altered, for the tiny European expeditions that began to venture down the western coast of Africa at about the same time would have been no match for this combination of merchant and military organization. But, the emperors called the expeditions to a halt in 1433. The costs seemed unacceptable, given the continuing expenses of the campaigns against the Mongols and the desire to build a luxurious new capital city in Beijing. Confucian suspicion concerning merchants surfaced as well. This decision left the door open for a new Western European surge, which began to take clear shape by the mid–fifteenth century.

West Europeans had several bases for this unprecedented advance, despite their backwardness during the postclassical period. They had merchant skills and a vigor-

HISTORY DEBATE

Causes of Global Change by 1450

It is easy to see that world conditions were changing rapidly by the fifteenth century. Western Europe, although still backward in many respects, was beginning to extend its reach toward new power—a long process that would last into the nineteenth century. What were the key causes of such global change? Here is where the debate lies.

The most conventional explanation focuses on the features of Europe itself, including some new ones. Christianity provided a missionary spirit. Feudal wars accustomed Europeans to fighting and schooled them in the importance of gaining an advantage over rivals. The new Renaissance, a cultural movement, gave Europeans greater confidence in the powers of individual effort and generated more interest in secular, rather than purely religious, goals (see Chapter 14).

This argument may be supplemented by focusing on the traditionalism of societies outside Europe. Carlo Cipolla, writing about European expansion, notes how the Chinese, for example, simply refused to follow Europe's technological gains, because innovation would threaten the established social structure, with scholar-gentry on top, and anticommercial Confucian values. Again, Europe can be seen as unique.

A different argument focuses on changes in world conditions that almost accidentally gave Western Europe an advantage. The Mongol era provided Western Europe with a chance to imitate Chinese technology, without actually experiencing invasion (an obvious contrast with Eastern Europe or even the Middle East). After the Mongol era, new barriers to overland international trade shifted attention to ocean routes—another boon for Western Europe. Europe was motivated to seek change not necessarily because of a distinctive culture, but rather because of certain acute economic liabilities. It simply did not have the goods to exchange for the spices and other Asian products it had come to cherish, so it needed to find sources of gold. It also feared dependence on Muslim merchants, particularly as Ottoman power showed a revival of Muslim political strength, so it looked for alternative sea routes. According to this world view, changing world forces, not special European qualities or strange Asian blindspots, were the center of primary attention.

Which historical approach seems most plausible? Are there ways to combine them?

ous iron industry. They had a missionary Christian religion, an active military tradition, and a host of internal rivalries that could propel traders and kings alike to seek advantageous gains by successful ventures abroad. They also had some problems. They feared the new Turkish empire. Their upper classes had a taste for Asian luxuries and spices that the European economy could not easily afford. During the postclassical period, this trade lay largely in Muslim hands, with Europeans transporting the goods only in the Mediterranean. Now it seemed desirable to find more direct access, without the Muslim intermediary. Europe's economy, furthermore, generated few goods that Asians wanted. They supplied some tin, wool, and salt, but the balance had to be paid for in gold. Europe had no real gold supply; this was another reason to push into new territories, in the hope of finding rich holdings. Finally, Europeans by the fifteenth century were able to assimilate some of the technologies that had passed their way thanks to the Mongol empire and even to improve on them. They had cannons and gunpowder; they possessed the compass; they were advancing in the design of sailing ships.

Initial European attempts to find routes to Asia and gold began earlier, in the postclassical period. As early as 1291, an expedition from the Italian port city of Genoa sailed into the Atlantic seeking a westward route to the "Indies," but the expedition was never heard from again. During the fourteenth century, Italian sailors reached islands in the Atlantic—the Canaries, the Madeiras, and possibly the Azores. There they established sugar plantations, importing African slaves to do the work—a sign of the system Europeans would soon develop further.

Spanish expeditions also ventured as far as the northwest Atlantic coast of Africa. However, such voyages were limited by the small, oar-propelled ships used in Mediterranean trade, for they could not press far into the oceans. During the fifteenth century, however, round-hulled ships were developed for the Atlantic, and the Europeans also began to use a compass for navigation—an instrument that they copied from the Arabs, who in turn had learned of it from the Chinese. Mapmaking and other navigational devices improved as well. Western Europe was ready for its big push.

THE END OF TRANSITION: POSTCLASSICAL TO EARLY MODERN

By 1450, the world had changed in many ways from just three centuries before. The Arabs, who had provided the first global civilization, were in partial eclipse. Major empires in the Americas were tottering. The reverberations of Mongol conquests continued, particularly in central Asia, Russia, and India, although the Mongols themselves were in retreat. New players in the game of international influence were beginning to emerge. The powerful influence of world religions continued, but this theme was no longer center stage. The clearest constant, aside from regional continuities in China and elsewhere, was the importance of international contacts. And, the greatest contribution of the postclassical period to world history was the creation of a regular international network affecting most of Asia, Africa, and Europe. The definition of the network changed, as Arabs yielded to Mongols and Mongols to Chinese as effective chief administrators of the network. However, its importance steadily intensified. What was about to happen, after the postclassical period closed, was a reformulation of the network itself, broadening to include the entire world for the first time in history.

For the Mongol period generated different effects in various parts of the world network. Even direct Mongol control, for example, affected Russia differently from China. Japan, spared invasion, gained in self-confidence in relation to the rest of the world. Mongol incursions added to instability in the Middle East. Western Europe benefited from new contacts, as learning opportunities, without facing a direct threat. Sub-Saharan Africa continued its international interactions—Mongol leaders wore headdresses made from monkey skins imported from East Africa—but was not directly affected by the Mongols, in terms of new contacts or new threats. Its stability contrasted with other regions in the network. These variations had obvious impact in the next stages of international contact, after the Mongol era had passed.

SUGGESTED WEBSITES

On the great emperor Kubilai Khan, see *http://www.ccds.charlotte.nc.us/~nwhist/china/tarwat/tarwat.htm*; on the Mongol heartland in Central Asia, see *http://pma.edmonton.ab.ca/vexhibit/genghis/intro.htm*; on Marco Polo, see *http://www.korcula.net/mpolo/index.html*; on the Renaissance, see *http://www.lib.virginia.edu/dic/colls/arh102/index.html*; on Black Death, see *http://history.idbsu.edu/westciv/plague*.

SUGGESTED READINGS

A substantial literature has developed on the Mongol interlude in global history. The most readable and reliable biography of Chinggis Khan is René Grousset's *Conqueror of the World* (1966); see also his *The Empire of the Steppes* (1970), and Peter Brent's more recent *The Mongol Empire*. Berthold Spuler's *The Mongols in History* (1971) makes some attempt to gauge the Mongols' impact on world history. T. Allsen's *Mongol Imperialism* (1987) provides the best account of the rise and structure of the empires built by Chinggis Khan and his successors. See also Richard Frye, ed., *The Heritage of Central Asia: From Antiquity to the Turkish Expansion* (1996).

For specific areas, see George Verdansky's *The Mongols in Russia* (1953). Morris Rossabi's recent *Kubilai Khan: His Life and Times* (1988) on the Mongols in China, James Chamber's *The Devil's Horsemen* (1979), and Denis Sinor's *History of Hungary* (1957) provide good accounts of the Mongol incursions into eastern and central Europe. The fullest and most accessible summary of the links between Mongol expansion and the spread of the Black Death can be found in William H. McNeill's *Plagues and Peoples* (1976). Finally, on international contacts, see Jerry H. Bentley, *Old World Encounters: Cross-Cultural Contacts and Exchanges in Pre-Modern Times* (1993), and J. L. Abu-Lughod, *Before European Hegemony: The World System* A.D. *1250–1350* (1989). For a recent debate, see Frances Wood, *Did Marco Polo Go to China?* (1996).

A New World Economy, 1450–1750

INTRODUCTION: THE NEW THEMES IN WORLD HISTORY

Between 1450 and 1750, world history developed a new framework. The centerpiece was a huge transformation of the world network that had developed during the post-classical period. It should be no surprise that the leading society in the new international economy now was Western Europe, rather than the Middle East or China. The rise of the West rested on several factors, but the new naval technology ranked high among them. A second change involved the incorporation of the Americas in international exchange. This had immense impact on the Americas but also, particularly through the spread of American foodstuffs like corn and potatoes, on the rest of the world. A third change involved, quite simply, the increasing importance of international commerce and the growth of internal trade. Several societies saw their basic political and social structures altered by their place in world trade, whereas commercial relationships affected life in an even broader range of civilizations.

This new global age saw many other changes besides a redefinition of the world economy. A host of new empires formed, not just those that evolved from Western Europe's new colonial outreach. Individual civilizations experienced significant innovations, like the new cultural influences in India or the expansion of Confucianism in Japan. Changes of this sort left their mark even later on, defining varied opportunities in both the nineteenth and twentieth centuries.

This new period in world history is usually called "early modern" because of the importance of many of the new features, including the world economy, in establishing a framework for developments in the past 200 years. The early modern period began with the rise of the West, the opening of the Americas to international contact, and the surge of several new Asian empires along with Russia—all occurring soon after 1450. It ended around 1750, when the West began to experience a further transformation—known as the Industrial Revolution—that would alter world relationships yet again.

257

The Postclassical World in Transition, About 1400 C.E.

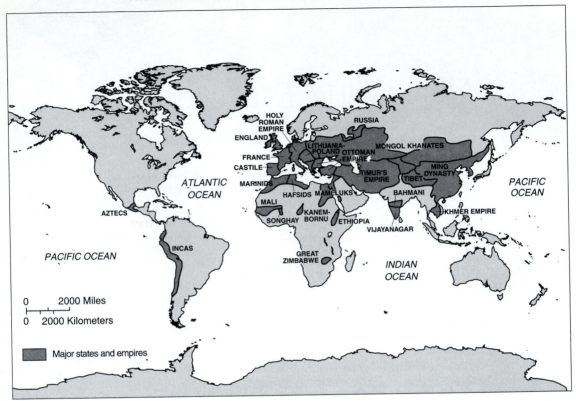

THE RISE OF THE WEST

Between 1450 and 1750, the West, led initially by Spain and Portugal, then by Britain, France, and Holland, gained control of the key international trade routes. It established colonies in the Americas and, on a much more limited basis, in Africa and parts of Asia.

At the same time, partly because of its new international position and the growing impact of commerce, the West itself changed rapidly, becoming an unusual kind of agricultural civilization. Commerce began to alter the social structure and also affected basic attitudes toward family life and the natural environment. A host of new ideas, some of them advocated by religious reformers, created a novel cultural climate in which scientific principles became increasingly more important; the scientific revolution gradually reshaped Western culture as a whole. More effective political structures emerged by the seventeenth century, as Western monarchs began to introduce bureaucratic principles similar to those pioneered long before in China.

A vital facet of the early modern period, then, consisted of the West's expansion as an international force and its simultaneous internal transformation. Like the previous world-class civilization, Arab Islam, the West developed a diverse and dynamic culture and society, which were both the results and causes of its ascending international position.

THE WORLD ECONOMY AND GLOBAL CONTACTS

The world network established during the previous period of history intensified and took on new dimensions. This change involved more than the fact that the Europeans, not the Muslims, dominated international trade. It involved an expansion of the world network to literally global proportions, well beyond the geographical scope of previous connections. Far more of Africa, and above all the Americas, were brought into contact with other cultures and included in international exchanges for the first time. At the end of the period, in the eighteenth century, Polynesian and Australian societies began to undergo the same painful experience of integration.

Effectively, by 1750 there were no more fully isolated societies of any great size. The new globalism of human contacts had a variety of important consequences that permeated early modern centuries. The human disease pool became fully international for the first time, and peoples who had previously been isolated from the rest of the world suffered immensely from their exposure to diseases for which they had developed no immunities. The global network also permitted a massive exchange of plants and animals. Cows and horses were introduced in the Americas, prompting significant changes in the American Indian economy and fighting techniques. American food crops were exported around the world, bringing sweet potatoes, corn, and manioc (a plant grown for its root) to China, corn to Africa, potatoes and tobacco to Europe—innovations that in many places initiated great changes in agricultural production.

One result of this food exchange, through most of the world including Asia and Western Europe, was rapid population growth. World population had declined in the late classical period, then bounced back as people gained new resistance to contagious disease. Population growth in the postclassical period, in places like Europe, was significant. However, rates of increase during the early modern centuries, except in Latin America and Africa, reached unprecedented levels.

Even globalization, although its impact was vast, did not exhaust the changes wrought in the world network during the three centuries after 1450. Far more than in the postclassical era, the period between 1450 and 1750 saw a set of definite and highly unequal relationships established among a number of civilizations. During the postclassical millennium, 450–1450 C.E., a few areas had contributed relatively inexpensive raw materials and slaves to more advanced societies, notably China and the Islamic world; this was true for the West and parts of Africa and Southeast Asia. These unequal economic relationships did not constrain the "raw-materials-producing" societies too severely, because international trade was simply not of overriding importance yet. After 1450 or 1500, as Western commerce expanded internationally, the West began to establish relationships with a number of areas that produced pronounced dependence and subordination within the international economy. Areas such as Latin America depended heavily on sales to export merchants, on imports of processed goods, and on Western ships and merchants to conduct international trade. Dependence of this sort might have had political ramifications in creating weak governments open to foreign intervention. It encouraged the commercial exploitation of slaves and serfs. It even corresponded to several full-scale attempts to impose Western culture on some dependent nations. Much of the world, particularly in the great Asian civilizations, remained outside this set of relationships, but there was a growing tendency to draw closer toward it, as occurred in India and Indonesia by the eighteenth century when the level of Western overseas expansion increased further.

THE GUNPOWDER EMPIRES

The centuries after 1450 could also be designated "the age of the gunpowder empires." The development of cannons and muskets in the fifteenth and sixteenth centuries, through the combination of Western technology with previous Chinese invention, obviously spurred the West's expansion. Ship-based artillery was fundamental to the West's mastery of international sea lanes and journeys to many ports and islands. Nonetheless, gunnery was developed by other societies as well. The Ottoman Turks used Hungarian-built cannons in their successful siege of Constantinople in 1453. The subsequent Ottoman Empire relied heavily on land-based guns to supplement trained cavalry. The rise of a new Russian Empire after 1480 also built on the growing use of guns, and the Russian economy was subsequently reshaped to provide the manufacturing base for new military hardware. Three other key empires—the Mughal in India, the Safavid in Persia, and the seventeenth-century Manchu dynasty in China—relied on the strength of the new gun-supported land armies. Guns also played a role in Japanese and African history during the same period.

Clearly, guns supported important military changes that, in turn, supported new political organization—colonial empires in the case of the West and new land agglomerations through much of Asia and Eastern Europe and, to an extent, in Africa. New Asian empires counterbalanced the growth of Western power to a considerable degree. The rise of the Russian Empire ran the course of the entire period. Although not as important as the rise of the West, it was certainly a predominant theme, involving among other things the progressive elimination of an independent central Asia. For the first time since the development of agriculture, nomadic herding peoples ceased to be a major force in world history. The rise of the Ottomans and Mughals was a bit shorter-lived, but echoed through the first two centuries of the period and, in the case of the Ottomans, created one of the most durable empires known in world history. The new land-based empires affected a massive number of people and long overshadowed, at least in the eyes of most Asian leaders, the surge in the West.

COMMERCE AND ITS OUTREACH

This was also an age of world commercialization. Market exchange played an increasing role in shaping economic activity. The world remained predominantly agricultural, but agriculture was now modified more than ever by specializations that depended on market transactions, as well as by the activities of merchants and the lure of money. Heightened commercial activity was one of the means by which rising populations could be sustained in advance of major technological change in the means of production. Commerce not only spread knowledge of new foodstuffs but also allowed increased specialization in production that could heighten output, as some regions concentrated on goods they were best suited to grow or manufacture, relying on trade for other materials.

The intensification of international trade, under the sponsorship of Western traders but also involving merchants in other societies, played an important part in the general expansion of commerce. Not only did many Latin Americans produce precious metals and agricultural products for sale to the West, many other Latin Americans produced foods and clothes to sell to workers in the export sectors. Internal trade increased within Latin America, particularly by the eighteenth century. Similar patterns emerged in West Africa. Earlier international trade routes, oriented toward North Africa, were diverted to a new Atlantic commerce organized by European merchants. African kings and merchants organized goods to sell in this trade, particularly slaves, and received manufactured products, including guns, in exchange. Again, the West was encouraged in its own commercial expansion, as considerable profits could be realized in the slave trade; the Americas were transformed through the introduction of new African populations and a new kind of slavery; and Africa itself was diversely affected by the new exchange.

The spread of commerce went beyond these Western-dominated transactions, however. Both China and Japan witnessed the rapid growth of market exchanges within their own boundaries, as the production and sale of foodstuffs, beverages, and the like expanded. Chinese commerce gained also from the American silver it amassed through trade with Western Europe. A general trend—the Western-dominated international economy and its growth—was thus supplemented by some parallelisms in other parts of the world, where internal trade far outweighed international exchange. And, this meant not only surprisingly widespread commercial and urban growth, but also some broader social effects. In most cases without toppling the land-based aristocracy, merchants in a number of societies, not just the West, gained new influence. Growing trade also played a role in some societies (in the West but also, for instance, in Japan) in encouraging some groups to reduce their commitment to religion and other worldly goals in favor of a focus on secular pursuits. The expansion of commerce thus had wider reverberations in many parts of the world.

MAJOR CIVILIZATIONS

The redefining of the world economy—the intensification of commerce, the inclusion of the Americas, and the rise of the West with its new naval technology—affected each major civilization to some degree. Even more than during the postclassical period, it becomes important to ask the following: How was each civilization affected by the new global developments? How were relationships with the West defined? How were new foodstuffs utilized? How was commerce handled? These questions follow the new framework of world history during the early modern period, but

(text continues on p. 266)

TIMELINE: The Early Modern World

East Asia	Middle East (Ottoman Empire)	India and Southeast Asia	Latin America
1336–1573 Return of Japan to feudalism.	**1453** Capture of Contantinople.	**1498** Vasco da Gama (Portugal) to India.	**1501** Introduction of African slaves.
1368–1644 Ming dynasty.	**1520–1566** Suleiman the Magnificent.	**Sixteenth century** Portugal's acquisition of trading rights, some trading stations in Siam, Burma, Indonesia.	**1500–1519** Spanish conquest of West Indies, including Puerto Rico, Cuba.
1405–1433 Great Chinese fleets.		**Sixteenth century and later** Formation of Sikh religion.	**Sixteenth century** Church organization of Spanish colonies established; Jesuit and other missions.
		1510 Portuguese acquisition of Goa.	**1519 ff.** Cortés expedition to Mexico.
	1526 Capture of Hungary	**1526–1529** Babur invasion from Afghanistan.	**1521** Capture and destruction of Tenochtitlán; building of Mexico City.
		1526–1761 (officially 1857) Mughal empire.	**1531** Pizarro conquest of Inca empire.
			1527–1542 Viceroyalties established for Central and South America.
1542 Portuguese traders to Japan.			**1532 ff.** Spanish explorations of California and Pacific coast of North America.
1557 Macao taken by Portugal.			**1536** Spanish settlement in Buenos Aires.
1577–1598 Hideyoshi general in Japan; centralization.			**1542** Enactment of new laws forbidding Indian slavery.
1597 Ban on foreign missions.			**1549** First Portuguese government in Brazil.

Western Civilization	Russia and Eastern Europe	Sub-Saharan Africa
1300 ff. Italian Renaissance: i.e., Giotto (1276–1337); Petrarch (1304–1374); Leonardo da Vinci (1452–1519); Machiavelli (1469–1527); Michelangelo (1475–1514).		
1450 ff. Northern Renaissance. Erasmus (1466–1536).	**1462** Much of Russia freed by Ivan III (Ivan the Great) from Tatars.	
1455 First European printing press, Mainz, Germany.	**1480** Moscow region free.	
1494 ff. French and Spanish expeditions in Italy.	**1533–1584** Ivan the Terrible, first to be called tsar; boyar power reduced.	
1517 Luther's 95 theses; beginning of Protestant Reformation.	**1552–1556** Russian expansion in central Asia, western Siberia.	
1534 Beginning of Church of England.		
1541–1564 Calvin in Geneva.		*Sixteenth century* Spanish, Portuguese, and Dutch ports on West African Coast.
1519–1521 Magellan expedition around world.		**1562** Beginning of British slave trade.
1550–1649 Religious wars in France, Germany, Britain.		**1591** Fall of Songhai empire.
1588 Defeat of Spanish Armada by English.		
1618–1648 Thirty Years' War.		
1642–1649 English Civil War.		

East Asia	Middle East (Ottoman Empire)	India and Southeast Asia	Latin America
			1565 Rio de Janeiro founded by Portuguese.
	1571 Loss of Lepanto naval battle.		**1569** Catholic Inquisition established for Spanish America; limitation of intellectual freedom.
1600–1868 Tokugawa shogunate.		**1608** First trade concessions from regional princes granted to England.	**1612** Wider colonization of Brazil begun by Portugal.
1635 Japanese travel abroad forbidden; policy of isolation.		**1627–1668** Jehan emperor; tolerance for Hindus reduced.	
1644 Suicide of Ming emperor.		**1632–1653** Taj Mahal built.	
1644–1912 Qing dynasty.		**1641** Capture by Dutch of major spice trade center in Indonesia; beginning of control of island of Java.	
1662–1722 Emperor Kang Hsi.	**1683** Failure of assault on Vienna.		
1727 Chinese-Russian frontier treaty.		**Seventeenth century** British and French forts on east coast of India.	
1774 ff. White Lotus society risings.	**1710–1711, 1736–1739, 1768–1774** Wars with Russia and Austria; loss of Balkan and central Asian territory.	**1658–1707** Aurangzeb emperor; high taxes, intolerance against Hindus; rise of Hindu resistance.	
1784 Chinese persecution of Jesuits.		**Eighteenth century** Mughal decline; rise of Sikh state (1708 ff) and states of southern India.	**1717 ff.** Spanish colonies established new provincial capitals.
	1729 First Muslim Arabic printing press.		**1720** Occupation of Texas by Spain.
		1744, 1756–1763 French-British wars in India.	**Eighteenth century** Several popular rebellions in Spanish colonies and by Creoles.
		1756 "Black hole" of Calcutta.	
		1764 ff. British control of Bengal.	**1794** Haitian uprising against France led by Toussaint L'Ouverture; independence and end of slavery there.
	1798 Brief capture of Egypt by Napoleon.		

Western Civilization	Russia and Eastern Europe	Sub-Saharan Africa
Seventeenth century Scientific revolution. Galileo (1564–1642); Newton (1642–1727).	**1604–1613** Time of Troubles.	**1626 ff.** French coastal settlements.
1643–1715 Louis XIV in France; absolute monarchy; wars (1667–1668; 1672–1678; 1688–1697; 1701–1713).	**1613–1917** Romanov dynasty. **1637** Russian pioneers to Pacific.	**1650 ff.** Intensification of slave trade. **1652** Dutch colony on Cape of Good Hope.
1688–1690 Glorious Revolution in Britain; parliamentary regime; some religious toleration; political writing of John Locke.	**1649** Law enacted making serfdom hereditary. **1689–1725** Peter the Great.	
Eighteenth century Enlightenment. Voltaire (1694–1778).	**1700–1721** Wars with Sweden. **1703** Founding of St. Petersburg.	
1712–1786 Frederick the Great of Prussia; "enlightened despotism."		
1756–1763 Seven Years' War: France, Britain, Prussia, Austria.		**1713** Right granted to Britain to import slaves to Spanish colonies.
1775–1783 American Revolution.		**Eighteenth century** Regulation of regional slave trade by West African kingdom of Fon.
		1760 ff. Fanning out of Dutch in South Africa.
	1762–1786 Catherine the Great.	**1770 ff.** Encounter with Bantu farmers; conflict for land.
	1773–1775 Pugachev revolt.	**Late Eighteenth century** Increase in Muslim conversions in Sudan region.
	1772, 1793, 1795 Partition of Poland.	**1754–1818** Founding of Islamic kingdom (in present-day Nigeria) by Usman dan Fodio.
	1785 Laws enacted tightening landlord power over serfs.	

the answers still vary. Because of prior traditions and new, separate developments, each civilization related to the global framework in distinctive ways. Western Europe by no means exercised uniform authority around the world; in many places its explicit influence, during the early modern period, remained negligible.

Furthermore, developments within each civilization, independent of the global framework, also caused important changes. On the one hand, some societies displayed great dynamism during the fifteenth and sixteenth centuries, only to trail off later; their new problems affected their regions' history during this period and subsequently as well. However, other societies developed important new political and cultural resources during the period, which would have an impact later.

The global framework intensified within the early modern period as well. By 1700, the West's activities were looming larger not just in key areas such as the Americas, the Asian island groups, and the coast of West Africa, but in Asia and Eastern Europe as well. A new Russian urge to selectively copy certain aspects of Western culture and the establishment of growing British control in parts of India were two indicators of this shift. Even Japan, which had responded to the new world economy by effective isolation, began to show new, albeit modest, openness, rescinding a ban on translating Western books.

By 1750 it is fair (with all the advantages historians have of knowing how the story turns out) to note that civilizations which were not in a position to react effectively to the West's new world role were verging on decline—whereas a mere century before, this would have been a considerable distortion of a more complex international balance. After 1750, in large part because of another major transformation within the West—the emergence of a revolutionary industrial economy—the theme of Western predominance took on new meaning, which is why the period of world history changes at this point once again.

Western Civilization Changes Shape in the Early Modern Centuries

14

Western Europe changed in many ways during the early modern period: compare a summary of the year 1750 with that for 1450. Europe's world position, its political structures, its social structures, and its culture had all shifted profoundly. "Big changes" in this period include the replacement of feudalism with national monarchies; greatly increased commercialization and the shift away from serfdom to wage labor; and a decline of traditional popular beliefs plus the rise of science. These themes must be charted through a variety of internal movements like the Protestant Reformation or the eighteenth-century Enlightenment. Why did Europe change so rapidly? What continuities can still be traced back to the postclassical period?

BASIC CHANGES

Between 1450 and 1750, Western European society went through a series of profound transformations. Each century produced at least one major new current. The fifteenth century featured the Renaissance, which began indeed a bit earlier in Italy and then spread to northern Europe. In the sixteenth century, the Protestant Reformation upstaged the continuing impact of the Renaissance, breaking the unity of Western Christendom; the Catholic Reformation, in turn, responded. Political turmoil dominated the first half of the seventeenth century, but still more profound change resulted from the scientific revolution, which was one of the most basic reorientations of intellectual life in the history of any civilization. Finally, during the first half of the eighteenth century, the Enlightenment extended the principles of the scientific revolution to generate new views of politics and society, indeed new views of human nature itself.

Thinkers during the Enlightenment professed embarrassment at the very existence of the medieval period, which seemed to them so remote and backward in contrast to their own sophisticated world. Such a view was, in fact, too extreme, as well as unfairly demeaning to the achievements of medieval society: The heritage of the Middle Ages was still visible in political, intellectual, and economic life. There was no question, however, that Western civilization showed a marked ability to change its focus.

So much seemed to be changing, in fact, that it is sometimes difficult to identify coherent directions in the period as a whole. Transformation was not neat and tidy:

267

Different movements overlapped, like the Renaissance and the Reformation. Some events represented a resurgence of earlier values. The Reformation, for example, stemmed in part from a very medieval piety, although it had quite nonmedieval results. Although it is important to gain a sense of specific developments, it is also possible to observe general trends. Various movements tended to strengthen the central state in European monarchies, but for different reasons. Historical processes led, even more clearly, to a significant transformation of Western intellectual and artistic life, with the ultimate result a decline in the religious approach to understanding the world and the eventual substitution of a rational, scientific framework. Trends of this sort were gradual, often complex, usually incomplete. But, they gave shape to a vibrant period in Western history.

This was also a time of fundamental change in Western economic and social life. Developments in these areas were just as important, in fact, as the overall intellectual revolution and indeed more important than political change. The Western economy became commercialized in an unprecedented way, and technologically—for the first time—the most advanced in the world. The European family took on unusual dimensions, and its importance in certain aspects of Western life grew.

Between 1450 and 1750, political, cultural, and economic shifts involved Western civilization increasingly in the larger world. Traders and explorers in overseas colonies brought back new techniques and cultural values. Even more obvious, from 1500 onward, Western society drew increasing wealth from its global contacts. In turn, based on its new internal dynamism, Western Europe began to influence other civilizations in a variety of ways.

PATTERNS OF EARLY MODERN WESTERN HISTORY

THE RENAISSANCE

The spotlight in Western history, around 1400, was on Italy. This region had never fully embraced medieval customs, especially feudalism. The peninsula was largely organized in terms of city-states, some ruled by kings, others by aristocratic or merchant councils, still others by military tyrants. Many city-states had extensive trade and cultural contacts with other parts of the Mediterranean. From these exchanges, especially with Byzantium, Italian scholars gained a new appreciation of Greek and Latin literature. At the same time, growing commercial wealth encouraged cities like Florence and Venice to create new artistic styles to celebrate their exciting achievements.

From Italy's mixture of trade and scholarly and artistic endeavor arose the movement known as the Renaissance, which took shape in the 1300s. It started most clearly as a literary and artistic movement. Writers such as Dante, Petrarch, and Boccacio—all three writing in Italian as well as the traditional Latin—began to address more strictly secular subjects than had been popular in the Middle Ages. Petrarch wrote love sonnets to his Laura; other poems praised his own valor in climbing mountains—a new sign of individualism and pride in human achievement. Boccacio wrote earthy stories of love and lust, and although he later recanted, professing his devotion to religious faith, his earlier writings won a wide audience. In art, Giotto developed a new sense of perspective, allowing three-dimensional portrayals of nature. Both writers and artists began to copy classical styles, writing of and painting gods and goddesses and human scenes, rather than strictly Christian motifs; their work thus reflected increasing realism.

Seldom has an age produced as many cultural "greats" as did the Renaissance in Italy. A host of architects designed churches and public buildings in classical styles, renouncing the Gothic aesthetic. Leonardo da Vinci advanced the realistic portrayal of the human body in art, even painting pictures of medical dissections. Michelangelo's statues offered graphic displays of human musculature. Overall,

World Profiles

Maria Portinari

Maria Portinari (b. 1456) was the wife of a Florentine banker (Tommaso, c. 1432–1501) who made a fortune as a representative of the Medici banking family in Bruges, Flanders (now Belgium). The image here shows her richly but somberly dressed. Her slightly melancholy expression may have seemed appropriate in terms of religious piety, for the Renaissance in northern Europe set a strong spiritual tone for laypeople. Historians have also realized that the Renaissance, striking as it was in terms of cultural innovation, may have led to a deterioration in the position of upper-class women, treated increasingly as ornaments and kept apart from most of the new sources of learning. How might a woman like Maria Portinari have reacted to the changes sweeping through Western Europe during the fifteenth century?

This portrait of Maria Portinari is by the Flemish master Hans Memling. (The Metropolitan Museum of Art, Bequest of Benjamin Altman, 1913, 14.40.627)

Italian Renaissance art, developed from the fourteenth through the early sixteenth centuries, stressed themes of humanism—a focus on humankind as the center of intellectual and artistic endeavor. The humanistic concerns spread also to music, where elegant choruses sang of love, drink, and the beauties of nature. A new interest in human history also emerged, and several Renaissance historians, using a newly critical approach to past documents, challenged traditional church claims in such areas as the origins of the papacy.

The new spirit extended also to political theory. Writing around 1500, the Florentine Niccolò Machiavelli described what a ruler must do to gain and maintain power: how to use cruelty, how to sway public opinion. Machiavelli combined a detailed knowledge of Italian politics of his time with the use of Greek and Roman examples—a characteristic Renaissance mixture.

The Italian Renaissance had flourished in part because Italy was free from the medieval political forms that continued to influence much of the rest of Europe. During a good deal of the Italian Renaissance, France and England were locked in their Hundred Years' War. Then late in the fifteenth century the larger monarchies started to gain strength. France and Spain looked greedily upon the weak Italian city–states and embarked on wars of conquest in the 1490s. Italian trade also began to decline as interest shifted away from the Mediterranean, to the Atlantic trade routes that France, Spain, and England soon dominated.

However, as Renaissance creativity faded in its Italian birthplace, it passed northward. Northern artists directly copied the new themes and styles of the Italians. Palaces in the classical style became the rage among northern rulers like Francis I of France, who increasingly fancied themselves patrons of the arts. Northern humanists

Classical themes and styles in the Italian Renaissance: "Birth of Venus" by Botticelli.

gained growing knowledge of Latin and Greek literary and philosophical sources; soon they turned to writing in their own languages. Typical northern humanists, like Erasmus in The Netherlands, were more religious than some of their Italian counterparts, but shared their interest in human affairs and a pure style. The Renaissance spirit also prevailed in such sixteenth-century writers as England's Shakespeare and France's Rabelais; they addressed a wide variety of earthly subjects, with an emphasis on human passions and drama. Their works, and those of Spain's Cervantes, developed new literary traditions in their respective nations.

The northern Renaissance had political implications as well. Renaissance kings increased the pomp and ceremony within their courts and tried to expand their power. Francis I claimed new authority over the operations of the Catholic Church in France. Leading monarchs from the Tudor dynasty in England, particularly Henry VIII and Queen Elizabeth I, ruled with firm hands. They encouraged trading companies and colonial enterprises, and even passed laws on how to deal with the poor. During the Renaissance, monarchs also cultivated a more open interest in wars of conquest than their medieval predecessors. England engaged in a lengthy effort to conquer Ireland; France invaded Italy and tried to construct alliance systems to counter the power of Spain and the Holy Roman Empire, both ruled for a time by a single royal family, the Habsburgs. Francis I even allied briefly with the sultan of the Ottoman Empire; the alliance meant little in practical terms, but showed that political interests had gained ascendancy over traditional Christian hostility to Islam.

THE RELIGIOUS UPHEAVAL

Political and economic patterns in Renaissance Europe, however, were soon embroiled in the currents of the next major change—the Reformation. In 1517, a German monk named Martin Luther nailed a document containing 95 theses to the door of a church in Wittenberg. He was specifically protesting claims made by a papal representative that the buying of indulgences for money would advance salvation. For Luther, the idea of indulgences became an utter perversity; according to his reading of the Bible, salvation could come only through faith, not through works and certainly not through the money that the Renaissance popes sought for the upkeep of their own expensive court. Luther's protest, rebuffed by the papacy, soon led him to challenge most of the traditional Catholic sacraments and the authority of the pope himself.

The stand taken by the German monk gained wide support. Many Christians believed that the Catholic Church had become too corrupt and many of its practices meaningless. Some Renaissance intellectuals welcomed Luther's use of original documents, like the Bible, and also his nationalistic defiance, as a German, against religious rule from Rome. A number of individual rulers liked Lutheranism because it broadened their authority; they could direct Lutheran churches without the interference of still-powerful popes. Some ordinary people, finally, saw in Lutheranism an opportunity to speak out against their poverty and the landlords who dominated their lives, although Luther did renounce the idea of popular protest. As Luther firmly rejected Catholic attempts to undermine his influence, Lutheranism spread widely in Germany and also Scandinavia.

The Northern Renaissance emphasized greater introspection and spirituality: "Melancholia" by the German painter Albrecht Dürer. (The Metropolitan Museum of Art, Fletcher Fund, 19.73.85)

Once Christian unity was breached, other Protestant groups evolved. In England, Henry VIII established the Anglican Church, initially to challenge papal attempts to enforce his first marriage, which had failed to produce a male heir. (Henry would ultimately have six wives in sequence; he had two of them executed.) Henry was also attracted to some Lutheran doctrines. His son and his daughter, later Queen Elizabeth, were Protestants outright, so the Anglican Church became increasingly Protestant in doctrine as well as a separate form of church government. Still more important were the churches inspired by Jean Calvin, a Frenchman who established his base in the city of Geneva. Calvinism insisted on God's predestination, or prior determination, of those who would be saved; nothing humans did, and certainly no sacraments, could win God's favor. At the same time, those elected to God's grace had the obligation to encourage others to behave morally and seek knowledge of the

Bible. Calvinist ministers became moral guardians and preachers of God's word, not special sacramental representatives of the deity. Like other Protestant ministers, they could marry. Calvinism sought the participation of other believers in local church government; it also promoted wider popular education, so that more people could have direct access to the Bible (which various Protestant groups now translated into the vernacular languages). Calvinism was accepted not only in parts of Switzerland but also in Germany and France, where it produced strong minority groups, and in The Netherlands, England, and Scotland.

Beginning about 1550, the Catholic Church, although unable to restore religious unity, reacted to Protestantism. Church councils not only condemned Protestant doctrine, they also communicated a message of greater religious concern to the pope. A new order of monks, the Jesuits, became active in politics, education, and missionary work, helping to strengthen the faith of most Catholics in Italy and Spain and to regain some territories initially open to Protestantism, such as Hungary. The result was a revivified Catholic Church.

The rise of the Protestant churches triggered a long period of religious war in Europe. During the second half of the sixteenth century, France was the scene of major battles between Protestant and Catholic groups. The conflict ended only with the granting of tolerance to Protestants in 1598. Catholics and Protestants waged war recurrently in Germany, although several negotiations were held in the hope of dividing Germany among Catholic and Protestant states. In 1618, the Thirty Years' War broke out, in which foreign powers as well as Germans fought over their religious beliefs. The Spanish monarchy, self-appointed chief defender of the Catholic faith, tried to aid its co-religionists, whereas Swedish armies assisted the Protestant cause in a war so bloody that it reduced Germany's economic activity and its population level for many decades. The war ended with Spain's power reduced and a reluctant agreement to permit religious division among the German states. Religious passions helped fuel a war between The Netherlands and Spain, in which the former ultimately won its independence. Religious strife simmered in England during parts of the sixteenth century, until Queen Elizabeth imposed a peace under a rather tolerant Anglican Church; strife erupted again in the 1640s, contributing to a civil war in which Calvinists fought Catholic sympathizers. Eventually, the Anglican Church was restored, but with tolerance for other Protestant groups. The English Civil War ended formally in 1660, but the full settlement, including limited religious toleration, was reached only in 1688–1689.

For the most part, the Reformation, which had dominated Western political as well as religious history during the greater part of the sixteenth century, was assimilated in Europe by the first half of the seventeenth century. Even the Thirty Years' War in Germany was as much a battle among national monarchies as it was a religious dispute. Thus, France during that war sided with Protestant forces in order to weaken its enemy Spain. Although Protestantism and revived Catholicism had a lasting impact on not only the religious map but also social and economic life, the battles among Christian groups no longer set the agenda for events in Europe itself. By 1650, it was becoming clear that Western Christianity was permanently divided, and unintentional repercussions of the Reformation began surfacing in business and family life.

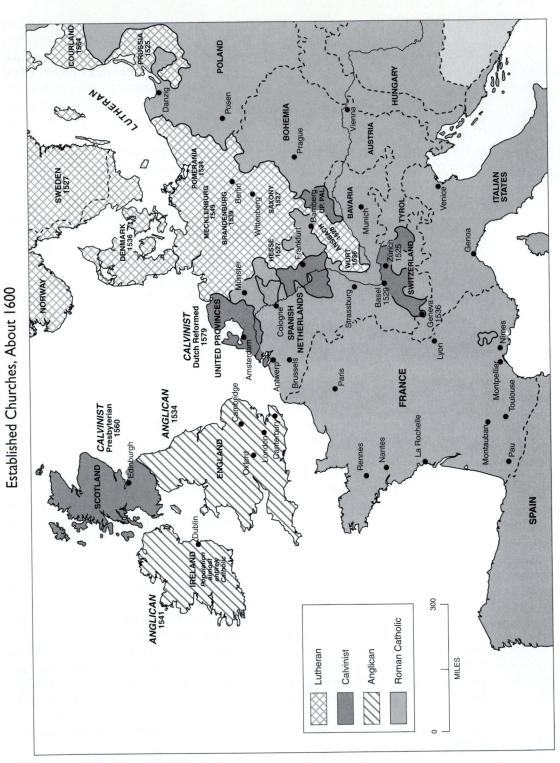

Established Churches, About 1600

NORWAY

SWEDEN
1527

COURLAND
1564

PRUSSIA
1525

LUTHERAN

Danzig

Posen

POLAND

DENMARK
1536

Iceland

POMERANIA
1534

MECKLENBURG
1549

BRANDENBURG
1539

Berlin

BOHEMIA

Prague

HUNGARY

Vienna

AUSTRIA

Wittenberg

SAXONY
1527

Frankfurt

HESSE
1527

Münster

Cologne

SPANISH
NETHERLANDS

BAMBERG

UP. PAL.

BAVARIA

Munich

TYROL

Zürich
1525

SWITZERLAND

Basel
1529

Geneva
1536

Venice

ITALIAN
STATES

Genoa

CALVINIST
Dutch Reformed
1579

UNITED PROVINCES

Amsterdam

Antwerp

Brussels

Strassburg

WÜRT
1536

Paris

FRANCE

Lyon

Nîmes

Montpellier

Toulouse

Pau

Montauban

La Rochelle

Nantes

Rennes

SPAIN

CALVINIST
Presbyterian
1560

SCOTLAND

Edinburgh

ANGLICAN
1534

ENGLAND

Cambridge

Oxford

London

Canterbury

ANGLICAN
1541

IRELAND
Population
almost
entirely
Catholic

Dublin

Lutheran

Calvinist

Anglican

Roman Catholic

MILES

0   300

274

In this context, during most of the 1600s, attention shifted to culture and politics. In culture, the leading development was the spate of new scientific discoveries, culminating in the great physical laws as advanced by Isaac Newton. Scientists learned how gravity works; they determined that the earth was not the center of the universe, but rather rotated around the sun; they discovered how blood circulates in the human body. Perhaps most important, they developed a coherent understanding of how the scientific method functions, through a combination of rational hypothesis, empirical testing through observation or experiment, and final generalization in theory or law. Far more than the Renaissance, the scientific revolution of the seventeenth century produced a fundamental reorientation of Western intellectual life.

THE RISE OF THE MONARCHIES

During the same period, leading Western monarchies gained new organizational power. With Spain in growing eclipse, after a century of glory in defense of the church and as Europe's major colonizer in the New World, France emerged as the bellwether nation. The French monarchy decisively defeated the remnants of feudal political forces during the seventeenth century. After 1614, the kings stopped summoning the national parliament. The greatest French monarch of this period, Louis XIV, also rescinded the toleration of Protestants. No group was allowed officially to limit the monarch's power. This political system, perfected under Louis XIV, was called, appropriately enough, "absolute monarchy." Louis, dubbing himself the Sun King, extended his patronage of the arts. He built sumptuous palaces, where the nobles competed for royal favor instead of cultivating their independent power base in the provinces. Military administration improved, as Louis' advisors built better forts and established ways to supply provisions to troops in the field. Louis set up military hospitals and even a military pension plan. Absolute monarchy also meant increasing attention to economic controls, mainly in the interest of securing greater tax revenue. The state tried to encourage exports and regulated manufacturing within France.

Absolutism was copied in a number of other countries. Particularly noteworthy was the rise of monarchies in central Europe along absolutist lines. Prussia, long a backward regional state in eastern Germany, began to strengthen its administration and expand its armies, gaining new power among the various German states. The Habsburg monarchs, although still claiming to be Holy Roman Emperors, worked to develop a solid monarchy in Austria. After Habsburg forces managed to repel the armies of the Ottoman Empire, by 1700 their rule extended to Hungary as well.

One of the clear purposes of the new absolute monarchs was to wage war. Louis XIV conducted several major wars, extending France's boundaries in the north and east. It took a coalition of other powers, including England, Holland, and some of the German states, to keep his ambitions in check. In the eighteenth century, France and England fought several times, although mainly in their colonies in North America and India. Prussia and Austria also fought, with Prussia winning important new territory. The idea of recurrent battle among the national monarchies and alliance systems designed to prevent any one European power from becoming dominant gained increasing ground.

The pattern of absolute monarchy continued into the eighteenth century. The French monarchy, exhausted by the wars and ruinous taxation of Louis XIV, was weaker than before, but despite numerous reform movements no new political system emerged. Prussian administration became more efficient. The Prussian kings, led by the able Frederick the Great, tried to improve agricultural production and extend education, while maintaining absolute political power and emphasizing military strength. Rulers like Frederick, because of their reform interests and their fascination with new political ideas, liked to call themselves enlightened despots rather than absolute monarchs, but the difference was not substantial.

Absolutism, enlightened or otherwise, was not the only political form to surface in Europe during the seventeenth and eighteenth centuries. In Britain and The Netherlands, parliamentary monarchies developed that built more clearly on older postclassical traditions through which kings would be checked by some kind of assembly. In England, the power of Parliament had been curbed during the reign of the strong Tudor kings of the sixteenth century, but the institution had not disappeared. Then, when less able monarchs in the seventeenth century tried to introduce taxes without parliamentary consent, supporters of Parliament joined religious dissidents in attacking royal power. One king, Charles I, was executed during the English civil wars of the 1640s, and for a time England was ruled by a military dictatorship. The monarchy, restored in 1660, again tried to defy Parliament while flirting with Catholicism. It was this combination that resulted in a final settlement, in the so-called Glorious Revolution of 1688–1689. A new king was crowned, under parliamentary authority, establishing the principle that Parliament, not the king, had supreme power in the realm, although royal power remained considerable through the eighteenth century. The crown could not suspend laws, levy taxes without parliamentary consent, or maintain a standing army in times of peace. The assembly was to meet regularly rather than depending on the king's summons. Parliament itself remained a largely medieval body, with a hereditary House of Lords and a House of Commons, whose members were elected by small numbers of voters. Campaigns for parliamentary office after the Glorious Revolution involved few questions of principle and a great deal of bribery. But Parliament had unquestioned authority, and no English king's power could be considered absolute, although it remained extensive throughout the century.

Thus, Western civilization, now divided by religion, was for a time divided by political systems as well. Absolute monarchs not only ruled without parliaments, they also created governments with larger bureaucracies and greater functions than the government of England (united with Scotland in 1700 to form Great Britain). At the same time, absolute monarchies were in some ways less flexible than the parliamentary states. They depended on efficient rulers, not always produced by heredity, and they tended to provoke discontent if their wars were unsuccessful or their taxes too high. Popular dissatisfaction mounted particularly in France during the eighteenth century and would result in massive revolution in 1789. Ultimately, through this revolutionary current, a greater degree of political unity would return to Western society. Until then, the absolutist and parliamentary impulses were largely separate, and both were important in expressing significant aspects of the evolving Western political tradition.

After the turmoil of the religious wars, it was the development of the new political systems and the recurrent military conflicts that gave the clearest superficial shape to Western history from the early 1600s until the 1750s. Ironically, the new divisions within Europe only spurred Western influence in other parts of the world. Catholics and Protestants, not content with their internal rivalry, spilled over into rival missionary efforts in Asia and the Americas. National monarchies battled overseas as well. Prussia and the Habsburg monarchy fought in Europe alone, but by the eighteenth century, Britain and France were prepared to wage war on virtually a worldwide basis. Thus, the last of the strictly monarchical wars in Western history, called the Seven Years' War in Europe for the good reason that it lasted from 1756–1763, saw Prussia defeat an effort by Austria to restrict its growing power, while Britain and France battled on three continents. Even earlier, English-Dutch, English-Spanish, and French-Spanish conflicts over territory and control of the seas had encouraged the formation of new European colonies in various parts of the world. Seemingly endemic tensions in Western society were now affecting the wider course of world history.

POLITICAL INSTITUTIONS AND IDEAS

The growth of the power and efficiency of the national state was the key political trend in early modern Europe. The Renaissance encouraged the greater splendor and ceremony, including artistic patronage, of the ruler's court. Renaissance interests also tended to weaken religious restraints on political power; even the Renaissance papacy acted more like a secular government, concerned with amassing wealth and acquiring art objects, than like a religious institution. Except in the Italian city–states, new government structures were not developed during the Renaissance, but there was a change in tone and motivation.

The Reformation enhanced the power of the state quite simply by weakening that of the church. Even Catholic monarchies, like those of France or Spain, gained because the Catholic papacy during the Reformation depended on them for support. Jesuit advisors, although devoted to the Catholic cause, also helped secular rulers increase their power base. In the Protestant camp, Lutheran kings and princes and the English monarch as head of the Anglican Church took over control of church government directly.

Still, before 1600, important medieval patterns persisted in politics. In particular, the aristocracy retained considerable power. Many church disputes, like the religious wars in France, found some aristocrats using the Protestant cause to support their claims against the monarchy. Revolts by nobles occurred again in France in the 1660s, when Louis XIV was a child, but this was a last gasp. The English civil wars featured land-owning gentry backing the parliamentary cause against the king—whose main defenders were also land-owning aristocrats. But, the political power of the nobility finally declined. Many landowners could not keep pace with economic change, and they depended for their livelihood on securing government jobs. Improvements in the quality of guns and cannons weakened aristocratic military power, although for the most part leading army commanders were appointed from the ranks of the nobles. The aristocracy was by no means dead as a political force, even aside from the parliamentary system in England, which gave landowners great power. However, in most monarchies, the balance had shifted decisively to the kings.

As stronger monarchies emerged, culminating in absolutism and enlightened despotism, bureaucracies became more sophisticated. French kings began to appoint regular administrators of provincial districts, who could manage the court system, supervise roads and other public works, and oversee the collection of taxes. Many bureaucrats were drawn from middle-class ranks, which helped check aristocratic power. The steady improvement in military organization gave kings larger and more reliable armies than ever before in Western history. These forces were used not only to fight wars but also to repress popular protest at home. New measures like the provision of regular uniforms for troops, introduced widely by seventeenth-century kings, symbolized the increasing professionalism of military forces.

New state functions developed. During most of the seventeenth and eighteenth centuries, the reigning economic theory, called mercantilism, held that states should provide the basic framework for the economy, to promote tax revenue and make sure that other nations did not gain an advantage. England and Holland, as well as the absolute monarchies, practiced a mercantilist system. They levied tariffs on imported goods, tried to encourage the growth and activity of their merchant fleets, and sought colonies to provide raw materials and a guaranteed market for manufactured goods. Some governments even built factories to foster national industry and discourage imports from foreign producers. In the eighteenth century, enlightened kings like Frederick the Great also tried to introduce new crops and farming methods and to stimulate population growth, held to be a vital source of military strength.

Louis XIV's palace at Versailles. Built as a lavish tribute to the absolute monarchy, Versailles demonstrates the symmetrical, classical style predominant in seventeenth- and eighteenth-century Western Europe.

Many governments broke down local internal barriers to trade, again for the sake of the national economy. State-sponsored road building increased. Here were important extensions of Western ideas of what the state should be responsible for. While economic activities were valued mainly for their impact on military capability and international competition, some rulers were starting to believe that one of the duties of government was the promotion of national prosperity.

During the early modern period, the growth of state powers and functions propelled the leading West European governments toward the front rank of all governments in the world, in terms of the resources they commanded and the ways in which they could control relatively large territories. Some of the Western measures, of course, duplicated earlier advances in administration introduced in places like China. It was also true that Western governments could not rival the territorial size of the great empires of the day. But, they did have more effective contact with their national units than many of the Asian empires maintained with their more diverse holdings. Popular loyalty to kings, and some hints of national identity, especially where the formation of national churches was concerned, supplemented the institutions of the monarchy. This period was, in sum, an important stage of state-building and organizational efficiency in a number of Western nations. The state still did not have regular contacts with ordinary people but popular protests began to suggest the expectation that government should help the disenfranchised in times of need.

The practical limits on the power of the expanding states of early modern Europe were buttressed by increasing ideological attacks, for political theory grew in importance as an expression of Western culture. A few theorists, to be sure, supported the absolute monarchs. In addition to Machiavelli's frank appraisal of how to use raw power, there emerged a "divine right" school of thought which held that kings derived their power directly from God and were accountable only to Him. This theory differed from traditions in some other civilizations, which claimed that the king or emperor was himself divine, but such a distinction meant little in practice.

Nonetheless, divine right theory was not the dominant approach in Western political theory of this time. Machiavelli himself, in his longer works, wrote of the importance of councils to balance a ruler's power. From the Renaissance onward, classical examples were cited, from Athens and republican Rome, to show the importance of representative institutions to express some popular sentiment and curb the excesses of kings. Calvinist writers, building on the experience of self-government in local churches and eager to protect their "true" faith against hostile governments, also developed theories about the limited powers of kings and states. The most significant theoretical statements arose in England in the aftermath of the civil wars. John Locke believed that basic political power lay with the people, who could withdraw their approval, even through revolution, if a ruler behaved arbitrarily. According to Locke, peoples' rights to life, liberty, and property should be protected against the state. These ideas were embraced, during the eighteenth century, by Enlightenment writers in France and elsewhere, many of whom advocated the founding of parliaments on the English model and even the drafting of formal constitutions to ensure individual rights and provide additional constraints on royal power.

In other words, as some of the traditional limits on kings declined and royal power expanded notably in many countries, some new restraints were being suggested. The fact that England provided an alternative model of government structure was vital in this ideological movement. But, the theories themselves were even more important, as many people in France came to believe that absolute monarchy was an inappropriate political form. Some ideas, not just of upper-class parliaments but of genuine popular political rights, were advanced, and ordinary people began to share similar beliefs. During the English civil wars, and again in the 1760s, popular movements arose in Britain to demand direct political representation for the common folk.

Along with growing government power, then, came a new statement of ideas that governments should be controlled and limited—a significant restatement, in other words, of a recognizable Western political tradition.

THE FERMENT IN WESTERN CULTURE

Renaissance humanism added important new elements to Western culture, in part, of course, by reviving classical styles and values in literature and art. The aesthetic value of the arts, rather than their service to religious goals, gained new attention. The Reformation and the Catholic response to it represented a distraction, to some extent, from this movement. Protestant churches were characteristically sparse and unadorned compared to the great Catholic cathedrals, the idea being that artistic images should not detract from a focus on God's great power. Church music assumed a vital role, and Luther himself wrote some well-known stirring hymns. In fact, Renaissance-inspired artistic themes continued even as religious conflict spread. Shakespeare's plays, for example, showed little interest in religious subjects in their evocation of political drama and human comedy and tragedy. Then, in the seventeenth century, classically inspired art and literature gained a new lease on life. In France, a series of powerful dramatic writers, led by the playwright Racine, used classical themes to directly express human emotions. Architecture and painting similarly borrowed classical motifs and scenes—although with some new decorative embellishments, in what is called the Baroque style.

More fundamentally, the Renaissance and Reformation, although very different in specific focus, promoted important new cultural values. Individualism was one such value. Renaissance writers emphasized the power of the individual. The concept of the "Renaissance man" expressed the conviction that talented human beings could excel in many fields and take legitimate pride in their own accomplishments. Reformation theology, to be sure, carefully placed God's power above human capability. But, Reformation writers also talked of the importance of a direct relationship between the individual and God, without the mediation of priests and sacraments. Although Protestant churches, in fact, exercised significant control over the moral and religious behavior of their flocks, individuals were encouraged to think on their own about their relationship to God.

Writers of both the Renaissance and Reformation spoke of the importance of the past, the source of stylistic inspiration or religious guidance. Scholars from both periods turned to a critical examination of historical documents as a key source of truth. Particularly during the Renaissance, the idea of human progress also began to surface. Renaissance writers believed in their superiority over medieval authors, and some wondered whether a more general advance in human knowledge and aesthetic sensibility was not underway.

Finally, secular interests gained ground. Renaissance writers incorporated humanistic themes in their works, although most continued to accept the importance of religious values as well. Reformation theologians were adamant in their hostility to purely secular concerns. However, by undoing Christian unity and producing a series of religious wars, the Reformation led many people to question whether the church was as important as medieval thinkers, or Reformation leaders themselves, had claimed. Even by the late sixteenth century, some writers, like Michel de Montaigne in France, emphasized that tolerance and peace were far more vital than any effort to establish a single religious truth. Western Christianity had long depended on the idea of religious uniformity. This is not an essential belief in a religious society; most Asian civilizations had long generated more religious diversity or promoted tolerance. In the West, however, Christianity since the Roman Empire had produced a passionate commitment to a single truth, with alternatives seen not just as wrong but as dangerous. Early Protestant leaders maintained this view; Calvin even had heretics executed. But the fact was that religious unity no longer existed, and given this challenge to the particular Western religious tradition, it was probably inevitable that secular values would become prominent.

The Renaissance and Reformation also drew more people than ever before into contact with formal ideas. Renaissance intellectuals were very interested in promoting education, although primarily for the elites. They wanted the upper classes to gain a new appreciation of classical literary styles and philosophies, and they set standards for upper-class education that have lasted, in Western society, into our own century. It was also during the Renaissance that Western society developed the printing press, a technique well advanced in Asia but new to the West and now improved by the use of movable block type. (Paper also became common in the West at this point, although the first papermaking factory, copied from the Arabs, had been established in the thirteenth century.) Printing was first used by its German inventor Gutenberg to produce Bibles, but by the end of the fifteenth century, printing presses were publishing a variety of Renaissance materials. Then, with the Reformation, printing presses spread to the literate public the theological disputes that consumed Western religious leaders. Most people still could not read, but the rate of literacy began to rise, particularly in Protestant areas, and those who could read now had a variety of styles and viewpoints to consider.

It was during the seventeenth century, however, that the real break in Western culture occurred, thanks in large part to the scientific revolution. Important artistic work continued. So did significant endeavors in theology, both Protestant and Catholic. The most widely published works were sermons and other religious tracts. Western culture, in other words, remained vigorously diverse, even contradictory. However, it was the rise of science that provided the most significant single theme.

The scientific revolution consisted of new knowledge, particularly about physics and astronomy but also about biology and chemistry. It consisted of new instrumentation to measure the heavens and examine microscopically the creatures of the earth. The movement became increasingly defiant of past wisdom. Scientists who proved that old ideas about an earth-centered universe were wrong were also showing up the glaring inadequacies of ancient knowledge. Many found these claims shocking, precisely because a belief in ancient wisdom was so deeply ingrained. Galileo, who insisted on the heliocentric universe, was forced to recant his claims by

This shop in Italy shows the early printing press in the West and Renaissance technology at work.

the Catholic Church. Nonetheless, the idea of progress in knowledge through experiment and critical thinking steadily gained ground. In France, René Descartes boldly set out to reexamine all past wisdom, his theory being that nothing should be assumed correct simply because of tradition. Skepticism was the order of the day among vanguard intellectuals; by the 1680s, this approach was being directly applied to religion, as writers sought to disprove beliefs in miracles and other Christian claims.

The European scientific revolution built on the current of direct observation and experiment that had begun in the later Middle Ages, with work on optics and other subjects. In the sixteenth century, this current began to swell. It was then that a Polish monk, Copernicus, used astronomical observation and mathematical calculation to prove that the Hellenistic belief in the earth as the center of the universe was wrong; rather, the earth moved around the sun. His finding was taken up shortly before 1600, when a great deal of astronomical observation began, from Italy to Scandinavia. Scientists developed a new understanding of the principles of planetary motion. Again using a combination of observation and experiment, Galileo and others began to generate theories about the impact of gravity, proving experimentally that Aristotle was incorrect in claiming that heavy bodies fell more quickly than light ones. Here was another blow to the dominance of traditional wisdom. Scientists shifted to an emphasis on what new truths they could discover.

Although work of this sort greatly advanced the knowledge of physics, biology too gained ground. Better instrumentation and observation led to a more accurate understanding of the human anatomy. The Englishman William Harvey showed

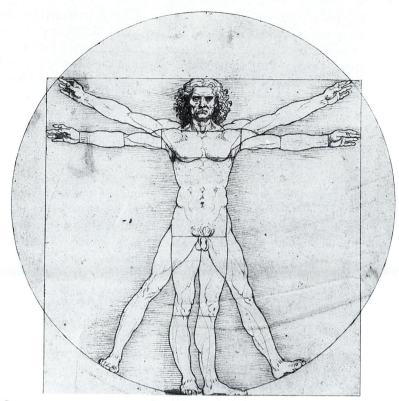

Renaissance art often reflected the emerging scientific revolution: anatomical sketches by Leonardo da Vinci.

how the blood circulates. Other scientists studied the behavior of gases. Thus, by the mid–seventeenth century, the Western world was responsible for a veritable explosion of knowledge about the physical universe. As part of this process, many intellectuals came to challenge the idea that learning was best approached through a reverence for tradition, for experiment was seen as an alternative, and sometimes more accurate, path to truth.

The scientific revolution also applied to science much of the rationalism that had informed Greek and then medieval scholastic thinking. Here was a crucial link in Western intellectual life, even amid great change. Most scientists believed that they could do more than disprove old theories and discover new data. They believed that they could formulate general laws of natural behavior—that there was a correlation between human reason and the orderliness of the universe. Here, the physics of Isaac Newton late in the seventeenth century seemed to culminate a long quest. In three basic laws, Newton established how physical motion operated, on earth and throughout the universe: A physical body preserves its momentum in a straight line unless forced by outside pressure to deviate; change of motion is proportional to the impressed force and takes place in the direction to which the force is applied; and to every action there is always an equal reaction. Additional work on the law of gravity showed why the planets remain in orbit and explained why objects fall at the same speed. Laws of this sort could be mathematically expressed, and Newton and others added to not only scientific theory but also mathematical knowledge, particularly in the area of calculus.

What had occurred, by 1700, was a real intellectual revolution in the West, and the establishment of a central scientific approach that no civilization had ever before ventured. The importance of a scientific outlook in Western history after the late sixteenth century therefore raises the obvious comparative question: why the West? Several other civilizations had produced significant scientific achievement. Byzantium preserved Hellenistic science, although it did not advance it and encourage scientific work elsewhere in Eastern Europe. Important science in India and the Middle East was ultimately limited by the rise of narrower religious concerns and, at key points, by political instability. China poses a more interesting case still, for the Chinese preserved a long tradition of elaborate empirical work. Unlike the West, of course, China had little contact with scientific discoveries outside its borders; its intellectual pursuits lacked the exciting challenge of mastering Greek and Arab learning. Chinese thought also tended to stress ethical knowledge over elaborate inquiry. Chu Hsi's emphasis on knowledge might have encouraged scientific inquiry, but it was modified by traditional Confucian stress on the individual's values. Chinese science itself differed from the Western approach in its more complete empiricism—its lack of large-scale, rationalistic attempts to fathom general laws of nature. Thus, despite extensive biological and physical data, the Chinese did not promote an overall belief that science was key to a basic understanding of the universe. Finally, we will see that at the time Western science began to surge, Chinese intellectual life was becoming more stagnant, a fact that would, ironically, encourage Chinese scholars to ignore Western scientific achievements for some time.

Western science involved popularization as well as basic discoveries. Information about the new science spread widely among the educated public. Scientific societies were founded to promote research. Many business and professional people began to dabble in science, finding new species of plants and animals and participating, however humbly, in this exciting expansion of knowledge. Popularized tracts explained scientific laws and advanced the idea that knowledge was progressing and reason, not faith, was the key to understanding how the physical world works.

Through scientific ferment, which simply grew as time passed, religion declined in importance in providing a basic intellectual framework. Rationalistic science became more vital in shaping habits of thought than ever before, in any civilization. Without necessarily eroding the importance of art, it did supersede creative expression as the foremost cultural influence; as one result, the late seventeenth and eighteenth centuries were not particularly significant in terms of stylistic developments, except in music. Scientific thought was heralded as the way to knowledge. And, rationalism would generate steady progress in the development of such knowledge, as intellectual leaders gradually turned away from a belief that classical learning was the basic path to truth. It was thought that rationalism might have other beneficial effects as well. Scientific writers like Francis Bacon, in England, argued that further discoveries would lead to technological improvements, making life easier and more rewarding.

These ideas gained ground during the eighteenth century. Scientific work continued. Chemists discovered much about the functions of oxygen. Biologists acquired increasing knowledge of a variety of animal and plant species. The science of psychology began to take shape, as scholars studied the workings of the human mind.

More important still was the effort to apply the principles of the scientific revolution to discussions of human nature and human affairs. Enlightenment thinkers, centered in France but operating in many countries, continued to popularize science and to attack errors of faith and superstition. They also developed a number of social sciences by writing of political and economic systems. The basic idea was that rational laws could be applied to social as well as physical behavior, producing an understanding of how humankind throughout the world operates. The Scottish philosopher Adam Smith, in his *Wealth of Nations,* thus posited a number of clear principles of economic behavior, based on the notion that people act according to self-interest and, through competition, will work to promote economic advancement if they are not distracted by government interference. This was a compelling statement of the doctrine of laissez-faire, that private initiative rather than state intervention promotes economic progress. Smith's work was also a ground-breaking treatise on social science as it suggested that general models of human behavior can be rationally derived.

In addition, Enlightenment thinkers believed in the inherent goodness and rationality of human beings. Progress in knowledge convinced them that more general human progress was also possible. Children can improve through education; old-fashioned methods of discipline were ridiculed. Criminals can become useful members of society if treated humanely; traditional methods of punishment were replaced or outlawed. Political life can improve if people are free, and the state does not try to force religious conformity and pays some attention to popular demands. The Enlightenment did not, in fact, produce a single political theory. Many writers were attracted to the idea of enlightened despotism, believing that a reform-minded ruler could produce social progress. Others talked of the importance of constitutions and parliaments. But, they all agreed that political life, like other aspects of life, could be reformed, through rational calculations and a belief in the essential goodness of human nature. Late in the Enlightenment, during the 1780s and 1790s, this kind of thinking even produced statements of socialism, arguing that property laws should be reformed in the name of equality, and of feminism, asserting that women as well as men should participate in political life and benefit from legal reforms.

The Enlightenment, then, served as the intellectual origin of a number of modern impulses in Western society. It set the stage for modern political movements, from liberalism through socialism. In emphasizing secular rather than religious thinking, it outlined a rationalistic approach rooted in social science that continues to describe this part of the Western intellectual world even today. It promoted a host of humanitarian reform movements. Most basically, by extending and translating the results of the scientific revolution, it established the framework for modern Western intellectual life. There were changes to come, to be sure. Most Westerners no longer think in precisely the same terms as those of the Enlightenment. However, many of the issues and fundamental approaches of the Enlightenment remain current. Simply put, the modern way of thinking, in Western society, took shape between about 1680 and 1750.

The Enlightenment hardly resulted in unanimous approval of its basic beliefs. A broader dissemination of some of the basic ideas was still to come. Numerous Christian writers objected vigorously to Enlightenment thinking, and they had many followers. Nonetheless, the Enlightenment was a popularizing movement. Leading writers, like the Frenchman Voltaire, who argued for human freedom and against church domination, became wealthy through the widespread sale of their works. From the aristocracy to the urban artisanry, many people were aware of at least some of the Enlightenment claims. Huge publishing ventures, like the *Encyclopédie* in France and later the *Encyclopaedia Britannica* in England, tried to summarize all relevant human knowledge in Enlightenment terms, with an emphasis on science and social science and a pronounced interest in technological improvements. Furthermore, the Enlightenment was essentially a Western-wide movement, striking chords in not only France and Britain but also Italy, Germany, Scandinavia, and the British colonies of North America. In this sense, it rivaled the earlier spread of Christianity in providing a common cultural framework for Western civilization.

TRANSFORMATIONS IN ECONOMIC AND SOCIAL LIFE

THE ROLE OF COMMERCE

During the early modern period, a steady expansion of commerce, along with significant changes in culture, helped transform Western life. Renaissance leaders were proud of the commercial bustle in their cities. Reformation thinkers also tended to favor trade. Luther and Calvin actually influenced the public to discard the traditional belief that merchants might be pursuing false values. Since ordinary people could have direct links with God, the duties and tasks of everyday life were not seen as contradicting religious purposes. Of course, God came first, but commercial success could be construed as proof that God's favor had been won. Not all Protestants became fervent entrepreneurs, however, and Catholic business activities grew as well. But, there was some relationship between the spread of Protestantism and the increasing interest in commerce. Finally, the expanding monarchies encouraged merchants to form powerful trading alliances. State backing helped organize great merchant companies to trade with Russia, India and Southeast Asia, and the Americas.

Commerce was also stimulated by the new supplies of gold and silver brought back from the New World, particularly from Spain's American colonies. During the sixteenth century, these precious metals produced a price revolution in Europe. As the supply of money rose on its traditional gold-and-silver base, the production of foods and manufactured goods could not keep pace, and the result was rapid inflation. Rising prices encouraged merchants to take greater risks, because they could borrow money with the understanding that it would be worth less when they had to pay it back. Capitalists also saw the profits to be made in trade with far-flung parts of the world. Asian spices commanded handsome prices. From the late sixteenth century onward, grain from Poland and Russia and furs, sugar, and tobacco from the Americas were imported at increasingly rapid rates, all through trade organized by European merchants.

Commercial expansion began to focus greater attention on Europe's manufacturing base. Growing wealth at home produced new markets for goods, and there was also a need to produce goods to sell to foreign markets. Although most production remained in artisan hands, a significant expansion of domestic manufacturing took place under capitalist auspices. Merchants in this system provided raw materials, particularly textile fibers, to workers scattered in rural settings, who spun and wove the fibers into cloth on simple machines; their products were then collected and paid for, and sold by the merchants on a wide market. Even in the artisan system, commercial expansion created a growing gap between guild masters and their journeymen; as masters pressured their workers to produce more, many journeymen became a permanent paid labor force manufacturing items like books, guns, and metal tools for wide market sales.

European technology steadily improved in this climate of economic expansion. Better mining techniques allowed the increased production of iron and coal. Better mill wheels facilitated the processing of grains. Textile equipment, although still manually guided, was also becoming more sophisticated. By the seventeenth century, European technology had no peer in the world in most branches of production, and the pace of change continued to be high. Early in the eighteenth century, the first steam engine was devised in England to pump water out of deep mine shafts. And in 1733, the Englishman James Kay invented the flying shuttle, which automatically interwove fibers to make cloth; with this new system, one weaver could now complete the work of two, although the looms were still powered by hand.

Improvements in agriculture were somewhat slower in coming, but the expansion of commerce and the growth of cities encouraged increasing numbers of farmers to produce for the market. Late in the seventeenth century, Dutch farmers began to experiment with new crops that would replenish the fertility of the soil without necessitating periods of fallow, in which nothing could be grown. The Dutch, hard-pressed to support a large population in a small land, also developed new methods of draining swamps and constructing dikes to keep out ocean tides. Interest in agricultural improvement spread further in the eighteenth century, and many societies were organized to disseminate knowledge of new crops and fertilizers and new machines to sow seeds.

The tide of economic change must not be exaggerated, however. Most people continued to use rather traditional methods, in both agriculture and manufacturing. Most people still did not depend heavily on market sales for their livelihood. The merchant class expanded, but it did not yet command the highest social levels. Many, indeed, still aspired to become aristocrats in their own right, for money-making alone did not provide adequate prestige. Nonetheless, Western Europe became more substantially commercialized than ever before. Enlightenment thinkers, generally hostile to the aristocracy, which they saw as an idle class, praised hard work and profit-making, a sign that social values were changing even before the social structure had been revolutionized.

One clear effect of commercial expansion was that Europe's wealth increased. An Englishman, writing in the late 1580s about village life, "noted three things to be marvelously altered in England within his own sound remembrance." First, farmers' cottages had more chimneys, which meant they were bigger and better heated. Second, beds and pillows had replaced straw mats for sleeping. And third, pewterware, instead of wooden utensils, was used for eating. With time, the list of advances in the standard of living continued to expand. By the early 1600s, French peasants began to consume wine fairly regularly with their meals. This was a sign of greater wealth, and also of the growing market production of wines, which could not be effected in every area of France. By 1700, ordinary people in Western Europe were consuming coffee, tea, and sugar—all imported goods that they had to buy on the market and that they therefore had to have enough money to afford. By this time, European farmers and artisans had far more objects in their possession—tools, furnishings, and the like— than any other people in the world.

However, new wealth was by no means evenly distributed. Some parts of the Western world were richer than others. Material standards lagged in Germany, in part because of the devastation of the Thirty Years' War. They also lagged in Spain, where merchant activity remained rather low despite the influx of wealth from the colonies; most Spanish gold passed to the vigorous merchants and banks of northern Europe. Social disparities also intensified. As a core group of farmers or peasants increased in size—the people who could sell to urban markets and whose standard of living thus rose—the poverty of those without property also grew. Western Europe by the seventeenth century faced significant problems of poor relief. Almshouses and other institutions designed to aid the poor, but also to isolate them, were one common result. The existence of growing pockets of poverty amid rising wealth represented another important theme for European society; it is a social contradiction with which Westerners are still grappling today.

Social and economic change also produced recurrent unrest. Many journeymen resented the growing power of guild masters and formed associations to promote their own interests. The first strikes in Western history occurred during the Renaissance. Riots were even more common, continuing a theme from the later Middle Ages. Peasants periodically rebelled against ever-steeper exactions from landlords. Both rural and urban riots commonly arose when grain and bread were in short supply. Considerable popular unrest accompanied the tensions of the Reformation. French peasants rose in many regions during the 1590s, in the aftermath of the religious wars. They attacked their landlords, who "had reduced them to starvation, violated their wives and daughters, stolen their cattle and wasted their land," while urban merchants with whom they had to trade sought "only the ruin of the poor people, for our ruin is their wealth." Popular unrest also surfaced during the English civil wars, with farmers and urban workers organizing to demand political rights and economic reforms. These uprisings produced an amazing series of revolts around 1648, in not only England but also southern Italy and elsewhere. Protest declined somewhat during the next decades, partly because population growth, which had been substantial during the sixteenth century, leveled off. But, the early modern period was not a peaceful time in Western society, even aside from the recurrent wars.

THE ROLE OF THE FAMILY

Social change also involved the Western family. During the fifteenth and sixteenth centuries, the characteristic structure of the family began to shift, producing a "European-style" family that was quite different from the patterns of most other agricultural societies. The contributing factors were simple. First, common people began to marry at a rather late age—about 27 or 28 (members of the aristocracy, in contrast, married much earlier). And, a rather sizable minority of ordinary people never married at all. The reason for these developments was a desire to protect family property against the demands of too many children. Late marriages led to reduced birthrates, so that a given family would not have more than three or four children living to adulthood. While understandable, such a system required considerable self-control and family supervision, for it meant that young people passed many years between puberty and the point at which heterosexual activity was generally permissible—in marriage. Tensions increased between young adults and older parents, for economic independence and marriage normally depended on the death or retirement of the elderly. Suspicion and fear led many older people to prepare careful contracts to spell out what support they would receive from their children if they turned over their land. The new family pattern also promoted greater interaction between men and women. Men remained officially and legally the heads of their families. But with the emphasis now on rather small units, a husband and wife and their children, economic cooperation between men and women increased. Generally, the new family structure shielded Europeans from the population density that had long been a fact of life in East Asian and Indian society.

During the seventeenth century and beyond, changes in the quality of family life contributed to earlier structural shifts. Europeans began to spend more leisure time within the family environment. Meals at home became more elaborate than before. This was partly the result of growing wealth, but it also involved some explicit choices. Women became the family agents who regulated its social life, preparing more intricate dishes and presiding over mealtime ceremonies and conversation. Here was a new aspect of Western family life that continued to gain in importance until very recently.

Family affection was also increasingly encouraged. Seventeenth-century Protestant writers stressed the importance of love as an ingredient of family life. As one English minister put it, "Keep up your Conjugal Love in a constant heat and vigor." This growing emphasis on the family as a center of emotional pleasure, which spread to Catholic areas by the eighteenth century, resulted in significant transformation. Fostered by religious developments, it may also have been a reaction to rapid social and economic change in the wider environment; families were seen as a comfortable and reliable refuge. Here, too, themes were set in motion that perpetuated to recent times. There were implications, finally, for the treatment of children within this new family environment. By the late seventeenth century, many writers were advocating love, rather than harsh physical discipline, as the means of raising children. They developed the revolutionary idea that parents owed children certain rights and protections, rather than espousing the traditional belief that children were obliged to accept whatever their parents might impose. The implications of all this change where women were concerned was not so clear. Their role in the family other than as bearers of children improved, but opportunities narrowed; in Protestant areas, the abolition of religious orders made marriage even more important for women.

Changes in family life, along with the shifts in broader economic and social structure, reveal a society that was beginning to alter some very basic patterns. Fundamental features of daily existence, even human emotion or at least its recommended expression, were taking new forms. Here was a potential source of further change as well. As an example, if parents began to change the way they treated their children, spanking them less often, drawing them more actively into an orbit of parental affection, these children might mature into somewhat different kinds of adults. During the eighteenth century, child-rearing practices changed still further. Widespread Western practices of swaddling young children—wrapping them tightly so that parents could work without worrying about their coming to harm—began to disappear. Children were more free, receiving more active adult care in place of physical restraints. These changes, widely urged by Enlightenment writers, who believed that children would improve through better treatment, had significant implications for Western adults. If child-rearing became more free, might adults not also seek greater liberty?

CONCLUSION: HOW EARLY MODERN TRENDS IN THE WEST INTERRELATED

The various trends of early modern Western society did not neatly mesh. There was overlap, to be sure. Commercial development and economic expansion were encouraged by some of the ideas of the Renaissance and Reformation, although not always intentionally; economic change also was the catalyst for some of the key values of the Enlightenment. Increased interest in carefully planned organization showed in business ventures, publishing, and government bureaucracy. Even more amorphous values, such as greater individualism, related cultural and religious movements to capitalism and possibly to family organization—the family was seen less as an economic institution, more as an emotional bond among individuals.

On the other hand, different currents had varied results, and many key shifts were slow and uneven. Changes in beliefs and the economy, however, added up to a major strain on people at various levels. One key symptom was a wave of witchcraft trials that occurred in many parts of Western Europe, and ultimately New England, from the late fifteenth century until the middle of the seventeenth century. Europeans had long believed in witches and magical powers, but they had never considered these forces to be such ominous threats as they did during these decades, when witchcraft trials sent hundreds of accused people to death and involved many thousands in mounting hysteria. Many factors were behind this sweeping fear. New anxieties about the poor were one cause, since many of the accused were among those bypassed by the growing prosperity. Protestant–Catholic divisions, shaking convictions about where religious truth lay, contributed to the fear. So did uncertainties about the changing roles of women and the elderly in the family (most accused witches were female, said to be "used by the devil," and a disproportionate number were elderly), and also new confusions about how to respond to sickness (whether through doctors or by superstitious remedies). A new belief system was taking shape in Western society, but its early stages left many people insecure and fearful.

Just as the witchcraft hysteria stemmed from a variety of intense concerns generated by change, so the end of the witchcraft trials signified the continuing spread of new ideas about how to understand the world. Growing numbers of officials and

UNDERSTANDING CULTURES

A Revolution in Popular Culture

The big cultural developments of the early modern period may seem abstract. The rise of Protestantism and Catholic reaction, the printing press, the scientific revolution are easy to list, but what did they mean? And particularly, what did they mean beneath the level of a formal intellectual life?

Historians have increasingly realized that between about 1600 and 1750, some huge changes occurred in the ways most ordinary people thought about quite basic aspects of life. Here are some examples:

- In 1600, many peasants did not bother naming children until age 2, because so many died. When parents did name infants, they often reused the names of children who had died. In 1750, naming occurred soon after birth, names were not reused, and many parents chose unusual, more distinctive names. This is a concrete example of the new individualism.
- In 1600, young people when they kissed often bit each other hard. In some regions, young men claimed possession of a woman by urinating on her dress. By 1750, kissing became a more private and gentler experience, and biting declined. Here are some concrete examples of changing attitudes about love and emotion, and about the family.
- In 1600, when a valued object was lost, ordinary Europeans turned to cunning men, who used magic sticks and incantations to find the misplaced object. By 1750, cunning men no longer existed, as part of the growing (although still not complete) trend against magic. Instead, people visited official lost-and-found offices, at least in cities, or advertised in local newspapers. Attitudes toward the natural world and social environments were changing.

These examples are just a few. Under the impetus of new commercial levels and new family forms, as well as growing literacy (thanks in part to printing), religious and scientific change, people were thinking differently. There was no organized movement, like a major religion, behind this great cultural change, although the Enlightenment may be viewed as somewhat missionary in its attempts to undermine what it termed common superstition. The work of historians also results from change, for example, in providing cultural bases for later developments in politics and industry. The transformation of culture raises basic questions about cause, result, and participation (who still believed in the old ways). It also raises questions about how Europeans, armed with some of these new ideas, would view the rest of the world.

ordinary people simply stopped believing that witchcraft was a real phenomenon, capable of disrupting the laws of nature. Although beliefs in witchcraft persisted and a few trials continued into the eighteenth century, the craze ended in most places by the 1680s. The spread of Enlightenment ideas in later decades, although again not universal in a society in which most people still could not read, was a further sign that the Western outlook was shifting in some common directions.

For all its tensions and confusions, the fact remained that by the eighteenth century, Western Europe had created a distinctive kind of agricultural society, compared to the traditions of the other great civilizations of the world. Its unusual qualities stemmed primarily from the changes that had been occurring since the late fifteenth century at almost all levels of social activity. The West was unusually commercial, unusually scientific, and shaped by family structures that encouraged property control and considerable individualism. And, not accidentally, Western society was simultaneously extending its influence to the rest of the world, despite political organizations that were in many ways inferior to the world's great empires of the time.

SUGGESTED WEBSITES

For Renaissance art and daily life, refer to *http://history.evansville.net/renaissa.html*; on the life of Martin Luther, see *http://luther.de/legenden.html* (in German). English version: *www.luther.de/e/legenden.html*.

SUGGESTED READINGS

For an overview of developments in Western society during this period, including extensive bibliographies, see Sheldon Watt, *A Social History of Western Europe, 1450–1720* (1984), and John Merriman, *History of Modern European Civilization*, Vol. I (1996). Charles Tilly, *Big Structures, Large Processes, Huge Comparisons* (1985), offers an analytical framework based on major change; see also Tilly's edited volume, *The Formation of National States in Western Europe* (1975), and Fernand Braudel, *Civilization and Capitalization*, 3 vols. (1952). Coverage of the Renaissance and the religious transformations can be found in J. F. New, *The Renaissance and Reformation: A Short History* (1977); K. H. Kannenfeldt, ed., *The Renaissance: Medieval or Modern* (1959); J. Atkinson, *Martin Luther and the Birth of Protestantism* (1981); D. Knowles, *Bare Ruined Choirs* (1976); J. H. Plumb, *The Italian Renaissance* (1986); O. Chadwick, *The Reformation* (1983); Steven Ozment, *The Age of Reform, 1520–1550* (1980); and Hubert Jedin and John Dolan, eds., *Reformation and Counter Reformation* (1980). On the important changes in science, consult H. Butterfield, *Origins of Modern Science* (1965), and A. R. Hall, *From Galileo to Newton, 1630–1720* (1982). Crucial political changes are addressed in G. Clark, *Early Modern Europe from about 1450 to about 1750* (1960). Europe's economic development is treated in R. L. Reynolds, *Europe Emerges: Transition Toward an Industrial World Wide Society 1600–1750* (1972), and R. Ehrenberg, *Capital and Finance in the Age of the Renaissance* (1948). On important transformations in popular life and behavior during the period, see Peter Burke, *Popular Culture in Early Modern Europe* (1978); P. Ariès, *Centuries of Childhood: A Social History of Family Life* (1965); P. Stearns, ed., *The Other Side of Western Civilization*, vol. 2, 6th ed. (1999); and Merry Wiesner-Hanks, *Women and Gender in Early Modern Europe* (1993).

The West and the World: Discovery, Colonization, and Trade

15

FOCAL POINTS *Western Europe's growing role in the world brought new influences and new constraints to a number of areas. These developments can be studied in sequence. What were the sources of Europe's new strength? What areas came under particular European influence, and why were other areas—such as most of Asia—less affected? How did Europe reshape aspects of sub-Saharan African society, and what aspects were left relatively untouched? Why was Europe's influence in the Americas so much greater than in Africa? What were the characteristics of the new civilization that began to emerge in Latin America? To what extent was it different from European settlements in North America?*

THE BASE OF NEW EUROPEAN POWER

Why does a civilization begin to ascend within the ranks of the various cultures of the world, gaining new power and importance? The question is hardly less complex than the issue of why civilizations decline. In the case of the West, in its rise to world prominence after 1450, the problem was enhanced by some of the civilization's overall drawbacks: here was a society still politically divided, often locked in internal wars and intense social unrest, with a relatively small total population. How could it, in the space of a few centuries, seize control of the world's oceans and some of its richest lands?

The answer to this question involves two kinds of factors: those that are measurable and material, and those deriving from culture and outlook. On the material side, the West, even as it launched its systematic explorations of the Atlantic in the fifteenth century, was gaining in technological sophistication. It was not yet the world's most advanced society in overall technology, but it was fast moving in that direction. It certainly had superiority over sub-Saharan African and American Indian cultures in manufacturing and agricultural know-how. More specifically, Western skills in shipbuilding and navigation, aided by refinements in the compass and other directional devices, were at a high level and would improve steadily to the point that, by the sixteenth century, they surpassed those of East Asia. More specifically, West Europeans had been quickest to develop high-quality gunnery, using the knowledge they gained of Chinese gunpowder to forge a weaponry that was awesome by the standards of the time (and more than a bit terrifying to many Europeans, who had reason to fear the new destructive power of their own armies and

293

navies). The West would maintain its weapons advantage over all other civilizations in the world into the twentieth century, and even today its arms technology is among the most highly developed. A crude but possibly accurate explanation of the West's rise, then, would focus simply on its technological edge in the art of war and intimidation.

However, sophisticated weaponry and other technological superiority may not have been the whole story. We have seen that Europe's problems, including an unfavorable balance of trade with Asia and the fear of Muslim power, created some special motives for Western leaders. East Asia had some comparable technological leads, surpassing the West not in weaponry but in navigation during the fifteenth century, but it chose not to exploit these advantages in a quest for new power in the wider world. Outlook, as well as material means, had to play an important role in the West's rise. Earlier civilizations that had influenced wide sectors of the world beyond

HISTORY DEBATE

The West as World Leader

The view of the West's new role in the world has undergone some striking transformations in recent decades. Old history textbooks—in the West, of course—used to picture Columbus as a clear hero, opening the New World to progress. But in an age of anticolonialism, new views of Western ascendancy have shifted the picture. Columbus brought disease and dominance to the Americas, and European exploitation would gradually worsen the environment as well. What is the most accurate historical evaluation?

Historians have also compared Westerners with another previous world power, the Arabs. Both world powers seized slaves and interfered with local cultures; both could look down on other peoples; both encouraged economic imbalances in world trade to their own profit. Other comparisons are even more unflattering. Christians were often less tolerant than Muslims had been. The West seized more territory by force and was more likely to seek complete surrender in war than the Arabs. In some quarters, West-bashing has become a popular intellectual pastime. Even aside from these negative interpretations of Western conquests, questions about Western motives and culture remain important. At the same time, of course, new technology gave the West greater powers than the Arabs had enjoyed, and some results may have reflected this new imbalance rather than simple greed. Finally, at various points and in some areas, growing Western influence (even when resented) may have had some beneficial effects, aside from the growing profits in Western coffers.

their borders, notably classical India and then Islam, had usually possessed an active merchant spirit, and certainly the West had this in abundance from its medieval and Renaissance–Reformation heritage. In Christianity, the West also had a religion eager to spread the truth to nonbelievers, even by force. Trade and Christianity would typically go hand in hand in the West's new rise. The specific culture of the Renaissance may have contributed as well. Certainly, it was no accident that the first discoveries in the Atlantic occurred during the Renaissance, when some Europeans were experiencing a new thirst for achievement and knowledge. The zeal of a Henry the Navigator to penetrate the unknown and the sheer adventurism of a Christopher Columbus related closely to other Renaissance enthusiasms. Finally, even the divisions within Europe pushed all the many vying civilizations toward a new world role. National monarchies soon competed for discoveries and colonies, as part of their overall rivalry.

The period of discovery and early colonization was an exciting example of Western power and daring. It also changed some key patterns of world history, which means that it must be assessed not only from the standpoint of European efforts, but also in terms of impact on the cultures it affected. Here, several zones developed, ranging from the Americas—where the European arrival began quickly to change basic cultural patterns toward creation of new civilizations or outright assimilation with the West—to East Asia, where European activities made little difference to the historical patterns of the next several centuries. Between these two extremes were several societies: Africa, where European contact caused important alterations in some regions but had little impact on others; India and the Middle East, where Western pressure grew but without undermining earlier traditions; and Russia, whose own new quest for power was colored by knowledge that the West had forged ahead.

PATTERNS OF EXPLORATION AND TRADE

When West Europeans began to venture forward into the wider world, their knowledge of where they were going was surprisingly scanty. To be sure, Viking adventurers from Scandinavia had crossed the Atlantic in the tenth century, reaching Greenland and then North America, which they named "Vinland." But they quickly lost interest, in part because they encountered Indian warriors whose weaponry was good enough to vanquish the intruders.

As we have seen, scattered expeditions from Spain and Italy into the Atlantic dotted the later Middle Ages, but they had no specific results. It took new technical knowledge, particularly the navigational devices imported from Asia, and growing problems, in the form of new needs to reach Asia directly and to seek gold as payment for the desired Asian products, to permit a more systematic effort in the fifteenth century.

The initiative began in the small kingdom of Portugal. The rulers of this country had just finished driving out the Muslims, who still threatened from North Africa. This threat, and the surge of energy that sometimes accompanies the expulsion of an occupation force, prompted the Portuguese during the fifteenth century to look for conquests in Africa. Portugal's rulers were drawn by the excitement of discovery, the harm they might cause to the Muslim world, and a thirst for wealth—for European legends of gold in Africa and elsewhere were abundant. This was not a matter of mere greed; Europe's lack of gold for its trade with Asia was becoming a serious problem. A Portuguese prince, Henry the Navigator, directed a series of expeditions down the African coast and outward to islands such as the Azores. Beginning in 1434, the Portuguese began to journey down the African coast, each expedition going a little farther than its predecessor. They brought back some slaves and perpetuated the tales of gold that they had not yet been able to find.

Later in the fifteenth century, Portuguese sailors ventured around the Cape of Good Hope, planning to find India and also the African east coast, which was thought to be the source of gold. They rounded the Cape in 1488, but weary sailors forced the expedition back before it could reach India. Then, after news of Columbus's discovery of America for Spain in 1492, Portugal redoubled its efforts, hoping to stave off the new Spanish competition. In 1497, Vasco da Gama's fleet of four ships reached India, with the aid of a Muslim pilot picked up in East Africa. The Portuguese mistakenly believed that the Indians were Christians, for they assumed the Hindu temples they encountered to be churches. And, they faced the hostility of Muslim merchants, who had long dominated trade in this part of the world. The Portuguese nonetheless managed to return home with a small load of spices.

This success set in motion an annual series of Portuguese voyages to the Indian Ocean. One expedition, blown off course, reached Brazil, where it proclaimed Portuguese sovereignty. With growing experience, both Portuguese and Spanish expeditions became increasingly comfortable with voyages in the South Atlantic and the Indian Ocean. Portugal began to establish forts on the African coast and also in India—the forerunners of such Portuguese colonies as Mozambique, in East Africa, and Goa, in India. By 1514, the Portuguese had reached the islands of Indonesia, the center of spice production, and also China. By 1542, a Portuguese expedition also arrived in Japan, where a Christian missionary effort was launched that met with some success for several decades.

Meanwhile, only a short time after the Portuguese quest began, the Spanish reached out with even greater force. Here too was a country only recently freed from Muslim rule, full of missionary zeal and a desire for riches. The Spanish had traveled into the Atlantic during the fourteenth century. Then in 1492, in the same year that the final Muslim fortress was captured in Spain, the Italian navigator Christopher Columbus, sailing in the name of the new Spanish monarchy and its rulers, Ferdinand and Isabella, set off on a westward route to India, convinced that the round earth would make his quest possible. As is well known, he failed, reaching the Americas instead and mistakenly naming their inhabitants "Indians." Although Columbus believed to his death that he had sailed to India, later Spanish expeditions indicated that he had voyaged to a region to which Europeans and Asians had not traveled before. One expedition, led again by an Italian initially in Spanish service, Amerigo Vespucci (see p. 300), gave the New World its name. Spain, eager to claim this American land, won papal approval for Spanish dominion over most of what is now Latin America, although a later treaty awarded Brazil to Portugal.

Finally, a Spanish expedition under Ferdinand Magellan set sail westward in 1519, passing the southern tip of South America and sailing across the Pacific, reaching the Indonesian islands in 1521 after incredible hardships. It was on the basis of

Discoveries in the Fifteenth and Sixteenth Centuries

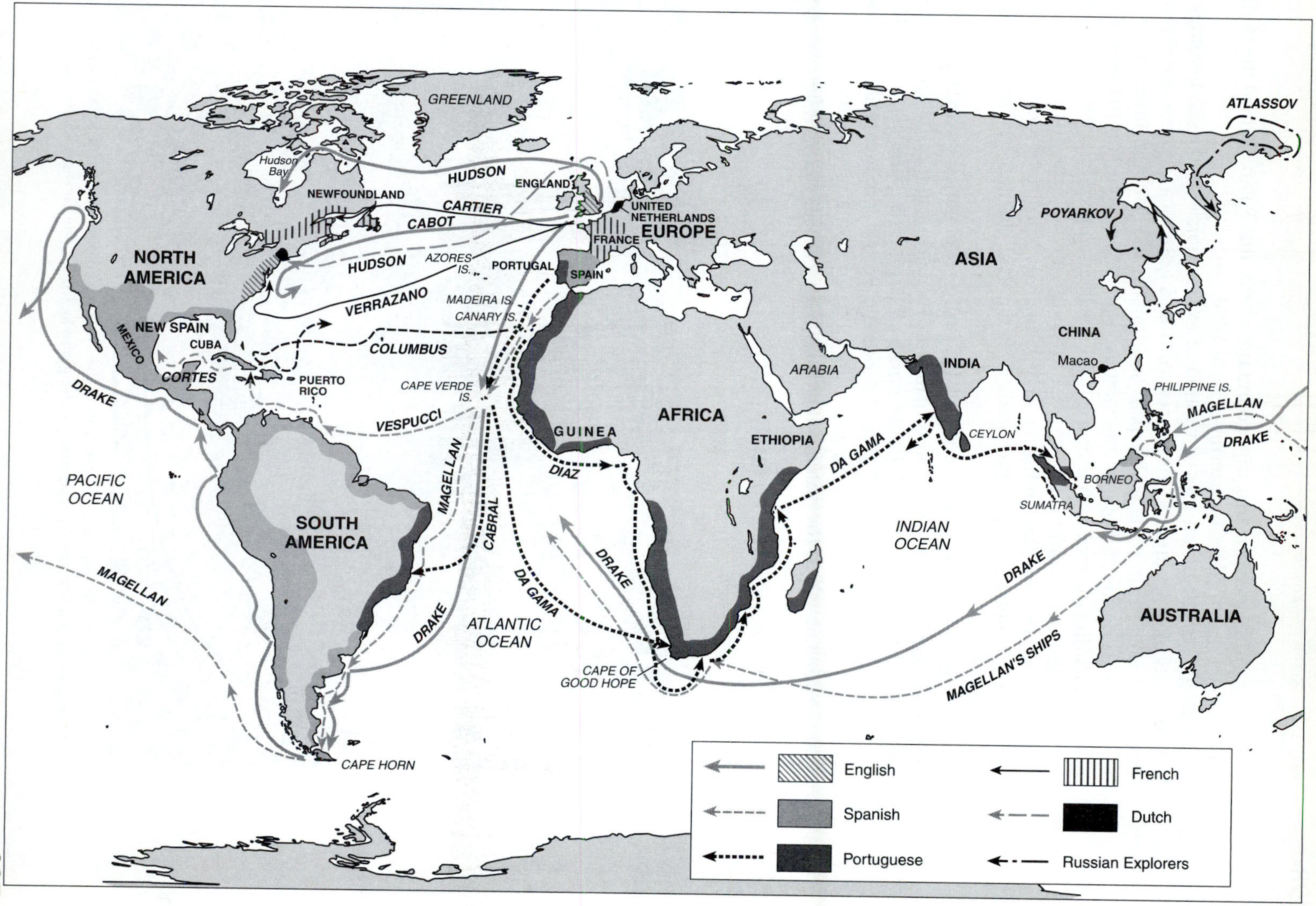
GREENLAND
ATLASSOV
Hudson Bay
HUDSON
ENGLAND
NEWFOUNDLAND
CARTIER
CABOT
UNITED NETHERLANDS
FRANCE
EUROPE
POYARKOV
NORTH AMERICA
HUDSON
AZORES IS.
PORTUGAL
SPAIN
ASIA
VERRAZANO
MADEIRA IS.
CANARY IS.
NEW SPAIN
MEXICO
CUBA
COLUMBUS
CHINA
Macao
CORTES
PUERTO RICO
ARABIA
INDIA
PHILIPPINE IS.
DRAKE
CAPE VERDE IS.
AFRICA
MAGELLAN
VESPUCCI
GUINEA
ETHIOPIA
CEYLON
DRAKE
DA GAMA
PACIFIC OCEAN
DIAZ
BORNEO
MAGELLAN
SUMATRA
SOUTH AMERICA
CABRAL
INDIAN OCEAN
DRAKE
MAGELLAN
DA GAMA
DRAKE
AUSTRALIA
DRAKE
ATLANTIC OCEAN
CAPE OF GOOD HOPE
MAGELLAN'S SHIPS
CAPE HORN
English
Spanish
Portuguese
French
Dutch
Russian Explorers

this voyage, ultimately the first trip around the world, that Spain claimed the Philippines, which remained Spanish territory until 1898.

Portugal emerged from this first round of exploration with coastal holdings in various parts of Africa and the Indian port of Goa; a lease on a Chinese port, Macao; short-lived interests in trade with Japan; and, finally, the claim on Brazil. Spain asserted its hold on the Philippines and various Pacific islands, and on the bulk of the Americas. During the sixteenth century, the Spanish attempted to assert these claims through military expeditions to Mexico and South America. The Spanish also held Florida in North America, and ultimately launched expeditions northward from Mexico into California and other parts of what later became the southwestern United States.

Later in the sixteenth century, the lead in further exploration passed to northern Europe. In part, this resulted because Spain and Portugal were now busy ruling their new territories; in part, it was because northern Europeans, particularly the Dutch and the British, improved the design of oceanic vessels, producing lighter, faster ships than those of their Catholic adversaries. Britain won a historic sea battle with Spain in 1588, in which the British navy and adverse weather routed a massive Spanish Armada. From this point onward, the British and Dutch, and to an extent the French, vied for dominance on the seas.

Ship technology in the expanding West. This is the *Vittoria*, the only one of Magellan's five ships that completed the first circumnavigation of the globe in 1522. (The Granger Collection)

French explorers first crossed the Atlantic in 1534, reaching Canada, which was claimed in France's name. French voyages increased during the seventeenth century, as various expeditions pressed down from Canada into the Great Lakes region and the Mississippi valley.

The British also turned their attention particularly to North America, starting with a brief expedition as early as 1497. The English hoped, in vain, to discover a northwest passage to India, but in fact accomplished little beyond an exploration of the Hudson's Bay area of Canada during the sixteenth century. England's serious expeditions commenced in the seventeenth century, with the colonization of the east coast of North America.

The Dutch entered the picture after winning independence from Spain and quickly became a major competitor with Portugal in Southeast Asia. The Dutch sent a significant number of sailors and ships to the region, ousting the Portuguese from the Indonesian islands by the early seventeenth century. Voyagers from The Netherlands explored the coast of Australia, although without much immediate result. Finally, toward the middle of the seventeenth century, Holland established a settlement on the southern tip of Africa, mainly to provide a relay station for its ships bound for the East Indies.

Dutch and British exploration and trade were government-sponsored, but unlike the Spanish and Portuguese expeditions, and to some extent the French, they owed much to the private initiative of merchant groups. The Netherlands, Britain, and France all chartered great trading companies, like the Dutch East India Company or the British firm of similar name. These companies were given government monopolies of trade in the regions designated, but they were not rigorously supervised by their own states. Thus, semiprivate companies, formed by pooling merchant capital and amassing great fortunes in commerce, long acted almost like independent governments in the regions they claimed. For some time, a Dutch trading company virtually ruled the island of Taiwan, off the coast of China; the British East India Company played a similar role in parts of India during much of the eighteenth century.

TOWARD A WORLD ECONOMY

By the sixteenth century, then, West Europeans had gained control of most of the world's seas. They were moving freely across the Atlantic Ocean and with some regularity across the vast Pacific as well—the first time in world history that an endeavor of this magnitude had ever occurred. The Europeans did not displace all Asian shipping from the coastal waters of China and Japan, nor did they completely monopolize the Indian Ocean; in East Africa, Muslim merchants remained active. But, Muslim and Hindu traders were now confined to regional specialties; they did not command the chief routes. In the Mediterranean, finally, where European power had been growing even earlier, the Spaniards inflicted a decisive defeat on the navy of the Ottoman Empire, in the battle of Lepanto in 1571; with this setback, any hope of a new Muslim rivalry to European naval power ended. By this time, the greatest competitors Europeans faced were other European states, and their battles would pepper world history from this point until the mid–twentieth century. By the sixteenth century, European traders even shipped products from one part of Asia to another, making profits by handling goods with which Europe had no direct involvement at all. World trade and its expansion lay largely in Western hands.

Into the eighteenth century, however, the Europeans' power, although astonishing by their own or anyone else's previous standards, was a sea power, and sea power had limits. Only in rare special circumstances were the Europeans able to penetrate inland, far from the protection of their ever-improving ship's cannon. The major exception, of course, was in the Americas, where the Spanish gained continental control and the English and Portuguese important regional centers. Elsewhere, the European grasp extended mainly to islands—with the control of major parts of the

World Profiles

Amerigo Vespucci (1451–1512)

Amerigo Vespucci is the only person in world history to give his name not to just one whole continent, but two. Vespucci was a talented Italian navigator in Spanish, then Portuguese, service who, on the heels of Christopher Columbus, crossed the Atlantic to the New World and charted some of the coast of North America. Like Columbus, he was a tireless self-publicist, who reached out to Europe's educated readership with information about the New World and his country's accomplishments. Vespucci's first name was applied to the continents of the Western Hemisphere, because his charts showed that whole continents, and not just strings of islands, were involved. Vespucci is here portrayed in association with the new scientific and technical devices beginning to capture European imagination, important to the voyages of discovery. He holds an astrolabe that, by measuring the altitudes of stars, allowed calculations of latitudes and times. What other symbols helped promote the new European surge and Vespucci's own exaggerated reputation?

"Vespucci Studying the Stars" *by Stradanus.*

Indonesian islands the most significant achievement—and scattered port cities. Even in Africa, where the Europeans had greater influence than they did in most parts of Asia, European control was mainly coastal until after 1800. In the Middle East and Eastern Europe, Westerners seized no territory at all, although their trading influence was actively felt; in East Asia, even their commercial efforts were kept to a minimum after a brief initial flurry.

Hence, outside the Americas, the Europeans affected but did not dominate major civilizations. We will examine their influence and its limitations in subsequent chapters. Even in India, until the eighteenth century, European presence and the seizure of a few coastal cities were fairly minor incidents, hardly rivaling the ongoing presence of a Muslim government in a largely Hindu population.

It is important, then, not to exaggerate the significance for world history of what the Europeans liked to call their age of exploration. There was no question of their new strength, but until about 1800, when the situation changed, they were not yet directing the world stage.

Nonetheless, Western Europe was beginning to shape new global economic contracts, which brought them great advantage and affected economic activity in many other parts of the world. Europe's wealth increased rapidly because of profits drawn from the Americas, Africa, and even Asia. The Europeans never uncovered the golden treasures they had hoped for, but they did gain access to vast supplies of gold and particularly silver in the New World. Spain was the chief initial beneficiary of this wealth within Europe, but bankers and merchants in northern Europe soon profited even more substantially. With the new supply of precious metals and resulting control of shipping, the Europeans were able to turn the balance of world trade in their favor for the first time. Spice and tea plantations in southern Asia began to produce for the growing European market on terms of trade set no longer by the rarity of their products but by the buying power of the West.

Then, as Europeans used some of their wealth to improve their own manufacturing base, they increasingly offered manufactured products to the world market—guns, cloth, and metal wares—instead of precious metals alone. The division was deliberately fostered by the policies of the Europeans themselves, whether as governments or as giant trading companies. The reigning theories of mercantilism urged seventeenth- and eighteenth-century Europe to monopolize as much manufacturing as possible, leaving other parts of the world to specialize in agricultural production or mining. By the eighteenth century, several parts of the world were producing raw materials or foodstuffs for a Western market and receiving more sophisticated and expensive manufactured goods in return. Russia and Poland sold grain; Africa, slaves; the Americas, sugar, silver, and tobacco. These goods, because they involved less processing, tended to command lower prices than did Europe's own products. And so a global economy was being shaped in which much of the world sold goods (generated by cheap labor) to the West, which sold more expensive items and in whose ships the goods were exchanged. Here was the beginning of a division in the world economy between have's and have-not's, which echoes to the present day.

The impact of this division could run deep. Basic labor systems increasingly responded to economic position. Western Europe required labor flexible enough to participate in growing manufacturing; hence, it increasingly developed a wage-labor force, often ill-paid. Areas dependent on producing raw materials, particularly where workers were in short supply because of disease, relied on compulsory labor systems, like slavery or extensive serfdom, that could keep costs down for unskilled work. Gender was affected. In many areas, men were responsible for an increasing amount of production for sale, relegating women to domestic tasks. New slave traders preferred men: two-thirds of all African slaves sent to the Americas were male, and this extended systems of polygamy in Africa itself as a means of dealing with an overpopulation of females.

However, this was only the beginning of an international economy dominated by the West. Most people were not deeply affected by the new patterns of trade. The Chinese were far more heavily influenced by new foodstuffs brought by European traders, by the seeds and tubers they introduced from the Americas, than by Europe's economic position within the world community. Most Asians, Russians, Africans, and even many American Indians were not drawn into production for the world market as yet, although it is true that Europe's financial influence reached farther than their ships. Here is another factor, along with outright European contacts, to be considered in contemplating the development of major civilizations between 1450 and 1800.

In three major cases, however, European influence did penetrate farther, even in the early modern centuries, so that major alterations in historical patterns resulted. Developments in sub-Saharan Africa, Spanish or Latin America, and North America revealed the extent of Western penetration and an emerging New World economy to reshape politics, culture, and individual lives.

AFRICA

It was long assumed, by prideful Westerners, that African history did not really begin until the coming of the Europeans. This of, course, is nonsense; African culture had evolved to a significant extent before Europeans journeyed down the Atlantic and, more to the point, it continued into the nineteenth century to develop apart from European influence. However, Europeans did have profound effects on a number of regions, and this new factor must be linked with other trends to describe African diversity after about 1500.

European exploration of Africa was limited by several factors. Transportation barriers were as great for them as for Africans; it was hard to move inland from the coast, particularly in the thickly forested areas. Moreover, the main rivers were not navigable for any distance. Disease also hit the Europeans hard for they lacked the immunity to tropical diseases that Africans had developed over time. Most important, the political powers of most African kingdoms were sufficient to block European entry until the nineteenth century. To be sure, the great African empires ended with the fall of Songhai late in the sixteenth century; in the south, there was nothing to match the earlier Zimbabwe. But, regional kingdoms flourished, some old, some rising for the first time. This meant that in most instances Europeans had to negotiate carefully with African leaders, offering real value in exchange for value received; with a few exceptions, they could not seize territory.

Here, for example, is how a Dutch representative described the king of the West African kingdom of Benin (where the Dutch traded actively during the seventeenth century, replacing the Portuguese as principal European contacts):

> I saw and spoke to the king of Benin, in the presence of his great counsellors. He was seated on an ivory throne under a canopy of Indian silk. He was about forty years old and of lively expression. According to custom I stood about thirty feet away from him. So as to see him better I asked permission to draw closer. He laughingly agreed.

The representative was also awed by the splendor of the palace, as big as the stock exchange in Amsterdam, supported by "wooden pillars encased in copper, where the victories of the kingdom are recorded."

European activity, however, did make a difference in Africa. The Portuguese and then other Europeans, particularly the French, established forts and urban settlements along the western coast, usually leased or made available by other arrangement with local rulers. With this base, the Europeans altered West African trading patterns. They encountered many valuable goods in Africa—cloth and iron items—but their main interests lay in gold, ivory, and slaves. They found African merchants as well as political rulers to be demanding negotiators, but they did have goods to offer in return: cloth, iron tools, and above all muskets. European imports reduced African craft production, which disrupted the economy severely. Dependence on weapons imports also brought change. Not infrequently, Europeans participated as allies in wars among African kingdoms, where their firepower could spell the difference in outcome. These trading activities brought new contacts to West Africa, drawing the region into a European-dominated world economic network and away from traditional trade routes across the Sahara to North Africa. The presence of Western trading stations on the coast also had an effect on some urban Africans, leading to a limited number of conversions to Christianity.

West Africa was more specifically and deeply affected by the growing Atlantic slave trade, which began in the sixteenth century but intensified greatly after about 1650. West African slaves were purchased by sea captains from Holland, Britain, and particularly France, to be sold in the North and South American colonies and the West Indies. Slavery was not new to this region of Africa, as many states had held troops captured in battle as slaves. But, the European demand transformed a traditional practice beyond recognition. Between 1500 and the end of the slave trade in the nineteenth century, as many as 12 million Africans may have been taken away as slaves. This exodus, one of the greatest and most terrible forced movements of peoples in human history, devastated some regions of West Africa, which lost population rapidly and found it difficult, in the absence of sufficient younger workers, to maintain traditional economic levels. Nonetheless, some West African states profited from the slave trade, at least in the short run. The actual capture and sale of slaves to European merchant sailors was almost always handled by African agents, who traded slaves for guns, gold, and other goods. One new, unusually centralized state, the Fon kingdom of the eighteenth century, organized all its dealings with Europeans in a

Patterns of Eighteenth-Century Slave Trade

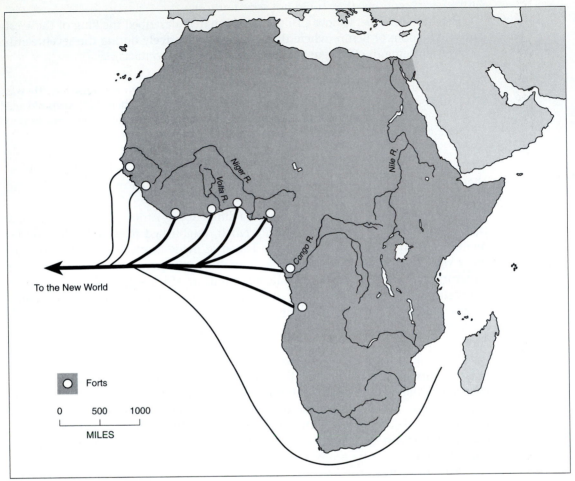

single location, to minimize contact between Europeans and inland Africans. The state carefully regulated and taxed the slave trade, controlling the import of firearms and ammunition.

Thus, the impact of the massive slave trade on West Africa was mixed and not simply the result of unchallenged European profiteering (although there were huge profits to be made from the exchange, even after the African agents were paid; this was one source of rising merchant wealth in Western Europe). Many parts of West Africa came to depend on the slave trade for their own economies. However, the long-term damage from it was done. African birth rates grew more slowly than those of most other societies throughout the nineteenth century, in part as a result of sheer population loss. Economic development was surely slowed down, although it is hard to say exactly how much change would have resulted had the slave trade not interfered. In addition, relations among West African kingdoms grew more warlike and chaotic, as various states clashed to gain slaves, and others armed to prevent raids. Destabilization was not complete, and again there was variety, depending on how a given kingdom handled negotiations; indeed, some West African kingdoms deliberately stayed out of the slave trade altogether. But, there is no question about the serious impact this practice had on West African history for more than two centuries.

There was also no question about the harsh life slaves were soon forced to endure, and the inhuman circumstances to which they were often subjected upon capture:

> As the slaves come down . . . from the inland country, they are put into a booth or prison, built for that purpose near the beach, all of them together; and when the Europeans are to receive them, they are brought out into a large plain, where the ships' surgeons examine every part of every one of them. . . . Such as are allowed good and sound are set on one side, and the others by themselves; these rejected slaves are called Makrons, being above 35 years of age, or defective in their lips, eyes or teeth, or grown grey. . . . Each of the others passed as good is marked on the breast with a red-hot iron, imprinting the mark of the French, English, or Dutch companies so that each nation may distinguish their own property. . . .

World Profiles

Olandah Equiano

Olandah Equiano was one of the few enslaved Africans able to later write about his experiences. He was born in a Nigerian village, Isseke, in 1745, to a wealthy, slave-owning family. He was kidnapped by slave traders and in 1756 taken to Barbados and then Virginia. Finally able to buy his freedom from a Quaker master, he went to England in 1767. By this point, he was both literate and well read. He became active in the antislavery movement, publishing his memoirs in 1788 as a protest against the entire institution of slavery. Equiano poignantly described his desperate feelings when he and his sister were tied up and put in sacks, and then separated from each other. He detailed the greater brutality of European slave shippers, compared to his initial African captors, and the ordeal of imprisonment among strangers and the frightening voyage to an unknown land with little hope of return. This account was one of the first in a wave of memoirs by former slaves and part of a growing movement against the system on both sides of the Atlantic. What kind of antislavery arguments would work best, in the context of eighteenth-century Europe?

Olandah Equiano.

Typically, a week after capture, the voyage across the Atlantic began, a terrifying, foul experience in which as many as half the slaves would die. For the survivors, a life of servitude in a strange land was the reward.

Slave trading also disrupted another part of the western coast, in the territory of Angola, which came under increasing Portuguese control. The Portuguese, initially interested in precious metals, soon concentrated on capturing slaves for trade with Brazil. Ruling Angola outright, through corrupt local officials, they produced growing chaos in this region for centuries. Here, in contrast to the picture farther north in present-day countries like Nigeria, there was no question of some compensatory benefits from the European quest for slaves; Angola simply suffered.

Finally, the southern end of Africa was affected greatly by European exploration. Holland established a small colony on the Cape of Good Hope in 1652, to help supply its ships bound for Asia. This community of *Boers* (the Dutch word for farmers) soon escaped Dutch control, fanning out on large farms in a region still lightly populated by Africans. The Boers clashed with local hunting groups, enslaving some of them. Later, after 1770, they came into increasing contact with Bantu farmers, initiating a long struggle for control of the region that still affects the nation of South Africa today.

European influence on African history between 1450 and 1800 was thus intense but, for the most part, regional. It set new forces in motion in southern Africa and Angola, and strongly affected the economic and political life of West Africa without, however, overturning all previous patterns.

Other parts of Africa were scarcely affected by the West during these centuries. Ethiopia, although Christian and in some contact with Portuguese missionaries, remained aloof. East Africa had little to do with Europeans; here, trading patterns were still oriented toward the Middle East, and both Africans and Arab traders pushed into the eastern interior in search of agricultural products and slaves. The slave trade to the Middle East and North Africa also expanded in the early modern period; totalling perhaps three million people, it remained more modest than its Atlantic counterpart.

Overall, the patterns of African culture remained much as before. Politically, most of the continent was organized in regional kingdoms, with rulers who allied with local leaders and operated as divine monarchies. Most Africans remained polytheistic, although Islam was a potent force in the Sudan region. Late in the eighteenth century, conversions to Islam began to increase in this area, as the religion became a popular force and not simply an elitist movement. Scholars like Usuman dan Fodio (1754–1818) argued against the traditional policy of living tolerantly alongside nonbelievers. Usuman and his followers, active in Muslim scholarship and law, conducted several holy wars in the western Sudan, winning over many ordinary people and producing a number of well-organized new states.

In another continuing trend, Bantu migration southward persisted. This movement, as noted, would bring Bantus into conflict with Dutch settlers. The severe crowding it produced in Bantu lands by around 1800 prompted Bantus to begin organizing into more coherent political units.

Finally, although African economic life was deeply affected by European trade at least in some key regions, there was no massive change in economic forms or technologies on the continent overall. Europeans did import corn seeds from the New

World, which were adopted by many African farmers and thereafter used as a food staple. But, perhaps because of the slave trade, the crop did not result in a significant population increase at this point; indeed, relative to world population growth, the African share actually decreased.

In sum, major changes occurred in Africa between 1450 and 1800. Some of these changes were of European origin or represented African reaction to European contacts, but others were quite distinct, resulting from Islam or Bantu migration. No single force mobilized more than individual regions of the continent; beneath the surface, important traditional patterns of politics, art, belief, and social organization largely persisted.

COLONIZATION IN LATIN AMERICA: THE BIRTH OF A NEW CIVILIZATION

European impact on the Americas was far more significant than that in Africa: here, the Europeans began to alter basic patterns as early as the sixteenth and seventeenth centuries, creating a new civilization in Latin America and extending Western civilization to the eastern seaboard colonies of North America. The natives' lack of iron weapons and their vulnerability to disease, often with devastating consequences, created a context far different from Africa. African independence long contrasted with the growing European colonies in the Americas. The colonization process, of course, also brought the Americas into mainstream world history and linked the two continents to the emerging world economy on conditions set mainly by the Europeans themselves.

In Central and South America and the West Indies, Spanish efforts to follow exploration with outright conquests began early in the sixteenth century. The chief goals were God and gold: The Spanish hoped to tap what they believed was the vast wealth of the new lands—their appetites having been whetted by the rich ornaments they encountered among groups like the Aztecs and by a taste for myth. And, as the most powerful Catholic state, soon heavily influenced by the active Jesuit order, Spain planned to win new converts to Christianity. Expeditions led to the occupation of leading West Indian islands, including Cuba, starting in 1512. Soon after this, a small army under Hernán Cortés conquered Mexico from the Aztecs. Although pockets of American Indian resistance remained in parts of Central America until the later seventeenth century, Spanish control was essentially complete by 1550. By this point, the empire extended loosely into parts of what are now the southern and southwestern United States.

From their colony in Panama, the Spanish moved into South America. They took over the northern part of the continent fairly easily, conquering loosely organized American Indian cultures. In 1531, an expedition attacked the Inca empire, inspired by tales of its many treasures. Intense combat was necessary to seize Peru, but the Spanish commander, Pizarro, ultimately prevailed. From this base, other missions extended along the Andes mountain chain, finding the Amazon River and seeking the silver mines of Bolivia. Spanish expeditions also moved into Argentina, founding a

Latin America by the Eighteenth Century

FRENCH COLONIES

ENGLISH COLONIES

ATLANTIC OCEAN

Gulf of Mexico

NEW SPAIN

Mexico City

BRITISH HONDURAS

CUBA (Spain)

SAINT DOMINIQUE (France)

SANTO DOMINGO (Spain)

JAMAICA (Britain)

CARIBBEAN SEA

PACIFIC OCEAN

Bogotá
NEW GRANADA

Orinoco R.

(British after 1803)
DUTCH GUIANA

FRENCH GUIANA

Equator

GALÁPAGOS IS.

Amazon R.

BRAZIL

ANDES MTS.

Lima
PERU

Rio de Janeiro

BUENOS AIRES OR LA PLATA

Santiago
Buenos Aires

Montevideo
La Plata R.

PATAGONIA

	Spanish
	Portuguese
	British

0	1000	2000

MILES

FALKLAND IS.

CAPE HORN

settlement in Buenos Aires in 1536. Only at the end of the sixteenth century, how-ever, did the Spanish really begin to colonize Argentina, introducing cattle raising and other forms of agriculture once the thirst for quick riches had somewhat dimin-ished. Finally, early in the seventeenth century, the Portuguese began to journey in-ward from small coastal settlements in Brazil, taking effective hold of much of the vast interior territory.

The conquest of Latin America, complete in outline during the seventeenth century, was amazingly swift. This was no well-coordinated, carefully planned venture. Many expeditions, such as Pizarro's against Peru, were essentially mounted by groups of adventurers or private merchants. And, all the campaigns, even those sponsored by the Spanish government, were small. How did they conquer such a vast territory so easily?

Superior technology was, of course, a key. The Indians lacked not only guns and cannons but also horses and metal weapons of any sort. The Europeans also profited from civil wars and dissent within Indian ranks. Hostility to the Aztecs provided Cortés with many Indian allies at first. The Inca empire was weakened by internal warfare shortly before Pizarro's arrival. Trickery played a role: Many Spanish commanders initially negotiated treaties with Inca, Aztec, and other leaders, only to violate the agreements at the earliest opportunity, often putting their erstwhile allies to death. And, the hold of the Europeans was not at first thorough. Many Indian villages were untouched by a Spanish or Portuguese presence for decades; many local Indian leaders were given considerable autonomy so long as they pledged loyalty to the new colonial government.

However, in scarcely more than a century, the Spanish had leveled the leading American Indian civilizations, destroying their political structures and obliterating their formal cultures. Their task was aided not only by their desire to impose "civilization" on non-Christian peoples, but also by the diseases, particularly smallpox, that they brought with them. Indians, so long isolated, had no resistance to these scourges. The result was plagues that resembled those at the end of the classical and postclassical periods in Eurasia, but even worse. Within less than a century, 90 percent of the Mexican population had been wiped out; entire populations on the West Indian islands vanished. Overall, as has been noted, 80 percent of the previous Indian population of North and South America would die as a result of disease. The resulting vacuum Europeans increasingly tried to fill.

LATIN AMERICAN CIVILIZATION

After the conquest period, the Spanish and Portuguese settled down to the construction of new political and religious institutions and a new economic framework for their vast colonies. The result, during the seventeenth and eighteenth centuries, was essentially a formative period for a new, Latin American civilization, closely tied to Europe but also distinct in significant ways.

Politically, this new civilization was characterized by the rule imposed from the outside by the monarchies of Spain and Portugal. European-born men held virtually all of the administrative positions, in what became significant bureaucracies. Two main provinces were created, called "viceroyalties"—one administered from Mexico, the other from Peru. Later, the huge South American holding was further divided, with new centers in Argentina and Colombia. In theory, this governmental system was highly centralized. In fact, the territories were much too vast for effective central control, which meant that church leaders, estate owners, and villagers had considerable latitude. Latin America would long be characterized by a gap between seemingly strong political authority and the actual weakness of the state in relation to local regions and to institutions like the village and hacienda.

One result of the gap between government claims and the reality of very lax state control was a sense that government power ought to be increased, that this was the chief problem in Latin American society. Even in the eighteenth century, Spanish colonial administration tried to expand its authority, and the quest would continue into the nineteenth and twentieth centuries as well. A second result was that the centralized system, however superficial in reality, prevented much participation in the new society, as most colonials were firmly barred from governmental activity. Spain further tightened the monopoly of Spanish-born appointees in the later eighteenth century, resulting in new grievances among the native-born Creoles.

Culturally, the leading feature of the new society was a fervent and pervasive Catholicism. Far more than the Spanish and Portuguese governments, the Jesuits and other missionaries moved actively among the common people, working hard to undermine the influence of earlier Indian religions and replace them with Christianity. Many Indian groups long remained isolated from this effort, but there was steady change. Mission schools, an extensive network of local churches, and the destruction of American Indian culture soon produced measurable results. The power and success of the new conquerors helped make the missionaries persuasive. But, they also offered a gentler religion with greater compassion for ordinary people than any of the religions the Indian civilizations of South and Central America had developed. Although American Indians resented the abolition of many ceremonies and even maintained some in secret, the elimination of human sacrifice and the power of the earlier priestly castes may have been welcomed by many. And, there were numerous opportunities for syncretism. Many Indians combined the notions of certain earlier gods or goddesses with Catholic saints, thus helping to transition change while producing a lively and distinctive religious art.

The Europeans also sought to introduce some features of their own wider culture. Major cathedrals were built in the Spanish Baroque style, and public buildings also followed European architectural models. Cities were established as islands of European order, building on the traditional belief in urban life that the Spanish inherited from the Romans and Arabs. Gridlike streets radiated from a central plaza, which was graced by a major church and a government building and jail. However, Westernized artistic culture was not yet advanced. Spanish-style religious paintings were attempted, but they did not match the vigor of Christianized Indian or mestizo designs. Literature was virtually nonexistent, as the Spanish authorities discouraged printing save in a few centers. Furthermore, American Indian artistic forms continued to survive, in pottery and textile design. This was not high art, but it was responsible for an important diversity in Latin American culture that would have more important effects in the future. Outside of the extension of Catholicism, then, Latin American culture was clearly in a formative stage but showed signs of some differentiation from purely European models.

Two kinds of economic activity coexisted in this early period of Latin American history. First, many Indians and *mestizos*—people of mixed Spanish and Indian ancestry—operated in a village or small-town economy, producing corn and other foods for largely local needs. The economic life of many Indian villages, even their

Franciscan mission cloister in Brazil.

communal ownership of the land, was left virtually undisturbed—although the Spanish eliminated the leading institutions of American Indian society, they did not eliminate all traces of this culture.

Along with this local village structure was an economy geared for export, and specifically for the profit of the Spanish and Portuguese. This economy involved mining operations, particularly in the Andes region, where 16,000 tons of silver were produced for Europe by the year 1650.

The market economy also promoted large landed estates established by the Spaniards or Creoles—Europeans born in the new land. The Spanish did not attempt to enslave many Indians, partly because of fierce resistance and partly because Catholic leaders, eager to protect their new converts, opposed such a policy. But, they did set up a network of large estates. As Indians died of European diseases, land was left vacant and often seized by mestizos or Spaniards, who benefited from the government authorization of such ownership. At first, it seemed that the original

The Portuguese Baroque style of architecture was used frequently in South America: San Francisco Church in Salvador de Bahia, Brazil.

Spanish conquerors might become a feudal nobility, but the Spanish government, aware of the importance of more central control, resisted this pattern save in a few areas. Nevertheless, many large estates resulted from land grants and seizures, particularly when a brief effort at the direct governmental distribution of Indian labor failed. Estate owners worked hard to command labor resources, increasingly scarce as the Indian population shrank. An early form of labor control, not necessarily corresponding to a single estate, was the *encomienda,* where the Spanish or Creole grantee was given rights over a certain percentage of Indian labor. This was one source of the labor used in silver and mercury mines in the Andes region; at its height, labor drafts generated 13,000 workers a year for the leading mine. More common still was the *hacienda,* a large estate on which a number of Indian villages were granted to a Spaniard, often one of the initial conquerors. Village inhabitants on the hacienda were required to pay tribute in goods (food and textiles) plus providing labor service. This system, which after a generation or two turned into effective ownership of the village lands, closely resembled the harsher forms of earlier European serfdom; the landlord provided some protection and a court system for his villagers, in return for payments in kind and almost absolute control over the farmers. Finally, in a few cases estate owners hired low-paid Indian or mestizo laborers, who were encouraged to go into debt and officially forbidden to leave until often impossible sums were paid off—again, a means of attempting to reduce rural freedom in order to address the twin realities of labor shortage and market opportunity.

Haciendas and the other estate forms did not, for the most part, produce for the export trade directly. But, they did yield grains and meats that were sold to mining centers and the growing populations of port cities and administrative capitals like Mexico City. Thus, a vigorous Latin American market agriculture developed, but on the basis of low-paid or servile labor under effective landlord control.

A somewhat different version of estate agriculture arose in the West Indies and some parts of the South American continent, particularly Brazil. Here the crops produced—tobacco and especially sugar—were intended for sale in Europe. These estates used hundreds of thousands of black slaves imported from Africa, initially in part because local labor was so scarce as a result of disease. Three times as many Africans were brought to Latin America and the Caribbean as to North America. Not only Spanish and Portuguese holdings, but also British, French, and Dutch West Indian islands, developed this slave-holding system. This was a slave-based economy on a scale never before known, the result of the commercial opportunities and appetites of the new global economy.

Latin America thus quickly developed an economy dependent on a world market, for which it produced agricultural and mining products; additional specialized commercial farming led to the development of mining and governmental centers. Relatively little manufacturing was undertaken, save for local needs; sophisticated

Indians in South America work gold and silver for the Spaniards: sixteenth-century woodcuts.

manufactured products and craft items were imported from Europe. Here was the most acute case of a European intrusion producing a dependent economy. Latin American landowners could reap tidy profits from their market sales, but for their success they relied on a low-paid, fully or partially enslaved, labor force.

Clear social divisions followed from this economic pattern, and they were enhanced by racial divisions. Spanish and Portuguese settlers were much less firmly racist than their English counterparts to the north. However, Latin American society was rather firmly split between a minority of political officials, mine owners, and landlords, and the majority of impoverished workers. The privileged classes were European-born or Creole; the masses were Indian, black, and—the largest group overall—mestizo. There were, of course, some local merchants and shopkeepers, but the size of this middling group was small. Almost all European trade was conducted by Europeans themselves.

Colonization and economic change inevitably affected gender relations. Although European officials tried to discourage intermarriage, the fact that most colonists and imported slaves were male inevitably encouraged sexual unions with American Indian women. Indian family arrangements were often disrupted, and the growth of the mestizo population accelerated. Marriage among African slaves was often forbidden—for example, in Brazil—which led to an additional set of sexual patterns.

As agriculture spread, based on local crops and also crops and animals introduced from Europe (cattle, sheep, rice, wheat), the Latin American population began to grow, despite the staggering effects of disease among the Indians. Prosperity increased also, during the eighteenth century, and many Creole owners became wealthy. However, resentment grew as well. Spanish and Portuguese policies were designed to keep Latin America subservient, and in the eighteenth century, would-be enlightened despots in both countries tightened controls over the colonies. The colonial administrations imposed heavy taxes on Latin American trade and limited it to a few ports and a handful of privileged companies. Contact with the more advanced economies of northern Europe was banned, although in fact some illegal trade developed, particularly with Britain, which was allowed to import slaves. Latin Americans grew increasingly restless under these limitations and also because of their exclusion from political rule. Many Creoles traveled in Europe and learned of the new political theories of the Enlightenment. In Colombia and other centers, new kinds of intellectual activity arose, as scientific discoveries and reform ideas were discussed. This intellectual ferment was modest, confined mainly to cities and Creoles, but, combined with the other, more widespread grievances, it was the basis for a series of wars of independence that produced the first massive slave revolt in Haiti, in 1798, and then swept across virtually the entire society between 1808 and 1820.

By the eighteenth century, a Latin American civilization was taking shape on the basis of ongoing popular traditions among many Indian peoples; new political, cultural, and technological influences from Europe; and the special conditions of the colonial economy and government. The civilization depended heavily on European models but it was not identical to Europe. Racial diversity, slavery and the estate systems, the nature of the export economy, and a popular culture combined with

World Profiles

Sor Juana Inés de la Cruz (1651–1695)

Sor Juana Inés de la Cruz was one woman in premodern times who rose to public prominence on the basis of her intellectual qualities and piety. An author, poet, musician, and social thinker, she was welcome at the viceroy's court in Mexico City. She represented the growing attempt to produce a European-style and predominantly Catholic culture in the new Latin American civilization. Like many Christian thinkers before her, she ultimately abandoned her wider interests, at the urging of her religious superiors, to concentrate on purely spiritual matters. Why did religion give some women a chance to rise in early modern world history? Were colonial conditions in the Americas more or less favorable to women in public life than to those in most established societies?

Sor Juana Inés de la Cruz.

Catholicism set it apart; so did the combination of wide governmental claims with limited actual authority over local conditions. Latin American civilization, still new, was also capable of important change. New cultural products, a more vigorous internal economy, and Creole contacts with the European Enlightenment all exhibited the spirit of innovation characteristic of the eighteenth century itself. In a different sense, a series of Indian risings in the Andes region, toward the end of the century, performed a similiar function, with leaders combining novel political demands with references to Inca heritage.

WESTERN CIVILIZATION IN NORTH AMERICA

French colonial holdings in Canada and along the Mississippi River, although vast on paper, were only lightly administered. Important French settlements were established only in parts of Canada. The French were far more interested in their West Indian islands, which produced so profitably for the European market. From North

America, they gained only some fur trade and some leverage against Britain's growing empire.

The British colonies along the eastern seaboard, however, were another matter. By the eighteenth century, three million Europeans had settled in these colonies, and a large number of African slaves had been imported as well. In the southern colonies a slave-holding estate system developed—producing rice, sugar, tobacco, and dyes—that in many ways resembled that of the West Indies and Brazil. Britain imposed some of the same limitations on all the colonies that Spain established for its Latin American holdings. Governors were appointed from Britain; taxes were high; manufacturing was discouraged as the British sought to protect their markets in the colonies and procure cheap raw materials and foodstuffs.

Nonetheless, the society that developed in the British colonies was far closer to Western European forms than was that of Latin America. The colonies operated their own assemblies, which provided considerable political experience; local town governments were also active. Despite British regulations, a substantial manufacturing economy developed, and the North Americans ran extensive trading companies and merchant shipping. North American products were less interesting to Western Europe than were those of Latin America and the West Indies. The southern colonies, to be sure, produced tobacco and later cotton, using slave labor, which served as the leading exports. And, southern planters imported expensive craft products from Europe. Here was a dependent economy quite similar to that of Latin America. But in New England and the Middle Atlantic colonies, aside from some furs and woods, there were no natural resources of great interest in the early modern world economy. These colonies were therefore left free to develop their own localized agriculture and also their own trading patterns, including merchant shipping and local manufacturing based on family businesses and wage labor. Britain did try to impose more characteristic dependency with new regulations and taxes in the 1760s, but by this point such attempts to control the colonies were too late; the colonial economy was not as advanced as that of Western Europe, but it demonstrated a somewhat similar range of activities, including growing merchant zeal.

The North American colonists' intellectual contacts with Europe were also vigorous. North America was closer to Europe than Latin America was. The tie with Britain gave North Americans access to one of the most dynamic centers of political theory and scientific inquiry in the Western world. Hundreds of North Americans during the eighteenth century contributed scientific findings to the British Royal Society, and discussion groups among American intellectuals were active as well. North American literacy rates were quite high, which encouraged participation in a European-derived intellectual life. In contrast, Latin America's ties to Spain, where Enlightenment activity was more modest, limited its access to the new intellectual currents of Western civilization.

British, and to an extent French, North America thus evolved less as a separate culture than as part of Western civilization. There were vital differences, of course. The North American colonies did not produce a full aristocracy, of the sort that still dominated West European society; this fact gave the values of merchant groups and free farmers freer rein. Colonial governments were also weak, by European standards, with few functions beyond defense and a rudimentary system of law courts. In

The World After 1763

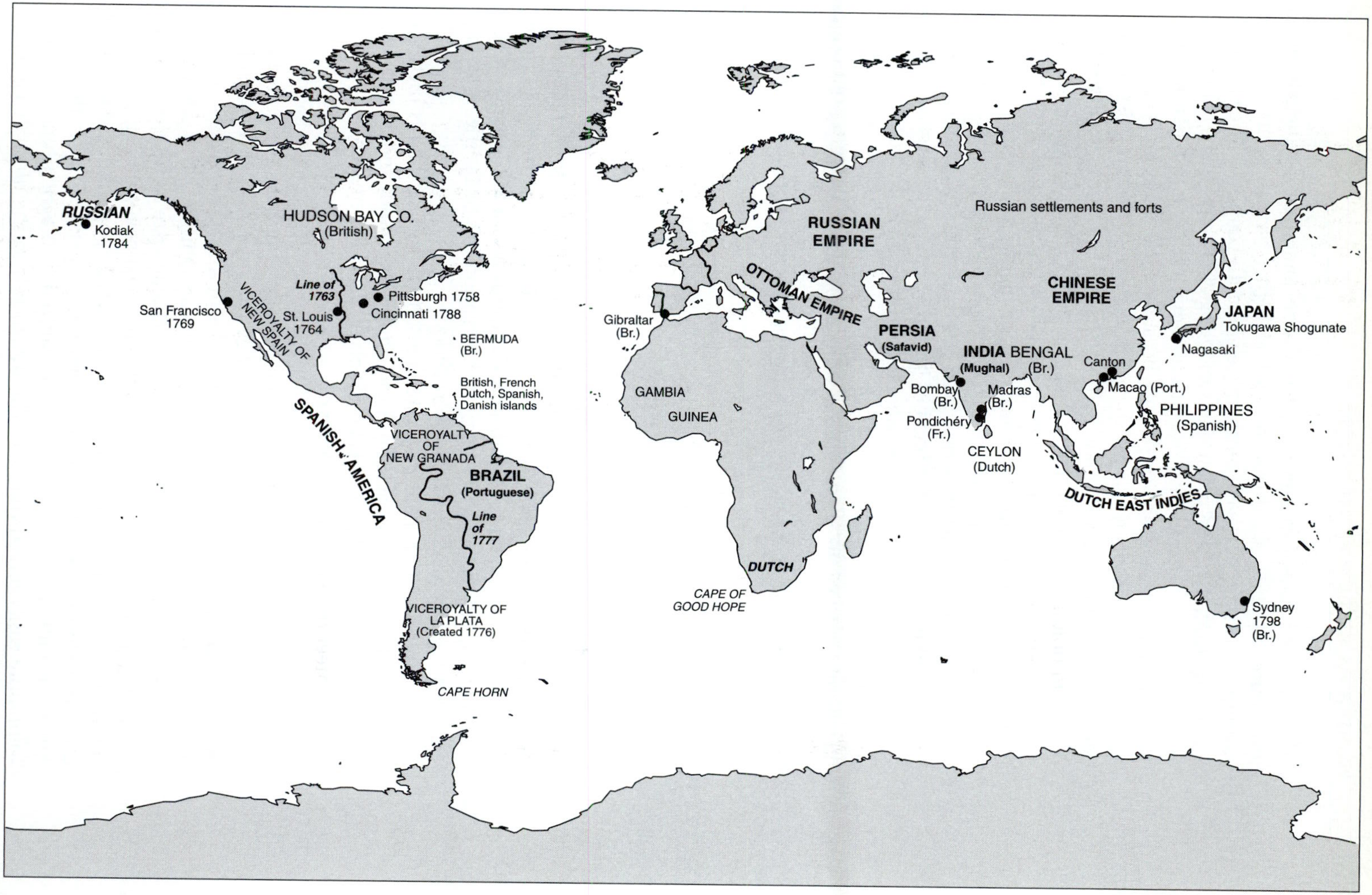

RUSSIAN EMPIRE

CHINESE EMPIRE

JAPAN
Tokugawa Shogunate

Nagasaki

Russian settlements and forts

PHILIPPINES
(Spanish)

Macao (Port.)

Canton

DUTCH EAST INDIES

Sydney
1798
(Br.)

INDIA BENGAL
(Mughal)   (Br.)

Madras
(Br.)

Bombay
(Br.)

Pondichéry
(Fr.)

CEYLON
(Dutch)

PERSIA
(Safavid)

OTTOMAN EMPIRE

DUTCH

CAPE OF
GOOD HOPE

GAMBIA

GUINEA

Gibraltar
(Br.)

HUDSON BAY CO.
(British)

Pittsburgh 1758

Cincinnati 1788

BERMUDA
(Br.)

British, French,
Dutch, Spanish,
Danish Islands

BRAZIL
(Portuguese)

Line
of
1777

VICEROYALTY OF
LA PLATA
(Created 1776)

CAPE HORN

VICEROYALTY
OF
NEW GRANADA

Line of 1763

St. Louis
1764

VICEROYALTY OF
NEW SPAIN

SPANISH AMERICA

San Francisco
1769

RUSSIAN

Kodiak
1784

317

addition, North American family patterns were somewhat distinctive. Blessed with more abundant land, North Americans had higher birthrates than their European counterparts during the seventeenth and eighteenth centuries. They treated children with greater care; thus, the practice of swaddling children was less common in British North America. Americans also placed somewhat greater emphasis on the family as the center of emotional stability, perhaps because of the strangeness of their surroundings. Most important of all, the North American colonies did establish a slave-holding system that, although concentrated particularly in the South, would strongly affect the history of the whole region—even after slavery was finally abolished.

North Americans were conscious of their distinctiveness. They lacked Europe's elaborate art and great cities, although by the eighteenth century, the imitation of European artistic forms was well under way. Americans felt somewhat inferior to Europe, but rejoiced in what they perceived as their greater freedom (slavery aside) and a more youthful vigor. But, the habit of imitating Europe remained strong as well. In fact, the British colonies were so similar to Europe that the course of their history would closely resemble that of the rest of the expanded Western world. Even when the colonies rebelled, in 1776, they did so in the name of Western political ideals and proceeded to establish a government that, although it maintained certain distinctive features, remained clearly within the range of Western political values.

NORTH AND SOUTH AMERICA:
REASONS FOR THE DIFFERENCES

Western penetration of the Americas from 1450 to 1800 thus had two leading results. It created an important although distinctive version of Western civilization in North America. It created an essentially new civilization, albeit one with unusually close ties to Western patterns, in South and Central America and Mexico. Because of its size and economic role, Latin American civilization was by far the more important in world history during the early modern period.

How and why did these two outcomes differ? Part of the distinction rests with differences between Spain and Portugal, on the one hand, and Britain and northern Europe, on the other. Spain was an intensely Catholic country, with a fervent missionary movement, but it was somewhat removed, particularly after 1600, from the mainstream of European intellectual life. Spain lacked a substantial merchant class of its own, which contributed to the Latin American emphasis on landed estates rather than elaborate commerce. Spain's tendency toward centralized control discouraged extensive political life in the new colonies. Latin American civilization, although still not fully formed, thus emerged with a political tradition, an economy, and a social structure quite different from what came to characterize its northern neighbor.

Latin America also developed a different racial balance from that of the English colonies. Disease decimated the American Indian population everywhere, but because of its prior size, substantial concentrations persisted in Latin America. North American Indians were also less fully organized into agricultural societies and they were more easily forced to move. The Indian role in the ultimate culture and social structure of North America was not great. In Latin America, in contrast, particularly in Central America and the Andes region, the values and labor contributions of a sizable Indian population played an ongoing role. The rise of a large mestizo population, virtually unknown in the more racially conscious English colonies, added to the differentiation. Latin American civilization resulted, in part, from a fusion of Western and Indian peoples and social forms; it also had a much larger African slave contingent. North America saw a much more straightforward extension of Western values over small, often badly treated and segregated Indian and African minorities.

From these early differentiations, Latin America and what became the United States and Canada were to follow largely different historical rhythms. To be sure, struggles for independence occurred almost simultaneously. The North American colonies (apart from Canada) rose first, and most of Latin America, inspired in part by this very example, soon followed. But from these wars came quite different results, in the political features of the new nations and in their economic base, as the new United States quickly joined Western Europe in industrialization, whereas Latin America remained in a more dependent position in the world economy.

CONCLUSION: THE WORLD ECONOMY REVISITED

Like all major developments in human history, the rise of the Western-dominated world economy resulted in both gains and losses. It tended to increase economic inequalities among civilizations. Latin America and major parts of Africa, drawn into the world economy as producers of largely unprocessed goods that depended on cheap labor or slaves, had scant reason for rejoicing, although individuals in these societies profited along with the Europeans. Furthermore, the inequalities of the world economy tended to be self-perpetuating. In some basic respects, Africa and Latin America remain dependent economies to this day, unable to control their own economic destinies; in many respects, the West continues to benefit from this sort of relationship. Only the English colonies of North America, on the fringe of dependency into the eighteenth century, managed to break free and become part of the dominant economy of the West.

The world economy also unleashed a new profit motive, through the spread of commercial capitalism. This motive, although capable of generating large-scale exploitation, also supported technological innovation as another means of increasing production at low cost. Before long this thirst, backed by the capital already earned in world trade, would produce vast changes in manufacturing methods, which in turn yielded measurable benefits even beyond Western society.

Before this occurred, however, other civilizations in the world, not fully caught up in the world economy but nonetheless affected by it, had to define their own relationship to the West and new patterns of trade. Some, like China and the Middle East, were not strangers to commercial capitalism, although they had not before encountered it on such a scale. Because of previous economic and technological strength, and strong political structures and distinctive values, most of Asian and Eastern Europe remained partly aloof to the world economy well into the eighteenth century, participating to a degree but not engulfed by it. However, such civilizations, too, faced the prospect of change, even if they resolved otherwise.

SUGGESTED WEBSITES

On the lives of early European explorers, see
http://www.win.tue.nl/cs/fm/engels/discovery/index.html; on the interactions between Spanish conquerors and North American Indians, see *http://www.FloridaHistory.com.*

SUGGESTED READINGS

Excellent discussions of Western exploration and expansion are C. M. Cippolla, *Guns, Sails and Empires* (1985), and J. H. Parry, *The Discovery of South America* (1979). Important recent work includes Alan K. Smith, *Creating a World Economy: Merchant Capital Colonization and World Trade, 1400–1825* (1991); Michael Pearson, *Port Cities and Intruders: The Swahili Coast, India, and Portugal in the Early Modern Era* (1998); and James Tracy, ed., *The Rise of Merchant Empires* (1990), and *The Political Economy of Merchant Empires* (1991). See also C. R. Boxer, *Four Centuries of Portuguese Expansion* (1969); W. Dorn, *The Competition for Empire* (1963); Alfred Crosby, *The Columbian Exchange: Biological and Cultural Consequences of 1492* (1972); C. A. Bayh, *Indian Society and the Making of the British Empire* (1988); and D. K. Fieldhouse, *The Colonial Empires* (1971). See also J. H. Elliott, *The Old World and the New, 1492–1650* (1970), and J. K. Thornton, *Africa and the Africans in the Making of the Atlantic World, 1400–1800* (1997).

On Latin America, consult James Lockhart and Stuart B. Schwartz, *Early Latin America* (1982); Lyle N. Macalister, *Spain and Portugal in the New World* (1984); Eric Williams, *Capitalism and Slavery* (1964); J. Fagg, *Latin America* (1969); S. J. Stein and B. H. Stein, *The Colonial Heritage of Latin America* (1970); and A. Lavin, ed., *Sexuality and Marriage in Colonial Latin America* (1989).

On the slave system, O. Patterson, *Slavery and Social Death: A Comparative Study* (1982), and D. B. Davis, *Slavery and Human Progress* (1984), are both useful. On other key topics, consult Nancy Farriss, *Maya Society under Colonial Rule* (1984); Louisa Schell Hoberman and Susan Migden Socolow, eds., *Cities and Society in Colonial Latin America* (1986); and Stuart Schwartz, *Sugar Plantations and the Formation of Brazilian Society* (1985). On the slave trade, see James Rawley, *The Transatlantic Slave Trade* (1981); Roger Anstey, *The Atlantic Slave Trade and British Abolition* (1975); Paul Lovejoy, *Transformations in Slavery: A History of Slavery in Africa* (1983); Patrick Manning, *Slavery and African Life* (1990); and Joseph Miller, *Way of Death* (1989).

Readable texts on the West and Asia and Africa include Paul Bohannan and Philip Curtin, *Africa and Africans,* 3rd ed., (1988); Martin Hall, *The Changing Past: Farmers, Kings, and Traders in Southern Africa* (1987); Leonard Thompson, *A History of South Africa* (1990); A. Hyma, *The Dutch in the Far East: A History of the Dutch Commercial and Colonial Empire* (1942); and S. D. Pen, *The French in India* (1958). See also K. N. N. Chaudori, *Trade and Civilization in the Indian Ocean* (1985). A provocative although controversial overview of the development of a new global economy is Immanuel Wallerstein's *The Modern World System,* 2 vols. (1980). For source reading, see P. Curtin, ed., *Africa Remembered: Narratives by West Africans from the Era of the Slave Trade* (1967). On colonial North America, see Jack Greene and J. R. Pole, eds., *Colonial British America: Essays on the New History of the Early Modern Era* (1984). For impacts on women, see Merry Weisner-Hanks, *Christianity and Sexuality in the Early Modern World: Reforming Desire, Regulating Practice* (2000).

The Rise of Eastern Europe

FOCAL POINTS

Russia both expanded territorially and changed greatly during the early modern centuries. What were the main directions of change? How was Russia's position in 1750 different from its standing in 1450? Russia developed new contacts with the rest of Europe during this period, but only some of its changes were similar to those of the West. What aspects of Russian society remained distinctive, and why? Russia should be compared to other societies also. Like the Ottoman and Mughal empires, discussed in Chapter 17, Russia developed a new multinational state during this modern period. Why was it relatively more successful than its counterparts in creating a more durable land-based empire?

FACTORS IN RUSSIA'S EARLY MODERN RISE

Along with Africa and the Americas, Russia and Eastern Europe were dramatically affected by the rise of the West during the early modern period. By the eighteenth century, some smaller regions, such as Poland, produced cheap grains for export to the West, using serf labor in a fashion not unlike the estate systems in Latin America. The Russian story was different, however. In contrast to the Americas, where local populations had little choice, Russian leaders deliberately chose to imitate certain Western ways. This pattern began haltingly in the sixteenth century and then accelerated during the eighteenth century. Explicit choice did not preclude important tensions as the Russian economy experienced still more Western influence and cultural reactions followed some attempts at imitation. Nonetheless, Russia's relation to the West remained unique.

One reason for the distinctiveness lay in the new trend toward expansion, initiated in the fifteenth century, that to begin with had nothing to do with the West. Russia's dynamism increased long before it had significant contacts with the West. The West was later courted, although very selectively, to help maintain the surge of expansion.

What causes a civilization to rise? The question, now a familiar one, remains complex. Western civilization expanded on the basis of a diverse but distinctive culture, which produced an aggressive, conquering spirit and a rapidly improving technology. Russia's case, coincident in time, was different. Shaking off Mongol domination, the Russians embarked on a policy of conquest without a major technological impetus.

321

Russia shared some expansionist thinking with the West. Both might have looked back to the precedent of the Roman Empire as an example of what societies could do when they were truly great. Both were Christian, and although the Russian missionary spirit was perhaps less active than that of the West, Christianity may help explain a common desire to achieve new victories. However, Russia long lagged behind the West technologically; it remained backward by Western standards into the twentieth century. It lacked the merchant tradition or commercial expertise of the West; indeed, Russia during the early modern period depended considerably on Western-directed trade patterns. In these respects, Russian differences from the West increased in the early modern period.

Russia did have a large and gradually growing population. It occupied a strategic geographical location, hovering between Europe and Asia, surrounded, except in the north, by few natural barriers. This position made it vulnerable to invasion, as the Mongols had proved, but it also facilitated expansion when the Russians decided to follow the Mongol example. Russia also had the advantage of some excellent natural resources, although its climate placed certain limits on agriculture. Russia's iron ore spurred manufacturing and weaponry. Furs and timber could be traded not only with the West but also with Asia, which helped fuel expansion.

The early modern period saw an elaboration of characteristic Russian social and political institutions. Earlier, Russian civilization had been barely defined. Now, building on many precedents, it was more fully formed. And, it became increasingly important as the Russians constructed one of the world's great empires.

PATTERNS OF EARLY MODERN RUSSIAN HISTORY

Russia's emergence as a new power, first in Eastern Europe and western Asia and ultimately on a still larger scale, depended initially on its winning freedom from Mongol (Tatar) control. Mongol influence had not reshaped Russian institutions significantly, although many Russians had adopted Mongol styles of dress and social habits. Most Russians remained Orthodox Christians; most maintained a separate identity from that of the Mongols. Moreover, local Russian princes had continued to rule, although paying tribute to their Mongol military overlords. It was the duchy of Moscow that served as the center for the Russian liberation effort, beginning in the fourteenth century. Under Ivan III, or Ivan the Great, who claimed succession from the Rurik dynasty, a large part of Russia was finally freed after 1462. Ivan organized a strong army—giving the new government a military emphasis it would long retain. He also capitalized on Russian and Orthodox loyalties—that is, a kind of nationalism along with religion—to win support for his campaigns. By 1480, Moscow had been freed from Mongol control and acquired a vast territory running from the borders of Poland, in the west, to the Ural mountains.

It was under Ivan that Russian beliefs in an imperial mission took on a new shape. Ivan's marriage to the niece of the last Byzantine emperor prompted him to proclaim himself the protector of all Orthodox churches and also to insist that Russia had succeeded Byzantium as the "third Rome." Accordingly, Ivan entitled himself tsar, or Caesar—the "autocrat of all the Russians." The next important tsar Ivan IV, or

Ivan the Terrible, attacked the Russian nobles whom he suspected of conspiracy; many were killed. But, Russian expansion continued nevertheless. Ivan III and Ivan IV encouraged some peasants to migrate to the lands seized from the Mongols and other groups, particularly in the south, along the Caspian Sea, and in the Urals. These peasant-adventurers, called Cossacks, were true Russian pioneers, combining agricultural skills with impressive military prowess on horseback. During the sixteenth century, the Cossacks not only completed their conquest of the Caspian Sea area but also, early in the century, moved across the Ural Mountains into Siberia, beginning the gradual takeover and settlement of these vast plains.

Russian expansion occurred despite the setbacks the Russian economy and culture had suffered under Mongol rule. Russia had become almost entirely agricultural, its earlier urban and merchant past largely forgotten. There was little trade and only localized manufacturing; although some commerce developed with Central Asia, creating regional economic ties, subsistence agriculture predominated. Not only peasants but also many landlords lived under poor material conditions. Rates of illiteracy were unusually high for an agricultural society, and artistic and literary production had almost ceased. In this situation, Russia was open to new influences from Western Europe, with its expanding commercial powers. Ivan III had been eager to launch diplomatic missions to leading Western states as a symbol of Russia's renewed independence and a sign that it wanted contact with the Western network of international relations. During the reign of Ivan IV, British merchants established trading relations with Russia, selling manufactured products in exchange for furs and raw materials. Soon, outposts of Western merchants were established in Moscow and other centers.

Ivan IV's death without an heir set off the Time of Troubles, early in the seventeenth century, in which Russian nobles, the boyars, attacked tsarist power; several neighboring states, including Sweden and Poland, captured Russian territory. However, in 1613, a noble assembly chose a member of the Romanov family as tsar; this family would rule Russia until the great revolution of 1917. Michael Romanov drove out foreign invaders and restored order, although the power of the nobles limited the tsarist government until late in the seventeenth century. Even amid some confusion, however, Russian military efforts continued; successful wars against Poland resulted in the annexation of the Ukraine, including Kiev, and extended Russian boundaries in southeastern Europe to the Ottoman Empire.

A second Romanov, Alexis, restored tsarist autocracy by abolishing the assemblies of nobles and claiming new authority over the Russian church. Alexis was eager not only to gain power, but also to purge the Orthodox Church of many of the superstitions that had developed during Mongol rule. His reform movement, however, antagonized some Russians, who were known as "Old Believers"; their resistance to church reforms caused thousands of them to be exiled to Siberia or southern Russia, where they extended Russia's colonizing activities. Alexis also developed cultural as well as economic contacts with Western nations.

Alexis's son, Peter I, or Peter the Great (1689–1725), greatly expanded his father's work. He was an energetic leader of exceptional intelligence. A giant himself, standing 6 feet, 8 inches tall, he was eager to reform his giant nation still further. He traveled widely in the West, incognito, seeking Western allies for a crusade against

Turkish power in Europe. He even worked as a ship's carpenter in Holland, gaining an interest in Western science and technology and bringing back scores of Western artisans with him to Russia. Politically, Peter defended tsarist autocracy firmly, vanquishing revolts with great cruelty. In foreign policy, Peter attacked the Ottoman Empire without significant results, and then warred with Sweden, winning extensive Russian territory on the eastern coast of the Baltic Sea and reducing Sweden to the status of a second-rate power. Russia now had a "window on the Baltic," including an ice-free port, and from this time onward became a major player in European diplomatic and military conflict. Peter the Great, in accordance with his desire to reform Russia in some Western directions, commemorated Russia's emergence into the European diplomatic orbit by moving his capital from Moscow to the new Baltic city, which he named St. Petersburg.

Internally, Peter's reforms concentrated mainly on streamlining Russia's bureaucratic and military apparatus and increasing central control under the tsar. He improved the organization and weaponry of the army and, with help from Western advisors, created the first Russian navy. New munitions factories and shipyards facilitated this effort, and a substantial iron industry developed: Russia would not come to depend on the West for weapons production. Peter eliminated former noble councils, establishing a set of advisors under his control and a specialized set of ministries in their stead. The central government appointed provincial governors, and although town councils were elected, here too a tsar-appointed magistrate served as the final authority. The church was placed still more firmly under state control, with the tsar as head of the church and a committee of bishops, under his direction, responsible for running religious affairs. Peter's regime rationalized law codes and extended them throughout the entire empire. The tax system was reformed, and taxes on ordinary Russian peasants steadily increased. Finally, the bureaucrats who ran the government were given special training, and Peter relied on non-nobles as well as nobles in his search for the best possible talents.

Peter the Great thus sought to create a state and military force that could compete with those of his rivals and peers in Western Europe. He also introduced some additional reforms designed to make Russian manners—particularly those of the aristocracy—more Westernized. Edicts were issued requiring nobles to shave off their beards and wear Western dress; in symbolic ceremonies, Peter removed the Mongol features, for instance, long sleeves, of nobles' garments. Women in the upper classes were encouraged to become less isolated. Upper-class women could attend theater and ballet, as in the West. Peter abolished a wedding tradition whereby the bride's father handed a whip to the groom, symbolizing the transfer of male power. Russia even imported the custom of Christmas trees, from Germany. These reforms were more than cosmetic. They were designed to enhance Russia in Western eyes and to jolt the noble class out of their established routine.

This was, however, a very selective process of Westernization. Although the education and culture of the aristocracy were profoundly altered (enhancing the tsar's control along with Westernizing much of the ruling class), the conditions of the masses were not significantly changed. Peter had no desire to initiate wage labor, as opposed to serfdom, in Western Europe. Nor was he interested in the parliamentary monarchies of the West. Nor, finally, did he wish to fully imitate the Western econ-

Tsar Peter the Great cutting off the beard of an Orthodox Old Believer. This eighteenth-century cartoon shows the westernization of hair styles.

omy. His technological borrowing focused on heavy industry and munitions. He did not encourage a massive merchant class or a major role in the world economy. Westernization increased Russia's economic contacts with the West, as not only technology but artistic items had to be imported, paid for by growing raw materials and grain exports. Russia was an unequal partner in this trade, which was handled for the most part by Western trading companies. But, the bulk of the Russian economy remained outside this orbit, focusing on agriculture and limited trade with central Asia; it remained far different from its counterpart in the West.

Peter's death in 1724 was followed by several decades of weak rule, dominated by various power plays among army officers who guided the selection of several ineffective emperors and empresses. Peter III, the nephew of Peter the Great's youngest daughter, reached the throne in 1762. He himself was retarded, but his wife, a German-born princess (see p. 326) who changed her name to Catherine, soon took matters in hand and continued to rule as empress after Peter III's death. Catherine—later, Catherine the Great—flirted with the ideas of the French Enlightenment, summoning various reform commissions that did very little. In fact, her goals continued to be those of her illustrious predecessors: to centralize power under the crown and enlarge Russia's territory. She put down a vigorous peasant uprising, led by Emelian Pugachev, who was subsequently executed. She used the Pugachev rebellion as an excuse to extend the powers of the central government in regional affairs, while confirming the nobles' control over most of the land. Catherine resumed Peter the Great's campaigns against the Ottoman Empire, with much greater success; she won new territories, including the Crimea, bordering the Black Sea. Catherine also accelerated Russian interference in Polish affairs, finally agreeing with Austria and Prussia to divide, or partition, this once vigorous state. Three partitions of Poland, in 1772, 1793, and 1795, finally eliminated Poland as an independent state, giving Russia the

World Profiles

Catherine the Great (1762–1796)

Catherine the Great was one of the most important rulers in Russian history and the only woman in their number. A German-born princess, she married Peter III, who was mentally impaired, and soon took over effective control of the government. She continued to rule as tsarina after Peter III's death. True to her own origins and the legacy of Peter the Great, Catherine continued a program of Westernization. In the 1762 portrait shown here, she appears fully dressed in Western fashion—although with a military emphasis that was no accident. Catherine also maintained more distinctive Russian traditions and was not willing to allow Western influences to weaken her autocratic power. Many of her reform moves, as a result, were mere facades. Catherine was also responsible for laws that gave nobles more power over their serfs and, at the end of her life, for banning Western contacts and Western-inspired writings during the French Revolution. In addition to her impact on Russian history, which included successful expansion, Catherine was one of the most lively personalities of world history, her person inspiring numerous stories and myths of great and varied sexual appetites. Even with the advantages of noble birth and marriage, what qualities would a woman need to make this kind of mark in history?

Catherine the Great, woman of uncommon power.

lion's share of the spoils. Finally, Catherine speeded the colonization of Russia's holdings in Siberia and encouraged further exploration, claiming the territory of Alaska. Russian explorers even moved down the Pacific coast of North America into what is now northern California, while tens of thousands of pioneers spread over Siberia.

By the time of Catherine's death, in 1796, Russia had passed through slightly over three centuries of extraordinary development. It had freed itself from all traces of foreign rule; had constructed a strong central state; and perhaps most important of all, had extended its control over the largest land empire in the world at that point.

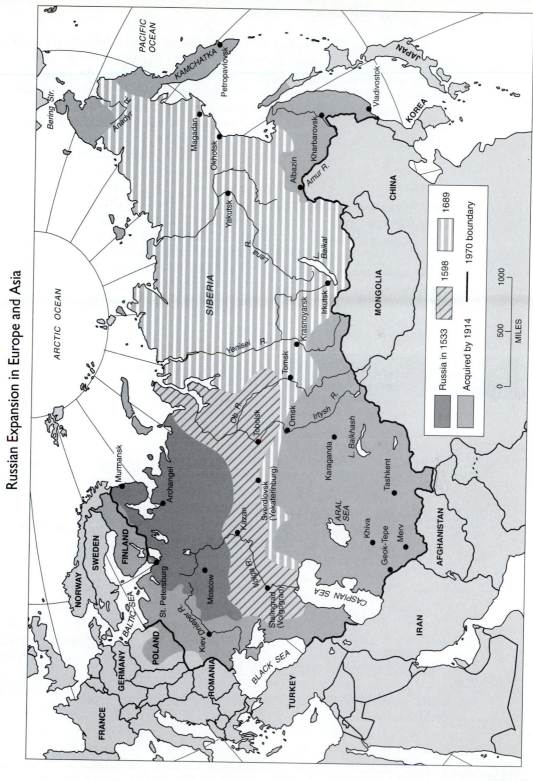

Russian Expansion in Europe and Asia

Russia's expansion had followed three basic directions. First, it had moved east-ward, into the vast stretches of Siberia, most of which had previously been inhabited by hunting-and-gathering peoples. This expansion had brought Russia to China's borders, which were regulated by the eighteenth-century Amur River agreement. Russia's thrust into East Asia was bolstered by vigorous, sometimes forced, coloniza-tion; being "sent to Siberia" was no twentieth-century invention, as thousands of Old Believers and other dissidents could attest. Siberia also offered new lands for agri-culture; colonization not only added to Russian resources but also benefited some of the colonizers.

The second direction of Russia's expansion was toward the south, into central Asia. This expansion brought Russia to the borders of the Ottoman Empire, and Rus-sia's increasingly successful rivalry with this empire was a key factor in Ottoman de-cline. Russia's central Asian holdings resulted in Russian control over a number of di-verse ethnic groups, mostly Muslim. This control was again enhanced by vigorous colonization by the Cossacks, bringing not only Russian rule but also a strong ethnic Russian presence into this region. Russian occupation of central Asia eliminated once

HISTORY DEBATE

A Russian Civilization?

Historians continue to wonder how best to fit Russia into the larger patterns of world history. A traditional impulse among Western historians was to include Rus-sia as part of overall European history from the fifteenth century onward. In the 1970s, even at the height of the Cold War, a French leader said that Russia was at least as European as England was. However, Russia has never been fully Western (although, of course, it may become so in the future, as many Russians currently hope and as others fear). In the fifteenth and sixteenth centuries, even as Italian artists and technical advisors were brought in, Moscow's high culture remained Byzantine; libraries, although still small, were filled with Byzantine books, mainly re-ligious. Social structures remained dramatically different from those in the West. Russia was also heavily influenced by Central Asia. The tsar called himself the khan of the north, to impress Central Asian peoples, and took oaths of loyalty from this region on the Quran. Central Asian models long guided the bureaucracy. Clearly, Russia emerged as a civilization under mixed influences, which it would continue to blend even when more extensive, although selective, Westernization began. The is-sue of how European Russia was, aside from geography, depends on what factors we use to determine the basic nature of a society.

and for all this region's long-standing role as a center of periodic invasions directed at other parts of Europe and Asia.

Finally, Russia moved westward along the Baltic and into Poland. By 1796, Russian borders met those of Prussia and Habsburg Austria; most of the smaller nations of Eastern Europe had been eliminated. Here, too, Russia assumed control over the government of many minority peoples, including various Slavic groups, some Germans, and many Jews. And, the Russian empire propelled itself into the mainstream of European diplomacy, winning alliances at various points with a number of Scandinavian and central European nations and increasing both naval and overland access further into Europe.

Russian expansion was by no means complete by 1800. Further efforts to expand extended in all three directions. The Russian government had established a clear and successful tradition of careful military aggrandizement. Segments of the Russian people had demonstrated a vigorous pioneering spirit, which took them into new, sometimes hostile lands, quite like the settlers of North America during the same period. Not too long after 1800, a French aristocrat, Alexis de Tocqueville, commenting on the dynamism of the new United States, compared American growth to that of the world's "sleeping giant"—Russia. He predicted that these two pioneering nations would someday emerge even more strongly in world affairs, and that they resembled each other, in their exuberant growth, more than anyone yet realized. His foresight was impressive.

RUSSIAN POLITICAL INSTITUTIONS

Russia's political structure was firmly autocratic, a centralized government under the tsar. This structure had been suggested in earlier Russian history, through Byzantine example and the Orthodox tradition of church-state unity; it was further enhanced by the military government's need to expel the Mongols and by the example of the Khans. Russia's steady territorial expansion was aided by such a strong central government and, in turn, served to bolster the regime.

Russian tsars did not, to be sure, develop extensive direct contacts with ordinary Russian subjects, although they claimed to be "fathers" to their people. Newly acquired territories were often run for a time rather separately from tsarist control, by freedom-minded Cossacks. Only gradually did the tsarist government regularize all their holdings. Most peasants were ruled by noble landlords, particularly during the seventeenth and eighteenth centuries. They had scant access to tsarist courts, but rather were confined to a judicial system directed by their own landlords. Peasants on a given estate regulated their own mutual relations through village governments, which tried to settle land disputes and other matters on the basis of communal tradition. Because of the power of landlords and the importance of village, or *mir*, governments, Russia was in some ways quite decentralized, as Latin America was becoming although without the colonial overlay. At this point, the Russian empire could not compare to its Chinese counterpart in size or the varied functions of its bureaucracy.

However, the tsars did wield great power, and by the eighteenth century there was no formal institution to check their power. Like China, for example, but unlike the Western monarchies, the tsars established a secret police to prevent dissent and to supervise the bureaucracy itself. The Chancery of Secret Police was initially established by Peter the Great and survived, although under different names and with changing functions, until the late twentieth century.

One key to the tsars' great power rested in their special relationship with the nobility—the Russian boyars. At the end of the period of Mongol rule, the boyars possessed extensive land holdings and hereditary titles. There was potential here for significant aristocratic defiance of the tsar's wishes. Periodically, as during the Time of Troubles, this kind of opposition did develop; it had some institutional base, for a time, in the councils of nobles called to determine tsarist succession. But, Russians had no tradition of feudalism to compare with that of the West. Furthermore, Russia's rapid expansion allowed tsars to grant additional lands to new nobles, whose loyalties were more firmly tied to the crown. Here was a key way in which military expansion strengthened tsarist rule and encouraged the tsars to continue seeking more territory. From Ivan III onward, tsars steadily pressed both new and old nobles to serve the state as military commanders and bureaucrats; they were not allowed to develop separate political loyalties. Thus, Russia's aristocracy differed crucially from its counterpart in the West, since it viewed itself as an extension of the state rather than as a force of partial opposition. Later tsars, such as Peter the Great, in promoting new bureaucrats to aristocratic ranks, reinforced this state-service orientation. They could not tamper with social structure, lest they offend their aristocratic allies.

In many ways, the expansion of the tsarist state resembled the rise of the absolute monarchy in Western Europe. Indeed, Peter the Great deliberately copied some of the organizational and military structures of states like Prussia. In the West, as in Russia, aristocratic power declined in relation to that of the central state. The collapse of the nobles' councils in Russia was reminiscent of the long period in which the French Parliament was not convened. The seeming resemblance between their government and that of much of the West encouraged rulers like Catherine the Great to dabble in the Western theories of enlightened despotism. Nonetheless, similarity was not identity. Russia lacked the church-state division and the feudal and parliamentary traditions that still flourished in the West. It did not generate the constitutional political theories that developed in the West during this period, and indeed Russian rulers were at pains to censor literature incorporating this kind of Western thought. It was not astonishing then that when political revolution rekindled the idea of limiting monarchical power in the West, from 1789 onward, Russia stayed resolutely apart.

Russia's efforts at partial Westernization, not surprisingly, confirmed the empire's autocratic tradition. Under Peter the Great and Catherine the Great, change came from the top down. It increased the hold of the tsar over the nobles, while genuinely seeking to retrain them. No Western monarch treated the aristocracy in such a superior manner, as Peter did in patronizingly and publicly ridiculing the traditional costumes of his boyars. None tried to impose education on them, as Peter did in requiring that all nobles and other bureaucrats learn mathematics. Russian bureaucratic procedures and culture may indeed have benefited from this forced dose of Westernization, in the form of better schools, increased literacy, and more science. But, it was clear that this kind of reform movement reflected and enhanced the special place of an autocratic central government in Russian political life.

RUSSIAN CULTURE

For most Russian people, culture during the early modern period meant the Orthodox religion and traditional forms of oral expression—the heroic epics, the rich musical life, the often witty proverbs designed to explain life's vagaries. The carefully structured rituals of the Orthodox Church and the worship of many saints allowed ordinary Russians to pray for victories or for protection from disease and famine. They represented the focal point of an elaborate system of festivals, more numerous in Russia than in the West, in which feasting and celebration contrasted with the ordinary, often harsh, routine of work. Early modern Russia did not experience the change in popular culture that was occurring in the West.

Russian cultural traditions revived in many ways after the Mongol period. From the fifteenth to the seventeenth centuries, icon painting became increasingly distinctive as a Russian art form. From individual heads of saints and the Holy Family, Russian painters moved to more abstract and complex religious scenes. In literature, the tradition of narrative histories and chronicles written by monks resumed.

During the early modern period as a whole, however, Russian culture was marked by important tensions—between popular tradition and elite tastes, and between Westernizing tendencies and a desire to define special Russian characteristics.

Under Ivan the Great and Ivan the Terrible, Italian architects were summoned to design church buildings and the magnificent tsarist palace in the Kremlin in Moscow. These architects did not introduce Western styles without modification, however. They generated some fusion between Renaissance classicism and Russian

Russian religious art: icon of the Annunciation, Moscow school.

Miracle of St. George and the Dragon, early sixteenth century.

building traditions, producing the ornate, onion-shaped domes that became characteristic of Russian (and other East European) churches.

With Peter the Great and Catherine the Great, the desire to Westernize went even further. The leading aristocrats almost entirely embraced Western cultural influences. Many nobles during the eighteenth century spoke only French, and some did not know Russian at all. European artistic styles began to displace the icon-painting tradition; cultural forms such as the ballet were embraced so fervently that they became part of Russia's own heritage. Western-style schools encouraged a new interest in science and secular philosophy. The public buildings of St. Petersburg were carefully constructed in Western classical styles. Russia was at this juncture still absorbing Western culture; later, in the nineteenth century, Russians would make powerful contributions to the Western pool of literature, science, and music. At this point, before 1800, elite culture was largely imitative.

Furthermore, Western influence was by no means uniformly welcomed. Ordinary Russian peasants, even the provincial nobility, were largely unaffected by these developments. A growing cultural gap between the upper class and the masses developed that would be resolved only through revolution in the twentieth century. And, some literate priests and nobles protested Westernization in the name of an often

Steeple of the Preobrazhenskaya Church, showing wooden carving of characteristic Russian domes. (The Granger Collection)

vaguely defined Russian soul. One wrote to the tsar Alexis: "You feed the foreigners too well, instead of bidding your folk to cling to the old customs." A number of cultural leaders tried to articulate traditional or "patriotic" forms opposed to the new influences.

Russian culture during the early modern period thus saw important improvements represented by revitalized art forms and some fruitful mergers with Western styles. Literacy and schooling advanced, although only a minority of Russians benefited; few Russians entered an essentially Western intellectual orbit. But, this was not yet an integrated culture. While a revived interest in science and new forms of painting and architecture were significant influences in Russian intellectual life, the most enduring single legacy was a heritage of ambivalence about Russia's relationship to the West. Collectively, after a period of stagnation in their own nation's artistic development, Russia's cultural representatives were torn between a desire to imitate the West and a desire to define Russian values as different from and superior to those of the West. In one form or another, this ambivalence continues to characterize Russian cultural development.

ECONOMY AND SOCIETY IN RUSSIA

As Russia moved partially into a Western diplomatic orbit and appropriated a number of Western cultural forms, the empire's economy and society pushed in rather different directions. Here was one of the key signs that Russia remained a separate civilization, although with special ties to the West.

As the Western economy became increasingly commercial, Russia continued to be resolutely agricultural, save for the iron-manufacturing sector and the continuation of active trade in Central Asia. Its economic growth, although considerable, rested on the extension of its agricultural lands as the empire itself expanded, as well as on the increasingly effective use of vast mineral resources. Russia developed only a small merchant class. Indeed, aristocrats deliberately discouraged local merchants, who were seen as potential rivals. Growing trade with the West was handled by the communities of British, Dutch, and other Western traders from their enclaves in Moscow and St. Petersburg, although Russian merchants were more active in the overland commerce with Asia. Russian cities, as a result, were small, less than five percent of the total population.

Most Russian agriculture was designed for local consumption; few peasants were engaged in a market economy, and few even handled much money. Village artisans supplied most of the manufactured goods that the masses required and could not make themselves. Luxury items and more complex equipment were largely imported from the West. Village-level technology did not change rapidly.

Russia did, however, enter the world economy, and on somewhat better terms than areas like Latin America or even sub-Saharan Africa, despite the empire's rather backward economic condition after the period of Mongol rule. In exchange for Western goods and commercial services, including merchant shipping, Russia initially offered furs, along with timber supplies from its vast northern forests. Then, in the eighteenth century, the empire began to sell grain to the West, from the rich lands of the Ukraine and, later, Poland. Furthermore, Peter the Great used government officials to help organize a growing mining industry, so that Russia sold considerable quantities of iron ore to the West as well. Government-sponsored improvements in Russia's network of rivers and the development of St. Petersburg as a major Baltic port facilitated this process.

The government in Russia essentially took the place of merchant capitalists in organizing mining exports, just as it assumed the lead in sponsoring munitions factories and related iron-processing works. Here was an important extension of government functions under the tsars, from Peter the Great on, that helped Russia maintain some balance with the more commercially developed West. Russia used government regulation and unusually rich natural resources to avoid falling hopelessly behind in the world economy.

However, the key to Russia's economic advances lay in its reliance on unfree labor. Some slaves were used, into the eighteenth century, as war brought many captives. More important, however, was the pervasive and rigorous system of serfdom. As serfdom increasingly unraveled in the West, it became more rigid in Russia and other parts of Eastern Europe. By using cheap servile labor, Eastern Europe sought to participate in the world market, taking advantage of the West's growing demand for grains and minerals. Serfs worked most of the land, and the government also assigned serfs to the iron mines and metallurgical factories.

Ironically, prior to the Mongol conquest, Russian peasants had been mainly free farmers, with their legal position being superior to that of their Western counterparts. But after the expulsion of the Tatars, increasing numbers of Russian peasants fell into debt and had to accept servile status under the noble landowners when they could not repay their debt. From the sixteenth century onward, the Russian government actively encouraged this process. Essentially, the government offered the support of serfdom to the aristocracy, in exchange for loyalty. As new territories were added to the empire, this system of serfdom extended to areas where it had not been known before. By 1800, half of Russia's peasantry was enserfed to the landlords, and much of the other half owed comparable obligations to the state. Various laws passed during the seventeenth century tied serfs to the land; a 1649 act proclaimed the status of serfs to be hereditary, so that people born to this station could not legally escape it.

On landed estates, serfs were taxed and policed through their landlords and even bought and sold like ordinary property. Although the earnings of peasants varied somewhat and they sometimes used village governments for community regulation, most remained impoverished and ill-educated. And, the legal servitude of most peasants only increased with time. Although Catherine the Great sponsored a few model villages to exhibit an enlightened form of serfdom, she, in fact, turned over the rule of serfs to the landlords more completely than ever before. A law of 1785 allowed landlords to administer harsh penalties to any of their serfs convicted of major crimes or rebellion. Serfdom spread to new regions, with nobles granted other new rights. Here was proof positive of the vital political basis of serfdom, as Catherine garnered the loyalty of the nobles by giving them, in effect, rule over half of the Russian masses.

In Russian serfdom, not only on the landed estates but also in the mines, the key obligation was not payment in cash or payment in kind, although taxes were high and rising as the government needs for revenue increased. Labor service, the *obrok*, was the obligation that made economic sense of this system. Peasants owed up to a tenth of their yearly labor to their landlords or the state. This was the labor that produced the grain available for export and serviced the mines and factories.

Russia's distinctive social and economic system worked well in many respects. It produced enough revenue to support an expanding state and empire. It underwrote a wealthy upper aristocracy and its glittering, Westernized culture. It supported a far larger number of gentry, who lived more modestly and often resented the Western ways of the imperial court but who were nonetheless secure in their position and loyalty to the tsar. The system also promoted considerable population growth. Population nearly doubled in the eighteenth century, to 36 million people, and although some of this growth was the result of territorial expansion, most was due to a natural increase. For an empire that contained few regions of great fertility and where the climate was harsh, this was no small achievement, although periodic famines and epidemics continued to plague Russia into the twentieth century, for this was a poor land in many ways. But, there could be no question that the economy had advanced.

However, the Russian system suffered from important limitations. There was little incentive for agricultural improvements; most methods remained rather primitive.

Peasants certainly lacked the motivation, for whatever surplus they produced was not theirs. Landlords, inspired by Western advances in the eighteenth century, did form associations to exchange information on new crops and methods, but little was done to improve production on a large scale. Given the secure base in servile labor, there seemed little need for change. Indeed, pressure from landlords caused the government to enact measures against a growing system of peasant-run domestic manufacturing and trade in the eighteenth century, for the aristocracy feared that growing peasant wealth might challenge its rule. Thus, Russia did not experience a significant increase in internal commerce or consumer-directed production comparable to that occurring in the West.

Most important, the system generated recurring peasant unrest. Russian peasants, although mainly loyal to the tsar, harbored bitter resentments against their landlords, who were seen as having taken lands that rightfully belonged to the peasants. Periodic rebellions attacked manorial records, seized land directly, and sometimes resulted in the deaths of landlords and their officials. The Pugachev uprising was the leading eighteenth-century example of this kind of outburst. But there were others, and popular unrest would continue to swell into the nineteenth century. Peasants had more than a sense of grievance; they also had tight links to each other through village governments and traditions of communal support. They maintained strong family ties, extending among many relatives; the network of the Russian family was thus larger than that of the West, with less stress on a purely nuclear unit. Community and family bonds provided a political basis for action, and although the peasants were never successful against the power of the landlords or the military strength of the state, they could not be permanently repressed.

Not surprisingly, by the early 1800s, it was clear that Russia had a major "peasant problem." Not only by Western standards, but also in terms of economic advance and political order, it seemed increasingly clear that something had to be done about Russia's unfree masses. Also not surprisingly, it was very difficult for those in a position of authority or oppression to decide what to do.

CONCLUSION: THE WORLD'S FIRST EFFORT AT WESTERNIZATION

Russia, particularly during Peter the Great's rule and onward, was the first non-Western civilization to attempt a partial "Westernization." The country was geographically close to the West and shared some of the same religious traditions. It had emerged from the Mongol period aware of its backwardness and eager to employ Western models as a partial remedy. What Russian leaders had attempted, in Westernization from the top down, would be tried to some extent in other societies and is still being tested today. The Russians sought to adapt key Western forms, not to make their society entirely Western but to modify it in such a way that it could compete with the West militarily. Thus, the emphasis was on bureaucratic training and military organization and armament. However, there was some sense within Russia that yet more should be done, that cultural styles and even personal manners should move in Western directions; hence, the changes, among the upper classes, in styles of dress as well as art.

Nonetheless, Westernization represented a limited effort. It served to enhance the distinctive Russian autocracy, not to import the full, complex political culture of the contemporary West and certainly not to change the beliefs of the masses. Russia's leaders—like many later cultures in their attempts to Westernize—did not want to reproduce Western civilization wholesale. Small wonder that by the late eighteenth century, some intellectual dissidents, attracted by the West, pressed for further change—although other writers continued to urge the sanctity of Russian traditions.

Rather, the current of Westernization fed into the more general growth of the Russian state and empire. Limited changes were sufficient, in combination with Russia's vast size, population, and resources, to maintain the country's growing role in world diplomacy, challenging smaller nations in eastern and central Europe and China and the Ottoman Empire in Asia. In strictly economic terms, Russia's relationship to the Western-dominated world economy was not vastly superior to that of Latin America; in both cases, the terms of trade were not advantageous and any success depended on an unfree labor force. But in the military and political sphere, the story was quite different. Russia carved out one of the great landed empires in world history.

SUGGESTED WEBSITE

For a website on key individuals, go to
http://www.departments.bucknell.edu/russian.

SUGGESTED READINGS

Two important source collections for this period of Russian history are T. Riha, ed., *Readings in Russian Civilization,* Vol. II: *Imperial Russia 1700–1917* (1969), and Basil Dmytryshyn, *Imperial Russia: A Sourcebook, 1700–1917* (1967). Excellent general coverage is provided in N. Riasanovsky, *A History of Russia,* 4th ed. (1993); see also Otto Hoetzsch, *The Evolution of Russia* (1966). On more specialized topics, consult H. Kohn, *The Mind of Modern Russia* (1955); M. Raeff, *Peter the Great, Reformer or Revolutionary?* (1963); H. Rogger, *National Consciousness in Eighteenth Century Russia* (1963); and A. Kahan, *The Knout and the Plowshare: Economic History of Russia in the 18th Century* (1985). Peter Kolchin, *Unfree Labor: American Slavery and Russian Serfdom* (1987), is an important comparative study.

The Ottoman and Mughal Empires

FOCAL POINTS

Two great Islamic states were created during the early modern period, one covering much of the Middle East and the Balkans, the other much of India. Both the Ottomans and Mughals brought new influences to these regions, including great political and military strength. What were their major contributions? Both empires however, also began to decline during the seventeenth century. What were the symptoms of decline? Why did these empires begin to fade relatively soon after they had peaked? Why did the Mughal empire decline much more rapidly than its Ottoman counterpart? One result of Mughal decline was growing European penetration of India by the eighteenth century. This had not yet happened in the Middle East.

THE MUSLIM EMPIRES

The Ottoman and Mughal empires resembled Russia in establishing large landed holdings with new boundaries during the early modern period. They also, like Russia, included a host of different linguistic, ethnic, and religious groups. Neither empire, however, attempted Westernization during this period, even selectively. Early Mughal emperors had a tolerant interest in Western culture, including its religion, but there were few real attempts to imitate it; the Western intrusion into India later on was a matter of conquest and economic exploitation. Ottoman rulers, with minor exceptions, explicitly avoided borrowing from the West.

Both Islamic empires followed their own paths during most of the early modern period, introducing important changes that had little to do with the West or the world economy. Contacts with the West did increase with time, so that in contrast to East Asia a more substantial Western presence began to affect internal developments by the late seventeenth to early eighteenth centuries. Here again are distinctive cases, unlike either East Asian isolation or Russia's partial Westernization. Trends during the early modern period created important new patterns, ultimately shaping the relationship of these key regions to the larger global framework.

The evolution of the Middle East and India after 1450 revolved around the rise of two new empires, one brought by the Turks to the Middle East, the other by Turkish-Mongol conquerors who ruled over the Hindu majority in India. (A third Islamic empire, the Safavids, developed for a time in Persia.) The Muslim empires provided new political and military solidity to their Asian territories. Under the Ottomans, the previous political decline of the Arab caliphs was reversed. Under the early Mughals, India achieved a degree of political unity rarely before attained.

The Ottoman and particularly the Mughal empires were not, however, as solidly based as those of China and Russia. The Mughals represented a minority religion as well as a foreign political force. The Ottomans, though sharing religion with the Arab majority of their empire, were also outsiders, who looked down on the Arab population for their political and military weakness. Perhaps, as a result, neither of these new empires created an integrated culture. Important cultural developments occurred, but earlier religious and artistic traditions persisted. Nor did either empire generate lasting economic strength. The earlier commercial glories of India and the Arabs were not recaptured, and economic conditions tended to stagnate. Both empires were partially drawn into the European-dominated world economy on decidedly disadvantageous terms. Finally, both empires began to decline well before 1800. In India, this resulted in direct European penetration during the eighteenth century. The Ottoman Empire remained intact, but by 1800, it was on its way to becoming what the Europeans called a "sick man" in world affairs.

THE OTTOMAN EMPIRE

THE EXPANDING FORCE OF THE NEW MIDDLE EASTERN STATE

The Ottoman Empire had taken shape during the several centuries before the early modern period, although its complete development followed the Turkish conquest of Constantinople in 1453. Turkish groups had been moving into the Middle East, from their original lands in central Asia, for some time. They served in the armies of the caliphs and as advisors. This interaction spread Islamic belief and knowledge of urban cultural styles and government even to those Turks still in central Asia.

The Osmanli group of Turks, or Ottomans as they became known by Europeans, were not one of the original Turkish peoples involved in Middle Eastern affairs. Their movement into the region came later, stimulated in part by the rise of the Mongol empire in Asia during the thirteenth and fourteenth centuries. Large numbers of migrants took over lands at the northern rim of the Middle East, in the country that is now Turkey—the only part of the Middle East that was heavily populated by Turks—where they became an agricultural people. Regional Osmanli leaders, exhibiting their military abilities, began to challenge both the Arabs and Byzantines. The Ottomans were fervent warriors, spurred by intense Islamic beliefs and a tightly knit military. By the fourteenth century, their leaders began to call themselves sultans, as they settled in the plains of Anatolia, the heartland of present-day Turkey. The first sultan, Orkhan, established a new army, called "Janissaries," in order to fight remnants of the Byzantine Empire in southeastern Europe. He had already conquered some European territory by 1400. The Ottomans viewed this conquest of Christian lands as a virtual crusade, and during the 1390s they captured Serbia, Bulgaria, and Greece. Already, the Ottoman Empire was the strongest state in the Middle East in the wake of the collapse of the Abbasid caliphate.

Nonetheless, the chief prize was Constantinople itself, the capital city of eastern Christendom. Several Turkish sieges failed before Sultan Mehmet II, known as "the Conqueror," finally succeeded in 1453, aided by the use of a huge cannon and the strict discipline he imposed on his troops. The Turks set up their imperial capital in what was now a Muslim city, renamed Istanbul. Soon after this, the Turks conquered Arab Syria and also took control of the Greek islands and the last Byzantine settlements around the Black Sea. By 1517, Egypt was vanquished, the last of the regional Arab kingdoms that had survived the fall of the caliphate. The Ottoman Empire was thus heir to both Arab and Byzantine lands, establishing one of the largest empires the Middle East had ever known and one that proved to be the last great attempt at unification in the region which has occurred to the present day.

During the sixteenth century, Ottoman conquests continued. The sultans conquered part of Persia and much of the southern Arabian peninsula. They pursued territories in Europe, attacking several Italian cities and conquering Hungary after a victory in 1526. In 1529, they besieged the Habsburg capital city of Vienna, in Austria, although this effort failed. They also captured islands in the Mediterranean. The conquest of the island of Cyprus in 1571 led to the establishment of a Turkish settlement that coexisted uneasily with the Greek majority, a tense situation that persists to this day. Minor conquests continued until 1715, although in most respects the highwater mark of the empire as a conquering force was reached in the late sixteenth and early seventeenth centuries.

By this point, the Ottoman Empire embraced the whole of southeastern Europe to the Danube River. It included Tatar provinces in the Crimea as the Ottoman Empire stretched around virtually the entire circumference of the Black Sea. It encompassed most of the Middle East, with some Arab settlements in desert regions and the smaller Safavid empire in Persia alone escaping its grasp; it also controlled most of North Africa. Ottoman rule over the holy cities of Mecca and Medina gave the empire new religious force, and the sultans assumed the title of Caliph of Islam, implying a direct link to the Muslim faith. As Caliphs, the sultans required that their names be used in the prayers of the faithful in the mosques.

The Ottoman Empire, although of greatest importance in the Islamic world, played a crucial role in European history as well. In its hold over the Balkan lands of southeastern Europe, the Ottomans preserved this region from direct Western control; a minority of Balkan people converted to Islam.

The Ottoman Empire's success rested on two leading factors. The first, visible from the early Osmanlis onward, involved strong military organization and conquest. The Ottomans, like many other imperial conquerors, depended heavily on a fairly steady course of expansion, which gave military leaders rewards in the form of new territories, plus slaves to serve as troops. When conquests largely ceased, the empire became increasingly troubled.

The second factor, was Ottoman leaders' considerable tolerance for the various peoples in their vast realms like that of Arab conquerors before them. Mehmet II did not attack the Greek Orthodox Church; indeed, he appointed a new patriarch to provide separate religious government for this people. Christians were taxed more heavily than Muslims, and in the provinces of southeastern Europe, they were forced to perform labor duties and allow the conscription of some of their youth as soldiers. For the most part, Christianity remained strong in southeastern Europe and, as a minority religion, in parts of the Middle East, and individual Christians rose high in the Ottoman government. Jews were also widely tolerated, as the Turks again demonstrated their willingness to accept a multiracial and multireligious society. The Turks did harbor some disdain for their fellow Arab Muslims and decidedly favored Sunni beliefs over the Shi'ite minority. But on the whole, Arab Muslims, from ulema scholars to the ordinary faithful, were not disturbed in their religious practices. Many Ottoman sultans were personally pious, interested in religion and culture as well as military affairs.

The greatest of the Ottoman sultans, near the height of the empire's power, was Suleiman, who ruled from 1520–1566. Known as "the Magnificent" to European traders, who marveled at the wealth of his court, he was called "the Legislator" by the Turks themselves because of his interest in just and disciplined rule. Although not a joyful warrior—indeed, his portraits reveal a rather gloomy man burdened by the cares of his state—Suleiman did pursue a policy of conquest. It was under his rule that the kingdom of Hungary was conquered and new portions of the Middle East, particularly present-day Iraq, were won from the Persians. Suleiman also constructed a major Mediterranean fleet, hoping in this way to extend his challenge of the Christian West. He strengthened Ottoman control of North Africa, especially Algeria, and frequently raided Italian and Spanish ports. In his later years, Suleiman grew less interested in battle and concentrated on the building of new mosques. However, his life remained troubled, as he had to put to death one son to please his favorite wife, leaving her incompetent son as his heir.

Under Suleiman, the institutions of the Ottoman Empire assumed their fullest shape, forming a successful political system long capable of adminstering vast and diverse territories. In theory, this was an absolute state, claiming control over all wealth and property in the empire. Annual tax revenue was massive by the standards of Western kingdoms. Although all power officially rested in the sultan, he, in fact, delegated much authority to his chief minister, the grand wazir. The wazir and other leading ministers were able to accumulate their own considerable fortunes through bribery and graft, although they had to struggle against rivals and the sultan's power to retire—and often execute—them at any given moment.

The provinces of the empire were ruled by governors called "pashas," who paid for their office with an annual fee. A pasha of Cairo was said to have bribed the grand wazir with a large yearly payment in order to preserve his lucrative position. Under the pashas, most land outside the cities was parceled out in fiefs to Turkish and other Muslim landlords, who collected revenues and enforced the laws on a local basis. Under a levy, or conscription, system, each landlord was obligated to furnish soldiers to the sultan. Under this decentralized system, regional rulers and landlords were encouraged to milk their holdings for as much revenue as they could. There was no hereditary nobility, since in theory the sultan owned all the land. This fact initially gave sultans control over regional officials who owed their position to the central court, but it also promoted short-term exploitation of the provinces by officials eager to turn a profit while they could still enjoy it. Suleiman did prepare a centralized law code, which served as a unifying legal force throughout the empire until the nineteenth century.

The Ottomans expanded the early Arab use of slaves in the army and administration. Using slaves of Christian origin in the central bureaucracy, from the viziers on down, bypassed the Quran's prohibition on enslaving Muslims and also integrated non-Muslims who formed a majority in the empire for its first 200 years. Government slaves were carefully educated, alongside the sultans' own sons, and promoted according to merit and seniority. Here was another solution to the government of an agricultural society, different from both Chinese bureaucracy and feudalism. It made the Ottoman Empire the best governed state in the world well into the sixteenth century.

The army itself was the main unifying element throughout the empire. In addition to the landlord levies, sultans like Suleiman directly controlled the force of Janissaries, who were recruited from the families of Christians, particularly in southeastern Europe, in what amounted to an annual slave tax. These young men were taken from their homes at an early age, converted to Islam, and trained to become fierce and able soldiers. They seldom numbered more than 15,000, because the sultans feared that they might otherwise grow too powerful; indeed, Janissary revolts troubled the empire periodically even so. Forbidden to marry, the Janissaries were expected to remain loyal to the sultan alone, from whom they received good pay and many other benefits. And until the eighteenth century, when their fighting spirit declined and their interference in internal politics increased, the Janissaries did indeed serve the empire well. The Janissaries were normally well disciplined and remained an excellent fighting force, particularly in battles with European Christians, which were still seen to an extent as holy wars.

The Ottoman navy, on the other hand, was rather limited. Although it operated in the eastern Mediterranean, it could not wrest control of the Mediterranean from Italian and Spanish forces. The empire lacked a large merchant marine, a fact that weakened its efforts on the seas. It used slaves as oarsmen; they had little interest in battle save as a chance to escape. Although the navy gained brief prominence under Suleiman, it soon declined and then was virtually eliminated by the defeat at European hands in the battle of Lepanto in 1571. After this point, Turkish naval activities were confined to the eastern coast of the Mediterranean, where they mainly protected existing Ottoman provinces.

Even at its height, the Ottoman Empire displayed some important weaknesses. It ruled over the oldest commercial economy in the world, but it did not sponsor significant economic advance. As the focus of world trade moved away from the Mediterranean, the empire was obviously at a disadvantage. Great efforts were exerted to sustain the magnificent city of Instanbul. Most farming was done by serfs, who were routinely exploited by greedy landlords and regional governors. This system did not encourage agricultural productivity. The Turks were not greatly interested in commerce. Most regional trade was conducted by Arabs, Greeks, and Jews, who maintained an active urban economy. The empire's role in the larger world economy declined. Once Europeans learned to sail around Africa directly to Asia, the position of the Middle East as an intermediary between Asia and Europe became less important. Trade between the Middle East and Europe lay largely in Western hands, and a growing colony of Western traders emerged in Istanbul.

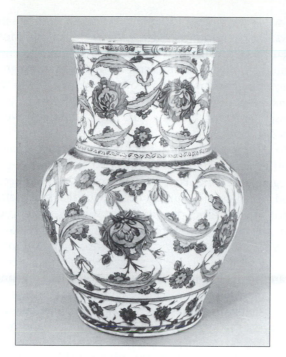

This Turkish artifact of the sixteenth century maintained earlier Islamic styles of art. (The Granger Collection)

The empire embraced and encouraged a lively religious life, although the most renowned Islamic scholars were more often Arab than Turk. The building of mosques and palaces stimulated architecture and crafts, which maintained earlier Arabic styles for the most part, although to some extent Persian influences were also evident. Decorative arts, including rich carpets and fine metal work, flourished. But, there was little new literature, particularly in Turkish; Arab poetry continued, but as in the later days of the caliphate, mainly in a religious vein. Arab schools and universities concentrated primarily on religious instruction and the complicated scholarship of Islamic law. Egypt served as the cultural center for Arab intellectual life, but most Egyptian writers devoted their efforts to compiling older works and commenting on them, or preparing biographies of ancient Muslim holy men. The rich and diverse cultural traditions of the earlier Arab civilization at its height were not revived. In the sixteenth century, Turkish literature began to develop, as sultans encouraged the writing of state histories highly favorable to those in power and as Turkish poets and songwriters copied Persian and Arabic verse. Much Turkish writing was devoted to accounts of the life of the prophet Muhammed and leading dervishes, confirming the heavily religious orientation of Middle Eastern culture.

The Ottoman Empire remained, in part, a military movement. Turkish leaders continued to esteem military virtues above all, although they often tempered their commitment to warfare by pursuing religious concerns and the enjoyment of art. The Turks had little interest in the dull work of the bureaucracy. Most administrative posts under the sultans were held not by Turks, but by East Europeans—mainly Slavs and Greeks—and by Jews. Only a minority of the wazirs were Turkish. Most of the literate bureaucrats were Europeans, Christian Armenians, and Jews. Decentralized rule combined with strong military power held this empire together, although high taxes, forced labor, and military recruitment caused discontent, particularly in southeastern Europe, where the Turks became cordially detested.

Despite its weaknesses, however, the Ottoman Empire enjoyed over three centuries of power, from its dynamic beginnings in the fourteenth century until well after the defeat at Lepanto. This is hardly a record of failure, for it compares favorably with the glory days of other military empires such as that of Rome.

Ottoman decline began late in the sixteenth century, although it became readily apparent only a hundred years later. The quality of individual sultans deteriorated after Suleiman. Many ruled for only brief periods; a few were mentally incapacitated. Many devoted themselves to sensual pleasures, surrounded by large harems of concubines. Palace intrigues and military interference increasingly dominated the Ottoman state, which perhaps helps account for the poor political performance of those who became sultans. Periodic reform efforts, to tighten central control and reduce the corruption of regional governors, had no permanent effects, although they helped sustain the regime. Religious and local institutions supplemented the government by providing courts, charity, education, and public works—another reason the system survived.

During most of the seventeenth century, the empire held onto its territory. Its control over North Africa (aside from Egypt) weakened, in part because of the declining navy. North African states became small principalities and were the source of considerable piracy until the nineteenth century. However, Western powers, caught up in their own colonial expansion, had no interest in a direct attack on Ottoman lands.

The Ottoman Empire made one last attempt at conquest in 1683, in a new assault on Vienna. For 3 months, a huge Turkish army laid siege to this city, until a mixed German and Polish force drove them back. Soon after this, the Austrian Habsburg emperor, in a loose alliance with the Russian tsar Peter the Great, attacked the Ottomans. Austrian troops drove the Turks from Hungary, inflicting the worst defeat the Turks had suffered since the early days of the Osmanlis. From this point onward, the Ottomans were on the defensive in southeastern Europe and central Asia. In the eighteenth century, Russian attacks pushed them from the northern coast of the Black Sea, while Austria also gained some territory in Serbia.

During the eighteenth century, the quality of internal government deteriorated further. Control over provincial governors declined; a few governors even rebelled against Constantinople. Many governors became increasingly corrupt, using their rule as a means of acquiring vast personal fortunes. Taxation, earlier restrained by some central regulations, grew heavier. Popular discontent increased, although there were no vast uprisings. Arab involvement with intense Muslim piety, under the leadership of Sufi mystics, helped limit the impact of protest, expressing hostility to the existing order but through attention to religious rather than political goals.

As the power of the empire waned, Europe's economic penetration of the Middle East began to intensify. Even before, Western traders, led by the French, had won special privileges from the sultans, establishing merchant colonies that were exempt

The Ottoman Empire at Its Height and in Decline, 1683–1923

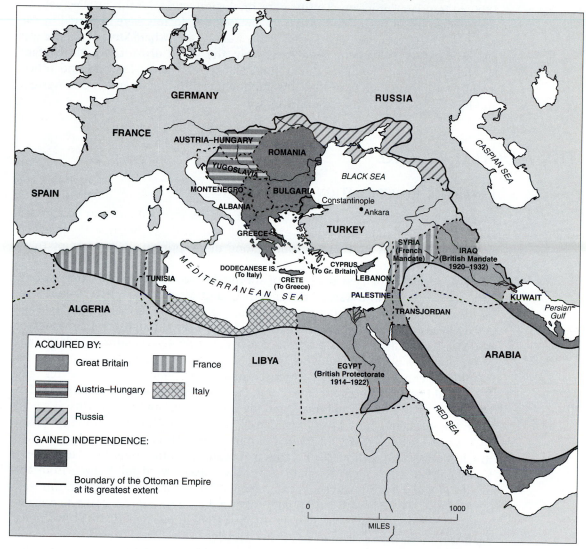

from Ottoman law. French, British, and Dutch groups thrived in not only Constantinople but Syria and Egypt as well. The West also had some cultural impact, as Middle Eastern Christians, particularly those in Lebanon, sought new ties with the Catholic Church. Christian printing presses were set up in Arabic, although they were banned by the Turks for Muslims until 1729.

For the most part, Turkish political leaders and Arab cultural leaders remained uncertain in reacting to the declining strength of their civilization, although officials were aware of the specific problems this decline posed. There was no successful effort at political reform until after 1800. Muslim cultural figures were convinced of their superiority over their European neighbors. No attempts were made, again until after 1800, to translate European scientific or technological works, for this intellectual current seemed irrelevant in Muslim eyes. A few Western doctors were imported by the sultans—which was ironic, because medicine was one area where Muslim science was just as good as its Western counterpart—but the larger disparities with Western Europe were simply ignored. The cultural blanket of Islamic legalism and other-worldly faith continued to protect this important civilization, even as both Western and Russian interests in the region increased.

THE MUGHAL EMPIRE

INVASION, CONSOLIDATION, AND DECLINE

India during the fifteenth century was locked in its recurrent pattern of regional states. The Delhi sultanate, which earlier had provided Muslim rule for much of northern India, was now merely one among many principalities, most of them headed by Hindu princes.

This situation changed as a result of another invasion early in the sixteenth century, the last echo, in a way, of the great period of Mongol conquests. Babur, a regional chieftain in Afghanistan and a Muslim, was of mixed Turkish and Mongol ancestry. Beginning in 1526, he used the familiar passes through the mountains of northwestern India to mount a war of conquest, within 4 years bringing a large part of the northern plains under his control.

Babur's conquests benefited obviously from India's political division, as regional states could not join forces effectively. But, Babur himself was no ordinary raider. His vision was a new empire, for himself and his descendants, not plunder. He was a bold often cruel general, but a lover of gardening and poetry who wrote a long memoir that showed real sensitivity for the rest of humankind. He cherished books and liked to select prize volumes from the libraries that came under his dominion. The dynasty he established was called "Mughal," from the Persian word for *Mongol;* from the wealth of Babur and his successors came the English word *mogul.* However, this was, at the outset, a regime with serious political purposes, not simply a luxury-loving enterprise. To solidify his new dynasty, Babur carefully avoided acts of intolerance against Hindus, whose customs he studied closely.

Babur's chief heir, after a brief period of confusion under a weak son, was his grandson Akbar, who took charge in 1555. Initially winning only a portion of Babur's empire, Akbar soon conquered one of the largest empires ever established in India, recalling the former days of the Maurya dynasty. Akbar's awe-inspiring achievements gained him the respect of many Europeans, who named him the "Great Mughal." Akbar was brave almost to the point of foolhardiness. As a boy, he liked to ride his own fighting elephants; he reveled in the hunt, once killing a tiger with his sword in single combat. He was also an excellent marksman—and guns spread to India initially through Muslim influence. But, Akbar was also a cultivated man, a book collector and patron of painting and architecture. Mughal culture reached its peak under his rule. Furthermore, Akbar carried the tolerance of Hinduism to an unusual extreme, marrying a Hindu princess and allowing Hindu women in his court to practice their religion openly, an unprecedented act for a Muslim ruler. He even listened to Portuguese Jesuit missionaries who reached the west coast under his regime, although he himself never converted. Akbar seems to have had a vague notion of sponsoring a new religion that would blend Hinduism and Islam, although it never had much of a significant following.

Akbar's empire built on a combination of great military force and careful administration. His army numbered 140,000 troops at its height, a massive number for the age, far greater than the forces of the leading European powers. At the same time, he established a clearly defined bureaucracy, divided into specialized ministries to deal with finance, law, and military affairs. Akbar's administrative reform drew on practices in Afghanistan that were refined by his Hindu chief minister. Eighteen provincial governors, called subahdars, administered the major regions of his empire. Akbar united virtually the whole of northern India and began the conquest of the Deccan

Mughal book painting: late sixteenth-century hunting scenes. (The Granger Collection)

region in the south. His legal system sought to moderate what he saw as some excesses in Hindu customs; thus, he attempted to ban sati, the practice of suicide by widows, and he forbade child marriage by insisting on a marriage age of 16 for boys, 13 for girls. Akbar also endeavored to create a common language for his empire, enabling his scholars to produce the synthetic mixture called Urdu, or Hindustani, which provided a vehicle of communication for his bureaucrats and ultimately spread to a large minority of his subjects, particularly Muslims. Urdu forms one of three major languages, along with English, on the subcontinent today. Above all, Akbar and his subordinates developed an efficient system of military recruitment and taxation, the latter based on landed property. Even with the huge demands of his government for revenue, prosperity increased in northern India. Muslim rule provided India with not only stable government, but also new products such as paper. India continued an active regional trade with southeast Asia in spices and other products, even as Western shipping spread.

Akbar's reign was the high point of Mughal rule in India, yet the empire survived until the nineteenth century. Akbar's immediate successors, although less able than he, maintained the policy of conquest; during the first half of the seventeenth century, the empire reached its greatest size through gains in the south. Patronage of the arts continued. Mughal portrait painters flourished, and some influences from Western art crept into their works—as in the halos painted around the heads of the emperors themselves. Mughal art had a distinctive style, different from Middle Eastern tradition, as the use of portraits demonstrates. In architecture, the Muslim heritage, including the use of decorative motifs, loomed larger. Under the emperor Shah Jehan I, who ruled from 1627–1658, the great tomb called the "Taj Mahal" was built. Designed by a Turkish architect, it required 14 years to construct; initially intended for Jehan's favorite wife, it also served as a shrine for Jehan himself and is still rated one of the two or three most beautiful buildings in the world. Thus, in painting and architecture, as in the development of Urdu, the Mughals contributed greatly to India's artistic and cultural legacy.

The political structure of the empire, however, began to unravel during the mid–seventeenth century. Jehan departed from the tradition of toleration for Hindus. Hindu officials still served in his bureaucracy, and the emperor patronized Hindu poets and musicians, but many Hindu temples were demolished. Jehan also attacked Portuguese settlements in the east (near present-day Calcutta), although his huge army had great difficulty subduing a force of merely 1000 troops, whose superior weaponry foreshadowed later Western power on the subcontinent. Many Christian churches were destroyed, and thousands of Christian converts were killed. Taxes were increased to cover the growing expenses of the luxurious court. Many peasants were forced off the land because of escalating taxes and rural crime became a growing problem.

Tensions increased under Jehan's son Aurangzeb, the last important Mughal ruler (1658–1707). Aurangzeb, who seized power by imprisoning his father, did manage to reduce taxation. But, he intensified the attacks on the Hindu majority in the name of Islamic law. More temples were destroyed, and taxes on Hindus were raised. Hindus who sought bureaucratic service normally had to convert to the Muslim faith. Hindu resistance, not a major factor in most of the empire previously, now

UNDERSTANDING CULTURES

Reactions to Western Values

By the eighteenth century and certainly since that time, the ways individuals and groups have reacted to what they perceived as Western culture form an important part of world history. The basic subject of reactions to other cultures was not, of course, new. But, extensive contact with the West was, and it was occurring at a time when, given the rise of science and the Enlightenment, Western culture was itself changing rapidly. It may be tempting to assume that, once exposed to modern Western values, peoples in Asia and Africa would enthusiastically embrace them, but not surprisingly, that's not what usually happened. Many people not only preferred their established cultures but also found specific Western beliefs particularly objectionable.

If you were a not-very-religious Muslim in the eighteenth century who had the unusual opportunity to visit England, what criticisms would you emphasize?

Abu Taleb Khan was an Indian Muslim, born in 1752, who visited London late in the eighteenth century, hoping (in vain) to find work in the colonial administration. He was not a strict Muslim—the chance to drink wine in England pleased him—and obviously he was not at all typical of the time. He liked many aspects of England, including the women, whom he found quite beautiful and, although unveiled, more strictly disciplined than the women back home. But, he also had several serious criticisms of English culture, which he carefully listed in a travel account he wrote, in Persian, when he returned home.

Point one: The English whom Abu Taleb met were not religious enough, and they indeed were "positively inclined" to atheism. Abu Taleb found this particularly true of the lower classes, who were dishonest and stole a lot.

Point two: The English were too proud and blindly confident, and they also, point three, had a "contempt for the customs of other nations," greatly preferring their own. Abu Taleb found that the English ridiculed his clothing as well as his religion, and he was deeply offended.

Finally, point four, the English displayed an undue "passion for acquiring money," again a sign of the lack of proper balance in values. Some not only lusted after worldly riches, they also were not generous, another obvious fault.

Again, few Muslims at this time had the chance to meet the English firsthand. But, Abu Taleb's comments are interesting, in expressing Muslim values compared to some genuine trends in late-Enlightenment England. Were Abu Taleb's criticisms those you anticipated in thinking about a non-Westerner's possible objections to Western culture?

The Mughal Empire in India

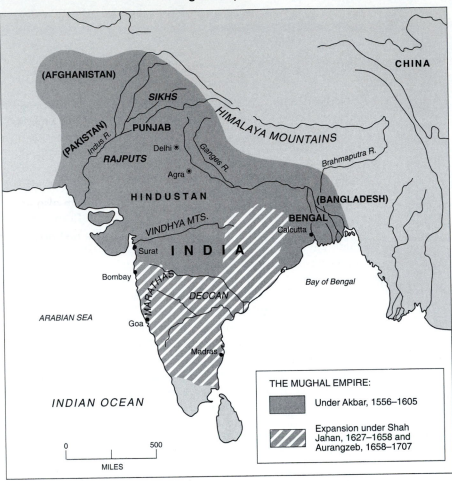

increased. This helped to rally regional princes in the south, who prevented the further conquest of the Deccan region. A new Hindu leader in the south, Shivaji, generated something akin to Hindu nationalism in forming a new Deccan state against which Aurangzeb battled in vain until his death.

Another important center of resistance arose in the northwest. Here, a new religion had evolved in the sixteenth century, in part as a reaction to earlier Muslim influence. This Sikh religion was closely related to Hinduism, although it was held by its leaders to be inspired directly by God. The Sikh faith combined Hindu practices and beliefs with a more activist approach. Sikhs abolished the caste system in their religion, creating a military brotherhood dedicated to a vigorous role in the affairs of this world, including something like a holy war. The contemplative side of Hinduism was played down, although Sikh temples maintained many Hindu rituals, and a belief in reincarnation persisted. As the Mughal Empire weakened, Sikhs established a regional realm of their own that lasted until 1849. Not only fierce fighters, the turbaned Sikhs were active in business and agricultural improvements. They formed an important religious minority in India from the seventeenth century onward, along with the larger Muslim group.

By the time of Aurangzeb's death, India was divided into essentially three major states—the Mughal Empire itself, the largest, plus the new state in the Deccan, and the Sikh empire. Several smaller states survived in the south, while European settlements—Portuguese Goa, but also British and French ports—dotted both the east and west coasts. Within the Mughal Empire itself, Hindus and Muslims were increasingly in conflict. Many Hindus withdrew into their own communities, fervently embracing their religious rituals in order to preserve their identity in a state they could no longer actively accept. Under Aurangzeb's eighteenth-century successors, Mughal administration became increasingly conservative and inefficient. Not only did political control become more lax, but India's educational system also declined as a result of Hindu isolation and Mughal inattention, and the economy deteriorated. Merchants suffered under the taxation of the later Mughals, who had no love for commerce. Indian technology—like that of much of Asia by the seventeenth and eighteenth centuries—stagnated.

Mughal art: Jahangir embracing Nur Jahan. Compare this to the earlier Indian styles shown in Chapters 3 and 7.

In sum, an empire that had commenced with great brilliance and promise declined with extraordinary rapidity. Intolerance seems to have been a key to the downfall, along with the continued ability of most Hindus to retain their faith. In this situation, Mughal rulers became increasingly beleaguered and ineffective.

WESTERN INTRUSION

Growing weakness and division in eighteenth-century India provided an unintended invitation to more active European intervention. Western merchant companies were drawn increasingly into Indian political affairs, to provide what they saw as necessary stability for their commercial operations. This was the most important impact of the new world economy on Asia in the early modern period. This motive for intervention was enhanced by conflicts among the European groups for influence on the subcontinent and particularly by the recurrent battles between England and France. Although European forces were small, their superiority in weapons gave them centralizing power in a divided region.

By the eighteenth century, Portugal's role in India was minor; the colony at Goa remained, but Portugal was too weak to reestablish other centers after the Mughal attacks. Dutch power was also declining, as the Dutch were preoccupied with administering their important holdings in the Indonesian islands. France and Britain had both established toeholds on the subcontinent during the seventeenth century, winning port rights by bargaining with local princes. The British East India Company operated a station at Calcutta, which gave them some access to the great wealth of the Ganges valley. The company had enormous influence over the British government and, through Britain's superior navy, excellent communication on the ocean routes. Their French rivals, in contrast, had less political clout at home, where the government was often distracted by purely European wars. The French were also more interested in missionary work than the British, who were long content to leave Hindu customs alone and devote themselves to commercial profits.

French-British rivalry raged bitterly through the middle decades of the eighteenth century. Each side recruited Indian princes as allies. Outright warfare erupted in 1744, and then again during the Seven Years' War. British officials had become alarmed at growing French influence with local princes. They were also roused in 1756 by the capture of Calcutta, by an Indian official, who imprisoned English captives in a "Black Hole"—an underground chamber originally used as a jail by the English themselves; many English officials suffocated. The East India Company's army recaptured Calcutta and then seized additional French and Indian territory, aided by generous bribes distributed to many regional princes. French power in India was decimated, and England was committed, without plan or clear intent, to the administration of the region called "Bengal," which stretched inland from Calcutta. Soon after this, the British also gained the island of Sri Lanka (Ceylon) from the Dutch. Although the British military force remained small, its superior weaponry, including field artillery, had proved decisive in battles with Indian rulers. At the same time, more sophisticated naval power allowed Britain to outdistance its European rivals. Thus, from 1764 onward, a British empire in India was truly launched. Along with Indonesia and the Americas, India became one of the great territorial acquisitions of the West prior to 1800.

The complete history of British India did not begin until late in the eighteenth century, when the British government took a more active hand in Indian administration, supplementing the quasi-government of the East India Company. Indeed, before 1800, British control of the subcontinent was incomplete. The Mughal empire survived, although it was increasingly powerless, as did other regional kingdoms including the Sikh state. Britain gained some new territories by force of arms, but was also content to ally with local princes without disturbing their internal administration, again until after 1800.

However, British, and to an extent French and Dutch, commercial activities in India did have an important effect even before the full implications of India's new colonial status were clear. Throughout the eighteenth century, much of India was increasingly drawn into the world trading patterns dominated by the West. Like Indonesia, but unlike the Americas, India offered a well-developed manufacturing economy along with a vast population and solid agricultural base. European merchants were eager to exploit India's wealth, but were concerned that India not compete with their own manufacturing capabilities. Early in the eighteenth century, Britain began to levy high tariffs on the import of cotton cloth. This was one of India's chief industries, but it was just getting started in Britain. By limiting Indian access to a British market, London effectively reduced India's opportunities in world trade. British-made goods, including textiles, were widely sold on the subcontinent, while hundreds of thousands of Indian textile workers began to lose their jobs. In turn, the Indians exported gold and also agricultural products, such as tea, which were grown on commercial estates staffed by low-paid wage laborers. British agents also assumed growing command over Indian textile production, dictating wages and conditions to the workers, while the British East India Company claimed Indian gold as payment for their costs of administration.

These exploitative economic policies were not Britain's final statement on Indian affairs. As the British Empire matured after 1800—and particularly after 1830—economic relations with India became less one-sided. In this early period, however, India was clearly added to the list of world territories that helped feed European wealth. An eighteenth-century Indian account described the climate of exploitation:

> But such is the little regard which they [the British] show to the people of this kingdom, and such their apathy and indifference for their welfare, that the people under their dominion groan everywhere, and are reduced to poverty and distress.

To be sure, some Indians welcomed British rule as an alternative to intolerant Muslim control. And many, particularly those in the independent kingdoms that still, in 1800, governed over half of the subcontinent in loose alliance with British administration, were scarcely aware of the British presence as yet. But the initial impact of European, especially British, operations deepened India's decline from the high point of Mughal rule. The Hindu religion, still the fundamental cultural resource for the majority, had ceased to spark vigorous philosophical and artistic statements. India's schools and universities were inactive. Manufacturing stagnated, and the level of prosperity reached under Akbar was never regained.

Basic structures—the family, the village, and the caste system—still organized daily life effectively. However, the subcontinent had suffered yet another foreign-imposed regime, the Mughals, whose ultimate political legacy involved the embittered relations between Hindus and Muslims and its own decline. And as the eighteenth century drew to a close, India experienced yet another administration imposed from the outside. British rule relied on superior military technology rather than the sheer numbers of its forces, as earlier Muslims had. The British concentrated more on commercial purposes, in contrast to the Muslim tendency, at least ultimately, to focus on religious gain. But in many ways, the British occupation confirmed what was now a well-established Indian tradition of long-suffering subjugation and control by outside forces, secure in the belief that basic local and religious structures could be preserved and were unable in any event to offer an effective political or military alternative. It could not be predicted, in 1800, whether British rule would finally overturn this aspect of the Indian tradition.

CONCLUSION: THE RISE AND DECLINE OF ASIAN EMPIRES

The rise of the great early modern empires in India and the Middle East, dazzling though they were, had not prevented the relative decline of both regions in the face of the rapid change and expansion of Western civilization. Partly because of the persistence of cultural and political traditions, partly because of the institutions of foreign military rule, neither Indian nor Middle Eastern civilization remained actively innovative, in their technology or intellectual life, between 1600 and 1800. The conditions of most ordinary people, the bulk of them peasants, changed little. Taxes rose, especially under rapacious Ottoman governors, and economic conditions deteriorated somewhat—most obviously in India—but the basic framework remained the same.

This pattern was not totally different from that of China during the same period. Here, too, we will discuss a growing stagnation, even as the West continued to develop rapidly. Here, too, there was relative decline as a result. But in the Middle East and particularly India, the outcome of relative decline was more quickly visible. Neither civilization was able to mount a policy of strict isolation. In both cases, European merchants dominated in growing numbers. Also unlike the Chinese, the Ottomans were unable to establish any durable agreement with expanding Russian forces, in part because the Russian heartland was closer, and in part because Russian appetites for warm-water ports and contact with Middle Eastern Orthodox Christians were more vigorous than vaguer interests concerning expansion against China. Despite outside pressures and the example of imaginative individual leaders like Suleiman and Akbar, the Ottoman and Mughal empires were no more eager than the Chinese to undertake significant internal reform. For Muslims, a reluctance to copy the West, so long viewed as culturally barbarian, was at least as great as a similar sentiment in China.

The results of first relative, then absolute, decline began to emerge after 1700. The growing British hold over much of India was the most dramatic sign that internal weakness plus Western ambition was a powerful combination. But, the Middle East was vulnerable as well. In 1798, a small naval expedition under a discontented French revolutionary general, Napoleon Bonaparte, sailed to Egypt and conquered the province after brief fighting. This was a minor episode in the European history of the time, and the French were indeed soon routed by British naval forces as Napoleon returned to France to pursue grander scenarios. But to Muslims, the shock waves were profound, as they came to realize that even a minor European excursion could now topple a proud Ottoman province. The question of a Western threat for the Turks and Arabs and of Western domination for the Indians was becoming paramount by 1800, despite the important political strengths that had surfaced in the sixteenth and seventeenth centuries. Indian and Middle Eastern responses, after 1800, would differ widely. However, for a moment both civilizations seemed caught in a similar midposition, among the ancient civilizations, between the expansive rise of the West and Russia and the proud isolation of East Asia.

SUGGESTED WEBSITES

For virtual visits to Ottoman palaces, see, *http://www.ee.bilkent.edu.tr/~history/topkapi.html*; for a simulated interview with Akbar, on his methods of rule, go to *http://itihaas.com/medieval/akbar2.html.*

SUGGESTED READINGS

On the Middle East, L. S. Stavrianos, *The Ottoman Empire: Was It the Sick Man of Europe?* (1957), offers some cohesive interpretations of key issues. For comprehensive surveys, see Stanford Shaw, *History of the Ottoman Empire and Modern Turkey,* Vol. 1, 1280–1808 (1976), and Peter F. Sugar, *Southeastern Europe Under Ottoman Rule, 1354–1804* (1977). For India, see M. Prawdin, *The Builders of the Mogul Empire* (1963); P. Spear's *Twilight of the Mughals* (1951) provides additional insight. On Mughal cultural development, consult Gavin Hambly, *Mughal Cities* (1968). For an excellent overview, see Ira Lapidus, *A History of Islamic Societies* (1988).

The Isolation of East Asia

FOCAL POINTS

China and Japan both consciously decided to isolate themselves from extensive Western contact and the emerging world economy. Why did they do this? Did they suffer from this decision in the early modern period? Apart from isolation, however, China and Japan embarked on radically different courses from the sixteenth century onward. China emphasized stability, drawing on its elaborate political and cultural traditions. Change came, particularly through growing cities and internal commerce and rapid population increase, but it was not fully acknowledged. Japan, in contrast, redefined a number of its institutions and cultural emphases. Why did Japan and China differ at this point, and what were the implications of these differences for the future?

The response of East Asia to the West and the new world economy differed greatly from the reactions that developed in Russia during the early modern period. At the same time, the East Asian situation differed from that of the Muslim empires as well. China, Japan, and Korea made absolutely no attempt at Westernization, although Japan briefly flirted with the idea. But, there was little intrusion from the West, in contrast to India. Geographically most distant from the West, operating in a culture much more accustomed to proud isolation, East Asia stood apart from the rest of the continent. Nonetheless, this was an important period in the region's history, as different sets of trends took root in China and Japan.

Both China and Japan responded similarly to the growing level of international contacts under Western auspices after the fifteenth century: They chose to try to ignore it. Their decisions were reached separately, for Chinese and Japanese societies, although rooted in some common patterns, remained distinct. Japan decided on isolation quite explicitly, after a brief and intense interaction with Western influence. China's decision came more by default. After an impressive move toward greater international involvement in the fifteenth century, China's leaders withdrew in favor of greater concentration on traditional cultural and economic patterns. Westerners were not entirely banned, but they were treated as an insignificant and decidedly inferior group.

The East Asian choice of isolation was in many ways unsurprising. This had long been the most remote of the major European and Asian civilizations, although Japan had, of course, vigorously utilized influences from China within the civilization's confines. None of the East Asian societies normally sought major expansion, which further limited the relevance of Western example. What was novel after 1450 was that isolation, when it arose, stood in direct contrast to the growing smallness of the world—the fact that all other societies were being drawn into an increasing network of contacts to at least some degree. East Asia's option to stand apart was entirely viable, in the sense that the separate societies continued to function well. Indeed, China benefited greatly from world trade; into the eighteenth century; isolation was not complete. But, the policy of isolation raised problems for the more distant future, for by the eighteenth century, East Asian civilization no longer possessed sufficient dynamism to maintain the pace set by other areas of the world, particularly the West, on its own. By standing apart, it fell behind.

Although Japan and China were both largely isolated, however, their patterns during the early modern period were not identical. Here, the importance of purely regional developments must be recognized, along with the larger relationship to the world economy. Japan changed more than China did, in part through the belated utilization of its Confucian heritage. As a result, by the eighteenth century, Japanese government and society were more vigorous internally than their Chinese counterparts.

CHINA: THE RESUMPTION OF THE DYNASTIES

Mongol rule in China turned out to be no more than a painful but passing episode, lasting from the later part of the thirteenth century until 1368. Chinese resentment of the Mongols as barbarians confirmed their suspicions of the world outside their boundaries. In fact, the Mongol episode paid tribute once again to the historic assimilating power of Chinese culture. The Mongol rulers used the bureaucracy, rather than destroying it, for the simple reason that they, like earlier invaders, could think of no better administrative system. Kubilai Khan, himself a Buddhist, supported Confucian scholarship, although Confucianists did not return his affection. Trade actually increased, as contacts with Muslim traders expanded. Chinese culture continued to experiment with new forms, particularly new dramatic and musical styles for urban audiences.

Although Chinese vitality seemed unaffected by Mongol rule, resentment increased, especially when serious flooding pushed the peasantry to revolt. Revolutionary forces drove out the Mongols, to the northern plains of Mongolia, in 1368. A rebel leader, born of peasant stock, seized the Mongol capital of Beijing and proclaimed a new Ming, meaning "brilliant," dynasty, which was to last until 1644.

It was the Ming dynasty that early on experimented with great trading expeditions through the Indian Ocean and then in 1433, suspended these voyages, on the grounds that the effort was too costly for what it yielded to China. The initiative was noteworthy, but the decision to return to relative isolation was in many ways more important to China's course during the early modern period. Other expenses, for a dynasty bent on building a splendid capital while protecting China from any Mongol resurgence, helped prompt the decision. However, the withdrawal reflected other more important factors, beginning with a preference for traditional expenditures rather than distant foreign involvements. Chinese merchant activity continued to be extensive in Southeast Asia. Chinese trading groups established permanent settlements in the Philippines, Malaysia, and Indonesia, where they contributed to the cultural diversity of the area and maintained a disproportionate role in local and regional trading activities into the twentieth century. But, China's chance to become a dominant world trading power was lost, at least for some centuries, with a decision that in essence confirmed the relatively low status of commerce within the official Chinese world view.

To Western eyes, accustomed to judging a society's dynamism by its ability to reach out and acquire new territories or trading advantages, China's decision may seem hard to understand, the precursor to some inevitable decline. In Chinese terms, of course, it was the brief trading flurry that was unusual, not its cessation. And, China did not obviously suffer from its decision to pull back. The government carefully regulated contacts with the West, permitting trade only through the Portuguese-controlled port of Macao. Ming emperors consolidated their rule over the empire's vast territory, although there was more factional fighting in the imperial court than had been true in earlier dynasties. The bureaucracy functioned well, as the Ming sent out representatives to guard against corruption by local officials. Internal economic development continued as well. Industry expanded, with growth in the production of textiles and porcelain. Ongoing trade with Southeast Asia enriched the port cities. Agricultural production and the general population both increased. Cultural activity focused on summarizing expanding knowledge in medicine, agriculture, and technology; on maintaining the interest in drama and poetry; and on pursuing philosophical training in Confucianism.

Historians of China have characterized the Ming period in terms of the importance of "change within tradition." The phrase aptly summed up developments under Ming rule, after the trading expeditions ceased. Chinese society evolved within frameworks previously established. There were no intellectual breakthroughs, no basic alterations in social structure, with the continued preeminence of the educated gentry-bureaucrat group. The expansion of trade, and the rise of a group of "overseas Chinese" merchants in Southeast Asian cities with close ties to the homeland, did not shake the earlier social priorities. Family structure remained similarly stable, with an emphasis on patriarchal control, reverence for elders and ancestors, and the provision of male heirs.

Traditional also was the decline of the Ming dynasty, early in the 1600s. Emperors grew weaker, the bureaucracy more corrupt, while peasant unrest increased under the impact of population pressure. Rebellions and roving gangs of bandits became widespread. A popular rebellion caused the last Ming emperor to hang himself. This internal disorder attracted invaders from southern Manchuria, who in 1644 established a new dynasty, the Qing (sometimes called Manchu), which lasted until 1912—the last royal house to rule China.

Again traditionally, the Qing (or Pure) dynasty started out with a flourish. The Manchurian emperors were foreigners in the eyes of most Chinese, and they maintained a separate military establishment to support their regime. But on the whole, their rule quickly took on familiar patterns, with a substantial reliance on the bureaucracy, which remained in Chinese hands, dominated by the educated scholar-gentry. The emperors also encouraged Confucianism. Like most early dynasties, the

Qing initially expanded the empire's territory. They pushed the Mongols still farther north and extended the empire into Muslim central Asia; they also took over the supervision of Tibet. Finally, they conquered the offshore island of Taiwan, which had previously been ruled by trading officials from a Dutch East India Company. This expansion, directed by the able emperor K'ang Hsi from 1662–1722, revealed the successful merger of Manchurian military skill and Chinese administrative expertise. K'ang Hsi himself mastered the Confucian classics and sponsored important cultural competitions, endearing him to the Chinese scholar-gentry class.

K'ang Hsi and his eighteenth-century successor also worked on increasing government centralization—another common impulse of vigorous early dynasties in the Chinese tradition. Central schools for training would-be bureaucrats expanded, and a Grand Council was established to direct the bureaucracy and process the mountain of paperwork resulting from the regular reports of local and provincial administrators. Carefully formulated regulations specified the punishments for local rebellions. Village leaders were held responsible for individuals within their community who committed crimes or tried to evade legitimate debts. Chinese society remained the most closely regulated and the most centralized in the world. Local and central administrations intertwined, and there was no real separation, as in the Western tradition, between public and private concerns.

During this vigorous period, the Qing dynasty continued to regulate European contacts with China. K'ang Hsi negotiated a border agreement with the expanding Russian empire, on the Amur River, that was to last until 1850. This checked Russian expansion into Chinese territory, although the Russians continued to move eastward into Siberia. Small numbers of Jesuit missionaries had been allowed into China since the sixteenth century, from Western Europe, mainly because they brought useful scientific and technical knowledge, including superior clocks. For their part, the missionaries were careful to adopt many Chinese ways, approving ancestor worship and wearing Confucian clothing. In the eighteenth century, the government, growing less secure, began to persecute the small number of Christians in China.

The Chinese outlook toward limited Western contacts was symbolized by its reaction to the Portuguese community set up on Macao. Although some officials wanted to force the Portuguese out, the dominant view was that it was safe to leave them there because they could be so closely supervised. Indeed, it would be easier to control them in this single center than to try to monitor their activities on the high seas. As one viceroy put it:

> Our military forces can watch over the foreigners by just guarding the surrounding sea. We shall know how to put them at death's door as soon as they cherish any disloyal design. Now if we move them to the open sea, by what means could we punish the foreign evil-doers and how could we keep them in submission and defend ourselves against them?

Cultural contacts with the West, or indeed with any other civilizations outside the traditional Chinese orbit, thus reached only modest levels by 1800. Some conscious policies of regulating foreign merchants and missionaries combined with great confidence in the superiority of Chinese ways to produce this result. Western demand for Chinese luxury products increased, which meant that China acquired a

Christian missionary (a Bajan Jesuit) in China, seventeenth century. Jesuits proceeded cautiously, respecting Chinese culture.

great deal of New-World silver in exchange. However, there was no extensive interaction with the West throughout this process. Efforts by Britain and other Western countries to open further trading contacts were consistently rebuffed. An English representative in 1793 was treated as if he brought tribute from an inferior state. He was forced to kow-tow (to bow by kneeling and knocking one's head on the floor), as the subject-state envoys from countries like Korea or Vietnam were required to do. And then the emperor, rejecting the representative's request for more trade, wrote a long, patronizing letter to King George III explaining that China had no need of English goods.

CULTURAL AND SOCIAL TRENDS: SOME NEW PROBLEMS

Although there was no reason to suspect in 1800 that China was on the eve of some unprecedented difficulties, going beyond the usual decline of a dynasty, significant problems in the empire occurred under the Qing even before this point. These problems were not initially political; the institutions of government remained secure. But, they raised important issues nevertheless.

In the first place, Chinese culture even under the early Qing seemed to stagnate. The Qing themselves, as foreign rulers, favored traditional expressions as a means of proving their sympathy with Chinese ways; thus, the emphasis on the classics of Chinese literature and philosophy, already extensive, increased. By the eighteenth century, most educated Chinese turned to collecting older examples of art and expounding literary criticisms of ancient works, rather than seeking to create new styles. The amount of cultural effort was great; many bureaucrats and other educated people painted nature scenes or dabbled in calligraphy and poetry writing. But, the goal was decidedly uninspired, with trivial themes emphasized and traditional styles rigidly defended. Similarly in philosophy, attention focused on expounding past principles and offering extended commentary on what had been written in earlier periods. Thus, the earlier Chinese ability to blend a reverence for tradition with an interest in promoting new styles and stimulating new thinking seemed somewhat stultified.

The Chinese economy, for its part, did not break fundamental new ground either. Revealingly, after the early Ming advances in navigational devices, the Chinese produced no significant technologies during the Ming and Qing dynasties. It was not a matter of decline. As in the arts, Chinese levels of achievement remained high, and Chinese craft products, such as porcelain (which became known simply as *china* to the Europeans), were greatly valued. However, an earlier ability to build on past accomplishments seemed to have been lost.

One key symptom of the new outlook toward technology showed in the Chinese reaction to European superiority in weapons. The Chinese were perfectly capable, in

Scholar and crane returning home, fifteenth century. Note the similarities to earlier Chinese styles (illustrated in Chapter 9).

the sixteenth and seventeenth centuries, of building cannons as good as the Europeans had, even though they had not pioneered their design. But, in fact, they did not care to; the subject did not interest them greatly, and they were content to assemble inferior muskets and small guns, confident that their strength on the land was sufficient to keep any European threat at bay. To be sure, the Chinese had never been as interested in military advances as in manufacturing technology, but their earlier creativity in the whole area was demonstrably slipping.

The interruption of China's tradition of innovation in basic technology did not, indeed, prevent continued internal economic development, supported by both the government and private business interests. During the late Ming and early Qing dynasties, manufacturing, city growth, and internal trade surpassed all previous levels. China's strong production base and extensive market activities help explain why, well into the nineteenth century, the nation could largely ignore Western goods, leaving Western merchants casting about for items to trade for sought-after Chinese products such as silk cloth and porcelain. However, China's economic surge did not bring fundamental economic transformation of the sort that might have generated new manufacturing technology. Much production lay in the hands of rural cottage artisans whose low wages discouraged more elaborate capitalist arrangements. And by the mid–eighteenth century, the economy itself began to stagnate, bringing renewed poverty and distress. Why did China not make a fuller turn to new economic forms?

The Chinese upper class had, of course, always esteemed traditionalism and looked rather scornfully at purely economic activity; such a viewpoint, nonetheless, had not prevented earlier technological or commercial advance. The increasing centralization of the government under Qing rulers, who were more cautious than their Han or T'ang forebears, may have been a cause as well.

One important and novel factor in the stagnation of certain key areas of Chinese society was a rapid increase in population levels, from the late Ming dynasty onward. Between 1600 and 1800, the Chinese population more than doubled, from 150 to over 300 million people. China's well-organized agriculture and the strong cultural emphasis on high birthrates, in order to produce male heirs in the family, had long encouraged population growth. Many dynasties had previously declined when such growth outstripped available resources, creating greater poverty. Usually, however, population levels would then level off, but this did not happen during the late Ming and early Qing periods. Agricultural techniques were advanced enough to maintain a large but impoverished population. Cultivation of some crops brought in from the Americas by European traders and missionaries, particularly corn and the sweet potato, added to the agricultural production that could support high population levels. New strains of rice, which grew more rapidly than older varieties, achieved the same end. As a result of these crop changes, China began to shift from a society in which population sometimes outstripped resources, to a society chronically challenged by its population levels.

Population pressure, in turn, had two clear effects, quite apart from the great poverty of many Chinese peasants and urban workers. First, it made political unrest a greater threat than had usually been the case except when dynasties were losing their grip. And second, it diverted resources that might have been used to encourage further manufacturing or trade to a desperate effort to sustain the vast population. The empire's economic flexibility was reduced by the need to devote so much labor and land to agricultural subsistence. This may be the clearest cause of the lack of innovation in the economy and possibly even in the culture.

By the late eighteenth century, massive poverty and slow economic growth began to surface as clear political problems. The Qing government found it increasingly difficult to collect adequate taxes. Collection efforts, along with grinding misery, also began to produce a new series of popular revolts. Peasants in many regions formed secret societies. An uprising by one such society in the 1790s, the White Lotus, was vanquished only with great difficulty. At the same time, the Qing dynasty was showing signs of internal decay: Military virtues waned among the Manchu generals, who preferred more luxurious living, and court officials became more corrupt, siphoning off money from the state. This kind of decline normally prefaced a period of growing instability and, ultimately, the rise of a new dynasty. Greater disorder came, without question, in the nineteenth century, but for once in China's long history a new regime, not a new dynasty, was the ultimate result.

Stagnation and political problems were not the only feature of Chinese society under the Qing. Some interesting changes occurred in popular culture, as Confucian leaders managed to persuade more and more peasants to abandon older beliefs in magic and superstition, and to use doctors instead of shamans in cases of illness. This shift in outlook, somewhat similar to changes occurring in the West during the same period, differentiated China from most agricultural societies, where popular religion had yet to be disturbed. The scholar-bureaucrats also pressed peasants and city dwellers to standardize the worship of local gods and goddesses. The practice of celebrating various deities and building temples to them had persisted from the classical period or before, along with other belief systems, and the government long tried to bend this popular faith toward loyalty to the state. Certainly, in 1800, the Chinese government remained easily able to regulate China's contacts with other cultures. European influence, most notably, remained no greater than it had been two centuries before, and European traders were powerless to escape government supervision. Only developments after 1800 would break this stalemate, to China's disadvantage.

JAPAN AND THE ORIGINS OF ISOLATION

Japanese social forms were less firmly set around 1450 than those of China, so it is not surprising that Japanese history shows more movement, more basic changes, than the evolution of its giant neighbor. However, the Japanese did come to share one basic concept with the Chinese: The outside world was a risky and inferior place, best kept at bay.

Japan was touched only indirectly by the Mongol invasions. The failure of the two great Mongol attacks bolstered Japanese confidence in the god-protected superiority of their own society even over that of China, which now lay under foreign thrall. But, the defense effort was very costly to the ruling government of the shogun; it contributed to the fall of this essentially feudal monarchy in 1338. Japan returned to a stage of regional feudal governments, of the warlike daimyos and their samurai supporters. A central government remained in form only. In fact, disorder and warfare, punctuated by some peasant rebellions, continued until 1573. A host of classic campaigns, celebrated in legend and more recently in Japanese films, dotted this period, in which samurai fighting techniques and codes of honor were perfected.

Despite disorder, the Japanese economy continued to progress. Because the daimyos were well aware of the importance of prosperous agriculture for their own tax revenues, they promoted irrigation efforts and improved methods of farming. Trade also grew, and the use of banking and money expanded. Daimyo supervision of trade established a pattern of government-business collaboration that in many ways has remained to the present day.

Japanese culture continued to develop as well, again creating durable new forms. The Zen strain of Buddhism, stressing calm meditation and a love of nature, predominated in religion, although there were many Buddhist sects and Shintoism still guided family ceremonies as well. Zen Buddhism encouraged an interest in ritual, as demonstrations of the simplicity of true beauty and as signs of self-control. Tea ceremonies and flower arrangements were important parts of family and social life. The Zen spirit also influenced art, leading to a focus on simple but dramatic representations of nature.

In literature, adventure stories and poetry continued to dominate. Soon after 1600, a new poetic form, the *haiku*, or 17-syllable verse in a 5–7–5 pattern, became popular. Although this was a new style, it maintained the East Asian tradition of carefully enunciated rules of poetry and an interest in the clever play on words. Composing haiku became a favored pastime among all social classes.

Japanese garden style: Sanbro-In Temple, Kyoto, laid out under Hideyoshi at the end of the sixteenth century. The pond, waterfall, and bridge show the move toward a disciplined nature.

By the mid-1500s, however, the Japanese combination of feudal warfare and economic and cultural creativity was eroding. Feudalism could no longer contain the forces at work in Japanese society. A rising merchant class complicated the feudal pattern. Armies of peasant soldiers were sometimes able to beat samurai swordsmen—just as common bowmen in Europe had ultimately dislodged the feudal cavalry. Furthermore, Portuguese traders reached Japanese shores in 1542 and, although they were initially welcomed by a people who had once before learned from others, their presence encouraged a desire among more conservative cultural and political leaders to develop a stronger government that could regulate foreign intrusion. And, the guns and cannons the Portuguese brought obviously threatened the fighting traditions of the samurai. Many regional daimyos tried to ally with the foreigners to gain a weapons advantage; the result, for a time, was simply further disorder. In the long run, however, the advent of gunpowder increased the possibility of greater governmental centralization. As the Japanese quickly learned to manufacture their own muskets, the fate of the feudal system was sealed.

The end of feudalism came in the form of several brutal wars at the conclusion of the sixteenth century in which a successful general, Hideyoshi (see p. 367), emerged victorious. Hideyoshi was able to reestablish centralized rule by using the allegiance of the daimyos. Thus, the feudal classes remained in Japan but were once again overseen by a national administration. After Hideyoshi's death, a general from the Tokugawa family took over the office of shogun and completed the process of centralization. A "great peace" settled on Japan, after more than two centuries of internal warfare.

This new centralization caused a reassessment of Japan's contacts with the outside world. Hideyoshi contemplated a policy of foreign conquest to keep the warlike samurai busy—a policy later renewed by Japan after 1890. However, an attempt to invade Korea failed, as Chinese armies supported their vassal government there, and this convinced the new Japanese government to concentrate instead on its own unique territories.

The Portuguese come to Japan, sixteenth century.

Hideyoshi and the early Tokugawa thus turned to what they saw as the problem of Western influence. Initial Western contacts had been welcomed not only for the guns and navigation technology the Westerners brought, but also, among some Japanese, for the religious message of Christianity. Interested in learning from foreign example and impressed by a religion that seemed to accompany military and trading success, several thousand Japanese converted to Catholicism in the port cities where Europeans clustered, during the late sixteenth century. But, Japan's new rulers looked harshly on this development. They feared European power and thought that where Western religion went, political control might not be far behind. When the Spanish government established military outposts in the Philippines, to enhance the missionary effort there, Hideyoshi's fears deepened. In 1597, he banned all foreign missionaries, crucifying 9 of them and 17 of their Japanese followers.

Western weapons seemed at least as great a threat as Christianity. The new central rulers feared the results of independent daimyo access to Western firearms. Rather, they sought state control over guns, while also protecting samurai warrior values. To do this, they needed to restrict foreign trade.

The Tokugawa shogunate completed the destruction of Christianity in Japan. It severely curtailed Western trade as well. Only merchants from The Netherlands were allowed in Japan at all—Holland was feared less than Spain or Portugal because, being Protestant, it was not linked to what seemed to the Japanese an ambitious and powerful papacy. And, Dutch traders were confined to one isolated, carefully controlled port (Nagasaki). Even Chinese merchants were supervised. In 1635, the Japanese themselves were forbidden to travel abroad, and those already overseas were not allowed to return home. Finally, the government prohibited the construction of large, seagoing ships; only vessels for coastal trade were permitted. Japan, even more so than China, was ostensibly cut off from the outside world. A nation that had once eagerly imitated foreign example, and would do so again in the nineteenth century, pulled back on this occasion. European ways seemed too foreign, and too inferior, to be allowed free play, and attacking outside influence was a useful way of cementing new national loyalties after the long period of disunity.

The policy of isolation combined with the regulation of military technology, now that foreign items could not be imported. The shogunate deliberately turned against guns, preferring to preserve the Japanese social structure. Only a few could be manufactured each year—sometimes no more than nine for the whole country. Even more than in the Ottoman Empire, where printing was long shunned, Japan decisively rejected the idea that new technology is always good technology.

In isolation, Japan proceeded to construct effective political forms and completed the development of a national culture, sponsoring considerable social change while seeming to maintain older values. Unlike the earlier Kamakura shogunate, the Tokugawa rulers depended less on personal ties with feudal lords and more on an efficient bureaucracy imbued with Confucian values. The warrior aristocracy was given great social prestige, including special privileges in law, and special costumes, although in fact there was no fighting to be done. Although warrior values and military training continued to describe the samurai ethic, upper-class bureaucrats learned the importance of administrative efficiency and training—Confucian principles that gained ground during the seventeenth and eighteenth centuries. This was

World Profiles

Toyotomi Hideyoshi (1536–1548)

Toyotomi Hideyoshi was an outstanding military leader who extended earlier sixteenth-century efforts to tame the power struggles among the daimyos in favor of more centralized, orderly rule. The son of a peasant, Hideyoshi, used his military acumen to rise to power in Japan; he then parlayed even greater diplomatic talents into the creation of a string of alliances with the daimyos that resulted in a central state by 1590. Hideyoshi, unlike most Japanese leaders before or after, dreamed of wider achievements as he contemplated ruling China and even India (despite, or perhaps because of, knowing little about either place). He did launch two abortive attacks on Korea, the last still in progress when he died. More important, Hideyoshi also launched the campaign to limit European and Christian influence in Japan. Hideyoshi's hopes to pass power to his son were dashed as the Tokugawa family seized control and his plans of overseas expansion were dropped. Nevertheless, he had contributed greatly to changing the course of Japanese history. How does Hideyoshi compare, in achievements and goals, to other great military leaders in world history who rose from the ranks?

This portrait reflects the military might and confidence that spurred Toyotomi Hideyoshi's achievements. (The Granger Collection)

an important period of cultural change in Japan, as Confucianism, and therefore secular interests, increasingly dominated intellectual life. The rapid spread of Confucian education and literacy disseminated the new cultural interests by the nineteenth century. Thanks to extensive schooling, literacy (at 25 percent among adult men) was far higher than in any society outside Western Europe and North America.

Although confined to internal trading, merchant activity flourished during the Tokugawa period. The government favored commerce, but was somewhat scornful of the merchant class. Great trading houses emerged, selling rice, textile goods, metals, and liquor all over Japan; some of these big family firms still operate in Japan today.

Feudal Japan Under the Shogunate, Sixteenth Century

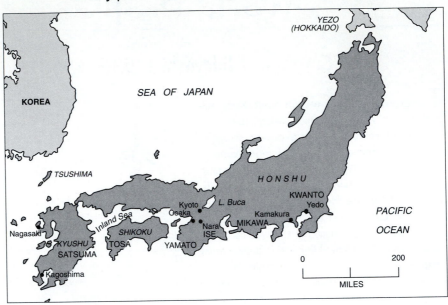

This was a key period for the development of banking and merchant experience in Japan. Japanese agriculture advanced as well, becoming more technologically sophisticated than any other system in Asia. Japanese farmers learned about crop specialization and the better use of fertilization; they also became increasingly accustomed to producing for sale on the market. Although economic growth slowed somewhat after 1700, Japan had the most advanced commercial economy in the world after that of Western society. In another important development, population size was controlled in the eighteenth century, in contrast to the situation in China. Many peasants practiced infanticide of unwanted—and particularly female—children.

Japanese literature and art remained vigorous under the Tokugawa, who supervised cultural life to prevent disorder. Enthusiasm for haiku poetry and the stylized *No*-theater continued. Literacy and book publishing spread. As in China, the growth of cities—particularly the capital city, Edo, which had a million inhabitants by 1700—encouraged a flourishing entertainment industry. Professional women entertainers, called geisha, or "accomplished persons," specialized in singing and dancing for male clientele. A new form of drama, Kabuki, developed in the eighteenth century, more popular in its portrayals than the *No*-forms; Kabuki theater remains active in Japan today. Not surprisingly, the varied artistic endeavors and continuing isolation of Japan produced a heavy emphasis on the nation's uniqueness and superiority, the forerunner of a cultural nationalism that still runs strong in Japan.

Japan thus emerged, by the eighteenth century, as an unusually diverse society, tolerating more internal tensions than China. Feudal and Confucian elements coexisted: An official lack of interest in commerce belied rapid commercial expansion; Buddhist spiritual fervor could survive in the face of a national emphasis on controlled expression and secular education. These tensions contributed to the dynamism of Japanese society, which had unquestionably advanced under the policy of isolation.

Indeed, by the eighteenth century, the policy of isolation was itself slightly relaxed. Some Japanese were allowed greater contact with Dutch traders in the port of Nagasaki; a few scholars learned Dutch and became familiar with Western advances in military technology and medicine. These early exchanges helped prepare the way for the fuller adaptation of Western ways in the nineteenth century. At the same time, they whetted the appetites of those few Japanese aware of the gap between their society and the West; Japanese backwardness in scientific and medical knowledge seemed particularly galling.

There were problems by 1800. Japan did not experience the kind of population pressure that burdened China, although its islands were severely crowded. But, Japan's commercial agriculture resulted in a division between land-owning peasants and landless paid laborers, whose discontent produced periodic revolts. On the whole, however, Japan's strengths, generated by the important developments of the early modern period, would help explain the nation's extraordinary reaction to challenges in the nineteenth century, when isolation finally had to be abandoned completely. The contrast with the looming crisis in China was marked, but there were some new concerns, and these too help explain why Japan became more open to the possibility of more radical transformations.

CONCLUSION: VITALITY AND TENSION IN EAST ASIA

East Asian history between 1400 and 1800 was no mere record of isolation. Although during this period the civilization was set apart from wider currents of world history, these were centuries of considerable internal change. Change meant new political dynasties, but also new cultural and economic forms, particularly in Japan. It also meant some new problems, such as the over-population that surged in China. The role of tradition was strong as well, in Japanese culture and its sense of national identity, in Chinese politics and society more generally.

East Asia's lag behind Western levels of technology and military organization during these centuries would leave the civilization vulnerable after 1800. It might have been preferable if the society assimilated or reacted to European styles more gradually, to the extent necessary to keep pace with European power. This was the sentiment that inspired China's communist leader in 1984 to claim that the Ming-Qing period of isolation—as well as a more recent, brief attempt to insulate China from foreign contact—was a mistake. However, in our own day, it seems clear that East Asian civilization, or at least significant portions of it, has been most successful in developing competitive alternatives to Western ways. In this sense, the period of isolation, as a time for solidifying traditions apart from the distraction of foreign influences, may not have been totally ill-conceived. Certainly, the decisions to sever ties with the West allowed East Asian societies to continue to follow their own complex dynamic for a final few centuries, before confronting some of the larger currents of modern world history.

SUGGESTED WEBSITES

On palaces and cities under the Ming, see *http://chinavista.com/beijing/gugong/!start.html;* on the Tokugawa capital, see Edo, *http://www.us-japan.org/edomatsu/Start/frame.html;* on the Tokugawa, see *http://www.namos.co.jp/aichi-hatsu/english/ittop.htm.*

SUGGESTED READINGS

An excellent collection of sources is W. T. de Bary, ed., *Sources of Chinese Tradition* (1966); close to source reading, offering fascinating insight into Chinese provincial life, is Jonathan Spence, *The Death of Woman Wang* (1979). Larger studies of China in the early modern period include J. D. Spence and J. E. Wills, Jr., eds., *From Ming to Qing: Conquest, Religion and Continuity in Seventeenth Century China* (1979); Albert Chan, *The Glory and Fall of the Ming Dynasty* (1982); Roy Huang, *1587: A Year of No Significance; The Ming Dynasty in Decline* (1981); Jonathan Spence, *The Memory Palace of Matteo Ricci* (1984) and *The Search for Modern China* (1990); and J. K. Fairbank, ed., *The Chinese World Order: Traditional Chinese Foreign Relations* (1968). On Japan, consult Peter Duus, *Feudalism in Japan* (1976); H. D. Harootunian, *Toward Restoration: The Growth of Political Consciousness in Tokugawa Japan* (1970); and E. O. Reischauer, *Japan: The Study of a Nation,* 3rd ed. (1981). Noel Perrin, *Giving up the Gun* (1979), is a fascinating account of shogun policies on weapons and trade. On the much-debated, important topic of peasant conditions in the Tokugawa shogunate, see H. Bix, *Peasant Protest in Japan, 1590–1884* (1986).

The World's First Industrial Period, 1750–1914

INTRODUCTION: THE INTERNATIONAL IMPACT OF INDUSTRIALIZATION

Toward the end of the eighteenth century, Western Europe began to change in several fundamental ways. Most apparent, a new economic and technological system took shape in Britain that would ultimately replace agriculture. British industrialization spread to other parts of Western Europe early in the nineteenth century and also to the new United States. New political doctrines and institutions also began to emerge in Western Europe and the United States, with fundamental beliefs about how the state should operate and what kinds of laws and social structures were appropriate. Previous changes in Western culture, plus the successful position Europe had already assumed in the world economy, now combined to generate even more sweeping transformations.

Although these developments initially concentrated in Europe and North America, they had major implications for the rest of the world. Western Europe's power, already on the increase, soared still further, beginning in the late eighteenth century and extending until 1914. Until 1850, Western Europe even maintained its edge in population growth rates, applying equally significant human resources (see Table V.1). Never before had a single civilization wielded such worldwide influence.

The world economy, already well defined, gained new importance as well. More parts of the world were drawn into production for export markets that Europeans dominated, whereas Western manufacturing expanded its output and its impact on sales to other societies. Two changes were particularly important. First, areas like Latin America and India, already producing raw materials, accelerated their manufacturing, but fell further behind in living standards because of the need for cheap labor. Western industrialization heightened the consequences of economic dependency for key regions, partly because it displaced even more local manufacturing. Second, areas

371

TABLE V.1 ✦ ESTIMATED POPULATION OF THE WORLD AND THE CONTINENTS, 1650–1850 (IN MILLIONS)

Continent	1650	1750	1800	1850
Africa	100	95	90	95
Asia (excluding Russia)	327	475	597	741
Latin America	12	11	19	33
North America	1	1	6	26
Europe and Asiatic Russia	103	144	192	274
Oceania	2	2	2	2
World total	545	728	906	1171

Source: Adapted from Dennis Wrong, *Population and Society* (New York: Random House, 1969), p. 13.

once barely affected by the Western-dominated world economy, like East Asia and the Middle East, were now forced to deal with this reality.

Growing dependency could be stark. During the early nineteenth century, the African production of vegetable oil for export reached 40,000 tons. However, then the use of petroleum (first in Pennsylvania, in 1860), Indian production of nut oil, and Australian and Russian production of fats cut into the price. So, Africans had to increase production still further, but at steadily falling prices, and to lower wages, just to maintain meager export earnings.

Industrialization also furthered European military advantage in the world by increasing weapons production and innovation. By 1850, Europe could defeat almost any rival on land as well as on the seas.

Overall, two of the key trends of the early modern period—economic and military—thus intensified. European influence escalated in a new imperialism that brought many additional areas under Western control. Variants of Western civilization spread to parts of the world particularly open to European immigrants, notably the United States, Canada, Australia, and New Zealand.

Europe's industrialization did more, however, than enhance preexisting trends. As the West came to rely more on wage labor supplemented by machines, and as new humanitarian ideals gained ground, Western leaders attacked the institution of slavery worldwide. The Western-dominated Atlantic slave trade ended, and slave systems within the Americas came to an end through the first three quarters of the nineteenth century. Pressure on African and Middle Eastern slavery also reduced the institution in these areas. The labor systems of many parts of the world, in other words, were dramatically challenged by new Western standards, backed by growing imperialist muscle. Africa had to redefine its world economic role as a result.

To be sure, the end of slavery did not end all negative forces in the work world. Low wages had coercive power, particularly when backed up by loans or required company stores that tied workers to a firm. Indentured contracts revived, particularly for Asian workers brought to southeast Asia, the Caribbean, and Hawaii. Over a million people from China and India were transported as indentured labor between 1850 and 1914. Still, the widespread elimination of formal, lifelong slavery was a historic change, as part of the dynamic economy and population movement of the long nineteenth century.

New beliefs spread on a global basis. Mass nationalism first arose in Europe itself, as a means of expressing new secular loyalties and supporting political change. Latin American people used a budding nationalist sentiment as one of their motives in demanding independence from Spain or Portugal. By the second half of the nineteenth century, nationalism spread to the Middle East, India, and elsewhere. Nationalism challenged many local and religious attachments. It focused new attention on the state (or on a desire for political independence) and wider changes needed to make one's nation a viable force in the modern world.

Because of growing Western power and the challenge of industrialization, a wider set of international forces influenced individual societies during the nineteenth century than had characterized the early modern period. Every society faced the necessity of coming to terms with the expanding world economy and Western imperialism—the impossibility of isolation, the worldwide growth of market labor instead of slavery or other traditional work systems, and the growing spread of nationalism all signaled the presence of these new international forces. Every society now had to ask questions about what changes must be contemplated in order to gain or maintain independence and to adapt to an industrially driven world economy.

New international forces, however, did not produce uniformity from one society to the next. Traditional beliefs and institutions continued to shape different responses. One of the reasons for nationalism's success lay in its ability to combine new political impulses and loyalties with devotion to older, distinctive values. Forces within the nineteenth century itself impacted different societies in different ways. Some places became new colonies; others freed themselves from colonialism; still others faced growing Western intrusion without the indignity but also without the protections of colonial control. As before in world history, tracking the different responses to the growing array of international contacts constitutes a major analytical challenge. On the surface, the extended nineteenth century seems perhaps the simplest of all world history periods, because it did not break fully with the trends of the early modern period. Its basics included the expanding world economy, Western imperialism, spreading nationalism, and other efforts to adapt to Western-dominated change. Nonetheless, the ways individual societies combined these factors and reacted to them involved considerable complexity. Careful comparison remains essential. The world by 1914 was much different from what it had been in 1750, but it was hardly more uniform.

Western Civilization	East Asia	Middle East	India and Southeast Asia
c. 1770 Invention of steam engine by Watt.			
1775–1783 American Revolution.		**1793** Failure of sultan's efforts at military reform.	
1787 Constitutional Convention, Philadelphia.		**1798** Napoleon's Egyptian expedition.	
1780 ff. Industrial Revolution.			
1789–1799 French Revolution.			
1793–1794 Radical phase.			
1799–1815 Reign of Napoleon.		**1811 ff.** Reforms in Egypt by Muhammed Ali.	
1800–1850 Romanticism in literature, arts.		**1820–1829** Greek war for Independence.	
1815 Congress of Vienna.			
1820 Revolutions in Greece, Spain.	**1820s** Growing Western trade with China.	**1826** Dissolution of Janissaries by Sultan Mahmud II.	**1825 ff.** Extension of Dutch control over interior of Indonesia.
1830 ff. Rise of liberalism, nationalism.	**1839–1842** Opium Wars in China.	**1828–1833** Russian-Ottoman War.	**1827–1829 ff.** Reorganization of British rule in India, development of Civil Service, new legal codes.
1829–1837 Jacksonian period in United States; universal white male suffrage.		**1830** Takeover of Algeria begun by France.	
1830, 1848 Revolutions several European countries.		**1830 ff.** Steamship routes established in eastern Mediterranean and Persian Gulf by Britain, France.	
1832 British Reform Bill.		**1839** Ottoman reform attempt.	
1848 ff. Writings of Karl Marx.			

Russia and Eastern Europe	Latin America	Sub-Saharan Africa
		1787 ff. Sierra Leone founded as British colony for freed slaves.
	1808 Formation of governing junta in Venezuela.	*1807–1834* Abolition of Atlantic slave trade.
	1810 Leadership of Mexican revolt by Hidalgo.	
	1810 Independent government in Argentina.	*1814* Acquisition by British of Dutch South Africa.
	1811 Proclamation of independence; Bolivar leadership.	*1821* Extension of British rule in West Africa.
1812 Failure of Napoleonic invasion of Russia.	*1814* Regain of control by Spain.	*1822* Liberia founded as colony for freed American slaves.
1815 Poland acquired by Russia in Treaty of Vienna.	*1821* Independence regained in "Gran Colombia."	*1830 ff.* Formation of firmer Bantu governments in southern Africa.
1825–1855 Heightening of repression by Tsar Nicholas I; increase in secret police.	*1814 ff.* Wars of independence led by San Martin in Chile, Peru.	*1835–1837* Great Trek of Boers; clash with Zulus.
1829 Full autonomy gained by Serbia within Ottoman Empire; fuller independence achieved in 1856; complete independence granted in 1878.	*1821* Proclamation of Mexican independence by conservatives.	*1840 ff.* Increased Protestant missionary activity.
	1822 Pedro emperor of Brazil.	
	1823 Independence of United Provinces of Central America.	
1830–1831 Polish revolt put down by Nicholas.	*1825–1850* Consolidation of new nations; division of Gran Colombia, Central America.	
1831 Full independence gained by Greece.	*1829–1852* Manuel de Rosas caudillo in Argentina.	
	1833 ff. Santa Anna leader in Mexico.	
	1836 Independence of Texas.	

Western Civilization	East Asia	Middle East	India and Southeast Asia
1859 Darwin, *Origin of Species.*	**1850–1864** Tai Ping Rebellion.	**1853** Russian Ottoman War.	**1850 ff.** Development of railroad in India.
1859–1870 Italian unification.	**1853** Perry expedition to Japan.	**1854–1856** Crimean War.	**1852–1853** British war with Burma; growing influence gained by Britain.
1861–1865 U.S. Civil War.	**1857–1859** Second Opium War.	**1856** Ottoman reform attempt; new rights for Christians.	**1855** Growing British influence over Siam; trade opened by treaty.
1864–1871 German unification.	**1867** Mutsuhito emperor of Japan.	**1869** Completion of Suez Canal.	**1857–1858** Sepoy mutiny, India.
1867 Unification, dominion status for Canada.	**1868–1912** Meiji period in Japan.	**1876** Promulgation of Ottoman constitution, guaranteeing individual freedoms, establishing parliament.	**1858 ff.** British reform of government in India.
1870 ff. Spread of compulsory education laws.	**1872** Universal service in Japan.	**1877** Lapse of constitution.	**1858 ff.** Takeover of Indochina begun by France.
1870–1879 Institutions of French Third Republic.	**1890** New constitution, legal code in Japan.	**1877–1878** Russo-Turkish War; independence gained by new Balkan nations.	**1861** Establishment of advisory councils, with Indian representation.
1871–1914 Highpoint of Western imperialism.	**1894–1895** Sino-Japanese War.	**1870s** Growing Western control over Egypt.	**1864** Indians allowed in upper Civil Sevice.
1871 ff. Rise of socialist movement.	**1896 ff.** Chinese students abroad.	**1881** Occupation of Tunisia by France.	**1885** Formation of Indian National Congress.
1879–1907 Alliance system: Germany-Austria (1879); Germany-Austria-Russia (1881); Germany-Italy-Austria (1882); France-Russia (1891); Britain-France (1904); Britain-Russia (1907).	**1897–1899** Chinese port concessions gained by Western nations and Russia.	**1882** British protectorate over Egypt.	**1885–1886** British takeover of much of Burma.
1881–1889 German social insurance laws enacted.	**1899–1901** Boxer Rebellion in China.	**1888** Construction begun on Berlin-Baghdad railway.	**1886** Steel industry begun in India.
		1896 ff. Rise of Young Turk movement.	**1896 ff.** More formal British control of Malaya (completed 1914).

Russia and Eastern Europe	Latin America	Sub-Saharan Africa
	1844–1846 Mexican-American War; occupation of Mexico by United States; upper California, New Mexico acquired by United States.	**1854 ff.** Expansion of French from Senegal.
1854–1856 Crimean War.		**1857–1863** French exploration in Congo basin.
1856 Gain of virtual independence by Romania.	**1858** First Benito Juarez government in Mexico.	**1960** German trade station established in Cameroons.
1861 Russian emancipation of serfs.	**1861–1867** French intervention in Mexico.	**1861** Beginning of British expansion in Nigeria.
1864 Abolition of serfdom by Romania; little land obtained by peasants.		**1867** Discovery of South African diamonds; increase in import of Indian laborers.
1860s–1870s Additional reforms by Alexander II in judiciary, local zemstov government.		**1875 ff.** Explosion of European imperialism in Africa.
1865–1876 Russian conquests in central Asia.		**1876** Congo claimed by Belgian king.
1867 Alaska sold to United States by Russia.		**1878 ff.** New Catholic missions set up.
1875–1878 War with Ottoman Empire, gain of new territory.	**1876–1911** Porfirio Diaz caudillo in Mexico.	**1878 ff.** Expansion of British, French interior expeditions in West Africa.
1878 Independent Bulgaria created.	**1880 ff.** Growing commercialization of Latin American economy.	**1899** Nigeria a full British colony.
1881 Anarchist assassination of Alexander II.	**1870–1888** Guzmán Blanco caudillo in Venezuela.	**1877–1879 ff.** New missionary efforts in east Africa; curtailment of East African slave trade.
1881 ff. Growing repression in Russia; attacks on minorities.	**1889** Republic of Brazil; abolition of slavery.	**1879** Defeat of Zulus by British.
1884–1887 New gains in central Asia.	**1898** Spanish-American War; acquisition of Puerto Rico by United States; protectorate over Cuba.	**1880** Acquisition by French of separate Congo colony.
1884 ff. Beginnings of Russian industrialization; Sergei Witte the leading minister; completion of trans-Siberian railway.		**1884** Organization of German treaties by Karl Peters to gain Tanganyika.
1898 Formation of Marxist Social Democratic party.		

Western Civilization	East Asia	Middle East	India and Southeast Asia
			1896–1899 Revolt against Spain in Philippines. **1898** U.S. capture of Manila. Defeat of Philippine independence movement by United States
	1904–1905 Russo-Japanese War. **1910** Annexation of Korea by Japan. **1911** Chinese revolution. **1912** Fall of last (Qing) dynasty.	**1911** Occupation of Morocco by France; takeover of Tripoli (present-day Libya) by Italy. **1918** Collapse of Ottoman Empire.	
1914 Beginning of World War I.			

Russia and Eastern Europe	Latin America	Sub-Saharan Africa
		1886 Discovery of South African gold; development of railway.
		1892 ff. Expansion of East Africa Company into Uganda.
		1890s–1905 Uprisings in West Africa (Ashanti); in Sudan, Tanganyika (Muslims and animists).
		1899–1902 Boer War.
	1903 U.S.-backed revolt in Panama; independence from Colombia.	**1901 ff.** Development of railway in East Africa.
1904–1905 Loss by Russia of war with Japan.	**1904–1914** Construction of Panama Canal by United States.	**1904** Great insurrection in German Tanganyika, defeated with 20,000 troops.
1905 Revolution in Russia; peasant reforms and Duma.	**1905 ff.** Growing U.S. political and military intervention in Central America, Haiti, and Dominican Republic.	
1912–1913 Two Balkan wars.	**1911** Beginning of Mexican Revolution.	
1917 Russian Revolution; abolition of tsarist regime; Bolshevik victory.		

The First Industrial Revolution: Western Society, 1780–1914

FOCAL POINTS

The industrial revolution was the predominant development in Western Europe during the nineteenth century. What was this economic transformation? How did it alter European politics, culture, social structure, and family life? Along with industrialization came a host of new political movements associated in particular with the great French Revolution of 1789. What were the goals of these movements? How did they change European life, and what impact might they have outside Europe itself? New approaches in science and art constituted a third area of innovation. Western Europe was the scene of vast changes during the nineteenth century, and the focus of inquiry must be on what these changes were and how they related to each other.

THE NATURE OF INDUSTRIALIZATION

The industrial revolution transformed agricultural society much as the Neolithic revolution had once transformed hunting-and-gathering cultures. Associated with this economic and technological upheaval in Western Europe and North America was the development of new political forms, ushered in by a variety of revolutions in many countries. Industrialization and political change also introduced major shifts in cultural life and basic social relationships, including class structure, family roles, and the locations of people's homes and work. The West did not lose all touch with its traditions in this sweeping process, but it was forced to reshape those traditions it retained.

This chapter deals with the transformation of the West itself, including the causes of change that evolved from previous developments in Western society, before proceeding to its global impact. With industrialization, the West traded in the social and intellectual currents of the early modern period and the capital amassed from its control of world trade, in order to produce a society, the likes of which had never been seen before in world history.

WHAT INDUSTRIALIZATION WAS

PATTERNS OF INDUSTRIALIZATION

Typically, when we examine major historical periods within a civilization, political or cultural developments hold center stage. Thus, there are centuries during which new political organizations seem to dominate other activities, and other centuries in which new religions, scientific innovations, or shifts in popular beliefs are the primary focus. In nineteenth-century Europe, however, economic change must be studied in advance of other features; economic change meant, above all else, industrialization.

In its essence, the industrial revolution consisted of a fundamental shift in technology and power sources. Instead of relying on human and animal power for virtually all production, the industrial revolution substituted fossil fuel power, first by means of coal to drive steam engines and later with electric and internal combustion engines. Along with the revolutionary power sources came new production equipment that could apply power to manufacturing (and later to other activities), with less dependence on human effort. Spinning jennies wound fiber into thread, applying steam or, in the early days, water power through gear transmissions. The flying shuttle was adapted to steam engines for weaving. Hammering and rolling devices allowed the application of power machinery to metallurgy. And although, in early industrialization, textile manufacturing and metallurgy, along with coal mining, received the greatest attention, engines were also used in sugar refining, printing, and other processes. The industry of machine building arose to construct engines, looms, and presses—the new tools of production. Machine building was greatly aided by the American invention of interchangeable parts, initially introduced for the manufacture of rifles.

The technological breakthrough spread quickly to communication and transportation. The development of the telegraph, steam shipping, and the railway, all early in the nineteenth century, provided new speed in the transport of information and goods. These inventions were vital in facilitating Western domination in world affairs.

Innovations were applied to agriculture, particularly after 1850, with new harvesting and planting equipment and gasoline-powered tractors. Scientific farming methods also produced artificial fertilizers and new strains of seeds and livestock. Technology also reached offices, through typewriters and cash registers, and homes, with sewing machines and refrigerators, although again, the major changes surfaced in the later nineteenth century onward. By this point, virtually all kinds of work had been altered by new equipment and power sources.

Furthermore, technological change was a recurrent process once the industrial revolution was launched. New generations of equipment displaced earlier machines. By the late nineteenth century, when the United States assumed the lead in technological advances, many power looms were sufficiently automated for one weaver to operate 16 or more looms, in contrast to the one or two looms per worker in earlier decades. Metallurgy was transformed, beginning in the 1850s, by new blast furnaces that increased the capacity for refining iron ore and allowed the automatic reintroduction of minerals to convert iron into steel. Coal mining, although less open to modernization, saw the introduction of engines to move ore and then cutting devices to use in the pits. Clearly, the industrial revolution may be linked to no single change in methods, but to successive waves of innovation.

Along with revolutionary inventions came major changes in economic organization. Manufacturing was becoming concentrated in factories, rather than in small

Power loom weaving in a cotton textile mill, 1834.

shops. With steam equipment, it was necessary for workers to cluster around the en-gines. Even apart from technological requirements, there were advantages to be gained from grouping larger numbers of workers: Both discipline and specialization increased. Finance, too, became more sophisticated. New equipment and factories re-quired growing investments. Banks began to play a greater role in funding industry. Corporations grew, particularly after 1850, to sell shares to large numbers of in-vestors. In industrial economies, big firms assumed a dominant position. Even in sales, small shops increasingly faced the competition of department stores and mail-order houses. Thus, the fundamental characteristics of economic organization were concentration, bureaucracy, and impersonality.

CAUSES OF INDUSTRIALIZATION

The industrial revolution first took shape in Great Britain, where key inventions, in-cluding the steam engine, had been introduced by 1780. British developments were quickly copied and other inventions added, so that by the 1820s most of Western Eu-rope and the new United States were actively engaged in the early stages of the in-dustrial revolution as well. Indeed, during the nineteenth century, the United States and Germany caught up with Britain, particularly in their emphasis on coal and iron production. The first industrial revolution was thus a Western-wide phenomenon, despite some interesting regional variations within the West.

The position the West had acquired in the world economy provided an active framework for the industrial revolution. European nations gained large amounts of capital from their colonial trading activities, including the slave trade. Businessmen also learned that there were markets for processed goods, which helped motivate them to devise new and cheaper ways to produce such goods. The privileged position

"Westward the Course of Empire Takes Its Way": Railroad across the North American continent. (Currier and Ives lithograph)

of the West in world trade unquestionably explains why it was this society that first introduced industrialization and why it long maintained an industrial lead over other areas.

The internal causes of the industrial revolution were exceedingly complex, a fact that helps explain why many societies continue to find it difficult to complete the process the West first introduced. The factors that went into the West's industrial revolution range from a massive population increase, which forced many workers to accept factory jobs simply because they had no alternative, to new ideas and a business mentality that made some industrial entrepreneurs positively eager to introduce risky changes. Material resources and capital constituted other Western advantages in pioneering the industrial spirit.

Industrialization built on many of the trends in Western society prior to the 1780s. The new technologies were related to the rise of science. James Watt, the inventor of the first manufacturing steam engine, worked closely with scientists at the University of Glasgow. During the nineteenth century, the link between the economy and science grew closer, as university chemists worked on developing new dyes, fertilizers, and explosives. More widely, the outlook accompanying the rise of science promoted beliefs in change and control over nature that guided many manufacturing innovators even without specific exposure to formal science.

Industrialization required capital and a willingness to take risks. Western experience in colonial trade had encouraged a daring merchant spirit that was now applied to manufacturing. The colonial trade and earlier improvements in agriculture and domestic manufacturing had resulted in considerable capital, available for investment in the new equipment. Industrialization also required favorable natural resources, particularly coal and iron ore; parts of Europe and North America had these in abundance, along with rivers and canals that facilitated transport even before the rise of the railroads.

Along with science, an openness to risk and change, the availability of capital, and a massive increase in population growth spurred the industrial revolution in Western Europe. Beginning early in the eighteenth century, the population began to soar, rising between 50 to 100 percent in all Western nations before 1800. The population revolution was itself caused by relatively peaceful conditions, a temporary decline in epidemic disease, and, above all, the introduction of new foodstuffs brought from the Americas. Europeans had initially hesitated to try new foods, but by 1700 they began to convert rapidly, particularly in their adoption of the potato into their diets. The use of new foods caused agricultural production to rise and the death rate to drop, which in turn allowed more offspring to live to adulthood and have children of their own. Hence, the population boom in a civilization that, unlike Asia, had not been particularly crowded previously. Population pressure rose rapidly, forcing many people off the land and creating a labor force for the new cities and factories. It also spurred merchants to take new risks in order to provide for their own growing families. The population revolution thus helps explain the timing of the West's industrial revolution as it combined with other factors.

Adding to population pressure was a new spirit of consumerism. Many people, in countries like Britain, sought new forms of pleasure and identity in buying fashionable clothes and furnishings. Shopkeepers learned new methods of advertising and sales gimmicks, to fuel this process. The acknowledgment of early consumerism was a major advance in historical knowledge, and it explains the existence of new markets that could convince manufacturers to innovate in the interests of increasing production.

In several Western countries, full industrialization also depended on political change. In general, industrialization relied heavily on private capitalists, who built the new factories and offices. But, governments played a role as well. In the United States, government provision of free land was vital to the development of the railroad network; in France and Germany, governments built rail systems outright. At the same time, governments had to abandon certain traditional practices in order for industrialization to occur. They could no longer, for example, defend the guild system, which tended to restrict technological innovation and the free movement of labor. Nor could they continue to defend slavery. Political revolutions in France and its neighbors, and the Civil War in the United States, served a vital function in establishing governmental systems favorable to industrialization and promoting a sense among government officials that industrialization was a good thing. Although a host of factors, such as the bitter moral debate over slavery, entered into U.S. political conflicts, a key ingredient was the clash over how the economy should be organized, with the North urging mobile wage laborers tied to rapid technological change. In the 1861–1865 Civil War, Northern industrial strength provided a vital edge, and in turn after the war U.S. encouragement of rapid industrialization increased.

HISTORY DEBATE

Consumerism and Industrialization

Until about fifteen years ago, historians thought they completely understood the relationship between Western industrialization, which was a major new production system, and the advent of a society in which the consumption of goods played a transforming role in defining the economy and personal goals. Industrialization came first, and only later did output reach levels at which people gained both the time and money needed for mass consumption.

Major discoveries in recent years, however, demonstrate that the first stage of a consumer society arose in places like England during the eighteenth century. New shops opened, advertising and sales gimmicks gained ground, and ordinary people began to place new meaning on acquiring goods, particularly clothing and furniture. New levels of consumption helped cause industrialization, which then accelerated consumerism to yet another stage. What historians still debate, however, is why consumerism arose in advance of major new production levels. Enjoyment of products from the world economy, like sugar, played a role. So did prior changes in social structure, which created more fluid boundaries in which people sought to establish identities by wearing stylish clothes. So did a decline in religious fervor. But, the precise causes remain to be established through fresh historical inquiry.

Industrialization was no simple development, even in its first, Western home. Many people resisted the changes in habits and the new, materialistic values it promoted. A complex set of causes, ranging from population growth to the dissemination of modern ideas, was needed to generate wide adoption of the new inventions and forms of organization.

EFFECTS OF INDUSTRIALIZATION

The economic effects of industrialization did not end with the rise of the factory system and the new equipment. Industrialization produced new wealth. With machines, productivity per worker rose rapidly. Even with the equipment available by 1800, a single worker using steam-driven spindles, for example, could produce as much thread as 100 manual spinners. Not all improvements in productivity were this vast, and the resulting new wealth was not evenly distributed. However, there was no question that, with industrialization, the West, already a wealthy society by world standards, became richer. Expanding wealth brought major changes in living standards and a desire for further improvements. By the later nineteenth century, the apparatus of a consumer society expanded further, as factories turned out growing

Industrialization of Europe, 1910

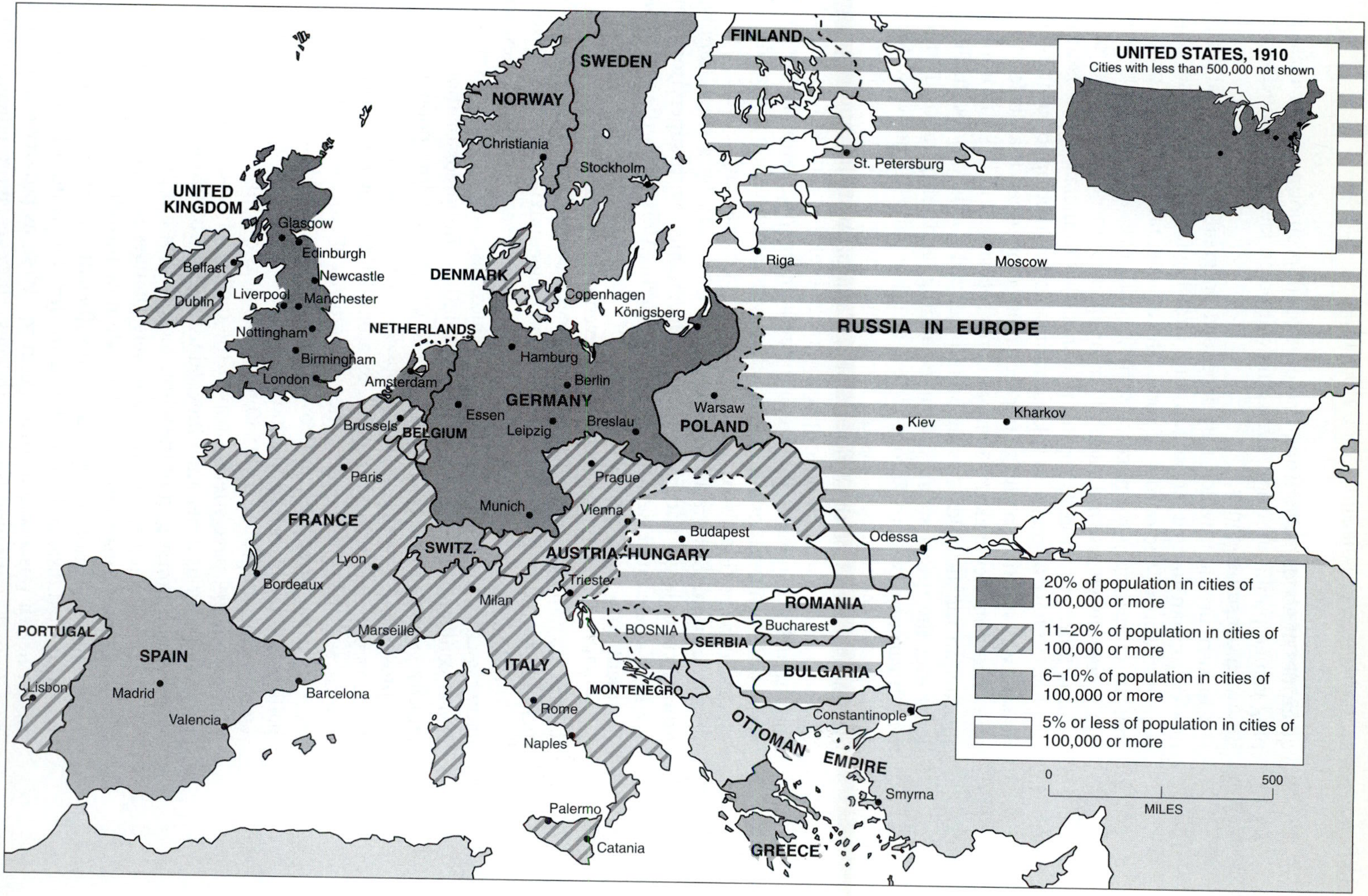

UNITED STATES, 1910
Cities with less than 500,000 not shown

Legend:
- 20% of population in cities of 100,000 or more
- 11–20% of population in cities of 100,000 or more
- 6–10% of population in cities of 100,000 or more
- 5% or less of population in cities of 100,000 or more

MILES
0   500

Labels on map:

RUSSIA IN EUROPE

Moscow
St. Petersburg
Riga
Kharkov
Kiev
Odessa

FINLAND

SWEDEN
Stockholm

NORWAY
Christiania

DENMARK
Copenhagen

POLAND
Warsaw
Königsberg

GERMANY
Hamburg
Berlin
Breslau
Leipzig
Essen
Munich

NETHERLANDS
Amsterdam

BELGIUM
Brussels

UNITED KINGDOM
Glasgow
Edinburgh
Newcastle
Manchester
Liverpool
Nottingham
Birmingham
London
Belfast
Dublin

FRANCE
Paris
Lyon
Bordeaux
Marseille

SWITZ.

AUSTRIA-HUNGARY
Prague
Vienna
Budapest
Trieste

ROMANIA
Bucharest

SERBIA

BOSNIA

MONTENEGRO

BULGARIA

OTTOMAN EMPIRE
Constantinople
Smyrna

GREECE

ITALY
Milan
Rome
Naples
Palermo
Catania

SPAIN
Madrid
Valencia
Barcelona

PORTUGAL
Lisbon

387

quantities of goods. Advertising also developed, promoting a new mass press. Shopping gained public attention; even a new disorder, kleptomania, reflected the obsession with consumer goods.

Industrialization, which had depended on greater agricultural output through new crops, transformed farming in turn. Growing factories and cities required major improvements in the output of food. The average farmer had to produce more, so that an increasing percentage of society could live and work off the farms. New equipment, fertilizers, and scientific techniques promoted the spread of market agriculture. More and more European peasants tried to increase their landholdings and employ landless laborers, to take advantage of market opportunities. This kind of peasant was still tied to village traditions, but more open than before to production growth and money-making. Some peasants specialized in dairy farming or vegetable production for the cities, buying more processed goods as a result. Finally, particularly after the rise of steam shipping, canning, and refrigeration in the later nineteenth century, Western Europe looked to other parts of the world for some of its food. Grain imports from Eastern Europe were surpassed by the highly productive commercial farms of the United States, Canada, Australia, and Argentina—where technological change far outstripped peasant levels—and meat was imported as well. Industrialization reduced the size of the agricultural population in the Western world while transforming economic life for those who remained on the farms.

Industrialization also created new needs for management skills and the handling of information. Early factories were small, often run by a single family. But with growth came larger and more complex hierarchies, with supervisors directing the workers, a sales staff, secretaries, and file clerks. Along with the spread of large department stores, the rise of management created an expanding white-collar work force, which by 1870 had growth rates even more rapid than those of factory labor. Like factory workers, white-collar employees were highly specialized and closely supervised according to rules designed to encourage maximum productivity.

Another effect of industrialization was the development of cities, and particularly big cities located at transportation hubs, near coal fields, or as banking and political centers. During the industrial revolution, hundreds of thousands of people, mostly young, migrated from country to city, prodded by population pressure and the prospect of new better-paying jobs. By 1850, for the first time in history, half of Britain's population lived in cities. By around 1900, the same was true of Germany, France, and the United States. The rapid growth of cities placed tremendous stress on existing urban structures and governments. Many early industrial cities suffered appalling conditions in housing and sanitation. Gradually, however, aided by industrial wealth, cities improved; by 1850, the worst was over in the West, as cities began to process sewage, pave streets, inspect the quality of food and housing, and provide parks and various other amenities. Adjusting to urbanization—or failing to adjust—was an important aspect of the whole industrialization process.

Closely related to urbanization were changes in health conditions. In agricultural societies, urbanization on the scale now introduced by the West would have been impossible, not only because of insufficient food supplies but also because cities had long bred disease. Indeed, during the first two-thirds of the nineteenth century, urban health was a serious problem in the West, as poverty and inadequate sanitation caused continuing high death rates. However, more efficient urban organization, particularly in the provision of better treatment of sewage and purer water supplies, plus related gains in medical knowledge through the development of the germ theory of disease, caused significant health improvements after 1880. Child death rates, especially, began to drop rapidly. Instead of a third of all children dying before adulthood, by 1900 the figure was down to less than 20 percent and falling fast. Here was another important use of the wealth, technical knowledge, and organizational skills that resulted from the industrial revolution.

The industrial revolution, itself primarily a transformation in technology and economic organization, had wide-reaching effects on where people lived, how healthy and well off they were, and what jobs they had. The transformations engendered by industrialization were not sudden, nor were they uniform. Early factories were small, and the large factory run by a hierarchy of supervisors and managers was only a development of the later nineteenth century. Many groups continued to work along rather traditional lines, well into the industrial revolution. Artisans still produced luxury products and even some necessities such as housing; most women employed in the cities worked as domestic servants, with their jobs remaining largely traditional. But change, if sometimes gradual and uneven, was the primary characteristic of the West's industrial century. Even artisans faced pressures to become less creative and more efficiency-minded in their work, while their overall importance was eclipsed by rising factories. By 1900, most people in the West were not working at the same jobs their great-grandparents had performed in 1780; they were not living in the same place; they did not engage in the same recreational activities. In 1780, most people had worked in or near the home; by 1900, most work was separate from the home. In 1780, most people had used traditional herbal remedies when ill, viewing hospitals as places where the desperately poor went to die; by 1900, many people in the West were beginning to rely on hospitals and doctors regularly and to believe that many age-old health problems could and should be eliminated. Here were some human measures of the change that the industrial revolution had produced.

PATTERNS OF WESTERN HISTORY, 1780–1900

Industrialization was a large, subterranean, often faceless process that altered the shape of Western society between 1780 and 1900. Particularly in its early phases, Western people were not always aware of exactly how their lives were changing. The concept of an industrial revolution itself arose only late in the nineteenth century, after the most basic changes had already taken place in the West. Along with industrialization, and more noticeable to most articulate observers, came a compelling number of political and intellectual innovations that produced a seemingly endless series of dramatic events.

THE PERIOD OF REVOLUTION, 1789–1848

The period began with a series of political revolutions, starting with the Revolutionary War in North America in the 1770s, which led to the formation of the United States. Americans, stirred by the liberal political values of the Enlightenment and pressed by new British restrictions on trade and political autonomy, engaged in the first modern struggle for national independence. They established a republican form of government, with a decentralized federal system and wide male suffrage. U.S. ties to Europe remained close, which enabled Americans to pick up quickly on European industrialization; European investment in the United States also supported economic change and expansion, while growing waves of European immigrants provided much of the necessary labor.

The American Revolution helped inspire a more sweeping revolution in France, starting in 1789. This great event resulted from an absolute monarchy grown inefficient, the power of Enlightenment ideas, and the discontent and confusion brought about by population growth and rising commerce in advance of outright industrialization. The French Revolution was the first of many struggles, in various parts of the world, that would stem from pressures to change that could not be contained within traditional political and social structures. Morover, the French Revolution, although not fully successful, did alter the political and legal framework of French society and, through conquest and imitation, that of much of the rest of Western Europe.

The French had grown restless under an absolute monarchy that was no longer effective and unable to produce meaningful reforms. Many French people resented the powers of the church and the aristocracy. Population pressure added to the discontent, as did the growing popularity of Enlightenment ideas. Although France was not yet industrializing, groups of peasants and artisans were already hostile toward the increasingly commercial spirit of many merchants and farmers; they saw revolution not as a blow for new political forms so much as a way to regain older values. This complex mix came to a head in 1789 when the king, Louis XVI, strapped for funds, had to call a meeting of the Estates-General, the former medieval parliament that had not met for 175 years. Business and professional people, inspired by the Enlightenment, were unwilling to meet as a separate estate, giving greater power to the aristocracy and clergy as the first two estates; peasants in many parts of France also rose against the remnants of manorial obligations. The great political revolution of modern Western history was underway.

The revolution went through several stages. For 2 years, relatively moderate leaders tried to set up a constitutional monarchy, which would protect the freedoms of the press, religion, and assembly. The idea was to scale down the power of the church, while abolishing serfdom and the guilds, thus abolishing the underpinnings of traditional social structure. The government divided up many of the estates of the aristocrats, making France a country of peasant owners. The Constitution of 1791 proclaimed the legal equality of all French people, as opposed to the traditional idea that different social groups had different rights of heredity. A parliament was established with the vote confined to the relatively wealthy—a strong suggestion that middle-class rule, based on the power of money, was replacing aristocratic rule, based on legal privilege by birth. But, partly because of opposition inside France and attacks by foreign monarchies, the revolution turned steadily more radical. Many aristocrats and other opponents were killed in what was called, somewhat grandiosely, the Reign of Terror (1793–1794); radicals executed the king and proclaimed a republic. The power of the central government increased over traditional local bodies; every man was allowed a vote. The most important result of the revolution's radical phase was the organization of a new, mass conscript army—now that citizens were equal, they had equal obligations to serve—which helped the revolutionaries gain new territories in western Germany, the Low Countries, and elsewhere. This successful war spread many of the revolutionary principles to larger parts of Western Europe.

The radical phase of the revolution was soon overturned, and in 1799 a military dictator, Napoleon Bonaparte, took charge of France. There followed 15 years of recurrent fighting, as Napoleon sought to carve out a European empire. Within France, Napoleon confirmed revolutionary law and promoted new secondary schools to recruit talented bureaucrats. Napoleon's conquests outside France weakened the manor system and advanced the idea of equality under the law throughout much of Western Europe. Wars during the revolution and under Napoleon also encouraged considerable popular nationalism. The French, armed with their new political rights, became enthusiastic about being citizens of France; Germans and Spaniards, angered by Napoleon's invasions, grew more nationalistic in opposition. Nationalism supplemented the efforts of Europe's monarchies to put down the dangerous revolutionary upstart. Britain was a consistent enemy of France, with Austria and Prussia frequent opponents of Napoleon. And the tsar of Russia, now intervening more in Western affairs than ever before, also played an important role in the final alliance that vanquished Napoleon. An attempt by Napoleon to invade Russia, in 1812, ended in disaster. As Russian forces retreated, the French armies followed and were subsequently caught in the frozen hold of a Russian winter; here was a sign of how much Russian military organization and size had changed since the days of the Mongols. The allies finally conquered France and exiled Napoleon in 1814–1815. A glittering diplomatic gathering, the Congress of Vienna, then tried to reassemble Europe's pieces.

For the next 30 years, Europe seemed dominated by conservative attempts to contain the forces that the revolution had unleashed. The monarchy was restored in France, and some, although not all, of the revolutionary legislation undone. The Catholic Church, vigorously allied with the antirevolutionary cause, gained new rights in France and elsewhere—however, it never recovered the vast property lost during the revolutionary period. Conservatism was buttressed by a new intellectual current, called Romanticism, which opposed Enlightenment values. Romantic writers and artists wished above all to express emotion; they disdained the cold rationalism of the eighteenth century. They adored Gothic styles and medieval adventures. Some Romantic theorists went further, opposing Enlightenment political values in the name of religion or the mystical collective power of the state, which, they felt, should not be constrained by constitutions or individual rights.

Although conservativism gained new ground, the old order that had existed before the French Revolution and the Napoleonic Wars could not be recaptured. The Congress of Vienna, for example, did not restore the small states into which Italy and Germany had been divided; it thus encouraged Italian and German nationalists to hope that their respective countries could be unified outright. At the same time, liberals in France and elsewhere wanted to regain revolutionary achievements such as constitutions, parliaments, wider voting rights, and full religious freedom. And a new, small group of socialists began to encourage protest in the name of economic equality. Thus, Western Europe was besieged by periodic efforts at agitation. Conservative leaders, headed by the tsar and the Habsburg monarchy, with its able minister Prince Metternich, tried in vain to keep the lid on popular unrest. Revolutions broke

Romantic nostalgia: Corot's painting of the harbor at La Rochelle, nineteenth century.

out in Spain, parts of Italy, and then Greece after 1820, with the Greeks winning independence from the Ottoman Empire. Again in 1830, further revolutions developed, leading to a new monarchy in France with a more liberal air, independence and a liberal monarchy for Belgium, and upheaval elsewhere. A final series of revolutions, in 1848, swept over much of Western Europe. It destroyed manorialism in Germany and Austria, encouraged Italian and German nationalists without, however, winning unity, and unseated the monarchy in France, this time for good.

A few Western countries were exempt from the tide of revolution. Britain, although strongly conservative in its opposition to the French Revolution, already had a parliamentary system. Popular protests sought political and social liberalization. In 1832, a reform bill gave most middle-class people the right to vote, and other reforms extended fuller religious tolerance, even to Catholics and Jews; regulated women and child workers in the factories; and granted new powers to city governments in improving material conditions. British politics became increasingly liberal, without revolution. Scandinavian governments also granted new powers to their parliaments and widened suffrage. In the United States, where revolution had already produced a constitutional republic and protection for individual liberty through the Bill of Rights, further pressures for political change were met, in the Jacksonian era of the 1830s, by reforms such as the secret ballot and extension of voting rights.

The revolutionary era in the West ended with the uprisings of 1848. There has been no major political revolution in this civilization since that time. The assurance of food supplies, prevention of famine, and stronger police forces contributed to the end of Western revolution, as did various political changes. On the surface, the revolutions of 1848 were political failures. Liberal leaders, eager for new rights and parliaments, grew afraid of the demands of the growing urban masses. Urban workers, pressed by the crowding and upheaval of early industrialization, sought economic reform, and a few fought for socialism as a means of creating economic equality. Socialists argued for group control over property and production, often urging governmental attacks on capitalist ownership and capitalist values. Revolutionaries were divided still further in many countries by their nationalist interests. German nationalists, for example, often wanted unity more than liberal political reforms. Amid these divisions, the forces of the traditional monarchs reasserted themselves, chasing revolutionaries from Hungary to Italy. In France, a nephew of the great Napoleon won popular election as president and soon established a new empire. The new or restored regimes proceeded to create police forces that helped stamp out political agitation.

THE POSTREVOLUTIONARY ERA AND NATIONALISM, 1848–1871

Political repression was not the whole story after 1848. The revolutions had won new freedoms for the peasantry, in their complete abolition of the manor system. Most of Western Europe now became a region of small peasant farmers; the aristocracy, although still powerful, was weakened. Furthermore, government leaders began to realize that concessions were necessary in the political arena, if a new round of revolution was not to begin. So, they granted constitutions and new powers to parliaments, plus a widened suffrage; these changes contented many liberals. Conservatism, in other words, became more adaptable. Two particularly flexible conservatives also worked to meet nationalist demands. In Italy, Count Cavour, the leader of a regional state in the north, engineered a series of wars beginning in 1859 that freed Italy from Austrian control and unified the entire peninsula. Otto von Bismarck, a Prussian politician, followed by orchestrating three regional wars, from 1864–1870, that unified the states of Germany. His final war, against France, also led to the downfall of Louis Napoleon's empire and the establishment of a new republic.

By 1870–1871, then, with the unification of Italy and Germany, political and diplomatic changes in Western Europe had delighted most moderate nationalists. The new nations, and also Habsburg Austria-Hungary, had constitutions with some real protection for personal liberties, including religious freedom; they had parliaments with some real power over the budget. Germany even offered universal male suffrage, although the measure was qualified by a complex voting system. France, newly republican, also confirmed universal male suffrage. These developments, along with continued reforms in other states—as in Britain, where suffrage was extended in 1867 and 1884 so that a majority of men could vote—seemed to satisfy most Westerners sufficiently that basic issues of political structure no longer dominated the scene.

The United States also addressed a fundamental issue of political structure in the same period, through the Civil War. The preservation of the Union and the abolition of slavery did not end important political divisions in the United States or the continuing problems faced by the black minority. As in much of Europe, political change was qualified by conservative principles. Thus, while Germany granted parliamentary rights but kept basic sovereignty in the hands of the monarch, who appointed the state's chief ministers, the United States abolished slavery but then allowed new kinds of legal discriminations against black citizens after the Reconstruction period. However, such changes reduced internal friction, another of the adjustments that brought revolution to an end throughout the West and resolved some long-standing issues related to political and legal structures.

Western society had thus gone through several political phases by 1871: outright revolution and upheaval, dominated by the French Revolution and Napoleon (1789–1815); conservative–liberal contest (1815–1848); and consolidation, under the auspices often of flexible conservatives (1849–1871). This last period had produced several sharp conflicts and the bloody American Civil War, which was the first war to signal the importance and destructive power of armies backed by industrial arsenals. The era of Romanticism had ended in the West, and with it some of the more visionary political efforts; politicians now preferred hard facts and cold steel to enthusiasms either revolutionary or conservative. Bismarck, in fact, talked of having created the new, united Germany through "blood and iron."

"THE SOCIAL QUESTION," 1871–1914

Between 1871 and 1914, most Western governments were concerned with protecting the gains and compromises of earlier times. There was no major war within the Western world, although rivalries spilled over into struggles for colonial empires elsewhere. Germany's unification and the consolidation of the United States brought these powers increasingly to the fore, which automatically generated new tensions by altering the balance of forces in the West. One result was a new system of diplomatic alliances, as Germany sought to protect itself by linking with Austria and Italy, whereas France, eager to regain territories lost to Germany in 1871, gradually constructed its own alliance with Russia and then Britain. Diplomatic maneuvering among the leading Western powers won growing attention by the end of the century; it would ultimately, in 1914, help lead to unprecedented world war.

The final decades of the century saw two major developments in the internal politics of Western nations. Governments began to react more clearly to the pressures and problems of industrial society, taking on new functions. Many countries followed Germany's example and maintained mass conscript armies even in peacetime. Most countries extended a national system of compulsory education. National—or, in the United States, state—governments also took on new functions in inspecting factory conditions, setting housing standards, and the like; many began to provide health services to the poor. A number of governments, finally, led by Bismarck's Germany in the 1880s, passed social insurance laws, granting some state-sponsored protection against financial problems caused by illness, accident, or old age.

The expanded functions of governments were prompted in part by new political pressures, the second important domestic political development. Socialist parties arose everywhere after 1871. Many were inspired by the doctrines of Karl Marx, who had worked out his theories between 1847 and 1870. Socialist parties urged major reforms to protect working people; their goal was an alternative to capitalism that would provide economic equality. Some advocated revolution to reach this goal, but in fact most Western socialists worked within the political system, seeking to obtain power by a majority vote. Careful political organization and wide appeal made socialist parties the strongest single political force in countries like Germany and an important third force, along with liberals and conservatives, in Britain, France, and (until after World War I) the United States.

The rise of socialism and the new functions of governments made what was called "the social question"—what to do about poverty and working-class demands—the leading domestic political issue in the last decades of the nineteenth century. Political alignments around this issue overshadowed the year-to-year shifts in parliamentary votes or presidential elections, as this level of politics became relatively routine. Thus, after a series of earlier periods in which the *form* of government had been the leading issue, Western politics settled increasingly into debates about the *functions* of government, the role of government in the reshaping (or preventing the reshaping) of society; and, with growing urgency, about the role of government in international affairs, as the armies and arsenals of the Western nations were mobilized around a tense network of diplomatic rivalries. Some observers believed that divisions over the social question encouraged Western governments to think in terms of diplomatic initiatives that could unite their nations, thus distracting them from new signs of unrest.

WESTERN POLITICAL INSTITUTIONS IN THE INDUSTRIAL REVOLUTION

The age of revolution in Western society recalled earlier political traditions in this civilization by calling for new balance against the power of the monarchy. However, this traditional impulse was reshaped by new political ideologies and the demands of an industrializing society. The result was a new kind of government, neither medieval nor absolutist in structure.

Nationalism constituted one new force, fed by revolutionary beliefs in popular government and reactions to French invasions. Nationalists argued that the state should be linked to a single basic culture—a "national" culture, which should override minority differences within the society and should clearly delineate each nation in relation to others. Nation–states were partly invented—national cultures were not, in fact, so clearcut—but the association of a state with a dominant language, literature, and history proved to be a powerful mix, first in Europe, then elsewhere in the world. Nationalists could either call for allegiance to existing territorial states, as in revolutionary France, or, as in Germany, they could claim ethnic cultural unity and urge its political expression. In Europe, nationalism fed the long-standing military and economic competition among states and ultimately encouraged a growth in the power of the state.

Liberalism also became a major political force throughout the Western world. Liberals believed that governments should be controlled, not by institutions such as the church or groups such as the aristocracy, but by constitutions and assurances of individual rights. Their efforts led to the establishment of wide freedoms for religious practice, assembly, and the press by the 1870s; even trade unions won the right to organize and strike. Liberals also believed in the importance of powerful parliaments, elected by at least part of the population and representing not estates, as in the medieval institutions, but the whole nation.

Although liberalism was particularly shaped by Enlightenment values, including the beliefs in progress and human rationality, and the possibility of improving the human condition, it was also affected by ongoing industrialization. Some liberals argued that the poor should fend for themselves. But, social problems created by arduous factory labor and crowded cities prompted most practicing liberals to advocate some limited social reforms, as in regulating the work hours of women and children. The growing political awareness of the urban masses also inspired many liberals to demand a democratic voting system.

The result of liberal and popular pressure, through the decades of revolution and reform, was a new structure for most Western states. By the 1870s, the Western political framework involved parliaments, based on wide voting rights, that served as the source of most legislation and acted as a check on executive authority. Monarchies had either been abolished, as in France, or greatly reduced in power. The political activities of the Catholic and Protestant churches had been radically scaled down, and most governments no longer believed that they should perform significant religious functions. It is important to realize that Western governments varied in the extent to which they had embraced liberal goals; the new German state, for instance, was notably less liberal in structure and intent than the governments of France, Britain, and the United States. And, there were important political movements in many countries that opposed liberal values in the name of the older principles of monarchy and aristocracy. Nevertheless, despite variety and opposition, liberal values had significantly reshaped Western politics during the nineteenth century, among other things creating more similar political forms among the major Western states than had existed during the seventeenth and eighteenth centuries.

One key result of the development of liberal institutions was the rise of modern political parties, designed to organize members of parliament and to campaign for popular votes. In the United States, both major political parties espoused broadly liberal goals, although they differed significantly at important points of American history—for example, on the issue of slavery. In most European countries, liberal political parties competed with more conservative groups. By the 1870s, most conservative parties had added nationalist appeals to their political agenda, using this new force to advocate a strong state and military. Nationalism also gained force from the disruptions caused by industrialization. As people moved to the cities from their local villages, they were open to new loyalties, and a fascination with national achievements often served this purpose well. Finally, particularly after 1870, socialist parties began to grow, adding a new element to the political spectrum of most Western countries. Socialists were wary of nationalism and found liberalism too limited, although they largely accepted the importance of parliamentary institutions. Socialists pressed for major legislation on behalf of working people, and their revolutionary rhetoric often frightened liberals and conservatives. Nowhere, by 1914, had socialists won major positions in government, but their growing power helped generate new legislation to address important social questions.

Western politics, then, involved not only new political institutions, but also a multiparty system embracing a wide variety of political opinions. These views, expressed through a host of new "isms"—liberalism, socialism, nationalism, and formal conservatism—coexisted uneasily, and some politicians questioned the ability of the parliamentary system to manage all the forces it had unleashed. But, most groups accepted at least tentatively the possibility of working within the system, seeking to win enough votes to enact the government measures they sought. Continuing changes in voting rights opened the way to additional issues. A rising feminist movement in many countries by 1900 pressed for women's right to vote; this was mainly an issue for the future, but several American states did grant female suffrage, and Scandinavian governments did so shortly after 1900. Here was an important extension of the idea that basic political power should rest with the people themselves, expressed through equal voting rights.

Along with new constitutional structures and parties, the modern Western state assumed important new responsibilities and created the bureaucracy to carry them out. Some old functions were, of course, dropped or reduced, including the support of a single official religion and of aristocratic privilege. Governments after 1848 had also stopped defending the rights of groups such as guilds to establish work rules. But, the new tasks of government were more extensive than those that were abandoned; one sign of this was that government staffs and budgets grew steadily, with rare exceptions, throughout the nineteenth century.

Western nations now clearly recognized their duty to encourage economic growth. Some used tariffs to protect particular industries. All supported the spread of railroad and canal networks. Governments also took on the function of mass education. All Western governments by the 1870s not only operated primary and secondary schools but also required attendance to at least age 12. Schools had as their role the teaching of useful economic skills to promote agricultural and manufacturing productivity. They also vigorously preached national loyalty, hoping the national literatures and histories would instill a new consensus among its citizens. Mass education was a new phenomenon, and levels of literacy, reaching 80 to 90 percent in Western society by 1900, had no precedent. The idea of the state, rather than the churches, serving as main educator was also novel. In addition, governments gained new contact with citizens through the practice of universal military conscription. The draft was used only in wartime by the United States and Britain, but even so military forces grew larger than ever before. Since most male citizens spent a period in military service, as in France and Germany, they experienced firsthand the new power of the modern state—and, of course, had yet another occasion to learn national loyalties. Finally, as we have seen, governments began to take on responsibility for providing some protection for the health and well-being of all citizens. Laws regulating working conditions and consumer rights, efforts to build sewers and other public-health facilities, and social insurance measures were important signs of the new welfare functions of the Western state.

To meet the new demands, the Western state not only expanded its bureaucracies, it also began to recruit according to talent. Secondary schools in many countries

World Profiles

Mary Wollstonecraft (1759–1797)

Mary Wollstonecraft was one of the world's first explicit feminists. Her book, *Vindication of the Rights of Women* (1792), applied the doctrines of the ongoing French revolution to women's issues and effectively launched the modern women's movement not only in her native Britain, but also throughout the Western world.

Wollstonecraft was the daughter of a tradesman who abused her mother and squandered his own inheritance. She early rebelled against some of the conventional practices applied to women, and her first writings addressed the lack of occupations open to them. She frequented radical circles in London and followed a deliberately unconventional lifestyle —bearing two children out of wedlock. (She died after the second birth; her daughter Mary Shelley is the author of *Frankenstein*.) Her sometimes shocking behavior caused subsequent feminists to shy away from citing her literary examples until a full century later. What combination of personal characteristics and more general social forces would prompt such a radical life and outlook at this time?

This portrait, by John Opie, shows Wollstonecraft as a powerful woman with a trace of sadness. She may have been pregnant with her second child at the time.

served particularly to train future bureaucrats. All Western governments introduced civil service examinations by the 1870s—imitating practices long ago developed in China. Although most upper bureaucrats still came from the aristocracy and wealthy business and professional groups, there was a new chance for ordinary people to rise on the basis of academic achievement and test results.

The Western state, as it had emerged by 1914, embodied some interesting tensions. Liberal structures implied controls on government power, through bills of rights and parliamentary limits. However, government functions and bureaucracies had grown, often with the blessing of liberals themselves. This tension was, in important ways, a restatement of older Western ambiguities about the state. It also reflected the fact that different political groups disagreed about the state's proper role. The tension over the state and its limits would continue to color Western history into the twentieth century.

WESTERN CULTURE IN THE INDUSTRIAL CENTURY

The nineteenth century produced a bewildering variety of intellectual movements. Major novelists abounded: Dickens, Austen, and many others in Britain; Hawthorne, Melville, and others in the United States; Balzac, Zola, and others in France. Poetry was slightly less important, as was drama, but here too literary production soared, and with it a host of new styles. In the arts, Romantic painters focused on pastoral scenes, and then, in the last decades of the century, impressionists challenged old traditions of literal representation in their attempt to use the canvas to convey the essence, rather than the surface reality, of what the eye beholds. Interestingly, the nineteenth century did not produce a distinctive architectural style; revived Gothic buildings predominated, but there was also classical and even Byzantine imitation. Science continued its advance, with major strides in biology, notably Darwin's theory of evolution; in electricity and magnetism as well as other aspects of physics; discovery of the germ theory in medicine; and important innovations in applied chemistry.

Industrializing society, as it generated growing wealth, almost naturally produced a growing array of cultural expressions. New money built new churches, new public buildings, new art galleries, and new laboratories. Industrial technology directly aided science, in promoting devices such as the X-ray machine or more powerful telescopes. New wealth also supported growing numbers of artists, even if many of them struggled lifelong with poverty. Inventions such as the camera and discoveries in optics also powerfully influenced artistic styles—impressionism rebelled against the camera's literalness, at the same time using new knowledge of how the eye perceives color. Rising literacy along with growing wealth supported new legions of writers; authors like Dickens directly serialized their novels in middle-class newspapers, where payment by the word encouraged a rather long-winded writing style.

The role of religion in determining the intellectual agenda continued to decline. Christian faith remained important in the nineteenth century, even as the political role of organized churches waned. Many new churches were built, and Western society funded a vast missionary effort. In the United States, religion retained a particularly lively function, as revivals and immigrant churches powerfully shaped American culture. Religion faded more definitively as a popular force in Europe, where nationalism and socialism provided competing loyalties; here, however, Christianity continued to sustain many people. But as a formal intellectual force, religion was less vigorous even than in the age of Enlightenment. Few leading writers cared greatly about the nature of God or the fine points of theology.

Western society continued to reshape its intellectual heritage. This effort involved two major elements: first, ongoing work within the rational, scientific tradition of the Enlightenment, and second, a vigorous artistic statement that new styles were essential to capture the meaning of life and provide an alternative to scientific modes of thought.

The Enlightenment heritage persisted, as we have seen, in political theory. Liberal writers modified Enlightenment beliefs. They no longer argued in terms of natural right, preferring instead to talk in terms of what was useful. However, they maintained the traditional beliefs that individuals were rational, education was worthwhile, and scientific and industrial progress was desirable. Most socialists also clung to Enlightenment beliefs. Karl Marx, the leading theorist of the entire century, used a historical rather than a strictly rationalist basis for his grand scheme. To Marx, history changed on the basis of who controlled the existing technology, or means of production. Class struggle resulted, with those in control fighting those below. In modern society, the middle class had wrested power from the aristocracy, but had created a new class enemy, the property-less proletariat, or working class. This class would grow until revolution became inevitable. But once the proletarian revolution had occurred, an Enlightenment-style utopia would result. The state would wither away, as each individual would be able rationally to determine his or her own interests; goods would be distributed according to need; class struggle would vanish once the vestiges of the middle class had been eliminated. More prosaically, most socialist theorists agreed with liberals about the basic goodness and rationality of humankind and the importance of material progress, education, and science.

In addition to liberal and socialist theory, the rationalist tradition was also kept alive through scientific inquiry. Indeed, as scientists learned about new fertilizers and health measures, science became more firmly linked than ever before with the idea of progress on this earth. On the more theoretical level, science advanced on every front. The great contribution was Darwin's evolutionary theory. On the basis of careful observation, Darwin argued that all living creatures had evolved into their present form through the ability to adapt in a struggle for survival. Biological development could be scientifically understood as a process taking place over time, with some animal and plant species disappearing and others evolving from earlier forms. Darwin's ideas clashed with traditional Christian beliefs that God had created humankind directly, and the resulting popular debate, on the whole, weakened the intellectual hold of religion. The picture of nature that Darwin suggested was far more complex than the simple natural laws of Newton. Nature worked through random struggle. However, Darwin confirmed the idea that scientists could advance knowledge, and his theory was compatible with the idea that natural laws encouraged progress.

The social sciences also continued to advance, on the basis of observation, experiment, and rationalist theorizing. Great efforts went into compilations of statistical data concerning populations, economic developments, and health problems. Sheer empirical knowledge about the human condition had never been more extensive. At the level of theory, leading economists tried to explain business cycles and the causes of poverty; social psychologists studied the behavior of crowds. Toward the end of the century, the Viennese physician Sigmund Freud began to develop his theories of the workings of the human unconscious, arguing that much behavior is determined by impulses but psychological problems can be relieved by rational understanding. Like many other scientists, social scientists complicated the traditional Enlightenment view of nature and human nature by studying the animal impulses and unconscious urges of human beings. However, they continued to rely on standard scientific methods in their work, believing that human behavior can be rationally categorized,

Bucolic romanticism: landscape by the British painter Constable, early nineteenth century.

and most of them asserted that ultimately human reason would prevail, as manifested in appropriate economic, political, or personal behavior.

The artistic vision developed by the nineteenth century was rather different. To be sure, many novelists realistically portrayed human problems, believing that their efforts could contribute to reform. Artists, as we have seen, were aware of scientific discoveries. Beginning with Romanticism, however, many artists looked to emotion, rather than reason, as the key to the mystery of life. They sought to portray longings and even madness, not calm reflection. They also deliberately endeavored to violate traditional Western artistic standards. They proclaimed their freedom from the traditional rules characterizing drama or poetry. This impulse was taken up, after Romanticism declined around 1850, by new artists who attempted to defy literal representation itself. Leading poets shunned conventional rhymes and meters, writing abstract, highly personalized statements. Artists and sculptors sought suggestive images, while later nineteenth-century composers began to work with atonal scales that defied long-established conventions in music. Some artists talked of an art for art's sake—that is, art that had it own purposes, regardless of the larger society. Other artists and philosophers rejected rationalism outright, stressing the power of impulses or the human will.

The new split in Western culture, between rationalists and nonrationalists, had institutional overtones. By the late nineteenth century, most scientists and social scientists worked in or around universities. Western universities, in a virtual eclipse since the end of the Middle Ages, now revived as great research centers that also trained society's elite. This model of the university developed first in Germany and spread quickly to France, the United States, and to a lesser extent Britain. Many artists, in contrast, worked outside any institution. Artistic communities, called "bohemian" by respectable middle-class observers who distrusted the artistic life style, developed in most major cities, with the community in Paris the most glittering. Most artistic patrons preferred older styles, particularly in painting and music. But, modern art continued to grow, its lack of clear standards and its defiance of ordinary taste and tradition clearly expressing an important aspect of Western culture in the modern age. It was revealing that in an age of great economic change, Western culture did not rely simply on existing artistic traditions as an anchor. The same individualism and secularism that helped spur business competition spilled over into culture, prompting many artists to seek alternatives to ordinary values, scientific modes of inquiry, and the sheer ugliness of the industrial environment itself.

INDUSTRIAL SOCIETY

Industrialization left a decisive mark on the shape of society in Western nations. In combination with the legal changes ushered in by the decades of revolution, it produced a new social structure. Position in society was increasingly determined by property and earnings, plus the level of education one had achieved. Former measures, such as birth, legal privilege, and purely landed estate, declined. In this new social structure, wealthy business executives and professional people gained growing prestige, at the expense of aristocrats and old merchant families. In the United States, where an aristocracy had never seriously existed and the Civil War decimated the land-owning class in the South, the middle class reigned supreme. In most European countries, aristocrats continued to wield cultural and political influence, but they no longer dominated the social pyramid. Middle-class culture, evincing a broadly liberal faith in science and education and a passion for respectable, restrained behavior, increasingly set the social tone. The ranks of the middle class grew, with the expansion of business and the rise of professions such as engineering, law, and medicine, in which individuals could claim unique expertise on the basis of special knowledge, training, and licensing.

The second leading social class of modern Western society consisted of urban workers, particularly in the factories. This group, far larger than the middle class, had scant property and much lower earnings. It did not accept all middle-class values, but was nonetheless influenced by their powerful expression in the popular media, notably books and newspapers, and the school system.

Not everyone fit into the basic middle-class/working-class division of industrial society, even aside from the important remnants of an aristocracy at the top. Artisans clung to older values, in some countries even hoping for a restoration of the guild system; they merged only gradually and incompletely with the new working class. The rural population, still massive, continued to reflect the distinctive features of a peasant tradition and agricultural life. Even here, however, the division increased between peasants or farmers who owned their land and employed others, on the one hand, and a growing number of landless laborers, on the other.

The rise of white-collar workers added another, newer complexity to the modern Western social structure. Like workers, secretaries and telephone operators owned little property. Although they needed some education to perform their jobs, they could not claim professional status. But, white-collar workers did share styles of dress and values with middle-class people. They liked to think—usually incorrectly—that they or their children could rise into the managerial or professional ranks.

Family life was powerfully affected by industrialization. Family responsibilities changed, although gradually. The family ceased being the main center of production, as work moved outside the home. But, the family gained or enhanced some other functions. It served as a consumer unit; most major purchases were effected within the family, and a new division of labor freed some family members—mainly housewives—for the important and time-consuming tasks of shopping, now that families did not make most of their own goods. Much leisure time was spent with the family. Holidays more and more became family occasions rather than community affairs. The idea of family vacations spread, first in the middle class and then, in the form of day-long excursions, to workers. The family also became the center of emotional gratification. Family members were supposed to love each other. Although this ideal of family life was articulated most directly by the middle class, who believed that the family should be a haven against the stress of the outside world, workers also reflected similar sentiments. Courtship became increasingly romantic; at least in the working class, the importance of sexual pleasure deepened. Ironically, this emphasis on emotional satisfaction produced a noticeable growth in the divorce rate, with the United States taking the lead. As families declined as units of economic activity, it became more possible and perhaps more necessary to dissolve marriages that were not providing personal gratification.

Changes in family functions had vital implications for the roles of family members. The man was increasingly seen as the breadwinner, with his earnings from work his main responsibility. Married women were largely kept out of the formal labor force; in the middle class, even most girls did not work. According to middle-class family ideals, women were to serve as the exponents of culture and the moral center within the family. This gave them a new significance, as women in fact came to dominate child rearing and the household more fully than before, but it also removed them from many public activities, since women lagged far behind men in political rights. Industrialization raised important questions about women's roles. Women were given new esteem, and their educational gains were more rapid than those of men although women started from a lower position on this scale. In the working class, moreover, women were vital to the labor force, as girls worked in factories, as domestic servants, and later as clerks and public school teachers. However, in day-to-day activities, married women were increasingly separate from men. The rise of feminist movements, seeking expanded rights and opportunities for women, reflected the anomalies of this aspect of the Western family.

Attitudes toward children changed as well. Most middle-class children were expected to learn, not earn. Working-class children, on the other hand, were essential to the operation of early factories, maintaining the traditional assumptions that children should contribute to the family economy. But, many people from all classes objected to the factory conditions to which children were exposed, particularly the fre-

HISTORY DEBATE

Conditions of Women

Historians continue to disagree on what happened to women in Western industrial society. There are disputes of interpretation: Traditionally, historians saw laws that limited women's hours of work as humanitarian gains. But, feminist historians note that these laws made it less attractive to employ women and formed part of a new emphasis on the importance of the male breadwinner. Women were now supposed to maintain sexual respectability, but this power had a downside, for respectable women were not supposed to be sexually eager.

There are disputes of emphasis. Women were pushed out of the urban labor force, particularly after marriage. However, they were given greater moral esteem and power within the home. Women provided the "essential elements of moral government," and it was assumed that their purity would overcome men's baser impulses. Educational gains for women did not result in equality, but they increasingly eliminated gender gaps in literacy.

Even feminism, rising in the second half of the nineteenth century, becomes controversial in this discussion. Did it result merely from new and old inequalities, or did it reflect women's new cultural status and other gains such as a reduction in family size? Is the nineteenth century to be seen as the triumph of a new form of patriarchy, or as a crucial albeit complex stage of women's liberation?

quency of accidents; in fact, as machines became more complex, children's usefulness declined. Moreover, the advent of compulsory education took most young children out of the labor force. Most adolescents still worked in 1914, although in the United States a high-school education became more commonplace, even among working-class youth. Parents grew concerned with fostering their children's learning ability. Their emotional expectations of children also increased, their hope being that such attention and the resulting affection would compensate for the fact that offspring had become a greater economic burden. At the same time, parents' roles in children's lives decreased, and interaction among young people in schools heralded the development of separate generational cultures by the end of the nineteenth century. Being a child in the industrial West was different from being a child in a traditional agricultural society, but it was not necessarily easier.

The final impact of industrialization on the family involved population structure. In what is called the "demographic transition," Western families quickly reacted to the population boom of the eighteenth century by reducing their birthrates. Birthrates began to fall gradually in the United States and France as early as 1790. The middle class led the way in this demographic transition. Middle-class culture emphasized the importance of sexual restraint, and most middle-class people married fairly late. Gradually, a birthrate limit spread to the working class and peasantry, although under the new demographic regime, poorer families, on average, had larger families than the middle class—the reverse of traditional patterns. With children now an expense and parents expected to provide careful supervision and training to children, large families began to decline. By 1914, the average Western family included only three to four children. By this point, the medical advances that would almost eliminate deaths in childhood were underway, making birth control even more imperative. Most families relied mainly on sexual restraint for this purpose, although new contraceptive devices became more common, particularly after the vulcanization of rubber in the 1830s; the incidence of abortion also increased. Thus, by 1914, the industrial, demographic regime was clearly in place in the West, with lower birth rates than ever before in human history, combined with low mortality rates for children as life expectancy steadily rose. This new demography produced important changes in family life and the roles of women, now that mothering required less effort than before; it also produced considerable tension given the need for sexual restraint. The new demography had wider consequences too, as the population of the West began to decline in relation to that of other parts of the world.

Despite all these changes, the family thrived in Western society, adapting new purposes and roles as old ones dwindled but also maintaining some traditional functions. Change itself was often concealed. As new household equipment made women's work easier, standards of household cleanliness increased so the effort involved in housekeeping, in fact, remained the same. Mothers were praised despite the decline in the birthrate—the U.S. Congress, for example, enacted Mother's Day soon after 1900. Of all the traditional institutions from agricultural society—the village, the guild, even the church—the family survived the best. However, it did change, and Westerners worried out loud about the stability of this basic institution, as they continue to in the present day.

Along with social structure and family, popular culture altered its shape under the effects of industrialization. Growing literacy, exposure to political campaigns, and increasing wealth—at least, for most by 1914, slightly above subsistence—all had an impact. Ideas about the value of education, science, and technology spread more widely, and the gap between popular and elitist values narrowed by 1914.

However, industrialization imposed a general strain on society, as do ongoing changes in technology and business organization. The nature of work shifted, and probably its quality deteriorated. Before the industrial revolution, work for most people had been a social act, punctuated by gossip and naps, accomplished within a family context. With the rise of factories and offices, work was not only taken out of the home, it also became increasingly regimented. Shop rules forbade workers from singing, chatting, or wandering about. The pace of work quickened, as workers' efforts were routinely timed by a clock. In addition, more people were supervised by strangers than ever before; they performed specialized tasks, rather than creating whole products.

These changes were hard to integrate, and many would argue that they have not been fully assimilated even now. In the early stages of the industrial revolution, particularly before 1850, the impact of new work forms was intensified by the rapid decline of popular leisure traditions. Festivals virtually vanished. As communities dissolved through migration to the cities, these highly local events were hard to maintain. Furthermore, the middle class disapproved of festivals as a threat to public order and sheer waste of time; the newly created police forces actively discouraged such public gatherings. Middle-class leisure consisted chiefly of useful activities, like family reading or piano playing, that would showcase cultural achievement and train the young. This utilitarian definition of leisure was not accepted by many workers, but they had few alternatives. Tavern drinking became one of their major pastimes (one that middle-class temperance reformers fought in vain) because it provided a glimmer of former sociability.

Many workers protested the changes in their lives. The decades of revolution depended heavily on working-class protest in the name of older work values, with artisans taking the lead. Workers also sought to cushion the impact of industrialization on their own lives, by taking time off from their jobs or changing employment with great frequency, to the fury of middle-class managers. Gradually, however, workers found some solace in the concept of instrumentalism; they recognized that they could not necessarily control the quality or conditions of their work, but would accept their job's constraints for the sake of rising earnings. In other words, work became an instrument to other things. After 1850, working-class protest, although it increased as workers became better organized, largely changed from attempts to control the job itself, to demands for shorter hours and higher pay. The worker looked forward to new economic benefits, rather than backward to older values. At the same time, new recreational outlets arose. Popular reading, vaudeville theaters, and professional and amateur sports proliferated in Western society after 1870, for various social groups. The new leisure was highly commercialized, signaling the growth of a consumer society. Sports also served to discipline people for the workplace, as they learned team cooperation and obedience to the rules imposed on every modern sport; sports also served to condition possible future soldiers. Some critics at the time and even today have blasted the new sports culture, its emphasis on pleasure seeking and physical release, and wondered if leisure was as satisfying and expressive as it should be, given the limits of industrial work. Whatever its quality, mass leisure was a uniquely modern creation and a vital part of the new culture spawned by industrialization. And, some games, like soccer football, first developed in industrial England, would spread around the world much faster than industrialization itself.

CONCLUSION: GAIN AND STRAIN IN INDUSTRIALIZATION

In 1900, heralding the advent of a new century, many Western newspapers looked back on the past century and found it satisfactory. Improved health conditions, new wealth, greater political freedom, more education—all suggested an improved quality of life, one that was getting better. Great change had unquestionably occurred, but by 1900 many people were becoming accustomed to it, bolstered by their belief in progress. Only a few groups in Western society, such as the new immigrants to the United States, were confronting urban, industrial life for the first time.

However, change had brought strain as well as apparent progress, and it continued to do so. An aristocratic German general, a Catholic bishop, and an old-fashioned New England intellectual would all take issue with the idea of progress, seeing the values that were lost as more important than the material gains. From other vantage points, many workers, particularly those who could find no meaning at all in their work, and many feminists would also quarrel with the idea of progress, hoping that their satisfaction or ideals would some day come to fruition.

The strains within Western society spilled over into the West's world role. Industrialization brought new power to Western society, which it used to gain more complete control over more areas of the world than ever before. But, the use of power was tempered by the need to alleviate tensions at home from those who looked back to a better past and those who pressed for more radical reforms for the future. The combination of power and uncertainty produced the great wave of European imperialism, which brought Western power to every corner of the globe. Imperialist expansion reflected not only business success, but also the desire of aristocratic officers and Christian missionaries to find new arenas for their values, in keeping with their vision of power.

In turn, groups from China to Latin America, although proud of their own cultures, recognized that they had to copy some features of industrial society if they wanted to prevent total Western domination. A key question was, which aspects of the Western industrial process had to be, and could be, imitated: Was it just the military technology and organization, or the wider economic revolution, or did Western-style politics, or art, or changes in women's roles also inextricably enter the process? Western history between 1789 and 1914 had brought profound transformations to one of the world's major civilizations; it also established a complex model for others to ponder.

SUGGESTED WEBSITES

On industrial workers, see *http://applebutter.freeservers.com/worker/index.html*; on working women, see *http://www.womeninworldhistory.com/lesson7.html*; on Marxist ideas and the great Marxist anthem, the International, go to *http://www.anu.edu.au/polsci/marx/marx.html* (which includes a very clear RealAudio file of the "Internationale" sung by an Irish folk-singer accompanied on the guitar). For a website on the British working class, see *http://www.history.rochester.edu/pennymag*; a rich site on the French Revolution is *http://chnm.gmu.edu/revolution*; on James Watt, see *http://homepages.westminster.org.uk/hooke/issue10/watt.htm*.

SUGGESTED READINGS

Fine studies of the early industrial period include Phyllis Deane, *The First Industrial Revolution* (1980) (on Britain), and E. J. Hobsbawm, *The Age of Revolution: Europe 1789–1848*

(1962) (on Europe generally). See also Peter N. Stearns, *The Industrial Revolution in World History* (1998). An excellent recent study highlights Europe by comparison: R. Bin Wong, *China Transformed: Historical Change and the Limits of European Experience* (1997). A more general survey of the social history of the period is Peter N. Stearns and Herrick Chapman, *European Society in Upheaval: Social History Since 1750,* 3rd ed. (1992); a more interpretive study is Barrington Moore, *Social Origins of Dictatorship and Democracy* (1966). For more specialized aspects of industrial change, see L. Tilly and J. Scott, *Women, Work and Family* (1978); E. A. Wrigley, *Population and History* (1969); F. D. Scott, *Emigration and Immigration* (1963); and E. P. Thompson, *The Making of the English Working Class* (1963). On leading developments in political history, a useful volume is R. R. Palmer's *The Age of Democratic Revolution: A Political History of Europe and America, 1760–1800* (1964); a good text survey is John Merriman, *Modern European Civilization*, Vol. 2 (1996). See also Harvey Graff, ed., *Literacy and Social Development in the West* (1982); Albert Lindemann, *History of European Socialism* (1983); and David Kaiser, *Politics and War: European Conflict from Philip II to Hitler* (1990).

The Settler Societies: The West on Frontiers

FOCAL POINTS

The nineteenth century saw the development of important societies in North America, Australia, and New Zealand. These societies were largely populated by Europeans and maintained close ties with European traditions. They were called settler societies as a result. However, they were also affected by frontier conditions and by interactions with other minorities, indigenous peoples, and, in the case of the United States, Africans who had been imported as slaves. Abundant land encouraged commercial farming; there was little peasant agriculture. What were the main features of these new societies? How did their cultural patterns differ from those of Western Europe? The economic influence of these societies increased steadily, as they developed commercial agriculture and mining and, particularly in the United States, an important industrial base. What other impacts did the rise of a "frontier West" have on the world at large?

COMPARISON WITH WESTERN EUROPE

The rise of the West, including its dynamic industrial growth and steady rise in population through much of the nineteenth century, benefited several overseas regions, who in turn received the majority of their populations and much of their political and cultural inspiration from Europe. The new United States, Canada, Australia, and New Zealand built on Western traditions, but they had to combine them with the values of more diverse peoples—native inhabitants, plus, in the case of the United States, African slaves and a small but important stream of Asian immigrants. These countries also faced frontier conditions long since eradicated from Europe, and in this respect they more closely resembled contemporary Russia and Latin America. These evolving centers became increasingly important in world history from about 1870 onward, when their economic growth generated growing agricultural (and, in the case of the United States, industrial) exports.

The settler societies differed from Europe in several key respects. They did not have an established aristocracy or a peasant class. Innovative, profit-minded farmers increasingly dominated the agricultural market. They were not as wealthy as their European counterparts, although their standards of living were high; they depended greatly on capital investments from Europe. These people were not as culturally creative as Europeans, looking to them for most basic styles, although a regional art and literature took shape during the nineteenth century (mainly in the United States).

The settler societies escaped some of Europe's political tensions, establishing democracy relatively early, but they faced specific political problems of their own—as, for example, in the American Civil War between the antislavery North and the slave-holding South.

The settler societies also followed many of the same trends Western Europe did during the nineteenth century, being affected by liberalism, nationalism, and (to a lesser degree in the United States) socialism. They underwent a demographic transition that cut their birthrates. Family patterns and women's roles were redefined in a similar fashion. Western-style science held a firm place, along with currents of thought derived from Romanticism. Industrial technologies spread quickly. Canada, New Zealand, and Australia relied heavily on mineral and/or agricultural exports, but they were well rewarded because of their rich resources and use of advanced technology. Canada, as its vast territory was linked by a rail network in the later nineteenth century, also began an industrial revolution of its own, and Australia and New Zealand had important regional factory centers. The United States, importing its first equipment from England before 1820, began industrializing rapidly, particularly as it participated in railroad and heavy industrial development. On the basis of its economic power and political independence, the United States even began joining in European-style imperialism by the 1890s, taking over islands in the Caribbean and assuming rule over the Philippines and other Pacific island territory.

Residents of the settler societies—aside from the native peoples whose numbers and power declined rapidly—had something of a love-hate relationship with Western Europe. They recognized their affinity and dependence and in many ways felt part of Western civilization, although the connection was not yet acknowledged, but they were also proud of their differences and realized that their tasks of settlement and state-building differed from those of the mother countries. In addition, the United States maintained a tradition of isolation from Europe's diplomatic squabbles, while it tried (not always successfully) to discourage European intervention in the Western Hemisphere from the Monroe Doctrine (1823) onward.

THE UNITED STATES

After the American Revolution, the constitutional structure of the new United States was established in 1789. The republic launched a period of consolidation—interrupted by the War of 1812 with England—and westward expansion, as the new nation acquired the Lousiana Purchase from France in 1803. Democratic voting systems, with rights for free males, were widely completed by the 1820s. The nation's federal system led to a fairly weak central government, and many major developments were the result of state action or business initiatives. Thus, the Erie Canal, which helped link the Midwest with the East coast, was sponsored by New York State. However, the federal government was heavily involved in further westward expansion and warred with Mexico to acquire Texas in the 1840s. Within the federal government, there was also a growing tension between the Northern states and the slave-holding South, which culminated in the Civil War.

American culture began to take shape before the Civil War, personified by many New England writers and thinkers and a smaller group of painters and musicians. Also before the Civil War, new waves of European immigrants, particularly from Ireland and Germany, added to the size and mix of the American population.

The North's victory in the Civil War led to a new period of consolidation. Efforts to reform the South, beyond the abolition of slavery, were largely abandoned by 1877, as the United States settled into a succession of undistinguished presidencies and relatively modest basic divisions between the two major political parties. Settlement of the western territories continued, amid recurrent Indian wars. The pace of industrialization increased, and labor agitation led to new unions, strikes, and occasional political assassinations. Waves of immigration from southern and Eastern Europe brought much-needed labor to the nation's growing industries, and by 1914, the growing migration of African Americans from the South increased urban populations as well.

U.S. entry into the world economy, as more than a source of cotton or an investment opportunity, began in the 1870s. Massive agricultural exports combined with significant industrial ventures abroad. Several American companies, like the Singer Sewing Machine Company and International Harvester, established subsidiaries in Europe and Russia. American arms manufacturers sold weapons abroad after the Civil War's end, including among their clients a newly opened Japan. Although still importing technologies from Europe in such industries as the manufacture of chemicals, the United States contributed a number of inventions, including major developments in the uses of electricity. Even more significant were American innovations in the management of labor, where the democratic system sponsored new ways of regimenting large groups of workers. American initiatives in time and motion studies, designed by industrial engineers to speed the work process, and then the assembly line, spread widely to other industrial societies after 1900.

America's diplomatic expansion showed in not only imperialism, but also its growing involvement in other international issues; President Theodore Roosevelt, for example, sponsored the conference ending the 1904–1905 war between Russia and Japan. American cultural influence was more modest outside its borders, although the introduction of the skyscraper in Chicago soon after 1900 suggested the new union and power of art and technology. Individual American artists and scientists went to Europe to learn and sometimes made their mark as creators or thinkers, but in most cultural arenas the United States remained largely a borrower.

NEWER EUROPEAN SETTLEMENTS

At the same time as the United States expanded, Canada, Australia, and New Zealand also filled with immigrants from Europe and established parliamentary legislatures and vigorous commercial economies that placed them effectively in the general orbit of Western civilization. Like the United States, these new nations looked primarily to Europe for cultural styles and intellectual leadership. They also followed common Western patterns in such areas as family life, the role of women, and the extension of

HISTORY DEBATE

Exceptionalism

For over a century, most approaches to U.S. history have emphasized the distinctiveness of American society—its "exceptions" to the norms of European history (or, presumably, any other history). American exceptionalism features arguments that the United States was unusually democratic, or unusually open to social mobility, or unusually free from political division. An exceptionalist argument can also be used in a less benign fashion: the nation as unusually racially divided or harsh to factory workers. Exceptionalism is, of course, a comparative statement, although many historians have not bothered to compare their observations. Should the United States be regarded as a separate civilization? If so, how can one account for similar dates and patterns of industrialization, demographic transition, feminism? Should the United States be viewed as a somewhat unusual but definite part of Western civilization? If so, how can one account for the unusual per capita rates of American violence (well above European levels from the late eighteenth century to the present), the unusual hostility to the state as an active force in society? The comparative problems run deep, and they have not yet been resolved.

In terms of world history, the ongoing debate over American exceptionalism raises additional issues. If the United States differs from Europe, how much does it resemble other frontier societies, like Australia or Latin America? As the United States gained a growing world role (particularly in the twentieth century) did it behave differently from previous European great powers, like Britain, and if so, how? Finally, did the United States grow more or less different from West European nations, as it became more industrial and a great power, and as Europe became more fully democratic?

mass education and culture. Unlike the United States, however, these nations remained part of the British Empire, although with growing autonomy.

Canada, won by Britain in its wars with France during the eighteenth century, had been preserved from the uprisings of the American Revolution. Religious differences between French Catholic settlers and British rulers and settlers troubled the area recurrently, and a number of revolts occurred early in the nineteenth century. Determined not to lose this colony in addition to the United States, the British began to grant increasing self-rule after 1839. Canada was permitted to establish its own parliament and laws, while remaining under the umbrella of the larger empire. Initially, this system applied primarily to the province of Ontario, but other provinces were gradually included, creating a federal system that describes Canada to this day. French hostilities were eased somewhat by the creation of Quebec, a separate province, where the majority of French settlers remained. Massive railroad building, beginning in the 1850s, brought settlement to western territories and a great expansion of mining and commercial agriculture in the vast plains. As in the United States to the south, new immigrants from southern and particularly Eastern Europe poured in during the last decades of the century, attracted by Canada's growing commercial development and spurring even further gains.

Britain's Australian colonies originated in 1788 when a ship deposited convicts to establish a penal settlement at Sydney. Australia's only previous inhabitants had been the aborigines, a hunting-and-gathering people who were in no position to resist European settlement and exploration. Unfamiliar European diseases and guns took a predictable toll. By 1840, Australia had 140,000 European inhabitants, based mainly on a prosperous sheep-growing agriculture that provided needed wool for British industries. The exportation of convicts ceased in 1853, by which time most settlers were free immigrants. The discovery of gold in 1851 led to further pioneering, which resulted in a population of over one million by 1861. As in Canada, major provinces were granted self-government with a multiparty parliamentary system. A unified federal nation was proclaimed on the first day of the twentieth century. By this time, considerable industrialization, a growing socialist party, and significant welfare legislation had developed.

New Zealand, discovered by the Dutch in the seventeenth century and explored by the English in 1770, began to receive British attention after 1814. Here the Polynesian hunting-and-gathering people, the Maoris, were well organized politically. Missionary efforts converted many of them to Christianity between 1814 and the 1840s. The British government, fearful of French interest in the area, moved to take official control in 1840, and considerable European immigration followed. New Zealand settlers relied heavily on agriculture (including sheep growing), selling initially to Australia's booming gold-rush population and then to Britain. Wars with the

This depiction of sheep-washing in the Australian outback shows one of the export staples of the Australian economy and the nation's frontier expansion, from the nineteenth century onward.

Maoris plagued the 1860s, but after the Maori defeat generally good relations were established, with Maoris winning some representation in Parliament. As in Canada and Australia, a parliamentary system was created that allowed the new nation to rule itself as a dominion of the British Empire, without interference from the mother country.

Like the United States, Canada, New Zealand, and Australia each had distinct national flavors and national issues. These new countries were far more dependent on the European, particularly the British, economy than was the United States. Industrialization did not overshadow commercial agriculture and mining, even in Australia, so that exchanges with Europe remained unusually important. Nevertheless, these countries followed the basic patterns of Western civilization from this point onward, from political forms to key leisure activities. Currents of liberalism, socialism, modern art, and scientific education, which described Western civilization to 1900 and beyond, thus largely characterized these important new countries.

It was these areas, finally, along with the United States and parts of Latin America, particularly Brazil and Argentina, that received new waves of European emigrants during the nineteenth century. Although Europe's population growth rate slowed after 1800, it still advanced rapidly on the basis of previous gains—that is, as more children reached adulthood and had children of their own. Europe's expansion was, in fact, greater than Asia's in percentage terms until the twentieth century, and Europe's export of people helped explain how Western societies could take shape in such distant areas.

CONCLUSION: SPECIAL FEATURES OF SETTLER SOCIETIES

The extension of Western society through most of North America as well as Australia and New Zealand depended on the fortuitous absence of large previous populations, compounded by the continued ravages of Western-imported diseases on the indigenous people in these locations. Other parts of the world, more thickly inhabited, had quite different experiences under the impact of Western influence and some outright settlement. The spread of the settler societies also reflected the new power of Western industrialization. Huge areas could now be populated quickly thanks to steamships and rails, while remaining in close contact with the Western home base in Europe. The expansion of the West revealed the power of Western values and institutions, as colonists deliberately introduced most of the patterns that had prevailed in Europe, from parliaments to Western-defined standards for women and children.

SUGGESTED WEBSITES

On the revolutionary war in America, see *http://www.revwar.com*; on Eli Whitney, the controversial American inventor, see *http://www.eliwhitney.org/ew.htm*.

SUGGESTED READINGS

On U.S. history, in addition to several excellent textbooks with good reading lists (e.g., Gary Nash and Julie R. Jeffrey, *The American People: Creating a Nation and a Society* [1990], and James Kirby Martin, et al., *America and Its People,* 2nd ed. [2001]), see Eugene D. Genovese, *Roll, Jordan, Roll: The World the Slaves Made* (1974); Thomas Cochran, *Frontiers of Change: Early Industrialization in America* (1981); Steven Mintz and Susan Kellog, *Domestic Revolutions: A Social History of American Family Life* (1988); and Albert W. Niemi, *United States Economic History* (1987).

On Canada, Australia, and New Zealand, see J. M. Bumstead, *A History of Canada* (1992); Alastair Davidson, *The Formation of the Australian State* (1991); Charles Wilson, *Australia, 1788–1988: The Creation of a Nation* (1988); and Miles Fairburn, *The Ideal Society and Its Enemies: Foundations of Modern New Zealand Society, 1850–1900* (1990).

World Economy and Western Imperialism: Africa and South Asia

FOCAL POINTS

European industrialization, supplemented by the growing industrial power of the United States, inevitably transformed the world economy. Merchants ventured forth from the industrialized nations, seeking markets and raw materials all over the world. Pressure to participate in world commerce increased everywhere. Previously isolated economies, like Japan, now had to interact with the West. Economies already selling to the West now had to increase those levels of export; this was the case in Latin America. The attack on the slave trade was another force calling for innovation. Industrialization also prompted the West to acquire new colonies, particularly in Africa and Asia, and to intensify its colonial control of places like India. Ironically, Western nations did not mostly trade with their own colonies, but they nevertheless sought secure resources and military bases. For the areas involved, new Western control brought massive change. How did heightened colonialism affect India? What was the impact of Western domination in Africa? What kinds of resistance to the West developed? Think of Western intrusion and national resistance as forces for change. How was India different, as a result, in 1900 from what it had been in 1780? How was Africa beginning to alter its previous patterns?

CHANGING THE WORLD ECONOMY

Even aside from the new frontier societies, the industrial revolution greatly changed the relationship between Western civilization and the rest of the world. New patterns became most obvious toward the end of the nineteenth century in a frantic burst of imperialism, but in fact, events had been taking shape for many decades as industrialization's impact took hold.

The links in the world economy expanded steadily. New and speedier shipping played a vital role, making the crossing of the oceans a matter of a week or two rather than months. At the same time, railroads reached into continental interiors. More rapid communication, provided by the telegraph and later the telephone and the wireless, transmitted an unprecedented amount of information about business conditions around the globe. Levels of international trade rose as a result. By the 1830s, many industrial concerns were opening branch offices in major cities in various parts of the world.

416

Along with the great increase in volume came some alterations in the nature of the world economy. The industrial revolution gave the West new quantities of manufactured products to sell, including factory equipment, locomotives, and steamships. The West had already sold manufactured goods to other societies, but its capacity was now literally revolutionized, as was its intense need to find available markets for its soaring output. Europe and North America also had capital to export, particularly after 1850. Earnings from early industrialization begged for profitable investment outlets; although domestic economies provided some of these, there was an avid search for opportunities, at higher interest rates, in less industrialized areas. The development of the U.S. West, including the rapid expansion of a railroad network, owed much to British and French investment, but significant capital also went to Latin America, Africa, and Asia—at a price. Western investment in Russia also increased rapidly.

New Western opportunities to export industrial products and capital were matched by growing needs for imports. There was one huge change: Slaves were no longer necessary. The transatlantic slave trade was abolished between 1807 and 1834, mainly on British initiative; as of the latter date, slavery was ended in the British colonies. In succeeding decades, slavery was abolished in the Americas and elsewhere.

Cheap labor, however, continued to be essential. Nonindustrial societies intensified their commitment to food exports, as Europe's urbanization and growing wealth increased the market for both staples, like wheat and beef, and specialty products, like coffee and sugar. The need for raw materials became even more intense. Western transportation and recreational requirements opened a wide market for rubber, for example, which could be produced only in tropical areas. Growing production of steel made certain rare alloys vital, whereas other metals (such as copper) and chemicals were sought outside the West as well.

In brief, with the important exception of the end to massive international slave trading, the world economy proceeded along the lines previously established: The West supplied more expensive manufactured products, while most of the rest of the world exchanged food and raw materials. The earlier result—a fundamental economic advantage to the West—persisted as well, particularly because until 1900 most of the world's trade was handled by Western ships and merchant firms. However, the new volume of economic exchange made the disparity between the West and most other civilizations far more significant than it had previously been. Spurred by Western merchants and capital, producers in other regions found themselves more deeply affected by the world economy than ever before. Huge numbers of Latin American peasants, for example, were now drawn into the production of coffee or hemp for ropemaking, and away from their traditional village agriculture. The influx of Western capital into mining, transportation facilities, and market agriculture literally around the world also increased the direct involvement of millions of people in the international economy. There was another significant change: no part of the world could now isolate itself from Western commercial pressure.

The solidification of the world economy was recognized and furthered by new European-sponsored economic arrangements, from the 1850s onward. International regulations facilitated telegraphic links; the new Postal Union systematized worldwide deliveries of mail.

HISTORY DEBATE

Causes of the Abolition of Slavery

In 1833, arguing for the abolition of slavery in all British colonies, the British Colonial Secretary explained the need in terms of the "liberal and humane spirit of the age." For over a century, historians echoed this explanation. It was new, humanitarian ideas that led to the abolition of slavery, in places like Britain, France, and the northern United States, after centuries of acceptance.

Then in 1944, a West Indian historian, Eric Williams, took a radically different approach. He claimed that it was not humanitarianism at all, but economic self-interest, which explained the shifting viewpoint. British and other industrial capitalists were now in a position of power where the world economy was concerned. Slave economies were fading within this context. It was not idealism, but simple materialism that now put slave owners on the defensive.

More recent work, by historians like David B. Davis and Seymour Drescher, has complicated this picture even further. Drescher has shown that the slave economies were still very profitable apart from slavery, so it was not simple materialism that prompted the institution's abolition. Davis argues, however, that industrial capitalists now needed to defend wage labor, being imposed (amid great hardship) on European workers themselves. To do this and distract workers from their own plight, they attacked slavery. Again, material self-interest rather than humanitarianism ruled the day, but such an analysis is complex. Drescher defends humanitarianism a bit more, but contends that it was popularized among artisans and other people frightened by the industrial economy, who used abolitionism to bolster their own sense of morality.

The current effort, then, is to combine a recognition that there were new humanitarian arguments involved in this historic change, with a belief that key changes in the capitalist economy were involved as well.

Can you think of other debates about the extent of idealism vs. material self-interest in explaining historical change?

Two other points are worth mentioning: First, during the nineteenth century as a whole, as abolitionism spread in the nations of the Americas, rapid world population growth made it relatively easy to replace the slave trade with imported workers from Asia and Europe. Second, although slavery was increasingly abolished, it was often replaced with systems that were still coercive to some extent. For example, immigrant workers might be tied by indenture contracts. Company stores might place workers in debt, so they could not legally leave or change jobs. Practices of this sort continue into our own time.

How do these points affect the idealism vs. materialism debate?

The expansion of the global economic structure under Western control was a basic force in world history throughout the nineteenth century, affecting all other civilizations. Its impact was enhanced by the new surge of outright imperialism, based on growing European appetites and new military technology such as the repeating rifle. Western European nations and the United States claimed huge chunks of territory, from the islands of the Pacific to the interior of Africa. Land previously acquired, particularly in India and Southeast Asia, was now more closely controlled, as Europeans had both the military and organizational means and the economic need to go beyond port cities and loose alliances with regional governments in the interior. The expansion of a Western empire and the subsequent changes in its nature bore most heavily on three non-Western regions: sub-Saharan Africa, India, and Southeast Asia. But, the threat of imperialist control, along with the expansion of the West's world economic role, affected all civilizations by 1900, accentuating the problem of what to do about the power and example of the West.

This chapter examines the new imperialism and the areas it most directly touched; the following chapters consider the varying reactions of other civilizations to what became, by 1900, a set of common themes in modern world history.

THE REASONS FOR IMPERIALISM: MOTIVES AND MEANS

At the end of the eighteenth century, the empires of Western nations consisted of North and South America, save for the newly independent United States; India, although the process of British control had yet to be completed; the islands of Indonesia; and scattered port holdings, particularly in parts of sub-Saharan Africa. The bulk of the Latin American empire was lost soon after 1800, through wars of independence; this civilization nevertheless remained closely tied to the Western economy.

By 1900, Western empires included all the 1800 holdings outside Latin America plus most of the mainland of Southeast Asia, as the French conquered Indochina (present-day Vietnam, Laos, and Cambodia), while Britain seized Malaya and effectively controlled Thailand and Burma; plus the entire continent of Africa with minor exceptions, the most important of which was the proudly independent kingdom of Ethiopia; Australia and New Zealand; and the various Pacific islands including Hawaii, Samoa, and Tahiti, which were divided mainly among Britain, France, Germany, and the United States. Western nations also had colonies along the coast of China, holdings on the eastern coast of the Arabian peninsula, and a growing influence in Persia, Afghanistan, and parts of the Ottoman Empire. Britain proudly claimed that the sun never set on its empire, because of its worldwide span, and to many other Westerners the world seemed, for all intents and purposes, a Western holding. Never before had so much territory been acquired in so little time.

During the nineteenth century, moreover, the Western concept of empire changed. Most earlier colonies had been regarded primarily as market outposts. Catholic powers, notably Spain and Portugal, had thought also in terms of Christian conversion, which extended European control in Latin America and the Philippines.

The British colonization of the eastern coast of North America had also been an important exception to the common pattern. Outside the New World, limited control for trading purposes described the Western approach. After about 1800, this guiding viewpoint began to change rapidly. Trade alone was not enough when new market agriculture, transportation networks, and investment outlets had to be established. The redefinition of the world economy alone suggested more extensive penetration. Furthermore, Europeans and North Americans began to develop a greater sense of cultural superiority. Protestant groups now joined Catholics in seeking missionary contacts. More generally, Westerners began to claim a clearer mission to bring civilization to the peoples of the world—civilization, of course, being as the West defined it. The English poet, Rudyard Kipling, described a widely held sentiment in arguing that the West had such superior moral and political values that it had a responsibility—the "white man's burden"—to reshape the rest of the world. Missionaries brought not only Christianity, but also Western styles of dress and approaches to education and medical care. Business managers, convinced of the inferiority of "native" ways, tried to tell non-Westerners how to work and organize their businesses. Imperial governments sought to redefine marriage customs, caste systems, and tribal politics. In both old colonies and new, European imperialism now meant an effort to establish effective government and supervision over wide areas.

Why did Western imperialism change and advance into so many new parts of the world? The West's growing technological sophistication assumed a major role although colonialists also played on ethnic and other divisions in the societies they conquered. European imperialism in Africa can be explained in large part by the ability of Western ships, steam-propelled, to navigate up the previously impenetrable African rivers. This allowed contacts with the interior that no people, including Africans themselves, had ever before achieved. Steam-driven iron boats were also basic to the European penetration of China. Western facility in weaponry continued to increase, even as Africans and Asians gained access to old-fashioned rifles. By the late

Fight between the German army and native troops in Tanzania: early twentieth-century African art.

nineteenth century, Western soldiers were armed with repeating rifles, which did not require separate reloading and thus represented a huge advantage. The introduction of the machine gun was another fundamental step. Winston Churchill, later the British prime minister, described an 1898 battle near the Upper Nile, pitting a small British force armed with 20 early machine guns against 40,000 Muslim troops:

> The infantry fired steadily and stolidly, without hurry or excitement, for the enemy were far away and the officers careful. Besides, the soldiers were interested in the work and took great pains. . . . And all the time out on the plain on the other side bullets were shearing through flesh, smashing and splintering bone . . . valiant men were struggling on through a hell of whistling metal, exploding shell, and spurting dust—suffering, despairing, dying.

When the battle ended, 11,000 Muslims and 48 British soldiers were dead, and the British had conquered the territory now known as the Sudan.

If technology, backed by medical advances that allowed Westerners to avoid contracting many tropical diseases, accounts for a key part of the Western advantage, particularly in Africa but to an extent elsewhere, it does not explain the motives for the new imperialism. Gains resulting from the industrial revolution, including technology but also improved organization, better health care, and expanded literacy, fed the growing belief that the West was superior to the rest of the world, with a right and duty to rule. This attitude now combined with Christian beliefs in religious superiority, a current that had been evidenced in earlier Western expansion attempts from the Crusades onward. Economic motives played a prominent role as well. Not only were Europeans eager for markets and raw materials, they were also anxious about the stability of their own changing economy. Even confident U.S. business leaders sought secure markets and supplies through colonies or, in Central America, semicolonies. Many people believed that domestic sales and supplies were insufficient for an economy which depended on growth. They also saw imperialism as a way to excite and divert ordinary people who might otherwise join in social protest—and indeed imperial conquest did arouse popular passions in Europe and the United States, aided by the stirring headlines of the new mass press.

Certain groups in the West, left behind in the rush to industrialize, found solace in their empires. Aristocrats, increasingly displaced at home, could win prestige as imperial bureaucrats, living the good life while ruling the natives. Christian missionaries sometimes experienced greater satisfaction in preaching to the heathen than in facing the gradual decline of religion in their own lands. Individual adventurers, tired of the increasingly bureaucratic life of industrial corporations, found excitement in seeking fame and fortune in distant places. In various ways, then, imperialism expressed social tensions generated by industrialization, as well as the power that the industrial revolution provided.

The most direct factors in the imperialist scramble, however, were the claims and rivalries of various states in the West. Nationalist loyalty motivated many explorers and adventurers, like the German Karl Peters, who staked Germany's claims to Tanganyika in eastern Africa, because of his desire to see his country assume its rightful place among the great powers—and who operated at first without official state backing. Patriotic assertions prompted European governments to intervene on behalf of individual missionaries or business entrepreneurs, who could not be tampered with lest national honor be impugned. Above all, chauvinist rivalries spurred new states to claim a share in imperial glory and old states to protect their existing holdings through expansion. Britain acquired many new colonies—such as Egypt, which guarded the quickest route to India after the building of the Suez Canal—to defend old ones against possible rivals. France sought additional territory in North Africa to protect its first North African colony, Algeria. Newly imperialist countries included Italy, which won important territory in North Africa; Belgium, which acquired the vast Congo region; Germany, which displayed its greatness by taking possession of two major African colonies plus areas in China and the Pacific. And to this list may be added the United States, which tended to oppose imperialism in principle, in part because of a long preoccupation with overland expansion to the west and in part because of its own national experience as a colony, but which in fact acquired extensive Pacific holdings, including the Philippines, won from Spain in the Spanish-American War in 1898, and several West Indian islands, most notably Puerto Rico. The appearance of new imperialist nations heightened a growing French desire, after 1871, to gain colonies to compensate for defeat at Germany's hands back home in the Franco-Prussian War. The various pressures for conquest, which developed particularly after 1870, added to the belief that every available territory should be claimed as quickly as possible, for the sake of national security and national glory. Ironically, this same spirit of heedless rivalry would later intensify conflict in Europe, when, after 1900, all available lands were taken and attention returned to competition nearer home.

IMPERIALISM IN INDIA AND SOUTHEAST ASIA

The new European imperialism focused particularly on conquering relatively populous territories that had important traditions of their own. It involved, in other words, ruling millions of other people and encountering considerable resistance in the name of established values. Most of the new colonies received European administrators and some business entrepreneurs, missionaries, doctors, and teachers, but few ordinary settlers. Important Italian immigration occurred in parts of North Africa, and some Europeans established themselves in the rich agricultural lands of East Africa as a new and privileged minority, but these were exceptional patterns.

European imperialism in Asia was completed—with the British conquest of India and extension of influence to Thailand and Burma and the French takeover of Indochina—without in any sense drawing these regions into the orbit of Western civilization. Revealingly, Christian missionary efforts in India and Southeast Asia had little success, winning only small minorities of converts—a clear sign of the continued validity of traditional cultures. The new imperialism had a vital impact nevertheless. In India, Britain's rule had far more sweeping consequences than most previous periods of foreign control, including the recent Mughal empire. Indeed, India and Dutch Indonesia became showcases for the kind of penetration that nineteenth-century imperialists sought. With such colonization, in turn, came important resistance, which itself established new patterns while confirming some older cultural values. One important result was that British rule lasted a considerably shorter time than had previous foreign occupations. This fact suggests some interesting features about the British commitment, which never evolved into a fully Indian regime, while also revealing important changes in the Indian political tradition itself, which became less tolerant of foreign rule.

INDIA

As Britain completed its conquest of India during the first half of the nineteenth century, it began also to take a more active hand in Indian affairs. Control by the British government substantially replaced that of the East India Company, and at the same time the respect British officials had for Indian culture declined. India became a place to change, to Westernize. Thus, laws (not totally unlike those of the early Mughals) sought to limit child marriage and religious sacrifices; Hindu converts to Christianity were rewarded with government jobs.

British rule during most of the nineteenth century had a significant impact on Indian politics. The very fact of unification of the entire subcontinent was a major

British colonial officials at Delhi. A herald reading a proclamation that declares Queen Victoria empress of India. (The Granger Collection)

development. British rule permitted considerable autonomy for individual areas, with regional princes allowed to maintain governments under British advisors, but a uniform code of laws, derived from British precedent, was imposed over the entire country. Administration became steadily larger and more efficient. Direct taxation, based on land values, replaced earlier regional collection. Britain established tax levels it regarded as equitable; however, the fact that it gathered taxes directly, rather than using regional lords and village headmen, who in earlier times determined taxes based on how much their clients were able to pay, meant that taxes tended to rise—a source of considerable discontent among Indians who were unaccustomed to dealing with government without intermediary patrons. Britain also established a civil service, based on an examination system. Top officials were always British until 1864, and mainly so thereafter, but lower-level officials were drawn from high-caste Hindus, who were thus exposed to Western administrative ideas.

British rule had considerable cultural impact as well. Although relatively few Indians converted to Christianity, new missionary pressures prompted Hindu leaders to reexamine their own practices. They tended to downplay the worship of lesser gods, although this custom continued at popular levels, and to emphasize the monotheistic elements of Hinduism. This reaction was similar to that which had greeted earlier Muslim influence. It involved an attempt to adapt traditions to the standards of India's new leadership.

Still more important, for Indian culture, was a British-sponsored school system, seen as vital to reversing the decline of Indian education that had occurred under the later Mughals. British-sponsored secondary schools and universities were bent on teaching Western values. As one British liberal put it: "The great end should not have been to teach Hindu learning, but useful learning." This meant increased emphasis on science and technology, not totally foreign to Indian traditions in any event, and modern (mainly European) history. Many schools taught their subjects in English, which meant that English became a second language among many upper-caste Hindus and Muslim leaders.

Economic development was another British target. During the 1850s, the British began to construct railroad and telegraph systems. The new facilities aided the administration and military control of the vast country, but they also brought some prosperity. The governor general stated, in 1853:

> A system of railways . . . would surely and rapidly give rise to the same encouragement of enterprise . . . and some similar progress in social improvement that have marked the introduction of improved and extended communication in various kingdoms of the western world.

By 1900, India had over 26,500 miles of rails, plus a number of new roads and canals. Britain also encouraged better agricultural methods, again along Western lines, and some industrial development. The subcontinent was no longer seen as a colony simply to exploit, but as a place where substantial economic activity could be pursued.

Socially, the British sought to change the caste system. Britain allowed different castes to mix in prisons and on trains, and lower-caste members could sue upper-caste people in British courts.

Railroads in India: change in an established civilization. This is a railroad station near Calcutta, 1867.

The British also tried, although cautiously, to alter conditions for women. The biggest short-term impact of such attempts actually was an increase in women's economic difficulties, by reducing traditional manufacturing jobs. However, this ramification was not clearly understood, as respectable women were, according to the Western viewpoint, no longer supposed to work. Disdain for Hindu customs led to more explicit changes, as British observers claimed that, "Nothing can exceed the habitual contempt which the Hindus entertain for their women." British officials attacked female infanticide and the practice of sati, and some Indian reformers soon joined the call for change. Colonial administrators also sought to modify marriage laws, by allowing widows to remarry. Here too was a theme that would continue to inspire Indian reformers, including later nationalists.

The British presence had mixed results. Many measures did not reach the Indian masses, who remained largely illiterate and wedded to traditional family and religious practices. The caste system persisted for the most part. On the other hand, some Indians, particularly those educated in the upper schools, welcomed aspects of the Western occupation. Rammohun Roy blasted traditional education and praised the British for promoting "a more liberal and enlightened system of instruction, embracing mathematics, natural philosophy, chemistry, anatomy, with other useful sciences."

Important resistance developed as well. Many Indians detested the more efficient tax collection, looking back fondly on the days when they could count on the informal patronage of local elites. Upper-caste Indians resented attacks on the caste system, and many lower-caste people also preferred traditional demarcations, disliking what they perceived as the demeaning treatment of the upper castes. Hindus and

Muslims alike were suspicious of Christian missionary efforts and certain aspects of the new schools. Muslims also resented British preference for Hindus in government posts; they increasingly saw themselves as a beleaguered religious minority rather than, as in many past centuries, a ruling group. Rumors abounded, amid fears and resentments about British influence. For example, many Indians spread the word that colonial officials would not only allow widows to remarry, against Hindu custom, they would force them to. From various sources, then, tradition encouraged hostility to the new Western administration.

This antagonism led to one of the great nineteenth-century uprisings against Western imperialism. The Sepoy Rebellion of 1857 pitted Indian soldiers in the imperial army, numbering about 200,000, against 16,000 British troops stationed on the subcontinent. Many sepoys were of high caste and resented British officers. They also were disgusted by European customs such as eating beef; they insisted on traditional religious practices, for which the British refused to provide facilities. The incident that touched off the revolt was the greasing of bullets to fit in a newly introduced rifle. Animal fat was used for grease, and rumors spread among Hindu troops that the grease was from cows, among Muslims that it was from pork—in both cases, a highly offensive practice. Mutiny resulted, and for a time the rebels held the city of Delhi and much of north-central India, massacring many English families. British reinforcements broke the mutiny in 1858, aided by the fact that most Indian civilians had not joined the protest.

Britain responded to this challenge by introducing limited political representation for Indians, through local governments; they also established an advisory legislative council. Thus, some Indians gained new experience in parliamentary matters. Britain also ruled that no native of India should be barred from any job or office because of skin color or religion, and while Indians advanced only slowly into the upper reaches of bureaucracy, there were some gradual improvements. The number of Indians with civil service experience grew steadily. Britain also increased centralized supervision of the Indian regions, encouraged English-language education, and attempted new social reforms including the abolition of slavery (never a very extensive institution in India since the classical age). In other words, pressures to Westernize intensified, as Britain stepped up its efforts to alter the colony without undue repression.

During the later nineteenth century, moreover, the Indian economy began to develop in new directions. Many estate owners and peasants were encouraged to grow crops for a world market. During the American Civil War, for example, the production of cotton in India increased to compensate for the decreased availability of cotton in the American South. Some factories also were opened, in textiles and metallurgy, and directed by Indian entrepreneurs using equipment imported from Britain. In 1886, Jamshedi Tata, an Indian from a wealthy Bombay family, established a large steel plant in western Bengal, near India's richest coal and iron deposits. Although still dependent on imported machinery, the Indian steel industry began to export some of its products soon after 1900. Industrial development remained rather localized, and no full industrial revolution was underway, but change was taking place.

Economic transformation was a double-edged sword in India, however. British efforts to encourage higher agricultural production, including the sponsorship of large irrigation projects to reduce traditional problems with periodic droughts, stimulated rapid population growth in an already crowded country. Government attempts to introduce some Western medical procedures, through inoculations and sanitary reforms, worked to the same end. India's high birthrate, linked to the traditional desire to have enough sons to protect parents into their old age, rose further, and the death rate, although still high by Western standards, declined. Population growth seriously limited the effects of economic development, as did continued competition from British factories that displaced hundreds of thousands of traditional manufacturing workers; the prosperity of the average Indian did not increase.

Many Indian traditionalists continued to resent British practices. At the same time, a new opposition force emerged among educated Indians concerned about their own national identity but also influenced by key Western political and educational values that, in their view, argued against undemocratic foreign rule. Several Indian newspapers sprang up, resulting in lively political discourse. The first Indian National Congress, with Hindu and Muslim delegates drawn mainly from the ranks of civil servants, met in 1885. Its initial demands were modest, focusing on greater opportunities for Indians in the imperial bureaucracy. From this base, a nationalist sentiment spread among educated groups, particularly Hindus. This represented a new loyalty in Indian history, cutting across caste, regional, and to some extent religious lines. Nationalism encouraged Indians to think in terms of growing political freedom as well as a culture independent of Western influence. Successive National Congresses became increasingly vigorous in requesting reforms. They focused not only on civil service jobs, but also on British economic control, seeking the creation of an India that could advance to the ranks of industrial nations on its own. As one 1910 speaker stated: "India has come to be regarded as a plantation of England, giving raw products to be shipped by British moguls in British ships, to be worked into fabrics . . . to be re-exported to India by British merchants." Here was a resentment of the Western-dominated world economy that would echo through the twentieth century in many civilizations.

Indian nationalism imitated European, and particularly British, political beliefs, while insisting on India's special qualities. Nationalist leaders opted for an inclusive definition of nationalism—including various religious, racial, and social groups—unlike the narrower ethnic nationalism that had developed in Germany. Key questions of precise definition, however, were overshadowed by the obvious need to reduce British control.

Before 1900, Indian nationalism did not pose a major threat to British rule. Periodic riots by peasant groups, against taxes or census taking (seen as a government plot to raise taxes), or in the name of traditional religion, were a greater problem, resulting in the assassination of several British officials.

India by 1900 was by no means Westernized, but it had altered substantially because of both British initiatives and the new interests of Indian leaders themselves, particularly in education, nationalist politics, and industrial management. Indian cultural vitality had in many ways increased, spurred by the revival of Hinduism and active use of traditional artistic and literary styles. At the same time, gaps had opened between Indian leaders, mostly upper caste in any event and now exposed to Western ideas and Indian nationalism, and the masses of Indians who revered traditional forms and viewed changes largely as impositions—new taxes, new and often poorly paid wage labor—by British or Indian masters.

SOUTHEAST ASIA

Many developments in Southeast Asia resembled trends in India—as had long been the case. The regional politics of this area continued, as different European powers controlled different countries. There was no substantial redrawing of the religious map, although a minority of Southeast Asians, particularly in French Indochina, converted to Christianity. In Dutch Indonesia, the government built railroads and created a Dutch-language education system for the elite, along with a growing bureaucracy and new tax structure. New laws attempted to regulate the planters' use of native labor on the large estates devoted to export production. Essentially manorial controls, involving significant rights over peasant labor, were converted after 1870 to a wage labor system.

Particularly during the second half of the nineteenth century, increasing numbers of Southeast Asian peasants were drawn into a market economy, employed as workers producing goods ranging from spices and tea to rubber, for sale on the world market. Many of these goods commanded relatively low prices and, as a result, the system depended on low wages.

Imperial governments, as in India, began to introduce Western-style administrative measures. Bureaucrats busily collected census data. The independence of local leaders, including village headmen, was reduced. New police forces attempted to regulate crime and local unrest. As in India, more efficient administration and some agricultural improvements led to population increases, putting new pressure on available land.

Nevertheless, although traditionalists bitterly resented many European impositions, there was little systematic protest against imperialism before 1900. Nationalism was slow to surface, although soon after 1900, Indonesian civil servants sought greater equality with Dutch officials. Some local peasant uprisings occurred, expressing the need for land and resentment against tax collection, and in Indonesia a movement to renew Islamic fervor took shape. But, the main wave of protest against European control, as in India, still awaited the future.

IMPERIALISM IN AFRICA

New Western penetration of sub-Saharan Africa became a dominant force only after the 1860s. During most of the nineteenth century, African history essentially followed an established route, with scattered innovations, although economic changes were significant. In the northern region, below the Sahara Desert, Islam continued to spread through the popular missionary and holy war movement that had evolved in the later eighteenth century. A literature began to develop in Swahili, East Africa's written language linked to Islam. Later in the nineteenth century, the dissemination of Islam was furthered by Western imperialism, for Islam was seen as a vital, well-organized religion that had the merit of not being Western. Even before this, Islam attacked many African cultural traditions as superstitions in the regions it touched, much as Western and Middle Eastern popular beliefs had been challenged by monotheism some centuries before. This process, in turn, helped launch a painful but exciting redefinition of African civilization to which Western imperialism would ultimately contribute as well.

In West Africa, before imperialism took firm hold, Britain and France gradually acquired new port territories. Britain, for example, took over the key city of Lagos, in what is now Nigeria; France, the city of Dakar, in Senegal. In European-controlled

Imperialism in Africa

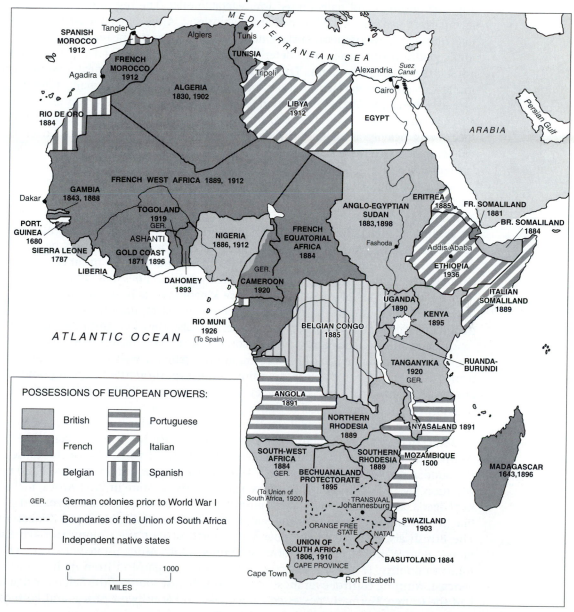

POSSESSIONS OF EUROPEAN POWERS:

- British
- Portuguese
- French
- Italian
- Belgian
- Spanish

GER. German colonies prior to World War I

- - - - Boundaries of the Union of South Africa

Independent native states

0   1000
MILES

port cities, a small number of Africans converted to Christianity and had other contact with Western values. Some began to think in terms of developing African states along liberal political lines, although this remained as yet a dream. The West African economy was badly disoriented by the end of the slave trade, while Western abolitionism led to new ventures in the interior as expeditionary forces sought to root out remaining slave traders. The end of the international slave trade also resulted in efforts to compensate for the lost slave revenue by novel exports. Slave shipments to the Middle East continued, but a new export agriculture also developed, featuring crops like peanuts and palms (used for vegetable oils). The response of Africans to new markets has been called a "peasant revolution." Although some Africans benefited from this development, enslavement within the continent increased. The economic position of women also deteriorated; the growing use of women as slaves enhanced patriarchal systems. These changes foreshadowed the greater world economic exploitation of Africa under imperialism. Finally, two small states were formed, Liberia and Sierra Leone, by freed slaves from the United States and British West Indian colonies, respectively. The freed slaves formed an elite governing group, which was heavily influenced by American and British governments, over the African majority in these states; here was another source of new Western influence in this region.

Greater change occurred in southern Africa. The migration of Boer settlers from the Cape province increased when Britain acquired control of this colony from Holland during the Napoleonic Wars. Boer farmers conducted many battles with African forces through the 1830s, gradually enlarging their own zone of settlement. At the same time, Bantu groups north of this zone faced crowded conditions because of their own population growth. The result was the formation of a number of tightly knit regional monarchies, organized along the traditional lines of a divine monarchy with highly ceremonial rule. Some of these kingdoms, such as the Zulus in Natal (now a state in South Africa), developed well-organized military forces, able to hold their own against not only other Bantu states, but also the Boers until the late 1880s.

In sum, most of sub-Saharan Africa continued patterns of regional government, mainly under a divine kingship, and traditional religion well into the later nineteenth century. Scattered European gains, more export-oriented farming, and the growth of Islam constituted new forces in some regions. On the other hand, there was no sweeping technological or political transformation.

Then came the new imperialism, bursting into this civilization with full force after 1870. To many European leaders, as well as many Africans, its force seemed bewildering. The British foreign minister lamented in 1891, "I do not know the cause of this sudden revolution, but there it is." And there it was, indeed. By conquest and negotiation, by 1900, Britain had developed an extensive empire in West Africa, including Nigeria, and a north–south axis running from South Africa toward Egypt and embracing the modern nations of the Sudan, Kenya, Uganda, Zambia, and Zimbabwe. The British also conquered the Boer states north of its Cape Colony through the bloody Boer War of 1899–1902, forming a united South African state with a large European minority. France concentrated on east–west expansion from its holdings in Senegal, winning control over most of the territory just south of the Sahara. Belgium had the Congo, Germany possessed Tanganyika and Southwest Africa, and Portugal increased its control over Angola and Mozambique.

World Profiles

John Mensah Sarbah (1865–1910)

European imperialism created complex pressures for new African leaders. John Mensah Sarbah chose a path of utilizing Western standards in defense of African rights. A member of the Fante tribe on the Gold Coast, in the area now known as Ghana, Mensah Sarbah was a scholarly man who trained in English law and was the first African from his region to be admitted to the English bar. Mensah Sarbah used English constitutional arguments to claim that the British had no right to rule the Gold Coast and were consistently violating established African laws. He actively urged expanded responsibilities for educated Africans who could preserve Africa's traditional communal virtues. His multivolume *Fanti National Constitution* (1906) followed from his elaborate research on customary law. He also founded several organizations designed to protect traditional African rights to land ownership, and his arguments did secure African land titles in British legislation of 1898. Mensah Sarbah thus worked in two worlds, an early example of a leader striving to unite Western methods and African goals. Was this a more effective approach than outright violent opposition to imperialism?

John Mensah Sarbah

These new empires were not won without hard fighting. France and Britain both faced bitter resistance from Muslim forces below the Sahara, leading to battles such as the one Winston Churchill described (see p. 421). Full subjugation of this region occurred only in the late 1890s, because Muslim armies were well organized, if poorly armed, and consumed with a spirit of jihad, or holy war, against the intruders. In both their colonies, Germans met with vigorous African resistance, which was vanquished only by brutal massacres in which tens of thousands of Africans were killed. European intervention was compounded by frequent insensitivity toward local customs, as the imperialists tried to export or destroy religious symbols and some of the ceremonial apparatus of the divine kingship. In West Africa, for example, a British governor provoked a war when he tried to seize the traditional Golden Stool of the Ashanti king, to send back to Queen Victoria.

The consequences of new European rule in Africa were dramatic, although colonialism by no means overturned all African customs. As in India, Western institutions were only one among many forces at work. Furthermore, by 1914, the European regimes were barely in place, and much of the impact of the West would become clear only later. Different imperialist countries followed somewhat different policies in their colonies. France, for example, was eager to educate an African elite in Western ways, whereas Britain concentrated more on basic education and medical care for a larger number of people while discouraging the formation of a new elite. However, some main lines of development were emerging by 1914, across the new political divisions of the continent.

The first consequence was the new political units themselves. Africa had always been divided, but now it was broken up into states artificially created by accidents of European competition and timing. None of the colonial states had any clear precedent. Many mixed different tribal, language, and religious groups that had long been rivals. A few regional kingdoms persisted under British supervision in southern Africa, and Ethiopia remained independent, defeating Italy in an 1896 war. Otherwise, however, the map of the civilization was entirely, and from an African standpoint arbitrarily, redrawn. European administrations tried to impose Western concepts of property law, sanitary regulation, and police on their new domains. Few Africans by 1914 were included in the new imperial bureaucracies.

The cultural impact of the Europeans was initially limited. Intense missionary activity created an important Christian minority in many parts of Africa, which added to the culture's religious diversity. But, most Africans remained polytheist or, in the north, Muslim. Some combined Christianity with traditional beliefs, like the witch doctors who converted but still prayed to other spirits for protection, relying on Christianity for favor in the afterlife. Knowledge of a European language spread among an educated minority, along with growing familiarity with Western science and some Western political ideas.

The economic impact of the Europeans was far greater than their cultural influence. The new rulers were eager to make the most profit from their colonies. Small numbers of white settlers claimed the most fertile land, a process already established in southern Africa and now applied to East Africa as well. Colonial administrations imposed new taxes, which forced many Africans to seek paying work on European-owned plantations and mines simply to obtain money in an economy that had previously relied heavily on barter. Colonial officials in some cases requisitioned labor directly, enforcing their demands by brutal physical punishments including dismemberment. In general, Africans working the mines and the estates suffered harsh conditions—including frequent brutal physical punishments—and of course low pay. Europeans did improve port facilities and other aspects of the communication and transportation system, although there was much less railroad construction, in the difficult African terrain, than in India or Southeast Asia. New medical facilities to combat traditional tropical diseases were also of some benefit, and the African population began to increase. Still, by 1900 and even beyond, the main economic results of European control were largely exploitative, as Africa supplied food and minerals—copper from the Congo, gold and diamonds from South Africa—to the Western market from the sweat of miserably paid laborers.

Most Africans, however, were not directly caught up in the institutions of imperialist rule. Village agriculture changed slowly, and other village institutions persisted; European ability to reach most Africans directly was quite limited in a vast and diverse continent where, even with European technology, communication remained difficult. At the same time, the relatively recent nature of European conquest hampered ongoing African reaction. Nationalist movements and other forms of resistance would come, but by 1914, the bloody defeat of initial opposition efforts was a setback to further response.

COMPARING COLONIES

Colonialism brought many similar experiences to otherwise different societies. Foreign rule raised some common issues, as did the subjection to an economic system dominated by industrial Europe. However, colonies often differed in their responses, depending on prior culture and institutions and variations in European policy.

India, with a major religion of its own and extensive experience of outside control in the past, adjusted its culture more selectively than did Africa; there were fewer Indian religious conversions, for instance. Indian civilization also had a longer time to come to terms with Western control, in comparison with the more sudden domination of Africa and the ensuing shock among local populations. Sub-Saharan Africa, by 1900, was beginning to experience the more systematic loss of traditional values, particularly in some areas where Christian missionaries had made advances. The rawest economic exploitation of India occurred around 1800. But in Africa, the European exploitation of resources and labor only increased from the 1890s onward. Competition among European states also affected conditions in Africa, in contrast to India by this point. Although European beliefs in their racial superiority affected policies everywhere, the impact was sharper in Africa than India. Such differences impacted the colonial experience during the nineteenth century itself, and also native reactions later on, when independence became a viable possibility.

European imperialism had a worldwide impact, as a threat if not always fact. The balance of power among the civilizations of the world was dramatically shifted not only by European control of major civilizations—India, Southeast Asia, and Africa—but also by the extension of essentially Western societies to North America, including the U.S. Western frontier as well as Canada, and to Australia and New Zealand.

In India and Southeast Asia, and ultimately in Africa, the fact of European control shaped vital questions of change and adaptation. New Western rule, efficiently administered, brought major innovations, including new political boundaries and new levels of commercialization. It was clear that the colonized societies were not going to become Western. Their traditional cultures were too deep-rooted, their populations and territories too vast; European ambivalence about reforming the natives and seeing them as inherent racial inferiors, as children to be disciplined by wiser

Western parents, also limited the process of Westernization. However, European oc-cupation did provide direct tutelage in Western ways, allowing leaders in southern Asia, and later in Africa, to decide what concepts they wished to borrow, which ones they wanted to reject. One idea to that was assimilated, if only to give shape to what may have been an inherent desire for independence, was nationalism, as was already evident in India. Through nationalism, leaders attracted to some Western patterns, and others eager simply to restore preimperialist traditions, could at least briefly join together in a fervent demand for independence. Imperialism clearly generated its own resistance, and this interplay would dominate much of the history of the twen-tieth century.

Nevertheless, imperialism also uprooted a host of traditional economic, social, and cultural patterns. An independent India or Africa would not go back to preimpe-rialist ways of life. Imperialism also resulted in new political problems in uniting or dividing earlier units. It brought economic benefits, in the form of improved trans-portation and agricultural methods, along with the often harsh use of local labor and integration of colonies into a Western-dominated world market. Population growth posed its own new challenge to the economies of Africa and southern Asia. Limited medical advances, such as inoculations, swamp-draining, and other disease-control measures, had a tremendous impact, just as Western population growth was ebbing. In 1914, the major question for Indian or Nigerian or Indonesian leaders was clear: How should we respond to Western rule? But, imperialism raised wider political, eco-nomic, and cultural concerns also, which would outlast the struggle for indepen-dence in setting an agenda for world history well into the twentieth century and beyond.

Many similar issues would also affect those parts of the world not subject to full imperialist control, such as China and the Ottoman Empire, or newly freed from it— Latin America, for example. Would outright imperialist rule help or hinder a civiliza-tion in addressing problems of population growth, imbalance in the world economy, and new political tensions? Was India, to use the clearest example, better off for hav-ing experienced an intense if relatively brief period of Western rule, than China, which faced Western depredations without the possible benefits of Western influ-ence? Imperialism provided a shock to the civilizations that came under its full sway in the nineteenth century; its impact and the reactions it provoked conditioned the history of these areas even after independence was won.

SUGGESTED WEBSITES

On the causes of imperialism, see *http://www.fordham.edu/halsall/mod/modsbook34.html;* for an African nationalist perspective, go to *http://www.anc.org.za/ancdocs/history/misc/isandhlwanaa.html;* on American imperialism in Asia, see *http://smplanet.com/imperialism/toc.html.*

SUGGESTED READINGS

Excellent general surveys of nineteenth-century imperialism and its causes include Winifried Baumgart, *Imperialism* (1982); D. K. Fieldhouse, *The Colonial Empires* (1968); and Bernard Porter, *The Lion's Share: Short History of British Imperialism, 1850–1970* (1975). See also C. H. Peake, *European Colonial Expansion since 1871* (1941), and the imaginative study by Michael Adas, *Machines as the Measure of Men* (1989). On specific areas and imperialist powers, W. Baumgart, *Imperialism: The Idea and Reality of British and French Colonial Expansion* (1982), is an excellent discussion. On Africa, worthwhile sources include Colin Turnbull, *The Lonely African* (1971); A. Moorehead, *The White Nile* (1971); Woodruff D. Smith, *The German Colonial Empire* (1978); Walter Rodney, *How Europe Underdeveloped Africa* (1982)—a vital study; R. P. Masani, *Britain in India* (1961); and M. D. Lewis, ed., *The British in India: Imperialism or Trusteeship?* (1962). See also C. A. Bayley, *Indian Society and the Making of the British Empire* (1988). On peasant resistance, refer to J. Scott, *The Moral Economy of the Peasant: Rebellion and Subsistence in Southeast Asia* (1976). On women's conditions, see Clare Midgley, ed., *Gender and Imperialism* (1998).

The Middle East and China in the Imperialist Century

FOCAL POINTS

China and the Ottoman Empire were two great states that had to consider a variety of changes under Western pressure. Unlike Africa and India, they were not, for the most part, directly taken over as colonies. Their position in the world did, however, change greatly from what it had been during the early modern period. What were the major signs of new Western impact? What were the principal responses of Chinese and Ottoman leaders and were they adequate in the face of the Western challenge? Neither China nor the Ottoman Empire managed to recover their former vigor during the nineteenth century, but Ottoman leadership on the whole reacted more fully. In what ways was China more damaged by Western exploitation and internal decline? What were the most significant Ottoman adjustments?

CHANGE AND RESISTANCE

The Islamic Middle East and China, although quite different as civilizations, displayed similar reactions to the heightened pace of the world economy and the threat of Western imperialism during the nineteenth century. Neither the Middle East nor China came fully under Western control, in part because of the continuing strength of their governments and in part because Western rivalries canceled each other out, so that no one imperialist power could win predominance. Their patterns thus differed from those of southern Asia and sub-Saharan Africa. But, both areas lost territory and increasingly felt the threat of further takeovers. Nonetheless, the Middle East and, particularly, China responded sluggishly to the transformations in the wider world during most of the nineteenth century, and both lost additional ground as a result. Change came, but haltingly. Traditionalist leadership and a long habit of looking down on foreigners, in the Chinese case, or Westerners, in the Muslim case, delayed vigorous reactions. Late in the nineteenth century, however, new forces arose in both societies ardently seeking fundamental reforms that would make their societies more competitive with the West and more like the West in certain ways. This outlook set the stage for a much more active period of development during the twentieth century.

China and the Middle East, then, followed a nineteenth-century pattern somewhat in between the societies under outright imperialist control, like India, and those that were stimulated during the century itself to radically new kinds of responses.

Ironically, it was China's East Asian cousin, Japan, that provided the most successful example of the latter type of approach. This means that China and Japan diverged increasingly despite shared traditions. Latin America, which was another "in-between" case, must be handled separately from China and the Middle East because its civilization was still in formation during the nineteenth century.

THE MIDDLE EAST

THE ATTEMPT TO MODERNIZE EGYPT

The Middle East began the nineteenth century with a fascinating initiative, although one that ultimately failed. The Ottoman Empire had been rocked, in 1798, by Napoleon's successful invasion of Egypt. When Napoleon was forced out, by British pressure plus Napoleon's own ambition, an Ottoman military officer named Muhammed Ali took over Egypt as a virtually independent ruler, and indeed the Ottomans never did fully regain control of this vital province. At points, Muhammed Ali also conquered areas of the Arabian peninsula adjacent to Egypt, although he was blocked by not only Ottoman resistance but also British fear of any strong power in this region so close to key routes to India.

As ruler of Egypt, Muhammed Ali represented one of the first non-Western leaders, and certainly the first in the Middle East, to adopt a self-conscious mission to modernize his society in Western terms. Unlike Peter the Great, Muhammed Ali never visited the West, but he greatly admired Western achievements and also realized that he must try to match some of them if he was to preserve the independence of Egypt. Under his sponsorship, Western, and particularly French, advisors flooded the country to aid in education, technology, and science as well as military affairs.

Muhammed Ali saw the need to alter traditional economic patterns. Although unable to spur outright industrialization, he did introduce agricultural improvements and, in particular, developed an active export market for Egyptian cotton. The hold of landlords, traditionally uninterested in innovation, was weakened. Muhammed Ali also established a printing press and sponsored the translation of many Western books on science and technology into Arabic. In addition to using Western teachers, he sent a number of Arabs to study abroad. French became a second language to educated Egyptians. Despite these many developments, Muhammed Ali was unable to break through either the hold of tradition on much of Egyptian society or the limitations imposed by Western dominance of the world economy. Egypt became increasingly dependent, for export earnings, on the Western market for cotton; it thus had to compete with other producers of cotton, including the southern United States and India, and its cotton did not always command favorable prices. Its export earnings were frequently insufficient to pay for the machines and military equipment that Muhammed Ali sought, so his regime was increasingly forced to go into debt to Western banks. Here was a tragic irony, repeated many times in many countries, in the Middle East and elsewhere, throughout the nineteenth and twentieth centuries. Governments seek to modernize, adopting new armaments, industrial machinery, and often an array of public buildings and urban amenities. But, these innovations, designed to spur independence, cost money, at a time when the economy remains sluggish. Hence, nations must face the temptation to borrow, which gives foreign banks new powers to supervise policy in the interest of protecting their loans. Muhammed Ali, in sum, managed to change Egypt, but he saw Western control steadily increase; by 1849, when he died, he was bitterly disappointed in his limited achievements. His efforts stand more as an early example of an attempt to adapt in response to Western standards than as a successful revitalizing regime.

Furthermore, the bulk of the Middle East remained largely immune to Muhammed Ali's influence. The Ottoman Empire reacted to growing Western pressure and the de facto loss of Egypt in much more limited terms. The sultans established somewhat more centralized controls over great estates, in the interests of ensuring higher tax revenues. The sultan Mahmud II (1808–1839) dismantled the corrupt Janissary corps. This group had long since lost its military skills and morale, and had turned to political intrigues while living well from state revenues. Mahmud II created a separate, modern artillery corps armed with a European cannon; on this basis, he was able to eliminate the Janissaries and develop a new officer group eager to rival Western military organization and technology.

DECLINE OF THE OTTOMAN EMPIRE

These reforms, focusing on military structure primarily, were not sufficient to revive the decaying Ottoman Empire or to limit growing Western strength in the region. Important provinces of the empire were lost during the first half of the nineteenth century. Not only Egypt (although it technically remained a province until 1914) but also the North African states of Algeria, Tunisia, and Libya (Tripoli) became independent; these last regions had never been fully integrated into the empire in any event. Piracy from the North African shores provoked a military response from Europe and also the United States, which attacked the "shores of Tripoli." In 1830, France began its outright conquest of Algeria, the first of many European takeovers in this area. On the Arab peninsula new, religiously inspired rebellions against the Ottoman Empire broke out, although with the help of Muhammed Ali, they were defeated. Finally, the European provinces of the empire became increasingly restless, inspired by the example of liberalism and nationalism in the French Revolution. In 1820, a major war for independence erupted in Greece, which after a decade, and with wide if informal support from Western Europe, won its independence. Nationalist agitation also stirred in Romania and Serbia, putting new pressure on the Ottoman regime.

West European economic influence in the Middle East intensified during the first part of the nineteenth century. Outside the boundaries of the Ottoman Empire, on the east coast of the Arabian peninsula, Britain established a number of protectorates to limit piracy. London established steamship routes between India and eastern Arabia; by the 1830s, Britain and France operated steamship routes across the Mediterranean to Egypt and the Ottoman Empire itself. Thus, Middle Eastern shipping and foreign trade lay increasingly in Western hands. British companies even operated some river shipping within the Ottoman Empire. Western economic power severely limited the revenue capacity of the empire, which was barred from taxing foreign enterprise. World economic position, in other words, greatly constrained the Ottoman political response.

Finally, pressure on the Ottoman Empire continued from yet another traditional source—the surging Russian empire. Several regional wars occurred between Russia and the Ottomans during the first half of the nineteenth century, resulting in a loss of territory. Russia could have gained still more save for the intervention of France and Britain, who now had their own stake in this region and feared Russian dominance. The Crimean War of 1854–1856 resulted from British-French opposition to further Russian expansion in the Mediterranean, and indeed the Russians were defeated. Another Russo-Turkish war occurred in 1877–1878, and again only Western intervention prevented Russian dismemberment of the empire, which lost new territory even so.

By this point, the Ottoman Empire itself was little more than the puppet of forces beyond its control. The empire was not fully carved up only because the Europeans and Russians could not agree on the spoils; each power feared that the others would gain too much. The Middle East was too close to Europe to allow the kind of free-for-all that ultimately occurred in Africa; the danger of all-out war was too great. So, the empire survived until 1918. Various sultans continued to tinker with reforms. Occasionally, they granted constitutions, in an effort to follow Western practices, but in fact the rule of the sultan and the bureaucracy remained unchecked. Slavery was abolished in 1908—quite late, of course, by some standards. Substantial military reforms concentrated much of the impetus for change within the ranks of the armed forces. Many Ottoman officers were trained in Europe, and European—particularly German—advisors were brought in to improve technology and modernize military administration. However, the Ottoman army remained weak and relatively backward, in part because military reforms were unable to transcend the loose political organization and largely agricultural economy. Tax revenues and morale were both inadequate to provide new vigor to the Ottoman state as a whole.

Hence, the empire continued to lose territory on its fringes and suffer growing Western economic penetration. Nationalist uprisings in the Balkan area, supported by Russia and some of the Western powers, produced a network of small, independent states by the end of the 1870s: Serbia, Romania, and a few still smaller states joined Greece. As a result of further Balkan agitation, which led to an independent Bulgaria, the Ottoman Empire had, by 1914, lost almost all hold in Europe, save for a patch of territory including Constantinople.

Direct imperialist conquest in North Africa also continued, although this region, of course, had already been lost to the Ottomans. In 1869, a French company completed construction of a canal through the Isthmus of Suez, the narrow strip of land that had connected North Africa and the Middle East. By using the new Suez Canal, European ships could save immense time in reaching the Indian Ocean, by sailing from the Mediterranean to the Red Sea rather than around Africa. Egypt's importance increased because of its new strategic position. Britain, anxious as always to safeguard its interests in India, began to interfere more and more in Egyptian affairs, mainly to preempt French influence. Heavy Egyptian debts to British banks provided an obvious opening. Britain was able to buy controlling shares in the Suez Canal and then, in the 1880s, established a protectorate over the Egyptian government; the Egyptian ruler became a virtual figurehead. In response, France took over outright control of Tunisia, and soon after 1900, Italy gained Libya; France captured Morocco. All of Muslim North Africa lay in European hands.

To the east of the Ottoman Empire, British and Russian representatives divided influence over the kingdom of Persia, while direct British hold over the small states of the eastern Arab coast continued. Within the empire itself, European interests gained increasing economic power. German businesses, backed by the government, constructed a major railroad linking Berlin to Baghdad. French and English merchants bought quantities of luxury items. In Turkey proper, a number of rug factories were established, utilizing machines imported from the West and displacing many traditional handworkers, to fill the growing markets of Western Europe and the United States, where Turkish carpets and other furnishings became the rage in middle-class homes in the later nineteenth century. Although some Turks and Arabs gained experience and wealth as factory owners or agents for Western companies, the new industry rested heavily on low-paid labor, and its basic directions were determined by Western merchants, not those in the Middle East itself. The Ottoman Empire, bounded by Western colonies, new and aggressive Balkan nations, and the ambitious Russian state, was no longer master in its own house.

The opening of the Suez Canal: the French Empress Eugénie on her way to the ceremonies.

THE RISE OF NATIONALISM

Although the Ottoman government proved unable to respond successfully to these new developments, several important events occurred that would shape Middle Eastern history in the twentieth century. A strong current of Arab nationalism began to emerge, directed against both European imperialists and the hold of the Ottoman state. In Turkey, a modernizing movement arose among younger army officers. Finally, some efforts were made to rouse new Islamic fervor.

In contrast to India, a large Middle Eastern nationalism did not take clear shape, although there were efforts to encourage patriotic loyalty to the Ottomans. Nationalism increasingly meant particularism, associated with a smaller region, like Egypt, or an ethnic-linguistic group, like the Turks.

Arab nationalism developed most vigorously in Egypt, where Muhammed Ali had first opened the way to growing European influence and example. There nationalism, in fact, emphasized Egypt more than Arabs in general, and a full nationalist statement would not emerge until the early twentieth century. Many educated Egyptians followed Muhammed Ali's goal in wanting to create a modern state and economy, along something like Western lines, but they also desired a proudly independent Egypt, inspired by the same nationalism they saw in Western Europe. Nationalism was a new force in the Middle East (as in India), in its quest for loyalty to secular states and specific peoples instead of Arabs or Muslims in general. Nationalism's newness for a time limited its appeal, particularly to peasant masses, but it did focus attention on the important twin goals of independence and political change. As the Egyptian government grew weaker and more indebted toward the middle of the nineteenth century, nationalist opposition increased. It was inflamed still further by a British takeover. Britain regularized Egyptian finances and helped sponsor some railroad construction and a massive dam on the Nile at Aswan, which increased the amount of water available for irrigation in agriculture. London also abolished slavery in Egypt and expanded the school system. However, these reforms did not daunt the new nationalism. Egyptian nationalists resented economic controls that, in their view, prevented full industrialization. They also resented the lack of political rights and the arrogance of many British colonial administrators. As mostly educated city dwellers, the nationalists were able to easily see firsthand the privileged position and luxury of foreigners in their own country.

Arab nationalism also sprang up elsewhere in North Africa, in response to new imperialist regimes. In Tunisia, for example, the French built port facilities, rails, and a telegraph and telephone system; they also introduced new schools and hospitals. However, they did not encourage much industry and were careful to retain control of most export trade. A handful of French settlers took over some of the most fertile land in the country. These developments, as well as the gap between French and Tunisian culture, were more than enough to stimulate nationalist concerns. As in Egypt, North African nationalism before 1900 mainly took the form of political rallies and newspaper diatribes—themselves new political experiences for the Arabs involved. Little nationalist rioting occurred. But, there was no question that a new political force was rising in this ancient region.

Some Arab nationalism also spilled over to the Ottoman Empire itself. A number of governors of Arab provinces, including the one that contained Mecca, flirted with nationalism; their loyalty to the sultan was questionable by 1900. In 1913, Arab nationalists were able to meet in Persia to discuss independence for Iraq.

Other kinds of nationalism also entered the field. A movement among European Jews, called "Zionism," arose in the later nineteenth century in response to European patriotic claims and new kinds of intolerance against the Jews. The Zionists argued that Jews should reestablish their homeland in Palestine, and by 1914, a number of Jewish settlers were entering the area. This current had no great political consequences as yet, but it would prove vital in the region's future.

Further north, in the Ottoman heartland, more serious reform currents from the early nineteenth century set the basis for Turkish nationalism. Even though the Ottomans lost the ability to rule their empire vigorously, they did introduce changes affecting Turkey proper. The strengthening of the military, following the courageous dissolution of the Janissaries, brought many Turkish officers into contact with Western training. University education was reorganized along Western lines, and the government launched new postal and railway services in Turkey. These changes were important, but they whetted appetites for more. Muslim leaders clashed with the Westernizing elite, and Sultan Abdul Hamid reestablished authoritarian rule after 1878. This was the context, around 1900, in which a number of younger army officers began to push for reform of the sultan's government and modernization of the empire. This movement of "Young Turks," as they were called, sought political rights similar to those promised in a constitution of 1876 that the sultan had quickly withdrawn; they wanted an end to political corruption and a more vigorous foreign policy. They demanded new limits on European economic activities in their land. As one Young Turk put it, "We follow the path traced by Europe . . . even in our refusal to accept foreign intervention." Young Turks participated in a number of violent attempts to overthrow the sultan's government, although without initial success.

The Young Turk movement was long unclear as to whether it wanted to revive the Ottoman Empire or form a modern nation–state in Turkey. It talked mainly of the empire, but the movement relied so heavily on Turkish pride and the imposition of Turkish force that it was, in fact, more narrowly nationalistic. Nonetheless, the movement proved to be the basis for the modern Turkish nation that emerged after the larger Ottoman Empire collapsed.

In 1914, the Middle East was caught between the pressures of imperialism and the structures of the Ottoman state, on the one hand, and the forces of a modernizing nationalism on the other. These latter forces, including the Young Turks, constituted an important new ingredient in the region, a sign of Europe's great influence but a symbol also of a vigorous desire for independence. Nationalism was not a native Middle Eastern development. The idea of breaking up the region into separate states, which even most Arab nationalists suggested in their concentration on Iraq, or Egypt, or Tunisia, had some precedent in earlier periods of regionalism in the Middle East, but it ran against the Islamic as well as the Ottoman tradition. The nationalists were not worried about precedent, however. They wanted not only independence, but also a new society, no matter how vague their definitions. They often embraced a reformist version of Islam, but they were positively hostile to the traditional social structure and educational system of their region. They wanted new political regimes, not only independence but also parliaments and voting rights. For them, as many admitted, the West was both the example and the enemy.

Most people in the Middle East were still peasants and only vaguely affected by the new currents. They remained faithful to Islam, educated in the laws and ceremonies of the Quran. Some were drawn into new economic endeavors, like the rug factories or cotton estates, but most continued to work by traditional methods and to rely heavily on village institutions. No serious change occurred in the lives of Middle Eastern women, still largely isolated in extended family households according to Islamic law; even in the upper classes, few women came into contact with Western ideas, as even imperialist regimes did not try to alter this basic feature of Islamic life. A few Muslim leaders talked of trying to adapt the religion to modern life, and to use Islam as a unifying force for the whole civilization against Western pressure and nationalism alike. Islam was not an unchanging force, although it embraced strong traditionalist elements. Several religiously inspired revolts broke out against Europeans in North Africa, and Islamic belief in the superiority of their religion continued unabated, easily sufficient to doom Christian missionary movements in the region. In this context, Islam conveyed anger and anxiety, a role that was to continue into the twenty-first century.

CHINA

China by the end of the eighteenth century had been able, proudly if not entirely realistically, to maintain its empire's isolation, which remained far more complete than in the days of Mongol rule, when Western travelers like Marco Polo had roamed widely through the vast country. The Chinese economy remained at this point largely self-sufficient, despite modest exports in return for gold. The Qing dynasty, although past its prime, was still functioning fairly smoothly in the hands of the fabled bureaucracy.

A mere 40 years later, China was forced to open its borders to new Western trading and cultural activities as a result of one of those imperialist wars barely noticed in Europe, involving handfuls of Western troops, which dramatically revealed the new balance of power between a declining imperial China and the industrial West.

From the 1820s onward, Western traders became increasingly insistent on gaining access to the vast Chinese markets and the products of Chinese artisans. As they became better established in other parts of Asia, such as India, they gained new knowledge of the profit potential of greater Chinese trade. Growing wealth at home spurred new demand for Chinese vases, porcelain, and other artifacts. At the same time, the Qing dynasty lost vigor rapidly, in a process familiar in Chinese history but now fatefully juxtaposed against the new Western strength. Local rebellions began to increase early in the nineteenth century. A major uprising, the Taiping Rebellion, arose in the 1850s. Led by a man who claimed to be the younger brother of Jesus Christ, the rebels sought traditional peasant goals: lower taxes and more land. Peasants were pressed by a rapidly rising population; simultaneously, the efficiency of the central government declined. The bureaucracy could no longer collect taxes effectively, and the quality of the imperial army deteriorated. This made unrest harder to put down and more difficult to prevent. The government struggled for years with the Taiping rebels, finally requiring Western military support to conquer them. Increasingly, the government was forced to rely on locally trained militias, but these forces, newly armed, often turned against the emperor as well, stepping up rebellion and banditry. The costs were staggering. Overall, the rebellion resulted in the loss of over 20 million lives, disrupting China even after the fighting ended.

The first clash between a waning empire and the greedy West occurred in the Opium War of 1839–1842. British merchants in India had been exporting opium for sale in China. Ironically, they still had trouble finding goods that would appeal to the Chinese market, because of the adequacy of traditional Chinese manufacturing; factory-made textiles, for example, had little appeal. So, opium was seen as an important item of exchange that would allow the West to pay for Chinese goods without offering valuable gold. However, the Chinese empire objected to the opium trade. Opium use was not traditional in China, and there was widespread knowledge of its harmful effects. Furthermore, the government continued to treat British representatives as annoying inferiors. A government effort to seize all opium in the harbor of Canton led to a fight with British sailors and an attempt to prohibit all British trade in the area. War followed, as the British blockaded the entire coast; the Chinese were powerless to resist because they had no effective navy. The Chinese finally yielded, paying for all British property they had destroyed, opening several ports including Canton and Shanghai to British merchants, and giving Britain the island of Hong Kong.

The defeat in the Opium War was a bitter blow to Chinese leaders, who would long remember not only the loss but also the fact that Britain was willing to fight for the right to export a substance that resulted in the addiction, albeit enslavement, of many Chinese people. But, bitter memories did nothing to stop further Western penetration. On the heels of British gains came France and the United States, demanding new trading rights. By 1850, foreign colonies existed in a number of ports. A second

British East India boats destroy Chinese junks during the Opium Wars period, 1841. Nineteenth-century line engraving. (The Granger Collection)

war, in 1857, led to the opening of still more ports and additional rights that allowed Westerners to trade and conduct missionary activity even in the interior. An Anglo-French army pushed to Peking, driving the emperor from the city, in order to enforce these concessions.

These early imperialist advances did not alter the basic direction of Chinese policy. The Chinese leadership still believed that traditional ways were best, seeing Western gains as temporary setbacks like other brief invasions that had occurred earlier in Chinese history. No new measures were taken to either imitate or counter Western developments. For their part, Western nations, led by Britain and France, were learning that China was a weak empire, not all that different from the Ottomans in basic strength, and hence an easy victim for any modern state with a good navy. Ironically, by the middle of the nineteenth century, the Chinese government was not particularly interested in copying Western military technology—in contrast even to the Ottoman regime. Chinese officers regarded technology as uninteresting, treating engineers with contempt as social inferiors. The reverence for tradition and for cultural as opposed to military or business concerns in the Confucian value system, plus the real weakness of the imperial administration at this point, combined to make innovation seem both undesirable and impossible.

Nonetheless, beneath the level of imperial administration, China was changing. Population growth continued, creating a great demand on the part of many peasants for land. A relatively small number of peasants even sought relief in emigration—an unusual development in Chinese history—as they were recruited by railroad or estate bosses in the United States and some parts of Latin America. This movement, however, had no real impact on continued unrest at home. At the same time, Western influence affected some Chinese as well. Missionary efforts converted small groups of Chinese to Christianity and promoted some wider interest in Western ways. More important, Western business activity in the open, or Treaty, ports helped sponsor wider economic development on a regional basis. The ports grew rapidly in population and wealth; they stimulated market agriculture and some manufacturing, even a few mechanized factories, in the surrounding countryside; and they gave some individual Chinese business executives experience with Western commercial methods, often resulting in profit-making zeal. A few entrepreneurs and Christian converts began to gain experience abroad, even attending foreign universities, although this was for the time being the merest trickle against the backdrop of centuries of isolation.

Western imperialists remained uninterested in trying to take over China directly, which would have been a difficult task and was unnecessary given their new access to Chinese trade. They even aided the Qing dynasty in putting down the Taiping uprising during the 1850s; Western regimes preferred a weak imperial administration to outright disorder. Given growing unrest over land, taxation, and corruption among many officials, the Qing dynasty became increasingly dependent on European—particularly British—assistance during the second half of the nineteenth century. Western advisors were employed to improve the army and also increase efficiency in tax collection—a real paradox for an empire with the greatest bureaucratic tradition in the world. The use of Western advisors signaled a new awareness of the need to change. Some Chinese officials grew more interested in Western weaponry—as one writer put it, "Learn the technology of the Barbarians in order to control them."

An English church in Shanghai, late nineteenth century: transporting Europe to China as literally as possible. Compare this style to the Jesuit approach in China, illustrated in Chapter 18.

However, there still was no commitment to significant reform. Indeed, after the Taiping Rebellion was finally crushed in 1864, the government directed most of its efforts to restoring the prestige of the emperor and traditional Confucian principles. The government even tore up a rail line built by private interests in the 1870s, in the hopes of maintaining traditional ways. Such actions showed a firm desire to avoid Westernization—indeed, some clashes with Christian missionaries occurred—but no grasp of what measures might be necessary to keep the Westerners out. Furthermore, the revival of traditional culture did not effectively deal with internal problems, as bureaucratic corruption increased and regional officials became harder to control. Some economic change occurred, in part because of Western influence in the port cities, but most Chinese manufacturing continued with traditional, hand-labor methods. The Chinese imported machine-made thread from Europe and the United States, but continued to weave cloth manually. A handful of Chinese bankers and merchants built prosperous enterprises in the port cities, but most economic patterns stagnated. Products exported to the West, like tea and craft goods, were generated by small-scale operations, not the big estates characteristic of India or Southeast Asia. China was moving only slowly toward the new principles of world commerce.

China, in fact, was faced with a situation that had no precedent. With the lone exception of Buddhism, foreign influence had never been seen as a source of inspiration—only as a nuisance to be outlasted through superior Chinese traditions. Most other cultures, including Japan, India, and even the Ottoman Empire, had more experience with selective borrowing. Chinese politics had long stressed not only tradition, but also the prevention of conflict; it was not well suited for promoting change. Bureaucrats saw no particular reason for new, Western-style efficiency, since they defined bureaucratic talent more in terms of cultural interests and the promotion of harmony. The expansionist, profit-seeking values of Western-dominated trade were also at serious odds with Chinese tradition, despite the vigor of many Chinese business executives even in the past. An old Confucian adage held: "Acknowledgment of limits leads to happiness." This was hardly the capitalist spirit. Added to these cul-

China and Japan in the Nineteenth Century

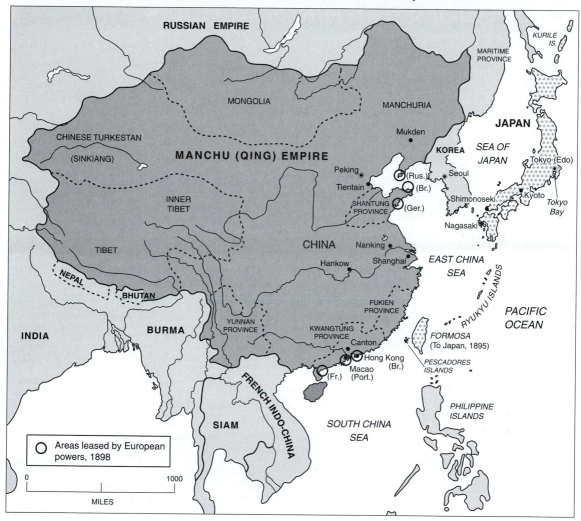

RUSSIAN EMPIRE

KURILE IS.

MARITIME PROVINCE

MONGOLIA

MANCHURIA

JAPAN

Mukden

CHINESE TURKESTAN

KOREA

SEA OF JAPAN

(SINKIANG)

MANCHU (QING) EMPIRE

Peking

Seoul

Tokyo (Edo)

Tientain

(Rus.)

(Br.)

Shimonoseki

Kyoto

INNER TIBET

SHANTUNG PROVINCE

(Ger.)

Tokyo Bay

Nagasaki

TIBET

CHINA

Nanking

Hankow

Shanghai

EAST CHINA SEA

NEPAL

BHUTAN

FUKIEN PROVINCE

PACIFIC OCEAN

RYUKYU ISLANDS

INDIA

BURMA

YUNNAN PROVINCE

KWANGTUNG PROVINCE

Canton

FORMOSA (To Japan, 1895)

Hong Kong

PESCADORES ISLANDS

FRENCH INDO-CHINA

(Fr.)

Macao (Port.)

(Br.)

PHILIPPINE ISLANDS

SIAM

SOUTH CHINA SEA

Areas leased by European powers, 1898

0   1000

MILES

tural impediments were the growing weakness of the reigning dynasty and the stark pressure of rapid population growth, which diverted resources and political attention from other issues. Thus during most of the nineteenth century, China changed less rapidly than not only the West or Japan, but also colonial India or Turkey.

This lack of change, in the context of nineteenth-century world history, meant an invitation to imperialism. France's conquest of Indochina from the 1850s onward was a blow to Chinese prestige, as Vietnam had long been an imperial protectorate. Russia, again on the advance, took over some territory in northern China in 1860.

The huge blow, however, came in 1894–1895, in a war with Japan. The Sino-Japanese War was triggered by a rebellion in Korea. Both Japan and China intervened to suppress this revolt. China had long treated Korea as a vassal state, whereas Japan,

UNDERSTANDING CULTURES

China's Nineteenth-century Sluggishness

A key task in exploring culture is to understand its role in causing other historical, or current, developments. But, cultural causation, although real, is difficult to measure. China in the nineteenth century provides an important case in point.

There is no question that China was slow to respond to Western intervention, despite a proud tradition of strength. The Confucian tradition—a core component of Chinese culture—is often blamed, not only by historians but also by subsequent Chinese leaders themselves. Confucianism did engender two weaknesses in China's responses to modern Western pressure: It encouraged traditionalism, as opposed to praising innovation, and it tended to downplay science in favor of more literary cultural emphases. Chinese bureaucrats, in resisting Western models, reflected these Confucian principles.

Nevertheless, other Confucian societies, notably Japan, did find it possible to modify but use the Confucian legacy as part of a commitment to change. Reduce the traditionalism and aversion to science, but keep the emphasis on group loyalty, obedience, and education, and a society could emerge with a strong basis for successful change. The basis would be perhaps different from that of the West, but no less effective.

Too much emphasis on culture, in China's case, may therefore be misplaced. Of course, there are other cultural components to consider, like the long-standing aversion to foreigners (Japan shared this perspective to a degree, although earlier it had successfully and very deliberately imitated China). But in addition to culture, maybe as important was the abusive manner of Western intervention, with its stress on opium trade, which hardly encouraged imitation. And, there was a period of ineffective government, as the Qin dynasty declined, plus massive population pressure. Cultural causation, and particularly Confucianism, need to be understood in a more complex context in contemplating China's nineteenth-century dilemmas.

now rapidly industrializing, sought new spheres of influence. Both China and Japan also wished to prevent Russian action in Korea. But, the two nations attacked each other as well, and Japan, with a modern navy, easily won—to the astonishment of literally the whole world outside of Japan. China was forced to yield not only Korea but also the island of Taiwan to the Japanese, plus the Liaotung peninsula. This region was regained only by the intervention of Western powers, who wanted no Japanese influence in China proper. China was shown to be a hollow power, unable to fend off its much smaller Japanese rival. This fact, plus concern about Japanese gains and the intense rivalry among the European states, which had by now consumed most of Africa and was searching for new pastures, produced a scramble for Chinese holdings.

The result, by 1900, was a series of new treaties giving France, Germany, Britain, and Russia long-term leases on a number of key ports and surrounding territories. This was not outright imperialist annexation, but it amounted to much the same thing as the imperial governments established their own local administrations. Russia also seized some additional northern territory outright. Western nations proceeded to expand their business influence from their new centers, building rail networks and setting up river shipping toward the Chinese interior.

At last, China started to decisively react. A new young emperor, Kuang-hsu, ordered military reforms, railroad building, and the extension of education. But, Tzu-hsi, the widow of the previous emperor, seized power in 1898 and canceled these reforms, executing several of the leaders of the Westernization movement. Tzu-hsi believed that China could still go its own way despite the presence of foreigners. She gave secret support to a society called the Righteous Harmony Fists, or Boxers, who began killing Europeans and Christian Chinese in 1899. The Boxer Rebellion was suppressed fairly easily by a combined European-American military force, and China was required to grant additional legal privileges to foreigners, making them virtually immune from Chinese jurisdiction throughout the country. Tzu-hsi herself established a Western-style military structure and updated the education of imperial bureaucrats.

But by this point, shortly after 1900, it was clear that the waning Qing dynasty could not master the three forces bedeviling China: internal problems of decline and population growth; imperialist pressure; and a new force among Chinese who were aware of Western ways and eager to "modernize" their country along partially West-

Western troops in the Boxer Rebellion raise the American flag on the Great Wall.

ern lines. From 1896 onward, a flood of Chinese students began to attend schools in Japan, Europe, and the United States, to gain access to the knowledge that their country so painfully lacked. They wanted to learn new technology, new science, and to an extent new organizational methods. In the process, they also learned about new political ideas, including nationalism but also liberalism, democracy, and socialism. There was no full agreement on what the new China should look like. Some reformers wanted only a limited imitation of the West, in purely practical matters; others desired a full parliamentary regime, new roles for women, an attack on Confucian tradition. However, there was agreement that change was essential and, increasingly, a sense that the existing regime had to go. Students returning from experiences abroad were joined by other students influenced by missionary schools or simply impressed by the growing translations of Western science and literature. Forced finally by defeat to open the gates to change, China's old regime could not contain the resulting flood.

CONCLUSION: THE NEED FOR FURTHER CHANGE

Even more clearly than the Ottoman Empire, China was poised on the brink of revolution by 1900. Population pressure caused more internal unrest in China than the Middle East, whereas the intellectual minority, newly aroused by Western ideas, was more excited in China than the Middle East, where Islam continued to exercise cultural control. Both areas, of course, suffered from weak imperial administrations and infuriating levels of interference from the Western powers and Russia. The resulting mixture was too unstable to last, and it did not survive. Revolution was to break out in China in 1911, ending the Qing dynasty the following year and installing a republic in its stead—ending the world's oldest imperial government. The Ottoman Empire crumbled in the aftermath of World War I, and the political cohesion of the Middle East was shattered as well. Both these developments highlighted the tensions that had developed as a result of internal change and external pressure, particularly during the last decades of the nineteenth century.

SUGGESTED WEBSITE

On Ottoman reform, see *http://landow.stg.brown.edu/victorian/history/dora/dora9.html*.

SUGGESTED READINGS

On the Middle East, see W. R. Polk and R. L. Chambers, eds., *Beginnings of Modernization in the Middle East: The Nineteenth Century* (1968); H. A. R. Gibb, *Modern Trends in Islam* (1947); Alan Palmer, *The Decline and Fall of the Ottoman Empire* (1992); and M. G. S. Hodgson, *The Venture of Islam* (1971). See also David Kusher, *The Rise of Turkish Nationalism* (1977), and P. J. Vatikiotis, *The History of Egypt* (1985). On China, an excellent short survey is M. Gasster's

China Struggles to Modernize (1983); for a related study, see Gilbert Rozman, *The Modernization of China* (1981), and Jonathan Spence, *The Search for Modern China* (1990). See also Immanuel C. Y. Hsu, *The Rise of Modern China* (1970); Mary Wright, ed., *China in Revolution: The First Phase* (1968); and Li Chien-nung, *The Political History of China, 1840–1928* (1956). A useful source collection is Ssu-yu Teng and J. K. Fairbank, *China's Response to the West: A Documentary Survey, 1839–1923* (1954).

The Development of
Latin American Civilization

FOCAL POINTS

Two main developments shaped Latin America during the nineteenth century. First came the wars of independence, which were part of the great revolutionary upheaval of the Atlantic world in the late eighteenth to early nineteenth centuries. How did the goals of independence relate to new political movements in the United States and Western Europe? What were the results of independence? Why was it difficult to form stable political societies after colonial controls were removed? Second was the force of the world economy dominated by Western Europe and the United States, which undermined most Latin American manufacturing and (particularly after 1870) pressed for its greater involvement with commercial agriculture and mining that would generate cheap exports. How did the effort to define new political systems and the pressures of the world economy combine in Latin America? How did they affect particular political movements such as liberalism, for example, in relationship to the Latin American masses? The nineteenth century also witnessed new efforts to define a Latin American culture: What were the principal directions in this regard?

PATTERNS OF LATIN AMERICAN HISTORY

During the century of imperialism, Latin American nations won independence, and the civilization as a whole further defined its identity. Latin America was seriously affected by the currents of imperialism, despite newly achieved independence, and it was even more severely constrained by the West's domination of the world economy. Ironically, Latin America's failure to free itself from dependence on Western-controlled economic patterns was one of the key signs that the civilization differed from that of the West. In politics and culture, Latin American leaders combined a deep devotion to many Western styles and values with some distinctive features that resulted from the civilization's racial diversity, its own colonial past, and the social structure which stemmed from a semicolonial economy. Thus, Latin America emerged as a civilization unusually tied to the West, not only through imperialism and economic dependency, but also through shared religious and political ideas—but one that forged its own character by blending Western influence with other currents. The result was a distinctive combination, in the nineteenth century and after.

Latin American history through the nineteenth century established much of the basic framework for this newest of the world's major civilizations. One of the primary challenges to nineteenth-century Latin America was the formation of new nations, where no clear precedent served to guide. These new nations were inevitably concerned with the establishment of territorial boundaries and with generating a leadership that could function despite the lack of prior political tradition. Hereditary rule, for example, made little sense in this context because there were no indigenous ruling families: Previous Indian regimes had long since been destroyed, and rule from Spain and Portugal was now ended as well. Along with new leadership, the nations had to set up legal structures and work to establish some kind of national loyalty. These were difficult tasks, yet for all their undoubted political problems, the new countries of Latin America achieved some success in addressing them during the nineteenth century. Other emerging nations in the twentieth century would face similar challenges and would adopt solutions like those pioneered in Latin America.

THE WARS OF INDEPENDENCE

The nineteenth century began with the wars of independence from Spanish rule. Conflict broke out at several points in 1810, and the drive for independence was essentially completed by the mid–1820s. There followed another 30 years of consolidation, when the boundaries of the new nations were largely set, amid considerable strife, and the broad outlines of internal politics established. This was a period of economic hardship throughout most of Latin America, as the wars of independence disrupted earlier trade patterns and consumed substantial tax resources. It is important to realize that the countries of Latin America were formed in a harsh economic context, when material distress heightened the possibilities of discontent and disorder. After 1850, economic conditions tended to improve, as the civilization underwent extensive commercial development—although such development brought new hardship to important segments of the lower classes. Further imbalance divided a wealthy minority of landowners and merchants from the low-paid masses, even though slavery was abolished. Political instability did not end in this final nineteenth-century period, but it did follow some clearly established lines. The late nineteenth century also saw new pressures from the outside world, in the form of the imperialist actions of Western nations, particularly the United States, and a massive wave of immigration from southern Europe.

The wars of independence—unquestionably the most dramatic events in Latin America's nineteenth-century history—had several causes. Example was one. The revolution that had produced the United States showed that European colonial authority could be defeated. The French Revolution of 1789 also provided an example of the principles of political liberty and nationalist loyalty. Latin American leaders, particularly those drawn from the Creole class, racially European but native to Latin America and often of considerable education and wealth, were keenly aware of what was happening in the Western world, and the new examples became inspirations.

The French Revolution and its Napoleonic aftermath, indeed, provided an opportunity for Latin American leaders. Spain, with a somewhat inefficient government already, became distracted by the new danger on its northern borders, as the Spanish monarch sought to prevent revolutionary uprisings in his own land. Then

Latin American Independence

Napoleon's armies invaded Spain, briefly establishing a regime that controlled most of the country. Neither this regime nor the beleaguered Spanish king Ferdinand had much time or resources to keep Latin American colonies in line. Ferdinand regained his throne in 1815, but by this point the drive for independence was well established. A later Spanish revolution, in 1820, led in fact by discontented troops about to be sent to put down colonial unrest, provided an additional diversion that allowed independence to be won.

Example and opportunity were fueled by serious grievances. In many regions, the colonial economy had depended on extensive slave-holding, and the slave population grew restless during the later eighteenth century. Material conditions and discipline were harsh. Many slaves expressed their discontent by fleeing; by 1800, over a quarter of all black slaves in Venezuela were fugitives, hiding out in self-governing communities in the jungles and mountains. Slave revolts also peppered eighteenth-century history in Latin America. In 1796, Toussaint L'Ouverture, a black leader in the French West Indian colony of Haiti, proclaimed outright independence. L'Ouverture, inspired by French revolutionary doctrines and eager to capitalize on France's own distraction by the war and revolution at home, not only ended Haitian slavery but also established the first black republic in the New World. Because most West Indian islands remained under Spanish, French, British, or Dutch control throughout the nineteenth century and beyond—although slavery was abolished during the middle decades of the century—Haitian independence did not have widespread repercussions. But pressure from discontented slaves was a more serious factor in the Caribbean and Latin America around 1800 than it was in the United States.

Indians and mestizos also had grievances. Many were bound to labor on haciendas run by Creoles, Spanish officials, or the church; others worked in the silver mines. Discipline was harsh, and there was little legal freedom. Most workers were forced to buy goods from estate stores and so suffered from a lack of economic options besides material misery. Revolts by Indian and mestizo estate workers had broken out in the 1770s, centered at first in Peru and spreading to Colombia. The insurrections attacked both the estates system and the high taxes levied by Spanish administrators. These uprisings, although they led to initial success, were ultimately defeated by a combination of military force and trickery. However, they did greatly contribute to the desire for greater freedom from Spanish rule.

At the top of Latin American society, another set of grievances existed. Creoles, often aware of Enlightenment ideals, resented their lack of political opportunity. Although Creoles had been part of colonial administration early in the eighteenth century, after 1750 Spain largely eliminated this role, returning to a policy of appointing only Spanish-born officials. These officials often disdained Creoles, which only added to this group's resentment. Creole merchants and professionals, moreover, disliked Spanish taxes and economic restrictions, which prevented legal trade with the more prosperous nations of Western Europe. As in the United States, revolt was fueled by regulations that seemed excessive and also arbitrary, since they were set without consultation, for the benefit of the mother country. It was Creole leadership that largely sparked the drive for independence. Indian, slave, and mestizo dissatisfaction did not play a direct role, save in Haiti, in part because popular revolts had been recently vanquished. The Latin American wars of independence were not, then, truly popular uprisings, calling social as well as political institutions into question. And while the resulting regimes changed some economic conditions, abolishing slavery in a few cases, such as Mexico, and weakening the estates system for a time, the social system of colonial Latin America, with its pronounced divisions between Creole owners and mestizo, Indian, and black workers, remained largely intact.

The first blow in the war for independence occurred in Venezuela in 1810, when the Caracas city council debated whether it owed loyalty to the new Napoleonic regime in Spain. The council decided on disobedience and urged other city councils

World Profiles

Simón Bolívar (1783–1830)

Simón Bolívar was perhaps the most well-known and revered leader for independence in Latin America, often compared to George Washington in the North. Like Washington, Bolívar was born into the upper classes, a wealthy Creole officer with close intellectual ties to Europe. He developed a passion for national freedom and republicanism, and his fervor plus real military skill catapulted him to leadership of the Caracas-based independence movement in 1810. He was able to mobilize diverse support and won a series of victories against the Spanish in Venezuela, Colombia, and Ecuador between 1817 and 1822. Running the new country, Gran Colombia, was more difficult, however, and as it broke up into smaller nations, Bolívar became bitterly disillusioned. "America is ungovernable," he said, and "those who have served the revolution have plowed the sea." His principles remained firm, nevertheless, and he (again like Washington) refused popular efforts to crown him as king. Why is it often easier for individuals like Bolívar to mobilize forces for national independence than to govern the new nation after victory?

Simón Bolívar (1783–1830) the great liberator.

to do likewise. King Ferdinand's government in flight from Napoleon, was greatly displeased by these actions, even though they were technically directed at his French enemy; he declared the new regimes in revolt and ordered the death of its leaders—an order he was powerless to enforce. The new administration in Venezuela promptly established its own army and proclaimed its independence, drawing up a constitution modeled on that of the United States and the French Declaration of the Rights of Man. Spanish forces were able to put down this regime in 1812, but their harsh retaliation against early leaders engendered further opposition. Simón Bolívar, a wealthy Creole trained in the Spanish army and deeply influenced by Enlightenment ideas (see p. xxx), now took leadership of the northern independence movement, rather like George Washington in North America, with whom he was often compared. Several years of fighting ensued, in which Bolívar assembled an army composed of many former British, Irish, and German soldiers, along with Creole nationalists and some Indian troops. By 1819, Bolívar was strong enough to defeat the Spanish army; he proclaimed a new republic, called Gran Colombia, which united Venezuela and Colombia. Spanish attempts to recapture this nation, hampered by its own 1820 revolution, ultimately failed. Bolívar's armies invaded Ecuador, adding this province to his country.

In 1810, independence movements sprang up in the south as well. In Buenos Aires, a provisional regime was formed with a strong liberal element. An army was organized, ultimately under the leadership of another able Creole general, José de San Martín. This army established a full-fledged government in Argentina and also aided the independence movement in Chile. Again, Spanish attempts to recapture these territories after 1815 were defeated, and the rebel armies also invaded Peru.

The final center of the independence movement took place in Mexico and Central America. Two priests, Miguel Hidalgo and José Morelos, led a lower-class rebellion of Spanish-speaking Indians and mestizos against the constraints of the hacienda system in 1810. Some Indians even talked of an Aztec government. The violence of the lower-class rebellion persuaded Mexico's Creoles to remain loyal to Spain until 1820. At this point, however, Spain's own weakness convinced the Creole elite that they should take matters in their own hands, so they would not end up powerless against further social upheaval. Hence, they supported an independent Mexico, hoping to create a monarchy that would attract a European prince. Finding no takers, a conservative Mexican emperor was crowned in 1822. Here was a clear case of decisive action, as Creole landlords in defending their own elite position, severely limited the social impact of freedom movements. Mexico's choice also foreshadowed political patterns in other Latin American areas, when strongman rule would be seen as essential support for the elite against possible lower-class radicalism.

Independence for the Central American areas south of Mexico initially assumed more liberal lines. Centered in Guatemala, the movement proclaimed a United Provinces of Central America in 1823, with a constitution closely modeled on that of the United States.

No war was needed to bring independence to the final major nation of Latin America, Brazil. Threatened by Napoleon, the Portuguese ruler had fled to Brazil; when he was able to return to Portugal, in 1815, his son, Pedro, remained as regent. Portugal then tried to reimpose colonial controls over Brazil, but Brazilian leaders, now accustomed to a government based in Rio de Janeiro, resisted. Pedro joined this movement, proclaiming Brazilian independence in 1822 with himself as emperor.

By 1825, then, virtually all of Latin America was free from colonial rule. Small European holdings persisted on the northeast coast of South America and in one part of Central America; and, of course, the bulk of the West Indies remained in European hands. Nonetheless, the spirit of freedom prevailed elsewhere.

THE PERIOD OF CONSOLIDATION

Following the intense activity of the liberation movement, a period of consolidation set in. Between 1825 and 1850, a number of the original nine new nations of Latin America split apart. Bolívar had cherished some hope of a political union among all the regimes, but this was clearly impossible because of disagreements among independence leaders, some of whom wanted to establish monarchies while others sought liberal republics. Similar kinds of disputes, plus personal rivalries, then divided even the original states. Gran Colombia fell apart by 1830, splitting into Colombia, Venezuela, and Ecuador. A brief union between Bolivia and Peru failed, in part because the stronger states of Argentina and Chile sought to avoid a powerful neighbor. The United Provinces of Central America had dissolved into five small states by 1840. Finally, a number of border clashes between some of the new nations marked this early period.

The period of consolidation also saw considerable instability in internal politics. Liberals dominated most governments, advocating free trade and a federal government system, but their policies were too idealistic. Debates soon surfaced between advocates of a central government and federalists. Mexico, for example, seesawed between the two systems, with one leader, the colorful general Santa Anna, taking contradictory positions at different points. Liberal rulers sought parliamentary institutions and religious freedom, whereas conservatives wanted to protect the church and upper classes; the latter controlled most regimes between 1830 and 1870. Many new governments were hampered by the lack of extensive political experience of the Creole group. Because Spanish administrators had so systematically excluded the Creoles, save at the level of city councils, few leaders could be found who knew how to operate a government. In this situation, military leaders, drawn from the independence armies, often played an unusually large role. They had a power base and organizational skills. They also characteristically enjoyed the support of landlords, who were eager for forceful military action against peasant unrest. But, factional fighting plagued the military as well, leading to frequent coups and revolts. During the nineteenth century, for example, Bolivia experienced 60 revolts and coups, Venezuela 52. Lack of previous political activity, the important role in internal politics taken by the military, and the obvious lack of agreement on political principles ensured considerable instability for most Latin American nations. Even Brazil, under the steady rule of the Emperor Pedro and then his son until 1889, ultimately followed this pattern, as a republic was proclaimed that soon generated battles among liberals, conservatives, and army leaders.

By 1850, however, despite instability and dispute, many new governments managed to establish some key institutions. New legal codes were written, based largely on Spanish precedent. A number of countries opened school systems and assumed the task of developing port facilities and other public works. Few regimes set up particularly effective bureaucracies, and personal corruption played a frequent role in Latin American affairs. However, the military hierarchy helped compensate for weakly developed civil administrations, and the promotion of military and police functions was obviously vital to the preservation of public order, in turn a cherished goal of the Creole landlords and also church officials.

Although political instability by no means ended after 1850, it is possible to recognize some changes by this point, as initial consolidation was completed. A number of individual nations emerged from early disputes with a forceful government ready to pursue vigorous policies. By 1840, for example, Chile had settled several key issues of political structure, and during a series of administrations under capable presidents,

Mexican *hacienda* owner with overseer, 1830. (The Granger Collection)

it was able to expand the education system, offer wider voting rights for parliament, and open new lands in the south through the defeat of Indian groups. A number of governments had also abolished slavery, although the institution would survive in Brazil until 1888.

More impressive than internal political consolidation was the achievement of relative stability in foreign affairs. Many Latin American states remained rivals, sometimes contesting border areas. Britain prompted the creation of Uruguay in the 1820s as a buffer between Argentina and Brazil. However, the Latin American map remained quite fixed after 1850. The only major changes, all provoked by the United States, involved the massive loss of territory by Mexico (Texas, the U.S. Southwest, and California). Later, a semiindependent Cuba was established, after the Spanish-American War in 1898, and then an independent Panama, also under U.S. influence, was carved from Colombia to promote U.S. control of the canal constructed through the isthmus there. A few wars dotted Latin American history in the later nineteenth century. Paraguay took on Argentina and Brazil in the 1860s, provoking great devastation, and Chile warred with its Andes neighbors in the 1870s, taking Bolivian and Peruvian territories. But for the most part, Latin America was free from major strife between nations—far more free, certainly, than Western Europe at the same time. The concentration of military leaders on their often repressive internal political role distracted Latin American countries from foreign exploits.

LATE-CENTURY TRENDS: DICTATORSHIP, IMMIGRATION, AND WESTERN INTERVENTION

No single political pattern describes Latin American developments during the late nineteenth century, but one significant trend was the tendency toward strongman rule. Venezuela, for example, went through three constitutions after 1870, but in fact was ruled mainly by a series of dictators, of whom the most successful was Antonio Guzmán Blanco. Mexico experienced a dizzying succession of changes before also settling into dictatorial rule. The final defeat of General Santa Anna had ushered in a period of liberal government under the Indian leader Benito Juárez. Juárez sought to reduce the power of the church in Mexican affairs and to extend a secular system of education; he also wanted to decrease landlord influence, although he pressed less vigorously in this regard than he had initially promised his Indian supporters he would. Even so, his efforts aroused the opposition of conservatives, who looked to France for help. During the 1860s, when France was eager to establish a new empire and the United States was divided by the Civil War, Mexico was ruled by an Austrian duke backed by French armies. However, these armies retreated and liberal insurgents captured and executed the hapless duke. Juárez returned, and with him another series of important liberal reforms. But on Juárez's death, a strongman regime was installed, under Porfirio Díaz, which lasted from 1876–1911. Díaz radically curtailed political rights, arranging for the assassination of major opponents. Even in Colombia, where a parliamentary regime had usually prevailed, a brief series of strongman governments assumed power after 1900.

The tendency to adopt strongman rule, amid the considerable shifting of regimes, was only one of the major trends in Latin American history during the second half of the nineteenth century. Liberals returned to power in most countries, after decades of conservative rule. They were eager for economic development and better, less constrained trade, but their policies were more authoritarian than before. Hence, a number of strongmen were actually liberal in orientation, like Porfirio Díaz in Mexico. Many regimes held regular elections but with very restricted voting rights, creating what some historians have called "oligarchic democracies."

A third theme, steadily accelerating after 1870, was the surge of commercial development. Estate agriculture spread, as Latin American leaders sought to take advantage of new European markets for beef and coffee. Extensive mining resumed: A silver boom arose in Mexico, while the extraction of copper and other products took hold along the Andes. This economic expansion was encouraged by increased foreign investment in Latin America. It was also supported by the interest of a number of Latin American governments, including dictatorships such as that of Guzmán Blanco in Venezuela, in extending roads and rail networks to the interior.

In several regions, a massive new wave of immigration provided the backbone for the commercial upswing. Many governments promoted immigration, often inspired by a belief that Indian and black labor could never be suitably trained in the ways of a modern society. The Argentine constitution even included a provision that "the Federal government will encourage European immigration," and by 1895, with three-fourths of all adults foreign-born, it had a far higher percentage of immigrants than the United States. The end of slavery in Argentina and Brazil, by the 1880s,

Benito Juárez (1806–1872)

Benito Juárez was one of those rare but particularly significant individuals in world history who rose from humble origins to gain an important role in society and then helped shape events. Juárez was a Mexican Indian who acquired an education in law and became a state governor. He was an avid liberal, eager to reduce the privileges of church and army and to promote economic change. After a liberal revolt in the 1850s, Juárez became president of Mexico and undertook a sweeping reform program including the sale of church property. He also backed a land reform act that restricted traditional communal land holdings among Indians in favor of private property; his hope was to spur modern, independent farming, but in fact, the lands were often purchased by speculators, leading to increased landlessness. Conservatives in reaction removed Juárez from power and installed a French-backed emperor whom Juárez opposed in the name of Mexican independence. Juárez returned to office but became increasingly autocratic in reaction to the previous period of instability. Juárez's personality and goals had made him a national symbol by the time of his death in 1872. His legacy, however, was more mixed than he would have wished. A period of strong government and economic growth followed Juárez, but social reform for the groups from which Juárez himself had risen proved more elusive. Why do leaders like Juárez sometimes fail to help their own people, despite a sincere desire to do so?

Mural showing Benito Juárez, by Diego Rivera, circa 1920.

created a new need for labor. Freed slaves encountered far less complete discrimination in Latin America than in the United States. More intermarriage occurred, as blacks added to the mestizo population, and light-skinned mestizos were not considered "colored" or black. However, considerable prejudice continued against dark-skinned former slaves and Indians. This created a favorable climate for the use of immigrant labor, which in fact decreased the number of job opportunities for former slaves in many regions. Latin American interest in immigration peaked just as population pressure in southern Europe crested. Hence, although some immigrants came from Britain and Germany, often bringing capital and organizational skills, the majority came from Italy, Spain, and Portugal. A small number of Asians, from China and Japan, also arrived. Immigrants provided labor for the expanding economies and rapidly growing cities. They also represented new markets for the foods produced by estate agriculture. Many settlers adapted readily to Latin American life, often intermarrying with Indians and mestizos. While immigrants promoted some European ideas, such as socialism, for the most part they accepted local beliefs, aided by the fact that many shared the Catholic religion with their new compatriots. Immigration thus brought important changes to Latin America, but it did not overturn established political or cultural patterns.

New problems with Western powers constituted the final major factor in late–nineteenth-century Latin American history. Western nations had not left Latin America alone during the consolidation period; their businesses had a major impact on economic life. Britain, which ruled the seas, also blocked the slave trade. France and occasionally Britain interfered militarily, and both Britain and the United States also officially discouraged outside intervention, although the United States consumed approximately half the territory of Mexico between 1830 and 1860, through the annexation of Texas and other lands won by war.

From the 1870s onward, however, foreign intervention increased. Heavy Western investment brought government action to enforce debt payments. British and French ships frequently threatened Latin American ports to compel fiscal reforms. U.S. ventures were still more significant. In addition to strong U.S. nationalist and imperialist sentiment, North American corporations acquired extensive estate and mining holdings and often called for military and diplomatic support against local reform movements. U.S. influence bore particularly heavily on governments in Mexico and Central America, although there were also important conflicts with Chile and other states. Through the war with Spain, the United States acquired the island of Puerto Rico directly and established a protectorate over Cuba. The building of the Panama Canal resulted in new pressure, leading to Panamanian independence from Colombia, under U.S. auspices. And shortly after 1900, the United States began a policy of frequent military intervention in unstable countries in Central America and the West Indies, out of concern for its business interests in these regions. The problem of dealing with Western nations, especially the United States, began to rank high on the agendas of all Latin American states.

Events during the nineteenth century, and particularly after 1850, had established a number of distinctive regions within Latin American civilization. The great states of the south—Argentina, Uruguay, Chile, and Brazil—took the lead in the new prosperity of the late nineteenth century. They were most active in commercial development, and they also encouraged the highest levels of immigration. Several states, led by Argentina, prided themselves on their European airs. Buenos Aires became almost Parisian in its elegant boulevards, with stylish French and English shops serving the wealthy classes. Although Brazil had large black and Indian populations, the southern states were overall more European racially than was Latin America as a whole.

A second group of countries covered the Andes region—Bolivia, Peru, and Ecuador. Here, the percentage of Indian population was highest and the poverty greatest. Political instability and military rule were also somewhat more pervasive in this region than in Latin America generally.

Mexico, Central America, Colombia, and Venezuela all had sizable Indian populations, although the majority was mestizo. This region enjoyed some commercial expansion in the late nineteenth century. It was also the region most vulnerable to imperialist pressures, a major factor in the development of both foreign and economic policy.

Latin American regionalism, although significant, took shape amid a number of roughly common developments, from independence onward, and amid some widely shared patterns of politics and cultural life.

POLITICAL INSTITUTIONS AND VALUES

The instability of Latin American politics became notorious in foreign eyes, particularly in the United States. Frequent violence and the collapse of one regime after another encouraged people in the United States to look down on the Latin American political style, because stability and a consensus on basic values seemed the hallmark of U.S. political life, at least after the devastating Civil War. Latin American politics were certainly distinctive, responding to factors rather different from those that described Western politics during the same period.

Politically active groups in Latin America tended to divide, from independence onward, between liberals and conservatives. A small, mainly intellectual socialist movement arose in some places toward 1900, but it had yet to win political significance. Liberals, strongly influenced by their Western counterparts, stood for genuine parliamentary governments, constitutions, and civil rights, and a reduction in the power of the Catholic Church. They welcomed economic development and sometimes considered limited social or land reforms; they were eager to extend education. On the other hand, they had little commitment to social reform, often scorning or repressing peasant and Indian values, and they supported elitist economic interests. After 1870, they increasingly supported the notion of strong governments that could back economic development but also regulate aspects of popular behavior which the liberals found distasteful.

Conservatives, often attracted in the early days to the ideals of a monarchy, distrusted parliaments. They directly backed the power of the dominant landlord class and were less interested in commercial or industrial development than liberals. They also stood in firm defense of the rights of the Catholic Church, which maintained a powerful role in education and possessed considerable wealth and land.

Disputes between conservatives and liberals helped account for political instability. When they were not clearly resolved, as in Colombia and Venezuela in the late nineteenth century, changes in regime were particularly frequent. Generally, however, liberal victory in the 1870s ushered in a period of greater political calm—it has been compared to the general triumph of democratic regimes in Latin America in the late twentieth century. Liberals rarely gained a popular following, but they did ally with business interests and a growing urban middle class in promoting not only commercial expansion but also European-style urban renewal projects and efforts to improve public health and eliminate prostitution and other forms of crime.

Accompanying liberal and conservative conflicts was the frequency of strongman rule. *Caudillismo,* derived from the Spanish word for "leader," described this governmental form. Caudillos usually favored the conservative bastions of church and landlord but sometimes represented the liberal camp. Their tactics often cut through some of the conservative–liberal debate, if only by force. At times, some even worked for reform, scaling back church prerogatives and seeking economic development. By reducing liberal attacks on Indian or mestizo traditions and offering public works, some conservative caudillos garnered ardent mass support. But, all caudillos relied on force. They outlawed political opposition, regulated schools and newspapers, and used jails, police, and firing squads with abandon. Some, without question, were simply corrupt, lining their pockets and those of their cronies. Porfirio Díaz, the last Mexican caudillo, in addition to brutalizing his political opponents, encouraged landlords and U.S. investors to take over vast stretches of Mexican land, receiving extensive kickbacks in return. His government, indeed, sold off literally 20 percent of all the land in Mexico, much of it previously held by Indians and mestizo villagers.

In the nineteenth century, Latin American politics had little contact with the masses, except for the times it exploited them. Few liberals were ardent democrats; they shared a distrust of Indians and blacks. Liberal constitutions gradually increased the suffrage, but few liberals favored democracy; hence, mass political action was not an important feature of Latin America during this period. Liberals, indeed, were in some ways less sympathetic to mass interests than conservatives, which helps explain their limited popularity. Liberals stood for individualized property rights; they promoted rationality and different, typically grueling, work habits; they attacked tradition, including, of course, popular religious customs. Liberal caudillos like Porfirio Díaz brutally suppressed incipient trade union movements among urban workers. Other caudillos at times developed political symbols and public works projects that did have mass appeal. Even before 1850, for example, an early Argentine caudillo, Manuel de Rosas, won considerable popular support by requiring church prayers for his regime, and by the widespread use of his image and his political symbol, a red rose, in public places. De Rosas and many other caudillos, particularly during the decades of consolidation, often helped build a national consciousness among elite groups and the masses, even when they were by Western standards unusually repressive. The tensions between the articulate political forces in Latin America and the somewhat separate masses were one of many traditions established in the nineteenth century that would affect Latin American politics into our own time.

Most Latin American governments remained weak in the nineteenth century, even when caudillos officially claimed great power. The ability to regulate landlord

HISTORY DEBATE

Is Latin America Western?

In 1997, a large number of Latin American historians, mostly but not exclusively from the United States, debated on the Internet whether Latin America should be judged a "non-Western" civilization. A few argued that Latin America should be viewed as part of the West because it shared a Western language and active participation in a common literary and artistic culture. Latin America is also the only society outside Western Europe and the United States/Canada/Australia/New Zealand where political liberalism gained widespread support in the nineteenth century.

Others, however, objected. Some argued that parts of Latin America—a city like Buenos Aires, a group like the middle class—were Western, but other key parts—the poor, or a city like Tucuman—were not. Costa Ricans may view themselves as Western, but the Quechua speakers in the Andean highlands would not. The majority of the debaters argued that the solution to the question was not to decide whether Latin America was Western or not, but to avoid the use of the term Western. For these historians, the term implied a certain "superiority," and in their view such an interpretation did not reflect an accurate picture of any society. They further attacked the related tendency of many historians to lump together many civilizations in a "non-Western" category, as if a culture's not being Western was a coherent feature. Finally, they argued that Latin America should be seen as a syncretic civilization, combining many influences—but that other civilizations, including Western Europe, were also syncretic. Interestingly, broad discussions of social and economic features did not loom large: The debate focused on culture and whether one was sympathetic or not to the viewpoint of Latin America as a Western civilization.

or foreign business interests, or even, in some cases, roving bands of criminals, was limited (as was true to some extent in the United States). This was the context in which, after 1870, liberals often advocated greater state powers in the interests of economic development, government-sponsored education, or regulating Indians.

CULTURE AND THE ARTS

The Catholic Church continued to provide one of the key cultural bonds throughout Latin American civilization. The institution operated schools and charitable facilities for the poor, in addition to maintaining its political role. Church ceremonies and buildings provided aesthetic as well as spiritual experiences for Latin Americans from almost all social classes and racial groups. Latin America thus remained largely separate from the assaults on religion as an intellectual and cultural force that arose in Western civilization during the same period, although liberals generated fierce attacks on the church as an institution. Debates such as that over Darwin's theory of evolution, in its implications for Christian belief, had little echo in Latin America. Indeed, Latin American culture, even at elitist levels, remained relatively disinterested in science. Although in most countries, universities were established by 1850 that gradually developed some scientific and medical training, science remained less prestigious in this civilization than in the West, with its contribution to the general culture less significant.

Latin American culture was framed not only by religion but also by class structure. A considerable gap divided educated Latin Americans from the largely illiterate masses. A few governments, particularly in the southern region or under regimes such as that of Juárez in Mexico, made strides in promoting literacy. Argentina's literacy rate, 22 percent in 1876, jumped to 50 percent by 1895—the highest of any Latin American nation. These developments, along with a growing prosperity, help explain why cultural activity increased in Latin America during the later nineteenth century. Nonetheless, most formal intellectual activity still played to what was, by Western standards, a limited audience.

Culture was also shaped, again especially in the southern region, by the immense popularity of Western trends. Latin America developed no architectural style of its own during this period, in part because those who could afford major building projects thought in terms of replicating what they had seen in Paris or Madrid. Many artists and writers patiently reproduced European-style portraits and novels for an eager, wealthy audience. And, even intellectuals who cultivated originality did not think in terms of an entirely independent Latin American culture, as they kept careful tabs on European, and particularly French, styles.

However, formal culture in Latin America, especially in literature, did achieve a distinctive tone. Poetry played an important role. Many poets were retained on university faculties, and in general, poetic expression became more vigorous in Latin America, in comparison with other literary output, than in the West. A number of women writers contributed to the impressive body of work in poetry. Using Romantic styles, a number of poets and novelists also tried to convey the popular themes and concerns within their own civilization. They wrote of the frontier, Indians, and slave life. Many were politically radical, using literature to spur social reform. They were joined by many historians and folklorists, who strove to describe the special features of the Latin American experience and its racial diversities. Finally, a number of writers, both conservative and radical, sought to convey something of the spirituality of life, and particularly Latin American life. In the 1890s, one Uruguayan novelist, Enrique Rodo, who achieved wide popularity in Spanish-speaking countries, highlighted what he perceived to be the special virtues of his civilization over the materialism and mediocrity of Western culture, most notably in the United States.

Along with formal culture, a vigorous popular art continued to flourish. Many Indian weavers and potterers used traditional themes, designs, and vivid colors in their work. Festivals, even when organized around Christian celebrations, provided Indians and former Africans with an opportunity to participate in lively folk dances. Popular dance music, using Spanish instruments such as the guitar but traditional

The European look: section of Buenos Aires in the late nineteenth century.

Indian or African melodies and rhythms, included the fast-paced tango and samba—styles that would later have an influence in Western popular culture as well.

Overall, despite the limitations of poverty, illiteracy, and frequent political repression, a vibrant cultural life emerged at various levels of Latin American society. As in politics, Latin Americans worked toward a distinctive amalgam of Western styles and their own customs and values. Artistic expression became a vital facet of the maturing civilization.

ECONOMY AND SOCIETY

Economic and social patterns in Latin America most clearly separated this civilization from that of Western Europe and the United States, and indeed accounted for many of the distinctions visible in politics and culture. For the most part, dynamic sectors of the Latin American economies arose as suppliers to the West; manufacturing was weakly developed throughout most of the nineteenth century, except for the peasant production of cloth and other simple items for local use. Since colonial times, Latin America's great export facilities had been geared for the sale of goods in the Western-dominated world economy; this orientation endured after independence, which helps account for the long hold of slavery in a few states such as Brazil. As many regions became commercially active in the second half of the century, Latin American dependence on Western markets and a low-paid labor force actually increased.

The first half of the century produced bleak economic news for much of Latin America. The wars of independence disrupted previous economic activities. Because few of the new regimes attempted significant land reform, most commercial production remained in the hands of great estate owners; nonetheless, there was a good deal of confusion because of unrest and the disruption of trade with Spain. The abolition of slavery in places like Mexico and Venezuela led to the erosion of a prime source of cheap labor that was not quickly replaced, with taxes rising to support growing armies. Furthermore, boundaries in several countries were drawn without regard to earlier economic patterns. Thus, Bolivia and Peru, centers of the great silver mines, were cut off from the rich agricultural plains of Argentina. More serious still was the decline in the production of precious metals, particularly in the Andes region, which reduced the availability of one of Latin America's chief exports. At the same time, independence opened Latin American markets to industrially produced cloth and tools from the West, especially Great Britain, which overwhelmed many local suppliers. Poverty among urban workers increased, and rural manufacturing was nearly eliminated.

By 1850, as we have seen, conditions often improved. There were exceptions, however—poverty increased in Mexico under Porfirio Díaz even as economic development advanced. Large estate owners, some of them foreign, tightened their grip on the Indian and mestizo labor force. But, many Latin American countries developed a key cash crop or mineral specialty that allowed them to capture a growing export market. In Cuba and part of Central America, the production of sugar was a primary focus. Brazil concentrated on coffee, and in 1889, the country produced 56 percent of the world's coffee; by 1904, the figure had risen to 76 percent. Argentina exported beef and wheat from vast ranches; Chile focused on copper and nitrates, Bolivia on tin. Mexico became a leading petroleum producer after 1900, spurred by U.S. investments and much foreign ownership. These concentrations on food and raw materials were highly vulnerable, however. Latin American production increased rapidly, but this risked flooding the market and thus lowering prices and total earnings. Brazil, for example, faced a devastating slump in coffee prices around 1900. The environment in many countries was also affected by deforestation and the promotion of crops like coffee that were not native to the region.

At the same time, demand for products manufactured in the West tended to grow rapidly. Upper-class Latin Americans, often possessing new revenue from trade, mines, or estates, wanted European luxury items. They quite consciously backed the growth of export sectors as the basis for their style of life. Further, the railroads and ports that governments sought to promote required imports of equipment from the United States and Europe. Latin American nations accumulated rising foreign debts when their exports did not match their imports. Government indebtedness led to frequent Western intervention, which often averted bankruptcy but never addressed the problem of a basic economic imbalance.

Outright foreign economic control compounded the problem. Britain led in investments to Latin America during this period, but the United States and other Western nations were also heavily involved. Foreigners owned many of the most lucrative estates and industries. In Díaz's Mexico, they purchased a great deal of land; in Colombia and Chile, they owned most railroads, banks, and mines. Western investments brought frequent pressures on Latin American governments to protect Western property. They deprived Latin America's struggling business class of a full range of opportunities, for top management remained in foreign hands. And, they removed much-needed profits from the region altogether.

Finally, the economic development that did take place in the later nineteenth century, whether foreign-based or not, created intense pressures on the lower classes. While Latin American dependence on the world economy was not new, it had previously coexisted with village agriculture. Into the 1880s, many Indians and mestizos operated village farms adequate for local subsistence needs. They were able to work according to traditional rhythms and organize frequent festivals, replete with dance, song, and drink. This pattern yielded quickly to the growing commercialization of the Latin American economy during the last decades of the nineteenth century. In virtually every region, more land than ever before was consumed by large estates. Indians, accustomed to community ownership, were forced to sell out to individual owners. In Mexico, for example, a law of 1894 ruled that land could be declared vacant and open to purchase if legal title to it could not be produced, but few Indians had such title, relying on traditional terms of use rather than modern notions of property. In Colombia and elsewhere, governments, often in liberal hands and eager to promote economic growth, opened new territories to bidding, which in fact displaced many traditional villages not regarded as having property rights. Other peasant owners were simply defrauded by shrewd speculators, or encouraged to go into debt. Some of the new estates embraced thousands, even millions of acres; one Mexican estate was as large as West Virginia.

The peasants, once displaced, encountered still further indignities. They had little choice but to work on the large estates, where they were paid low wages or, even more commonly, paid in kind and kept permanently in debt. Virtual serfdom spread, as workers were not allowed to leave the land until they had paid their debts, and not allowed to earn enough money to have any hope of making these payments. Furthermore, hard-driving commercial estate owners tried to spur greater zeal on the part of workers. They clamped down on traditional festivals, regarded as a sheer waste of time. This was a pattern not entirely different from the pressures earlier placed on European or U.S. industrial workers, for a real commercial revolution was underway. But, Latin American peasants suffered far less freedom and far more poverty than most Western workers, for the economy, because of its weak position in the world markets, depended on exploited labor. Investment in new equipment, which might have provided an alternative to cheap labor, lagged. And, although many estate and mine owners worked conscientiously to expand production, as opposed to the stereotype of idle drones living in luxury with no attention to management, the gap between the wealthy, mainly Creole or foreign, land-owning classes and the impoverished masses grew ever wider.

Finally, many former peasants, forced off the land, sought refuge in the growing cities, where they faced competition for jobs from new immigrants from Europe. A large, often miserable property-less class spread in the cities, pitting sprawling slums

Mexican rebels on the march toward Xochamilcu, August 15, 1914.

on the outskirts against the impressive upper-class districts nearer the center of town. Because industrialization was slow, there were relatively few factory jobs to absorb the newcomers. Aided by foreign capital and European immigrants, countries like Brazil did develop some industries in food processing, textile, and metallurgy. However, the numbers of workers these industries employed were small, as Western competition continued to cut into the available markets for manufactured goods. Hard-pressed governments had few resources to devote to welfare programs, so urban poverty and shantytowns grew unchecked.

The Latin American masses were not quiet under this new assault. The organization of urban trade unions was difficult, because of widespread misery and sheer confusion; government oppression also complicated any protest efforts. However, peasant uprisings to seize land and escape the commercially driven work routines became common from the 1880s onward; indeed, they persist in many areas even today. Peasant rebellions were not regular occurrences, for peasants were usually repressed and could not be supported by legal organizations. But, they also proved impossible to put down permanently. Countries like Mexico, Bolivia, and Colombia faced major revolts every 10 or 20 years. Rural banditry also increased in many regions, recruiting displaced peasants and winning the quiet support of even larger numbers, who saw the bandits as expressing their discontent and hatred of landlords. Finally, rates of individual violence were high in many countries. Essentially frontier conditions existed in many places, as the formal presence of a central government was sporadic at best. Hence, many peasants took vengeance into their own hands. High levels of violence also reflected the deep grievances of landless peasants whose cheap labor sustained Latin America's production for trade.

Latin America during the late nineteenth century thus generated a paradox of rapid change and continued vulnerability in the world markets. Many sectors of the economy were out of Latin American hands. Emphasis on agriculture and mining continued, with only halting industrial development. Cities grew, but without a vigorous manufacturing base. Social structure remained oddly traditional, with great estate owners at the top of the heap, masses of peasants and property-less workers at the bottom, and a small middle class in between. Slavery had been abolished, but poverty and near-serfdom replaced it not only for many blacks but also for Indians, mestizos, and many immigrants as well. Family structure remained rather traditional, with a strong emphasis on the inferiority of women. Many lower-class women, in fact, entered the labor force, both on estates and in the cities, but officially and legally their place remained subordinate to men at virtually all social levels.

CONCLUSION: TENSION AND CREATIVITY

The tensions of Latin American society help explain the importance of strongman governments and the diverse roles of religion, through the late nineteenth century and beyond. One country, Mexico, was on the verge of revolution in 1900, driven by the unusually heavy hand of Porfirio Díaz and the extensive exploitation of Indian and mestizo labor. However, most of Latin America would long avoid outright revolution, although not recurrent protest, as army, church, and sometimes foreign intervention combined to keep the lid on unrest. Efforts by artists and intellectuals to voice the yearnings of the masses or to provide a spiritual identity distinct from Western values gained growing significance. Latin American civilization was formed under many unusual difficulties and under the strong tutelage of the more powerful West, yet it managed to generate not simply an array of problems but also a unique flavor that blended diverse traditions with the creation of new countries and rapid economic change.

SUGGESTED WEBSITE

On the web, the life of José San Martin is examined at
http://www.pachami.com/English/ressanmE.htm.

SUGGESTED READINGS

A useful collection of sources is B. Keen's *Readings in Latin American Civilization* (1955). For discussions reflecting recent scholarship, see T. Skidmore and P. Smith, *Modern Latin America* (1984); the book's only drawback is its concentration on single national or regional cases. See also David Bushnell and Neil Macauley, *The Emergence of Latin America in the Nineteenth Century* (1994), and Fernando Henrique Cardoso and Enzo Faletto, *Dependency and Development in Latin America* (1979), which disagree on the issue of dependency. On political patterns, see Tulio Halperin Donhi, *The Aftermath of Revolution in Latin America* (1973), and Claudio Veliz, *The Centralist Tradition in Latin America* (1980). On key topics, see E. Bradford Burns, *Poverty or Progress: Latin America in the Nineteenth Century* (1973); Herbert Klein, *Bolivia* (1982); June Nash and Helen Safa, eds., *Sex and Class in Latin America* (1980); and Charles Berquist, *Labor in Latin America* (1986).

Russia and Japan: Industrialization Outside the West

24

FOCAL POINTS

Among societies outside the West or the settler societies, Japan and Russia alone launched industrial revolutions by the late nineteenth century in response to a Western challenge. Why were they able to do so? What factors allowed Japan, unlike China, to adopt a process of rapid change? Both Russia and Japan needed to introduce other reforms besides new economic policies: What did they emphasize? In what sense did Japan "prepare" its industrialization more thoroughly than Russia? The early industrial revolution had many effects in Russia and Japan similar to those in Western Europe a bit earlier. Were there any marked differences? Did Japan become "less Japanese," Russia "less Russian" as they consciously imitated Western industrialization?

THE SPREAD OF INDUSTRIALIZATION

Both Russia and Japan escaped full Western economic dominance during the nineteenth century. Russia remained backward by Western standards, and its leaders grew painfully conscious of this fact. Even after 1900, its economy depended heavily on Western trade, technology, and capital; only revolution, in 1917, would seriously alter this situation. However, Russia had displayed dynamism in previous centuries despite an economic lag, and this pattern persisted during the nineteenth century. Russia continued to expand, although it met Western and, at the end of the century, Japanese resistance at key points. The nation gained territory in central Asia and the Far East, and it achieved important influence over new, small states in southeastern Europe. Finally, the Russians began to sketch their reaction to the Western example of industrialization. Without becoming Western, Russia tried to alter its social pattern to conform to the requirements of an industrial society, and by 1890, it had launched the early phases of a real industrial revolution.

The response of Japan was even more striking. Continuing its policy of isolation until the 1850s, when Western pressure forced new contacts, the Japanese then rapidly transformed their basic political and social institutions, generating initial industrialization and a military reform that soon made Japan Asia's leading power. These events more clearly than ever before divided Japan from its Chinese neighbor, although in fact they still shared many cultural and artistic customs. For a time, indeed, the Japanese seemed bent on imitating everything Western, as the tradition of isolation made it difficult to sort out which Western habits were essential to economic and

473

military strength and which were optional. But no more than Russia did Japan become Western: A key aspect of both Japanese and Russian development was an ability to industrialize without sacrificing all the distinctive features of their societies.

Japanese and Russian efforts form the first examples of what can be called "latecomer" industrial revolutions, in that they began after the West had established a pronounced lead in the process. Latecomer industrialization involved certain factors that had not been necessary in the West. Capital was hard to come by for essential investment; neither Japan nor Russia had the West's advantage of prior colonial and merchant wealth. Unfamiliar technology must be mastered. There may be an inevitable tendency for the government to assume a greater role in latecomer industrializations than was true in the West, to amass scarce resources through taxation and to guide manufacturers in the adoption of foreign techniques. At least this was clearly the case in both Russia and Japan, where, in any event, previous political structures made a strong government seem logical. Latecomer industrialization may also impose greater strain on the population involved, because change is even more abrupt than it was in the West, where innovation caused enough tension even without these additional factors.

Although sharing both the ability to respond strongly to Western example and some common features of the latecomer pattern, Russian and Japanese initiatives differed in crucial respects. Russian efforts to change, and failures to change rapidly enough, produced a revolutionary climate by 1905 when the first Russian revolution broke out. Japan avoided revolution in a literal sense, although in some ways revolutionary transformation was imposed from the top down after an intense internal struggle in the 1860s. At the same time, Japan shifted its traditional policies more radically than Russia, in not only industrializing so rapidly but also adopting an aggressive diplomatic stance quite foreign to its own precedents.

Neither Russia nor Japan was fully industrialized by 1914; both would continue to lag behind the West for some decades still. Nevertheless, the nineteenth-century breakthroughs were crucial in both countries. They ultimately had an influence even beyond national borders, in showing people in other parts of the world that Western economic tutelage was not the only way to produce change, and that a strong response could keep Western imperialism at bay.

RUSSIA

CONSERVATISM AS AN ALTERNATIVE TO THE WEST

The first half of the nineteenth century saw relatively little change in Russian culture and society. Russian leaders were indeed proud of their seeming immunity to the revolts and tensions that plagued Western Europe during the same period. After the defeat of Napoleon's armies, the Russian state viewed itself as one of the guardians of conservative order in Europe. Its acquisition of new territory in Poland at the Congress of Vienna, in 1815, furthered its long-standing interest in expansion. The Russian tsar Alexander I flirted with liberal ideas, and a few reforms were introduced, notably to improve the training of Russian bureaucrats. But, neither the authoritarian state nor the tight system of Russian serfdom was seriously altered.

In December 1825, a minor revolt broke out, led by Western-minded army officers who wanted to see their country change. The Decembrist revolt was easily vanquished, but it inspired the new tsar, Nicholas I, to embrace more outright conservatism. The repression of political opponents increased, as the secret police expanded. The press and schools were tightly supervised. What political criticism survived did so mainly in exile, in places like Paris and London, and with little impact on Russia itself. In 1830–1831, Nicholas I brutally put down a nationalist uprising in Poland, led by Catholics and liberal aristocrats who chafed under foreign rule. He also intervened in the revolutions of 1848, sending troops to Hungary in 1849 to help the Habsburg monarchy restore their government. Russia itself remained untouched by the revolt and agitation that spread virtually throughout Western Europe.

Although the situation in Russia seemed calm, the country was, in fact, falling further behind the technological and economic levels of the West. Russia responded to Western industrialization initially by a further tightening of labor obligations of the serfs, so that the great grain-growing estates would have more to export. Individual factories did sometimes use Western equipment, but there was no significant change in overall manufacturing or transportation methods. Russia remained a profoundly agricultural society based on essentially unfree labor. Russian aristocrats, conscious of the West's greater dynamism, attempted to conceal the differences by their enthusiastic embrace of European cultural styles, remaining up-to-date on the latest styles in dress, dance, or painting, but this important cultural current did not close the economic and social gap between the two societies.

This gap was dramatically highlighted by an apparently minor war in the Crimea, in the mid–1850s. Russian leaders had continued to peck away at Ottoman holdings in central Asia, maintaining what was by now a traditional foreign policy interest. However, British and French power in the Middle East constituted a new force of opposition. When Nicholas provoked war with the Ottomans in 1853, the Western countries came to the sultan's aid. Essentially because of industrialization, which provided superior equipment and relatively rapid transport, the Western forces, far from home, prevailed over the Russian army in its own backyard. This was a severe blow for a regime that prided itself on military dynamism.

The Crimean War resulted in the greatest event of nineteenth-century Russian history, the emancipation of the serfs. Some aristocratic landlords were no longer sure that serfdom provided the most profitable system of labor. Many Russian leaders were also concerned with the periodic peasant uprisings, against their lack of land and freedom, that continued to punctuate Russian history even after the collapse of the great Pugachev Rebellion. Some upper-class Russians were swayed by ideals of liberty and humanitarianism, finding serfdom wrong in principle. But above all, Russian leaders, including the new tsar Alexander II, wanted to rid Russia of a social system that seemed to be holding it back in relation to the West. If Russia were to develop a more dynamic economy, it needed workers that were free to move to cities and factories. It needed to encourage better methods even in agriculture, which the easy reliance on servile labor prevented. It needed, in sum, a partial revolution from above.

THE BEGINNINGS OF INDUSTRIALIZATION

The decision to emancipate the serfs came at roughly the same time as, in the United States and, shortly before, in Brazil, the decision to free slaves. Some of the motives, including humanitarianism and a desire to convert more fully to a free labor market, were also similar. No more than slavery did rigorous serfdom suit the economic needs of a society that could hold its own in modern world trade.

In some ways, the emancipation of the serfs in 1861 was more generous than the liberation of slaves in the Americas. Although aristocrats retained part of the land, including the most fertile holdings, the serfs got most of it—in contrast to slaves who received their freedom but nothing else. But, Russian emancipation was careful to preserve essential aristocratic power and above all the tight grip of the tsarist state. The serfs obtained no new political rights at a national level. They were still tied to their villages until they could pay for the land they were given—the money from such a redemption going to the aristocrats. Many peasants, as a result, could still not travel freely or even sell their land, although some became more mobile. High redemption payments, in addition to state taxes, kept most Russian peasants miserably poor. Emancipation did bring change; it helped create a larger urban labor force. However, it did not spur a revolution in agricultural productivity, as most peasants continued to use traditional methods on their small plots. And, it did not bring contentment; indeed, peasant uprisings became more rather than less common, as hopes for a brighter future now seemed dashed by the limits of change.

Alexander did, to be sure, introduce further reforms during the 1860s and 1870s. He created local political councils, the *zemstovs,* that had a voice in regulating roads, schools, and other conditions. The zemstovs gave some Russians, particularly middle-class people like doctors and lawyers, new political experience, but they had no influence on national policy, where the tsar resolutely maintained his own power and that of the extensive bureaucracy. Alexander liberalized legal codes and created new courts. Reformers modernized the army, by encouraging promotion by merit and other organizational changes. Recruitment was extended, and many peasants learned new skills, including literacy, through their military service.

These adjustments, like emancipation itself, were important. They imitated some Western principles; the new law codes, for example, provided milder punishment for crimes and enforced equality before the law. However, they were not designed to create a Western society: They did not attack the fundamental power of the aristocracy and modify political authoritarianism. The reforms were sufficient to spur the beginnings of Russian industrialization. They were not sufficient to provide a stable social base for economic upheaval. Political as well as peasant unrest increased and provoked a return to more repressive measures.

From the 1870s onward, Russia began to construct an extensive railway network. It served as a vital link in the giant country—the establishment of the Trans-Siberian Railroad, connecting European Russia with the Pacific, was the crowning achievement of this drive, largely completed in the 1880s. Railroad facilities were also necessary to integrate Russia's wealth in coal and iron and to bring these resources, in turn, to markets—Russia's river system, running south to north, was not particularly useful in this regard. Moreover, rails aided Russia's drive to export grain, essential for earning capital to purchase Western machinery. The rail system, finally, helped spur a modern coal and metallurgical industry, for although some key equipment had to be purchased from the West, the government stimulated native industry as much as possible. By the 1880s, when Russia's railroad network had almost quintupled compared to 1860, modern factories had sprung up in Moscow, St. Petersburg, and several Polish cities, and an urban working class was growing at the same pace.

Russian industrialization was not unopposed, however. Quite apart from impoverished factory workers, who soon proved susceptible to revolutionary doctrines, some Russian leaders worried about the unsettling impact of this Western force. But, industrialization appealed to the widespread desire to catch up with the West. It allowed further Russian territorial expansion in central Asia and northern China, for rails enabled Russia's massive armies to be moved more quickly and established technological superiority over many Asian states. Furthermore, Russian industrialization flowed in part from the authoritarian position of the state. Railroad development was a state-run operation. Many factories were also state-run, and the government oversaw some of the industrialization effort.

Under Count Witte, minister of finance from 1892–1903 and an ardent economic modernizer, the government enacted high tariffs to protect new Russian industry, improved its banking system, and encouraged Western investors to build great factories with advanced technology. As Witte put it, "The inflow of foreign capital is . . . the only way by which our industry will be able to supply our country quickly with abundant and cheap products." By 1900, approximately half of Russian industry was foreign-owned and much of it foreign-operated, with British, German, and French industrialists taking the lead. Witte and others were confident that government controls could keep the foreigners in line, rather than converting Russia into a new imperialist playground, and for the most part, they seemed correct. By 1900, Russia had surged to fourth rank in the world in steel production and was second to the United States in petroleum production and refining. Russian textile manufacture was also impressive. Long-standing Russian economic backwardness was beginning to yield.

This was still, however, an industrial revolution in its early stages. Russia's world position was a function more of its great size and population, along with rich natural resources, than of really thorough mechanization. Agriculture remained backward, as peasants had neither the means nor the motive to change their ways. Literacy was gaining and peasant habits did begin to change—for example, thanks to urban contacts, the rules of courtship relaxed, with more sexual overtones permitted—but agricultural methods lagged. This, in turn, retarded the growth of cities and made periodic famine a recurrent threat. Many Russian factories were vast—the largest, on average, in the world—and an urban artisanry also gained ground in fields like printing. But, the urban labor force, although expanding rapidly, was still a minority, and many workers had yet to convert to new work values. Nor did a powerful business class arise in Russia. Government controls and foreign investment produced industrialization without a surging middle class. Some Russian entrepreneurs showed impressive dynamism, and the number of businessmen and professionals increased, but Russian industrialization did not engender the kind of assertive, self-confident middle class that had arisen in the West. Industrialization was, in sum, still tentative, and it was definitely proceeding along distinctive lines in Russia.

THE FOUNDATIONS OF REVOLUTION

The nation's early industrialization increased the already fearsome tensions within the society. Peasant discontent, although not a constant force, continued to rise. Famines regularly provoked uprisings. Peasants, who deeply resented aristocratic estates and the redemption payments and taxes that burdened them, were also pressed by rapidly growing population levels, which augmented land hunger. Along with the peasantry, many educated Russians, including some aristocrats, clamored for revolutionary change. Their goals and motives varied, but in general they wanted political freedoms while maintaining a Russian culture different from that of the West, which they saw as hopelessly plutocratic and materialist. Upper-class radicals claimed that a spirit of community lay deep in the Russian soul, which could serve as the basis for an egalitarian society free from the injustice of the capitalist West. Many Russian radicals were anarchists who sought the abolition of all formal government. Although anarchism was not unknown in the West, it took on particular force in Russia in opposition to unyielding tsarist autocracy. Many anarchists turned to extremely violent methods, forming the first large terrorist movement in the modern world. Terrorism, in the form of assassinations and bombings, seemed an essential approach given the lack of other political outlets. It appeared that anarchist–terrorist tactics often focused more on destruction than on coherent political goals for the future. As the anarchist leader Bakunin put it:

> We have only one plan—general destruction. We want a national revolution of the peasants. We refuse to take any part in the working out of schemes to better the conditions of life; we regard as fruitless solely theoretical work. We consider destruction to be such an enormous and difficult task that we must devote all our powers to it, and we do not wish to deceive ourselves with the dream that we will have enough strength and knowledge for creation.

Not surprisingly, the recurrent waves of terrorism merely reinforced the tsarist regime's resolve to avoid further political change, in what became a vicious circle in late–nineteenth-century Russian politics.

By the late 1870s, Alexander II pulled back from his reform interest, fearing that change was escalating out of control. Censorship of newspapers and political meetings tightened; many dissidents were arrested and sent to Siberia. Alexander himself was assassinated by a terrorist bomb in 1881, and his successors, while escalating the effort to industrialize, continued to oppose further political reform. New measures of repression were also directed against minority nationalities, as a conservative nationalism, hostile to internal minorities and Western influence alike, swelled in praise of Russian values. The Poles and other groups were carefully supervised, and persecution of the large Jewish minority increased, resulting in many executions and seizures of property; as a consequence, many Russian Jews emigrated. In general, moreover, the late–nineteenth-century tsars sponsored a vigorous drive to impose Russian culture and language on the minority peoples. They thus tried to Christianize many Jewish children by force, while forbidding Poles and other minorities from using their own language for public purposes. In response, many minority nationalist movements spread on an underground basis, joining the anarchists in their energetic, if illegal, resistance to the tsarist regime.

One final political current arose by the 1890s. A number of radical leaders, drawn from the same educated circles as the anarchists, were attracted to the Marxist doctrines that were being disseminated in the West. Largely underground or in exile, Marxist groups formed, committed to a tightly organized proletarian revolution. Although the Marxist movement remained small, its ideas took hold among some urban industrial workers, who chafed under the harsh conditions of the early factories and the illegality of ordinary trade union activity.

By 1900, the contradictory currents in Russian society may have made revolution inevitable. While the forces demanding change were not united, and while extensive police work and military repression kept most uprisings in hand, the combination of pressures may have been too powerful to resist. Peasants had little concern for the more formal political ideas; indeed, anarchist efforts to reach out to the people in previous decades had been largely ignored. Marxists and anarchists, in fact, often disliked each other, for indeed both their methods and goals were different. The small middle class, interested in some political voice but not eager for full-scale social upheaval, was yet another piece on the complex Russian chessboard. Revolution did come in 1905, after Russia had suffered another disastrous and surprising military defeat, this time at the hands of Japan, who opposed further Russian expansion in

Shooting of strikers in St. Petersburg, January 1905. This sort of bloodshed helped launch the revolution of 1905.

Searching passersby in Riga during the Revolution of 1905.

northern China and Korea. Defeat unleashed massive general strikes by urban workers and a tumultuous series of peasant insurrections. In response, the tsarist regime relaxed the constraints of the postemancipation rural system, allowing peasants greater freedom to buy and sell land and operate independently of redemption payments and village controls. However, a halting pledge to appease middle-class sentiment by creating a national parliament, the Duma, was soon dashed by renewed political repression; the Duma became a hollow institution, satisfying no one. And, no gains were offered to the Marxists at all. The prospect of further revolution loomed large and then became reality when Russia plunged into yet another conflict—World War I—hoping that battle would bring new territory and distraction from internal stress. The gamble failed and, in 1917, one of the great revolutions in world history took place.

THE CULTURE OF EASTERN EUROPE

Many smaller East European countries followed patterns similar to those of Russia during the later nineteen century. New nations such as Romania, Bulgaria, and Serbia, free from Ottoman control, liberated the serfs, but amid restrictions that retained the bulk of the land for the aristocracy. Parliaments were established on superficially Western lines, but they had little power and were based on very limited voting rights.

Most of the smaller East European nations industrialized less extensively than Russia and remained even more dependent, as agricultural producers, on Western markets.

Despite economic problems and political tensions, however, Eastern Europe, including Russia, enjoyed an impressive cultural surge, a final ingredient in the complex developments that accompanied reactions to Western industrialization. Many Western artistic styles were appropriated. Russian and other East European novelists and essayists wrote in the Romantic vein, glorifying national ways; the Russian novel enjoyed unprecedented popularity in the hands of writers such as Tolstoy, Turgenev, and Dostoyevsky. Composers like Tchaikovsky brought Romanticism to music. Modern art currents in the West also found an echo, as abstract painting and atonal music took shape in the hands of Russian practitioners soon after 1900. East European intellectuals also participated in the scientific developments of the later nineteenth century. The important experiments on conditioned reflexes conducted by a Russian physiologist, Ivan Pavlov, advanced the understanding of unconscious responses in human beings.

In many ways, then, Eastern Europe seemed to be drawing closer to the West in cultural activity, continuing a pattern visible since the time of Peter the Great. Combined with growing industrialization and some political impulses borrowed from the West, including Marxism, it seemed possible that, despite its political peculiarities, Russia might produce a version of Western civilization, just as it had moved into the Western diplomatic orbit in many respects.

However, East European culture remained ambivalent about the West. Although some intellectuals were ardent admirers of Western culture, others used only partially Western styles to comment on the distinctiveness of the Russian or Slavic spirit. Many novelists joined political conservatives in finding a unique soul in their people, which, they felt, should be exalted and protected against Western influence. Romanticism, in its East European manifestation, encouraged a vigorous set of cultural and political nationalisms, designed to capture the glories of Russian, or Ukrainian, or Serbian peoples. A Pan-Slavic movement arose also—particularly in Russia, which claimed leadership of Slavic Europe—that argued for Slavic unity against the more materialistic and individualistic West.

Furthermore, the masses in Eastern Europe, mainly peasant, remained firmly attached to older traditions, including the Orthodox religion, different from those of the West and the partially Westernized upper classes. Popular culture changed through the impact of growing literacy, rising urbanization, and military service, but it did not merge with the popular culture of the West. Indeed, popular resentment against growing Western influence, including the power of foreign capitalists, would be yet another revolutionary rallying cry during and after World War I.

By 1900, then, Russia and much of the rest of Eastern Europe represented a distinctive amalgam of tradition and change. Principles of authoritarian rule remained virtually unaltered, but they now joined with diverse political opposition concentrated for the most part on sweeping revolution rather than purely liberal reforms. The tradition of territorial expansionism, although checked by resistance from the West and Japan, still ran strong. Pan-Slavic sentiments indeed encouraged new Russian influence in southeastern Europe. Massive social change had resulted from emancipation and early industrialization, but East European society continued to be more agricultural and in many ways more traditionalist than its Western counterpart. Finally, a larger ambivalence toward Western values persisted. East European intellectuals contributed creatively to general European artistic and scientific work, but a desire to define distinctive features, to resist full Westernization, remained all-important in many quarters, both elitist and popular. Eastern Europe was, in sum, developing its own pattern of change as it entered the industrial age. This pattern would soon embrace a distinctive kind of revolution as well.

JAPAN

Even more than Russia, Japan faced new pressure from the West during the 1850s, although it took the form of a demand for more open trade rather than outright war. After a tense debate during the 1850s and 1860s, Japan's response was more direct than Russia's and, on the whole, more immediately successful. Despite the long history of isolation, Japanese society was better adapted than Russia's to the challenge of industrial change. Market forms were more extensive, reaching into peasant agriculture; levels of literacy were higher. Japan, nevertheless, had to rework many of its institutions during the final decades of the nineteenth century, and the process produced significant strain. The result, by 1900, was different from both purely Western patterns and the more obvious tensions of Russian society.

On the surface, Japan experienced little change during the first half of the nineteenth century. The Tokugawa shogunate remained intact, although there were signs that it was becoming less effective. The shogunate ran the country through a combination of central bureaucracy and alliances with the regional daimyos. It also encouraged some business interests and provided a central banking system. Japanese culture still relied heavily on Confucianism, and participation in Confucian schools grew rapidly. Traditional artistic and dramatic styles remained lively. The interest in Western science that had developed among a small number of scholars continued, through eighteenth-century contacts with the Dutch trading outpost in the port of Nagasaki, but no technological breakthroughs occurred. The Japanese boasted a productive agriculture and considerable rural manufacturing, but there were signs of economic stagnation, particularly in a growing number of peasant riots against poor conditions. Nevertheless, there is no reason to believe that Japan was on the verge of significant change before change was thrust upon it.

The Opening of Trade

In 1853, the American commodore Matthew Perry arrived with a fleet in Edo Bay, near Tokyo, insisting through threats of bombardment that Americans be allowed to trade. In 1854, he returned and won the right to station an American consul in Japan; two ports were opened to commerce. Britain, Russia, and Holland quickly won similar rights. As in China, this meant that Westerners living in Japan would be governed by their own representatives, not by Japanese law. Other privileges soon followed, along with a few military skirmishes. Leading Western nations simply insisted on their need and right to trade, as part of the expanding world economy, while also seeking fishing rights in Japanese waters. For several decades, they limited Japan's ability to decide on its own tariffs. Russian pressure was a problem as well, as the nation's eastward expansion had already produced a few small clashes over control of islands in the North Pacific.

Some Japanese had already grown impatient with strict isolation. More important was the now obvious fact that Japan could not compete with Western navies and so had to defer to their interests. But, many Japanese leaders, including conservatives who feared Western influence, wanted to strengthen their government in order to control their nation's future. Their interest caused them to bypass the shogun and appeal directly to the emperor for support. Long secluded as a religious figure, the emperor now began to gain power.

In the 1860s, a political crisis came into the spotlight, involving a clash between many samurai and the shogunate. The crisis was marked by attacks on foreigners, including one murder of a British official, matched by the Western naval bombardments of feudal forts. Virtual civil war broke out in 1866 as the samurai eagerly armed themselves with surplus weapons from the American Civil War, causing Japan's aristocrats to finally come to terms with the sheer power of Western armaments. When the samurai defeated a shogunate force, a number of Japanese finally were shocked out of their traditional reliance on their own superiority, with one author arguing that the nation was, compared to the West with its technology, science, and humane laws, only half-civilized.

This multifaceted crisis came to an end in 1868, with the proclamation of rule by a new emperor named Mutsuhito, whose regime was soon called "Meiji," or "Enlightened Rule." Backed by some samurai leaders, the new emperor managed to put down the troops of the shogunate and gradually built up support, establishing his capital in Edo, now named Tokyo. The crisis period had been shocking enough to allow further changes in Japan's basic political structure—changes that went much

Commodore Perry's "Black Ship" as seen by the Japanese, 1854.

deeper at the political level than those introduced by Russia from 1861 onward. With the chief ministers actually taking the major initiative, the imperial government sponsored three decades of rapid change, designed to make Japan competitive with the West and thus save national independence in what was, for Japan, a radically new and perilous environment.

The key to the Japanese response was heightened governmental centralization. Meiji leaders abolished feudalism, as the regional lords surrendered their land rights to the government. Ministries in the central government now directed national policy in a surprisingly quick political adjustment. And, the ministers in the Meiji period were committed to further reform, as a government-sponsored reshaping of Japanese society was underway. Such reshaping, however, did not call into question the Japanese belief in not only their independence but also the basic superiority of their culture. An early Japanese visitor to the White House wrote a self-satisfied poem that captured part of the national mood:

We suffered the barbarians to look upon the glory of our Eastern Empire of Japan.

INDUSTRIALIZATION IN RESPONSE TO THE WEST

The Japanese combination of rapid adaptation and firm belief in the validity of their own values and institutions may explain the distinctive Japanese response in matching Western pressure without outright revolution and full-scale Westernization. Japanese leaders carefully blended economic political change with existing institutions and values.

Reform interests, in the Meiji period, focused on several targets. A new army was established, modeled on the German system. It was based on the universal conscription of young males. The training of officers improved, as new men replaced older feudal generals. Military armament was brought up to Western standards, and a navy was formed initially with the aid of Western advisors. The government also quickly introduced Western public-health measures, which promoted population growth.

Mass education spread rapidly from 1872 onward, for women as well as for men. Elite students at the university level often emphasized science, many of them studying technical subjects abroad. The rapid assimilation of a scientific outlook was a major new component of Japanese culture. Other cultural changes ranged farther afield: Fearful of embarrassment in Western eyes—a factor of growing importance in world history—the Japanese government even tried to outlaw homosexuality around 1900 and to increase differences in dress between boys and girls.

Reform also meant further political change. A new constitution took effect in 1890, again based on the German model. A two-house parliament, elected by men of property, served under the supreme emperor. The parliament did not develop extensive powers, as the emperor named his own ministers and controlled basic policy. But, several political parties competed for votes. The Japanese political style now combined centralized imperial rule with limited representative institutions; the combination gave great power to a new oligarchy of wealthy businessmen and aristocrats, who influenced the emperor and also pulled strings within parliament. This rule by an elite echoed earlier Japanese reliance on cooperation rather than competition in politics, as well as a tradition of considerable deference to the authority of the

HISTORY DEBATE

Different Confucian Paths

Japan and China were both societies strongly shaped by Confucian beliefs, yet Japan proved much more quickly capable of adaptation to change. Why? Some clues lie in prior cultural experience. China had been Confucian longer, and more people had a stake in preserving the emphasis on tradition and a nontechnical education. Japan already had imitated other cultures, as when it had turned to China during an earlier period, and had learned that one could engage in imitation without destroying all vestiges of one's own distinct culture. Its feudal traditions also encouraged a more prompt response to the West's military challenge. Its interpretation of Confucianism was different, hence, it had a more extensive educational system prior to Western influences (consider as another example of its intellectual open-mindedness the earlier "Dutch school" interest in Western science). Scorn for merchants was less intense; Confucianism in Japan had not led to as complete a subjugation of women.

Cultural factors may not provide the primary explanation for the new differentiation between China and Japan. Japan had the good fortune of a stronger government when interaction with the West occurred, and it also faced much less population pressure at that point.

Both China and Japan ultimately had to modify Confucianism. Both preserved elements of the Confucian heritage, but in very different twentieth-century political and economic systems. At the end of the twentieth century, however, some observers wondered whether the same heritage might draw the societies of East Asia, all now dynamic, into a renewal of more commonly shared patterns.

---

upper classes. Here was a clear case of blending Japanese values with Western-style institutions.

Above all, reform meant industrialization, with the government taking a far more active role than its Russian counterpart. New banks were created by the government to fund growing trade and to provide capital for industry. State-built railroads spread across the country, and the islands were connected by rapid steamers. Although Japan still relied heavily on home or small-shop production, particularly of goods like silk cloth that were widely exported, factory industry expanded steadily. Finally, the market emphasis on agriculture increased, as new methods were introduced to raise output to feed the growing cities.

Japanese state initiative not only built transportation and banking systems but also led to the government operation of mines, shipyards, and metallurgical plants. Scarce capital and the unfamiliarity of new technology seemed to compel state direction, which also served to supervise the many foreign advisors the Japanese required. Japan established a ministry of industry in 1870, and it quickly became one of the

The first Japanese Parliament meets, 1890.

key government agencies, setting overall economic policy as well as operating specific sectors. However, private initiative played a role as well. In textiles, private businessmen, many of them from older merchant families, ran the leading companies. In other industries, government concerns, tax-financed, were later sold to private interests, to the profit of the latter. Close collaboration between government agencies and private firms, especially big business concerns, early formed a hallmark of the new Japanese economy.

Although Japanese big business developed rapidly, early industrialization also depended on the massive exploitation of workers, particularly women workers. Tens of thousands of women were sold for labor service by fathers or husbands in the overpopulated Japanese countryside. They worked particularly in the silk industry, developed by the state on a labor-intensive basis to capture vital export earnings as Japan surpassed China in producing this luxury commodity.

CULTURAL AND SOCIAL-ECONOMIC EFFECTS OF INDUSTRIALIZATION

As had earlier occurred in the West, industrialization altered the existing social structure. Only a handful of aristocrats and people from the samurai warrior class entered the ranks of successful businessmen. A new elite was formed that embraced leading entrepreneurs for the first time, and while old merchant families contributed to this group, talented people from diverse backgrounds, including former peasants, now rose to the top. Among the masses, the rise of a huge, property-less class of urban workers was a new development. Both peasants and workers endured low wages and high taxes, as Japanese leaders used cheap labor to compete with Western enterprise and to amass the capital needed for further investment. And while the new elite did not cultivate the luxurious life style of Western business magnates, being content with lower profit rates, it did insist on retaining power. Unions and lower-class political parties, although they began to emerge by 1900, made only slow headway, and a militant socialist movement was outlawed without difficulty.

Many Japanese copied Western fashions as part of the effort to become modern. Western-style haircuts replaced the samurai practice of a shaved head with a top knot—another example of the fascinating Westernizing of hair throughout world history. Western standards of hygiene spread, and the Japanese became enthusiastic toothbrushers and consumers of patent medicines. Japan also adopted the Western calendar and the metric system. Few Japanese converted to Christianity, however, and despite fads imitating Western popular culture, the Japanese managed to preserve an emphasis on their own values. What the Japanese wanted and got from the West involved practical techniques; they planned to infuse these with a distinctively Japanese spirit.

Thus, in education, an initial surge of interest in Western schooling in the 1870s, which included the use of hundreds of European and American teachers, yielded in the 1880s to a reassertion of Japanese group loyalty and attacks on excessive individualism. New exposure to science changed culture, but the growing stress on nationalism provided a new focus for traditional beliefs in Japanese cohesion and distinctiveness.

Japanese family life retained many traditional emphases, as opposed to Western customs. To be sure, unprecedented population growth forced increasing numbers of people off the land, which disrupted families and caused the unusual reliance on women's work in industry. However, the Japanese were eager to maintain the traditional inferiority of women in the home. A new law promoted monogamy, but in practice mistresses were still widely accepted in the upper classes. The position of Western women seemed repellent. Official Japanese visitors to the United States were appalled by what they saw as the aggressive, domineering ways of women: "The way women are treated here is like the way parents are respected in our country." Standards of Japanese courtesy also contrasted with the more open and boisterous behavior of Westerners—particularly Americans. "Obscenity is inherent in the customs of

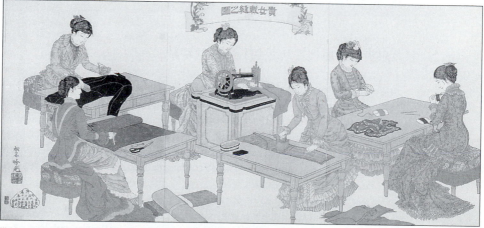

"Women of Fashion Sewing," Japanese woodblock print, 1887.

this country," noted another samurai visitor to the United States. Other basic features of Japanese life, including diet, were maintained in the face of Western influence. Japanese religious values were also distinctive. Buddhism lost some ground, although it remained important, and Confucianism was undermined through the new emphasis on science in the schools. But, Shintoism, which appealed to the rising nationalist concern with Japan's own unique mission and the religious functions of the emperor, won new interest.

By 1900, Japan's industrial success did not bring the country to Western levels, and the Japanese remained intensely fearful for their independence. Economic change, and the tensions as well as the power it generated, did however produce a shift in Japanese foreign policy. With only one previous exception, the Japanese had never before been interested in territorial expansion, but by the 1890s, they joined the ranks of imperialist powers. Partly this shift was an imitation of Western models, and at the same time it was an effort to prevent Western encroachment. Imperialism also relieved some strains within Japanese society, giving displaced samurai a chance to exercise their military talents elsewhere and providing symbols of nationalist achievement for the populace as a whole. The Japanese economy also required access to markets and raw materials. Because Japan was poor in many basic materials, including coal and oil for energy, the pressure for expansion was particularly great.

Japan's quick victory over China, in the quarrel for influence over Korea in 1894–1895, was a first step. Japan convincingly demonstrated its new superiority over all other Asian powers. Humiliated by Western insistence that it abandon the Liaotung peninsula, the Japanese planned a war with Russia as a means of striking out against the nearest European state. A 1902 alliance with Britain was an important sign of Japan's arrival as an equal player in the Western-dominated world diplomatic system. The Japanese were also eager to undermine Russia's growing strength in East Asia, after the completion of the Trans-Siberian Railroad. Disputes over Russian influence in Manchuria and Japanese influence in Korea led to the Russo-Japanese War in 1904, which Japan won handily on the basis of its superior navy. In 1910, Japan annexed Korea outright; it was now not only a modern industrial power, but a new imperialist force as well.

THE STRAIN OF MODERNIZATION

Japan's success by 1900 was amazing. Its victories over China and then Russia surprised virtually every observer outside of Japan. There is no question that Japan's rapid transformation, like its more recent success in becoming one of the most advanced industrial societies in the world, constitutes a unique achievement. Furthermore, the Japanese—unlike Russia or major parts of the West—prepared the groundwork for industrialization without the serious threat of popular revolution.

However, this achievement, even combined as it was with significant currents from earlier Japanese culture and political styles, had its costs. Many Japanese conservatives resented the passion that some Japanese displayed for Western fashions. Their concern helped ensure that Japanese women, initially the subject of some reform interest, would be mainly confined to family roles. Nevertheless, disputes between generations, with the old clinging to traditional standards, the young more interested in Western culture, were commonplace and very troubling in a society that stressed the importance of parental authority. Social tensions added to the strain, as expectations rose more rapidly than standards of living. Crowded conditions in the growing cities produced misery at least as great as in earlier Western slums. Rising divorce rates—Japan had the highest in the world by 1900—showed another kind of strain.

Some tension translated into politics, even with the narrow voting system. Political parties in Japan's parliament, called the "Diet," sometimes clashed with the emperor's ministers over rights to determine policy. The government frequently had to dissolve the Diet and call for new elections, seeking a more workable parliamentary majority.

Another kind of friction emerged in intellectual life. Many Japanese scholars emulated Western philosophies and literary styles. But in addition to an interest in more traditional forms, other intellectuals expressed a deep pessimism about the Japanese loss of identity in a changing world. Some wanted the government to become more fully Western; many were concerned about jobs, as universities tended to turn out more graduates than the economy could handle. But, the underlying theme was confusion about a Japan that was no longer traditional, but not Western either. What was it? Thus, some writers spoke of Japan heading for a "nervous collapse from which we will not be able to recover."

As an antidote to social and cultural insecurity, Japanese leaders urged national loyalty and devotion to the emperor, and with considerable success. The official message promoted Japanese virtues of obedience and harmony that the West lacked. School texts thus stressed:

> Our country takes as its base the family system; the nation is but a single family, the imperial family is our main house. We the people worship the unbroken imperial line with the same feeling of respect and love that a child feels towards his parents. . . . The union of loyalty and filial piety is truly the special character of our national polity.

Nationalism was a partially new force in Japan, and of course it was common in the West and other parts of the world in 1900 as well. However, Japanese nationalism built on traditions of superiority and cohesion, deference to rulers, and the new tensions generated by rapid change. It became if not a deeper force in Japan than elsewhere, at least one that played a unique role in justifying sacrifice and struggle in a national mission to preserve independence and dignity in a hostile world. Nationalism, along with the police's firm repression of dissent, certainly helps explain why Japan avoided the revolutionary pressure that plagued Russia, China, and other countries after 1900, and also the kind of unrest that had characterized early Western industrialization around 1848.

Japan's traditions thus enabled it to foster rapid change from above, without the need for a literal revolution to either purge the existing system or respond to the undeniable tensions that modernization produced. The result, by 1900, was a dynamic country newly powerful on the world scene, shaping a distinctive kind of industrial society. No other country would match its achievements for over half a century.

CONCLUSION: WORLD PATTERNS IN 1900

Western imperialism and new economic outreach, both backed by industrialization, had substantially altered world patterns during the nineteenth century. Significant divisions opened between societies directly under imperialist control and those, like China and the Ottoman Empire, touched by imperialism but technically independent. East Asian civilization split between China's sluggish response to the new world environment and Japan's surging modernization. Russia continued its own rise to greater power, now including early industrialization in this process. Latin America was another scene of important change, as political independence and cultural identity were combined with the growing commercialization of a dependent economy. Through imperialism and reactions to Western example, there were some common themes around the world, although they were very general. Educational systems spread in most societies. Traditional forms of unfree labor, including rigorous serfdom and slavery, largely disappeared, although low-paying and highly supervised wage labor on estates and in factories provided new employment for many workers.

Nevertheless, in 1900, it was the world's diversity that remained most striking, as it combined long-standing differences in cultural and political traditions with the newer variations produced by responses to Western imperialism and industrial example. Some of the divisions taking shape between industrializers including "early latecomers," such as Japan, and more dependent economies would have a continuing influence in world history into the late twentieth century. Other divisions, between an India open to forced Western influence and a more traditionalist China, would be complicated or superseded by later developments. What was becoming clear was the new set of divisions among civilizations, based no longer on evolving tradition alone, but on the response to new change and challenge.

SUGGESTED WEBSITES

On the emancipation of the serfs and later peasant life, see
http://russianculture.about.com/culture/ russianculture/msub23.htm;
on the formation of Meiji industrial policy, including an early industrial fair and Japan's wars with China and Russia, see *http://www.Meiji.com/index.html.*

SUGGESTED READINGS

A. Gerschenkron, *Economic Backwardness in Historical Perspective: A Book of Essays:* (1962), helps define the conditions of latecomer industrialization. Russian reforms and economic change are discussed in W. Blackwell, *The Industrialization of Russia,* 2nd ed. (1982) and Jerome Blum, *Lord and Peasant in Russia from the Ninth to the Nineteenth Century* (1961). On social and cultural developments, see Victoria Bonnel, ed., *The Russian Worker; Life and Labor under the Tsarist Regime* (1983); Barbara Engel, *Mothers and Daughters: Women of the Intelligentsia in Nineteenth Century Russia* (1983); and Jeffrey Brooks, *When Russia Learned to Read: Literacy and Popular Culture* (1987). On another vital area of Eastern Europe, see L. Stavrianos, *The Balkans, 1815–1914* (1963).

Japan in the nineteenth century is viewed from the perspective of modernization in R. Dore, ed., *Aspects of Social Change in Modern Japan* (1967). For a comparative view, see Peter

N. Stearns, *Starting School: The Rise of Modern Education in France, the United States, and Japan* (1997). See also W. W. Lockwood, *The Economic Development of Japan: Growth and Structural Change 1868–1938* (1954); J. C. Abegglen, *The Japanese Factory: Aspects of Its Social Organization,* rev. ed. (1985); Hugh Patrick, ed., *Japanese Industrialization and Its Social Consequences* (1973); Andrew Gordon, *The Evolution of Labor Relations in Japan* (1985); R. H. Myers and M. R. Beattie, eds., *The Japanese Colonial Empire, 1895–1945* (1984); and E. O. Reischauer, *Japan, the Story of a Nation* (1981).

World War I and the End of an Era

25

FOCAL POINTS

One of the most devastating wars of all time broke out in Europe in 1914. World War I had international significance and international causes. It marked the beginning of the end of Western Europe's world supremacy. Moreover, its causes also reflected other major changes, in Europe and elsewhere, that indicated significant shifts in the framework of world history.

World War I ended a major period in the world's history. This short chapter sums up the factors that led to the massive conflict. The same factors help explain why the conflict was so decisive.

Dramatic events are involved in the end of many eras in world history, of course. The collapse of the great classical empires might be compared to World War I, although this occurred over a far longer period of time. World War I had its own character, however. Although many Europeans launched the war almost eagerly, thinking it would lead to glory and power, the mood soon changed. By the war's end, many people knew that an age had ended. The causes of the war highlighted the century of imperialism, but they also led to the erosion of Europe's dominance.

Events soon after 1900 signaled an end to what some historians have called the "long nineteenth century."

Item: Women obtained the right to vote in several Scandinavian countries plus Australia, and feminist agitation heated up in other parts of Western society.

Item: Australia became fully independent in 1900, a symbol of the changing role of the European frontier societies in world history.

Item: A Chinese revolution in 1911 toppled the imperial system for the first time since the collapse of the Han dynasty. China was in the throes of massive change.

Item: A Mexican revolution began in 1910 that called into question some of the political and social arrangements that had been common in nineteenth-century Latin America.

Item: Japan's victory over Russia and the Russian revolution of 1905 signaled dramatic new power alignments and the potential for turmoil in one of the world's major empires.

Item: The outbreak of World War I in 1914 launched a conflict that would have massive effects in Europe and the Middle East, with important spillover in East Asia and the Pacific, Africa, South Asia, and North America. The war pitted Britain, France, and Russia against Germany and the Habsburg monarchy—the world's most heavily armed nations came to blows through rival alliance systems. Other areas joined as colonies of the European powers or independently through hopes of territorial gains or other advantages. By the time the war ended in 1918, the nineteenth-century world order had been severely disrupted, although many Western leaders, eager to return to what they called normalcy, refused to recognize this fact.

The causes of World War I hardly sum up all the major trends that had emerged by the end of the nineteenth century, but they capture a fair number. The specific trigger for the war lay within the small nations of southeastern Europe, recently independent from Ottoman control. Ottoman weakness had created a vacuum of power in this region that continues to this day. The new Balkan states, all highly nationalistic, frequently quarreled among themselves, conducting two regional wars before 1914. Russia and the Habsburg monarchy vied for influence in the area, hoping to distract their own peoples from internal tensions. Russia sponsored Slavic nationalism, whereas the Habsburgs, with large and restless Slavic minorities, tried to suppress the same force. In 1914, a Serbian nationalist assassinated a member of the Habsburg royal family. Austria threatened war, but Russia backed Serbia. Then the larger European alliance system came into play: Germany feared abandoning Austria lest it face Russia and France alone. France and, more reluctantly, Britain decided they had to support Russia. Rigid diplomacy and fervent nationalism among all the European great powers parlayed a regional crisis into full-scale war. Europe's alliance system, combined with growing military rivalry and massive armaments, thus trapped the major powers into decisions that led inevitably to war.

Larger issues were at play, as the causes of war revealed massive fault lines in Western society. Huge weapons industries had evolved in all the powerful European nations, partly because of imperialist rivalries, partly to ensure sales to influential industrialists. Arms races—particularly navy-building competitions and especially between Britain and Germany—enhanced public anxiety and made it more difficult for nations to compromise when disputes broke out. Russia, Germany, and France all had rigid strategic plans that encouraged prompt military action—in the hope, which proved completely illusory, of delivering quick knockout blows to the enemy.

Imperialism itself had created a growing sense in Europe that aggressive expansionism was normal state policy. But by 1914, the opportunities for further colonies were essentially exhausted, and the fervor that had gone into empire building now turned back on Europe itself. Politicians had increasingly pointed to nationalist triumphs as a means of wooing voters, and the habit persisted. Russia and Austria-Hungary, keenly aware that they had fallen behind in imperialist races, hoped for triumphs that would divert public opinion.

European political and military leaders also worried about broader social tensions within their societies. Labor unrest was mounting, joined in some cases by feminist agitations and other repressed groups such as, in Britain's case, the Irish who increasingly pushed for independence. Many officials worried that internal difficulties would erode national power—believing that it would be wisest to engage in war now, while strength was still high. Others argued that a successful war would unify the population, reducing the strength of socialist dissent. Ordinary people, bored or oppressed by industrial life, saw war as an exciting option—unaware of how devastating industrial warfare would actually be. Boys in various social classes had been raised on a diet of toy soldiers and aggressive sports—war seemed a glorious prospect in societies in which the importance of masculinity was asserted but not always easily expressed. The enthusiasm for war, in sum, drew on a number of tensions and anxieties created by industrial society.

Europe's decision to embark on a war also reflected its position in the world, strengths and weaknesses alike. Europeans were feeling at least vaguely threatened by the rise of societies outside their borders. Japan's industrial and military surge, plus stirrings in China, made some European nationalists talk of a new "yellow peril" that might displace Western supremacy. U.S. economic rivalry was keenly felt. British observers, greeting the new century in 1900, wondered if their days of easy empire were numbered, given new rivals and the sheer numbers of its colonial peoples. Oddly, given Britain's strength, but revealingly, they looked forward to the new century with real dread. These anxieties might, of course, have prompted a new European unity, in order to protect their general interests, but national divisions ran too deep for this. Instead, countries concerned about their future turned to the familiar, nationalist military response. In essence, Europeans worried about their world position

Women help their men carry heavy rucksacks to the station during Germany's troop mobilization. Their rifles are decorated with flowers.

but at the same time they assumed a position of assured dominance, believing it was safe to engage in internal conflict. This assurance would lead, among other things, to a rapid impulse to extend European warfare to the colonies themselves and to use colonial troops on the European front. The result was a genuine world war and one that would redefine world alignments.

But war in an industrial age, and in the changing world context, had itself changed. Although many Europeans entered this conflict optimistically, assuming a quick and glorious end, World War I resulted in unprecedented dislocation and a host of unforeseen consequences. A new period in world history was baptized in blood, as the most powerful civilization tore itself apart.

CONCLUSION: A WORLD HISTORY WATERSHED

Even more than the fall of Constantinople to the Turks in 1453, World War I constituted an event that reshaped world history. Along with other developments, such as upheaval in East Asia, it furthered a realignment of power in the world. The war also promoted other shifts, such as changes in gender relations in Western society, that had been taking shape more gradually. The Western powers would seek to return the world to its prewar condition after the great conflict ended, but their success was both fleeting and superficial. A new age was brewing.

SUGGESTED WEBSITE

On World War I, see *http://www.WorldWarI.com*.

SUGGESTED READING

On the causes of World War I, see James Joll, Origins of World War I (1980), and K. Robbins, *The First World War* (1984). For a wider view, see Eric Hobsbawm, *The Age of Extremes: A History of the World, 1914–1991* (1996), and G. Barraclough, *An Introduction to Contemporary History* (1968).

PART
VI

The Contemporary World

INTRODUCTION: KEY CHANGES IN THE TWENTIETH CENTURY

With the dramatic, often violent events that unfolded between 1900 and 1918, headed by World War I itself, the twentieth century marked a new phase in world history. The transition was bathed in blood. Several even larger themes, apart from the war, also distinguished the twentieth century from the previous period.

The virtually unchallenged rise of the West, which along with the related development of a genuine world economy formed the central theme of world history from 1450 to around 1900, ended in the twentieth century. The change was not immediately clear. Much of the first half of the century marked the end of the old order rather than the visible shaping of the new. Nonetheless, three trends came together to end the West's continued dominance. First, various regions gained ground in the West in military terms. Second, parts of eastern Asia, particularly Japan, became industrial equals to the West, undergoing much more rapid economic transformation than the West itself experienced after 1900. Finally, the age of Western imperialism ended with a wave of decolonization that established independent nations throughout the Middle East, southern Asia, Africa, and the islands of the Pacific and the Caribbean.

Quite simply, developments in the twentieth century reversed several basic trends in world history, most of which had existed since the fifteenth century:

- The West's clear military supremacy, initially established through naval gunnery and then increased by industrial armaments, began to fade. Not only the military strength of powers like the Soviet Union and, for a time, Japan, but also new methods of warfare, particularly guerrilla tactics developed in places like Vietnam and Algeria, made military operations more difficult for Western armies.

New wealth allowed many nations to acquire modern armaments sufficient to deter easy Western invasions.

- The West's near monopoly on world trade dissipated. Several areas generated more rapid economic growth rates, allowing them to catch up with the West. Even many poorer regions developed dynamic industrial sectors that made them competitive and also reduced their dependence on the West for manufactured goods.

- Decolonization obviously reversed the long period of growing territorial acquisition by the West. Growing Western weakness and a desire to concentrate on rebuilding one's own society combined with growing demands for independence that echoed around the world. Here, tensions between the world wars set the stage for the rapid establishment of new nations between 1946 and the mid–1970s.

The diminishment of Western power was not the same, to be sure, as outright Western decline. The expanding strength of the United States helped to qualify any notion of a complete setback in the West. So did new signs of economic and political vigor in Europe, particularly after 1945. Throughout the century, some observers claimed to see symptoms of the kind of decay in the West that had earlier toppled the Roman Empire or led to the more subtle deterioration of Arab civilization. Although such forewarnings might turn out to be justified, they remain speculative. What is demonstrable is that the balance among societies began to alter during the twentieth century and Western dominance of the world lessened.

Western culture continued to exercise worldwide influence, which further complicates an assessment of the West's relative decline. Western intellectual standards in science and modern art still define many fields, although researchers and artists from many societies now participate in these fields. In the field of modern architecture, for example, architects from Japan, Latin America, and elsewhere now gained world-class status, but major styles still reflected their Western origins. The West, including the United States and Europe, also set international standards in popular culture, from sports through music, costume, and film. One of the key issues in twentieth-century world history involved the reactions of different societies to Hollywood movies, fast foods, or Anglo-American rock music. Changes in the cultural balance around the world, in other words, lagged behind the redistribution of power, although new religious currents by the 1970s signaled attempts by several societies to counteract Western influence in this area too.

Issues of power were not the only items on the new agenda of the twentieth century. It also witnessed an unprecedented increase in the world's population. By 1970, there were more people living than had ever reached adulthood in the entire previous history of the human species. World population nearly tripled in the first three quarters of the century. Improved border controls by newly efficient governments and international organizations helped control devastating plagues. Swamp drainage, insect control, and basic sanitary measures reduced other traditional killers. Although dire hunger persisted, advances in agriculture enabled greater numbers of people to be fed adequately. Falling death rates, though at varying levels in different regions, not only increased population outright but also allowed more people to reach adulthood and have children of their own. Despite the fact that per capita birthrates did not rise, overall birthrates did. The result was a massive number of people, whose lives easily compensated for the devastation of twentieth century wars, with hundreds of millions to spare.

Massive population growth helped account for a number of other key developments across the world. Urbanization proceeded rapidly in most civilizations. Individual cities in Asia and Latin America easily outstripped the Western giants in size. The growth of Tokyo, or Shanghai, or Mexico City involved huge movements of people. New migrations also occurred across the boundaries of nation and civilization. The West began to attract millions of immigrants from other societies—particularly southern Asia and the Middle East, Africa, and Latin America. The world population explosion also helps explain the frequent unrest of urban and rural masses in many twentieth-century societies.

The nature of war and diplomacy changed during the twentieth century. Imperialism had already established a world diplomacy, although of a one-sided sort; in the twentieth century, particularly after 1945, international diplomacy became a commonplace practice. Alliances were routinely formed, and broken, across civilization boundaries. Wars intensified in scope. They involved greatly heightened powers of governments, as many states learned to mobilize entire economies and to inflame national opinion as part of the military effort. Above all, wars became more violent. New technologies facilitated the killing of more people than ever before. World War I saw the introduction of tanks, submarines, long-range artillery, aerial bombing, and poison gas; World War II brought more massive aerial and naval clashes and the dawn of nuclear and missile warfare. After both world wars, diplomats and ordinary people alike operated amid an atmosphere of fear and uncertainty engendered by steady advances in weaponry.

The pace of many human endeavors quickened in the twentieth century. Air travel shrunk the globe even further than steam shipping had. Telephones, radios, and later, satellite and computer communications allowed the more rapid transmission of greater volumes of information across greater distances than ever before. Multinational companies, operating on all inhabited continents, became capable of transporting goods and people with unprecedented swiftness. Popular culture, particularly but not exclusively in industrialized societies, adopted the theme of speed. Olympic Games promoted competition in all sorts of speed-related sports. People ate faster; by the 1980s, most Japanese schoolchildren could no longer be bothered with chopsticks because the utensils made eating too slow, while fast-food restaurants cropped up in most major cities. Although speed was a factor first and foremost in transportation and communication, it also affected the way people thought and the stresses, often job-related, they imposed on themselves.

Finally, two major trends swept across many different societies in the twentieth century, creating parallelisms, although not full homogeneity, in regions otherwise as different as Germany and Korea. Political change constituted the first common theme. Almost all nations had different political systems, by 1994, from those that had been in operation in 1900. Some regions had gone through several different political systems, in fact. This widespread pattern meant that many societies had to develop new beliefs and defenses of their political legitimacy, while governments took on important new functions. Even the United States, which retained its basic system, redefined the role of the state from the 1930s onward.

The second change involved culture: Many people believed in different ideas, by the 1990s, from what their counterparts had embraced in 1900. In some areas, traditional religions were challenged, whereas in other regions, religious conversion topped the cultural agenda. As in politics, the point was not a common pattern but rather a common participation in change.

The twentieth century thus contained most of the standard characteristics involved in the advent of a new period of world history. The balance of power among civilizations shifted from what had prevailed in the previous centuries—hence, the relative decline of the West and the rise of new dynamism in places like Japan. Contacts among civilizations intensified, thanks to new technologies, new cultural diffusion as in the exchange of film and television, and new international organizations such as multinational businesses. The world became even smaller than it had been during the century of Western industrialization. Finally, a number of common themes spread around the world, inducing revisions of established political and cultural forms, the impact of unprecedented population growth, and the altered nature of war and diplomacy. Not since the fifteenth century had so many facets of the framework of world history altered direction.

In addition to these changes, of course, were a host of developments in individual civilizations. Russia, China, and, more briefly, Germany pioneered new forms of government controls. Experimentation in modern art and sleek architectural styles spread from the West to many parts of the world. The list of innovative trends and shattered traditions is long. They add up, in the view of many observers, to what one historian has termed "a world different, in almost all its basic preconditions," from that of the late nineteenth century.

Identifying major breaks in world history, and not just the history of a single civilization, is a tricky business. We have emphasized long periods: the birth of agricultural society; the elaboration of key classical civilizations; the expansion of civilization and the impact of the great religions; and the rise of the West and the development of a new global economy. We cannot be absolutely sure, living in what is at best the beginning of a new period, that a definitive new era has dawned, and we certainly cannot be sure of all its major characteristics. A mere 100 years is—and even allowing for a faster rate of change—a rather brief span of time by which to judge in world history terms.

Nevertheless, if the twentieth century does constitute a break in world history, as events and themes suggest, it is possible to speculate about the underlying dynamic that is evolving. The twentieth century marked the start of the industrialization of the world. The nineteenth century had seen the first industrial revolutions, to be sure, and their results were brought to the world by Western merchants and imperialists. But, the twentieth century saw full industrialization achieved in some areas outside Europe and North America, particularly in Eastern Europe and the "Pacific Rim," including Japan, and the beginnings of gradual industrialization elsewhere—notably in China, Southeast Asia, India, and parts of Latin America. The world was by no means completely industrialized by the 1990s, of course, and in some ways economic disparities among some major civilizations increased. However, the strivings for economic modernization and the adjustments to its impact now form a theme that literally encompasses the world.

Global industrialization, understood as a common process rather than a uniform economic system, underlies the other trends that can be identified, on an international basis, as distinguishing the twentieth century. It was the industrialization of Russia and Japan that most clearly ended the undisputed rise of the West in world affairs. Offshoots of mechanization, in new sanitation procedures and agricultural techniques, led to world population growth. Industry was behind the fearsome technologies of contemporary war, and it, of course, set the stage for the new theme of speed. Political changes resulted in part from growing industrialization, as new government functions both preceded and followed economic shifts; more traditional regimes, for the most part failing to keep pace, had to be replaced. Cultural changes, including new secular loyalties, followed from the development of more industrial economies. Traditional social structures often shifted as well, as aristocracies largely disappeared and peasantries declined, to be replaced by new kinds of managers and a growing urban working class.

Industrial growth also redefined the kind of global economy that had come to life in the early modern period and then intensified during the nineteenth century. The West no longer monopolized the top spot in the world economy as Japan claimed a share. And although some regions were still exploited for their raw materials and cheap labor, a larger number of nations reached a middle ground in world trade during the second half of the twentieth century. Rapid industrial growth, at 5–10 percent a year by the 1970s, characterized places like Brazil, Mexico, India, Turkey, and China. Rates of this sort could double industrial output every 10–20 years. Huge economic divisions persisted, and some areas still had only tiny industrial sectors. Nonetheless, significant industrial evolution was a genuine international trend. International trade and technological exchange became more important than ever before; societies that isolated usually suffered after a decidedly short time. However, the nature of the world economy was more complex, with a wider variety of roles, than in the simpler days of the nineteenth century when the West led the band and almost every other region danced to its tune.

Not all was new. Many developments, including even massive population growth, built on earlier trends. Modern war was foreshadowed by the American Civil War and by the sophisticated weaponry of the later nineteenth century. One can view the twentieth century as the beginning of a transition to a new stage of world history without denying that earlier developments had paved the way. The revival of traditional antagonisms between Christians and Muslims in central Asia and the Balkans in the 1990s reminded the world of just how many issues have their roots in the more distant past.

Furthermore, the major civilizations responded to the challenges of the twentieth century in different ways, in large part because of their distinctive traditions. Some developments, to be sure, became in fact international. It was possible to find examples of the same building styles, the same mode of dress, the same soft drinks, the same sports in most parts of the world. But, along with closer international links came varied reactions, depending on prior experience. Thus, although the monarchy lost its grip, several different political forms took its place. While the desire to industrialize spread, the economic system a given society would adopt, the kind of cultural change it would embrace, or the way it would define the roles of different family members, all varied widely. The world, although growing smaller, was not necessarily becoming more homogeneous; as a result, twentieth-century history must be interpreted as a combination of sweeping trends and particular reactions based on tradition. Each civilization changed, without question; even the West went through an important transformation of its earlier industrial order. However, it is important to recognize new and old distinctions among civilizations, as well as shared problems and responses.

THEMES, SUBPERIODS, AND CIVILIZATIONS

Looking at the twentieth century as the beginning of a new period in world history means asking some common questions about each major civilization. How did each area participate in cultural change and how did it react to Western influences in popular culture? How did change in each area relate to the redefined patterns of international trade and to what extent did the area gain greater control over its own economy? What impact did the major wars have, or the surge of world population? Did the area develop a new political style, and in response to what forces? How did responses to the common issues reflect the particular characteristics of each civilization, in relation to its own long history?

The twentieth century as a whole, and the histories of most of the major civilizations, must also be divided into three major subperiods, each relating to the unfolding of the new global framework. The period from 1914–1945 was clearly transitional. Western Europe and, to an extent, the United States suffered the agonies of war and economic dislocation, but Japan and Russia, although ravaged by war, solidified their industrial economies. Central governments strengthened in Latin America, while the nationalist challenge to imperialism surged forward in Asia, the Middle East, and Africa. From a Western standpoint, these were dreadful decades, but from other vantage points, they were decades full of new promise.

From 1945 onward, new political structures arose, as imperialism dissipated. New nations were built, while Japan and its neighbors in the Pacific Rim advanced economically. The "industrialization of the world," although very uneven, clearly moved ahead. But, these developments occurred under the shadow of the great cold war between the United States and the Soviet Union. Political and economic systems varied greatly depending on cold war alignments.

Finally, beginning in the 1970s, the cold war became less of a threat, coming to an end with the collapse of the Soviet system in 1989–1991. New diplomatic issues came to the fore, including a host of regional troublespots. Four other major trends shaped world developments at this point. First, industrial growth in virtually every society heightened the levels of global competition, while multinational companies established operations wherever they could find suitably trained but cheap labor (and, often, relaxed environmental regulations). New economic problems and new areas of growth resulted. Second, almost all societies decided to reduce the economic role of government in the interests of faster economic growth. The results varied, in part because the roles of government already differed, but on the whole the policy shift seemed to spur production while creating new gaps between the rich and poor within most societies. And, the decision itself constituted unprecedented, if not necessarily permanent, international agreement on basic economic goals and means. Third, a new enthusiasm for democratic political forms spread almost everywhere— although there were a few revealing exceptions. Never before had this political structure spread so widely, as many societies tried to replace authoritarianism or communism. Finally, religions revived in many areas, often in quite novel forms, resulting in new cultural tensions between secular and religious styles and commitments. These trends have continued boldly into the new century.

Chapters in this section return to each of the major areas of civilization. Here is an opportunity to see how forces from earlier civilizations interacted within the framework of the new period of world history. Some areas, to be sure, were divided in new ways. China and Japan followed different patterns in East Asia. The Middle East split between secular and religious states. Amid great change, each civilization sought to accommodate innovation with past traditions. All experienced the new international pressures of growing trade, migration, and cultural influence. The tension between regional traditions and globalism was obvious everywhere. The contemporary world continues to be shaped by the dynamic interplay between past and present.

World Events	Western Civilization	Soviet Union and Eastern Europe	East Asia
	1905 Einstein's theory of relativity formulated.	**1905** Revolution in Russia.	
	1910 First use of assembly line production.		**1911** Revolution led by Sun Yat-sen.
1914–1918 World War I.			**1912** Fall of Chinese empire.
1917 Russian Revolution.	**1918–1919** End of German empire, Habsburg empire.	**1917** Revolution in Russia. Bolshevik takeover in October.	**1916** Yuan Shi-h'ai named China's president.
1919 Formation of Communist International.	**1919–1939** Period of U.S. isolationism.		**1919** Former German islands in Pacific taken by Japan.
1919 Paris Peace Conference (Versailles); founding of League of Nations.			**1919 ff.** Growing regional warlord power in China.
	1920s Rise of fascism.	**1921** Lenin's New Economic Policy promulgated.	**1921** Formation of Chinese communist movement.
	1923 Fascist regime in Italy.	**1923** New constitution.	
	1920–1923 Rapid inflation.	**1927** Stalin in full power.	**1927** Communists expelled by Kuomintang.
		1928 Beginning of collectivization of agriculture, five-year plans.	
1929–1939 Worldwide economic depression.	**1929** Depression.		
			1934 "Long March" led by Mao Zedong.

India and Southeast Asia	Middle East	Latin America	Sub-Saharan Africa
1914–1918 Participation of Indian troops with Britain in World War I.		**1910–1917** Mexican revolution.	**1914–1918** Use of African troops in World War I; British takeover of German colonies.
	1915 ff. Rise of Arab nationalism, encouraged during World War I.	**1917** New constitution; nationalization of mineral rights.	
1919 British colonial reforms; limited representative government.	**1917** Promulgation of Balfour declaration, promising Jewish homeland in Palestine.		**1919** First meeting of Pan-African Congress; rise of African nationalism.
1920 Beginning of Gandhi's nonviolent movement.	**1920** Treaty of Sèvres, ending Ottoman Empire.	**1920** Obregón president; rise of National Revolutionary Party.	**1921 ff.** Sporadic religious and nationalist riots against European rule.
	1920 ff. Growth of Jewish settlement in Palestine.		**1924** Color bar bill backed by Afrikaner Nationalist Party in South Africa, limiting black–white social contacts.
	1922 Partial independence granted to Egypt by Britain.		
	1923 ff. Independent Turkey created by Atatürk; beginning of modernization drive.		
	1923 ff. Rise of independent Persia under Shah Riza Khan.		
	1935 Name changed to Iran.	**1929 ff.** Depression; rise of economic nationalism.	

World Events	Western Civilization	Soviet Union and Eastern Europe	East Asia
	1933–1939 U.S. New Deal.		**1931** Japanese invasion of Manchuria.
	1933–1944 Nazi regime in Germany.		**1932** End of political party government in Japan; rise of military rule.
	1938 Munich agreement; effort at British, French compromise with Hitler.		**1935** Further advance of Japan.
	1939 German-Soviet alliance.	**1937–1938** Great Purge conducted by Stalin.	**1937** New Japanese attack on China.
	1940–1944 Holocaust, slaughter of 6 million Jews.	**1939** Signing of Soviet-German pact.	
1939–1945 World War II.	**1940 ff.** Rise of women in labor force.	**1941** German invasion of Russia.	**1941** Pearl Harbor attacked.
1945 Atomic bomb dropped on Japan.	**1945–1948** Postwar reconstruction; new democratic regimes in France, Italy, West Germany; rise of welfare state.	**1943** Red Army pushes west.	**1942–1945** Momentum against Japan gained by United States.
1945 United Nations established.		**1945–1948** Soviet takeover of Eastern Europe.	**1945** Atom bomb dropped on Nagasaki and Hiroshima by United States; surrender of Japan; beginning of U.S. occupation.
1947 ff. Cold war begun between United States and Soviet Union.	**1948–1949** Berlin airlift.		**1945 ff.** Communist-Kuomintang war in China.
1948 ff. Decolonization; rise of new nations.	**1949** Formation of NATO.		**1949** Communist victory.
			1950 Start of Chiang Kai-shek's regime in Taiwan.
			1949 Korean War; U.S. intervention.
			1950 Chinese intervention.

India and Southeast Asia	Middle East	Latin America	Sub-Saharan Africa
1930–1931 Rioting in Indochina; rise of communist movement under Ho Chi Minh.		**1930** Military coup in Brazil; Vargas caudillo to 1945.	
1934 Philippine self-government increased by United States.		**1933** Power in Cuba seized by caudillo.	
1935 New British constitution for India.		**1934 ff.** U.S. "good neighbor" policies begun.	
1935 Nationalist victory in Siam; nation renamed Thailand.		**1934–1940** Cardenas president of Mexico; formation of Pemex.	
1937 Nationalist petition in Indonesia.	**1936** Syria promised independence by France.		**1936** Exclusion of blacks from South African voting.
1940 ff. Japanese invasion of Southeast Asia.	**1945** Syria and Lebanon fully independent.	**1945** Juan Péron president of Argentina.	
1946 Hindu-Muslim clash in India.	**1948** State of Israel declared.		
1946 Philippines independent.			
1947 India and Pakistan independent.			**1948** Full control of South African government gained by Afrikaners' independence from Britain and extension of apartheid.
1948 Sri Lanka and Burma independent.			**1953** Strikes by black workers barred by law.
1949 Indonesia independent.			**1959** Enactment of Bantu self-government law, setting up 10 homelands as the only legal black residences.

World Events	Western Civilization	Soviet Union and Eastern Europe	East Asia
	1950–1973 Growing economic prosperity.	*1951* Atom bomb developed by Soviets.	*1950 ff.* Rapid economic advance in Japan.
	1958 Establishment of French Fifth Republic.	*1953* Death of Stalin.	
1955 First meeting of non-aligned nations.		*1955* Formation of Warsaw pact.	
1957 Sputnik, first artificial satellite, launched by Soviet Union, beginning the "space age."		*1956* Stalinism attacked by Khrushchev.	
	1958 Founding of European Economic Community (Common Market).	*1956* Hungarian revolution and its suppression.	
		1961 Berlin wall erected.	*1960s* Mao's Cultural Revolution.
		1962 Cuban missile crisis.	
	1968 Student protests, in United States and Western Europe.	*1968* Revolt in Czechoslovakia and its repression.	*1969* Russian–Chinese border fighting.

India and Southeast Asia	Middle East	Latin America	Sub-Saharan Africa
	1950–1962 Complete independence of Arab states.		**1952–1959** Mau Mau terrorism against white landowners, Kenya.
1954 End of French war against Vietnamese nationalists and communists; independence and division of Vietnam.	**1952** Egyptian revolution, fall of monarchy.	**1953** Reformist regime in Guatemala unseated by United States.	
	1956 Egyptian seizure of Suez Canal.	**1955** Péron overthrown by military coup.	
1955 First meeting of non-aligned nations, under India's leadership.	**1956, 1967, 1973** Israeli–Arab wars.	**1966, 1976** Other Argentine military coups.	
		1959–1960 Castro's revolution in Cuba.	
		1960 ff. Independence achieved by most West Indies territories.	**1957–1980** Independence granted to most of black Africa.
			1957 Ghana independent.
	1962 Algeria independent.	**1960 ff.** Rise of liberation theology in Latin American church.	**1958** French colonies semi-independent, soon fully so.
		1961 Failure of U.S. "Bay of Pigs" invasion.	**1959** Riots leading to Congo independence (Zaire).
		1964 Military coup in Brazil.	**1965** Southern Rhodesia declared independent under white rule.
			1974–1975 Angola and Mozambique independent from Portugal.
1963 Beginning of authoritarian rule under Marcos in Philippines; military coup in Indonesia.			**1980** Rhodesia renamed Zimbabwe under black government.
1964 ff. Growing U.S. participation in North–South Vietnam war.			**1960–1963** Civil war in Zaire.
			1967–1970 Nigerian civil war.

World Events	Western Civilization	Soviet Union and Eastern Europe	East Asia
1973–1979 Increase in world energy prices promoted by OPEC. **1978 ff.** Widespread trend to more market economies, reduction of state role. **1989** End of cold war. **1989 ff.** Growing U.N. role in intervention in regional conflicts. **1988–1993** Widespread economic recession, rising unemployment: United States, Europe, Japan. **1990 ff.** Increased U.N. peacekeeping and relief efforts in Africa, Eastern Europe, Southeast Asia, Middle East. **1994** North American Free Trade Association. **1998** International environmental agreements in Kyoto.	**1970s** Introduction of microchip computer. **1979 ff.** New economic tensions. **1981** Reagan president in United States. **1990** German unification. **1992** End of economic restrictions within common markets. **1992–1993** Negotiations in extending Common Market toward single currency, etc. **1993** Full unification of European Economic Community (now known as the European Union). Maestricht treaty urges more coordination. **1994 ff.** Entry of Finland, Austria, Sweden to European Union. **1999** Single European Union currency, the Euro, begins.	**1979** Uprisings in Poland and their suppression. **1985** Gorbachev assumes power in Soviet Union; reform follows. **1988–1989** Liberalization sweeps throughout Eastern Europe; new constitutions, economic reforms; nationalist agitation in Soviet Union. **1988** New Soviet constitution; establishment of the Congress of People's Deputies. **1989–1991** Collapse of Soviet empire; new elections throughout much of Eastern Europe; Gorbachev selected as President. **1991** Collapse of Soviet Union, replaced by Russia and numerous European and central Asian republics; Yeltsin replaces Gorbachev. **1991–1996** Civil war in parts of former Yugoslavia. **1997** NATO invites Poland, Hungary, Czech Republic as members. **1999** Russia wars with Muslim region, Chechnya. **2000** Putin wins election as Russian president.	**1971** Partial Chinese–U.S. reconciliation. **1976** Death of Mao; more pragmatic regime in China. **1978** More market economy in China. **1980** End of U.S.–Taiwan treaty alliance; economic rise of Pacific Rim. **1984** British–Chinese agreement to return Hong Kong to China in 1997. **1988–1989** Growing student agitation for liberal political reform in South Korea; elected civilian government installed. **1989** Suppression of democratic protests in China. **1993** Split of factions within Japan's Liberal Democratic Party; Liberal Democrats fall from power in Japan. **1997** Hong Kong is returned to China. **1998** Asian economic crisis.

India and Southeast Asia	Middle East	Latin America	Sub-Saharan Africa
1971 Revolt in Pakistan; creation of independent Bangladesh.	**1970s** Rise of Muslim fundamentalism.	**1970** Chilean election won by socialist coalition.	**1980s** Growing problems of hunger in parts of Africa.
1973 End of Vietnam War.	**1977** Egypt–Israeli peace.	**1973** Allende murdered in U.S.-backed military coup; beginning of repressive regime of Pinochet.	**1989** DeKlerck charts a path of peaceful reform in South Africa.
1975 Control by North Vietnamese of all of Vietnam; movement into Laos and Cambodia.	**1978–1979** Iranian revolution. **1980–1988** Iran–Iraq war.	**1978** Agreement by United States to turn over control of Panama Canal.	**1984 ff.** New wave of black protest against South African apartheid.
1975–1977 Suspension of civil liberties in India; sterilization campaign.	**1981** Assassination of President Sadat of Egypt.	**1979** Sandinista revolt in Nicaragua.	**1990** Nelson Mandela released from prison.
1984 Assassination of Indira Gandhi by Sikh extremists; smooth transition of leadership to her son Rajiv.	**1982** Invasion of Lebanon by Israel. **1985** Withdrawal of Israel from Lebanon; Lebanon in chaos.	**1980 ff.** Growing U.S. involvement against guerrilla insurgency in Central America and Sandinista regime. **1980 ff.** New democratic current in Latin America.	**1990 ff.** Dismantling of apartheid. **1990** Several democratic elections in Kenya, other nations.
1986 Fall of Marcos regime in the Philippines.	**1990** Iraqi invasion of Kuwait.	**1980 ff.** International debt crisis in many Latin American nations.	**1992** U.N. intervention in Somalia famine.
1990 Economic reforms in India.	**1991** Gulf war against Iraq.	**1982** Argentina and Great Britain clash over the Falkland Islands (Malvinas Islas).	**1993** Agreement on democratic elections in South Africa.
1998 Testing of nuclear weapons tests in India and Pakistan.	**1993–1994** New peace movement. Palestinian autonomy in Israel. Israel–Jordan treaty.	**1983** United States invades Grenada. **1989** Sandinistas lose election in Nicaragua.	**1994** Election of Nelson Mandela as South Africa's president.
	1997 More moderate regime in Iran.	**1989** United States invades Panama, deposes General Noriega. **1990 ff.** Decline of insurgency in Central America; high economic growth rates in Brazil, Argentina, Mexico.	**1994 ff.** Democratic regimes in several African states. **1997** Insurgent army establishes new regime in Congo (Zaire).
		1997 Multiparty elections in Mexico.	**1999** Democratic regime in Nigeria.

The West in the Twentieth Century

The West suffered greatly during World War I and the years between the world wars, although some areas such as the United States were less deeply affected than others. New currents such as Nazism reflected and furthered the West's crisis. How can these new movements be explained? How much did they change the West? After World War II, the West in many respects rebounded, although it did not recapture its previous dominant role throughout the world. What older institutions and values did the West reemphasize? What were the main innovations in politics, the economy, and social structure that made the West different by the 1990s from what it had been in the late 1940s? Was there still a definable Western culture?

STRENGTH AND RELATIVE DECLINE

Although one of the themes of twentieth-century world history is the relative decline of the West, particularly in Europe, Western civilization has remained a standard-bearer in many ways. By the late 1980s, it still was the wealthiest society in the world. The artistic and popular cultural forms it has generated have had far more influence on other civilizations than those of any other single society. Western nations continue to set much of the tone for world diplomacy. One sign of the West's continued importance has been its role as a target for people in many parts of the world who dislike not only Western power but also the threat it poses to traditional values.

PATTERNS OF WESTERN HISTORY: 1914–1945

World War I, the explosive event that effectively opened the new century, had international repercussions. Britain and France used many troops from their colonies. Some fighting occurred against German holdings in Africa. The Ottoman Empire's alliance with Germany produced conflict in the Middle East, which, among other things, encouraged Arab nationalism while further weakening the Ottoman state; many nations, including Italy, hoped for big colonial gains in the Middle East after the hostilities ended. Finally, Japan entered the war on the side of Britain and France and seized a number of German territories in the Pacific.

513

The World of Western Dominance, 1914

Legend:

Europe
European colonies
Russia

British Dominions
Independent states, former European colonies
Independent regions under strong European pressure

Map labels:

PACIFIC OCEAN

JAPAN (The only fully independent state, not derived in part from Europe)

NEW ZEALAND

AUSTRALIA

PHILIPPINE IS. (USA)

CHINA

FR. INDO-CHINA

SIAM

DUTCH EAST INDIES

INDIA

INDIAN OCEAN

RUSSIA

AFG.

PERSIA

ARABIA

TURKEY

ETHIOPIA

AFRICA

SWEDEN

A.-H.

GER.

NORWAY

FR.

SP.

ICELAND

GREAT BRITAIN

PORT.

LIBERIA

UNION OF SOUTH AFRICA

GREENLAND

ATLANTIC OCEAN

CANADA

UNITED STATES

MEXICO

CENTRAL AMERICA

GUIANAS

SOUTH AMERICA

ALASKA

PACIFIC OCEAN

Nevertheless, the bulk of the fighting occurred within Europe, including European Russia. Germany invaded large parts of Russia, fueling the growing discontent that finally brought the 1917 revolution, which took Russia out of the war. Combat on the Western front, located mainly in France, was still more bitter. New weapons, including more effective artillery and tanks, led to the construction of defensive trenches, from which neither side could advance without huge casualties. Occasional offensive efforts cost tens of thousands of lives each day. The sheer loss of life and the frustration of nearly 4 years of virtual stalemate had a devastating material and psychological impact on the European combatants. Finally, in 1918, the exhausted allies managed to invade a still-more-exhausted Germany. The German emperor abdicated (as did the Habsburg ruler), and the war was over.

Picking up the pieces after World War I was extremely difficult, however. More than 10 million people had been killed in Europe. Vast amounts of property had been destroyed, and the European economy suffered a shattering blow through the loss of investments abroad and huge debts accumulated internally to fund the wasteful war effort. A peace conference was held at Versailles, its work divided between desires for revenge against Germany and the idealism represented by President Wilson of the United States. Idealism led to the establishment of the League of Nations, designed to promote international harmony in the future, and the creation of a series of new states in central and eastern Europe, from the territory of Russia, the Habsburg monarchy, and Germany. Poland resurfaced, along with other new Slavic states and an independent Hungary. The new states were weak, however, and this created a source of tensions in European diplomacy for the foreseeable future. The League of Nations, although not insignificant in world affairs during the next 15 years, proved largely ineffective as well. At the same time, motives of revenge resulted in huge reparation payments and a loss of territory for Germany, generating further resentments. Even the victorious allies were unsatisfied: France still feared its German neighbor, the United States pulled back from European entanglements into an unrealistic isolationism—not even joining the League of Nations, and Italy bemoaned its lack of success in acquiring vast new territory.

World War I and Versailles set the stage for the next two difficult decades of Western history. Diplomatic tensions eased somewhat during the 1920s, as Germany made some efforts to adjust to its reduced position, but fears and resentments still ran high. European and U.S. internal politics were largely ineffectual as a series of mediocre leaders gained power. Germany, now a republic, suffered at the hands of a number of groups who opposed democracy. Communist movements, linked to the Soviet regime that now ruled Russia, emerged to the left of socialist parties in many countries, serving as small but frightening revolutionary forces. The liberal middle sector of Western politics weakened, as many erstwhile liberals became more conservative in their desire to prevent major social reform. The absence of a strong center made effective government difficult, even in Britain, where the parliamentary tradition was particularly strong.

New political tensions might have been manageable had postwar economic trends not proved so disastrous. Many nations suffered from massive inflation during much of the 1920s, the result of wartime debts and postwar dislocations. Prosperity returned toward the middle of the decade and the United States, in particular, enjoyed an industrial boom. But in 1929, a major depression occurred, as banks failed

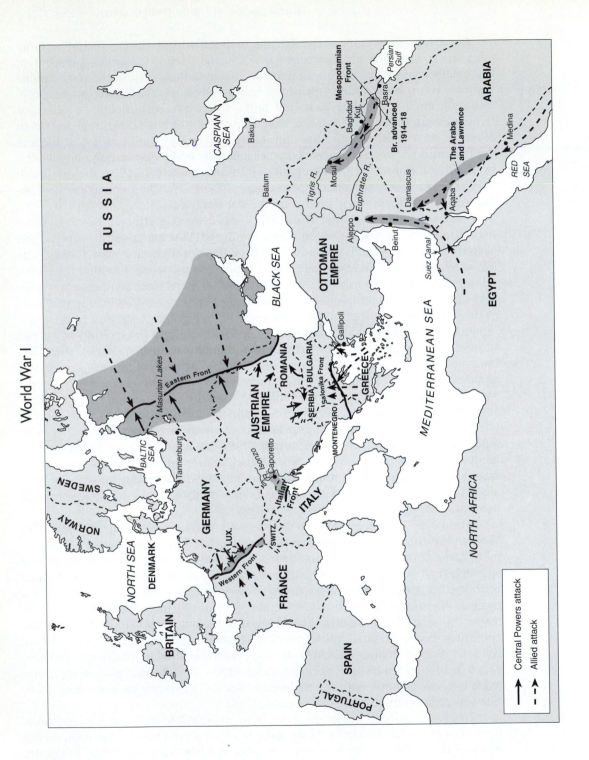

World War I

Central Powers attack
Allied attack

RUSSIA

CASPIAN SEA

Baku

BLACK SEA

Batum

Tigris R.

Mosul

Baghdad

Kut.

Basra

Persian Gulf

Mesopotamian Front

Br. advanced 1914–18

ARABIA

Medina

RED SEA

The Arabs and Lawrence

Aqaba

Damascus

Euphrates R.

Aleppo

Beirut

Suez Canal

OTTOMAN EMPIRE

EGYPT

MEDITERRANEAN SEA

NORTH AFRICA

Gallipoli

GREECE

Salonika Front

BULGARIA

SERBIA

ROMANIA

MONTENEGRO

AUSTRIAN EMPIRE

Masurian Lakes

Eastern Front

BALTIC SEA

Tannenburg

Isonzo

Caporetto

Italian Front

ITALY

SWITZ.

Lux.

Western Front

GERMANY

FRANCE

SPAIN

PORTUGAL

DENMARK

NORTH SEA

SWEDEN

NORWAY

BRITAIN

516

first in the United States and then throughout the Western world. The great depression resulted from a number of factors. Purchasing power was too low among many peasants and workers to sustain increased industrial production. Many peasants and American farmers faced a rapid decline in agricultural prices, due to overproduction; mechanized agriculture outstripped the demand for food in the Western world, and this limited farmers' ability to buy. Nonindustrial countries in Eastern Europe and many other parts of the world also saw prices for their raw materials tumble as their production increased faster than Western demand; this crisis also weakened markets for Western goods. High tariffs, imposed by many nations to protect their own economies, added to the difficulties of trade. In essence, Western productive capacity outran available markets. As a result, speculative investments finally proved hollow, causing the stock market crash and bank failures of 1929.

The ensuing depression was the worst in modern memory. Millions of workers lost their jobs. Wages plummeted, and insecurity spread even among those who were employed. Levels of production collapsed, as up to a third of the economic capacity of countries like Germany and the United States was idled by 1932. And although the worst of the depression was over by the mid–1930s, its traces remained strong throughout the rest of the decade.

Only a few Western governments responded constructively to this economic crisis. Scandinavian states increased government spending, providing new levels of social insurance against illness and unemployment and foreshadowing the modern welfare state. In the United States, Franklin Roosevelt's New Deal, from 1933 onward, enacted a number of social insurance measures and used government spending to stimulate the economy. The New Deal did not cure the American depression, but it alleviated the worst effects and provided new hope that forestalled major political pressure against the established order. Britain and France, however, reacted weakly to the economic catastrophe. Both countries continued to be plagued by inept leadership. They were also torn between socialist and conservative forces, and their allies on the political extremes; effective action seemed impossible.

The depression led directly to a fascist regime in Germany in 1933. Fascism was a product of World War I; the movement's advocates, many of them former veterans, attacked the weakness of parliamentary democracy and the corruption and class conflict of Western capitalism. They proposed a strong state ruled by a powerful leader, who would revive the nation's forces through vigorous foreign and military policy. Fascists vaguely promised social reforms to alleviate class antagonism, and their attacks on trade unions and socialist parties pleased landlords and business groups alike. The first fascist regime arose in Italy in 1923, and fascist parties complicated the political process in a number of other nations during the 1920s. However, it was the advent of the National Socialist, or Nazi, regime in Germany, under Adolf Hitler, that made this new political movement a major force in world history.

Hitler appealed to a country bitter about its defeat in war and unusually hard hit by economic disorder. He promised many groups a return to more traditional ways; thus, many artisans voted for Hitler in the belief that preindustrial economic institutions like the guilds would be revived. The middle class, including the leaders of big business, were attracted to Hitler's commitment to a firm stance against socialism and communism. Although Hitler never won a majority popular vote in a free election, his party did attain the largest single vote total by 1932. By this time, the effects

Nazi Party Congress in Nuremburg, Germany. The Führer is saluted by his "storm troopers," in a demonstration of the effective Nazi use of mass orchestrations.

of the depression were compounded by the weak, divided response of Germany's parliamentary leadership, in a country that had never fully accepted the validity of liberal political forms.

Once in power, Hitler quickly set about constructing a totalitarian state—that is, a new kind of government that would exercise massive, direct control over virtually all the activities of its subjects. Hitler eliminated all opposition parties; he purged the bureaucracy and military, installing loyal Nazis in many posts. His secret police, the Gestapo, arrested hundreds of thousands of political opponents. Trade unions were replaced by government-sponsored bodies that tried to appease workers with low pay by offering full employment and various welfare benefits. Economic planning on the part of government helped restore production levels, with a particular emphasis on the manufacture of armaments. Hitler solidified the power of his regime with constant, well-crafted propaganda, strident nationalism, and an incessant attack on Germany's Jewish minority. Hitler's hatred of Jews ran deep; he blamed them for various personal misfortunes and also for movements like socialism and excessive capitalism that in his view had weakened the German spirit. Obviously, anti-Semitism served as a catchall for a host of diverse dissatisfactions. Anti-semitism also benefited Hitler's cause by providing a scapegoat that could rouse national passions and distract the population from other problems. Measures against Jews became more and more severe, as Jews were forced to wear a letter on their clothing identifying them as Jews, their property was attacked and seized, and increasing numbers were sent to concentration camps. After 1940, Hitler's policy took an extreme turn, focusing on the total elimination of European Jewry. In this Holocaust, 6 million Jews were killed in the concentration camps of Germany and conquered territories; other groups like gypsies and homosexuals were targeted as well.

Hitler's policies were based on preparation for war. He wanted not only to re-coup Germany's World War I losses but also to create a land empire that would ex-tend across much of Europe, particularly toward the east into the territory of al-legedly inferior Slavic peoples. Progressively Hitler violated the provisions of the Treaty of Versailles, which had limited German rearmament. In 1936, he intervened in a civil war in Spain, on the side of fascist forces. Within 2 years, he had annexed Austria and seized part, then all, of Czechoslovakia. To all these steps, the other Eu-ropean powers responded only weakly. France and Britain were too divided to pursue a resolute foreign policy. They negotiated with Hitler at Munich in 1938, offering him part of Czechoslovakia in the hopes that this concession would satisfy his ap-petite, but their feeble attempt at appeasement merely inspired Hitler to further de-mands. The United States remained isolationist; the Soviet Union was worried but too isolated from potential Western allies, who feared its communism, to pose an ef-fective counterbalance.

WORLD WAR II

With nothing standing in his way, Hitler moved forward, forming an alliance with the Soviet Union in 1939 that allowed both powers to attack Poland. This act finally convinced Britain and France that they could no longer sit idly by, and war was de-clared in September 1939. Hitler was far better prepared for conflict than were his op-ponents, and during the first 3 years of the war, his forces, in alliance with Italy, swept over much of Western Europe. By 1942, Germany held France, Norway, the Low Countries, and the small Balkan states. However, an invasion of Russia in 1941, following the collapse of the brief alliance between Russia and Germany, resulted in Germany's armies being bogged down much as Napoleon's had been 130 years be-fore. Furthermore, the United States, goaded by the Japanese attack on Pearl Harbor, entered the war in December 1941 on Britain's side. Three years of bitter fighting in Europe, the Pacific, and elsewhere followed. The Russian armies gradually recovered, with some assistance in the form of armaments from the United States, and pressed inexorably toward Germany's eastern borders. American and British forces, aided by resistance movements against Nazi occupation, drove Germany first from North Africa, then gradually from Italy. In 1944, a massive invasion force moved across the English Channel into France, and within a year the allies entered Germany from the West. Hitler committed suicide, and the European war drew to a close.

Like its predecessor, World War II resulted in a massive loss of life. Russia and Germany were hardest hit, along with the Jewish population of central and Eastern Europe. Economic devastation was even greater than before. Hitler had drained the occupied countries of labor and productive goods, as part of his frenzied war effort. Massive bombing had destroyed many cities and factories, as well as transportation networks. For several years after the war, Western Europe was the scene of grinding poverty, massive movements of dislocated people, and seeming hopelessness.

The war also redesigned the European map more fundamentally than World War I. Russian dominance extended through virtually all of Eastern Europe. Only two countries in Eastern Europe preserved any real independence: Greece, which was aided by Britain and the United States in maintaining a noncommunist government,

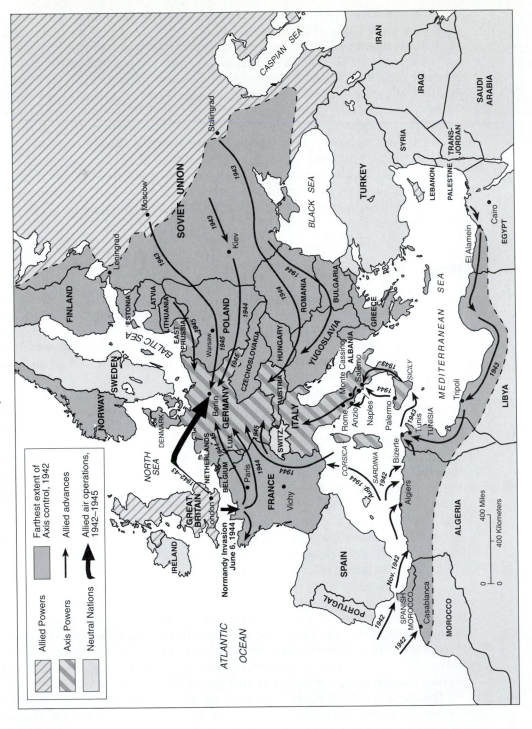

World War II: European and North African Theaters

Legend:

Allied Powers
Axis Powers
Neutral Nations

Farthest extent of Axis control, 1942
Allied advances
Allied air operations, 1942–1945

and Yugoslavia, which established a communist regime independent of Soviet control. Germany was divided. Initially, the Soviet Union, France, Britain, and the United States each occupied a zone of Germany. But, the three Western powers gradually allowed their zones to be united in an independent Federal Republic, whereas the Soviet zone converted into a communist state heavily dependent on Russian military support.

The new boundaries of Europe initiated a prolonged struggle between the Soviet Union and the United States, each with a network of European allies and dependencies. A "cold war" started in 1947, pitting the two postwar giants against each other. Russia, with its virtual empire extending into central Europe, saw the United States construct an alliance system among the leading Western states and retain a substantial military presence of its own to guard against possible Soviet attack. Here, within Europe's own boundaries, was the cruel result of half a century of disarray and violent internal struggle.

PATTERNS OF WESTERN HISTORY: 1950 TO THE PRESENT

To many observers, by 1950, the future of the Western world, or at least its traditional European base, seemed unbelievably bleak. If World War I had caused two decades of virtually unqualified confusion, could the consequences of a second conflict be anything but worse? In fact, the West seemed to recover both economic and political vigor in the decades after 1950; although the results were far from problem-free, they were certainly more constructive than the record of the years between both world wars.

Postwar Europe did not regain its previous diplomatic position. The dominance of the superpowers, the Soviet Union and the United States, continued. The United States formed the North Atlantic Treaty Organization (NATO) with most other Western governments in 1949, to oppose the Soviet threat; creation of the alliance ensured American influence over Western Europe in dealing with the Soviet Union. At the same time, weakened by world war and pressed by surging nationalist movements throughout the world, Western Europe lost most of its colonies, sometimes as a result of bitter struggle. India, Southeast Asia, and then Africa all gained independence. Although many Europeans resented this sign of decline, attempts to reassert some shadow of earlier authority largely failed. In 1956, for example, Britain and France tried to seize control of the Suez Canal from a newly independent Egypt, only to be forced into retreat as a result of Egyptian resistance and U.S. and Soviet pressure. Even aside from the great power of the United States as a representative of generally Western values, the West did not suffer perpetual diplomatic decline. Decolonization was largely accepted by the people of Western Europe, who did not attempt to hold out at the expense of political stability and economic growth at home. West European cultural and economic influence in many former colonies remained considerable. With time, leading European powers also gained a more independent voice vis-à-vis the United States. Although not military equals, individual states such as France were able to oppose American policies at key points.

Make no mistake: After World War II, the world's diplomatic framework decisively changed, and in many ways this transformation worked to the West's disadvantage. The balance of power within the West shifted to the United States. When the age of imperialism ended, the West's direct voice in Asia and Africa was dramatically lessened. The cold war between the United States and the Soviet Union meant that even the West's leading power could not set the tone for world affairs, instead facing a roughly equal rival. By 1951, when the Soviet Union developed the atomic bomb, it became clear that centuries of Western military superiority over all other civilizations had ended, and that Eastern Europe now shared this claim of strength. The fearsome power of modern weapons and the intense East–West rivalry left many Westerners concerned that a new war could destroy their own civilization and that of most other parts of the world. At times, diplomatic processes seemed to have escaped human control.

Nonetheless, the Western world itself remained free from war after 1945. Early cold war tensions, particularly over the new divisions of Germany, brought war scares. In 1948–1949, the Soviet Union blocked off the city of West Berlin, a western enclave within East Germany, and only a massive American airlift relieved the pressure on supplies. Colonial wars also involved the West. France lost a bitter war to retain its Indochinese possessions and then faced a long, ultimately unsuccessful struggle to keep Algeria. Finally, in 1949, the United States, with wider world interests now than Western Europe, became involved in a war in Korea and then, in the 1960s, in a long and disheartening struggle in Vietnam, both against communist forces. These regional wars were important, of course, but the fact remains that even major threats of war within the West now receded, as at least for a time the West became one of the world's more internally peaceful civilizations.

A key ingredient of the West's new diplomatic environment involved explicit West European initiatives to set its own diplomatic house in order after 1945, with some American encouragement. Eager to prevent further nationalist wars and also anxious to promote economic development, leading West European nations joined hands in economic cooperation. Initial moves to coordinate industrial policies led in 1958 to the formation of the European Economic Community, which promoted full-scale exchange across national boundaries. Although the Common Market, as it is called, ultimately broadened to include Britain, Ireland, Denmark, Greece, Spain, and Portugal, in addition to its initial members, West Germany, France, Italy, and the Low Countries, it did not become a single government. However, the organization did develop common policies and a common bureaucracy to oversee economic relations and, to an extent, coordinate other policies. Nationalist tensions receded to a lower point than ever before in modern European history. In 1993, the European Economic Community (now known as the European Union) created full tariff unity and planned further integration possibly involving a single currency and exchangeable rights of citizenship. The new currency unit, the Euro, was launched in 1999, even as additional countries moved closer to membership in the European Union.

More striking still were new economic and political trends. Particularly during the 1950s and 1960s, the doldrums of the interwar decades were reversed. Political tensions declined, while economic growth soared. Western society avoided major depressions, although there were years of slackening prosperity; most Western nations enjoyed a growth rate ranging from 2–8 percent per year. The West easily retained its lead over most other civilizations in terms of per capita prosperity, and indeed the gap between its wealth and that of many agricultural societies widened. Only Japan caught up in this regard. Within the West, mass affluence, now exhibited by widespread ownership of cars, refrigerators, and the now ubiquitous television set, reached unprecedented levels. The United States, whose population had achieved affluence earlier, found its prosperity rivaled by dynamic European countries such as West Germany and France.

Western economic development was spurred by the widespread transformation of leadership after World War II. In Western Europe, men and women who had fought in resistance movements against Nazism vowed to avoid the errors of the past and to create a new society. The influence of the older aristocracy was further reduced. Training for West Europe's elite now broadened to recruit more talented people from worker and peasant families, as support for higher education and the availability of scholarships increased. University education itself was revamped to focus on more technical subjects. A new generation of managers, with a redefined mission and educational background, brought new dynamism to the West in various fields.

During the crucial years immediately after 1945, Western society also forged new political institutions. Carefully wrought democratic constitutions were developed in West Germany and Italy, providing more stable parliamentary institutions than ever before. France revived its parliamentary system after the years of Nazi occupation; in 1958, government instability in the face of the paralyzing colonial war in Algeria prompted the nationalist leader Charles de Gaulle to engineer a new constitution, providing for a strong but democratically elected presidency overseeing parliament. Spain, Portugal, and Greece installed new democratic systems in the 1970s. Democracy and relative political stability were encouraged by the virtual destruction of the radical right in politics, discredited by Nazi excesses and defeat in war. Most Western countries had a strong conservative party fully committed to the democratic system. On the left, although significant communist movements remained in a few countries, reformist socialist parties, also committed to the democratic process and extensive personal liberties, won wide support outside North America. The communist minority itself declined by the 1980s. The new political spectrum thus provided a multiparty system, with leadership characteristically alternating between major parties, depending on the performance of the economy, but the spectrum was bounded by the commitment of most groups to the basic political process. Even communist parties in Western Europe relied mainly on election efforts, abandoning attempts at revolutionary agitation.

The political system was altered, finally, by the construction of more extensive welfare institutions. In France and Italy, coalition governments combining conservatives, socialists, and communists enacted new welfare programs between 1945 and 1948. These programs provided state-sponsored medical insurance, payments to large families, and greater regulation of working conditions. France and other countries also created more formal state economic planning, to guide in postwar recovery and then further industrial development. Between 1945 and 1951, Great Britain extended its welfare state under the leadership of the Labor Party. The British welfare state featured an unusually elaborate program of socialized medicine, with the government paying most medical bills from tax revenues; it also entailed government housing programs and other social measures. Most other Western nations extended their welfare and economic planning activities; Canada, for example, enacted a state-funded medical insurance program. Even the United States, which had a more restricted array of welfare programs than most other Western countries, initiated the Great Society measures of the 1960s, providing medical insurance for the indigent and elderly, expanding the social security system, and passing a number of laws to protect the rights of minorities and women.

The pattern of economic growth and political stability that took shape in the postwar West was disrupted in the late 1960s by a series of student protests, compounded in the United States by civil rights demonstrations and rioting among urban blacks. Campus unrest at major American universities focused on the war in Vietnam, which many students regarded as futile and immoral. Young people in Europe and the United States also targeted the materialism of their societies, seeking the embrace of more idealistic goals and greater justice. Student uprisings in France in 1968 created a near revolution. By the early 1970s, new rights for students and other reforms, combined with police repression, ended the most intense student protests. But, some ongoing political concerns, including feminism and environmental protection, entered the arena during the 1970s partly as an aftermath of the student protests; in some Western European countries, a terrorist movement, focused on the kidnapping of political and business leaders, and sometimes their assassination, caused anxiety as well. Economic growth also slowed during the 1970s, partly because of rising energy costs; in the late 1970s and early 1980s, the Western world faced its greatest economic recession since the postwar recovery. New leadership sprang up within the British Conservative Party and the U.S. Republican Party, seeking to reduce the costs and size of the welfare state to spur new economic growth. Additonal political currents arose in other Western countries, including new rightist parties and "Green" environmentalist movements.

Key problems intensified in the 1990s. Global economic competition hit the West hard. In Europe, the result was substantial unemployment, up to 12 percent or more, as goods requiring less skilled labor now came from elsewhere. The United States faced similar pressures but created a larger number of low-paying jobs; here, the new trend involved growing inequalities in income, greater than in any other industrial society. All Western nations, amid economic pressure, had to reconsider welfare state expenditures, and most cut back; again, the United States, with a smaller welfare system than most others, reduced protections for the poor most systematically. Various political changes accompanied these developments: More zealous conservatism surfaced particularly in the United States. Liberal and socialist movements in Western Europe as well as in North America developed a more moderate stance, less wedded to welfare traditions. A few new currents of protest developed: a racist, neofascist movement in France called the National Front, a surge of paramilitary groups in the United States on the far right.

Compared to the frenzy of the 1920s and 1930s, Western society after 1950 has been relatively free from traumatic events. Decolonization created tension; U.S. involvement in world diplomacy had produced a number of new concerns; the student movement of the late 1960s was an indictaion that all was not well in the affluent society. Cushioned by the rapid rise in wealth, however, the Western world remained considerably more free from major upheavals than most other civilizations in the

Youth antiwar protest: Washington, DC, 1967.

postwar decades. Indeed, boredom itself became an issue, as observers worried that the welfare state created too much security, and political apathy was so pervasive that many people no longer bothered to vote. In Western Europe, periodic terrorism reflected the discontent of a small minority against the calm of the existing system, whereas in the United States, declining voter participation raised questions about the vigor of the political process. Had Western society achieved a new harmony, or were the postwar decades a period of deceptive tranquility before a new storm?

WESTERN POLITICAL INSTITUTIONS IN THE TWENTIETH CENTURY

Two somewhat contradictory themes ran through the political development of Western society after 1900. On the one hand, the power of the state increased; on the other hand, a commitment to democratic and liberal values remained strong and, after 1945, gained ground.

The rising power of the state showed in both world wars. Governments in democratic nations such as Britain and the United States increased their regulation of economic activities, introducing rationing and the allocation of labor. Governments mounted massive propaganda campaigns to win the passionate loyalty of citizens to

HISTORY DEBATE

Convergence

The Western world split apart during the 1930s, between fascist and democratic systems. After 1945, however, European nations became more similar than ever (although not identical)—a phenomenon called *convergence*. Industrial growth reached countries like Italy. The results of World War II eliminated some German peculiarities, such as a rabidly conservative aristocracy. The spread of democracy was obviously a convergent development. So were key social trends, like an aging population and new roles for women. Nationalism declined. Growing West European unity both reflected and furthered the convergence phenomenon.

Convergence also reduced some key differences between Europe and the United States. On the West European side, the elimination of the traditional peasantry and the final demise of the aristocracy, along with rapid economic growth, made social and economic structures more similar on both sides of the North Atlantic. A prosperous Europe also opened the door to the consumer culture of the United States, providing a growing (if occasionally critical) market for American TV shows, fast foods, even a Euro-Disney. Because of new immigration, Europe also developed some racial tensions similar to those in the United States, although usually less severe. On the American side, the New Deal and World War II had created a stronger government, more like its European counterparts, but the United States did not develop as extensive a welfare state. Although American popular culture predominated, European contributions like the miniskirt and the Beatles moved easily across the Atlantic in the other direction.

Differences remained. The United States participated with Europe in more open sexuality, but the nation was more prudish; topless beaches, the norm in Europe, did not crop up in the West. American moralism also showed in an unusually intense antismoking crusade. The largest new distinction involved obvious differences in military policy. The United States, the world's greatest power, rapidly increased its peacetime army and armaments expenditures—spending rose 300 percent in the 1950s alone. American foreign policy, as a result, was more influenced by military pressures than was true in Europe, which often boasted of pioneering in a civilian society. Correspondingly, Europe depended on American military protection while its own global military capacity steadily diminished.

Different reactions to the economic pressures of the 1990s also seemed to contradict trans-Atlantic convergence. Western Europe was more reluctant to dismantle the welfare state or to accept growing gaps between the rich and poor, although it was affected by both trends. Convergence might not be permanent.

the military effort; enemies were pictured as the epitome of evil; newspapers were censored and the new media of radio and motion pictures were used to further intensify patriotism. The powers of wartime government helped inspire the totalitarian dictatorships of Nazi Germany (and also communist Russia). Nazism demonstrated that under stress, a major Western society could abandon liberal values in favor of a government dedicated to the destruction of all competing sources of power and the manipulation of individual citizens through mass education and propaganda. Authoritarian governments in some other states, such as fascist Italy and, after 1936, a semi-fascist Spain, also used new police and propaganda powers to repress opposition.

More generally, the rise of the welfare state throughout most of the West after 1945 represented a major extension of government power. Government expansion under the New Deal greatly increased the importance of the American state, which was then extended by the growth of military spending from World War II until the end of the cold war. Throughout the West, governments assumed the responsibility for providing some coverage of health-care costs, adequate working conditions, and protection against dire poverty. The United States, more fully committed to older liberal values that relied on individual initiative, stood slightly apart in this movement. But even here by the 1970s, 21 percent of total tax income was applied to social welfare payments. Expanding welfare functions and growing involvement in economic planning obviously broadened the role of the state in individual lives. Taxes increased, and so did the regulation of how employers could hire and fire, what crops farmers could plant, where poor people could live. Government bureaucracies expanded steadily.

The rise of the state has been balanced, however, outside the period of fascist regimes, by the West's continued devotion to a multiparty democracy and substantial freedoms of speech, press, religion, and assembly. The West has developed a mixed system, in which important governmental authority is combined with private enterprise. In the economy, for example, state planning has left the operation of most businesses in private hands. West European countries did nationalize some economic sectors, such as railroads and mines. The nationalization movement took place primarily during the period of recovery after World War II, but a French socialist regime extended nationalization again in the early 1980s. Even here, however, most businesses have operated through private decision making within frameworks partly established by government.

The extension of liberal, democratic systems after 1945 showed the continuing strength of parliamentary institutions in Western political culture. West Germany established a far more solid democracy than it had managed in the 1920s. Political debate has centered on significant disagreements between conservatives and socialists about the extent of the welfare state or diplomatic policy, but it has not called the system into question. Although conservatives dominated German politics through most of the 1950s and 1960s, and again in the 1980s and early 1990s, socialist leadership took power peacefully at a number of points. The 1989 collapse of the Soviet empire brought about German unification in 1991, partly because of extensive East German demands for democracy. By the mid–1980s, the Western world was more fully characterized by a single political system—liberal democracy—than at any time since the decline of feudalism. From Australia and New Zealand through North America to Western Europe, a tension between multiparty rivalry and personal freedom on the one hand, and powerful state planning, taxation, and welfare systems on the other, has constituted the core of modern politics. Alternative political ideologies such as fascism and even Marxism have declined.

The rise of a strong state democracy was accompanied by the decline of classic diplomatic and military issues in Europe. Old antagonisms between France and Germany or Britain and the continent declined. So did commitments to imperialism. Although West European governments participated in the cold war, military issues and expenditures receded. U.S. military concerns, however, increased, as did American diplomatic influence in European affairs—even after the cold war had ended, the United States continued to take a lead in new issues such as the strife in the former Yugoslavia. Tensions between the United States and Western Europe occurred at times, particularly during surges of French nationalism or when American policy became high-handed, but they were rarely acute—never reaching the pitch of the former nationalist rivalries within the West.

CONTEMPORARY WESTERN CULTURE

Western culture continued to display great vitality during the twentieth century, although at times it seemed to lack coherence. Artists and composers stressed stylistic innovation, against older traditions and even the efforts of the previous generation. Scientific work flourished, as the West remained the center of most fundamental inquiry in the theoretical sciences. However, complex discoveries, such as the principle of relativity in physics, qualified older ideas that nature can be explained in a few sweeping scientific laws. And, the sheer specialization of scientific research removed much of it from ready public understanding. Because no unifying assumptions represent the essence of formal intellectual activity in the contemporary West, neutral terms like "modern" or "postmodern" are used even in the artistic field. Disciplines that once provided an intellectual overview, such as philosophy, declined in the twentieth century or were transformed into specialized research fields; many philosophers, for example, turned to the scientific study of language, rather than writing basic statements about the nature of life and the universe. And although work in theology continued, among both Catholic and Protestant thinkers, it no longer commanded center stage in intellectual life. No emphasis was placed on an integrated approach, no agreement was reached on what constitutes an essential understanding of human endeavor.

The dynamism of scientific research formed the clearest central thread in Western culture after 1900. Growing science faculties commanded the greatest prestige in expanding universities; individual scientists made striking discoveries, while a veritable army of researchers cranked out more specific findings than scientists had ever before produced. In addition, the wider public continued to maintain a faith that science held the keys to understanding nature and society and to improving technology and human life. Finally, although scientific discoveries have varied widely, a belief in a central scientific method persists: form a rational hypothesis, test through experiment or observation, and emerge with a generalization that will show regularities in physical behaviors and thus provide human reason with a means of systematizing and even predicting such behaviors. No other approach to understanding in Western culture has had such power or widespread adherence.

The first scientific breakthrough of the twentieth century took shape with the discovery of the behavior of atomic particles. Experiments with X-rays and uranium produced the knowledge of electrons and the nucleus of the atom. At about the same time, by 1905, the work of Albert Einstein in Berlin transformed the former idea, central to Newtonian physics, of physical matter as a solid essence that behaved in absolutely uniform ways. According to Einstein's theory of relativity, space and time are not absolutes but are always relative to the observer measuring them. Einstein used time as a fourth dimension to explain behaviors of light and planetary motion that had been misstated in Newtonian physics. Radiation and other electronic activity are not regular, but occur in discontinuous waves. Increasingly complex mathematics, involving the abstract language of differential equations, was essential in understanding the actual behavior of both planetary bodies and particles within the atom. By the 1930s, physicists began to experiment with bombarding basic matter with neutrons, particles that carry no electric charge; this work was to culminate during World War II in the development of the atomic bomb. Research in physics continued after World War II with a combination of increasingly sophisticated observation, made possible by improved telescopes and then lasers and space satellites, and the complex mathematical theories facilitated by the theory of relativity. Astronomers made substantial progress in identifying additional galaxies and other phenomena in space; the debate about the nature of matter also continued.

Breakthroughs in biology have primarily involved genetics. The identification, in the 1860s, of inheritance characteristics received wide attention only after 1900. By the 1920s, researchers experimenting with the increasingly familiar fruit fly determined exact rules for genetic transmission. In the 1940s, the discovery of the structure of the basic genetic unit by British and American scientists, the famous "double helix" pattern of deoxyribonucleic acid (DNA), advanced the understanding of how genetic information is transmitted and can be altered.

Biologists were also responsible for major improvements in health care. New drugs, beginning with penicillin in 1928, revolutionized the treatment of common diseases, whereas immunization virtually eliminated scourges such as diphtheria. Findings on hormones and their connection to certain behaviors, leading in the 1920s to the science of endocrinology, also had widespread medical applicability. Genetics itself, by the 1970s, gave rise to a host of industries that utilized scientific principles to produce new medicines, seeds, and pesticides.

Nevertheless, the new science has also had some troubling features, even apart from its use in weapons of destruction and its sheer complexity. The physical world is no longer considered to be neatly regulated, as it had been by Newtonian physics. Genetics made it clear that evolution proceeded by a series of random accidents, not through any consistent pattern. The use of the rational, scientific method thus has not produced the kind of simple world view that it had resulted in a century or so before, and the ensuing uncertainties have influenced some artists in their attempts to convey an irrational, relativist universe. However, for most people in the West, the belief in progress, defined in terms of both better technology and a rational understanding of nature, largely persists.

The rational method, broadly conceived, also advanced in the social sciences from 1900 onward. The German sociologist Max Weber worked to characterize general features of institutions such as bureaucracies, for analysis and comparison. Many sociologists promulgated theories of human society, or aspects of it such as the behavior of elites, on the assumption that rationally conceived models captured the essential reality of human affairs. In economics, quantitative models of economic cycles or business behavior have increasingly gained ground. Work by the British economist John Keynes, stressing the importance of government spending to compensate for loss of purchasing power during a depression, played a great role in the policies of the American New Deal and efforts by European planners to control the economic cycles after World War II.

Like the sciences, the social sciences became increasingly diverse and specialized. Also like the sciences, many social scientists sought practical applications for their work. Psychologists became involved, for example, in not only defining and treating mental illness but also trying to promote greater work efficiency. Governments called on economic forecasting. Social science thus added to the impression of an explosion of rationally generated and useful knowledge, even when research pointed to deterministic or irrational aspects of human affairs. Most leading social scientists continued to emphasize the quest for consistency in human and social behavior. After World War II, the increasing use of mathematical models and laboratory experiments in the social sciences enhanced this emphasis.

Most twentieth-century artists, concerned with capturing the world through impressions rather than through reason or the confinements of literal reality, worked against the grain of science and social science. Painting became increasingly nonrepresentational. The cubist movement, headed by Pablo Picasso, rendered familiar objects as geometrical shapes; after cubism, modern art moved even further away from the tenets of normal perception, stressing purely geometrical design or other expressionistic techniques. The focus was on mood, the individual reaction of viewers to the individual reality of the artist. Musical composition involved the use of dissonance and experimentation with new scales; after World War II, a growing interest in electronic instrumentation added to this diversity. Because writers are, in fact, constrained by words, their stylistic innovation was generally less extensive. However in poetry, the use of unfamiliar forms, ungrammatical constructions, and sweeping imagery continued the movement of the later nineteenth century. Playwrights experimented with new types of staging and unconventional dramatic forms, often seeking to involve the audience in direct participation. In literature, the novel remained dominant, but it turned toward the exploration of moods and personalities, rather than the portrayal of objective events or clear story lines. A vast gulf grew between the scientific approach and the artistic framework as to how reality can be captured and, to an extent, what constitutes reality.

Many people ignored the leading modern artists and writers, in favor of more commercial artistic productions and popular stories. The gap that had evolved earlier, between avant-garde art and public taste, generally continued. Some politicians, including Adolf Hitler, campaigned against what they saw as the decadence and im-

This example of the cubist style is by Pablo Picasso, a leading figure in twentieth-century modern art, who was born in Spain but worked primarily in France. The painting, "Violin and Grapes" (*Ceret et Sorgues*), Spring–Summer 1912. Oil on canvas, 20 × 24 (50.6 × 61 cm). (The Museum of Modern Art, New York. Mrs. David M. Levy Bequest. Photograph © 1998 The Museum of Modern Art)

morality of modern art, urging a return to more traditional styles. And, certainly art did not hold its own against the growing prestige of science.

However, artistic vision was not simply a preoccupation of artists. Designs and sculptures based on abstract art began to grace public places from the 1920s onward; furnishings and films also reflected modernist themes. Most revealing of a blend between art, modern technology, and public taste was the development of a characteristic twentieth-century architectural style, the "modern" or "international" style. The use of new materials, such as reinforced concrete and massive sheets of glass, allowed the abandonment of much that was traditional in architecture. The need for new kinds of buildings, particularly for office use, and the growing cost of urban space also encouraged the introduction of new forms such as the skyscraper, pioneered in the United States. In general, the modern style of architecture sought to develop individually distinct buildings—sharing the goal of modern art to defy conventional taste and cultivate the unique—while conveying a sense of space and freedom from natural constraints. Soaring structures, free-floating columns, and new combinations of angles and curves were features that described leading Western buildings from 1900 onward. Following World War II, when reconstruction in Europe and the growth of the U.S. west and southwest provided massive opportunities for building, the face of urban space in Western society was greatly transformed.

There were a few unifying themes between the artistic and scientific approaches. A constant quest for the new was one feature, as artists sought new styles, scientists new discoveries. Furthermore, Western culture in the twentieth century, in both art and science, became increasingly secular. Individual artists, writers, and scientists might proclaim religious faith, but church institutions had long since lost control over basic style or content. In Western Europe, despite an important reform movement within the Catholic Church that abandoned traditional ceremonies in favor of more direct contact between priest and worshippers, religion played a minor role in both formal and popular culture. Regular church attendance tended to be of interest only to a minority—5 percent of the British population, for example, by the 1970s. In the United States, religion maintained a greater hold, and both church attendance and popular belief remained at much higher levels than elsewhere in Western society. The United States also witnessed, both in the 1920s and again after World War II, a greater variety of popular revival movements and attempts to use religion to maintain or restore traditional values. Here was a clear indication that, for some individuals, neither the artistic nor the scientific approach to understanding was fully satisfactory—and this became yet another ingredient in the cultural diversity and tension of Western society.

Western culture was not a monopoly of European civilization in the twentieth century. Western art forms, particularly in architecture, spread widely. The achievements of Western science, at least those related to technology and medicine, often had to be taken into account by societies seeking their own industrial development. Western arts and sciences were, by the same token, greatly enriched by many practitioners from other cultures—by Japanese artists, for example, or Indian medical researchers and computer scientists. Elements of Western culture thus became international, and in tracing their roots, we must link most accomplishments to a number of other civilizations. Yet no other culture, not even the Japanese, created quite the same balance between an overwhelming interest in science and an all-important concern for stylistic innovation and individual expression in the arts.

ECONOMY AND SOCIETY

During the twentieth century, rapid transformation characterized the economy and social organization of Western civilization. By the latter part of the century, some of the changes seemed almost as fundamental as those that had ushered in the industrial revolution two centuries before. The recurrent shifts in technology, economic organization, and social structure in Western industrial society had significant effects on the rest of the world as well, making it hard for industrializing nations to "catch up" to Western levels.

To begin with, economic change involved new products. During the first decades of the century, synthetic textile fibers, such as rayon and nylon, introduced variety into the clothing industry. Radios and, by the 1930s, early television brought instant entertainment and news into homes across the land (see Table 26.1). The automobile, although invented before 1900, increasingly became a consumer staple, first in the United States and then, after World War II, in Western Europe.

Economic change involved, in addition, new forms of organization. The growing role of the state in formal planning was one aspect of this. In the private sector, corporate business became increasingly common, furnishing giant companies with extensive funds for widespread investment. Older family enterprises declined further. By the 1920s and again after World War II, many corporations established an international base of operations. U.S. firms took the lead here, for the extensive American market provided both capital and experience in dealing with large markets. However, a number of European-based firms became multinational as well. They had marketing and supply offices, and production subsidiaries, on several continents. In domestic markets and to an extent internationally, the concentration of ownership among a small number of corporations was the rule. A multitude of aspiring automobile producers before World War I thus settled into a handful of big producers in most Western countries between the wars, and further concentration, including international operations, occurred after World War II. As one result, the Ford Motor Company manufactured cars in Britain and Germany, whereas German and French automakers stepped up operations in the United States, Mexico, and Brazil.

Agriculture experienced an organizational revolution of its own, particularly after World War II. In Western Europe, peasant farming gave way to cooperatives for purchases and sales; most small landholders acquired new market skills as well as modern equipment, making them more like rural business executives than peasants. In the United States, Canada, and Australia, great concentrations of land operation, called agribusiness, arose after 1950, as purely family farms became increasingly marginal. Organizational change plus improved machinery, seeds, and fertilizers steadily raised agricultural productivity in the Western world, although some worried about a decline in the actual quality of foods and also growing environmental damage from the chemical spraying and other measures designed to maximize production.

Refinements in organization also affected the structure of work. Early in the twentieth century, U.S. firms took the lead in developing ways to increase the pace of manufacturing by defining jobs and supervising workers more closely. By 1910,

TABLE 26.1 ◆ TELEVISION OWNERSHIP IN 1957 AND 1965		
Country	**1957**	**1965**
France	683,000	6,489,000
Germany	798,586	11,379,000
Italy	367,000	6,044,542
The Netherlands	239,000	2,113,000
Sweden	75,817	2,110,584

Sources: The Europa Year Book 1959 (London, 1959) and *The Europa Year Book 1967,* vol. I (London, 1967).

early forms of the assembly line system were in effect, pioneered at Henry Ford's automobile plant. Such operations had workers performing repetitious tasks with a minimum of motion and thought, becoming as much like the machines they worked with as was humanly possible. After World War II, assembly line procedures were modified by the use of more automated equipment, with machines themselves—including, by the early 1980s, robots—performing some of the most routine functions.

As it had since industrialization began, economic change meant new technologies. The growing use of the internal combustion engine in manufacturing and transport, and growing use of petroleum instead of coal for fuel, marked important steps early in the century. Coal mining, long a staple of Western industrialization, declined, and some regions, particularly Western Europe, became dependent on fuel imports since their own oil holdings were small. Faster and more mechanized equipment steadily increased manufacturing productivity. Early in the century, the production of machines was revolutionized by the use of automatic riveters, drills, and other equipment that provided the technological basis for an assembly line operation in what had been a craft industry. The production of chemicals and ubiquitous plastics required automated procedures for transporting, mixing, and molding ingredients. After World War II, a technological revolution took shape in communications and information storage as well, with the introduction of computers; in the 1970s, the development of the microchip made computers smaller and more flexible, and increased the speed and volume of information flow, while displacing conventional storage operations such as manual filing.

The economic advance of Western society was not, of course, without its setbacks. During the decade of the depression, many wondered if the economy could ever recover its former vitality. The two world wars resulted in immense loss and dislocation. The economic slowdowns of the late 1970s and early 1980s, with rising rates of unemployment and fierce foreign competition particularly from East Asia, raised anxieties anew. In the 1990s, global competition produced high unemployment in Western Europe, while inequality in income increased in the United States. Furthermore, not all Western nations fared equally well in the economic development process; previous leaders such as Great Britain fell behind. Australia and Canada produced large quantities of foods and minerals for export, which made them unusually dependent on the prosperity of more fully industrial centers like Japan or the United States, although they maintained considerable industries of their own.

Nevertheless, for the century as a whole, the theme of continued economic vitality and change remains valid. Western society was quick to recover from wartime destruction, for example, bouncing back rapidly from the bombings of World War II, a sign that basic industrial capacity and know-how accounted for considerable resilience once they were firmly established.

Yet another area in which economic change had an impact was the class structure of Western society. A basic division between the middle class and working class continued. But, the middle class was defined increasingly by its managerial skills and education, rather than property ownership; the working class became less distinctive as its affluence increased. In the United States, indeed, the majority of workers identified themselves as middle class, on the basis of earnings. Furthermore, increased mobility, particularly in the decades after World War II, blurred class lines somewhat.

Making the most of new educational opportunities, a number of people from working-class backgrounds entered corporate upper management and the top levels of government service, although they still formed a minority. Interestingly, social mobility in Western Europe soon matched that of the newer nations of the Western world, such as the United States, despite a more explicit class structure.

The greatest change in social structure, however, was the rise of workers in the service sector of the economy. The percentage of farmers, already small, dropped further. But by the 1920s, the number of factory workers began to stabilize as well, as production increased mainly through continuing mechanization. By the 1950s, it was clear that service work—that is, jobs involving steady interaction with people and the processing of paperwork rather than producing goods—was the wave of the future. Restaurant workers, health-care workers from hospital janitors to doctors, teachers, recreation workers—all rapidly expanded in number, as did the secretaries and salespeople needed in a bureaucratized, consumer-oriented economy. By the 1970s, over half of all workers in Western society were employed in the service sector.

Finally, again particularly after 1945, a new wave of unskilled workers entered the labor force, many of them immigrants. Western Europe drew hundreds of thousands of workers from the Middle East, North Africa, the West Indies, and Asia; immigration to the United States reached higher levels than ever before, drawing mainly from East Asia and Latin America. Not all the newcomers were unskilled, but many filled the ranks of agricultural laborers, maintenance workers, fast-food personnel, and other slots where pay was low and rates of unemployment often high. Many urban blacks in the United States also fit into this growing category, which often seemed tragically isolated from the prosperity and security of most sectors of Western society.

Like social structure, family life changed considerably during the twentieth century without being totally transformed. Birthrates remained relatively low. Western society experienced an increase in birthrates from the late 1940s until the early 1960s—the famous baby boom. The boom was caused by growing prosperity, after many families had delayed births during the depression, and in some cases in response to government aid to families. But even the baby boom, while it severely pressed schools, day-care facilities, and so on, produced relatively modest birthrates. And after 1963, the baby boom ended, with birthrates again dropping rapidly. Further decreases in death rates for most age groups, due to improved medicine and a new interest in exercise and fitness, have maintained the basic population pattern of the later nineteenth century: low birthrates and low death rates adding up to a stable or slightly rising population and a growing number of elderly people. The increase in the elderly population, while a significant burden on social security systems, has had only limited impact on families, as most older people in the Western world now live apart from younger relatives—a major change in residential patterns that began in the 1920s.

Western family life continued to emphasize the importance of close emotional ties, between spouses and between parents and children, along with a new emphasis on sexual satisfaction before and during marriage. The role of the family in recreational activities increased. The annual family vacation became a standard experience as time at work was shortened. After 1945, the advent of television made the home an attractive place to spend leisure hours.

Although family functions and family demography displayed striking continuities with the past, but with some interesting new twists, the roles of family members were revolutionized by new patterns of women's work. During World War I, with many men away in battle, women entered the labor force in vast numbers. This movement was largely cut off in the 1920s. But in World War II, women returned to the factories and offices, and after the war they tended to remain there. Increasing numbers of women in Western Europe and North America, now as well educated as men, with relatively few children to care for, and in a society where earnings bring self-fulfillment and power, sought an identity and income through work. At the same time, the rise of service occupations deemed suitable for women facilitated the movement of women into the labor force, while increased expectations—a desire for better housing, travel, or education—encouraged women to work. In all Western countries, women's participation in the labor force rose steadily, reaching roughly 45 percent of the total by the late 1970s. Women of all social classes were now working, and they were doing so after marriage and even during active motherhood. Their earnings lagged behind those of men, and in response to this, an active feminist movement seeking fuller equality sprang up by the 1960s. Nonetheless, the change in work patterns easily reversed the earlier trends of Western industrial society, in which women had been encouraged to concentrate on family life.

Women's work fostered greater equality in family decision making. However, although the authoritarian position of husbands declined, new roles for women brought great confusion as well, for all parties concerned. Household work was not always equally shared by men, even when women found their time at home with the family decreased. Child care was another key issue. Increasing numbers of children, particularly in Western Europe, were raised, in part, in day-care centers, one of the new functions of the welfare state. But, worry persisted about the quality of children's upbringing, as older values of maternal nurturing changed less rapidly than mothers' activities did. Many thus professed that mothers, at least those of young children, should not work.

Tensions of this sort easily fed concern about the family itself, a theme already raised during the industrial revolution. Many people complained about changes in family roles, claiming that children were receiving too little adult supervision and spending too much time in front of television sets. Certainly, the Western family became more unstable. Divorce rates rose during most decades of the twentieth century, with the United States leading the way. By the 1970s, one marriage in two in the United States, and one in three in Great Britain, ended in divorce. The fact that changing laws made divorce easier to obtain was merely a symptom of a growing tension between individual fulfillment and continued interest in family ties. The family has survived in the West and in many ways adapted to new functions. One of the reasons for rising divorce rates has indeed been the high expectations Western people have about the family, as they seek love, sexual pleasure, and freedom from dispute. However, there is no question that the concept of the family often failed in practice, and the resulting strains on and conflicts for family members occasioned great anxiety in the twentieth-century West.

Along with social structure and family, pleasure seeking became an important theme of Western society in the twentieth century, most obviously during the 1920s

Modern leisure: bathers at Coney Island beach and amusement park, New York, 1952.

and again in the affluent era following World War II. With growing prosperity and shorter working hours—by the 1940s, most people worked an eight-hour day—interests in leisure exploded. Mass media, including popular novels as well as movies, radio, and television, brought escapist entertainment to millions. Professional sports commanded growing attention, particularly soccer in Western Europe and football and baseball in the United States. Sex also garnered more open public interest than was the case during the nineteenth century. Birth control remained an essential consideration, but it was provided increasingly by artificial devices, not abstinence. And, a society concerned with pleasure and the consumption of goods found sex an important consideration. More revealing fashions, particularly those for women; the more open use of sexual themes in films and on television; and manuals devoted to teaching methods of greater sexual pleasure all marked this new chapter in Western history. Whether people actually experienced greater sexual pleasure than before is open to question, but there was no doubt of great public interest in the subject. Sex or sexual allure became a vital part of having fun and of selling products. To some observers, indeed, sports and sex seem to have taken the place that religion once held in popular Western culture.

The changes in Western society during the twentieth century—including technological advances as well as setbacks like the depression—caused considerable social tension. Burgeoning unionization and rising rates of strikes into the early 1950s expressed class conflict, as workers reacted to automation and the power of their middle-class bosses. However, with growing affluence and the rise of the service sector, where unionizing came harder, strikes and unions receded somewhat. Other protest movements, including the student risings in the 1960s and feminism, reflected social change, including discontent within the family. Overall, though, collective protest did not surge in the West. But, there were also more individualized signs of distress. Rates of violent crime increased in Western society after World War II, initially because of the dislocation of war itself but then as a result of new conflicts among youth and also racial minorities. For the most part, the United States had the highest per capita crime rates, but Western Europe faced an upward trend as well. The growing use of drugs was also interpreted as a reaction to boredom and the lack of meaning in Western life.

Western society, like Western politics and art, seemed enmeshed in a fundamental contradiction of the twentieth century. On the one hand, the society encouraged individualism. Children were raised to think of themselves as individuals, to rise above their parents' achievements if possible, to embrace new educational and employment opportunities. Leisure interests appealed to individual pleasure seeking. But, individualism was severely curtailed by the growing bureaucratization of society. Most jobs involved routine activities, controlled by an elaborate supervisory structure; individual initiative counted for little, in not only factories but also the offices of giant corporations. Leisure, appealing to individual self-expression in one sense, generally meant mass, commercially manipulated outlets for all but a handful of venturesome souls. By the 1950s, television watching had become far and away the leading interest of Western peoples, and most television fare was deliberately standardized. Individualism also came into conflict with the continued devotion to family bonds, as we have seen. Ironically, individualism and its manifestations often made collective protest against bureaucratization and routine extremely difficult.

To critics, inside Western society and without, late–20th-century Western society seemed confused, in constant conflict. Poverty and job boredom coexisted with affluence and continued appeals about the essential value of work. Youthful protest—as expressed in defiant styles of dress and jarring forms of music—family instability, and crime might be signs of a fatally flawed society. Rising rates of suicide and an increasing incidence of mental illness were other troubling symptoms. At the least, Western society continued to display the strains of change. People displaced by change or troubled by the rejection of former values, as well as people caught up in new styles but disappointed by their results, showed the tensions of adjusting to a society still in rapid flux.

CONCLUSION: A POSTINDUSTRIAL AGE?

Many people in Western society came to believe that they were facing greater changes than ever before, whether for better or for worse. By the late 1960s, a new concept of a "postindustrial" society took shape in both Western Europe and North America. It held that Western society was the leader in a transformation as fundamental as the industrial revolution had been. The rise of a service economy, according to this world view, promised as many shifts and changes as the rise of an industrial economy had precipitated. Control of knowledge, rather than control of goods, would be the key to the postindustrial social structure. Technology would allow the expansion of factory production with a shrinking labor force, and attention would shift to the generation and control of information. The advent of new technology, particularly the computer, supported the postindustrial concept, by applying to knowledge transmission the same potential technological revolution that the steam engine had brought to manufacturing.

Changes in the role of women paralleled the postindustrial concept, and some observers began to talk of a postindustrial family in which two equal spouses would pool their earnings for a high-consumption life style. Postindustrial cities would increasingly become entertainment centers, as most work could now be decentralized in the suburbs, linked by the omnipresent computer. Postindustrial politics were less clearly defined, although some noted that the old party structure might loosen as new, service-sector voters sought issues more appropriate to their interests. The rise of environmental and feminist concerns that cut across former political alignments might thus prove an opening wedge to an unpredictable political future for the West.

The postindustrial society was not an established fact, of course, even by the late 1990s. Important continuities with earlier social forms, including political values and cultural directions, suggest that new technologies might modify rather than revolutionize Western industrial society. It is clear, however, that Western society has taken on important new characteristics, ranging from age brackets to occupational structure, that differentiate it from the initial industrial patterns generated during the nineteenth century. And this fact, even if more modest than the visions of some of the postindustrial forecasters, raises an important question for the West and the world: How would a rapidly changing, advanced industrial society fit into a world that has yet to fully industrialize? How could the concerns of an affluent, urban, fad-conscious Westerner coexist with the values of the world's peasant majority?

SUGGESTED WEBSITES

On personal experiences in the Great Depression, see
http://www.sos.state.mi.us/history/ museum/techstuf/depressn/teacup.html;
on the Holocaust, see *http://www.remember.org*; on the feminist leader Simone de Beauvoir, see *http://members.aol.com/CazadoraKE/private/Philo/ Beau/USimone.html*;
for efforts at European union, see *http://www.eurunion.org*.

SUGGESTED READINGS

Important overviews of recent European history are Walter Laqueur, *Europe Since Hitler* (1982); D. A. Low, *Eclipse of Empire* (1991); Helen Wallace et al., *Policy-Making in the European Community* (1983); Alfred Grosser, *The Western Alliance* (1982); and R. Paxton, *Europe in the 20th Century,* 2nd ed. (1985). On the Holocaust, see R. Hilberg, *Perpetrators, Victims, Bystanders: The Jewish Catastrophe* (1992). Some excellent national interpretations provide important coverage of events since 1945 in key areas of Europe. See A. F. Havighurst, *Twentieth-Century Britain* (1982), and John Ardagh, *France in the 1980s* (1982). Volker Berghahn, *Modern Germany: Society, Economy and Politics in the 20th Century* (1983), is also useful. On post–World War II social and economic trends, see C. Kindleberger, *Europe's Postwar Growth* (1967); V. Bogdanor and R. Skidelsky, eds., *The Age of Affluence* (1970); R. Dahrendorf, ed., *Europe's Economy in Crisis* (1982); and Peter Stearns and Herrick Chapman, *European Society in Upheaval,* 3rd ed. (1991). On the welfare state, see Stephen Cohen, *Modern Capitalist Planning: The French Model* (1977), and E. S. Einhorn and J. Logue, *Welfare States in Hard Times* (1982).

On the relevant Commonwealth nations, see Charles Doran, *Forgotten Partnership: U.S.–Canada Relations Today* (1983); S. M. Lipset, *American Exceptionalism: A Double Edged Sword* (1995), which compares Canada and the United States; Edward McWhinney, *Canada and the Constitution, 1979–1982* (1982); and Stephen Graubard, ed., *Australia: Terra Incognita?* (1985). On the United States in the cold war decades, see Walter LaFeber, *America, Russia and the Cold War, 1945–1980,* 4th ed. (1980); Thomas Patterson, *On Every Front: The Making of the Cold War* (1979); David Oshinsky, *A Conspiracy So Immense: The World of Joe McCarthy* (1983); Richard Polenberg, *One Nation Divisible: Class, Race and Ethnicity in the United States Since 1938* (1980); Harvard Sitkoff, *The Struggle for Black Equality, 1954–1980* (1981); and William Chafe, *The American Woman: Her Changing Social, Economic and Political Roles* (1972).

Eastern European Civilization

27

The Russian Revolution and its aftermath dominated Eastern European history in the twentieth century. What caused the revolution? What were the principal changes it brought to Russia? What were the results of Russian power over the rest of Eastern Europe after World War II? How did communist society relate to earlier traditions in Eastern Europe? What changes resembled trends occurring within Western Europe and the United States? Why did the Soviet system fall apart in the 1980s and early 1990s? Based on current conditions and prior history, what is the future of this region likely to be?

NEW POWER FOR A NEW RUSSIA

During the twentieth century, Russia, while experiencing many of the events that also rocked the West, developed a distinctive kind of industrial society under a communist system. This society reflected earlier Russian traditions and the massive innovations produced by the revolution of 1917. Until the 1940s, the smaller nations of Eastern Europe stood apart from this system, but as the Soviet Union extended its military influence, they too were brought under a communist economic and political framework. The result was considerable unity, but also significant tensions in East European civilization as a whole. Then in the late 1980s, the whole communist system split apart, within Russia as well as its empire.

The fundamental transformation in Russian society during the twentieth century resulted from industrialization and the creation of a new social structure, freed from traditional aristocratic control and supported by mass education. The communist regime installed in 1917 was an instrument of change. Revolution itself resulted from the conflicts of a society in which population pressure, new political aspirations, and the early stages of Russian industrialization challenged older social and political forms without reforming them. As in France within the eighteenth century and China and other countries in the twentieth century, massive revolution was essential in responding to the initial forces of change and in opening the way for further shifts. However, the Russian Revolution did not alter every facet of society—no revolution does. The new Soviet political system, although vastly different from tsarist times, preserved the authoritarian tradition in Russian life, including many

541

specific institutions such as the secret police. An expansionist foreign policy continued as well, but it was one shaped by the results of two world wars. Russia's expansionism, combined with its new industrial strength, catapulted the country into superpower position, along with the United States, after 1945. Russia also preserved its long-standing ambivalence regarding Western culture, at once seeking to imitate features of the West but then trying to avoid its influence in the name of distinctive East European values. Thus, although science and a secular outlook gained ground in Russia, bringing it closer to modern Western culture in many respects, deliberate efforts to avoid Western artistic and popular cultural styles created divisions between the two civilizations. The events of 1989–1991 reopened the relationship to the West, redefining yet again the question of Russia's identity.

THE RUSSIAN REVOLUTION

The impetus behind Russia's 1917 revolution was its suffering during World War I. Russian forces encountered many defeats, particularly at the hands of the better-equipped German armies, and civilian conditions deteriorated dreadfully as the country sought to sustain the war effort. Food shortages and high prices spurred massive discontent. However, the underlying problems ran deeper. The government had refused to provide meaningful political rights, as the parliament (Duma) remained a shallow exercise. The tsar Nicholas II was both impervious to the legitimate grievances of the masses and stubborn; he surrounded himself with corrupt advisors who weakened the regime's reputation. Urban workers formed the clearest revolutionary class, as they were subjected to harsh conditions in the early industrial factories that only intensified the resentments they had harbored from their peasant background. But, middle-class liberals and the peasantry had grievances of their own, and a variety of revolutionary movements and factions, mostly operating illegally, were eager to channel any and all discontent. In essence, Russia constituted a traditional rural society being hurried into the industrial age at a dizzying pace, with an unresponsive political system—the formula for twentieth-century revolution.

In March 1917, strikes and food riots broke out in Russia's capital, and they quickly assumed revolutionary proportions, calling for not just material aid but a new political regime. A council of workers, called a "soviet," took over the city government and arrested the tsar's ministers. The tsar abdicated, thus ending the long period of imperial control. For 8 months, a liberal provisional government struggled to rule the country. But, liberalism was not deeply rooted in Russia, if only because of the small middle class, and the regime also made the mistake of trying to continue the war effort. Nor were liberals ready to grant massive land reforms, for they respected existing private property and thus disappointed the peasantry. So, a second revolution took place in November (October, by the Russian calendar) that soon brought the radical wing of the Communist Party—the Bolsheviks—and their dynamic leader—Vladimir Ilyich Ulyanov, known as Lenin—to power.

The Bolsheviks formed one of the smaller revolutionary forces in Russia, but they had the advantage of tight organization and a coherent plan of action. They also had, in Lenin, one of the great revolutionary organizers of all time. Although in exile during most of the early years of the twentieth century, Lenin had hammered out a distinctive version of Marxist theory, arguing that a country like Russia, even though not fully industrialized, could have a working-class revolution on the basis of a well-organized vanguard of the proletariat. This vanguard would operate in the proletariat's name, initially as a dictatorial force. Revolution was further possible, according to Lenin, because international capitalism had extended so widely in the world: Here was a powerful statement in the age of imperialism, facilitating Marxist movements not just against native capitalism, but against Western domination as well. Lenin built a cadre of trained, professional revolutionaries under his leadership. He dominated other Marxists, many of whom believed that Russia must first pass through a middle-class phase; he outmaneuvered other radical groups as well. His organization became known as the Bolsheviks, or "majority," even though they were, in fact, outnumbered. His most formidable opponent was the Social Revolutionary Party, which had anarchist roots and won wide appeal among the peasantry by arguing for the primary importance of land reform. During the early months of the revolution, Lenin also worked for peasant support, pressing for state control of all the land, and he gained growing influence among urban workers by backing their spontaneous revolutionary councils, the soviets. Above all, Lenin surpassed his rivals by calling for radical revolution immediately, rather than taking the cautious approach that most others advocated. As popular discontent persisted, with urban strikes and rural riots, Lenin's firm position won growing prestige. By October, Lenin had a majority in the leading urban soviets. On November 7, Bolshevik leaders seized power throughout the capital city, and a national Congress of Soviets established a Council of People's Commissars, headed by Lenin, to govern the state.

Bitter struggles remained after the Bolshevik seizure of power, however. Popular elections produced a majority for the Social Revolutionary group, but Lenin forced this party to dissolve, concluding that "the people voted for a party which no longer existed." The assembly was shut down, and the Bolshevik-dominated Congress of Soviets took its place; Russia was to have no Western-style, multiparty system. A greater problem was posed by massive resistance in various parts of the country. The Bolsheviks had only a vague notion of what to do after power was obtained. They ended the war effort, signing a humiliating peace treaty with Germany that cost considerable territory. And, they redistributed land to the peasantry. Gradually, they also nationalized basic industry under the Council of People's Commissars. But, tsarist generals fought the new regime in many regions, backed at points by troops from Japan, France, Britain, and the United States, all appalled at the radical regime that ruled Russia. Civil war raged for 3 years, until the communists managed to construct a powerful Red Army of their own and win widespread popular support against foreign intervention. Internal opposition, including competing revolutionary leaders, was gradually crushed, with numerous executions. Lenin also found it necessary to curry popular favor by issuing a New Economic Policy in 1921, which promised greater freedom for small businesses and peasant agriculture than the Bolsheviks had intended. Under this temporary policy, food production began to recover after years of widespread famine, and the regime had time to formulate the more permanent policies of the communist system.

Parade of the Red Army, Moscow, soon after the revolution.

By 1923, the Bolshevik revolution was an accomplished fact. A new constitution established a federal system of socialist republics, which gave minority nationalities some sense of freedom while preserving the dominance of ethnic Russians. The new nation was known as the Union of Soviet Socialist Republics, but firm Communist Party control over the state governments, and centralization of all basic decisions in the new capital of Moscow (moved from St. Petersburg, now named Leningrad, to provide a more Russian, less Western tone to the revolutionary state), formed the basis of an authoritarian rule more effective than the tsarist regime had ever been. The revolutionaries also began to concentrate more exclusively on Russian affairs, after a brief period in which great hopes had been pinned on promoting a communist revolution in other European states. The Bolsheviks maintained a Communist International Office (Comintern) to support and guide communist parties elsewhere, but their main focus was on building their own state.

The Russian Revolution was one of the most important transformations in human history. Building on widespread if diverse popular discontent and a firm belief in centralized leadership, the Bolsheviks beat back foreign intervention and avoided even a partial restoration of the "old regime," as had occurred in France after Napoleon. Although the Bolsheviks utilized features of the tsarist system, including its authoritarian principles, they managed to create a new political, economic, and cultural structure without serious internal challenge after the initial years of chaos.

PATTERNS OF SOVIET HISTORY AFTER 1923

Lenin died in 1924, and after a few years of jockeying, Joseph Stalin succeeded him as undisputed leader of the Soviet state. Stalin, with his base in the Communist Party, which now clearly dominated the new government, was a man of working-class background, with limited education and scant interest in theoretical Marxism, but he had a relentless obsession with power. Under his rule, Russia was to develop its own version of a socialist society—"socialism in one country," as Stalin put it, as opposed to the vision of worldwide revolution that had inspired many earlier leaders. By the time Stalin had fully eliminated potential rivals in 1927, Russia had advanced only slightly toward a socialist system, although its revolutionary momentum had not ended. Much of the land was in the hands of wealthy peasants, or kulaks, who seemed attuned to a profit-based market agriculture; even in industry, state-run enterprises and planning had only limited effect. Stalin devoted himself to a double task: to make the Soviet Union a fully industrial society, and to do so under the full control of the state, rather than private initiative. In essence, Stalin wanted modernization, but with a revolutionary, noncapitalist twist.

A massive program for collective agriculture began in 1928. Collectivization meant large, state-run farms, rather than individual holdings as in the West. Communist Party agitators pressured peasants to join the collectives. The vast majority of kulaks refused, but through threats and mass executions and deportations to Siberia, they were forced to submit. Agricultural production fell drastically as a result, and although it gradually recovered during the later 1930s, the Soviet Union was saddled with the persistent problem of lack of peasant motivation. Although collective farms allowed peasants small plots of their own and job security, they created an atmosphere of factorylike discipline and rigid planning from above that left many peasants reluctant participants.

The collective farm system did, however, facilitate control of the peasantry so that rural profits could be reduced, in favor of providing capital for industrialization, and excess workers could be forced into the ranks of urban labor. If Stalin's handling of agriculture had serious flaws, his approach to industry was in many ways miraculously successful. A system of five-year plans under the state planning commission began to construct massive state-run factories in metallurgy, mining, and electric power, to make Russia an industrial country without foreign capital or more than very limited foreign advice. The focus was on heavy industry, which built on Russia's great natural resources and also served to prepare for possible war with Hitler's Germany. This unbalanced allocation, which slighted consumer goods, was to remain characteristic of the Soviet version of an industrial society. Further, Stalin's ambitious hope to replace market forces with government choices led to many allocation bottlenecks plus a wasteful use of resources and labor, as production and supply quotas for individual factories were set in Moscow. However, there was no question that rapid industrial growth had occurred. During the first two five-year plans, to 1937—that is, during the same period when the West was mired in the depression—Russian output of machinery and metal products grew 14-fold. Russia had become the world's third industrial power, behind only

Germany and the United States. Russia's long history of backwardness seemed to have ended.

Along with forced industrialization, Stalin continued to maintain the police powers of the state. Opponents and even imagined opponents were executed. During the great purge of high party leaders in 1937–1938, hundreds of people were intimidated into confessing imaginary crimes against the state, and most of them were executed. Party congresses and meetings of the executive committee, or Politburo, became mere rubber stamps, and a zealous internal police, renamed the MVD in 1934, perpetuated an atmosphere of terror in Russian society.

Ironically, Stalin's purges had weakened the nation's ability to respond to the rising threat of Hitler, the self-proclaimed leader of anticommunism. Along with an understandable suspicion of the motives of the Western powers, this internal weakness encouraged Stalin to sign his pact with Hitler in 1939. The alliance bought some time for greater war preparation and also enabled Russian troops to attack eastern Poland and Finland in an effort to regain territories lost in World War I. Here was the first sign of a revival of Russia's long interest in conquest, which would be born out by the results of World War II.

The war itself was devastating for the Soviet Union. German invasions, although ultimately unsuccessful, brought massive death and hardship. Russia's new industrial base, hastily relocated to the Ural Mountains and beyond, proved vital in providing the material needed for war, along with some U.S. and British aid, but the effort was extremely costly. Great cities such as Leningrad and Stalingrad were besieged by the Germans for months, with a huge loss of life. The war heightened Russia's age-old fear of invasion and foreign interference, already enhanced by World War I and Western intervention during the revolution. However, as the Red Army pressed westward after 1943, finally penetrating to the Elbe River in Germany, there was new opportunity for aggrandizement as well. Russia was able to regain its former western boundaries, at the expense of nations like Poland; some small states, established by the Treaty of Versailles, were swallowed up entirely. Larger East European states were allowed to remain intact, but their regimes were quickly brought under the control of Communist parties backed by the Soviet occupation forces.

Most of the small nations of Eastern Europe had encountered serious problems between the world wars. They were mostly new, the product of particular nationalisms honored by the Versailles treaty and carved from the western parts of the Russian empire plus the now defunct Habsburg realm. Only in Czechoslovakia did a democratic, parliamentary regime achieve durable success. Most states, after a brief democratic experience, had turned to authoritarian rule under a monarch or army general. Land reform had been ignored in favor of continued aristocratic dominance. Bickering over boundaries had added to severe economic distress; industrialization lagged, and agricultural productivity actually declined. Then came the Nazi attack that easily overwhelmed the smaller, more backward armies of states like Poland. And this was followed, between 1944 and 1948, by effective Russian control. Through a combination of sheer military might and collaboration with local communist movements, opposition parties were crushed and an essentially Soviet political system installed in Poland, Hungary, Romania, Bulgaria, Czechoslovakia, and East Germany, in an unprecedented westward extension of Russian power. Only Yu-

Soviet and East European Boundaries by 1948

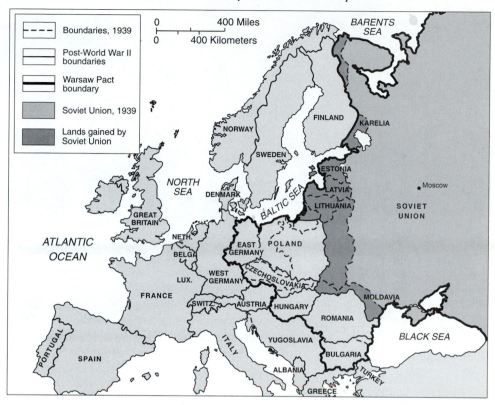

goslavia and Albania, with separate communist regimes, plus Western-oriented Greece escaped the new Soviet empire. Elsewhere, Russian-style agricultural collectivization and state-run industrialization began to take shape along with a single-party communist government. Ultimately, the Soviet Union forged the Warsaw Pact alliance of military cooperation, to confront NATO in the West.

Although the extension of Soviet control to the rest of Eastern Europe was the most dramatic diplomatic result of World War II, there were other significant developments as well. Russian participation in the late phases of the war against Japan presented the Soviets with an opportunity to seize some islands in the northern Pacific. Russia established a protectorate over the communist regime of North Korea, to match the American protectorate in South Korea. Russian aid to the victorious Communist Party in China resulted in new influence in that country for a time. In the 1970s, Russia gained a new ally in communist Vietnam, which among other things provided naval bases for the Russian fleet. Russia's growing military and economic strength gave the postwar Soviet Union new leverage in the Middle East, Africa, and even parts of Latin America. Communist ideology, attacking Western domination and capitalist exploitation, won wide followings in many parts of the world. The Soviet Union's superpower status was confirmed by its development of the atomic and

Uprising in Budapest, 1956: At this stage of a temporary victory, the citizens control a tank.

hydrogen bombs and deployment of missiles and naval forces to match the rapid expansion of U.S. arsenals. Russia had become a world power.

Internally, the Stalinist system remained intact during the first postwar years. The regime was supported by the growing cold war with the United States, which convinced many Russians that firm authority was essential to counter the new foreign threat. But Stalin died in 1953, and from that time onward no single leader gained comparable power. Choice of single leaders by ruling committees balanced various interest groups in the Soviet hierarchy—the army, the secret police, the bureaucracy of the Communist Party. The Soviet government had rigidified, with entrenched bureaucratic interests ready to defend their prerogatives, and no ruler could produce sweeping change. But in 1956, a new Russian leader, Nikita Khrushchev, attacked Stalin's dictatorial policies, blasting the late dictator's crimes against opponents. The de-Stalinization current roused great interest in the satellite states of Eastern Europe, chafing under Russian control. More liberal communist leaders arose in Hungary and Poland, seeking to create states that, while communist, would permit greater diversity and certainly more freedom from Soviet domination. In Poland, the Russians accepted a new leader more popular with the Polish people; among other results, Poland was allowed to halt agricultural collectivization. However, a new regime in Hungary was brutally crushed by the Russian army—de-Stalinization clearly had limits. Within the Soviet Union itself, de-Stalinization produced a reduction in the number of political trials and the most overt forms of police repression. But, the apparatus of the state, including the one-party system and centralized economic planning and control, remained intact.

After the furor of de-Stalinization, patterns in Russia remained unusually stable until the 1980s. Economic growth continued, but with no dramatic breakthroughs and with recurrent worries over sluggish productivity and especially over periodically inadequate harvests, resulting in expensive grain purchases from Western nations including the United States. A number of leadership changes occurred, as party chieftains aged and died, but such transitions occurred smoothly. Russian military development continued, including substantial troop deployment throughout Eastern Europe; the Soviets' world position was dramatized by leadership in many space probes and space flights, and by growing success in international athletic competitions, including the Olympic Games. The Soviet hold over Eastern Europe loosened slightly after the trauma of 1956, for heavy-handed repression cost considerable prestige. East European governments were given a freer hand in economic policy and allowed to experiment with greater cultural freedom in a limited sense. As a result, Hungary emerged as a state with considerable intellectual diversity and extensive consumer-goods industries. However, severe limits remained, as Soviet leaders insisted on basic political and military control of the border states. An attempt to create a more liberal regime in Czechoslovakia, in 1968, brought Russian army repression, while renewed agitation in Poland during the late 1970s, although controlled by the Polish army, was carefully monitored by Soviet leaders. Finally, in the one direct military thrust outside the postwar orbit, Russian troops entered Afghanistan in the late 1970s, to protect a regime friendly to Soviet interests against Muslim opposition. Russian foreign policy, in other words, while not literally imperialist, remained opportunistic and particularly bent on buffering Soviet borders against a potential threat, although Russia's only actual war after 1945 was in Afghanistan.

SOVIET POLITICAL INSTITUTIONS

The political system that the Soviet leaders built after the revolution, and then extended to the smaller states of Eastern Europe, maintained the authoritarian traditions of the tsar in many ways. Stalin's brutal treatment of opponents and his paranoid suspicion of potential rivals were accurately compared to the actions of tsarist predecessors such as Ivan the Terrible. Even forced industrialization, although it represented a dramatic shift in Russia's economic structure, bore the marks of Peter the Great's state-sponsored Westernization. Finally, the parliamentary system that evolved under Stalin, creating impressive-sounding institutions that were elected under Communist Party supervision, with no opposition tolerated, bore more than a small resemblance to the essentially powerless Duma that the last tsar had created to try to pacify liberal opposition. By Western standards, the Soviet Union had no more parliamentary power than the tsars had allowed, despite carefully worded constitutions and a universal suffrage system that, in fact, compelled most Russians to vote but offered no choice save the officially sponsored candidates and policies.

Nonetheless, the Soviet system was far more efficient and sweeping than tsarist authoritarianism had been. It utilized modern technologies, including rapid communications, and the experience of Western governments in mobilizing their societies during World War I. The Soviet system, like Hitler's Germany, was sometimes called a totalitarian government in that it sought to reach citizens directly, to shape their thoughts and actions and command their loyalties. Thus, it developed far more extensive functions than the tsarist regime had attempted. Under Stalin, control of virtually all of agriculture and industry, under state planning ministries, meant that the economy and the state were fully intertwined. Peasant garden plots, a few small shops, and an often extensive black-market system were the only economic forces that escaped state direction. The state was also responsible for cultural policies, and although this had been foreshadowed by the church-state links under the tsars, it had no full precedent. The communist regime tried to shape a secular population that would believe in the political doctrines of Marxism and embrace a scientific outlook on the world, monitoring artistic and literary styles as well as purely political writing. The educational system was greatly extended, yielding rapid gains in literacy and considerable access to higher education for talented students; this system, too, was designed to promote the state's vision of a loyal and productive citizenry.

Soviet leaders also constructed an elaborate state-sponsored welfare system. Able-bodied citizens, men and women alike, were required to work; the Soviets permitted no unemployment, although extensive underemployment often existed. But, the state operated medical facilities, day-care centers, and youth organizations, and provided payments to the disabled and elderly. Many of these programs were administered by Communist party organizations, including the loyal trade unions that were

"In Memoriam to Y. Gagarin." Painting of Yuri Gagarin, a leading early cosmonaut, by A. Shmarinov, member of the USSR Academy of Arts, 1971.

not permitted to strike but did mobilize many group recreational activities. Athletic clubs and beach resorts in southern Russia were among the state-run operations that cemented the welfare system. Far more literally than the welfare system developed in the West, the Soviet version embraced its citizens from cradle to grave.

Networks of political police and police informers attempted to ensure loyalty to the state, continuing and extending the tsarist tradition. All major operations, from youth groups to collective farms, were monitored by Communist Party members. Foreigners visiting Russia and Russian groups traveling abroad were carefully supervised. Groups and individuals suspected of dissidence were intimidated, often arrested. In the Stalinist era, in addition to the widely publicized purge trials and executions, millions of suspected opponents were sent to forced labor camps in Siberia. Under de-Stalinization, intimidation was moderated somewhat. Some opponents of the regime were allowed to go into exile, others were sent to psychiatric clinics; outright political executions became rare, but an atmosphere of considerable fear remained.

Along with policing came extensive positive efforts at persuasion and propaganda. The press and other media were strictly state-controlled, offering carefully filtered versions of the news. Massive banners, pictures of leaders, and patriotic parades stimulated devotion and a sense of identification with the regime. The Soviets intro-

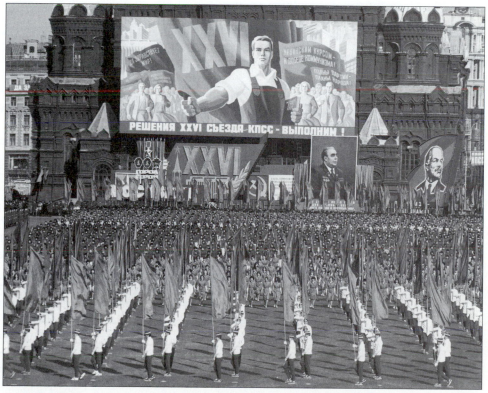

Parade of athletes and workers: Red Square, Moscow, May 1, 1981. May Day was a major civic celebration in the USSR and for workers' movements in many other countries.

duced a new set of holidays, commemorating the revolution and other anniversaries, including the international workers' day, May 1. Under Stalin, efforts to instill Marxist loyalty to the cause of the proletariat were blended with more traditional nationalism against foreign enemies, a powerful brew that unquestionably created a high level of commitment among many Russian people.

The construction of the Soviet state was in many ways a remarkable achievement. The tsarist precedent helped, but tsarist officials and church leaders were cast aside during the revolution, while a host of new functions were undertaken. The Soviets tapped vast reservoirs of popular talent and enthusiasm to construct their new bureaucracy. At the same time, this very creation became increasingly unwieldy. After important new access to political power for able workers and peasants in the 1920s, recruitment to the party and the bureaucracy increasingly came within the ranks of bureaucratic families, which favored their own. The Communist Party itself was effectively run by a top committee, the Political Bureau, or Politburo, consisting of 20 people who were the real rulers of the country. Decisions were made at the top tier, often in secret, and then transmitted to lower levels for execution; little reverse initiative, with proposals coming from lower bureaucratic agencies, was encouraged. Just as the new bureaucracy replaced the tsarist aristocracy in ruling the country, so it raised some of the same problems as a power elite often more concerned with self-perpetuation than innovation.

SOVIET CULTURE

As in politics, Russian culture in the twentieth century exhibited a fascinating blend of new elements, products of the revolution and industrialization, and more traditional themes.

Soviet leaders from the beginning viewed key features of traditional Russian culture as forces to be attacked and undermined. Religion headed the list. Although the new regime did not attempt to abolish the Orthodox Church outright, it greatly limited the church's outreach. Thus, the church could not give religious instruction to anyone under 18, and state schools vigorously preached that religion is mere superstition. The Soviet regime also limited freedom of religion for the Jewish minority, often characterizing Jews as enemies of the state in what was, in fact, a manipulation of traditional Russian anti-Semitism. The larger Muslim minority was given greater latitude, on the condition of firm loyalty to the regime.

The Soviet state also opposed the strong Western orientation of the nineteenth-century tsarist elite, although it should be pointed out that this preference had never widely touched the masses. Modern Western styles of art and literature were attacked as decadent. Earlier styles, appropriated as Russian, were maintained. Thus, Russian orchestras performed a wide variety of classical music, and the Russian ballet, although rigid and conservative by twentieth-century Western norms, commanded wide attention. Soviet culture emphasized a style of "socialist realism" in the arts, intent on glorifying heroic workers, soldiers, and peasants. A vigorous strand of modern art in prerevolutionary Russia was repressed under Stalin, in favor of grandiose, neoclassical paintings and sculpture. Russian architecture emphasized functional, classical lines, with a pronounced taste for the monumental, although various sorts of historical buildings were carefully preserved.

Russian literature remained diverse and vibrant, despite official controls sponsored by the communist-dominated Writers' Union. Leading Russian authors wrote movingly of the travails of the civil war and World War II, maintaining the earlier tradition of sympathy with the Russian people, great patriotism, and a concern for the eternal Russian soul.

The most creative Soviet artists, particularly writers, often tread a fine line between conveying some of the sufferings of the Russian people in the twentieth century and courting official disapproval. Their freedom also varied depending on the mood of Russia's leaders; thus, censorship eased after Stalin and then tightened again, although not to previous levels. Nonetheless, even authors critical of aspects of the Soviet regime maintained distinctive Russian values. Aleksandr Solzhenitsyn, for example, was exiled to the West after the publication of his history of Siberian prison camps, *Gulag Archipelago,* but found the West too materialistic and individualistic for his taste. Although barred from his homeland until 1993, he continued to seek some alternative to both communist policy and Westernization, clinging to his belief in the durable solidarity and faith of Russia's common people.

Along with an interest in the arts, Soviet culture placed great emphasis on science and social science. Social scientific work, heavily colored by Marxist theory, nevertheless produced important analyses of current trends and history. Scientific research was even more heavily funded, and Soviet scientists generated a number of

"In a Designing Office": socialist realism. Notice bust of Stalin at left of painting.

UNDERSTANDING CULTURES

The Impact of Revolution

Many major revolutions try to change culture, as part of creating the conditions for a better, or at least different, world. English Puritan revolutionaries, in the seventeenth century, passed laws to limit what they saw as immorality and a lack of religious zeal. Revolutionaries during the radical phase of the French Revolution hoped to create a new, civic religion to replace what they viewed as older superstitions.

Communist revolutionaries during the twentieth century often sought even more systematic cultural change. Their Marxist doctrine stressed that old cultures are tainted by an outdated and unjust economic structure and must be attacked. Religion, particularly, is, as Marx put it, the "opiate of the masses." At the same time, new cultural values must be created as part of building a perfect communist society in which people can govern themselves and contribute freely to the common good.

In Russia, this general approach meant a vigorous attack on traditional popular culture, especially religion. At the same time, new beliefs had to be constructed that were different from those of the contemporary—capitalist—West. This was one of the reasons for an emphasis on the new socialist-realist artistic style, to replace not only older styles but also to provide a clear alternative to "decadent" Western art. Education emphasized science and communism, in the hope of creating the desired new cultural values. Russian leaders even aspired to provide an alternative to the consumer culture of the West, which was seen as shallow as well as unjust because of the continued inequality within Western society at large.

The revolutionary approach to culture was extremely ambitious. It did generate some change, but its goals were impossible to pull off entirely. Thus, many artistic traditions, such as the ballet, coexisted within the new cultural effort; the past was only attacked selectively. In the name of protecting revolutionary culture, many intellectuals were jailed or worse, because they would not toe the party line. It was also impossible to prevent the influence of outside values, and by the 1960s, an awareness of Western consumer and popular culture caused increasing unrest, particularly among Russian youth. Finally, when the communist effort failed by 1989, Russian culture was severely impacted. The past was gone, although there was some effort to revive it. The culture of the future had failed. What new beliefs would fill this vacuum?

fundamental discoveries in physics, chemistry, and mathematics. At times, scientists also experienced the heavy hand of official disapproval. Biologists and psychiatrists, particularly, were urged to reject Western theories that called human rationality and social progress into question. Thus, Freudianism was banned, and biologists who overemphasized the uncontrollability of genetic evolution were jailed. But, Russian scientists overall enjoyed considerable freedom as well as great prestige. As in the West, their work was linked with advances in technology and weaponry.

Shaped by substantial state control, twentieth-century Soviet culture was neither traditional nor Western. Considerable ambivalence about the West remained, as Russian leaders shared Western enthusiasm for science while trying to redefine artistic styles and popular beliefs.

ECONOMY AND SOCIETY

The Soviet Union became a fully industrial society between the 1920s and 1950s. The rapid growth of manufacturing and rise in city populations to over 50 percent of the nation's total were measures of this development. Most of the rest of Eastern Europe was also fully industrialized by the 1950s. East European modernization, however, had a number of distinctive features. State control of virtually all economic sectors was one key element: No other industrialized society gave so little leeway to private initiative. The unusual imbalance between heavy industrial goods and consumer items was another distinctive aspect. The Soviet Union lagged behind in the low priorities it placed on consumer goods—not only Western staples like automobiles, but also housing construction and simple items such as bathtub stoppers. Consumer-goods industries were poorly funded and did not achieve the advanced technological level that characterized the heavy manufacturing sector. The Soviet need to amass capital for development, in a traditionally poor society, contributed to this inattention to consumer goods; so did the need to create a massive armaments industry to rival that of the United States, in a society still poorer overall. Living standards improved greatly, and extensive welfare services provided security for some groups that was lacking in the West, but complaints about poor consumer products and long waiting lines to purchase desired goods remained a feature of Soviet life. East European industrialization also paid little regard to the environment. Chemical pollution and the exhaustion of waterways endangered large stretches of the region; some estimates held that as much as 40 percent of Russian agricultural land became endangered, whereas over 20 percent of Soviet citizens lived in areas of "ecological disaster."

The communist system throughout Eastern Europe also failed to resolve problems with agriculture. Capital that might have gone into farming equipment was often diverted to armaments and heavy industry. The arduous climate of northern Europe and Asia was a factor as well, dooming a number of attempts to spread grain production to Siberia, for example. But, it seemed clear that the East European peasantry continued to find the constraints and lack of individual incentive in collective agriculture a deterrent to maximum effort. Thus, Eastern Europe had to retain a larger percentage of its labor force in agriculture than was true of the industrial West and still encountered problems with food supply and quality.

Despite the importance of distinctive political and economic characteristics, Eastern European society echoed a number of the themes of contemporary Western social history—simply because of the shared fact of industrial life. Work rhythms, for example, became roughly similar. Industrialization in Russia brought massive efforts to speed the pace of work and introduce regularized supervision. Incentive systems designed to encourage able workers resembled those used in Western factories. In the 1930s, the Soviets adopted a practice of rewarding the heroes of labor—workers who exceeded production quotas—with extra benefits and prestige. Along with similar work habits came similar leisure activities. For decades, sports provided excitement for the peoples of Eastern Europe, as did mass media such as film and television. Family vacations to the beaches of the Black Sea were cherished.

Russian social structure also grew closer to that of the West, despite the continued importance of the rural population and the impact of Marxist theory. The aristocracy ended. Particularly interesting was an increasing division of urban society along class lines, between workers and a better-educated, managerial middle class. Wealth divisions were not as great as in the West, to be sure, but the perquisites of managers and professional people—particularly if they were Communist Party members—set them off from the masses and their lower standard of living.

Finally, the Russian family had to cope with some of the same pressures of industrialization that the Western family experienced. Massive movement of people to the cities and crowded housing helped to undermine the nuclear family unit, as ties to a wider network of relatives loosened. The birthrate dropped. Official Soviet policy on birthrates varied for a time, but the basic directives became similar to those in the West: Falling infant death rates, with improved diets and medical care, plus growing periods of schooling and some increase in consumer expectations, made large families less desirable than before. Wartime dislocations contributed to a decline in the birthrate at various points as well. By the 1970s, the Russian growth rate was about the same as that of the West. Also as in the West, some minority groups—particularly Muslims in southern Russia—maintained higher birthrates than the Russian majority.

Patterns of child-rearing showed some similarities to those in the West, as parents, especially in the managerial middle class, devoted more attention to their children's education and ensuring good jobs for them in the future. At the same time, children were more strictly disciplined than in the West, both at home and in school, with an emphasis on authority that might have political implications as well. Russian families were never afforded the domestic idealization of women that had prevailed in the West during industrialization. Most married women worked, an essential feature of an economy struggling to industrialize and offering relatively low wages to individual workers. As in the peasant past, women performed many heavy physical tasks. They also dominated some professions, such as medicine, although they were far lower in status than their male-dominated counterparts in the West. Russian propagandists took some pride in the constructive role of women and their official equality, but there were signs that many women suffered the psychological burdens of demanding jobs with little help from their husbands at home.

By the 1970s, many Russians seemed satisfied with their political and social system. Police repression remained, but Stalinist excesses had been reduced. Pride in

Russian space and athletic achievements was coupled with a realization of the improvements in living standards and opportunity that had grown with the Soviet system. Many Russians also noted weaknesses in the West that enhanced their faith in their own institutions: Family instability, greed, and crime seemed lesser problems in the Soviet context, and only partly because the regime concealed accurate statistics. Except for the unpopular war in Afghanistan, Russian foreign policy had remained fairly prudent; American diplomacy could be construed as more unpredictable and warlike. In 1962, for example, the Soviets pulled back their missiles from Cuba, rather than risk outright conflict with the United States. Furthermore, of course, the Soviet system had partially isolated much of Eastern Europe, allowing only limited trade outside the communist system and only carefully regulated cultural contacts. The imagery of an "iron curtain" enclosing this civilization was not entirely an exaggeration.

THE EXPLOSION OF THE 1980S

Despite its many achievements, Soviet society began to come unglued by the early 1980s, opening a dramatic new chapter in East European and Central Asian history. The initial cause of this extraordinary upheaval lay in deteriorating economic conditions, intensified by the costs of a military rivalry with the United States. The Soviet economic system, after a strong growth rate in the 1950s and 1960s, stopped functioning well by the late 1970s. Industrial production began to stagnate and even drop, as a result of rigid central planning, health problems, and poor worker morale. Growing inadequacy of housing and common goods resulted, further worsening motivation. As economic growth stopped, yet cold war military competition continued, the percentage of resources allocated to military production escalated toward a third of all national income. This reduced the funds available for other investments or for consumer needs. Disease rates, infant mortality, and alcoholism all increased. Younger leaders began to recognize, at first only privately, that the system was near collapse.

Nevertheless, the Soviet system was not incapable of change, despite its complex bureaucracy. In 1985, after a succession of leaders whose age or health precluded major initiatives, a new, younger official rose to the fore. Mikhail Gorbachev quickly renewed many of the earlier attacks on Stalinist rigidity and replaced some of the old-line party bureaucrats. He conveyed a new and more Western style, dressing in fashionable clothes (his wife, Raisa, publicly did the same), holding relatively open press conferences, and even allowing the Soviet media to engage in active debate and reporting on problems as well as successes. Gorbachev also urged a reduction in nuclear armament, and in 1987, he negotiated a new agreement with the United States that limited medium-range missiles in Europe. He ended the war in Afghanistan and brought home Soviet troops.

Gorbachev proclaimed a policy of *glasnost,* or "openness," which implied new freedom to comment and criticize. He pressed particularly for a reduction in bureaucratic inefficiency and unproductive labor in the Soviet economy, emphasizing more decentralized decision making and the use of some market incentives to stimulate greater output. In many ways, Gorbachev's policies constituted a return to a characteristic Russian ambivalence about the West as he reduced Soviet isolation while continuing to criticize particular aspects of Western political and social structure. Gorbachev clearly hoped to use some Western management techniques and was open to certain Western cultural styles, without, however, intending to abandon the basic controls of the communist state. Western analysts wondered if the Soviet economy could improve worker motivations without embracing a Western-style consumerism or whether computers could be more widely introduced without allowing the free exchange of information.

Gorbachev also sought to open the Soviet Union to fuller participation in the world economy, recognizing that isolation in a separate empire had restricted access to new technology and limited the motivation to change. Although the new leadership did not rush to make foreign trade or investment too easy—considerable suspicion did persist—the economic initiatives resulted in symbolic changes, such as the opening of a McDonald's restaurant in Moscow, and a whole array of new contacts with foreigners.

The keynote of the reform program was *perestroika,* or economic restructuring, which Gorbachev translated into more leeway for private ownership and decentralized control in industry and agriculture. Farmers, for example, were given the chance to lease land for 50 years, with rights of inheritance, whereas industrial concerns were authorized to buy from either private or state operations. Foreign investment was newly encouraged. Gorbachev urged more self-help among Russians, including a reduction in the consumption of alcohol, arguing that he wanted to "rid public opinion of . . . faith in a 'good Tsar,' the all powerful center, the notion that someone can bring about order and organize perestroika from on high." Politically, he encouraged a new constitution in 1988, giving considerable power to a new parliament, the Congress of People's Deputies, and abolishing the communist monopoly of elections. Important opposition groups developed both inside and outside the party, wedging Gorbachev between opposing factions—liberals pressing for faster reforms versus conservative hard liners. Gorbachev himself was elected to a new and powerful position as President of the Soviet Union in 1990.

DISMANTLING THE SOVIET EMPIRE

Gorbachev's new approach, including his desire for better relations with Western powers, prompted more definitive results outside the Soviet Union than within, as the smaller states of Eastern Europe uniformly demanded greater independence and internal reforms. Bulgaria moved for economic liberalization in 1987 but was held back by the Soviets; pressure resumed in 1989 as the party leader was ousted and free elections were arranged. Hungary changed leadership in 1988 and installed a noncommunist president. A new constitution and free elections were planned, as the Communist Party renamed itself "socialist," and Hungary moved rapidly toward a free-market economy. Poland installed a noncommunist government in 1988 and again acted quickly to dismantle the state-run economy; prices rose rapidly as government subsidies were withdrawn. The Solidarity movement, born a decade before through the merger of noncommunist labor leaders and Catholic intellectuals, became a dominant political force. East Germany displaced its communist government in 1989, expelling key leaders and moving rapidly toward unification with West Germany, which occurred in 1990—a dramatic sign of the collapse of postwar Soviet foreign policy. Czechoslovakia installed a new government in 1989, headed by a playwright, and again sought to introduce free elections and a more market-driven economy.

Although mass demonstrations played a key role in several of these political upheavals, only in Romania was there outright violence as an exceptionally authoritarian communist leader was swept out by force. As in Bulgaria, the Communist Party retained considerable power, although under new leadership, and reforms moved less rapidly than in countries like Hungary and Czechoslovakia. The same held true for Albania, where the unreconstructed Stalinist regime was dislodged and a more flexible communist leadership installed.

New divergences in the nature and extent of reform in Eastern Europe were exacerbated by clashes among nationalities—as in the Soviet Union itself, where both Baltic nationalists and Asian Muslims raised new demands. Change and uncertainty brought older traditions to the fore. Romanians and ethnic Hungarians clashed, while Bulgarians attacked a Turkish minority remaining from the Ottoman period. In 1991, Yugoslavia, where an existing communist regime—although not Soviet-dominated—also came under attack, a bloody civil war developed from nationalistic disputes as Slovenia, Croatia, and Bosnia-Herzegovina proclaimed independence and then Bosnia divided among warring Serb, Croat, and Muslim factions. Czechoslavakia was peacefully broken up into a Czech republic and Slovakia.

Amid many conflicts and uncertainties, the Soviet empire was dismantled. Gorbachev reversed postwar imperialism completely, stating "Any nation has the right to decide its fate by itself." In several cases, notably Hungary, Soviet troops were rapidly withdrawn, and generally it seemed unlikely that a change of heart, toward an attempt to reestablish a repressive empire, would be possible.

RENEWED TURMOIL AFTER 1991

The uncertainties of the situation within the Soviet Union were confirmed in the summer of 1991, when an attempted coup was mounted by military and police elements. Massive popular demonstrations, however, asserted the strong democratic beliefs that had developed in the Soviet Union since 1986. The contrast with earlier Soviet history and with suppression of democracy in China 2 years earlier was striking. But, Gorbachev's authority ironically weakened. The three Baltic states gained full independence, although economic links with the Soviet Union remained. Other minority republics proclaimed independence as well, but Gorbachev struggled to win agreement on a continued economic union and some form of political coordination. By the end of 1991, leaders of the major republics, including Russia's Boris Yeltsin, proclaimed the end of the Soviet Union and a commonwealth of the leading republics in its stead, including the economically crucial Ukraine.

Amid the disputes, Gorbachev fell from power, doomed by his attempts to salvage a presidency that depended on the survival of a greater Soviet Union. His leadership role was assumed by Boris Yeltsin, who as president of Russia and an early

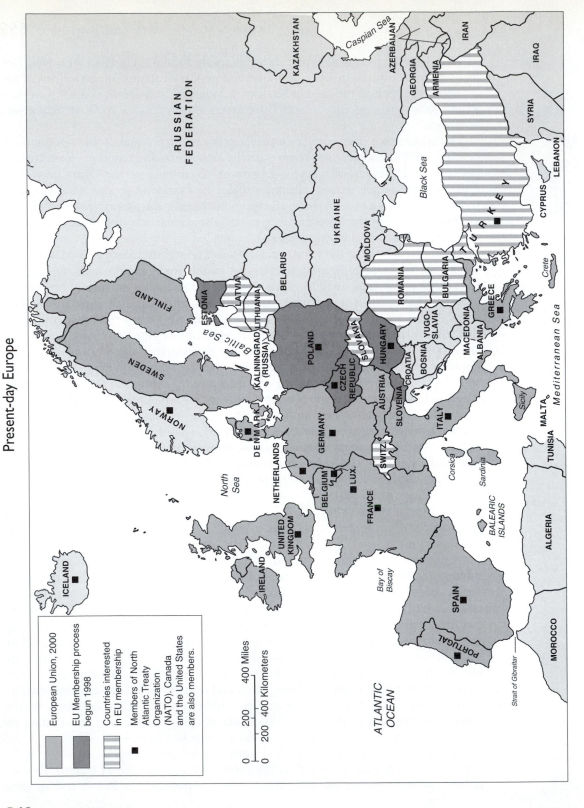

Present-day Europe

European Union, 2000

EU Membership process begun 1998

Countries interested in EU membership

Members of North Atlantic Treaty Organization (NATO). Canada and the United States are also members.

0   200   400 Miles

0   200   400 Kilometers

critic of communism now emerged as the leading, although quickly beleaguered, political figure in Russia.

Most of the now independent republics tentatively agreed to the resulting Commonwealth of Independent States. But, tensions immediately surfaced about economic coordination amid the rapid dismantling of state controls; about control of the military, where Russia—still by far the largest state—sought predominance, including nuclear control, amid challenges from the Ukraine and Kazakhstan (the two other republics that could claim nuclear weaponry); and about relationships between the European-dominated republics, including Russia, and the cluster of central Asian states. Unity within the former Soviet Union had largely ended, although Russia retained economic influence in Central Asia and close ties with some new Slavic states like Belarus.

The fate of economic reform was also uncertain, as Russian leaders hesitated to convert to a full market system lest transitional disruption further antagonize the population. Here again, more radical plans emerged at the end of 1991, calling for the removal of most government price controls. Economic conditions improved by the late 1990s; food suppplies, for example, were plentiful. However, inefficient state-run factories persisted. Government revenues dropped. New gaps between rich business groups and workers and retirees resulted in important tensions.

Political directions also became complicated. Russian leaders outlawed the communist party, in retaliation for its leadership of the failed coup, but an alternative party system emerged only slowly. Soviet citizens took delight in tearing down the old emblems of the revolution, including massive socialist-realist statues of Lenin. Even old tsarist flags and uniforms were trotted out for display. But, effective new emblems had yet to be generated. Nonetheless, in some republics, including central Asia, party leadership retained considerable vigor, and political strife in several now independent republics allowed the Russian army to regain some role. In Russia itself, Yeltsin quarreled bitterly with the parliament dominated by former communists, dissolving it by force in 1993. Communist politicians retained a strong following, whereas an equally vigorous, militaristic nationalist movement won some support. Yeltsin himself, struggling with personal problems, displayed inconsistent attitudes toward economic reforms and politics. Finally, regional conflict in Muslim areas within Russia, particularly the region of Chechnya, resulted in bitter fighting in the late 1990s.

CONCLUSION: UNCERTAIN FUTURES IN EASTERN EUROPE

Inevitably, Soviet and East European history in the late 1990s was dominated by the surprising events of the most recent period and by huge uncertainties about their futures. Certain stirring events made clear that much less had changed in this region during the twentieth century than had been recognized—even by Soviet citizens themselves. Soviet law had long trumpeted women's equality and, indeed, Soviet women played an important role in the labor force. However, inequality within the household continued, while the unavailability of reliable birth-control devices—a result of shoddy consumer goods production—resulted in a high rate of abortions. Soviet constitutions had featured a system of federated republics, but, in fact, central government control and Russian ethnic dominance spurred minority nationalism, causing new nationalist hostilities to develop. Indeed, nationalism, in Russia and among newly independent East European nations, threatened to profoundly divide the region. Religion also remained a vital force despite decades of secularization. Catholicism within the smaller nations and western republics of the former Soviet Union, and Judaism and Islam in central Asia made for important loyalties that could now be acknowledged.

Revolution and a totalitarian state had exerted only a limited impact despite theories of absolute control and undeniable police terror during key periods. The same system had done less to diminish a traditional attraction to Western values and standards than might have been imagined. Several East European states indeed rushed to proclaim a Western-style devotion to individual liberty as well as a market economy. In 1997, NATO granted membership to Poland, the Czech Republic, and Hungary, pulling them further into a Western orbit as the former border lands embraced the institutions and culture of the West. In Russia itself, although nationalist loyalties and economic lags might ultimately limit the country's openness to Westernization, in the long run it seemed unlikely that isolation could be resumed—a sign of both long-standing East European interest in the West and the new intensity of international contacts.

Amid a host of questions about the future, once the Soviet mantle of protection had been withdrawn, several key issues dominated any analysis of the new Eastern Europe and central Asia. The first involved sheer stability. Conversion to a market economy and a democratic political system was bound to be difficult. Many experts thought Poland, Hungary, and the Czech Republic stood an excellent chance to succeed, because of their relatively advanced industrial structure and unusually great contacts with Western cultural and political values. Prospects for southeastern Europe and Russia itself were less clear, and efforts to move toward market structures and abandon former Communist leadership were characteristically less rapid in these areas. Ethnic and religious battles seemed to promise more instability in the former Yugoslavia, central Asia, and possibly other parts of the Balkans.

The second issue involved traditionalist revivals. As communism fell in this region of the world, many people reembraced former loyalties, like religion or ethnic nationalism, because they had no other beliefs to follow. Would these more traditionalist impulses persist, or would a more Western-style, semisecular mentality develop? Although predictions are inherently best guesses, history did offer some guidelines. It was important to realize that the revolution of 1917, extended to the rest of Eastern Europe after 1945, would not be entirely undone. No one seriously called for a return to peasantry or the aristocracy, or an end to industrialization or mass literacy. Despite dramatic changes, there was no revolutionary dismantlement of the prior system; most of the new leaders in politics and business came from the communist bureaucracy and cautiously renounced their past. Specific features of the revolution connected to the communist system came under bitter attack, but not the more fundamental restructuring. This might facilitate democracy, compared to its fate in places like Poland between the wars. At the same time, history also warned against facile assumptions that this region would easily assimilate with Western society after some period of adjustment. Russians, for example, maintained their commitment to a more extensive welfare system, while attacking unattractive features of Western individualism like high crime rates and unrest among youth. Many resented profiteering, on the grounds of more egalitarian beliefs than were common in the West. Many disdained, for instance, the new influx of American "junk food," sold for high prices.

Finally, Russia's relationship to not just the West but also the wider world focused new attention on important questions. The Soviet empire, although somewhat closed to outside contact, had organized politics and economics in a huge part of Europe and Asia, building on the previous expansion of the tsars. Much of this was now undone. The empire had also played a vigorous role in world affairs, providing political guidance and economic and military aid to every continent. Economic failure eclipsed this role, at least for the moment. But, what world role would Russia and its neighbors now play? In the immediate aftermath of collapse, particularly after 1991, Russian leaders carefully supported most Western diplomatic initiatives. Was this likely to persist, given different traditions and interests? Would Russia, still industrial and still a territorial giant, renew contact with its long-standing, if variously defined, sense of mission? These are questions not yet answered, as Russia's new role continues to unfold as we begin the twenty-first century.

SUGGESTED WEBSITES

For websites on Lenin, see *http://soften.ktu.lt/~kaleck/Lenin/*; on leaders of the Soviet Union and Russia from Stalin to Yeltsin, see *http://home.mira.net/~andy/bs/index.htm*; for Alexander Dubcek, the Czech leader in the 1968 uprising, on changes in the former Soviet Union since 1991, see *http://www.learner.org/exhibits/russia*.

SUGGESTED READINGS

Recent Soviet history is examined in Martin McCauley, *The Soviet Union, 1917–1991* (1993); Richard Barnet, *The Giants: Russia and America* (1977); A. Rubinstein, *Soviet Foreign Policy Since World War II* (1981); Alec Nove, *The Soviet Economic System* (1980); Stephen Cohen et al., eds., *The Soviet Union Since Stalin* (1980); and Ben Eklof, *Gorbachev and the Reform Period* (1988). On the Russian revolution, see B. Wolfe, *Three Who Made a Revolution* (1955); D. Footman, *Civil War in Russia* (1962); and T. Skocpol, *States and Social Revolutions* (1979), a major interpretive effort.

Other areas of Eastern Europe are explored in Joseph Held, *The Columbia History of Eastern Europe in the 20th Century* (1992); F. Fetjo, *History of the People's Democracies: Eastern Europe Since Stalin* (1971); J. Tampke, *The People's Republics of Eastern Europe* (1983); Timothy Ash, *The Polish Revolution: Solidarity* (1984); H. G. Skilling, *Czechoslovakia: Interrupted Revolution* (1976), on the 1968 uprising; and B. Kovrig, *Communism in Hungary from Kun to Kadar* (1979).

On the early signs of explosion in Eastern Europe, see K. Dawisha, *Eastern Europe, Gorbachev and Reform: The Great Challenge* (1988). Bohdan Nahaylo and Victor Swoboda, *Soviet Disunion: A History of the Nationalities Problem in the USSR* (1990), provides important background information. An excellent recent study is Ron Brady, *Kapitalism: Russia's Struggles to Free Its Economy* (1999). On women's experiences, see Barbara Engel and Christine Worobec, eds., *Russia's Women: Accommodation, Resistance, Transformation* (1990).

East Asia in the Twentieth Century

28

FOCAL POINTS

In the twentieth century, East Asia divided between societies experiencing revolution and the establishment of communist regimes and those that maintained democracy or authoritarianism. The process of revolution was immensely disruptive in China and later Vietnam, but it yielded huge changes in the economy, society, and culture. What were the main stages of revolution and change? What earlier traditions were particularly attacked? Noncommunist East Asia, led by Japan but ultimately including other parts of the dynamic Pacific Rim, emphasized rapid industrial growth, although involvement in World War II created important new developments as well. Why was the Pacific Rim so successful economically? East Asia remained divided by 2001, but new Chinese and Vietnamese policies and a common Confucian heritage beneath the surface of formal politics began to call growing attention to the region as a whole.

THE CLASHING REGIONS OF EAST ASIA

In the nineteenth century, East Asia had been divided by the differing responses of Japan and China to Western pressures. These divisions continued into the twentieth century. Japan maintained an aggressive foreign policy that helped launch World War II and then developed one of the most successful economies in the world. China, in contrast, continued to struggle in order to industrialize. The giant nation was wracked by two revolutions, the second initiating a communist regime that resembled Soviet Russia in important ways.

Nevertheless, East Asia has maintained something of its own character. Japan, although an advanced industrial nation and a democracy, continued to differ from the West in many ways. China, although ultimately a communist society, showed marked variations from the Soviet model. It borrowed selectively from the Soviet example, somewhat as Japan had earlier picked and chosen from the West. There were some signs, also, that the unique characteristics of East Asia would propel much of the region, and not just Japan, into the ranks of fully industrialized nations by the early twenty-first century. Certainly, the rapid economic growth of South Korea, Hong Kong, and Taiwan, and the possibility that China itself might make the turn to full industrialization, has raised new discussion of East Asian "advantages" in the process of latecomer modernization. Finally, even amid great diversity, East Asian nations continue to interact. Japan's invasion of China in the 1930s colored the development of both nations. New economic exchanges by the 1970s again focused some attention on the links within this historic region.

East Asia in the twentieth century thus split between the Chinese communist pattern, shared to an extent by Vietnam, and Japan's rapid industrialization joined after the 1950s by other parts of the Pacific Rim, including much of southeast Asia. Both parts of East Asia continued to utilize former traditions of strong government and Confucian values, blending them with new ingredients—in China's case, outright revolution—to gain increasing impact in the world at large.

PATTERNS OF EAST ASIAN HISTORY

A CLASH OF CULTURES: REVOLUTION AND WAR

During the first two decades of the twentieth century, Japan continued its policies of rapid industrialization and imperialist expansion. The exploitation of Korea developed rapidly from 1910 onward. Japan's participation in World War I involved little major fighting, but provided it with a chance to acquire former German colonies in the Pacific islands. At the same time, Japan was not granted high status at the Versailles Peace Conference, which Japanese leaders found humiliating; internal pressure mounted for a more aggressive foreign policy that would compel the Western powers to recognize Japan's greatness. Internal stresses were also accumulating within Japanese society. A growing radical-socialist movement attempted to address working-class grievances, although it was successfully outlawed. Intellectuals continued the discussion of Japan's identity.

But as important tensions swirled in Japan, it was in China that more dramatic events occurred in the century's first decades. Growing Western penetration of the empire, combined with the government's sluggish response and the wave of students eager to see major reform, produced a revolutionary climate. A new republican movement sought to replace the age-old empire. Headed by Dr. Sun Yat-sen (see p. 566), the educated son of a poor family who had spent time in both British-controlled Hong Kong and Hawaii, the republicans believed that China should imitate Western principles of nationalism and democracy while introducing socialist policies to protect the people's welfare. Sun Yat-sen was no blind admirer of Western values; his emphasis on socialism was designed to guard against the excesses of capitalism and individualism. Nonetheless, he and his student followers advocated a radical departure from Chinese political traditions.

In 1908, the death of the dowager empress brought government promises of a written constitution and an examination of other aspects of Western government. But, these vague assurances were not enough to prevent widespread student rioting, which led to outright revolution in 1911. Sun Yat-sen hurried back from a trip abroad to head the provisional government, as the empire was ended in 1912.

The revolution demonstrated the weakness of the imperial regime, victim of the long decline characteristic of earlier Chinese dynasties but heightened by its inability to counter growing Western imperialism. However, although the old regime was easily displaced, the issue of what to do next was far less quickly resolved, for China was

World Profiles

Sun Yat-sen (1867–1925)

Sun Yat-sen was an important figure in twentieth-century Chinese history; he helped solidify the revolution that toppled the traditional imperial government. Dr. Sun failed, however, to create a fully successful alternative, becoming one of those world leaders in whose reach exceeds their grasp. Sun Yat-sen was born into a poor family near Canton, but he acquired an education at that point in history when students experienced new influences from the West and became resistant to Chinese traditions. Because of his opposition to the conservative imperial regime, Dr. Sun was forced to spend much time abroad, particularly in the United States, and he was thoroughly familiar with Western political thought. His writings proclaimed goals of nationalism, democracy, and ultimately socialism for a China that would be new, but not necessarily a victim of some of the social ills that plagued the West. These writings made him the hero of Chinese students educated overseas. When a revolution broke out in China in 1911, Dr. Sun rushed back to China from the United States and became its provisional president. At his insistence, no compromise was struck with the imperial regime, and China's boy-emperor resigned in 1912. Sun Yat-sen could not control the presidency, however, which passed to a military general. Dr. Sun formed the Nationalist Party (Kuomintang) to join forces with the military as part of an effort to organize a parliamentary state. However, these efforts to unite communists and conservatives in one movement failed with his death in 1925. China remained deeply divided for another two decades. Was Sun Yat-sen the best kind of leader to create a new state in China? What were the main barriers he faced in fulfilling his self-proclaimed tasks?

China's first great modern revolutionary, Sun Yat-sen.

not ready to spring into a modern, Western life style. Sun Yat-sen's movement had attracted student support because of its optimistic belief that China could regain its full independence and become politically like the West with no difficulty. However, the Chinese had never had direct experience with voting or representative bodies. The decline of the imperial institutions made it difficult simply to govern the country, much less reform it. The revolutionaries appointed a military general, Yaun Shi-h'ai, as president of the new republic, to conciliate the army and prevent foreign, particularly Japanese, intervention. The choice also reflected the fact that Sun Yat-sen and his colleagues had no government experience, and they proved to be indifferent administrators. But, the new president was no reformer; although he briefly tolerated an elected parliament, he worked to consolidate his own power as a possible future emperor. He was not capable of improving government efficiency, as tax revenues dwindled and Western influence expanded. In fact, China by 1916 was collapsing into a series of regional governments, headed by competing warlords, each with his own local army. Sun Yat-sen and his associates tried to counter the growing chaos by forming a political party of their own, the Kuomintang, but they gained influence only in part of China, mainly around the city of Canton. Thus, the 1911 revolution had destroyed key traditional institutions, but it had not created adequate substitutes for them. For this reason, revolution simmered in China throughout the next few decades, producing one deficient new regime after another until after World War II.

There was, briefly, a more hopeful interlude. During the later 1920s, the Kuomintang armies were able to subdue a number of the warlords. The regime also induced the major Western powers to renounce their claims on Chinese territories; the Western-controlled treaty ports thus returned to Chinese hands, with the exception of Portuguese Macao and British Hong Kong. Revolutionary leaders became more skeptical of Western political models and capitalist economics, and the values behind them, and the idea of a Chinese version of modern society gained ground. The new leader of the Kuomintang, Chiang Kai-shek, formulated a constitution that established authoritarian rule but was designed to lead the country to democracy. New laws also attacked traditional constraints on women in Chinese society, including the practice of footbinding; growing numbers of students attended modernized universities, some run by Christian missionaries, where Western-style science and social science were taught. Nonetheless, this period of renewal was short-lived. Chiang Kai-shek did not effectively rule the whole country, and the warlords soon resurfaced. Chiang's own government became increasingly opportunistic, making deals with warlords and business leaders rather than focusing on political reform, and the hope for a complete democracy increasingly dwindled. Furthermore, the Kuomintang faced another internal opponent in a strong communist movement, inspired by Marxism and the Russian Revolution. Driven out of the Kuomintang itself, the communists staged the heroic "Long March" to the distant Shensi province in the northwest, where they held out under the leadership of Mao Zedung.

It was in this confusion that Japan's path fatefully crossed China's once again, as Japan's industrial strength continued to grow. As in the Soviet Union, the 1920s and 1930s constituted an important second stage in the Japanese process of industrialization. Heavy industry expanded rapidly, as the Japanese developed their own machinery production and the use of electrical systems spread widely. With a growing and skilled labor force, mostly male, the Japanese also reconsidered earlier industrial policies. Many workers were given security of employment in return for hard work and loyalty to the firm, whereas the government itself increasingly combined worship of the emperor with nationalism in order to prevent social unrest. Political stability, however, proved elusive.

After a period of moderate politics, during the 1920s, in which Japan seemed to accept a multiparty political system, even allowing nonaristocrats to serve as prime ministers for the first time, Japan abandoned liberalism after 1930. The nation suffered severely from the early stages of the depression, as international trade plummeted. Dependent on exports for food and fuel, Japan saw unemployment rise steadily when the depression in the West reduced its available markets. The silk industry, long an export staple, suffered as Western synthetics like nylon cut into sales—a sign of Japan's continuing industrial vulnerability. Furthermore, population growth contributed to the pressure, as 65 million inhabitants were crowded into territory about half the size of the state of Texas. A million people a year were added through the combination of high birthrates and falling death rates.

Economic chaos, although short-lived, allowed Japan's military leaders, allied with conservative business and agricultural interests, to regain the upper hand in politics. This group rebelled against the cautious liberalism of the reigning politicians, using assassination and the threat of mass unrest as weapons. Japan's powerful but fearful oligarchy turned to an essentially fascist approach, foreign, in its violence and methods of intimidation, to Japan's political tradition. This transformation reflected not only the crisis of the depression but also the strains that rapid industrialization had placed on Japanese society—strains that did not produce outright revolution, but did lead the ruling oligarchy to its militaristic lines of defense. Parliamentary rule became increasingly shallow, as military leaders manipulated the politicians or, like General Hideki Tojo, held office directly. And, with this authoritarianism came renewed interest in foreign expansion, as the Japanese sought a sphere of influence in eastern Asia to deal with the nation's overproduction and overpopulation. The more aggressive foreign policy aided, and was aided by, Japan's quick rebound to renewed industrial growth.

In 1931, the Japanese launched an undeclared war on China, seizing the province of Manchuria and turning it into a satellite state. This was the first act of aggression in the interwar period that led toward World War II; Chinese leaders were unable to gain Western support, beyond moral condemnations of Japan, and this failure helped teach other rulers, such as Hitler, that aggression reaped worthwhile dividends. Chiang Kai-shek hoped to satisfy the Japanese by agreeing to the loss of Manchuria, but in fact the Japanese soon resumed their advance, extending control over additional provinces in 1935 and then in 1937 mounting a new war against China, which effectively continued until Japan's World War II defeat in 1945. Thus, China, already internally divided, faced 15 years of invasion and occupation. Vast stretches of the country were seized, many resources diverted to Japanese war industries, and millions of people killed or uprooted. Chiang's regime was driven from the great cities, but he was able to maintain control of many rural provinces. Both the warlords and communists now joined in opposition to the Japanese, the communists gaining prestige and important military experience through their role in the resistance.

Stalemated in China, Japan used the outbreak of war in Europe as an occasion to turn its attention to other parts of Asia. It seized Indochina from France's troops and then allied with Germany and Italy in a pledge of mutual military assistance. This alliance, along with continued expansion in Southeast Asia as the Japanese attacked Malaya and Burma, put the Japanese on a collision course with the United States, which as a Pacific power itself was unwilling to allow Japan to become a predominant force in the Far East. U.S. holdings in Hawaii and the Philippines, the fruit of earlier imperialism, convinced Japanese leaders that a clash was inevitable. Negotiations with the United States broke down with the American insistence that Japan renounce all lands acquired since 1931. It was within this climate that the Japanese attacked Pearl Harbor on December 7, 1941, and then in the following months seized American possessions in the eastern Pacific, including the Philippine islands. Only

World War II: Pacific Theater

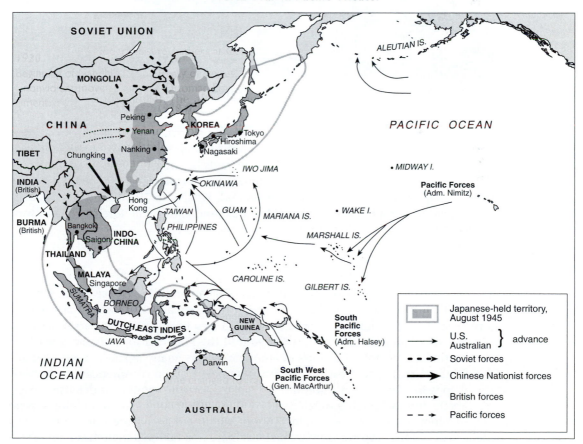

Hiroshima, 1945, after the first atomic bomb was dropped.

toward the end of 1942 did the United States begin to turn the tide, making the most of its superior level of industrialization. Scattered islands were reconquered, followed in 1944 by the Philippines, while massive air raids began an onslaught on Japan itself. Meanwhile American, British, and Chinese forces continued to bog down a considerable Japanese army on the Asian mainland. Finally, in 1945, the United States dropped atomic bombs on the cities of Nagasaki and Hiroshima, forcing the full surrender of Japan and a period of American occupation.

RETURN TO STABILITY IN JAPAN

The end of World War II separated the paths of Japan and China once again. Japan's imperialist surge ended, seemingly for good. It had been an anomaly in Japanese history in any event, and American-imposed changes in government personnel and limitations on military activity further reduced the potential for military adventurism. Victims of the only actual use of atomic weapons, many Japanese advocated an antimilitarist stance, whereas official Japanese policy accepted American protection against possible Soviet aggression rather than mounting a significant defense capacity directly. Internal politics were restructured as well, as American occupation forces helped produce a more liberal constitution, which enhanced the power of parliament, reduced the emperor from a religious figure to a national figurehead, and provided important safeguards for freedom of speech and press. Universal suffrage, first granted during the moderate period of the 1920s, was restored, and a number of political parties contested the major elections. In fact, a single party, the Liberal Democrats, held the reins of government throughout most of the postwar decades, but extensive political criticism and continued potential opposition affected its policies. Japan produced a new era of political stability, in which major concentration turned to economic development, as the Japanese soon entered the ranks of the world's most technologically sophisticated nations.

UPHEAVAL AND LATER REVOLUTION IN CHINA

With Japan's defeat, China emerged as the leading power in the Far East. Chiang Kai-shek was welcomed as a postwar leader, particularly by his U.S. allies; the Chinese were treated as a great power, along with Britain, France, the United States, and the Soviet Union, in forming the new United Nations. This was the first time an Asian nation had been accorded such status in Western-dominated diplomacy. However, the honeymoon was short-lived. Chiang was unable to assert a firm hold on China, for communist opposition began to mount.

The communist struggle with the Kuomintang dated back to the aftermath of China's first modern revolution. Inspired by the revolutionary atmosphere and also the example of Russia's Bolshevik success, a communist movement formed among students in Beijing between 1919 and 1921; the movement quickly came under the leadership of Mao Zedung, a librarian who was from a wealthy peasant family. Communists and Kuomintang collaborated for a time, both interested in establishing a revolutionary regime and opposing the warlords. But, the goals of the two groups were quite different, and Chiang Kai-shek expelled the communists in 1927, summarily executing anyone who wore the emblematic communist red scarf. Recurrent battles continued, for although the communists were weakened, they were not eliminated. Then a renewed military effort in 1934 culminated in the historic Long March, in which Mao led his followers to a remote northwestern province, where they built a strong reform movement among the peasantry and an independent power base. World War II gave the communists a chance to display their solid organization and guerrilla fighting techniques, and they also gained important new territory in their resistance effort against Japan.

By the war's end, the communists claimed to control over 70 million Chinese, with an army of almost a million. The Kuomintang, in contrast, had been exhausted in its war effort, as the Japanese had taken over the coastal cities where the movement had its power base. Economic problems and internal divisions and corruption further weakened the Kuomintang, which could not prevent communist guerrilla attacks and sabotage that undermined support for the existing regime. The communists offered not only successful military strategies but also a much clearer program of land reform to China's peasant majority than the Kuomintang, which increasingly seemed little more than a Western-dominated militarist group, its heritage from Sun Yat-sen mere rhetoric. Soviet aid to the communists also helped, whereas American support for the Kuomintang actually enhanced the government's organizational confusion. While Stalin had no love for the Chinese communists and Mao had long since diverged from the Russian model in peasant issues, a temporary union between the two was a critical factor in communist success.

Civil war between the communists and Chiang's armies broke out in 1945, and the Kuomintang lost ground steadily. Indeed, the speed of communist success surprised everyone, including the communists themselves. By 1949, the communists were in full control of mainland China. By 1950, Chiang had been driven to the island of Taiwan, which the communists could not capture because they had no navy. There, Chiang and his army imposed an authoritarian regime, while still plotting an eventual return to the mainland. But, in fact, the mainland now squarely belonged to Mao and the communists.

Communist victory, in turn, meant a second revolution in modern Chinese history—or a culmination of almost half a century of revolutionary agitation. The new rulers executed at least 800,000 political opponents and arrested many more. Their goal was to destroy all traces of China's forming ruling class—educated bureaucrats, landlords, and capitalists alike. In their place, the communists constructed a strong centralized state dedicated to economic modernization and social change. Five-year plans were issued, based on the Soviet model, to encourage heavy industry. Agriculture was collectivized, with peasant communes replacing traditional villages. With property seized from landlords, the revolution in the countryside reached major proportions. The government strictly controlled education and information, mounting a major attack on the various religions of China.

In its early years, Mao's regime maintained its close alliance with Soviet Russia. This alliance, plus a desire to assert China's traditional power in Asia, prompted the communist regime to resist U.S. advances in the Korean War. Divided between a communist north and noncommunist south after World War II, Korea had become a battleground in 1950 when the communists invaded the south. The United States came to the aid of its southern protectorate and then crossed into North Korea. This move resulted in massive Chinese intervention, which ultimately forced American retreat and a restoration of the previous Korean regimes and boundaries. China thus served notice that no outside power could claim East Asian dominance, in contrast to the humiliating decades of Western and Japanese imperialism. However, this same new strength soon caused a rift between Chinese and Russian communists. Mao began to attack post-Stalinist Soviet policy as a violation of true Marxism. Russian aid and advisors to the new Chinese regime were withdrawn, and tensions along the Soviet-Chinese border increased. Although ideological differences colored the new disagreement, it became clear that territorial disputes were an important consideration as well: The Chinese had not forgotten the earlier Russian seizure of some northern lands, whereas Russian rulers were keenly aware of the potential pressure of China's massive population on their sparsely peopled Asian republics. By the 1960s, the two giants of the communist world had become virtual enemies.

The rift with Russia prompted Chairman Mao to experiment with a different path to communism during the 1960s. Instead of five-year plans for heavy industry, Mao began to emphasize small-scale workshops in which intensive labor would substitute for advanced technology. Peasant communes stressed the need for a new Chinese personality, with common dining halls and large-scale propaganda attacking

Mao Zedung poster helps inspire election workers as they count the vote during elections to the National Peoples Congress.

the evils of traditional family ties and Confucian hierarchical values. Finally, schools were transformed into pure agencies of Maoist propaganda, and technical and scientific study was abandoned. Many teachers and other intellectuals were ordered to the countryside to perform agricultural work. During the 1960s, China seemed engulfed by this new revolutionary fervor, as Mao sought to solidify his power, to defy the Soviet model, and, above all, to attack many of the traditions of Chinese society, in order to produce a modern nation that was also free from the trappings of Western modernization or the bureaucratic conservatism of the Soviet Union. During this period of the Cultural Revolution, bands of youths were organized to attack any vestige of traditional hierarchy in schools, family, and even the army. As one manifesto proclaimed, "We are bent on striking down not only the reactionaries in our school, but the reactionaries all over the world. Revolutionaries take it as their task to transform the world."

The Cultural Revolution in China began to yield, however, by the late 1960s. Disruption of the schools and the attempt at backyard industry had worsened the Chinese economy. Pressure from the Soviet Union, including outright border fighting in 1969, prompted Mao to seek a partial reconciliation with the United States, which occurred in 1971. More moderate communist leaders also regained influence, and on Mao's death, in 1976, they assumed control. Under the leadership of Deng Xiaoping,

Peasants thrashing rice on an agricultural commune near Beijing.

the communist regime, although maintaining tight political authority, began to devote itself to intensive but rather conventional modernization efforts, stressing technical education and industrial development. In fact, an important student movement for democracy in 1989 was vanquished in favor of continued authoritarianism.

EAST ASIA TOWARD THE END OF THE CENTURY

The major events of East Asian history in the twentieth century may seem bewildering in their complexity. Japan moved from imperialism to modernization, from authoritarianism to democracy and a concentration on economic advance. China endured two revolutionary periods punctuated by Japanese invasion and, then, under the communists, three distinct periods: Russian-style consolidation, radical experimentation during the Cultural Revolution, and more pragmatic modernization since the late 1970s. Clearly, East Asian nations struggled for appropriate political forms during much of the twentieth century. Stability in Japan since World War II, and considerable stability in China since the end of the Cultural Revolution, suggest that such a goal has finally been achieved.

East Asia was also adjusting to new power alignments. Along with the period of conflict between Japan and China, the region was engaged in limiting Western influence and preventing major new Soviet gains. China's expulsion of special Western treaty rights, Japan's attack on Western-held territories, and China's Korean intervention all worked to this end, albeit in different ways. Although Soviet and American influence in East Asia remained considerable, there was little question by the 1970s that the region had regained substantial freedom of action. Internal conflicts subsided as well, so that since the end of the Korean War a period of effective peace took hold within the region. Tensions continued, to be sure: The regimes of North and South Korea faced each other across a precarious border; the Chinese People's Republic officially claimed sovereignty over a now separate regime on Taiwan; and China encountered tensions with Vietnam to the south. But compared to many other parts of the contemporary world, the region became fairly trouble-free—as it had so often been in earlier periods of history. Relative stability and a reduction in the turmoil that had marked the earlier decades of the century have given the major regimes of East Asia a chance to define their own characters.

JAPAN, INCORPORATED

Twentieth-century Japan, for all its transformations in political regime and foreign policy, displayed two consistent traits: an ability to combine adaptation to selected Western imports and technologies with a distinctive cultural identity, and a dynamism that brought the nation to world prominence first as a military force and then as one of the economic giants of the final decades of the twentieth century. The two traits were interrelated. Japan's skill in borrowing without a loss of identity, and its ability to utilize traditional characteristics such as strong group cohesion, had much to do with military and economic success. Such was Japan's impact that by the 1970s, along with continued Japanese interest in Western ways, came an almost obsessive Western eagerness to learn Japanese secrets, including traditional social traits that seemed so strikingly useful in an advanced industrial age. Western business and labor leaders began to make pilgrimages to Japan with some of the same zeal that Japanese students had displayed in their visits to Western nations during the previous century.

Japanese politics certainly blended modern democratic forms with traditional elitist ties. As in the Meiji era and to an extent during the authoritarian period of the 1930s, postwar politics were dominated by civil servants and business leaders. Although democratic suffrage prevailed and a number of political parties showed strength, the fact was that postwar Japan experienced no shifts in party leadership. Opposition groups were less important than factional jockeying within the Liberal Democratic Party. Few major policy shifts occurred after World War II. Only in 1993, amid growing evidence of business payoffs, did the Liberal Democrats split and lose their parliamentary majority, opening the possibility of more innovative politics. Up to this point, unusual stability in party dominance made Japan less similar to the Western political system than the constitutional structure would suggest. The other distinctive feature of the contemporary Japanese state was an unusual alliance with business interests toward the promotion of economic development and the expansion of exports. Government economic planning remained extensive, and business leaders willingly acquiesced to government production guidelines and other regulations; there was no sense of a division of interests between public and private

Contemporary Tokyo.

spheres, as still prevailed to an extent in the West. Small wonder that the coordination of economic policies produced the half-admiring, half-derisory Western label of "Japan, Incorporated."

Close business and political interaction resulted, in part, from the needs of a wartime economy and then postwar reconstruction. It was supported by Japan's precarious position in terms of resources, as the nation needed to import petroleum and most other vital raw materials, and so depended on active exports, which, in turn, the government helped promote. However, the interaction also followed from a long cultural tradition in which group cohesion was seen as the logical basis of society's functioning, a cohesion that easily blurred what Westerners saw as the lines between private enterprise and the role of the state. Government initiative also played a key role in ending Japan's rapid population increase. Once imperialist expansion ended, Japanese leaders realized that population must stabilize, and they used government, in the late 1940s and 1950s, to organize an active campaign promoting birth control and legalized abortion, which indeed reversed a century-long trend of demographic expansion. Unlike the West, where government policy had little to do with population trends and sometimes ran counter to such trends, Japan's more integrated political-social system allowed concrete action in a vital area of human behavior, which, in turn, encouraged more orderly economic growth and an improvement in living standards.

Important segments of Japanese culture were also oriented toward the goal of economic development. The extensive school system established during the Meiji period was further expanded. Japanese children were encouraged to achieve academic success, with demanding examinations for entry into the university becoming the primary goal of ambitious young men and women. Higher education, in turn, placed a major emphasis on technical and scientific subjects, although general research and teaching in the social sciences gained ground as well. Growing university enrollments, based on examination performance, thus recruited students on the basis of educational merit, creating one of the most open social systems in the world.

Japanese culture also preserved important traditional elements, however, providing aesthetic and spiritual satisfaction amid rapid economic change. Japanese films and novels recalled earlier history, including the age of the samurai warriors; they also stressed group loyalties, as opposed to individuality or strong assertions of personal will. An interest in rituals, including tea ceremonies and traditional costumes for recreation, remained an important theme as well. Japanese artists participated actively in the "international style" developed in the West, but they typically infused it with earlier Japanese motifs such as stylized nature painting. Japanese architects, also working in the modern style, incorporated traditional themes as well. Finally, both Buddhism and Shintoism, despite a largely secular culture, sustained religious forces in Japanese life. Overall, Japan during the twentieth century produced a blend of new cultural interests, many of which originated in the West, and older approaches, which allowed Japan, in turn, to make distinctive contributions to international artistic and scientific movements.

Particularly after World War II, however, it was through rapid economic growth that Japan made its clearest mark. Industrial development had continued at a steady pace through the 1920s, and again in the late 1930s, as Japan built upon its efforts during the Meiji era and produced a fully industrialized society. Then from the 1950s onward, the Japanese moved into the orbit of advanced industrial nations, easily surpassing the level of technological development current in Eastern Europe and challenging Western nations for world leadership. Beginning in the middle of the century, economic growth rates were among the highest in the world. By the 1970s, Japan became the world's chief producer and exporter of automobiles and many kinds of electronic equipment.

Japan's economic success rested on several factors. Wages remained lower than those common in the West, although living standards improved rapidly, particularly by the 1960s. The collaboration of business and government was supplemented by the large corporate combines, called *zaibatsu,* that emerged by the 1920s as a means of reducing competition within Japan itself. Business concentration took place in the West as well, but the mutual arrangements among large Japanese concerns, backed by government planning, went further still. The Japanese also cultivated an unusual degree of worker loyalty and diligence. Although some labor unrest occurred both in the 1920s and after World War II, strike rates were low by Western standards and Japanese workers were noted for their careful workmanship and productivity. In the large companies, workers were assured of job security; they could not be fired. They were often consulted on possible technical improvements. At the same time, businesses sponsored group exercises and other collective activities that increased worker morale. Japanese managers also showed less interest than their Western counterparts in high profits, while emphasizing group decision making and loyalty over individual ambition within a corporate hierarchy.

The Japanese approach to labor relations had some serious political and social costs, however. Many workers were forced to join company unions, as Japan's ruling oligarchy continued to find ways to undermine protest. Pressure to maintain high productivity was intense, and some workers who would not toe the line were forced to retire. Workers themselves were divided between those with job security and a large number, about 60 percent of the manufacturing labor force, including most working women, who faced more unstable market pressures. The *zaibatsu* system, effective in economic coordination, also helped suppress political competition, although less completely and arbitrarily than in the 1930s. But at least into the early 1990s, the Japanese way, in the eyes of a significant number of Westerners and many Japanese themselves, was a powerful economic instrument, creating unprecedented productivity and economic growth and a rising margin of exports over imports that steadily increased Japan's role in the world economy. Economic growth slowed in the 1990s, partly because of new global competition, but the nation remained a world powerhouse.

An additional element in Japan's economic success was the application of distinctive social relations to an advanced industrial technology. By Western standards, the Japanese seemed extremely nonindividualistic, loyal to group endeavors and not very concerned with personal reward or private expressions of discontent. Continued elaborate expressions of politeness, plus a heavy emphasis in the schools on the importance of patriotism, helped explain this unique national psychology. So did Japanese methods of child rearing. Children were encouraged to conform to group standards, among other things by the use of shame as a punishment for nonconformity—an approach in child rearing that the West had largely abandoned by the early nineteenth century. Japanese social solidarity showed even in the nation's legal practices. Lawyers were uncommon in twentieth-century Japan, for it was assumed that people could resolve certain issues on the basis of mutual agreement and that individuals had no reason to use the courts to protest the activities of neighbors or business leaders, or the government.

Not surprisingly, Japanese family customs and important aspects of personal behavior continued in ways that were significantly different from those of the contemporary West. Male authority remained preeminent in twentieth-century Japan. Relatively few women worked after marriage, and women's wages lagged well behind male levels—about 40 percent compared to the 70 percent that was common in the West. Women's role in the family, particularly in rearing young children, was heavily stressed. Japanese family structure stabilized after the high incidence of divorce around 1900, but it emphasized more than ever the domestic functions of women. Although a few Japanese feminists emerged, there was no movement comparable to that in Western society demanding new rights for women. However, Western influence showed, for example, in growing tolerance toward expressions of romantic love. In intimate life as in culture, Japan blended diverse ingredients. In the area of personal behavior, Japanese psychiatrists reported a distinctive pattern of mental illness. Problems of loneliness and alienation were far less significant than in the West, as the Japanese remained highly dependent, emotionally, on group activities. Conversely, in situations where individuals encountered competition alone, as in university entrance tests, stress levels were much higher than in analogous Western experiences. The Japanese also had their particular ways to relieve tension. Bouts of drunkenness were more readily tolerated than in the West, as a time when normal codes of conduct could be suspended. Businessmen had recourse to traditional geisha houses as a normal and approved activity.

Japanese popular culture was not static. Western influences permeated this area too. During the 1920s, Western styles of dress, sports, and music gained acceptance in the cities. Fashionable residents of Tokyo were even called "maden boi" and "modan garu" (modern boy or girl). The U.S. presence after World War II resulted in a growing fascination with the sport of baseball, and a number of professional teams were established. In the early 1980s, a new passion for television game shows, adapted from their American progenitors, took hold, although the Japanese typically altered the characteristic format of such shows to engender more elaborate humiliation (or shame) for losers. Romantic soap operas hit Japan with *Tokyo Love Story,* in 1989, quickly the most-watched TV show in the nation's history. In popular as well as formal culture, Western domination caused some concern among conservatives, who worried that important traditions—like the use of chopsticks—might be lost for good. But to Western eyes, the Japanese ability to assimilate imported culture within a distinctive context seemed far more striking.

As noted, Japan was not without its problems amid economic success. Many nations both in the West and Asia resented Japanese competition, often seen as unfair because the Japanese were slow to open their own markets to outside goods. Japanese dependence on imported oil and other products made the nation vulnerable to events in distant areas, such as the oil-producing Middle East. Pollution became an increasing problem with industrial growth and the rapid expansion of cities; traffic police, for example, often had to wear protective masks simply to breathe. New regulations after the 1970s did reduce pollution problems and helped generate growing environmental industries. Competition from other parts of Asia increased. Some Japanese experts, worried that the nation's economic vigor would prove fragile, wrote articles with such titles as "The Short, Happy Life of Japan as a Superpower," and growing unemployment plus sluggish production rates caused new concern by 1995.

THE COASTAL COUNTRIES OF EAST AND SOUTHEAST ASIA: THE PACIFIC RIM

A number of other East Asian nations developed an extensive industrial economy from the 1950s onward, although none could rival the advanced methods and accomplishments of Japan. South Korea, Taiwan, the British colony in Hong Kong, and, further to the south, the city-state of Singapore (whose population is largely Chinese) produced rapid economic growth. By the 1980s, Malaysia, Thailand, and Indonesia joined in. Most of these nations were long ruled by authoritarian regimes; political opposition was suppressed. Governments and business leaders collaborated to develop new factory industries, with an emphasis on both consumer goods and metallurgy. Growing exports earned revenues needed for the import of raw materials and advanced Western or Japanese technology.

As in Japan, the Pacific Rim states stressed national and group loyalties and limited what they saw as excessive individualism, including undue consumerism, which they considered to be wasteful and a threat to economic growth. Korean leaders emphasized traditional Confucian morality as part of this effort. The intent, as in Japan, was to change traditional values and social structures sufficiently to modernize the economy, but to preserve enough of these same values to avoid Westernization. The success of these nations suggested that East Asia, led by but not confined to Japan, was becoming the world's second industrial civilization, along with the West, as the region easily outstripped Eastern Europe. The prospect was made all the more probable by the region's ability to maintain the world's highest rates of economic growth during the 1970s and early 1980s. Greater openness to democracy was an important additional development in much of the Pacific Rim by the 1990s. A near revolution generated a more democratic regime in Indonesia by 1999, whereas greater political diversity in Taiwan contrasted that country with communist China. The Pacific Rim weathered a major financial crisis in 1998, but growth trends soon resumed.

CHINA UNDER COMMUNISM

China, the mother country of East Asian civilization, did not participate fully in the initial East Asian economic boom. The political system remained resolutely authoritarian. Once again, East Asia was a divided region, in politics and economic patterns, as the fits and starts of the communist regime in China abundantly demonstrated.

Communism took hold in China for a number of reasons. Historical accident played a role: The Japanese invasion distracted the Kuomintang and thus prevented a concerted attack on the communist forces and allowed the latter to consolidate their provincial power base. The inspired leadership of Mao Zedung was another important ingredient; as in Lenin's Russia, the communist revolution depended heavily on individual talent. Mao converted to communism during his student years, in 1918, seeing it as a means of challenging Western economic dominance while also facilitating fundamental changes within China itself. The all-encompassing belief system that Marxism provided played a role here as in the West and Soviet Russia. But, Mao adapted Marxism to Chinese circumstances early on, particularly in his emphasis on the power of the Chinese peasantry. He argued in 1927 that "the force of the peasantry is like that of the raging winds and driving rain. . . . The peasantry will tear apart all nets which bind it and hasten along the road to liberation." By promising land reform and conciliating peasants during the revolutionary struggle, Mao's forces gained crucial support in their war against the better-armed Kuomintang.

Although communism was a new force in Chinese history, with the goal of genuine revolution and not simply the seizure of power, it coincided with traditional features of Chinese society—as had been the case in the Soviet Union. The Chinese legacy of a strong state, with an elaborate bureaucracy, lent itself readily to a communist system, in which state power was further extended and in which government bureaucrats, although recruited from new sources and held to a new political faith, regulated large sectors of the economy and even family life. Mao's success, after the earlier failure of more liberal politics during the 1920s, was in this sense no accident. From the late 1940s onward, communist officials prevented political opposition, monopolized the main sources of information and propaganda, and abandoned all pretense of establishing a Western-style parliamentary regime. The Communist Party ruled the new People's Republic of China, and the party itself was dominated by Mao. Although the communist state was more efficient in its use of police and active promotion of political loyalty than the empire had been, there were some strong similarities between the two. Indeed, Communist leaders themselves soon found that they had recreated a complex bureaucracy that posed some of the same barriers to change that the old Confucian bureaucracy had. By the 1970s, appeals to bureaucrats to recognize the importance of new technologies and management methods became standard, as the Chinese continued to seek a reconciliation between a strong state authority and revitalized economic growth.

Mao's state and that of his more pragmatic successors was bent on transformation outside the political arena. China had been changing even before the communist revolution. During the 1920s, the port cities continued to expand, and factory industry took root. Modernized patterns of work and education gave a new voice to young people, weakening the Confucian tradition of ancestor worship. The importance of student groups expressed this shift. The position of women also began to change, as women in the cities acquired formal education and practices such as footbinding declined. More and more marriages were based on mutual affection rather than economic arrangements alone. Educational reforms brought even greater shifts in outlook, as science began to play a more significant role; many educated Chinese, at home and abroad, contributed actively to scientific and technological research.

The first-anniversary celebration of the founding of the People's Republic of China, October 1950: Workers carry hundreds of portraits of Mao in the parade.

Mao sought to extend and formalize the pattern of cultural and social change. He attacked Confucian values head-on. Harmony, ceremony, and ancestor worship were impediments to the liberation of China's masses, in his view. He encouraged the new importance of youth, the validity of attacks on established hierarchies and even on the authority of parents within the family. Officially, at least, revolutionary China mounted a far more sweeping attack on the traditions of its civilization than did the other societies of East Asia, including Japan. Plays, operas, and art embraced the revolutionary regime, abandoning older themes in favor of praise for the heroic peasant and worker and attacks on China's enemies, among them the United States. The commune system in the countryside, which placed children under the charge of nurseries long before formal schooling began, and limited young people's contact with parents, was designed to eliminate traditional values at their root. Here, Mao's regime went further than Russian revolutionaries had ever attempted.

Chinese habits, however, were not easily undone. The Communist regime dislodged the former landlord class, putting the land directly in the hands of the peasantry, who were then organized into state-directed communes. Agricultural production proceeded more smoothly than had been the case in Soviet Russia during collectivization. Foreign business interests and native capitalism were unseated in favor of state-directed enterprise. However, more subtle traditions, including family values and a tendency to venerate the elderly, seemed to persist. The Communist Party itself was soon dominated by older men, as Mao's group aged. After the furor of the Cultural Revolution, it was not clear that youth would become the new heroes in China. Women gained greater equality and participated actively in the labor force as had long been the case, but, particularly in the countryside, older traditions such as arranged marriages persisted. Other customs, such as extreme politeness and the careful control of emotions, proved durable as well.

Furthermore, Communist leaders were eager to utilize some traditional practices as an alternative to a simple imitation of the West. In health care, for example, teams of "barefoot doctors"—hygiene officials rather than formally trained medical specialists in the Western sense—were dispatched to numerous rural villages, where they were responsible for raising health standards without fully imposing the concepts of modern medicine. Traditional remedies, including acupuncture, were maintained along with Western-style hospitals.

The Communist regime had a mixed impact on the Chinese economy, particularly in the area of industrialization. State control furthered the accumulation of resources for mechanization, but resulted in some of the same problems of inflexible planning that plagued the Soviet Union. The sheer chaos of decades of Japanese invasion and then civil war, and the renewed turmoil of the Cultural Revolution, retarded economic advance. Furthermore, Chinese population growth continued at high levels. Mao wavered in his approach to this issue, at times believing that China's great resource, militarily as well as economically, lay in increasing numbers. However, as before, population growth consumed immense resources and produced widespread poverty. By 1979, China's population stood at 23 percent of the world's total, but the nation accounted for only 3 percent of the world's industrial product. Clearly, a full industrial revolution had yet to occur, although most observers agreed that the country was further along the path than most other agricultural nations.

Chinese leaders after Mao's death, especially under Deng Xiaoping, worked more single-mindedly toward the goal of industrialization. High-level technical and scientific training returned to the universities, after the disruption of the Cultural Revolution. The regime adopted an unprecedentedly rigorous policy toward the population problem, aiming at zero growth almost immediately. Marriage before the age of 25 was forbidden, and couples having more than one child were punished. Here, not only the policing apparatus of the communist state but also earlier traditions of state control over society combined to produce a startling reversal in social customs. Again, official policy and reality, particularly rural reality, may differ. There were reports that the new rigor produced a wave of female infanticides, as couples were more interested in producing male heirs. However, the regime claimed, with apparent justification, that the birthrate had radically slowed. Finally, the regime collaborated with Western and Japanese enterprises, seeking more advanced technology. Individual managers and also rural producers were given greater authority and some profit incentives to obtain higher output, as the communists sought a new balance between state control and individual initiative. Industrial development was given clear priority over military concerns, as China returned, more clearly than under Mao, to a position of largely defensive foreign policy. China's new leaders projected an essentially completed process of industrialization by the year 2000. Improvements in living standards, most notably in the cities, were an early and popular result of the new policies, and population growth rates stood at 10 percent a year by the 1990s. A rising pollution problem resulted as well, as Chinese cities filled with industrial gases referred to as the "yellow dragon."

China (and in its wake, Vietnam and North Korea) firmly resisted the democratizing trends of the 1980s that so altered Eastern Europe. Even as more democratic systems were installed in South Korea, Taiwan, and the Philippines, and in the face of their own massive student rebellion of 1989, Chinese leaders maintained an authoritarian regime. Russia's troubles in combining political and economic reform further convinced them that the toleration of dissent would be a significant mistake. The regime eagerly moved forward toward a more market-based economy, with profit incentives and private initiative along with state planning. Chinese exports soared in order to pay for new equipment and expertise from abroad. However, China insisted—as it had so often done in the past—on its own political formula. Assimilation of the former British colony of Hong Kong, from 1997 onward, exposed China to another dose of ardent capitalism, but also another set of issues concerning freedom of expression.

CONCLUSION: EAST ASIA AND THE WORLD

As the communist revolution spread across China, while Japan adapted to a more democratic political structure after World War II, the differences among East Asian societies seemed overwhelming. Even by the 1990s, the variations in levels of economic development and political forms constituted major distinctions not only between Japan and China, but also among the smaller nations as well. Japan, along with the leading Western industrial states, was a key participant in annual "free world" economic conferences, because of shared political concerns as well as world market interests. Countries like South Korea and Taiwan were less industrialized, although growing rapidly; they also faced periodic protest against their authoritarian political structures, which liberalized somewhat toward the end of the 1980s. On the other hand, China and Vietnam, still partially isolated, attempted economic reforms while maintaining their communist systems.

Over time, some enduring common features among East Asian societies have reemerged. An emphasis on strong social cohesion is one such element. China's communist regime seeks tight social solidarity, whereas Japanese values stress group ties from the family through the nation. From a common Confucian past, admittedly one much altered by recent events, East Asian nations also preserve an interest in ceremony and emotional restraint. They share a desire to develop or maintain industrial dynamism without necessarily becoming a carbon copy of either Western or Russian society.

Both China and Japan, although open to more international influences than ever before in their history, have continued to stand somewhat apart from other civilizations. Visitors to Japan report a polite but somewhat detached welcome, as the Japanese continue to honor the distinctiveness and superiority of their own culture, to which foreigners are rarely, if ever, fully admitted. China, although embarking on renewed contacts with the West after the vigorous attack on all foreign influences during the Cultural Revolution, continues to monitor outsiders closely, making it clear that selective imitation should not make the Chinese people fully tolerant of foreign ways. East Asia, more influential in the wider world by the early twenty-first century than at any previous point in history, has maintained its traditional ability to see the world through its own lens.

SUGGESTED WEBSITES

On leaders in Japanese industrialization, see *http://www.historynet.com/WorldWarII/articles/ 11963_cover.htm;* on the Korean War, see *http://socrates.berkeley.edu/~korea/koreanwar.html;* on Japan's economic boom after World War II, see *http://www.iss.u-tokyo.ac.jp/ Newsletter/SSJ1/gluck.html;* on leaders of the communist revolution in China, see *http://cnd-f.org/fairbank/prc.html.*

SUGGESTED READINGS

For an overview on China, see I. Hsu, *The Rise of Modern China,* 2nd ed. (1975). For an excellent interpretive study, using a modernization model, see G. Rozman, ed., *The Modernization of China* (1981); see also Wolfgang Franke, *A Century of Chinese Revolution* (1970). On the Chinese revolutions, J. Spence, *The Gate of Heavenly Peace: The Chinese and Their Revolution, 1895–1980* (1982), is invaluable; on the communist revolution specifically, Edward Snow, *Red Star Over China* (1968), is quite readable. Consult also, as a source, A. Freemantle, ed., *Mao-Tse Tung: An Anthology of His Writings* (1962). On developments after Mao, I. Hsu, *China Without Mao: The Search for a New Order* (1983), is worthwhile.

On Japan, an excellent cultural interpretation is E. O. Reischauer, *The Japanese* (1988). See also P. Duus, *The Rise of Modern Japan* (1976), and M. Howe, *Modern Japan: A Historical Survey* (1986), as well as H. Patrick and H. Rosovsky, *Asia's New Giant: How the Japanese Economy Works* (1976). An important specific topic is covered in R. Story, *The Double Patriots: A Story of Japanese Nationalism* (1973). Japanese economic success and its significance are addressed in Ezra Vogel, *Japan as Number One: Lessons for Americans* (1980). On the Pacific Rim, see Philip West et al., eds., *Pacific Rim and the Western World: Strategic, Economic and Cultural Perspectives* (1987); see also G. Rozman, ed., *East Asian Region: Confucian Heritage and Its Modern Adaptation* (1991), and Bruce Cuming, *Korea's Place in the Sun: A Modern History* (1997).

India and Southeast Asia

29

FOCAL POINTS

The first half of the twentieth century in India and Southeast Asia was dominated by the struggle against colonialism and the rise of nationalism. Why did the colonial powers finally yield? What were the goals of nationalists beyond national independence, and how did some of them disagree? India was noteworthy among the new nations for its ability to maintain democracy: What facilitated this political form? It also experienced important economic changes, as food production increased and new manufacturing sectors emerged. Amid change, what balance did Indians strike between traditional cultures and newer beliefs? What happened to some of the historical components of Indian society such as the caste system? Compared to China, was India helped or hindered by the fact that it did not undergo a real revolution?

INDIA AND SOUTHEAST ASIA FROM WORLD WAR I TO INDEPENDENCE

During the first half of the twentieth century, nationalist pressures built steadily on the Indian subcontinent and in Southeast Asia. Dislocations produced by World War II prompted the end of European controls. In a few cases—most notably Vietnam—the struggle to achieve independence continued well after World War II, but in most instances, including India, decolonization occurred quickly and without much further conflict with the former imperialist powers. Thus, the history of India and Southeast Asia since the late 1940s is characterized by the formation of newly independent nations and the establishment of their distinct political styles. India became the world's largest democracy, building on older political traditions as well as the legacy of British rule and nationalist struggle. Other nations on the Indian subcontinent and in Southeast Asia were more authoritarian in political structure, whereas Vietnam became communist. The earlier pattern of political division thus persisted in Southeast Asia, although in new forms. Problems of economic development also loomed large. Again, there was great diversity; a few new nations, such as Bangladesh, proved to be among the world's poorest. But in India itself, significant economic change took place, while parts of Southeast Asia pulled into the dynamic orbit of the Pacific Rim.

THE RISE OF NATIONALISM

India provided a key example of the growing struggle for independence after 1914, just as it would help lead the movement of new nations after World War II. Rising nationalism in much of Southeast Asia proved somewhat similar to patterns in India. Throughout southern Asia, indeed, the issue of national freedom moved to the top of the agenda during the years between the world wars. Problems in Europe weakened the hold of the imperialist nations, although they remained militarily dominant until the 1940s. Many Europeans became increasingly open to the idea that their colonies should work toward ultimate freedom. New currents in India and Southeast Asia provided an even greater impetus to nationalism. The example of the Russian Revolution and the Leninist concept that a massive social revolution was possible as part of the struggle against an empire also converted some Indian and Southeast Asian leaders. Outside Vietnam, where nationalism and Marxism were closely linked, Marxism had less impact in southern Asia than China, but it was a significant element nonetheless.

More important still was a new wave of peasant unrest in various parts of southern Asia. Peasant agitation resulted from growing population pressure combined with the more efficient tax collection and commercial agriculture that were part of imperialist rule. Peasants had their own idea of social justice, which included the more tolerant leadership of village headmen and greater access to land; they were rarely directly concerned with national independence, but their goals were compatible with liberation movements in that they resented the economic and administrative measures induced by outside rule.

Nonetheless, it was nationalism itself, gaining new vigor and popularity, that characterized the political history of southern Asia during the first half of the twentieth century. Copied from Europe initially, nationalism took on, if anything, greater importance in India and Southeast Asia. Here, it meant freedom from foreign domination and a chance to come to terms with the modern world while preserving important features of traditional civilization. In India, nationalism promised a kind of unity that the country had almost never known and a self-expression that had not been possible for many centuries. The Indian patriot Chittaranjan Das, writing early in the century, advanced the nationalist cause as follows:

> What is the ideal which we must set before us? The first and foremost is the ideal of nationalism. Now what is nationalism? It is, I conceive, a process through which a nation expresses itself and finds itself, not in isolation from other nations, not in opposition to other nations, but as part of a great scheme by which, in seeking its own expression and therefore its own identity, it materially assists the self-expression and self-realization of other nations as well: Diversity is as real as unity. . . . I contend that each nationality constitutes a particular stream of the great unity, but no nation can fulfill itself unless and until it becomes itself and at the same time realizes its identity with Humanity.

The idealistic fervor of southern Asian nationalism, and especially the form of nationalism that took root in India, was a real force on its own, quite apart from specific issues and grievances.

Indian nationalism was given direct impetus by the events of World War I. Three million Indian soldiers fought in British armies during the war. At the same time, taxes and food shortages at home created discontent, bringing new strength to the Indian National Congress and an alliance between the Hindu leadership of the Congress Party and the nation's Muslim League. This united front called for self-government within the British Empire. Britain did indeed establish new provincial legislative councils as a result, providing voting rights for 6 million of the nation's 250 million people; the councils had jurisdiction over such areas as education and public health. But, this 1919 measure was obviously half-hearted, indicating London's continued suspicion of India's ability to rule itself. The central government remained firmly in British hands, with advisory councils elected by only a million Indian voters. The British followed a classic pattern of offering enough reform to encourage new expectations—along with the excitement caused by World War I and the principles of national self-determination discussed at Versailles—but not enough to satisfy all. At the same time, the British tightened police measures against those they viewed as troublemakers. The new repression resulted in a wave of rioting across the subcontinent. Police anxiety even prompted clashes at Hindu religious festivals; in one such confrontation, 379 celebrants, all unarmed, were killed by British-led troops. Police brutality here, and in major labor strikes, heightened Indian nationalism and helped unite upper-caste leaders with large numbers of workers and peasants.

Popular agitation continued in the 1920s. An influenza epidemic and crop failures that killed 5 million people led to a wave of rural uprisings against landlords and moneylenders. Some urban protest developed as well, with strikes among textile and railroad workers; Marxist doctrines made some headway. This diverse discontent was grist for the nationalists' mill, as it served to pressure the British. Middle-class nationalists even discussed a boycott of British goods, to protest India's economic dependence.

THE NONVIOLENT STRATEGIES OF GANDHI

In this context of growing agitation, the emergence in 1920 of Mohandas Gandhi (see p. 510) as the leader and master tactician of the nationalist forces was a key development. Gandhi became an almost universally respected symbol of India's political awakening, the most important political figure in Indian history since the Mauryan and Gupta dynasties of the classical period. Gandhi had been born into a merchant family that also wielded great political influence in a small princely state north of Bombay, under British rule but shielded from the most direct Western pressure. His family had been devout Hindus, keenly persuaded of the importance of group loyalties. Gandhi himself studied law in Britain and practiced it for a time in South Africa, where he became keenly aware of the desperate plight of many Indians whom the British had imported as indentured laborers and who, like Gandhi himself, were often victims of brutal discrimination in public. Gandhi's reaction was not just one of indignation, but a deep search for a strategy by which the weak could overcome imperialist strength. His conclusion, drawn from his version of Hindu tradition plus other religious reading, was collective nonviolence in resistance to injustice. He organized a campaign of peaceful marches to protest discrimination in South

Africa, including nonviolent resistance to police attacks and arrest, which was successful in removing some of the most overt forms of discrimination against Indians in that colony.

Then, in 1915, Gandhi returned to India, and after a few years of reflection and experimentation with different tactics, he seized the opportunity provided by growing popular and nationalist unrest to mount a campaign of nonviolent resistance. Gandhi's great gift was to unite educated nationalist leaders with the rural masses, who saw in Gandhi an incarnation of deep spiritual values and whose own Hinduism was in accord with his emphasis on nonviolence. Gandhi told the Indian masses, who had long left the fighting to the warrior castes, that they too could be courageous:

> Wherein is courage required—in blowing others to pieces from behind a cannon, or with a smiling face to approach a cannon and be blown to pieces? Who is the true warrior—he who keeps death always as a bosom-friend, or he who controls the death of others? Believe me that a man devoid of courage and manhood can never be a passive resister.

Under Gandhi's leadership, the Congress movement became a mass political force for the first time, giving Indians a far greater taste of political participation than Britain's timid legislative experiments had allowed. Gandhi served also as a significant figure in a revived and revised Hinduism, in which ethical principles were stressed over both ceremonialism and the caste system.

Gandhi was also a master of tactics. His simple, holy style of life, which included a renunciation of sex, brought him the title Mahatma, or "saintly one." He could attack castes, and so please the masses and Muslims, while also wooing Brahmin religious leaders by praising tradition. He could converse with both striking workers and moderate reformers. He appealed to new public interests for women, urging them to abandon domestic isolation for the sake of national freedom. However, he did not renounce Hindu family ideals. Above all, his stress on nonviolence confounded British authorities, who found it difficult to respond with all-out repression. Gandhi was frequently arrested, but his sentences aroused so much mass furor—heightened by well-publicized refusals to eat during imprisonment—that he ultimately was released. Although Gandhi was not able to prevent periodic violence against British officials, he did direct most attention to peaceful mass disruption, refusals to pay taxes, and other tactics that were hard to counter. "We must voluntarily put up with the losses and inconveniences that arise from having to withdraw our support from a government that is ruling against our will." In this spirit, Gandhi and his followers boycotted elections, blocked trains by lying down on the tracks, and surrounded government buildings with thousands of quiet demonstrators so that officials had to walk over bodies in order to get to work.

By the 1930s, the British realized that they had to offer further reforms. However, a series of conferences with Indian leaders convinced the British that there was no way to please Hindus and Muslims, radicals and princes. Indeed, many Muslim leaders were increasingly antagonized, despite Gandhi's efforts at reconciliation, by the development of an Indian nationalism based largely on Hindu symbols and customs, and began talking of the need for their own nation, a "Pakistan," or "land of the pure," instead of a unified India. Britain also played its own role in encouraging Hindu-Muslim divisions, in spite of considerable Muslim support of Congress Party

World Profiles

Mohandas Gandhi (1889–1948)

Mohandas Gandhi was unquestionably the leading figure in India's independence movement and one of the most important individuals in twentieth-century world history. Trained in part in England, Gandhi later turned to modifications of Hindu tradition in his nonviolent mass protests against British rule. In particular, he attacked traditions of caste and the subjugation of women. He also projected an Indian alternative to modern society as it had developed in the West. He urged a craft-based, rather than factory- and common-based, economy. Gandhi's protest tactics worked, although his goals were less completely realized. Tragically he was killed by a narrow nationalist group hostile to tolerance for Muslims. How much did Gandhi shape and reflect a distinctive Indian experience, and would India's independence have occurred differently without his guidance?

Mohandas Gandhi.

goals. In this context, the British issued a new constitution, in 1935, that provided for a federal system of 11 provinces, each with an elected assembly and ministers responsible to it, with a British-appointed governor to oversee. At the center, a two-house parliament would have some real power, although British officials remained in charge of defense and foreign affairs. The vote was extended to 35 million people.

Although disappointed at the lack of full self-government, the Congress Party ran in the new elections and won majorities in most states. Gandhi himself advocated service in the new governments as long as the British did not unduly interfere, whereas more radical leaders, including Jawaharlal Nehru, preached continued resistance. But, all leaders agreed on the need for ultimate independence, and when Britain became unresponsive on this point after 1940, they refused to cooperate in the government's World War II effort. Gandhi, Nehru, and other leaders were arrested as a Japanese attack threatened, and Britain ruled India through military control until the war's end.

NATIONALISM IN SOUTHEAST ASIA

A similar national awakening developed in Southeast Asia during the 1920s and 1930s, although without such a compelling figure as Gandhi. In French-ruled Indochina, an advisory council was permitted, but, as in India, such halfway reforms proved insufficient. Rioting broke out in major cities in 1930–1931; although it was suppressed by force, nationalist agitation continued. Serious peasant outbreaks occurred as well, caused more by economic hunger, as the market for agricultural exports collapsed during the depression, than by nationalism. A significant Marxist movement also took shape under the leadership of Ho Chi Minh, who became an enthusiastic convert to Marxism while working as a waiter in Paris, finding it a faith that could sustain him in his country's long battle for national freedom. But amid the new unrest, the French were determined to preserve their power. A similar pattern prevailed in Indonesia. Dutch rulers granted local leaders half the seats in a national assembly, but when nationalist and socialist unrest spread against the limited reforms, the government responded by jailing the leaders—which only stimulated further agitation. In 1937, the nationalists petitioned the Dutch crown for dominion status within 10 years.

Nationalism and peasant unrest against lack of land and high taxes created new ferment in Burma and Siam, where British influence predominated. In Siam, nationalist sentiment prompted a successful attack on Western control of tariff policy and special legal rights for foreigners. The nationalists celebrated their achievement by renaming their nation Thailand, or "land of the free." Finally, nationalists attacked U.S. control over the Philippines, where a popularly elected legislature already had real powers. Although Americans talked of ultimate independence for this land, they also discriminated against native Filipinos, whom they tended to treat with the same racism that they expressed toward blacks at home. Thus, Filipino nationalism persisted, and it also was enhanced by the economic problems brought about by the Depression, as U.S. resistance to Filipino exports grew amid that crisis. In 1934, the U.S. Congress increased Philippine rights to self-government and promised outright independence in 1944.

Southeast Asian nationalism generally was stimulated by the results of World War II. Japanese control of the Philippines, Indochina, and other areas was often harsher than Western imperialism, but it demonstrated that the West was vulnerable and to this extent spurred hopes for ultimate freedom. When Tokyo surrendered, in 1945, to the allies, many Westerners prepared to return to the Southeast Asian plantations and social clubs as if nothing had happened, but, in fact, a new era had begun in the whole region. Imperialism, difficult in the 1930s, had now become impossible.

DECOLONIZATION AFTER THE WAR

Thus, it was not surprising that the current of decolonization, which would soon sweep the world, bore its first postwar fruit in southern Asia. With nationalist resistance already well established in places like India, most European powers, now exhausted, were unwilling to experience the trouble and risks of hanging on any further—even assuming that they could have done so successfully. The new Labor Party in Britain was positively eager to leave India after 1945, for the costs of operating a government there had become too great to bear. A crucial issue remained the split between Hindu and Muslim, which to the sorrow of leaders like Gandhi, occasioned bitter rioting as independence neared, but the deepest conflict was resolved in 1947 by the creation of two states, a Muslim Pakistan and a predominantly Hindu India. Religion-based nationalism triumphed over the larger territorial nationalism in the Congress tradition, although this tradition persisted in India along with frequent religious and ethnic challenges.

Britain extended its decolonization policy by granting freedom to Sri Lanka (formerly Ceylon) and Burma in 1948. Malaysia also won independence after the British successfully suppressed a communist guerrilla movement. The United States made good on its earlier pledge by freeing the Philippines in 1946, while retaining substantial military bases on lease. The Dutch retreat from Indonesia was somewhat less graceful, as there was an attempt to reconquer the territory after the end of World War II. However, this effort failed, and an independent Indonesia was recognized in 1949.

Only in Indochina was national independence seriously delayed after World War II. The French, particularly eager to reassert their military strength after their disastrous loss to Hitler's armies in 1940, were unwilling to recognize the strength or validity of the nationalist movement. They were aided by the United States, which was hostile to communism, especially after the success of the Chinese revolution, and eager not to "lose" another Asian region to their cold war enemy. Ho Chi Minh, however, proved to be a stubborn opponent, successfully organizing a guerrilla warfare that depended on widespread peasant support and was impossible to suppress by conventional tactics. A series of defeats suffered by French troops led to a peace settlement in 1954, which brought division between a communist North Vietnam and a noncommunist South Vietnam. The French also withdrew from Laos and Cambodia. North Vietnam soon began to press its southern neighbor, with aid from the Soviet Union and China. As South Vietnam faced guerrilla attacks, it turned to the United States for aid. American participation in the conflict escalated in 1964, after North Vietnamese ships allegedly attacked American vessels, and over the next 10

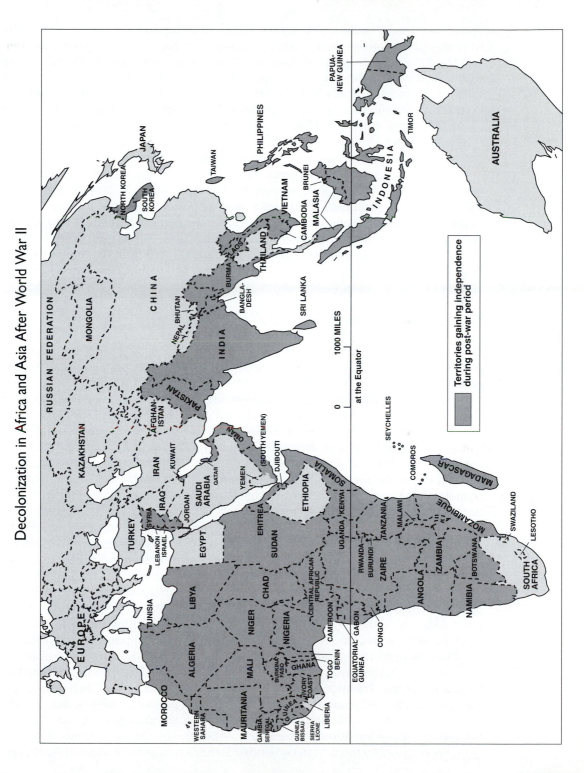

Decolonization in Africa and Asia After World War II

Territories gaining independence during post-war period

1000 MILES

0

at the Equator

years, more than 2 million U.S. soldiers were sent to fight in Vietnam. Despite massive American bombing raids, however, communist guerrilla forces gained ground, and the fighting also spread to Laos and Cambodia. Opposition to the war effort within the United States helped prompt peace talks, begun in 1969, which finally resulted in an end to the war in 1973. With U.S. forces withdrawn, and amid accusations from both sides about treaty violations, North Vietnam increased its troop levels in the South, and by 1975 it had gained full control of this region. A united, communist Vietnam then proceeded to impose military control over Laos and Cambodia, although these nations later regained a shaky independence.

The rise of a communist regional state in Southeast Asia was an extremely important development. The bitter warfare that had led to this state played a significant role first in French and then U.S. politics. More important, the same warfare resulted in massive devastation and loss of life within the region itself, creating long-lasting scars and severe problems of economic reconstruction. Military experience and a communist regime distinguished this part of Southeast Asia from the majority of the new nations, where independence had come earlier and with far less trauma.

SOUTHEAST ASIA AFTER INDEPENDENCE

The rise of nationalism during the first half of the twentieth century had provided most of southern Asia with such a compelling cause that the problems which independence itself would bring were often obscured. The focus was on freedom from outside control. Leaders were less clear about what would be constructed when and if the Westerners left. Most nationalists assumed a democratic, parliamentary structure—to this extent, they copied Western values. However, there was profound division among religious groups, as in India, and between educated leaders and the peasant masses. This could make democracy difficult. Nationalists were also typically vague about economic and social issues. Gandhi, for example, had little interest in economic development in the sense of industrialization. He was not opposed to factory production but insisted on preventing its dehumanizing effects on workers; at times, he seemed to prefer a stress on enhancing peasant agriculture and home-based manufacturing. But, other Indian leaders called for an aggressive drive toward economic modernization. Peasants, although often drawn to the nationalist cause, were far more interested in land and protection from world market fluctuations than in purely political reforms or economic modernization. Urban workers, poorly paid and badly housed amid the conditions of early factories, also pressed for greater social justice. Dealing with these various pressures, while also establishing the institutions of government, was an arduous task after the excitement of attaining national freedom.

The new or revived nations of Southeast Asia illustrated the range of possibilities and problems that followed from decolonization. Southeast Asian civilization had always been diverse. Traditional variations continued to be important, as differing religious and ethnic backgrounds determined distinctive policies. However, new distinctions now arose as well, as in the split between communist Vietnam and the noncommunist—sometimes anticommunist—policies of the other states of the region. With encouragement from the United States, a number of Southeast Asian governments formed a loose alliance to coordinate resistance to Chinese and Vietnamese communist influence and to discuss common economic interests. Nonetheless, this grouping was not a significant unifying force amid the region's fascinating cultural and political diversity.

Most Southeast Asian nations attempted to establish democratic parliamentary institutions after attaining independence, but most found these institutions impossible to maintain. Lack of political experience among the peasant masses, divisions within the population that prompted frequent rioting, and, often, the ambition of individual nationalist leaders tended to turn governments toward more authoritarian policies. In the Philippines, for example, a parliamentary system modeled on that of the United States lasted until 1963, when President Ferdinand Marcos seized full power, which he would retain, amid considerable corruption and political violence, for over two decades. The Philippine government faced attacks from communist guerrillas, which were mostly controlled. It largely avoided any effort at land reform; a wealthy elite dominated the country, sharing power with the military. The gap between rich and poor was significant, and there was little progress toward economic development. The government nevertheless received substantial U.S. aid and support, from postwar reconstruction onward, in part because of American concern for maintaining its military bases on the islands. Only in 1986 was the Marcos regime toppled, after trying to rig a new election, and replaced by a reformist regime that initiated more genuine democracy.

In Malaysia and the monarchy of Thailand, parliamentary institutions functioned somewhat more effectively than in the Philippines, and the repression of political opposition was less complete. By the 1970s, Thailand faced considerable pressure from the powerful Vietnamese armies on its northern border. Malaysia had earlier suppressed a communist guerrilla movement run mainly by the ethnic Chinese minority on the peninsula. Tension between native Malays and the Chinese minority continued to produce friction, however. It also made impossible a brief union with the city-state of Singapore, dominated by the Chinese; Singapore split off under a strong-willed leader bent on rapid economic growth and tight control of the city's population.

Burma, like Thailand a largely Buddhist nation still, opted for considerable isolation soon after independence, hoping to avoid the influence of both the West and communist nations. A series of generals ran the country, whose culture remained highly traditional, one of the only nations in the world that isolated so fully from broader international currents. Only a few indications of greater openness occurred in the late 1990s, as the country adopted the new name, Myanmar.

Indonesia gained independence under the leadership of Achmed Sukarno, who soon established authoritarian rule, in part, as a means of unifying a diverse population. A strong communist movement influenced Sukarno, but an outright communist uprising in 1963 was defeated and the army seized power, killing at least half a million communists and radicals. The military also attacked the ethnic Chinese minority, who were resented for their hold over merchant activity in the cities. Sukarno was forced out of power, and the army generals ruled with no pretense of democracy. Firmly Muslim, the new government supported Islamic law and customs, although without the rigor of some other nations in the Islamic orbit. The authoritarian regime did, however, attack several minority nationalities as it retained its hold against the currents of democracy into the late 1990s.

In Vietnam—first the North, after 1954, and then the larger nation after 1975—a political and social system developed with many similarities to that of China under Mao Zedung. Private businesses were seized, and land was taken from the large landowners and turned over to government-controlled communes. Vietnamese society was colored by the heavy toll of prolonged war, including the military outlays needed for the conquest of Cambodia against considerable resistance. The Vietnamese regime relied heavily on Soviet support, as relations with China soured. China had never welcomed a strong Vietnam and objected strenuously to the attack on Cambodia. Border tensions, including one brief war, further encouraged the strong militaristic tone of the Vietnamese version of communism. Economic development remained meager into the later 1980s, because of wartime dislocations and continuing military costs. By the 1990s, Vietnam followed China's policy of greater openness to the outside world and a more market-oriented economy, still combined with a strong communist state.

Except for Vietnam, and the Philippines until 1986, most Southeast Asian governments tried to combine an interest in social reform, including aid to the peasantry, with considerable private enterprise. A number of nations experienced noteworthy economic growth. More productive crops were developed in the 1960s as part of the Green Revolution, which brought the aid of Western science to bear on the food problems of agricultural countries, thus allowing most Southeast Asian nations to feed themselves. Particularly important were new strains of rice, which grew faster and had higher yields than those grown formerly. The Green Revolution favored wealthy farmers who could afford expensive seeds and fertilizers, but it did nevertheless help many nations regain self-sufficiency in food production. Even so, economic advance was modified by considerable population growth. Most Southeast Asian nations continued to depend heavily on raw materials and cash crop exports to the industrialized nations of the West or Japan, and this dependence brought the usual problems of low and uncertain incomes on the world market. Except in dynamic Singapore, full industrialization had yet to come.

INDIA AND PAKISTAN

India presented an unusual mixture of strengths and weaknesses as it attained independence in 1947. It lacked a consistently successful political tradition, having far more often been divided and/or ruled through outside conquest than by self-government. It embraced a wide array of regions, religions, and languages. Despite important pockets of modern industry, it had a largely agricultural economy pressed by a rapidly growing population. On the other hand, India had an unusually well established nationalist movement, which had a recognized and experienced leadership. Because of roughly two centuries of British rule, it also had been exposed to Western political ideas and institutions, including an effective civil service system.

The birth pains of the new nation were a severe disappointment to Gandhi and other nationalist leaders. Growing Muslim insistence on a separate nation met vigorous Hindu opposition, as Congress-style nationalism ultimately failed to override re-

Rioting in India against Muslim shrine.

ligious divisions, but massive violence during 1946 convinced both sides that unity was indeed out of the question. The nation of Pakistan formed two regions, the heartland being the northwestern portion of the subcontinent nearest the Middle East, where Islam had the strongest roots, with a second area in the northeast. Even partition was insufficient to prevent further religious antagonisms. In the weeks after independence, Hindus and Muslims battled each other, causing at least 100,000 deaths and forcing 3 million people to flee their homes to seek sanctuary with co-religionists in one of the two new nations. Gandhi and the Congress Party were powerless to stop the bitter hatred. When Gandhi started a fast to protest Hindu persecution of Muslims and to restore the "best friendship" between the two peoples, he was shot by a Hindu fanatic. Tensions with a Muslim minority continued to affect India. Furthermore, relations between the nations of India and Pakistan were hostile, with each eyeing the other warily and devoting hard-won tax revenues to military expenditures designed to keep the other at bay.

Pakistan followed a political pattern rather similar to that of the Southeast Asian nations. It adopted an authoritarian form of government in 1958, under military leadership. Even under these conditions, the nation proved unable to maintain unity

The Partition of South Asia:
The Formation of India, Pakistan, Bangladesh, and Sri Lanka

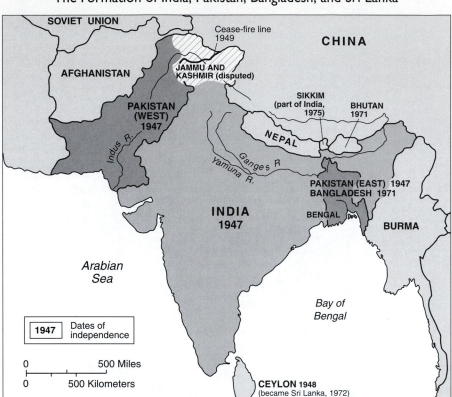

among its two main provinces, as East Pakistan constantly complained of neglect. In 1971, a revolt in the east produced the new nation of Bangladesh, the eighth most populous country in the world and one of the poorest. Pakistan itself, although less crowded, faced serious problems of economic development. Land reform was slighted in favor of supporting the regional elite. In the 1970s in an appeal to religious tradition, Pakistan's military government adopted increasingly rigorous Islamic laws. The nation also faced tensions with the Soviet Union as a result of the invasion of Afghanistan, and this too became a burden despite U.S. aid. More democratic elections occurred in the 1990s, but political stability was fragile and the army kept a watchful eye. A military regime returned in 1999, just after Pakistan tested its first nuclear bomb and as tension with India mounted.

India, which controlled the majority of the territory and population on the subcontinent despite the 1947 partition, developed a distinctive political and cultural pattern that combined tradition and change. Most striking was its ability to maintain democracy; indeed, India has been one of the few newly independent nations to preserve this political form with any consistency since World War II. Equally important was India's resolve to combine serious social reform with economic development and esteem for many aspects of Hindu culture.

Politically, India retained a federal system, which reflected the nation's regional diversity and the pattern set under British rule. Individual states had considerable power, although there were disputes with the central government at various points. The nation was ruled by the nationalist Congress Party with only two exceptions—in the late 1970s, when a coalition of conservative groups assumed office briefly, and again through the 1990s. However, multiparty competition was free and fierce, and freedoms of the press and association were not normally limited. Control of many state governments, indeed, passed to parties other than the Congress group, including the Communist Party. Congress Party leaders, although mainly drawn from the political elite, learned to campaign effectively among the masses, combining the prestige of high status with genuine popular appeal.

There were some questions about Indian democracy, to be sure. Congress Party dominance prevented a great deal of experience with partisan shifts at the central government level. As in the Japanese Liberal Democratic Party, more political maneuvering took place among factions within the dominant group than among different parties. India also experienced few leadership changes at the top. The first prime minister, the nationalist Jawaharlal Nehru, held power for 17 years. He was succeeded by his daughter, Indira Gandhi (no relation to Mahatma Gandhi). Although Indira Gandhi was initially selected by Congress Party stalwarts for her presumed susceptibility to manipulation, she proved to be a tough-minded leader who was very conscious of her power. Indeed, it was under her rule that liberal rights were suspended, from 1975–1977, as she tried to clamp down on a number of opposition groups and arrested many political critics. These policies led, however, to the Congress Party's defeat in 1977, which suggested that the curtailment of democracy within India was costly. New elections in 1980 restored Indira Gandhi to power, but there was no attempt to revive authoritarian rule. Regional disunity, however, remained a serious problem. Gandhi faced growing opposition from the minority Sikh religion, which demanded greater autonomy for the Sikh-dominated state of Punjab. This led in the early 1980s to renewed religious rioting, this time between Hindu and Sikh, and Indira Gandhi's assassination by Sikh militants. Her successor was her son Rajiv, which raised concern about a new dynasty ruling India; again, the formal institutions of a liberal democracy continued to function, doubtless solidified by some popular faith in the ruling family. Rajiv's assassination by southern Tamil separatists ended his family's reign. The Congress Party also yielded its control, but a new political coalition assumed power smoothly. India had produced four decades of strong political performance, suggesting that its democratic forms responded to traditions and needs alike and had become part of the nation's political heritage.

India also took the lead in establishing a distinctive diplomatic policy. The new nation remained friendly with its former British rulers and indeed participated actively in Commonwealth meetings to discuss mutual concerns with Britain, Canada, Australia, New Zealand, and the growing number of other former British colonies. At the same time, Nehru and his successors were firmly resolved to avoid entrapment in alliances that were irrelevant to India's needs. The government thus assumed the initiative in organizing interested non-Western nations in a nonaligned, or "third force," bloc that would seek to deal with both the West and Soviet Union while shunning military pacts with either side. The first meeting of this neutral group took place in 1955, and although the cohesion of the group oscillated, India persevered in establishing good relations with both the United States and Soviet Union, often lecturing the great powers on the evils of their competition. India itself faced diplomatic problems, particularly with Pakistan and, at times in the 1960s, with China as well. However, the nation avoided extensive involvement in issues outside its regional concerns, except perhaps for a sometimes moralizing rhetoric.

Congress Party leaders from Nehru onward were eager to remake their nation without losing its identity; independence and political power were not enough. Their vision differed somewhat from that of Mahatma Gandhi's in that they were more concerned with economic modernization and less disdainful of factories and sophisticated commerce. Nevertheless, Gandhi, too, had sought some changes in India's old order. Key targets in early legislation were the caste system and traditional gender relations, as India sought to institute equality under the law. The nation's constitution granted equality to women, including the right to vote, and allowed women to seek divorce and marry outside their caste. The caste system itself was outlawed. The government tried to encourage former untouchables to participate more fully in Indian society, by establishing quotas for "ex-untouchables" in the universities and government jobs. But, India's attack on these ancient social traditions was of necessity less forceful than China's war on ancestor worship and other family practices, for outright coercion or the formation of radical new institutions such as communes would have been incompatible with democratic forms. India had no revolution. Therefore, in fact, strong remnants of the caste system remained in India, although not enforced by law. Most government leaders were drawn from the traditionally higher castes, as were most of the growing numbers of university-trained professionals and managers. At the family level, the authority of men continued to be strong, particularly among the rural majority. Practices such as arranged marriages, often with the partners pledged during their teens and not even necessarily meeting before their wedding, continued to be widespread at all social levels.

In economic policy, India's leadership professed a nondoctrinaire socialism. This meant, in practice, considerable economic planning toward the allocation of scarce resources; it also meant government operation of key services such as airlines and railroads. But, substantial private enterprise remained as well. Government welfare services focused mainly on basic hygiene, as the nation's poverty prevented a more elaborate social security system. The government also encouraged widespread peasant landownership, dismantling some former estates and helping to clear new land toward this end. This policy, along with progressive taxation, reduced the economic power of the old princely aristocracy.

A key concern, even in the heady early days of independence, was economic development. Congress Party leaders had long wanted fuller economic equality for India, as a weapon against Western dominance. Furthermore, steady population growth virtually compelled attention to the issue of economic growth. Government planning and private enterprise, plus some foreign economic aid, promoted substantial growth during the 1950s; the national income expanded by 42 percent. However, the nation's population grew from 360 to 439 million during the same decade, which eliminated half the economic gain. During the 1960s, per capita income stagnated, and India was forced to import food to prevent starvation. This prompted greater concern for improved agricultural production. The government helped sponsor Green Revolution research on better seeds; it also promoted the widespread use of fertilizers and pesticides. These measures yielded impressive results; despite continued population growth, the nation remained self-sufficient in agriculture from 1970 onward.

The government also attacked the population problem directly. Under Nehru, official measures were half-hearted, but with a growth rate of 2.4 percent per year, it became increasingly clear that no serious improvement in living standards for the impoverished masses could occur without birth control. Indira Gandhi's government stepped up propaganda efforts, with slogans such as "A Happy Family Is a Small Family," and medical personnel provided free birth-control devices and procedures, including vasectomies for men. But, the campaign met massive popular resistance. Men and women alike feared to tamper with God's ways. Men worried that an operation such as a vasectomy would destroy their "male power," making them as docile as castrated animals. They also continued to value a large family as a sign of good fortune, seeking particularly a sufficient number of sons to ensure their own care in old age. Popular resistance to birth control helped prompt Indira Gandhi's suspension of liberties in 1975 as the government launched an effort to force poor men with large families to undergo vasectomies. This campaign stopped, however, in 1977, as the government returned instead to a policy of intense propaganda and widespread medical services. India's birthrate did begin to slow in the later 1970s, as people became more aware of family planning as an alternative to grinding poverty, but birthrates remained high.

Despite population pressure, which diverted extensive resources to increasing agricultural production and was unquestionably responsible for massive poverty in the countryside and crowded cities alike, India managed to resume its pattern of economic growth in the 1970s. Modern industrial technologies were applied to metallurgy and chemical production, creating pockets of advanced factory industry in a still agricultural nation. India produced cars and tried to limit imports. With ready technological interchange with the West as well as Soviet Russia, India for a time in the early 1980s surpassed the technological level of China. Modern factories as well as rising agricultural productivity accounted for a 4-percent annual growth rate in the years after 1975. By the 1990s, a significant software industry had emerged as well. India has remained vulnerable in the world economy, and its export performance has lagged despite important industrial sales in the Indian Ocean region. The nation's growth record fell well behind that of the Pacific Rim, particularly after the mid–1980s. But despite widely publicized problems, it has engaged in serious economic change. Efforts to reduce state controls to spur growth occurred in the 1990s, while training in computer science expanded.

Indian cultural life showed a predictable balance between new themes and old, but with a bias here toward the more traditional. India's leaders encouraged a rapid expansion of education, which gradually cut into widespread illiteracy. By the 1970s, literacy rates had doubled over the 1947 figure to 30 percent. At the elitist level, scientific training spread widely, and Indian researchers participated actively, in both India and foreign laboratories, to advances in physics, biology, medicine, and computer science. The Indian government even mounted its own space program. Cultural change was also encouraged, although particularly among the elite, by the continued reliance on the English language, which helped maintain India's openness to developments in Western culture. Congress Party leaders had hoped to promote

Hindi as a new national language, but regional resistance was so great that English remained the only language with countrywide currency in government, the universities, and the press. A number of leading writers also relied primarily on English. Because Indian universities produced more trained professionals than the society required, a large number of doctors and lawyers emigrated to Britain or North America, giving India further ties to the West, although at some economic cost.

At the popular level, however, traditional cultural forms predominated, albeit sometimes in new guises. An active film industry produced innumerable stories of adventure and romance, couched in the terms of traditional popular literature. Few foreign movies penetrated beyond elitist levels, while at the same time Indian films themselves almost never reached beyond the country's borders. Along with films, literature in the various traditional languages remained active, as did traditional artistic styles. Indian painters and sculptors did not participate widely in modern or "international" artistic developments, preferring to continue working mainly in older modes. Artistic imagery, both old and new, remained a vital part of Indian popular life, as did religion. Devotion to Hindu ritual and belief was widespread among the majority, and reverence for holy men continued to be a high priority.

Part of India's distinctiveness rested in the ongoing divisions between the elite and popular culture. The elite, drawn mainly from higher castes, were responsive to new educational opportunities as well as to the new outlets for political and managerial leadership. In this group, both men and women played a meaningful role, for here India's attack on gender divisions had a significant result. Women graduated from universities in growing numbers and held important government and professional positions. The elite did not become Western. Traditional patterns such as arranged marriages continued among this group, as did distinctive religious and cultural interests. However, there was significant change in elitist values, including significant contact with Western (particularly English-language) cultural and scientific

Movie poster in Bombay, featuring the actor Shashi Kapoor in the film *Deewangee*.

developments. Popular culture was quite a different matter, which helps explain the widespread resistance to government-sponsored measures such as birth control in the name of religion and family. India's masses did change, as a minority entered jobs in modern factories and a larger number altered some of their agricultural methods. But, change here definitely took place amid vigorous devotion to a number of earlier values. Distinctive religious and cultural interests showed even in basic outlook, as Indians preserved a greater place for imagination in their child-rearing practices, putting less stock than Westerners (or East Asians) on careful lessons in the distinction between pretend and "reality."

India's divisions were regional and religious as well as social. Lacking a highly centralized culture, India had long experienced religious diversity. Despite Mahatma Gandhi's hopes to use nationalism to transcend these differences and a long tradition of considerable tolerance, relations among Hindus, Muslims, and Sikhs grew more tense by the 1990s. Cultural change, including the partial secularism of the elite, challenged tolerance, leading to many clashes that threatened the stability of the government. A Hindu fundamentalist movement arose, calling on the government to promote Hinduism at the expense of other religions—a fascinating, perhaps ominous development, all the more interesting in that the use of the state was not, in fact, a Hindu tradition. Fundamentalist political power increased in the 1990s, and Hindu nationalists assumed control of the government, increasing military spending and nuclear development.

CONCLUSION: INDIA AND CHINA

Because India established an independent democracy just as China underwent its communist revolution, comparisons between the two Asian giants became commonplace. Which path would produce greater political success? Which path would prove most compatible with economic development? American observers initially pinned their faith on India, convinced that democracy and real modernization would ultimately go hand in hand. But just as India's democracy proved incapable of stemming population growth—and as India insisted on neutrality rather than an alliance with the West, to the annoyance of many Americans—opinion veered, and China often seemed the better bet. Indian traditions, including religious beliefs and a certain idealism coupled with the country's phenomenal population growth, now seemed less suited than forceful Chinese methods to the necessary reforms. As China became friendlier with the United States in a number of well publicized moves, enthusiasm for China's development prospects increased.

By the late 1990s, neither China nor India had managed to achieve a full industrial revolution in the style of Japan. At the same time, both have experienced significant economic change. Both have health rates and per capita income rates significantly above those in the poorest agricultural nations, with China, however, now in the lead. Both have seemingly vigorous governments, albeit with quite different institutions, styles, and problems. A comparison is complicated, to be sure, given our ignorance of some Chinese developments, as official control of information remains extensive. Nonetheless, it seems certain that, building on government tradition and communist zeal, China has become more effective than India in reducing its rates of population growth. Most experts assume that India will indeed surpass China as the world's most populous country soon after the year 2000. On the other hand, India has advanced more consistently in technological development and higher education, and it has also had more regular contacts with the outside world. Each nation, then, uses both distinctive traditions and distinctive current political forms to produce its own balanced mix of strengths and weaknesses. Ongoing differences between India and China recall different traditions established in the classical period, particularly in terms of political values and institutions but also attitudes toward the outside world. Later developments are also compelling examples of other important distinguishing factors: India's complex experience as a colony compared to the Western treatment of China, the fact that China had a revolution and India did not, perhaps even the different creative styles of Gandhi and Mao as seminal twentieth-century leaders. If China has ultimately gained the edge in economic growth, it may have suffered more in terms of cultural instability and dislocation.

SUGGESTED WEBSITES

On Gandhi, see *http://dwardmac.pitzer.edu/anarchist_archives/bright/gandhi/Gandhi.html;* on the life of Mohammad Ali Jinnah, the early leader of Pakistan, see *http://www.rediff.com/news/1998/sep/10jinnah.htm.*

SUGGESTED READINGS

India's recent political history is covered in J. Brown, *Modern India: The Origins of an Asian Democracy* (1985), and S. Wolpert, *New Oxford History of India* (1983). On specific topics, see J. Brown, *Gandhi's Rise to Power: Indian Politics, 1915–1922* (1978); F. Frankel, *India's Political Economy, 1947–1977* (1981); V. B. Singh, ed., *Economic History of India, 1857–1956* (1965); K. M. Panikkar, *The Foundation of New India* (1963); V. P. Menon, *The Transfer of Power in India* (1957); and A. de Souza, *Women in Contemporary India and South Asia* (1980).

A provocative general study of Asian politics, with particular reference to southern Asia, is L. W. Pye, *Asian Power and Politics: The Cultural Dimensions of Authority* (1985), which argues for the difficulty of using Western concepts to understand the Asian state. Eric Wolf, in *Peasants* (1966) and *Peasant Wars of the Twentieth Century* (1970), offers considerable coverage of this general subject within a South Asian context.

On Southeast Asia, D. G. E. Hall, *A History of South-East Asia* (1981), is a good survey; see also R. N. Kearney, *Politics and Modernization in South and Southeast Asia* (1974). Useful works on the Vietnam conflict are E. J. Hammer, *Struggle for Indochina* (1954); C. Cooper, *The Lost Crusade: America in Vietnam* (1972); and J. Zasloff and M. Brown, *Communist Indochina and U.S. Foreign Policy: Forging New Relations* (1978). An important study on recent Southeast Asian history, with larger theoretical implications, is James Scott, *The Moral Economy of the Peasant: Rebellion and Subsistence in Southeast Asia* (1976).

Excellent source reading on twentieth-century India is provided by various English-language novelists, who write directly of Indian life, although using Western languages as well as literary conventions. A well-known example is Rabindranath Tagore. More strictly contemporary authors are Kamale Markhndaya, Shanta Ramarao (on women), T. Shizasankara Pillai (on the south), and R. K. Narayan (on peasants). Also relevant is the work of novelist and essayist V. S. Naipaul, who is of Indian extraction but because he was raised in the West Indies writes as an outsider.

Middle Eastern Civilization in the Twentieth Century

30

The Middle East has been a center of recurrent international conflict in the twentieth century. Struggles against European colonialism yielded after the 1940s to frequent regional wars. What have been the main ingredients of conflict? The Middle East has also seen many changes, some of them similar to those in other parts of the world: New political regimes sought stability, various leaders promoted economic development, and new values took hold among many nationalists. Why did the Middle East, for the most part, accept neither democratic politics nor communism? Amid important departures from tradition, Islam remained a potent force, and it could motivate a reaction against certain kinds of change. What kinds of divisions over appropriate goals emerged in the Islamic nations? Were Islamic fundamentalists hostile to all signs of change?

CHANGES AND TENSIONS

Several major themes are interwoven in the most recent historical events of the oldest area of civilization in the world. Political unity in the Middle East, already tenuous during the nineteenth century, ended completely after World War I. A few subsequent efforts to revive larger segments, usually under the banners of Arab nationalism or Muslim brotherhood, failed. As new nations were carved out of the former territory of the Ottoman Empire, semiimperialist controls by various European states coexisted with the independence of several regional states between the wars. After World War II, the entire region gained independence. Divisions among Middle Eastern nations were compounded by a diversity of political forms. Monarchies arose in a few cases—virtually the only recent instances in which monarchy remained a serious political force in the twentieth century. Strongman regimes were even more characteristic. Some Middle Eastern states worked vigorously to modify age-old traditions, including the force of Islam, in the name of more secular goals. Others sought to preserve older values above all else.

Partly because of political divisions, the Middle East became the world's leading trouble spot after World War II. This status was not entirely new; already in the nineteenth century, the weakness and instability of the Ottoman Empire had resulted in conflict. The oil wealth discovered in the Middle East during the twentieth century gave the region new importance in the world economy, but it also attracted greed; this intensified the potential for outside interference in Middle Eastern affairs. Further, the creation of a new Jewish state after World War II produced a seemingly un-resolvable tension that provoked internal warfare within the region and a series of interventions from the leading powers in the cold war.

Finally, the Middle East generated an unusually complex pattern of reform efforts and counterreactions. A new regime in Turkey, installed in the wake of the collapse of the Ottoman Empire, provided the first of many secularization attempts that would succeed in producing some industrialization and agricultural development, as well as new systems of education and relationships both in society at large and within the family. Nonetheless, change came painfully in the Middle East, and a number of Islamic leaders, in the name of traditional ideals, helped mobilize reactions against the new trends. Thus, the Middle East produced a more bitter and overt clash between reformist and conservative forces than any other civilization in the contemporary world. Friction was often heightened by disputes over political form and rivalries among the new nations, adding greatly to the intricacy, and often the tragedy, of recent Middle Eastern history.

PATTERNS OF CONTEMPORARY MIDDLE EASTERN HISTORY

The Ottoman Empire's alliance with Germany during World War I opened the most recent chapter of Middle Eastern history. Britain and France worked to undermine Ottoman rule as part of their own war effort; they encouraged Arab nationalism, against Turkish control, and the British also vaguely promised Jewish leaders a new homeland in Palestine. Wartime pledges plus the ringing ideals of President Wilson at the Versailles Peace Conference prompted many Arab leaders to hope for outright freedom. Instead, they encountered victorious Western allies bent on extending imperialism to their region; not only Britain and France but also Italy and Greece were eager for new territory as the spoils of war. Thus, Middle Eastern nationalism was at once stimulated and frustrated, a dangerous combination.

REPLACING THE OTTOMAN EMPIRE

One point was clear, however: The Ottoman Empire could no longer be supported. Arab leaders, united in their hatred of the Turks, agreed on this point with European imperialists, who hoped to carve up the region for their own purposes. Arab uprisings were led by the chief magistrate of Mecca, Hussein Ibn Ali. Then at the war's end, French and British forces moved into the Middle East, the French taking over Syria and Lebanon, the British occupying Palestine, Jordan, and Iraq. The 1920s treaty of Sèvres proclaimed the end of the Ottoman Empire. Efforts to conquer Turkey itself failed, however. A Young Turk military leader, Mustafa Kemal, organized a Turkish resistance movement, defeating both Greek and Western invasion forces. Kemal's success resulted in new negotiations with the European powers and produced a 1923 treaty that created Turkey as a new, separate nation. This treaty not only ensured Turkish independence but also guaranteed the nation's continued strategic importance in European and Russian diplomacy because of its important geographic location.

Buoyed by his military and diplomatic success, Kemal unseated the sultan and proclaimed a secular republic in the new Turkey. Like Muhammed Ali in Egypt a century before, Kemal intended to lead the modernization of an Islamic nation, to achieve parity with the European states on their own terms. He carefully fostered a new Turkish nationalism separate from religious faith. He moved the country's capital from Istanbul to Ankara, in the Turkish heartland. Profoundly influenced by Western political ideas, Kemal introduced parliamentary institutions and a new voting system. But, his version of democracy was tightly controlled, with a single party—the People's Party—preventing any legal opposition. Like other notable Westernizers—including Peter the Great—Kemal believed that authoritarianism was an essential precondition of change, for the people had to be forced to accept reforms. Kemal, who took the name Atatürk, or "father of the Turks," vigorously attacked the hold of Islam. He abolished the religious caliphate and made the state secular. Civil marriage was required, and a secular school system was established. The regime outlawed many Muslim customs and symbols, including polygamy and traditional clothing—Western dress was mandatory. Sunday rather than Friday was proclaimed the national day of rest, and Muslim law was superseded by the laws of the state, which were modeled after Western codes. Arabic script was replaced with a Latin alphabet for the Turkish language, judged easier to learn and thus more appropriate for modern education. Against Islamic tradition also, Atatürk granted women the right to vote and to receive an education. A concerted effort to extend primary schools reduced illiteracy from 85 percent in 1914 to 42 percent in 1932.

The Middle East Before and After World War I Settlements, 1914–1922

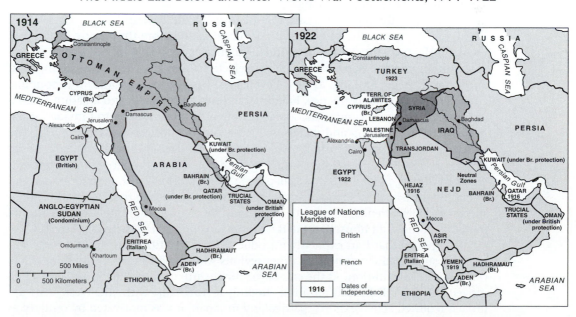

Atatürk's reforms, like those in Peter the Great's Russia or Meiji Japan, included stirring attacks on traditional clothing. It is important to recognize, and to explain, the passions involved. Here is how Atatürk framed his views on the fez, a traditional cap for upper-class Ottoman men: "It was necessary to abolish the fez, which sat on our heads as a sign of ignorance, of fanaticism, of hatred to progress and civilization, and to adopt in its place the hat, the customary head-dress of the whole civilized world, thus showing that . . . no difference existed between the Turkish nation and the whole family of civilized mankind."

Atatürk's regime also promoted industrialization. A number of factories were established under state guidance. Cities grew. Turkey vigorously pursued the training of engineers and other technical personnel, to make foreign experts unnecessary. At the same time, unions were forbidden to strike, in order to prevent any barriers to economic growth. By 1939, a year after Atatürk's death, the economy had advanced enough so that foreign railroad companies could be bought out—a major blow against lingering economic imperialism.

Atatürk's hopes were not entirely fulfilled, however. His power base was secure; nationalism unquestionably gained ground; traditional culture yielded to new interests in science and economic development. However, the rural majority was not entirely supportive of the new regime, as Muslim objections to secularism persisted. Many crusading schoolteachers reported persistent traditionalism—in their view, superstitious belief—among their students and village leaders. Atatürk's successors had to allow for this deeply rooted religious faith, as they slowed the pace of reform. Furthermore, although Turkey became a new nation and successfully maintained its independence, bolstered by the largest, best-disciplined army in the region, it did not fully industrialize. Economic growth was slow, poverty widespread. Despite the genuine revolution in Turkish politics and culture, this was no Japanese-style leap forward in terms of economic change.

Turkey was the most dramatic case of new Middle Eastern politics after World War I, but it was not the only one. Persia, dominated before the war by British and Russian influence, proclaimed new independence as well, shaking off British efforts to maintain control. Persian nationalists selected an army officer, Riza Khan, soon known as the shah, or king, as their new leader. The new ruler worked for economic change as well as independence, building rail lines and schools and creating a banking system. The government encouraged enough factory industry to provide for national needs in clothing and metals, reducing dependence on Western imports. The regime benefited from important oil revenues, developed by a British company under Persian license. In 1935, to signal the beginning of an era, the kingdom's name was changed to Iran. But, the shah was deposed during World War II, in favor of his son, in part because of efforts to gain advantages from both sides in the war. Islamic opposition to modern trends, along with hostility to the luxurious life style and dictatorial methods of the shah himself, created far more tension than persisted in Turkey.

One policy that Iran explicitly introduced from the 1920s onward deserves particular note, because countries in other regions would soon move in the same direction: import substitution. At the end of the nineteenth century, Russia and Japan had moved toward full industrialization, hoping to catch up with the West. This approach required active exports, particularly in Japan; it was motivated by military as well as economic goals. Import substitution suggested a more modest approach: build enough factory industry to reduce dependence on Western goods in areas like textiles and basic machinery (later, automobiles would be added to this list). Success here would give the nation more economic independence, although it might not become a world economic power. Turkey followed this policy to a degree, as did India after 1947; Latin American nations did the same from the 1930s onward. Successful import substitution would have its own impact on the world economy, and of course it did not preclude a more active export stance later on.

ASSERTIONS OF ARAB NATIONALISM

Although important new regimes arose in the northern Middle East, marked by commitment to reform and authoritarian rule, the bulk of the Middle East lay under European control during the 1920s and 1930s. North Africa, of course, was held as colonies by France, Britain, and Italy. The major areas of the Middle East proper, now taken over by France and Britain, were governed as League of Nations mandates, rather than as outright possessions, which implied some commitment to ultimate independence. Nevertheless, Arab indignation at this new foreign rule was a further impetus to nationalism. Riots and demonstrations forced Britain to recognize the technical independence of Egypt in 1922, and Iraq and Jordan soon followed, although in all these cases, Britain continued to regulate economic and military affairs. France made fewer early concessions to nationalism in its territories. It split Lebanon off from Syria, encouraging division between Christians and Muslims in Lebanon as well. And while Lebanon achieved independence under French protection, and Syria won promise of the same in 1936, European influence remained strong. Indeed, in oil-rich territories such as Iraq, European and U.S. companies quickly acquired ownership rights, which actually increased the Western stake in the region even as formal imperialism was declining.

Another key issue for Arab nationalists during the 1920s and 1930s was the growing Jewish presence in Palestine. Although Jews constituted a mere 11 percent of the total population of the region in 1914, Jewish emigration from Europe, encouraged by Zionist organizations and also by Hitler's anti-Semitic onslaught, increased the number of Jewish residents rapidly, to half a million by 1940. The Jewish population was still outnumbered by Palestinian Muslims and Christians, but Arab nationalists were alert to this threat to what they regarded as their land. They pressed Britain, as the mandate power in Palestine, to restrict immigration, but British policy in fact vacillated, failing to satisfy either Muslims or Jews. In the meantime, Jewish organization of agriculture and industry in Palestine, around communal farms known as kibbutzim, gained ground steadily, greatly increasing traditional productivity and developing new export crops such as citrus fruits.

Arab nationalism thus had a number of targets. Although nationalism became more intense, it was also a divisive force in the Middle East. Not only were nationalists distracted by the boundaries drawn among mandate territories, such as Lebanon and Syria, but they also disagreed about the future of the Middle East. Some, as in the new kingdom of Saudi Arabia, advocated traditional Muslim ways, whereas others talked of Western-style parliamentary democracy; still others, like the Iraqi Kamil

Chadrichi, preached an Arab form of socialism. Few groups in the Middle East were outright Marxists, for Marxist hostility to nationalism and religion, demonstrated by attacks on Islamic groups in the Soviet Union, was too severe even for most secular reformers. However, no single non-Marxist formula for a Middle Eastern future emerged.

Then came World War II, which further weakened Western Europe's tenuous hold on the region. Turkey remained carefully independent during the conflict, bent on developing its own state without distraction. But, much of the rest of the area was drawn into the hostilities, as German forces invaded North Africa and then faced defeat at the hands of the British-American alliance in 1942. More important was the sheer weakness of Britain and France after the war, which gave new hope to Arab leaders. France yielded to riots in 1945, abandoning all government powers in Syria and Lebanon. Britain followed suit, although this was delayed by its attempts to find a solution to Arab–Jewish conflicts in Palestine. Riots and terrorist attacks by the two groups and even against the British marked the period of 1945–1948. When the British finally pulled out of the area, the Jews simply declared a new state of Israel (May 1948), beating off an attack by the surrounding Arab countries and conquering more territory. Almost a million Muslim refugees were expelled from Palestine, creating a legacy of great hostility between the Arabs and Israel and its political allies, including the United States.

Defeat at Jewish hands triggered a revolution in Egypt, where the army colonel Gamal Abdel Nasser drove out the corrupt, pro-Western king in 1952. The goal was a secular, reformist state under one-party leadership. Nasser, who for a time spearheaded Arab nationalism generally, seized the Suez Canal in 1956, provoking a British-French-Israeli attack that managed to invade Egypt but was forced back by U.S. and Russian pressure, as the two superpowers were bent on courting Arab favor. A fully independent Egypt, which proved its technical competence by running the Suez Canal efficiently, was a major new player in the Middle East from this point onward. Nasser quickly demonstrated his reformist inclination internally by dividing the great estates along the Nile and awarding land to the peasants, thus ending the long-standing manorial system.

Arab independence was completely achieved between 1956 and 1962; the final North African colonies won their freedom as the states of Libya, Tunisia, Morocco, and Algeria. The key battle here focused on Algeria, a French holding since the mid–nineteenth century and symbolic, to many French leaders, of France's battered claims to greatness in the world of power politics. Nationalist agitation led to outright civil war for almost a decade, as the minority of European settlers supported the French army against a pattern of guerrilla attacks and terrorism that proved impossible to suppress. Finally, the French, rightly worried about the effects of the long, brutal struggle on their own internal political stability and national morality, pulled back, agreeing in 1962 to Algerian independence.

With independence achieved, through an assortment of individual states, the most coherent thread in Middle Eastern affairs remained the dispute between the Arab states and Israel. Israel's immediate neighbors were most directly involved, but other Arab leaders found Israel a convenient target to generate popular enthusiasms at home, and a genuine affront to Arab and Islamic authority in the region. For its

The Middle East Today

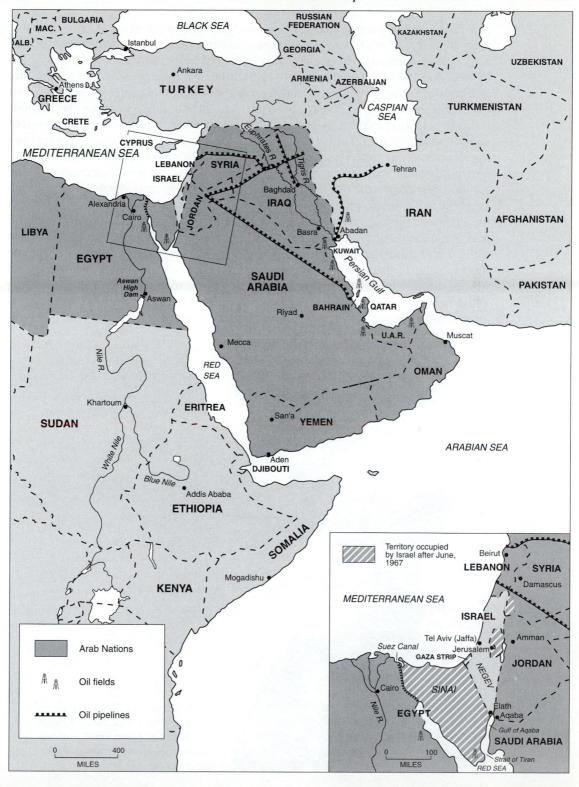

BULGARIA
MAC.
ALB.
GREECE
Athens
CRETE

BLACK SEA
Istanbul
Ankara
TURKEY

RUSSIAN FEDERATION
GEORGIA
ARMENIA AZERBAIJAN
KAZAKHSTAN
UZBEKISTAN
TURKMENISTAN

CASPIAN SEA

MEDITERRANEAN SEA
CYPRUS
LEBANON
ISRAEL

Euphrates R.
SYRIA
Tigris R.
Baghdad
IRAQ
JORDAN
Basra
Abadan
KUWAIT

Tehran
IRAN
AFGHANISTAN
PAKISTAN

Persian Gulf

LIBYA
Alexandria
Cairo
EGYPT
Aswan High Dam
Aswan

Nile R.

SAUDI ARABIA
Mecca
Riyad
BAHRAIN QATAR
U.A.R.
Muscat
OMAN

RED SEA

SUDAN
Khartoum
ERITREA
White Nile
Blue Nile
Addis Ababa
ETHIOPIA

San'a YEMEN
Aden
DJIBOUTI

ARABIAN SEA

KENYA
Mogadishu
SOMALIA

Legend

Arab Nations

Oil fields

Oil pipelines

0   400
MILES

Inset

Territory occupied by Israel after June, 1967

MEDITERRANEAN SEA

Beirut
LEBANON SYRIA
Damascus
ISRAEL
Tel Aviv (Jaffa)
Suez Canal
Jerusalem
GAZA STRIP
Amman
JORDAN
NEGEV

Cairo
EGYPT
Nile R.
SINAI
Elath
Aqaba
Gulf of Aqaba
SAUDI ARABIA
Strait of Tiran
RED SEA

0   100
MILES

part, Israel created a strong military force, with far more modern armaments than the Arab states could boast and an aggressive outlook designed to avoid any further scapegoating of the Jewish people. Wars broke out between Israel and its neighbors in 1967 and 1973. The first war led to substantial new Israeli-controlled territory, including the entire city of Jerusalem, regarded as a religious center by Muslims and Christians as well as Jews. Even apart from outright war, guerrilla attacks and terrorism were widely employed by Palestinian groups hostile to Israel, whereas Israel frequently retaliated with bombing missions against refugee camps suspected of harboring terrorists. In 1982, Israel invaded Lebanon in order to unseat Palestinian terrorists, producing literal anarchy in this nation as no group seemed capable of ensuring order. There were few bright spots in the seemingly unresolvable conflict over Israel. In 1977, the Egyptian president, Anwar Sadat, made a stunning gesture by visiting Israel in the hopes of negotiating a peace. Although this initiative reduced tension, it led to no overall settlement, since Israel refused to surrender most of the territories it had gained in 1967 and many Arab nationalists refused to recognize Israel's right to exist. In 1993, Israeli agreements with the Palestinians in some autonomous regions, followed by a 1994 peace treaty with Jordan, renewed optimism for settling a number of wider disputes. Tensions again increased after 1996 with the victory of a more right-wing party in Israel. The peace effort resumed in 1999, but then seemed to collapse in new violence in 2000–2001.

The Palestinian issue, 1979: Israeli soldier patrolling Arab village during a Palestinian general strike against Israeli-ordered expulsion of a mayor sympathetic to Palestinian independence.

In addition to the issue of Israel, questions of alignment with the world's super-powers were the focus of many nations in the Middle East. Israel was a firm Western ally, receiving significant financial and military aid from the United States. Turkey, anxious about its Soviet neighbor to the north, was also in the Western camp as a member of NATO. Most other Middle Eastern nations, however, oscillated in their alignments. Egypt's Nasser helped organize "neutral" nations in the world, along with India during the 1950s, as an alternative to an alliance with either side during the cold war. And, most Middle Eastern leaders would probably have preferred an essentially neutral course, so they could concentrate on foreign and domestic objectives of their own. However, Western influence continued to loom large. Western nations were often the target of attacks as allies of Israel, remembered imperialists, or capitalist exploiters. They were also valuable sources of arms, purchasers along with Japan of most of the oil produced in the region, and usefully hostile to Marxism. Most of the more conservative Arab states thus tended to develop relatively close ties with the West, whereas more secular regimes either alternated—like Egypt, which used Russian aid after the Suez war and later renounced it in favor of American support—or leaned toward heavy reliance on Russia, like Syria during the 1970s. Or, they tried to win support from both sides. In any event, competition between the cold war camps continued to weigh heavily on the Middle East, which could not resist substantial outside influence because of internal divisions and military and economic weakness. At the same time, great-power rivalry gave many states a chance to play off the two sides and thus gain room for independent maneuvers.

Two other factors played a considerable role in Middle Eastern events after the end of outright imperialism: local rivalries and efforts at economic coordination. A number of newly independent states clashed over territory or policy. Egypt and Libya developed a rivalry; Morocco and Algeria disputed territory; in the early 1980s, a particularly brutal and protracted war broke out between Iraq and Iran, over territory and also a fundamental policy dispute between a secular state in Iraq and the fervent religious revolutionaries who had seized power in Iran in 1978. Iraq's own expansionism led to the invasion of Kuwait in 1990; a subsequent alliance among Saudi Arabia, Egypt, Syria, and the major Western powers beat back the Iraqis while trying unsuccessfully to replace their strongman leader, Saddam Hussein.

Against this backdrop of frequent fighting, a few institutions of greater scope provided partial balance. The Arab League existed to help reconcile quarrels in the name of the larger ideal of renewed Arab unity. Periodic efforts to unite different nations surfaced; Syria thus briefly merged with Egypt. Although these attempts seldom had much substance, they served as a reminder that a higher political dream for the region persisted and might someday have greater impact. Finally, and more pragmatically, oil-producing Arab states, headed by Iran, Iraq, and Saudi Arabia, took the lead in forming OPEC (Organization of Petroleum Exporting Countries) in 1961, although there were important non-Middle Eastern participants as well. The formation of OPEC resulted from successful Arab and Iranian efforts to reduce the independence of Western oil companies operating in their region, as either nationalization or at least significant government supervision took hold. OPEC nations also attempted to coordinate production levels and pricing policies, and during the 1970s, they had considerable success in raising the price of oil and therefore the earnings of member nations. Here, at least briefly, was an important change in the customary dependency of raw material suppliers in the world market. By the end of the 1970s, however, competition from other regions and even among OPEC members, plus Western conservation efforts, reduced OPEC's effectiveness in maintaining revenues. Nevertheless, OPEC, along with individual efforts by wealthy Arab states such as Saudi Arabia to provide economic support to petroleum-poor states like Jordan and Egypt, again demonstrated that narrow nationalist rivalries did not alone capture the complexities of Middle Eastern politics. By 2000, coordination again improved, producing higher oil prices and revenues.

THE POLITICAL CULTURE OF THE MIDDLE EAST

THE NEW ROLE OF THE STATE

With growing nationalism and then independence, the states of the Middle East developed a number of similar functions. Most assumed new responsibility for providing systems of education; an economic infrastructure including roads, ports, and airlines; and some limited welfare programs. Most regulated foreign companies to some extent, and the region gained leverage against the West. Universities were created, teaching secular subjects along with or instead of the basic principals of Islamic faith. Even conservative regimes such as the Saudi Arabian monarchy spurred technical training. The new functions of government demonstrated the novelty of many of the forces impinging on this region during the twentieth century. What was happening in the Middle East, as elsewhere in the world, was a common pattern of political modernization, defined simply as the extension of government functions to new areas, like mass education and economic planning, and the attempt to focus new loyalty on the state. This effort may be viewed as an obvious development, but it was profoundly unsettling to some. Nationalism itself was a new loyalty, not an inevitable outgrowth of Middle Eastern tradition. Many Muslims believed that nationalism was irrelevant so long as pious Muslims controlled the government; thus, for example, it was unimportant that Arabs be ruled by an Arab government. By the same token, Middle Eastern nationalists had to tread very carefully in the area of religious devotion, insisting that nationalism did not contradict true belief and emphasizing a common interest in the glorious Muslim past, while urging some reforms in Islam itself. Definitions of nationalism also varied and clashed. Was a nation a region with boundaries established by Europeans after World War I? Should it embrace all Arabs? Should it be secular or Islamic?

Changes in government functions and the rise of nationalism did not mean Western-style political forms in the typical Middle Eastern states. Liberal democracy did not take hold in this region; here was another common denominator in the Middle Eastern political style. Along with China, the Middle East indeed proved to be the region most resistant to the spread of democracy in the 1980s and 1990s. The one consistent exception was Israel, where a parliament achieved great power and a multiparty system flourished. Even here, Israel's focus on military development and repression of its Palestinian minority at times clouded the nation's liberal vision, as did the power of extremist religious groups in winning government support for Orthodox Jewish practices.

Most Middle Eastern states either did not establish parliaments or, as in the more secular states, limited their effectiveness by preventing multiparty competition. Even Turkey, which periodically experimented with opposition parties and a fairly free press after World War II, often retreated into military regimes. A multiparty system did gain ground, producing the first woman prime minister in the 1990s. But, then victory by a pro-Muslim party caused the military to intervene in 1997 and install secular politicians, although on the basis of a party coalition in parliament. Elsewhere, monarchy or strongman rule normally prevailed. Islamic political tradition provided scant basis for liberal political values, whereas the tensions within Middle Eastern society convinced many leaders that their power could not be preserved within a framework of political competition. Most countries, then, imposed restrictions on the press, used political police extensively, and relied heavily on military support in an essentially authoritarian approach.

Nevertheless, there was no single vision of how the state should operate. A key division erupted between the monarchies—Morocco, Jordan, Saudi Arabia, Iran before 1978, and some smaller states on the Persian gulf—and the secular republics, where individual strongmen typically wielded power, often backed by a single political party. Most of the monarchs, while working for economic development, not only discouraged political opposition but also tended to support the existing social hierarchy and conservative Islamic social values. Saudi Arabia was the most extreme example. The country sought to use oil revenues to develop a wider industrial base as well as new cities and extensive education. But it also enforced traditional Arab dress and social segregation of women, as well as significant penalties for sexual misconduct or other violations of Islamic law. The government forbade women to drive cars, even though many had learned to drive during visits to the West. Most republics, on the other hand, although just as hostile to political opposition as the monarchies, sought to encourage not only industrial development and agricultural reform but also a more secular outlook. They worked for new educational and job opportunities for women, while discouraging traditional dress. Like Atatürk's regime, they tried to limit Islamic habits—such as fasting during the day for the month of Ramadan—that would affect economic productivity. A number of the republics worked toward a policy of what was called Arab socialism, designed to produce a society different from the West and the communist nations alike. Arab socialism meant regulations for business—particularly foreign-owned business—but not state control of the entire economy. It involved attempts to limit inequality, through heavier taxation on the rich and land reforms to benefit the peasantry. Arab socialism did not, however, represent a full-scale attack on religion or devotion to elaborate political doctrine; it was an impulse more than a well-defined movement.

THE RISE OF FUNDAMENTALISM

Political and economic change produced an important backlash in Middle Eastern political and cultural life, which became increasingly dominant from the 1970s onward. Furthermore, failures of reform—in the continuation of massive poverty—created pressure to use religion for protest. The spiritual power and pervasive legal framework of Islam explain why many people, ordinary peasants as well as religious leaders, were tempted to use their Islamic faith as a rallying point against change or for different kinds of reform, and especially against any signs of Western cultural influence. Thus, the Ayatollah Khomeini, ultimately the leader of Iran's 1978 revolution, reacted to educational change:

> Our universities must become Islamic. . . . They have served to impede the progress of the sons and daughters of this land; they have become propaganda arenas. Our young people may have succeeded in acquiring some knowledge, but they have not received an education, an Islamic education. . . . The universities do not impart an education that corresponds to the needs of the people and the country; instead they squander the energies of whole generations of our beloved youth, or oblige them to serve the foreigners.

Thus, a new Islamic fundamentalism took shape, after 1970, that in essence sought a return to original Islamic political ideals of a state committed to religious values and the enforcement of these values as its first priority. This was not pure traditionalism; fundamentalists used novel methods and often displayed an intolerance that was not characteristic of Islam in the past. Most leaders were urban-educated. But, there was a protest against change. Many Islamic scholars and other religious leaders, including the ulema scholars, raised important objections to trends in the Middle East (and also in neighboring Islamic societies such as Sudan, Afghanistan, and Pakistan). They viewed concentration on economic advance as evidence of improper priorities: Adherence to religious duties should come first. Westernized clothing—particularly for women and especially in recreational areas and on beaches—and other imports, including films, were attacked as scandalous and immoral. The

An Iranian revolutionary trains women in military skills.

tendencies of more secular states to promote education without a firm basis in religion and to cooperate with Christian Westerners were condemned, while Islamic purists also insisted on a more concentrated attack on the problem of Israel. In short, Islamic fundamentalists called for a restoration of many traditional values, including a reorientation of political actions.

Appeals for a return to traditional values have been a standard part of modern history in societies exposed to rapid change: They occurred in Christian societies during the nineteenth century, and they still occasionally surface in some parts of the West, including the United States. They also occurred, although on different terms, in Japan. Hindu fundamentalism echoed similar themes in India. However, the fundamentalist movement in Islam seems to have struck a deeper chord in the Middle East than analogous movements in other civilizations. Deeply committed Muslim groups emerged in most Middle Eastern states by the 1970s. Even in conservative Saudi Arabia, they exerted pressure on the regime to follow Muslim laws more faithfully. Thus, as the result of some court trials intended to set an example, adulterers were stoned or beheaded. A group of fundamentalists was responsible for the assassination of President Anwar Sadat, in 1981, although Egyptian policy was not greatly affected by the conservative current. Fundamentalist pressure in Pakistan prompted the military regime to introduce a new code of law more in line with Muslim tradition, providing, among other things, harsher punishments for such crimes as sexual immorality. In the 1990s, fundamentalist pressure increased in Turkey, although the military tried to curtail it. Algerian military rulers faced an even tougher battle with a larger fundamentalist faction, and a great deal of violence ensued between both groups. In general, Muslim fundamentalism added an important ingredient to the Middle Eastern mix, even when states largely resisted the pressure.

The greatest victory of the Islamic militants occurred in Iran. It was revealing that the most dramatic revolution in the twentieth-century Middle East was religious in spirit, unlike all other contemporary revolutions in the world. The Iranian revolution has been called, in fact, the first real "third world revolution," in that it sought not a special national path to modernization using ideas such as Marxism first created in the West, but a commitment to the ideals of Islamic law. The revolutionaries were zealous Shi'ites, a majority in Iran although a minority in Islam overall. Shi'ites had long been bent on creating a purer religious state, against what they saw as the errors of the Sunnites, the majority group of Muslims. This aspect of the Iranian struggle renewed a conflict that had existed for centuries within Islam.

The specific framework for the Iranian revolution involved a rapid reform program that had taken place in Iran, building on the efforts of the 1920s and 1930s, combined with brutal political repression. The shah's government, which with U.S. help had defeated a 1953 protest, had launched a crash program of modernization rather like that of Atatürk earlier in Turkey, but with the added development of substantial oil revenues and greater contact with the West. The regime supported education, including the training of many Iranians abroad, plus industrial and military development. These changes caused much discontent. The rural majority was neglected. Inflation ran high, for even with significant oil earnings, the country's many new projects were expensive. The shah's brutal repression of political opposition, through a powerful secret police, antagonized additional, liberal segments of

Iranian opinion, as did extensive corruption. Other grievances rested with the Muslim faithful. Islamic leaders were appalled at the new surge of Western influence, visible in the 100,000 foreigners who helped run the economy. They protested the resort areas developed for foreigners' use, where the use of liquor and skimpy bathing attire openly clashed with Muslim law.

Revolt broke out in 1978, forcing the exile of the shah early the following year. The new leader was the aged holy man, the Ayatollah Khomeini, who had long campaigned against the "godless and materialistic" regime of the shah. The revolutionary government quickly suppressed other discontented groups, including liberals and communists. It banned Western music, bathing suits, and liquor, and set out to create a holy Shi'ite state. Traditional dress, including a veil or *chadur*, was required of women. During the long war Iraq launched against Iran, leaders hoped to export its political principles to other Islamic states; the ayatollah talked of a new jihad, or holy war, that would unite the whole Middle East in a literal version of the Islamic state. A high level of religious and revolutionary excitement continued in Iran through the mid–1980s. Fundamentalists, mainly Shi'ites, were also active in the troubled nation of Lebanon, after the 1982 Israeli invasion, and they stirred elsewhere; in Syria, for example, a fundamentalist insurgency was vanquished, but only after considerable brutality. By the late 1990s, however, more moderate policies gained ground in Iran.

Fundamentalist reaction to change in the Middle East thus formed an important current in the late twentieth century. There was no way to determine its durability; certainly key states such as Iraq and Syria, as well as most North African regimes, managed to maintain their secular policies that were, in any event, not in full opposition to Islam. But, fundamentalists put massive pressure on governments, as in Algeria, along with being responsible for frequent acts of terrorism. Even the Soviet Union worried about a potential fundamentalism current among its own Islamic minority; this was one reason for the invasion of Afghanistan, to guard against a fundamentalist regime in this neighboring state. Debates over Islamic policy resumed in the new Central Asian republics that followed the Soviet collapse. Finally, the incompleteness of industrialization and divisions of outlook, even in well-established secular states such as Turkey, suggested that Islam and some aspects of a conventional reform program were not easily compatible. Again, Islam's spiritual hold, its emphasis on obedience to Allah, and its tradition of regulating social life in some detail, gave it an unusual role among world religions in the twentieth century.

By the late 1990s, it was not clear how important Islamic resistance and innovation would prove to be. Certainly, the continued strength of the Muslim faith added to the diversity of Middle Eastern politics in the later twentieth century. It also suggests the ongoing complexity of the process of change in this vital region, for Islamic fundamentalism has by no means been triumphant. Its surge reflects the fact that significant political and social change has already touched Middle Eastern civilization—for example, the gradual steady urbanization, bringing over 65 percent of the population of major countries like Egypt into the cities, away from rural roots and a different kind of economy. If Westernization obviously cannot capture the patterns of the contemporary Middle East, in politics and culture alike, no more so does an image of unaltered traditionalism.

The Iranian Revolution, 1979: anti-American demonstration, with posters of the Ayatollah Khomeini.

MIDDLE EASTERN CULTURE AND SOCIETY

One fully industrial country emerged in the Middle East after World War II: the state of Israel. The new nation, although severely pressed to defend its existence, benefited from extensive foreign aid, a deeply felt nationalism on the part of many of its citizens, and its experience in developing an industrial economy. Most initial Israeli leaders were immigrants. Hundreds of thousands of European Jews migrated to the new nation after the Nazi Holocaust of World War II. Substantial immigration from the cities of the Middle East developed as well, as hostilities between Arabs and Jews disrupted earlier patterns of tolerance and the new Israeli state served as a beacon for the Jewish faithful. With immigration came population growth and the infusion of a multitude of skills in business and manufacturing. Israeli commitment to industrial output and market agriculture, including extensive projects of desert reclamation, produced a dynamic economy that easily placed Israel among the most technologically advanced nations of the world. Although the new country faced economic problems, particularly because of heavy military expenditure, it had easily jumped the basic hurdles of twentieth-century economic development. The country turned increasingly to consumerism by the 1990s, which caused concern among religious groups and secular nationalists alike.

HISTORY DEBATE

Fundamentalism

Many Western experts on the Middle East caution great care in interpreting fundamentalism. They note that fundamentalist hostility to the West, particularly the United States, makes a sympathetic interpretation difficult. They especially urge that fundamentalism not be seen as a single movement. Not all fundamentalists oppose all change. Muslim tradition is perfectly compatible with commercial advance, for instance. Most fundamentalists accept certain kinds of change, including new technologies and the importance of mass education (although they seek a strong religious element in this education and the careful regulation of female dress). Even the effort to implement the laws of the Sharia is new, for such an attempt has never been initiated before. Further, fundamentalism addresses both traditionalist beliefs *and* discontent amid modern problems like massive urban poverty.

Another important question involves the relationship between this strong, growing current in Islam and religious change elsewhere. Related Hindu movements became more vigorous in the 1980s and 1990s, as we have seen. The collapse of the Soviet system resulted in the renewed vitality of Orthodox Christianity in Eastern Europe, while Protestant fundamentalists also worked for converts. In addition, religious pressures increased in Israel in the 1990s, particularly in the Orthodox Jewish stronghold of Jerusalem. Protestant fundamentalism, advanced by missionaries mainly from the United States, was the most rapidly growing new belief system in Latin America in the 1980s and 1990s. Islamic fundamentalism, in other words, played a special role in the Middle East and North Africa, plus adjacent territory in Pakistan and Central Asia. However, it may be viewed as part of a wider international current in the late twentieth century, which means that its explanation goes beyond strictly Islamic bounds.

Other observers, however, stress some specifically Islamic ingredients. They note the relevance of the long-time Sunni-Shi'ite rift and also Islam's extensive legalism, its host of rules and regulations, that make it harder for the faithful to accept certain kinds of social and cultural change than is true for other religions. Islamic law applies to so many aspects of life, from the position of women to one's daily schedule, that its mandates can clash with any modern reform drive. This provides a special basis for the more general temptation to defend tradition in the contemporary world. Interpreting fundamentalism, or any specific manifestation such as Islamic fundamentalism, clearly raises important questions and challenges.

In contrast, manufacturing, market agriculture, and levels of technology lagged in most other parts of the Middle East. Indeed, the gap in technological sophistication between Israel and its rivals was one of the bases of Israeli survival, as Israeli production of up-to-date armaments became a major industry. Variety among the Islamic states in economic conditions itself increased. The region embraces about 60 percent of the world's known petroleum reserves, but they are not evenly distributed. Nations with substantial oil production and small populations—among them some of the traditionally poorest desert states—suddenly surged to immense per capita wealth. The Persian Gulf state of Kuwait thus ranked in 1980 as the richest in the world in terms of average income. Saudi Arabia also rose to great wealth. Lavish new urban construction and extensive medical and educational services followed from oil revenues in these nations, particularly during the heyday of OPEC price manipulation. Regional manufacturing did gain ground, generating additional import substitution and a new minority of factory workers. However, although the oil-rich states struggled to invest their earnings in industries that could sustain a better-balanced economy and provide wealth even when oil production declined, they encountered serious difficulties. Many, indeed, invested substantial funds abroad, especially in the West, because there simply were insufficient productive opportunities at home. Lack of other resources, continued limitations in technical training and interest, a pronounced gap between rich and poor that restricts consumer demand—these were some general factors that inhibited the translation of oil wealth into industrialization. Heavy military expenditures also played a role, for these investments involved purchases from abroad rather than a stimulus to domestic production. When military expenditure turned into war, as in the Iran-Iraq conflict, the impact on economic conditions could be devastating.

Nations without oil wealth faced even more severe economic problems. Here, too, military expenditures and, in some cases, political instability limited economic development. Many countries were also burdened by significant population growth. Lack of available land haunted many rural people, whereas opportunities in the cities did not keep pace with need, even as urbanization accelerated. Muslim beliefs slowed conversion to new birth-control methods. A number of governments attempted massive projects to expand production. Egypt's President Nasser, for example, with substantial Soviet aid, orchestrated the construction of a huge dam at Aswan, on the Nile, designed to increase agricultural land through irrigation while providing low-cost electrical power for industry. The dam was also meant to symbolize Arab greatness and recall the glory days of ancient Egypt; thus, Nasser described the dam as "more magnificent and seventeen times greater than the Pyramids." Unfortunately, the Aswan project, although successful, did not keep pace with Egypt's population growth. Both the urban masses and peasant population of this key nation remained desperately poor.

New oil revenues, land reform, and some real growth in urban manufacturing did bring economic change to the Middle East, particularly after World War II. City populations outstripped rural populations in most countries as Middle Eastern urbanization levels exceeded those of India and China. However, outside of Israel, a breakthrough to a fully industrial economy has yet to occur, and standards of living in the larger countries tend to stagnate. One result was considerable emigration in search of jobs, as many Turks and North Africans sought work in Western Europe, whereas other Arab peasants took unskilled jobs, often at low pay, in the oil-rich states.

Middle Eastern culture, like the economy, also straddled the fence between tradition and change. Outside of Israel, few Middle Eastern artists participated in international styles. Most Muslim art continued to use traditional styles and themes, although "modern" architecture did find a place in the urban development of countries like Saudi Arabia and prerevolutionary Iran. Although some Western films were shown in the more secular nations, Islamic film-making remained largely separate from patterns developed in the West, partly of course for religious reasons. The Muslim world retained an active allegiance to traditional musical styles, relying, even for most popular music, on instruments and singing techniques different from those in the West. Although important work has been done in art and literature—an Egyptian novelist won the Nobel prize for literature in 1994, for instance—and also in Islamic theology and law, there was little sense of a revival of creativity that would recall the brightest periods of Middle Eastern culture.

Most Middle Eastern governments encouraged a growing interest in science. Nasser established a Supreme Science Council in Egypt, arguing that

> we have to keep up with the new world and new discoveries. We suffered so much in the past because we were left behind by the ages of steam and electricity. What suffering awaits those who fail to keep up with the new dawn will certainly be much greater than whatever we have experienced in the past. . . . In this world of breathtaking discoveries, to be left behind is to forfeit one's right to existence.

Although improved scientific training added an important dimension to Middle Eastern culture, it did not propel the region into the top ranks of scientific creativity; the Middle East remained heavily dependent on the West for basic scientific research. The dissemination of a scientific outlook to a larger population through the expanding school systems, along with growing literacy, established a basis for further change in the future, although at times this viewpoint clashed with Islamic fundamentalism.

Society in the Middle East reflected the growth of cities and the policies of reform-minded governments. It also reflected population pressure and, in places, the impact of war. But, there were important continuities with the past as well. Many Middle Eastern villages have changed only slowly. Some new agricultural equipment was introduced, and contacts with urban markets expanded. However, the pace of life and work remained recognizable in traditional terms. Although landlord dominance was reduced throughout most of the region, the gap between peasant masses and local notables was an important fact of life.

A key tension in Middle Eastern society involved the position of women. In a major break with the past, increasing numbers of women gained access to formal education. In the more secular states, such as Turkey, Egypt, Algeria, or Syria, many women also cast aside traditional clothing, abandoning the veil and adopting Western dress. Many governments tried to encourage new work patterns among women, seeing them as a vital resource for fledgling industrial economies. Thus, some women entered the ranks of factory and office workers. But, the economic and social segrega-

During the Iranian Revolution, a middle-class feminist demonstration.

tion of women remained severe. Work outside the home, and especially a commitment to professional jobs as doctors or lawyers, was widely disapproved of, and few women could hope to support themselves without family resources. The gap between male and female school attendance remained greater than in any other civilization. Male dominance within the household was still pronounced, and the relatively high birthrate both caused and reflected the domestic emphasis of women's lives. Conservative states like Saudi Arabia enforced even more pronounced separation between men and women, including severe penalties for sexual infidelity. And, the Iranian revolution showed that even reformist regimes like the shah's can yield to more traditional practices concerning women.

Again, the result was not uniform. Countries like Turkey had large numbers of "Westernized" women, wearing cosmetics and European-style clothes, active in urban jobs including politics and possessed of a secular education. They shared the streets with women in traditional dress, those enmeshed in a more traditional Islamic culture and family life. In a few cases, they also faced attack from the fundamentalist movement.

Moroccan shoppers wear traditional clothing, while looking at Western-style shoes.

CONCLUSION: A TROUBLED REGION

Many more question marks dot the appraisal of trends and prospects in the Middle East than is the case for other major Asian civilizations in the late twentieth century. The region has produced no unity in political forms. The existence of divisions and diversity is no novelty in Middle Eastern tradition, of course, as periods of chaos often punctuated efforts at unification in the past. However, there is certainly no clear end in sight to some of the fundamental conflicts that describe political and military life in the region. Disputes between secular reformers and Islamic fundamentalists continue to constrain many national governments and divide behaviors among women. The precise blend of tradition and change that will continue to define a Middle Eastern civilization has yet to be found. The civilization remains unique and faces a number of problems of significance to other parts of the world as regional wars spill over into wider tensions.

Perhaps the troubles of the Middle East will prove transitory. Once before, when the Arab caliphate declined but before the full hold of the Turks was secure, the region passed through many decades of disarray. Regional political units refused to coordinate their policies. An outside force—the Kingdom of Jerusalem established by European crusaders—seized a holy territory but could not easily be dislodged. Out of frustration, terrorist groups, called the Assassins, arose. However, this chaos did eventually subside, as a new wave of Turkish invasions, the Ottomans, engendered political unity and military strength, while preserving many distinct features of Islamic civilization, including considerable tolerance and regional diversity. History may, in some basic ways, repeat itself; certainly, this particular analogy is interesting. Nonetheless, analogies are never certain—Israel is no mere crusader state; economic development issues and basic disputes over politics complicate any earlier pattern—and this one, in any event, would take several more generations to work out. In the meantime, the Middle East, unquestionably dynamic in many ways, remains one of the world's trouble spots.

The collapse of the Soviet Union added to the complications facing Middle East politics, with the emergences of the new Muslim nations in nearby central Asia. These nations had their own problems: what kind of political system to establish, how to treat minorities like Armenian Christians in their region, and how to plan economic development in an area long used by Russia as a raw-materials center. They also had a new opportunity to reach out to their Muslim brethren. Iranian fundamentalists hoped to guide them back to their version of Islam. Diplomats from more secular Turkey tried to persuade them of the virtues of top-down reform. Questions about the eventual fate of Islam became no easier to answer, but gained even greater importance.

SUGGESTED WEBSITES

On Nasser and Egypt during the cold war, see *http://www.arab.net/egypt/history/et_nasser.html*; on Islamic religious reactions and the works of Hasan al-Banna of the Muslim Brotherhood, see *http://www.prelude.co.uk/mb/banna/message.htm*.

SUGGESTED READINGS

Several valuable sources are available on the Middle East in this period. See David Ben-Gurion, *Israel: Years of Challenge* (1963), and I. Khomeini, *Practical Laws of Islam* (1983) and *Islam and Revolution: Writings and Declarations of Iman Khomeini*, Hamid Alger, tr. (1981). Mahmud Makal, *Village in Anatolia* (1951), is an exceptionally interesting account of the tension between a modernizing Turkish schoolteacher and the environment and response in his village.

A useful overall survey is G. Lenczowski, *The Middle East and World Affairs,* 4th ed. (1980); see also Hain Faris, *Arab Nationalism* (1986), and Juan Coley, ed., *Comparing Muslim Societies* (1992). On specific national and diplomatic topics, J. C. Hurewitz, *A Diplomatic History of the Near and Middle East* (1956); W. Lacqueur, *Communism and Nationalism in the Middle East* (1956); N. Safran, *The United States and Israel* (1963); W. Lacqueur, *A History of Zionism* (1972); R. Cottam, *Nationalism in Iran,* rev. ed. (1979); K. Wheelock, *Nasser's New Egypt* (1960); E. B. Childers, *The Road to Suez* (1963); and Z. N. Zeine, *The Struggle for Arab Independence* (1960), are all useful works. See also E. Boserup, *Women's Role in Economic Development* (1974), which covers a vital aspect of Middle Eastern development (and also the patterns in other non-Western areas), although with a controversial theoretical framework. For information on the individual Muslim states, see Ira M. Lapidus, *A History of Islamic Societies* (1988). On fundamentalism, *http://abcnew.go.com/sections/world/islam/islam.html*.

Latin America in the Twentieth Century

FOCAL POINTS

Many Americans regard Latin America as a highly traditional area. In fact, the twentieth century resulted in a number of rapid economic and political changes worldwide, although Latin America retained a great deal of its distinctive cultural identity. Compared to 1900, Latin America in the 1990s was strikingly democratic: When and why did this political trend develop, and what political themes preceded the move toward democracy? Government responses to the depression of the 1930s form a particularly important, predemocratic turning point. Without becoming fully industrial, major regions of Latin America improved their position in the world economy. What are the main indications of economic change? How has Latin America balanced extremely rapid urbanization with some relatively stable family patterns? Has Latin American culture shifted as rapidly as the economic and political structure of the civilization?

THE LEADING THEMES

After 1900, Latin America maintained many of the characteristics it had developed during the nineteenth century. This society did not have to contend with the problems of new nationhood that preoccupied so many other parts of the world. Great-power intervention remained a concern, particularly because of the economic and military outreach of the United States in the Caribbean and Central America. Responding to North American influence was not a novel issue, however, although it took on some new twists, especially after World War II. Latin America also remained free from major warfare except for the 1932–1935 Chaco War between Bolivia and Paraguay. Nationalist rivalries existed and led to some conflict, but the region was far more peaceful, in terms of formal diplomacy, than most of its counterparts elsewhere in the world. There were no regional arms races, and military arsenals, although they expanded after World War II, were modest for the most part. Major internal violence was generally directed against peasant protesters and Indian minorities, as landowners and caudillos, or military dictators, sought to maintain their power.

Nonetheless, after 1900 there were new themes and strains in Latin American society. The revolution in Mexico, early in the twentieth century, reflected some of the same tensions that plagued China and Russia during the same period, although the revolution yielded a distinctive result. Latin American politics were redefined by

CHAPTER 31: *Latin America in the Twentieth Century*   **627**

the growing role of central states, beginning in the 1930s. Popular unrest in Latin America rivaled that of other peasant societies, although it did not always lead to significant political reform until the early 1980s, when a new democratic trend gained ground. The twentieth century, in sum, saw important new political contests and governmental forms.

A second area of change focused on economic problems. Issues of economic development inevitably assumed a new urgency, as growing numbers of Latin American governments, both democracies and caudillo-led authoritarian regimes, sought a more active economic role. Moreover, rising levels of population brought Latin America new social problems as the region became one of the most rapidly growing areas of the world. A number of societies further developed significant industrial sectors, undoing the economic weakness that had long characterized Latin America's place in the international economy in the past. Economic inequality, between a growing middle class and impoverished urban and rural groups, was considerable by world standards. New problems, but also new approaches, thus described economic patterns during this period.

Finally, the Latin nations continued to develop their distinctive cultural amalgam, blending styles generated in the West with a variety of local patterns. Indeed, the twentieth century proved to be a rich period in Latin American culture, with major innovations in painting, architecture, and literature. Even as economic and political tensions garnered attention, the cultural and religious creativity of the region suggests a civilization still actively expanding its range.

LATIN AMERICA IN TWENTIETH-CENTURY WORLD HISTORY

Latin America may sometimes seem a society apart. It did not participate significantly in the world wars, although the cold war had significant impact in the region. Nevertheless, international themes were vital. Industrial development coexisted alongside the older tradition of economic dependency. Most countries continued to depend, at least in part, on cheap exports produced by low-paid workers. Even the drug trade fits into the patterns of Latin American dependency in certain key respects.

Older racial issues had left their own particular legacy. Slavery was gone and explicit racism was less pervasive than in the United States. African-inspired cultural and religious movements gained wide audiences. But, the color of one's skin nonetheless counted. In societies like Brazil, with large black minorities, economic inequalities increased on racial lines.

Population movement was another important theme. Latin America and the Caribbean sent growing numbers of emigrants to the United States and Western Europe.

Cultural influences, finally, interacted in two ways. Latin America continued to import cultural forms, including different versions of Christianity. However, popular music, dances, and costumes from the area also became part of international culture, providing important variety. Latin American interaction with the wider world was thus vitally important.

Latin America Today

CANADA

UNITED STATES
OF AMERICA

ATLANTIC
OCEAN

Gulf of Mexico

MEXICO

Mexico
City

Havana

Nassau
BAHAMAS
HAITI (1804)
CUBA (1898)
DOMINICAN REP. (1844)
Santo Domingo
San PUERTO RICO (U.S.)
Juan
JAMAICA
(1962)
Port-au-
Prince
CARIBBEAN SEA
Port of Spain
BARBADOS (1967)
TRINIDAD & TOBAGO (1962)
GUYANA (1966)

PACIFIC
OCEAN

CENTRAL AMERICA
See Inset Below

Caracas
Georgetown
Paramaribo
VENEZUELA
(1811)
Cayenne
FRENCH GUIANA

Bogotá
COLOMBIA
(1821)
SURINAM
(1975)

Equator

GALÁPAGOS IS.
(Ecuador)

Quito
ECUADOR (1822)

Amazon R.

PERU
(1821)

BRAZIL
(1822)

Lima

Brazilia

| 0 | 1000 | 2000 |

MILES

BOLIVIA
(1825)
La Paz
Sucre

PARAGUAY
(1811)

Rio de Janeiro

CENTRAL AMERICA

JAMAICA
(1962)

GUATEMALA
(1821)
Belmopan
BELIZE (1981)

Kingston

CHILE
(1818)

Asunción

Guatemala

HONDURAS (1821)
Tegucigalpa

CARIBBEAN SEA

Santiago

Buenos Aires
Montevideo
URUGUAY (1828)

La Plata R.

Salvador
EL SALVADOR
(1821)
NICARAGUA
(1821)
Managua

ARGENTINA
(1816)

San Jose

*Panama
Canal*

COSTA RICA
(1821)
Panama

PACIFIC
OCEAN

FALKLAND IS.
(Br.)

PANAMA
(1903)

CAPE HORN

Dates indicate year of independence

PATTERNS OF LATIN AMERICAN HISTORY: THE MEXICAN REVOLUTION, 1910–1920s

Revolution in Mexico, from 1910–1917, was the great event of the early twentieth century in Latin America, although it directly affected only one major nation. The Mexican conflict articulated some of the same peasant grievances that simultaneously surfaced in Russia, as the peasantry was caught in the pressures of an expanding market agriculture while still lacking full access to the land. Discontented intellectuals also played a role, attacking a political regime seen as corrupt and inefficient—although in the Mexican case, the regime lacked the deep historical roots of the Russian or Chinese empires. Resentment against foreign economic influence, visible in China and Russia, played an even more obvious part in Mexico. And although the Mexican revolution produced no single leader of the stature of Lenin or Sun Yat-sen, it had its share of dramatic figures and, at least in a strictly political sense, proved more successful than its Chinese counterpart during the same period of time.

The specific roots of the Mexican revolution dated back to 1900, when a small group of intellectuals began to agitate against the authoritarian and corrupt regime of General Porfirio Díaz. The agitators sought democracy, a more liberal economic policy, and new restrictions on the church; the movement soon broadened to include social issues of concern to urban workers and the peasantry. Landless rural laborers, receiving low wages for work on land that had once been theirs but under Díaz had been seized by a small landlord class, were particularly restless. Their resentment focused on foreign owners; economic nationalism, or a desire to return control of economic life to Mexican hands against outsiders, especially U.S. investors, formed an important part of the revolutionary movement. Peasant leaders included Emiliano Zapata, whose motto was "Land and Liberty" and who saw revolution as the uprising of rural and urban workers against capitalist owners of all sorts. Bandit leaders were also active in some rural regions. Pancho Villa established something of a Robin Hood reputation, robbing the rich and befriending the poor. Revolution, in sum, drew on diverse groups with varied goals—as successful revolutions must always do.

Fighting broke out late in 1910. At first a moderate leader, Francisco Madero, came to the fore, arranging for a new presidential election after Díaz escaped the country. Madero thought too strictly in terms of political reform to satisfy the working class and peasant leaders, however, and the revolution soon escaped his control. Zapata, in particular, organized new revolts, which in turn terrified business interests, including many Americans; with U.S. backing, a military leader replaced Madero, executing him and many other rebel leaders. Revolutionary forces continued to operate, however, and in the south Zapata established a regional government of his own. In 1916, a change in U.S. policy lent support to a more moderate leader, Venustiano Carranza, who seized power in that same year. Carranza began to solidify key revolutionary gains. A new constitution, in 1917, proclaimed Mexican ownership of all mineral rights, thus reducing the role of foreign investment; land ownership was reserved for Mexicans, and many large estates were broken up, to the benefit of mestizo and Indian peasants. The power of the Catholic Church, which had supported Díaz and then the repressive regime that attacked Madero, was also restricted.

Carranza's reform goals were limited in practice, however. He showed little interest in a liberal political government, preferring to hold power directly; he did not, in fact, carry land reform too far. In 1920, revolutionaries pressed for new leadership; under the presidency of Álvaro Obregón, the long period of disorder drew to a close, and the results of revolution took clearer shape. Obregón continued the land redistribution in the south that Zapata had initiated; Pancho Villa and his bandit forces were bought off by the gift of a cattle ranch. Obregón moved slowly with further changes, however, lest conservative opposition overturn the new regime. Fearing U.S. hostility, he even allowed existing foreign owners to retain their holdings. Instead of a full attack on the social system, comparable to that in the new Soviet Union, Obregón preferred to concentrate on selective reforms that would encourage economic development. He advanced a widespread system of primary education that taught Spanish, and Mexican nationalism, to many Indians for the first time. The government worked actively on public-health measures and also expanded cultivable lands through irrigation. However, the regime did not try to seize control of the urban economy from business groups, nor did it unseat the entire landlord class. And although the Catholic Church found its political influence reduced, there was no effort to uproot it. Revolution in Mexico, in social terms, meant change but not upheaval.

Politically, the revolution during the 1920s ended the nation's long history of instability, creating a system that differed from both liberal democracy and caudillismo. A single political party, the PNR (National Revolutionary Party), dominated political life, coopting opposition leaders and vigorously repressing dissent. Presidents, who were selected from within the party and thus faced election with an assurance of victory, wielded huge power; some grew rich on public funds, much as old-style caudillos had done. Nonetheless, the new system prevented any one person from ruling the country permanently, for the presidency had to change hands every 6 years, and so the worst excesses of caudillismo were avoided. Furthermore, the PNR did withstand the process of regular elections and thus remained responsive to many wider concerns. At times, its rhetoric and slogans, which boasted of worker and peasant rights, outstripped its achievements. But, there was no question that the power of the traditional ruling classes was now limited by the PNR's desire to retain popular loyalty, or that foreign influence in Mexican affairs had been dramatically reduced. The regime's successful balance between forces old and new was reflected in its durability, amid only occasional, usually minor, political attacks. Into the mid–1990s, as the former PNR, now renamed the PRI, began to allow freer elections, Mexico has known considerably more political stability and considerably more independence in policy than many other Latin American nations—particularly those close to the orbit of the United States.

PATTERNS OF LATIN AMERICAN HISTORY SINCE THE 1920s

Unlike many revolutions, Mexico's had little spillover to other areas. For one thing, its sometimes chaotic course reduced its appeal. Nor did the revolution produce a single doctrine, like Marxism, capable of rousing support elsewhere. U.S. opposition to political radicalism also helped limit the revolution's impact in Central America.

Furthermore, although the revolution generated important reforms and encouraged a vigorous cultural movement, it did not propel Mexican economic development to new heights, nor did it lead to a full industrial revolution, again in contrast to the Soviet regime in Russia. Its social achievements were not great enough to draw discontented peasants elsewhere. For this reason also, the Mexican revolution failed to usher in a new period in Latin American history as a whole.

EFFECTS OF THE DEPRESSION: 1930–1950S

The worldwide economic depression of the 1930s had widespread, catastrophic effects on Latin America, which in turn triggered a new round of political turmoil. The value of Latin American exports decreased by a full two-thirds; the economy had depended on selling agricultural goods and minerals to the industrial nations of the West, which now simply could not afford to buy them. As unsold goods piled up in warehouses, poverty increased. No sweeping revolutionary movement resulted, although popular rioting broke out in many areas. But, the results of the depression encouraged the nation to press for fuller economic independence and to use government power to gain greater economic control. Various kinds of political regimes evinced this new, nationalistic concern.

The despair caused by the depression did encourage Marxist movements in several countries, including Chile and Brazil, but these were generally kept in check by firm military rule. A revolutionary movement in Peru produced a doctrine combining socialism, fierce anti-Americanism, and a stress on Indian cultural values; although it promoted agitation, it did not seize power.

The tide of economic nationalism proved more successful. Unequal land distribution, illiteracy, and poor production methods spurred a number of governments to take remedial action. Many of the regimes proved willing to run some industries directly, and most saw the need to regulate foreign investment and require foreign firms to employ Latin American managers. Most important, state-sponsored programs of import substitution increased the size of the industrial sector.

A series of populist leaders came to the fore in many countries, building multi-class alliances, including urban workers (whose importance was obviously growing).

In Mexico, a spirit of reform was rekindled by the election of Lázaro Cárdenas as president in 1934. Cárdenas seized foreign oil companies, establishing a state corporation, Pemex, to manage the industry. A series of land reforms broke up additional estates. Education spread and with it an effort to integrate Indian culture more fully into national life. A state bank was organized to encourage industry; as a result, Mexican production increased more rapidly than that of any other Latin American country from 1940–1960, although immense poverty persisted.

In Brazil, weak political leadership and deteriorating economic conditions led to a military revolt, headed by Getúlio Vargas, which produced a reasonably mild caudillo-style dictatorship that lasted from 1930–1945. Vargas abolished elections and parliament, while regulating the press and operating a secret police that kept the opposition divided. Deeply committed to economic modernization, Vargas hoped to free Brazil from its dependence on coffee exports. Under his administration, the state constructed important steel mills, and the nation began to produce most of the industrial goods it required. The Amazon basin was opened to agricultural development. Cities expanded, their centers graced by modern office buildings and apartment houses. Brazil remained a largely agricultural nation, but one capable of considerable economic growth.

The government of Chile responded to the effects of the depression without dismantling its liberal, parliamentary system. A state-run development corporation was established during the 1930s to provide funds and planning for industrial projects.

Other parts of Latin America reacted less forcefully to the economic and political stress of the 1930s. Poverty and static social and economic conditions were particularly apparent in the Andes nations of Peru, Bolivia, and Ecuador, with their large Indian populations. Here, as in a number of other countries, army-backed caudillos often ruled without great vision beyond the maintenance of power, amid recurrent rural unrest and frequent changes of regime.

Argentina was governed during the 1930s by a military and land-holding elite. Only in 1943 did real change take place under the populist authoritarian Juan Perón (elected president in 1946). Even more than Brazil's Vargas, Perón appealed to the masses with a policy of benefit programs. His government crushed free trade unions

Mass demonstration for Perón in Buenos Aires, with a heroic statue.

and opposition parties, while directing the main branches of the economy. Foreign-owned companies were bought out, and the power of former landholders was diminished by state controls over the price of their goods. Perón promoted the general thrust of economic nationalism, but with a populist twist—an effort at frenzied mass appeal that was suggestive of European fascism. The expense of Perón's massive welfare programs limited Argentina's real economic growth, even as popular loyalty to Perón remained high. A military coup in 1955 displaced the Argentine strongman, with an attempt to restore parliamentary democracy. But worried by the continued strength of Perónism and eager to ensure stability, the military took political control in 1966 and again in 1976, each time with vigorous police repression of opposition political forces.

REVOLUTION AND RESPONSE: 1950s–1990s

Despite important variations in political forms and economic development, by the late 1950s, there was considerable optimism about Latin America's prospects. Leading countries, including Mexico, post-Vargas Brazil, and post-Perón Argentina, were firmly bent on economic development, some social reform, and some degree of political freedom, if not usually through a full-fledged, multiparty system. Despite Marxist currents, radical political efforts had little appeal. U.S. opposition to anything that smacked of communism combined with the strength of conservative forces. A reform-minded regime in the Central American nation of Guatemala was unseated with U.S. aid in 1954, as the giant to the north briefly resumed the tradition of intervention of a half-century before. Nevertheless, the United States did not consistently oppose the nationalist policies that had emerged since the 1930s. A major social revolution in Bolivia in 1952–1953 produced significant agrarian reform. Although U.S. business interests exercised great power in many countries, Washington also welcomed the economic growth of nations like Brazil and Mexico despite the fact that considerable planning and investment on their part were involved. "Good neighbor" policies initiated during the 1930s, during Franklin Roosevelt's administration, took some of the rougher edges off U.S.–Latin American relations, although a profound disparity in power remained and much of the good neighbor rhetoric was purely cosmetic.

Hopes for a new level of stability were challenged by the revolution in Cuba. Long a U.S. protectorate, Cuba had suffered from weak political institutions. A strongman leader, Fulgencio Batista, had ruled since 1933, despite the great corruption of his regime. A pronounced gulf divided a rich minority from the impoverished masses, as in many Latin American nations, and although the Cuban economy was relatively prosperous, it depended dangerously on sugar exports to the United States. During the 1950s, a guerrilla rebellion arose against the Batista regime, headed by a magnetic leader, Fidel Castro. Castro's long-term political goals were unclear, but his attack on corruption and foreign influence, and his plea for land reform, constituted an important new revolutionary current, blending peasant grievances with explicit political concerns. Military victory came in 1959–1960. The new regime frightened away or expelled wealthy Cubans, while deteriorating relations with the United States followed from, and also encouraged, the increasingly communist orientation of the Castro government. The Cuban Communist Party, initially hesitant to do so, soon came to embrace Castro fully. A U.S. effort in 1961 to topple Castro failed miserably, leaving the new regime free to build a society along modified Soviet lines. State ownership combined with worker committees in factories, while the great sugar estates were confiscated and turned into collective farms. The new regime promoted greater racial equality. The result was, in many ways, a more complete revolution than had occurred in Mexico—and it also led, thanks to Castro's policies and rhetoric but also to U.S. response, to the development of cold war tensions within Latin American politics. Revolution in Cuba came to mean a close alliance with the Soviet Union, and a leadership cult evolved around the strong and persuasive personality of Castro.

The Cuban revolution did not have the unsettling effects on the rest of Latin America that its supporters had hoped for or its opponents had feared. Many Latin American governments maintained good relations with the new regime, rather pleased at Cuba's success in defying the North American giant but not eager to install a communist system in their own nations. U.S. policy shifted, in reaction to its failure to dislodge Castro, toward more significant economic aid to other Latin American countries, although momentum in this effort dwindled by the 1970s. A radical regime arose in Peru in 1968, but the reform results were meager, and military coups soon killed off most of the civilian revolutionaries. Much later, in 1979, a radical uprising in Nicaragua, with assistance from Cuba, unseated a U.S.-backed dictator. The new regime did promote land reform, seizing great estates (many of them owned by U.S. concerns), and enacted education and public-health measures. It also encouraged guerrilla movements in other Central American nations, notably El Salvador. During the early 1980s, the United States provided military aid and encouraged its own guerrilla activity in defense of more conservative regimes in the region. By the 1990s, peace had been largely restored as the regime sponsored, and lost, a democratic election.

The establishment of a communist system in Cuba encouraged a new round of authoritarianism in some other countries, as military and civilian leaders sought the fullest possible protection against any new subversion. Populist regimes also seemed to have failed by the 1960s in places like Argentina, whereas economic development increased internal disputes, often pitting workers against the middle class and elites. The resulting series of military regimes, although they did not affect every country in the 1960s, became increasingly common. Fear of communism encouraged the military regimes of Argentina, beginning in 1966. In 1970 in Chile, a Marxist-led coalition of communists, socialists, and radicals won a free election. No carbon copy of Castroism, the new regime proceeded to enact a number of key reforms, including nationalization of U.S.-owned copper mines and division of the great landed estates. This, in turn, provoked reaction from the middle and upper classes, and the conservative resurgence won U.S. support. A military coup toppled the reformist government, amid considerable bloodshed, and a strongly authoritarian dictatorship was installed that lasted into the late 1980s.

The spread of democratic systems began to overtake the surge of conservative military dictatorships in the 1980s, starting with the new Argentine regime of 1982. At first, the trend seemed merely a renewal of the oscillations long characteristic of Latin American politics. Free elections occurred in Brazil in 1984. A newly elected leader in Uruguay noted that "there are winds that blow in favor, winds that blow against. It is evident in this era the winds are favorable to democracy." Chile's authoritarian ruler yielded to democracy. Mexico retained one-party dominance, but contested elections became more common and opposition groups controlled some state governments; elections in 1997 were freer than at any point since the revolution. Paraguay, one of the classic authoritarian states, adopted democracy in 1993. At least for the moment, Latin American leaders decided that democracy spared societies the painful costs of repression and encouraged economic development. The surge resembled the rise of liberalism in the late nineteenth century, but it was not only democratic but less authoritarian. Amid changes in regimes and oscillations in the form of governments, Latin American political values unquestionably changed during the twentieth century, even before the democratic surge. More groups gained political consciousness. In Mexico and many of the Andes nations, Indians obtained new rights and political involvement. Women were given the right to vote for the first time in many countries—in Mexico, this occurred in 1954. By the 1990s, a significant minority of women served as elected officials in that country. The extension of education and the vote to property-less males was another important, although not necessarily continuous, tide in countries like Brazil.

Still more significant was the growing commitment of Latin American governments to programs of economic development, although there had been some precedents for this trend in the nineteenth century. By the 1950s, few caudillos remained who sought only personal power and riches for themselves and their followers. Cuba's Batista was one such leader; so was the Nicaraguan head of state deposed by a revolution in 1979. Most authoritarian leaders, like Perón or Vargas, now adopted a new stance, extending the functions of government in important new directions, whereas the same held true for the Mexican regime and expanding democratic systems at the end of the twentieth century.

The new-style authoritarian leaders might be just as brutal toward political opponents as their more traditional predecessors had been, but they were increasingly likely to sponsor economic planning, to encourage new technologies, and to regulate foreign investment in order to achieve greater economic nationalism. In most cases, their interest in development led to some concern for social reform, as authoritarian as well as liberal leaders moved to dismantle at least some of the vast landed estates and to provide some welfare protection for urban workers. Except for Cuba, no government sponsored revolutionary social reform during the twentieth century. However, with rare exceptions, governments did assume new functions, including the extension of education and public-health measures and the development of certain economic sectors. Here was a significant, evolutionary transformation of the Latin American political style under various constitutional arrangements. Authoritarian rulers might now appeal directly to popular support and engage in vigorous reforms unsettling to conservative interests.

The democratic current in the 1980s emphasized greater free enterprise. Governments sold off many state-run businesses, as the international emphasis on freer trade and capitalism strongly affected Latin America. Mexico, for example, reduced the government's role in the economy as part of its participation in the North American Free Trade Agreement (NAFTA) with the United States and Canada. Government

Urbanization: Belo Horizante, Brazil, 1967. Then only 70 years old, the city had over a million inhabitants.

activities remained extensive and in some areas, such as environmental regulation, they increased somewhat. Latin America did not return to the weak government structures that had predated the 1930s.

Partly because of more vigorous efforts on the part of government, leading Latin American nations also managed to become increasingly independent from outside influence during the twentieth century. The Mexican revolution did not eliminate foreign economic activity, but it unquestionably reduced U.S. ability to determine key political or diplomatic policies. The nationalization of some crucial foreign enterprises, inaugurated by Mexico's control of its oil industry, was embraced by diverse governments in several Latin American countries. In the Caribbean islands, many former colonies gained political freedom after the 1950s, leading to a number of new island nations formed from previously British and Dutch holdings. In 2000, the United States finally surrendered control of the Panama Canal to the nation of

Panama—another sign of the waning of the imperialism that had surged around 1900.

At the same time, Latin American independence was far from complete—again, a sign of continuity amid change. Cuba exchanged U.S. domination for Soviet influence in its economy and diplomacy. France, The Netherlands, and the United States still maintained some outright colonies, although they upgraded their status, as in the case of the Commonwealth of Puerto Rico. Britain maintained control of the Falkland Islands claimed by Argentina and rather easily vanquished a military uprising there in 1982. The ability of the United States to intervene in Central America, reasserted in the 1980s, remained an important factor, although it was not clear that such intervention could be as straightforward, or as successful, as in the past. Most important, the continued economic power of the United States and Western Europe, in the still dependent economies of Latin America, seriously qualified the general tendency toward greater national freedom and self-assertion.

LATIN AMERICAN CULTURE

In culture, even more clearly than in politics, the close interaction with the West left a definite mark, as Latin Americans participated vigorously in Western-initiated artistic developments of the twentieth century. However, this was no simple extension of Western culture either, for a new artistic and literary vigor resulted in a growing emphasis on distinctive styles and themes.

Most wealthy Latin Americans shared Western tastes in fashion, furnishings, and art. Throughout the twentieth century, a considerable market existed for Western imports of this sort, and some Latin American artists produced for this market as well. A number of Latin American composers made a mark in symphonic music after 1920, and major cities boasted orchestras performing a wide repertoire of Western-style music. Still more impressive was the region's contribution to modern architecture. Economic and political development encouraged new building in most Latin American cities, as hotels and office complexes sprang up in the sleek styles familiar in the West. Particularly breathtaking was the erection of an entire city, Brasília, constructed in the 1960s as Brazil's new capital; although criticized for its costliness, Brasília became a powerful symbol of modern architectural and urban-planning concepts.

Latin American initiatives in science lagged somewhat, as in the past. Major universities trained their students in science and technology, but the expense of elevating research to a more prominent position, and traditions in a civilization that still placed greater emphasis on the artistic and spiritual aspects of culture limited the overall importance of science in intellectual life, compared to other contemporary civilizations.

In art and literature, Latin America contributed vigorous twentieth-century styles, although with an ongoing link to Western influences. The Mexican revolution spurred innovative developments in painting. Two great muralists, Clemente Orozco and Diego Rivera, created numerous and powerful epics depicting the struggle of the Mexican lower classes from colonial days to the twentieth century. Their forceful human figures and stark colors emphasized the suffering and courage of agricultural

Mural by Diego Rivera. The subject is Mexico's Aztec past.

and factory workers, women as well as men. Their decision to paint wall murals, rather than conventional canvases, was a result of their social commitment to the public good, for their art decorated many public buildings and was not confined to museums or private collections. Both painters achieved international reputations. A number of other artists, from several countries, moved toward less representational styles after World War II, but an interest in the forms and coloration derived from Latin America's Indian and black heritage remained.

Contributions to Latin American literature, although at times constrained by political repression, involved both poetry and the novel. Major writers emerged in Chile, Mexico, Brazil, and Argentina. The Mexican revolution inspired realistic novels that dramatized the plight of Indians and other labor groups. Masterpieces of the Mexican revolutionary period include Mariano Azuela's *Los de abajo* (1916) and Martin Luis Guzmán's *El Aquila y la serpiente* (1928). The rise of Latin American fiction was symbolized by the award of three Nobel prizes for literature after World War II to Latin American writers. Major writers embraced many themes—history and anthropology, foreign domination including U.S. imperialism, and a strong current of fantasy that built on earlier poetic traditions. Both fantasy and stark realism, sometimes combined in the same novel, were intended to convey the special features of the Latin American experience; they represented a balance of subject matter different from twentieth-century European fiction. In addition to the use of Indian themes and a strong social awareness, Latin American literature often addressed problems of

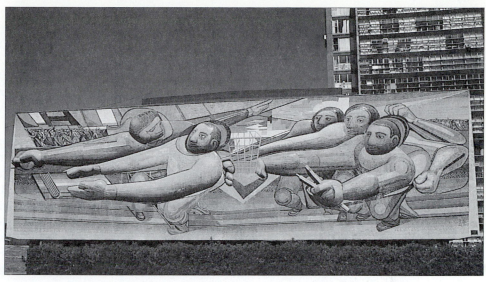

"Mural to Students" by Sequeiros, University of Mexico, Mexico City.

identity—the attempt to define this part of the world's culture amid strong European and North American influences. At the same time, Latin American and Western writers worked in similar styles as well as languages, and they shared the same body of literature and criticism.

A final feature of Latin American culture, both formal and popular, was its dynamic Christianity. Although the political power and wealth of the Catholic Church declined in some countries, such as Mexico, religion remained a much more pervasive force in Latin America than in Europe and North America. In terms of sheer numbers and pious devotion, Latin America indeed became the most significant Christian civilization by the mid–20th century, with 233 million people listed as Catholics—not all, to be sure, fervent believers—by 1985. Nonetheless, Latin American Catholicism was not simply a traditional force. From the 1960s onward, a new generation of priests and theologians was responsible for increasing social commentary, urging Catholic involvement in the cause of social and political reform. Some Catholic leaders aided peasant guerrilla movements, whereas sympathetic bishops pressured governments for improved welfare programs, land reform, and popular political rights. Statements about the church's social responsibility became known as "liberation theology." The new currents within Latin American Catholicism resulted in clashes with some authoritarian governments and also criticism from the papacy, which by the 1980s was not enthusiastic about political activism. Catholic debate formed another important channel for Latin American culture and additional evidence of a new level of intellectual vigor. Catholicism was itself challenged, however, by popular religions that mixed Christian and African elements—particularly in Brazil—and by a surprising current of conversion to fundamentalist Protestantism, creating a vibrant new religious minority. The advance of Protestantism, particularly among poorer groups seeking cultural outlets, was truly striking: by the late 1990s,

30 percent of the Guatemalan population was Protestant, and similar changes had occurred in Brazil. These developments complicated the society's cultural map but confirmed the unusual importance of religion in twentieth-century Latin America.

ECONOMY AND SOCIETY

Latin America experienced rapid social and economic change, particularly after 1950, although important traditions continued from the past. In most countries, the social division between rich and poor remained great; the wealthy minority controlled landed estates in many countries—in some cases, only 4 percent of the population owned 80 percent of the land—and also operated the leading commercial and manufacturing concerns. In many cities, luxurious mansions and life styles juxtaposed with mass squalor. The widespread employment of female domestic servants remained a standard prerogative of upper-class households. Social reform efforts, even in revolutionary Mexico, rarely did more than scratch the surface of such a basic division, although some changes occurred. Regional disparities remained considerable as well. The Andes nations were particularly impoverished. Argentina maintained its position as a significant exporter of grains and meats, but the Argentine economy was often hampered by political problems and a level of government spending that encouraged paralyzing inflation.

Another troubling continuity involved Latin America's inability to free itself from reliance on vulnerable export items. Despite concerted policy attention and some diversification, the civilization continued to depend on imported Western technology, and exports consisted disproportionately of agricultural goods like coffee, sugar, raw materials, and oil, all vulnerable to low and fluctuating prices. Furthermore, most Latin American nations, because of their poor earnings position in the world economy, remained heavily indebted to Western banks. Ambitious development programs often merely increased the debt, which by the 1980s severely burdened both richer and poorer economies within the civilization. Even Cuba, which defied tradition in many ways, proved unable to escape economic dependency, as it relied for its export earnings on sales of sugar to Eastern Europe and million-dollar-a-day Russian aid. The Soviet collapse brought new problems to the island that highlighted its failure to industrialize.

Nonetheless, many areas of Latin America gained new economic strength. Agricultural production improved in many countries, as new techniques, including the innovations of the 1960s, the Green Revolution, were adopted. Tourism expanded, resulting in foreign earnings and influences. Chile dramatically expanded its exports in commercial agriculture, gaining growing prosperity by the 1990s. Manufacturing output advanced, too, and the wealthier Latin American nations began to produce most of the industrial goods they required for normal consumption. Textile and metallurgical industries spread widely, and a few countries, headed by Brazil, began to export basic manufactured goods to other parts of the world, including the United States. Brazil also developed the world's fourth largest computer industry, specializ-

UNDERSTANDING CULTURES

Adapting Consumer Values

The pressure of foreign (mainly West European and U.S.) consumer forms and other societies' responses to them was one of the great cultural issues of the twentieth century and promises to remain one in twenty-first-century world history. Western consumerism stands for the importance of acquisition, secular values, and new products as a measure of personal and national success and modernity. Some groups deeply resist this kind of pressure, like Islamic fundamentalists who promote a religious alternative to consumer culture. Other groups gleefully join in, like the many Japanese who made McDonalds and the Disney theme park near Tokyo instant successes.

Nevertheless, a common response involves embracing a consumer trend while adding a distinctive regional twist. This is, in fact, a common pattern in cultural contact, involving the blending, or syncretism, of an outside model with local elements. But, it is particularly important to grasp this in terms of contemporary consumerism, because otherwise it becomes easy to mistakenly assume that the whole world, except for pockets of resistance, is largely becoming American.

The history of comic books in Mexico provides a specific example of such a pattern. Comic books were imported from the United States to Mexico as early as the 1930s, and they caught on quickly thanks to the prestige of U.S. products and the low levels of average literacy. However, comics were soon modified to meet Mexican standards of beauty and political values. Thus, one series noted: "He was no vulgar bandit, he shared with the poor who live under the lash of vile capitalism"—this was hardly a common theme in the United States at the same time. Macho exploits were touted, but there was also great emphasis on kinship and community ties; in contrast to American warriors, Mexican heroes were not loners. Indeed, they were often pitted against American villains, such as the "Invincible Jack Superman of Indianapolis," and in these imagined conflicts, the gringos lost almost every time. By the late twentieth century, comic books were read far more regularly in Mexico than the United States, precisely because Mexico had changed the medium to make it part of a national culture. Important local ingredients thus blended with the influence of American styles.

ing in less sophisticated computers than those from Japan or the United States, but ones deemed reliable in other less developed, less technologically advanced nations.

To be sure, advancing mechanization still fell short of a full industrial revolution. It did not bring Latin America to the levels of economic development being achieved in the Pacific Rim. The high birthrate, averaging between 2 and 3 percent annually after World War II, limited gains in the standard of living. Catholic hostility toward birth-control measures and the strong traditionalism of many Latin American families contributed to this growth in population, which in many countries literally consumed the gains in food and manufacturing production. One result of population pressure was the extraordinary rate of emigration, both legal and illegal, to the United States. Another result was a low-wage economy that induced many U.S., and some European and Japanese, firms to establish factories in Latin America for inexpensive exports to industrialized areas of the world.

Many Latin American countries, however, did make a turn to greater population control. Mexico, for example, underwent a demographic transition in the 1960s, resulting in markedly smaller families even though population expansion continued on the basis of earlier growth. Furthermore, the manufacturing gains—the evolution toward a more industrial society—engendered measurable improvements in living standards for many people. Brazil's economic growth, at 6 percent per year during some decades, increased both the middle class and urban working class. Many began to participate in new consumerism. By 1990, 22 percent of all Brazilians owned cars, 56 percent had televisions, and 63 percent had refrigerators. These gains, which were echoed in Mexico and elsewhere, surpassed levels in Eastern Europe or the Pacific Rim (apart from Japan). Not yet industrialized, Latin American economies were nevertheless carving out a distinctive position among the major societies of the world.

Both population pressure and industrial gains furthered the rapid urbanization of Latin America from the 1930s onward. Here too, the society held an unusual place, becoming more urban than most of Asia and Africa although less so than the industrialized societies. City growth was itself distinctive, combining new manufacturing with huge conclaves of dire poverty. The rural populations simply could not be accommodated in the countryside, particularly when the land was held in large estates. Cities provided some factory jobs to a privileged segment of the masses; to even more people, they offered some hope of occasional work plus charity or welfare.

In 1925, only 25 percent of Latin America's population was urbanized; by 1975, 60 percent lived in cities—in contrast to a mere 30 percent in China or India. Massive shantytowns arose in Mexico, Brazil, and elsewhere, as a largely unemployed population constructed houses out of cans and boxes. The world's largest city took shape in the Mexican capital, which had 3 million people in 1950 but an overwhelming 9 million by 1970, and 16 million by 1995 with projections of over 20 million by 2001. Excruciating problems of pollution as well as dire poverty resulted from this extraordinary urban development.

Population pressure and urban problems inevitably added to earlier social grievances, notably the unequal distribution of land and the gap between rich and poor, to produce recurrent popular protest. Rural rioting occurred in many countries in the twentieth century, even aside from the major revolutions. Peasant attacks on landlords paralyzed much of Colombia in 1947. Indian peasants formed guerrilla bands that controlled stretches of Bolivia and Peru in the 1970s and 1980s. A rural rebellion erupted in southern Mexico in 1994. Urban strikes and riots dotted the twentieth-century landscape as well. And, violence spilled over into other areas. Mass sports events often featured fights between partisan crowds. In countries like Mexico and Venezuela, murder rates were among the highest in the world.

Urban slums in Caracas, Venezuela. Migrants to the city stake out their unauthorized living spaces.

Nevertheless, there were strengths in Latin American society as well as fearsome tensions. Family structure remained tight, characteristically under male domination. Popular festivals and religious celebrations featured traditional dances and music and provided joyful release to many groups. The ability of Latin Americans to preserve family institutions and cultural forms in the face of rapid population movement to the cities set some limits on the worst confusions of social transformation, although the same traditionalism enforced limitations on the conditions of women under the sway of *machismo* traditions and a strong emphasis on sexuality. Amid problems common to many parts of the world—such as that of underemployment—Latin American popular culture retained a distinctive flavor.

CONCLUSION: TOWARD A GREATER WORLD ROLE?

Latin America has always occupied a somewhat ambiguous place in world history. The civilization first developed as one dependent on the West, a status still not fully shaken off. Although Latin Americans participate fully, if not always influentially, in the world economy, they have generated neither dramatic cultural forms nor catastrophic military upheavals of international impact. Nationalism and literary preoccupation with issues of Latin American identity follow from a sense of being ignored or misunderstood in the wider world. The United States, which continues to play a powerful role in Latin American affairs, stands particularly accused of ignorance and neglect.

However, the trends of Latin American history in the later twentieth century suggest an increase in the civilization's visibility. Latin America constitutes a growing share of the world's population. Its economic advance, although often troubled, places it in the middle rank of developing nations. Its importance in world religious life is on the increase. Some observers would add that the civilization's potential for social upheaval remains unusually great, although the twentieth-century experience has suggested a balance between unrest and conservative continuities. The directions of Latin America's future are at least as unclear as those of other major civilizations. Brazil and a few other leaders may soon make the turn to a self-sustaining industrialization—but hopes of this sort have been dashed before in the past century. Democracy may solidify Latin America, but the civilization's history reminds us that it also may not. In 2000, a new strongman leader in Venezuela and growing guerrilla warfare in Colombia highlighted democracy's fragility. But, the likelihood of growing international impact in the future seems high, as the twentieth century brought new self-consciousness and millions of new people to a civilization increasingly proud of its achievement, if still resentful of its economic dependency.

SUGGESTED WEBSITES

On the art of Diego Rivera, see *http://www.arts-history.mx/museomural.html*; on the Cuban revolution, see *http://www.neravt.com/left/allende.htm*; on revolutionary leaders, see *http://flag.blackened.net/revolt/mexico.html*; and the Cuban Che Guevara, see *http://pbs.org/ newshour/forum/november97/che.html*.

SUGGESTED READINGS

General coverage of twentieth-century Latin America is provided by Tulio Halperin-Donghi, *The Aftermath of Revolution in Latin America* (1973), and R. A. Humphreys, *Tradition and Revolt in Latin America* (1969); see also the Skidmore and Smith volume cited in Chapter 22. On economic dependency, see E. Bradford Burns, *Latin America: A Concise Interpretative History*, 4th ed. (1986). On revolution and other developments in Mexico, John M. Hart, *Revolutionary Mexico* (1987); R. D. Anderson, *Outcasts in Their Own Land: Mexican Industrial Workers, 1906–1911* (1976); and Jan Bazant, *A Concise History of Mexico from Hidalgo to Cardenas, 1805–1940* (1975), are helpful. Other key countries are covered in H. S. Ferns,

Argentina (1969); Robert Potash, *The Army and Politics in Argentina, 1945–1962* (1980); and E. B. Burns, *A History of Brazil* (1970). On the Cuban revolution, consult Hugh Thomas, *Cuba: The Pursuit of Freedom* (1971), and Carmelo Mesa Lago, *Revolutionary Change in Cuba* (1971). For economic patterns, important works include Celso Furtado, *The Economic Development of Latin America* (1970), and N. Sanchez-Albornoz, *The Population of Latin America* (1974); on women, see June Hahner, *Women in Latin American History* (1976). On labor, see Charles Berquist, *Labor in Latin America* (1986).

Sub-Saharan Africa: From Colonies to New Nations

FOCAL POINTS

African history during the twentieth century may be divided fairly neatly into three stages: the rise of nationalism amid ongoing European domination; the struggle for independence; and the particularly demanding issues of new nationhood during the past few decades. It is vitally important to understand the growing economic and cultural hold of colonialism during the first half of the twentieth century: How did the living patterns and beliefs of ordinary Africans change? What new problems did independence result in? What political forms were used to address these problems? Why did Africa's economic position in the world lag behind its political and cultural innovations? Africa was also the scene of cultural changes more diverse and complex than those of any other civilization in the twentieth century.

PATTERNS OF AFRICAN HISTORY IN THE TWENTIETH CENTURY

Africa south of the Sahara had been fully consumed by European imperialism only 20 years before the twentieth century began. For several decades after 1900, when other areas of the world were rousing to new nationalisms, African history continued to be characterized by the operations of the colonial governments and Western Europe's increasing economic impact. However, nationalism took root here as well, and after World War II it gained momentum. The result, occurring only slightly later than in most of Asia, was the independence of a number of new nations. From the 1960s onward, their efforts to establish the institutions and loyalties of nationhood represented the primary focus in the region. Problems of economic development, and in some areas recurrent famines and disease, complicated national politics. And, the continued existence of a powerful, white-dominated South African nation long cast its shadow over the continent.

Even before independence was achieved, and certainly after its first results were taken into account, issues of cultural identity and social and economic transformation played a vital role in the patterns of Africa. Imperialist policies brought fuller contact with the world economy and encouraged some internal economic development along with great dislocation. One result was a marked resemblance to earlier characteristics of Latin America, the other society most fully touched by Western economic dominance and cultural and political influence. African civilization, to be sure, was by no means obliterated to the extent that American Indian cultures had been. Nonetheless, Africa displayed patterns of economic dependency comparable to colonial and nineteenth-century Latin America, including a reliance on vulnerable cash crops and mineral exports; of tensions of new nationhood, including frequent reliance on authoritarian political forms; and even of considerable cultural innovation, the result of both Muslim and Christian missionary efforts that made this civilization, again like Latin America, the scene of great religious fervor and creativity.

Africans, on the other hand, were less closely linked to Western cultural styles than Latin Americans, and they faced more acute problems of defining their identity amid new or outside influences. And, Africa emerged from its brief colonial experience less developed—in terms of city size, literacy levels, amount of manufacturing and commercial agriculture—than any of the other major contemporary civilizations. Generating further change, particularly toward industrialization or a better-rounded economy, and adjusting to twentieth-century trends such as population increase and urbanization, have posed acute challenges for contemporary Africans. Efforts to combine cultural and family traditions with modernization reflect a desire to maintain a distinctive African character and to cushion the impact of new political and economic styles.

EMERGING NATIONALISM

World War I triggered some new currents in colonial Africa. Scattered fighting took place in the German colonies in the south, which were then taken over by the British, with one possession, South West Africa, or what is now called Namibia, administered as part of South Africa. The French used large numbers of loyal African troops in their European campaigns. Discussion of national rights after World War I encouraged a rethinking of the future of the African colonies. European diplomats spoke of their holdings as "a sacred trust of civilization" to help educate peoples "not yet able to stand by themselves under the strenuous conditions of the modern world." This outlook produced new efforts to better the standard of living of the colonial peoples by building local schools, hospitals, libraries, and so on. Belgium, known for its harsh exploitation in the Congo, shifted its policies significantly. Colonial-run police forces tried to prevent tribal warfare, and attention was paid to improving agricultural techniques.

Western imperialism did not change entirely, however. Assumptions of African inferiority continued. Schools reached only a minority of Africans, and they often taught details of European history and culture that made little sense in the African context. Belgian officials in the Congo, for example, insisted that educated Africans learn Flemish as well as French, although the language had little wider applicability, simply because the civilization back home and its language were regarded as the pinnacle of culture. Many schools were run by missionaries, including large numbers from the United States, who attacked local religious traditions in the name of Christianity; a Christian minority, both Catholic and Protestant, did develop in most colonies as a result. Most colonial governments allowed Africans to enter only the lower levels of the bureaucracy and military. French policy encouraged an African elite to enroll in schools in France and assimilate into French culture, but there was

African mission school run by Europeans. Probably from the Belgian Congo, 1920s.

little real concern for the African masses. Britain paid attention to a larger number, but reserved the upper ranks of administration for British officials. Few African soldiers could rise above the rank of sergeant. Thus, twentieth-century imperialism, although it involved new expenditures for the colonies—Britain may have spent more in Africa during the 1920s and 1930s than it earned there—remained very much an imposition from the outside.

Imperialism also resulted in continued pressure for economic change. In largely British-ruled eastern Africa, where population levels were low and prior political forms relatively loose, a wealthy minority of white colonists established estates on the rich agricultural lands of the plateaus, using African labor; other Africans preserved a hunting-and-gathering existence or worked as farmers on the less fertile lands. In western Africa, with more of its own commercial experience, African business entrepreneurs along with Europeans introduced cash crops, like peanuts and cocoa, for sale on the world market. Railroads and shipping lines also opened further access to raw materials. Belgium drew rubber, copper, and vital minerals from the Congo; British Rhodesia exported copper; South Africa mined gold and diamonds. Mining operations were owned and operated by Europeans, or by white South Africans, using poorly paid gangs of African labor. Thus, the ties of Africa to the world economy became more extensive, but largely on terms that reaped profits for Europeans.

The impact of this burgeoning economic activity on Africans was mixed. Some businessmen drew substantial profits while becoming accustomed to the ways of international commerce. In the boom years of the 1920s, rich business leaders in British West Africa acquired an extravagant life style: "Motor cars were purchased right and left, champagne flowed freely, and expensive cigars scented the air." This elite also participated in local elections, for governing bodies that had a limited voice over such issues as roads and public health. A far larger group of Africans were drawn into the emerging cities and the mining centers as laborers. Many traditions and family ties were disrupted by the move to the cities, particularly because women were often left behind. A tension began to develop, between older customs and the attractions of a partially Westernized urban life, that would influence African culture from this point onward. Finally, large numbers of Africans remained generally isolated from the economic transformation, in scattered agricultural or hunting settlements rarely reached by Europeans.

In South Africa, a special pattern of European–African relations continued to develop. Here, white settlers, some of English origin but primarily Afrikaners of Dutch extraction, were more numerous than in any other African region. Clashes between the English and the patriotic Boers, the name given to the Dutch settlers, intensified the friction. The Afrikaners increasingly supported the Nationalist political party, which talked of leaving the British Empire and vowed to keep black Africans, the majority, in a subordinate place. The party slogan was "South Africa: A White Man's Land." During the 1920s, the Nationalists sponsored the Color Bar bill to prevent blacks from holding skilled jobs. In 1936, blacks were excluded from voting in elections. White South Africans were gradually creating two separate societies, preventing any contact between whites and blacks save that between employer and unskilled laborer.

Nowhere, of course, did Africans have extensive political rights. What was unusual in South Africa is that representative institutions did exist but were reserved mainly for whites. In other colonies, voting rights, if any, were limited to an urban minority of Africans, and the bodies they elected had few powers and were dominated by whites.

African bitterness toward white rule broke out periodically. To promote black rights, a group ultimately named the African National Congress formed in South Africa as early as 1912. In 1921 in the Congo, a carpenter named Simon Kimbangu formed a religious movement with impressive rituals and revolutionary political doctrines, drawn in part from the Bible. His movement aroused considerable mass support until Kimbangu was arrested and executed. In Kenya a government clerk, Harry Thuku, organized the East Africa Native Association to protest a reduction in wages; his arrest, in 1922, on charges of sedition, led to a wave of riots.

Outright African nationalism developed only gradually. The experiences of the African elite, some trained at European universities, brought growing awareness of nationalist ideas. The Pan-African Congress met in Paris in 1919 to press for national independence, and similar meetings occurred periodically through 1945. Pan-African nationalism, bent on not only freedom from European control but also a glorification of the strengths and traditions of Africa and the hope for a new, unprecedented African unity, received powerful stimulus from the writings and political leadership of U.S. and West Indian black leaders in the 1920s and 1930s. Figures like the American Marcus Garvey, who sought new links with Africa as part of the black struggle for freedom in the United States, helped African nationalists, particularly in the British colonies, articulate their own strivings. However, the limits to Western-style education in Africa meant that nationalist ideas spread slowly. To many Africans, the concept of nationhood was an abstraction, compared to the known loyalties of the tribe and extended family. Even more than in the Middle East after 1918, most African colonies were arbitrary units, embracing many tribes and language groups with no precedent in Africa's earlier political history. Loyalty to these nations thus came hard. Nationalist leaders themselves debated inconclusively about whether to pursue a larger African unity, tribal units, or nation–states based essentially on colonial boundaries. This was a period of genesis for African nationalism, not, before 1945, a full flowering. Many individual leaders who would emerge after World War II developed their nationalist convictions during this period, however. For example, Jomo Kenyatta, educated at the London School of Economics and later in Moscow, began to write of the strengths of African traditions as opposed to Western materialism and corruption. Kenyatta would later lead the nationalist movement in Kenya and become its first president. Leopold Senghor, a Catholic native of Senegal who lived in Paris, learned of the cultural traditions of Africa and also admired the achievements of blacks from the United States and West Indies. He began to write of the beauties of *négritude,* or blackness, seen as a source of racial pride and confidence in black creativity, particularly within the arts.

The depression hit Africa hard. The region's growing dependence on the sale of low-price items like cocoa beans to the West, and on Western companies that directly organized raw-materials production was vividly highlighted. Loss of jobs and wages increased unrest and spurred the nationalist movement as strikes and riots attacked the power and greed of European and U.S. companies.

World War II heightened nationalism still further. A number of black leaders in French colonies supported the resistance movement against Nazi control of France. They felt real loyalty to France, but expected growing political rights in return. The rise of anticolonial movements in other parts of the world and the retreat of once-proud empires in Asia served as an obvious inspiration in Africa. For their part, European administrations recognized the need to work harder for social and economic improvements in Africa. France thus poured more money into its African colonies between 1947 and 1957 than it had done in the whole previous half-century. British leaders began to talk of ultimate self-government, suggesting that the role of the mother country was to now train its colonies in nationhood. Nonetheless, many Europeans seemed to be in no hurry to admit that Africans were ready to take over their own government. Their belief in African inferiority and a desire to hold fast to this one vestige of imperialism, while the rest of the empire was crumbling, posed obvious barriers. In many colonies, particularly in British East Africa, the demands of the influential white-settler minority also slowed change: How could this group be protected if colonialism came to an end?

European hesitation was met by a new generation of nationalist leaders, most of them trained in European or North American universities; many had experience in trade unions or local governments. They thought in terms of independent nations built on the basis of existing colonies: Ideas of African unity or a return to tribal organization now faded. The new leaders mounted mass rallies of urban Africans. Often arrested, they used imprisonment to dramatize their cause. Many also battled traditional African leaders, including the tribal chiefs, to whom the concept of nationalism remained foreign. Direct raids on European settlers, as in Kenya, added to the pressure from yet another source, as villagers and hunters protested the white control of the best lands.

THE TRANSFORMATION TO INDEPENDENCE

Between 1957 and the mid–1970s, the colonial era drew to a close. The country named Ghana arose first, based on Britain's western Gold Coast colony; Kwame Nkrumah was its nationalist leader. A schoolteacher, he had studied for a decade in the United States, where he was deeply influenced by both European socialism and American black nationalists who called for a rebellion against white domination. Returning to the Gold Coast in 1945, Nkrumah built a mass political movement among urban elements and commercial cocoa farmers with the slogan "Self-Government Now." Many of his followers saw independence as a key to a brighter future across the board, in which economic as well as political problems would be swept away by the searchlight of freedom. Nkrumah organized a series of riots and strikes, which landed him in jail; he dominated local elections from 1951 onward. Britain conceded the inevitable, and Ghana, drawing its name although not its boundaries from the historic kingdom, won its freedom in 1957.

Other British colonies in West Africa gained independence soon after. France sought to prevent a complete rift within its colonies, after its bitter experiences in Indochina and then Algeria, by granting commonwealth status to its 13 sub-Saharan holdings in 1958. African leaders deeply loyal to France supported this move, although Sékou Touré, a radical leader in the colony of Guinea, insisted on full independence immediately. The other nations gained national status in the early 1960s, but most retained close ties to France. Belgium lost the Congo in a series of riots in 1959—one of the only cases outside southern Africa where the granting of independence did not come peacefully. Britain's East African colonies also gained national freedom, despite the agitation of white settlers. Only in Southern Rhodesia did a major delay in independence arise, as the white minority broke away from Britain in 1965 and held out for over a decade against a guerrilla war conducted by black

Native Nigerians rehearse a traditional dance to prepare for independence celebrations, 1960.

nationalists, and against substantial diplomatic pressure from Britain and the United States. Here too independence triumphed, through the creation of a black-run government with assurances of white minority representation; in 1980, the new nation shook off its colonial name and took on another historic name—Zimbabwe. Finally, also in the 1970s, a change in the political regime of Portugal, along with significant guerrilla warfare and some backing from the Soviet Union and Cuba, led to independence for Angola and Mozambique. In the space of two decades, approximately 40 new nations had been born in sub-Saharan Africa.

The Challenges of New Nationhood

The ease with which most—although not all—former colonies had achieved their freedom was deceptive. Many Africans and Westerners alike expected great gains once imperialism had ceased to be a distraction. In fact, most African states found independence a greater challenge than the battle against European control had been. Although conditions varied widely in a civilization still quite diverse, most of the new nations were poor. Independence did not transform the economy or promote new power on the world market. In a few cases, as in the former Belgian Congo (renamed "Zaïre"), initial disorder disrupted trade patterns and caused the flight of Western managers and technicians, a situation that was only later repaired. Many new nations, like Nigeria, adopted policies of so-called "indigenization," or partial nationalization, which required that business and landed estates pass from European hands to majority African control within a decade or so. This approach, in seeking fuller national command over the economy, was understandable; indeed, it resembled the economic nationalist policies of Latin American countries in the earlier decades of the twentieth century. But, indigenization efforts had to be balanced against continued needs for Western technologies and capital. Nor could indigenization free most economies from the previous status of dependency. For many African workers, indigenization merely substituted African for European capitalists in a cash-crop or mining operation, as land was not widely redistributed and reliance on poorly paid labor remained extensive.

Leadership was also a problem in the new nations, along with agonizing economic issues. Some stirring nationalists proved inept or corrupt once in power—Ghana's Nkrumah was a case in point. Filling bureaucracies with competent staff was not easy when so few Africans had prior political experience. Here was one reason for frequent reliance on authoritarian rule, after brief attempts at parliamentary systems, as firm lines of control might compensate for political inexperience. The fact that army leaders had more organizational training—of the modern, bureaucratic type as opposed to the personalized, tribal sort—than most and national rather than local loyalties helps account for frequent periods of military control. However, this reliance on the army for effective leadership was no panacea. Many armies were run by generals who the year before had been sergeants; although some quickly learned the lessons of complex management, others were inefficient.

Many of the new nations faced periods of civil war soon after independence. This experience resembled that of Latin America and the United States in the nine-

The New Africa

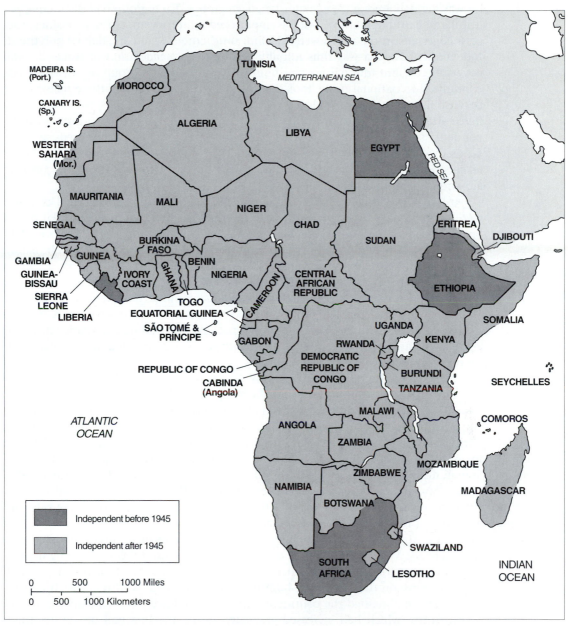

teenth century, but precedent was of little comfort. Divisions by tribe and language group made central administration difficult, in some ways more difficult than when Europeans had ruled. Leadership could now be ascribed to one group, which tended to antagonize other groups. The former British colony of Nigeria, in West Africa, dramatically illustrated a common problem. A large, populous nation, potentially one of Africa's wealthiest because of rich oil holdings as well as commercial farms, Nigeria was divided among three major language groups. Each group had distinctive political and cultural traditions—some emphasized military values, others business success. Nigerians in the north were Muslim; southerners were Christian or polytheist. Independent Nigeria was thus initially organized as a federation of three regional governments, but internal warfare resulted nevertheless. A group of army officers, committed to national unity, took control in 1965 and abolished these regions, but because most of the new leaders were from a single tribe, the Ibos, the result was a fierce attack by the Muslim north. The attempt by the Ibo region to form an independent state in 1967 led to 3 years of bloody warfare in which hundreds of thousands died of starvation. However, national unity survived, as the central military leadership held on and then made peace with the defeated Ibos through economic aid and local autonomy.

Internal warfare also surfaced in Zaïre, although in this case regional conflicts were heightened by Western and Soviet interference. With backing from European business leaders and military forces, a pro-Western dictatorship was ultimately established. Warfare between majority and minority tribal groups also plagued Zimbabwe after independence, although outright civil war was avoided. Another bloody clash between two tribes broke out in Rwanda in 1994. Tribal conflict and also hopes for political and economic reform led to an insurgent military movement in Zaïre in 1997 that displaced the aging dictator and restored the country's former name, the Congo. In general, the problems of joining nations that had no real tradition, which embodied a host of diverse, often antagonistic peoples, dominated African history after independence.

There were also other complications. Boundary disputes led to regional warfare in a few instances. Ethiopia and Somalia engaged in a bitter territorial quarrel in the late 1970s. The Pan-African Congress met periodically to resolve disputes, often with considerable success, and the civilization was far freer from warfare than the neighboring Middle East. Cold war tensions also affected the new nations. Soviet backing for Angolan independence included the provision of Cuban troops. The Ethiopian-Somali dispute was fueled by aid from both the Soviet Union and the United States, as first Somalia and then Ethiopia became Soviet allies. Most African nations tried with some success to stay clear of a firm alignment with either cold war side, but great-power rivalries could be an undeniable distraction.

South Africa proved to be one of the most intractable problems of the late twentieth century. White minority rule continued in this powerful country, long defying the movement toward black independence. South Africa boasted the only industrialized economy on the continent, built on unusual mineral wealth and rich agriculture; it also maintained the continent's strongest military force. Afrikaner power in South Africa, which had increased gradually during the first half of the twentieth century after the Boer War, culminated in outright victory in the 1948 national elections. The National Party ruled the country until 1994, seceding from the British Commonwealth in 1961. The Afrikaners progressively constructed a system called "apartheid," or separation, to keep the black majority in economic and political subjugation. In most public places, blacks were not permitted to use white facilities; intermarriage was forbidden; blacks, even when working for white-owned firms, were

Protesting apartheid: demonstration at the funeral of a riot victim shot by South African police, 1985.

required to live in segregated urban compounds; and many rural blacks were forced onto artificially created homelands, usually on the worst lands, where superficial self-government barely masked white control. Protests from a liberal white minority were silenced by police action and censorship, although moderate opposition was allowed to continue. Agitation from black groups, and also from Indian and mixed-race minorities, surfaced periodically, only to be crushed amid widespread brutality.

However, pressures from blacks for political rights and against an economic discrimination that confined them to unskilled jobs could not undo the existing system of apartheid. Unrest developed particularly among black workers in the urban compounds. Many parts of the world supported these actions, which also prompted some superficial concessions in apartheid policy during the 1970s, although in 1984–1986, a new series of bloody riots led to the reinstatement of martial law. Only at the end of the 1980s did a breakthrough begin, as a new white leader, de Klerck, negotiated with Nelson Mandela (see p. 656) of the African National Congress. Apartheid was legally dismantled and negotiations continued toward election-based universal suffrage with some protections for the white minority. Conditions remained uncertain, and violence between whites and blacks and among black groups continued to run high, but the long era of white domination ended. Mandela was elected president in the first elections based on universal suffrage, in 1994.

For most of sub-Saharan Africa, which remained rather separate from South Africa while denouncing apartheid, three themes dominated the decades after independence. First, national unity was successfully maintained. Administrations were extended over the new nations, school systems expanded, national loyalty preached through the government-dominated press and the ubiquitous transistor radio. In key

World Profiles

Nelson Mandela (1918–)

Nelson Mandela became the major nationalist leader in South Africa during the 1960s and 1970s. Despite the unusual features of the South African racial situation, Mandela's career in many ways resembled that of other early African nationalist leaders. Mandela was the oldest son of a chief in a Bantu tribe (the Tembu) and was raised as a nationalist. Active earlier on in the African National Congress youth league (the ANC, founded in 1912), he quickly became one of its most articulate spokespersons. Like other nationalists before him, he studied law, hoping to work toward the elimination of apartheid discrimination. With other leaders, he became more radical, supporting some terrorist activities in the early 1960s. This, in turn, brought repression; Mandela was arrested in 1962 and found guilty of treason at a major trial in 1964. He remained a prisoner until his release in 1990, despite increasing health problems. His dignity and statesmanlike interviews during the long imprisonment brought worldwide attention and support. Upon his release, he worked to forge unity among the native African population while pressing for political democracy and offering some pragmatic concessions to the governing white elite—a difficult combination, which Mandela worked hard to pull off. Nelson Mandela's extraordinary personal and public qualities are clear, but his full place in history awaits further definition as the situation in South Africa continues to unfold. In 1993, Mandela led negotiations for the first democratic elections in South Africa's history and shared the Nobel Peace Prize. He became president as a result of the elections, in 1994, and moved vigorously for national reconciliation. South African politics remained amazingly stable under his leadership. He retired in 1999 but continues to play a role as an international statesman. How can a nationalist leader, having suffered such injustice, rise above resentment in dealing with former enemies?

Nelson Mandela.

cases, as we have seen, secessionist movements were defeated, and with a few exceptions a full commitment to either side in the cold war was avoided.

Second, initial attempts to maintain democratic political structures were quickly abandoned. Despite Western expectations, in part because of the limited political experience that had been possible during the colonial period, virtually all the new nations dismantled parliamentary institutions, multiparty political systems, and guarantees of political freedom. In Ghana, Kwame Nkrumah soon jailed his political opponents and outlawed all parties save his own. His goal was a one-party state, capable of arousing the kind of loyalty that would hold together the nation and maintain his personal power. Nkrumah finally failed, victim in part of poor economic management that bankrupted the new nation, but he was replaced by military leadership. Most other African countries converted to either military rule or one-party systems that brooked no legal opposition. One-party governments arose in Kenya and Tanzania and in most of the former French colonies. Military rule predominated in Zaïre, Ethiopia, Liberia, and elsewhere. During the 1950s and 1960s, Africa experienced at least 70 attempted military takeovers (20 of which succeeded), and the pattern continued in later decades. Nigeria's military government turned power over to an elected civilian government in 1979, but another military coup soon followed.

The third theme of postindependence Africa involved determined efforts in many nations to promote economic change. Most of the new African leaders saw economic development as a vital expression of independence, an essential component to the national unity they worked hard and successfully to preserve. Such a goal proved far more compelling than Western-style liberalism, although its achievement remained elusive amid a particularly daunting set of economic and demographic barriers.

AFRICAN POLITICAL CULTURE

The almost uniform conversion of independent African states to authoritarian political structures in the later twentieth century is not surprising. Latin America and many Asian nations have shown a similar pattern in response to new nationhood. African political traditions, which so often emphasized the divine power of kings and had been shaped more recently by repressive colonial administrations, offered scant basis for a more liberal political approach in the Western or Indian sense.

African leaders, many personally ambitious and almost all eager to defend the unity of their new countries as the top political priority, found it hard to countenance opposition that seemed a personal affront and often expressed regional or tribal loyalties that threatened the nation. Success in maintaining unity—and the new African nations fared better in this regard than the initial Latin American nations had done in the first half of the nineteenth century—seemed to require strong police effort. Authoritarian rule also came naturally to many military leaders, who represented one of the more solid national institutions in most new nations. Many ordinary Africans, particularly in the fast-growing cities, placed great faith in the more charismatic leaders. Rural Africans might be less involved politically, but their loyalties, more traditional, corresponded to smaller segments of society such as family, village, and tribe, not to a national force of opposition. Although a number of Africans defended liberal values, the extent of support for parliamentary politics that helped forge an oscillation between liberal and authoritarian forms in the Latin American tradition did not surface, at least during the first decades of independence. And so, the authoritarian style went largely unchallenged until the 1990s, except for attacks by rival aspirants to authoritarian power.

Although authoritarian government in Africa characteristically meant attacks on opposition leaders, monopoly of the press and radio, and an emphasis on an internally strong army, other policies of authoritarian leaders varied widely. At one extreme was the brutal corruption of a number of leaders in Uganda, where at least two dictators used their armies to attack rival tribes and kill hundreds of thousands of civilians. This kind of brutality resulted in no stability, as rival claimants to power chased each other out of office with some frequency. Another authoritarian style involved emulation of the Soviet Russian example. Ethiopian Marxists, who took power after a revolt toppled the nation's ancient monarchy, talked in terms of a totalitarian state that would represent workers and peasants. But, the Soviet model was unusual in Africa. Few Africans found that doctrinaire Marxism described their political or economic conditions. Even in Ethiopia, the active power of the government, in an impoverished agricultural economy and amid great regional strife, hardly permitted the political controls of the Soviet state. A few kingdoms bordering South Africa, in yet another pattern, maintained some of the trappings of divine kingship, with rulers enjoying lavish ceremonies. Although not officially a king, the ruler of the giant state of Zaïre assumed the trappings of a divine kingship, stressing ritual demonstrations of power and receipt of tribute, along with a strong army, but the actual administration of government under his rule was very loose.

A number of nations with one-party systems achieved impressive political stability. Kenya faced tensions between two main tribal groups, but the ruling party created considerable unity and produced able leaders who transferred power without engendering strife. Kenya's capital city of Nairobi gained stature as the headquarters for several U.N. agencies and a meeting place for African organizations.

Several African nations pursued non-Marxist socialist policies, hoping to combine economic advance with social reform. In Tanzania, Julius Nyerere tried to build on African community traditions to create a distinctive form of rural socialism. The government supported village cooperation. Nyerere argued that "socialist societies in different parts of the world will differ in many respects . . . reflecting both the manner of their development, and their historical traditions." An African definition of socialism appealed to nationalist sentiment and reflected an unquestionable distaste, on the part of many Africans, for the greed and competitiveness of Western capitalism. Nyerere's practical policies in Tanzania, however, were hampered by poor economic management, and the country did not develop rapidly. Zimbabwe, although late in winning its independence, was a more hopeful example. Robert Mugabe, the prime minister, although a Marxist in theory, devoted himself to a program of practical reforms, which would redistribute some land and offer a degree of protection to manufacturing workers but would not antagonize the white minority or repel foreign investors.

Several West African governments made little reference to socialist ideas. Leaders in Nigeria supported private enterprise while also using government funds and planning to encourage further economic development. Great hope existed in the 1970s that government oil revenues could be channeled into industrial investment, although the decline of oil prices in the early 1980s threatened economic advance and resulted in widespread unemployment.

Early in the 1990s, a resurgence of democracy began to emerge. Although stable political regimes collapsed in some nations, like Somalia, Africa (including the now democratic regime in South Africa) was influenced by international trends and pressures toward more open political regimes. By 1997, 17 countries had installed freer elections with multiparty competition. Nigeria joined this list in 1999. The trend was still halting, but it suggested some interesting political potential for the future and the closeness of African ties with influences in the wider world. Tensions within the military persisted, however, partly because the end of the cold war reduced foreign aid and the weapons supply that had been used to placate the armed forces. Military coups continued. Several major states, such as Kenya, saw democratic elections set aside by authoritarian leaders, whereas the successful military movement in the renamed Congo resulted in a leader whose promises of future elections were at best tentative. The African definition of a stable political order that was not simply authoritarian proved to be no easy task.

AFRICAN CULTURE

Men and women who, as artists or writers, attempted to articulate African culture in the twentieth century faced an important contradiction. On the one hand, a widespread awareness existed of traditions that should be maintained, as a bridge between the civilization's past and its future and as alternatives to Western (or Marxist) styles. In this sense, contemporary African culture served many of the same purposes as cultural traditions in the Middle East or India. On the other hand, a defense of African culture has often involved the use of alien languages and forms of expression. For example, the novel, as a work of literature, did not evolve from the African heritage. Moreover, except for those who wrote in Arabic or Swahili, most novelists turned to Western languages—English, French, or Portuguese. They thus were detached from the African masses, many of whom remained illiterate, even as they tried to express and further guide public values. Here was a source of friction inherent to some extent in any formal intellectual life, in a culture that had long been largely oral. In Africa, the newness of many cultural outlets, particularly the educational system and the written word, posed a fundamental challenge to the preservation of vital traditions.

Indeed, one sign of the tension of intellectual life showed in the characteristic education of the small minority that passed beyond the primary level, in the independent African nations. African secondary schools preached nationalism and taught African history; to this extent, they departed from the conventions of the former colonial schools. However, the schools taught in Western languages, of necessity. They maintained a strong interest in European history and social science, as well

UNDERSTANDING CULTURES

The Question of Identity

During the twentieth century, intellectuals in a number of societies worried about what they called identity. They saw their societies changing rapidly, in part because of heavy influences from the outside world—particularly Western Europe and the United States. They did not necessarily object to all the changes, only the crucial loss of what was distinctive or traditional about their societies. With this, they further argued, came a loss of cultural value. The notion of identity is abstract, and certainly many people prefer newer identities as Western-style consumers or economic modernizers. But for some, including certain leading intellectuals, the concern was very real.

Africa was one of the centers of discussion around the issue of identity. Two examples highlight why identity seems to be of a particular importance in this part of the world. Nationalist leaders did not worry too much about identity when there was a common enemy—European colonialism—to attack. But once independence was achieved, nationalists faced several difficulties in the area of identity. First, their nations lacked traditions, for the boundaries had been defined by colonialists. Second, key tribal customs had to be opposed for they might undermine fragile loyalty to the new nations, which were usually made up of several groups. In contrast to the Middle East or India, there was no great religion to uphold with pride, as part of a valid tradition, for the religions that were spreading most rapidly, Islam and particularly Christianity, came from the outside. And third, certain cultural imports from the West—for example, science and medicine—continued to seem attractive. Where was identity in all of this? Some leaders emphasized a common African character, one that cut across national boundaries; ideas about blackness, or negritude, had a similar ring. Nationalists also stressed what they saw as key African virtues, such as communal and family loyalty as opposed to excessive individualism and exploitation; reverence for nature; distinct artistic styles; and a spirituality that transcended specific religions. Were these virtues enough to provide an identity to a people experiencing rapid change?

Chinua Achebe was a Nigerian novelist who wrote directly (in English) about the issue of identity. His book, *Things Fall Apart*, told of how traditional religion was undermined by Christian missionaries. He bemoaned the loss, although he could not bring himself to advocate a complete return to traditional religious practices, some of which now seemed either superstitious or cruel. Another novel, *No Longer at Ease*, discussed how even after Christianity, Western urban culture, with its emphasis on consumerism and sexuality, attacked traditional family values. Again, however, Achebe did not expressly advocate a return to the past. So, his work raised the question that still preoccupies many: Where does African identity lie?

as some Western science. Large numbers of British, American, and French school-teachers served the system, which was still linked to examination procedures in European countries. Zambia's standardized secondary tests, for instance, were prepared and graded in England. Despite the drawbacks, genuine progress resulted as the educated African leadership expanded. Nonetheless, the challenge to older cultural habits was far greater than in any other twentieth-century civilization.

An important group of African writers emerged after 1920. Crafting essays and poetry, but particularly the novel, these writers came to terms with a number of contemporary African issues. White South African writers, many critical of the policy of apartheid but deeply loyal to their homeland, wrote of the tensions and brewing trouble within their society. Black writers typically stressed the virtues of African traditions, pointing out that their people had a rich heritage long before Europeans arrived on the scene. The Senegalese poet and political leader Leopold Senghor thus criticized Western scientific traditions that separate humankind from nature; he advocated, instead, an African tradition of intuition about nature through experience in it. The Angolan Agustinho Neto praised the power of African culture, again attacking many Western standards and describing a unique black point of view. Jomo Kenyatta, glorifying tribal culture in Kenya, elevated the position of women in African society. A West Indian poet, popular in Africa, praised the new black consciousness of superiority over Western values:

> Hurrah for those who never invented anything hurrah for those who never explored anything hurrah for those who never conquered anything hurrah for joy hurrah for love hurrah for the pain of incarnate tears.

More soberly, Nigeria's leading novelist, Chinua Achebe, stated "the fundamental theme" of the rising group of African writers:

> . . . the African people did not hear of culture for the first time from Europeans; . . . their societies were not mindless but frequently had a philosophy of great depth and volume and beauty, . . . they had poetry and above all, they had dignity. It is this dignity that many African peoples all but lost in the colonial period, and it is this that they must now regain. The worst thing that can happen to any people is the loss of their dignity and self-respect. The writer's duty is to help them regain it by showing what happened to them, what they lost.

However, the new African novelists were not simply apostles of tradition and black pride. They also wrote of the anxieties that accompany modernization. Achebe's brilliant novels dealt with the corrosive effect of Western ideas, including Christianity, on powerful village characters. In his works, he examined the stress of city life on popular traditions and expressed the disillusionment of many African intellectuals with corrupt and power-hungry rulers, worrying that the masses "had become even more cynical than their leaders and were apathetic in the bargain." African culture, with writers like Achebe, combined traditional values with new forms of expression to present powerful dramas of a changing society.

African artists and craftspeople preserved a thriving legacy, working in older stylistic conventions largely apart from the "modern art" styles of the West, which, ironically, had been partly inspired by African forms. Design and decoration in village houses retained their distinctive quality. Sculptors continued to create powerful figures for both religious and aesthetic purposes. African dance and music remained lively art forms, both at the popular level and in formal government-sponsored troupes that toured internationally. African culture was not isolated, however, and many craftsmen and musicians interacted with the proponents of other styles. Some crafts, catering to tourism, pandered to Western ideas of what African art should be like.

The interactions that dominated twentieth-century African culture showed clearly in the area of religion. Africa remained a religious society, although in the cities secular values competed for center stage. Islam, which gained many new converts in the north and center, maintained a trajectory as the most rapidly growing popular

Modern African art showing traditional themes. Cameroon brass sculptures of two "juju men" wearing the costumes used at religious ceremonies. (The Granger Collection)

religion, claiming about 40 percent of all Africans south of the Sahara. Africa's Christian minority, almost as large, grew rapidly as well. Black Protestant leaders played a leading role in moderate resistance to apartheid in South Africa. African Catholicism assumed a growing role in the Roman church, as the first African cardinal was named and the pope visited the continent for the first time in the 1970s. Catholicism in Africa expanded more rapidly than in any other area, as the number of African Catholics more than doubled from 29 million in 1965 to 66 million in 1985. Christian and Muslim gains meant that Africa experienced the kind of growth of monotheism and new spirituality that had characterized civilizations such as Western Europe after the classical age. The result, as in these earlier cases, was both exciting and unsettling. New converts often retained former beliefs in part, for syncretism was common. African Christianity characteristically combined conventional Christian doctrine with traditional values—including, in some areas, a continued belief in polygamy and a definite scorn for Catholic celibacy—and traditional rituals. At the same time, outright polytheistic beliefs retained some vitality, in both the city and countryside. Traditional remedies were often used to treat disease, following the quite logically presented principles of spirit-caused illness and its cure. Popular religious leaders, some of them women, helped arouse fervor in several regional twentieth-century revolts, in which faith in divine guidance combined with worldly grievances against colonial rule or economic exploitation. A number of movements, focusing less on protest than on healing by prayer and the promise of the millennium, blended traditional animist creeds with ideas adapted from the Christian Bible. Overall, although religious diversity—and sometimes bitter conflict—continued, a general esteem for the applicability of religion to life, society, and nature continued to dominate African culture.

The surge of literary creativity and the complex religious transformations were not the only cultural innovations in twentieth-century Africa. Nationalist leaders obviously urged cultural change, away from purely traditional concepts; while attacking imperialism, they usually argued for the adaptation of some concepts from the West, including new kinds of science and medicine. However, they also tried to highlight important African qualities, such as community and family solidity. In the cities, other Western cultural influences, including consumerism, constituted yet another force, adding to changes in belief and creating complicated combinations of old and new.

ECONOMY AND SOCIETY

Changes in African culture, and particularly the spread of education and Western-language literature, raised some basic questions about the relationship between culture and social change. Even as praise for traditional styles and values resounded, there were signs of the unusually rapid disruption of many customary social forms. Writers like Achebe wondered whether the breakup of long-held beliefs had not weakened Africans' ability to find an anchor amid so much change. Other intellectuals, however, stressed the continuing validity of basic religious orientations and family ties, contrasting African strength in this regard with what they saw as the demoralization of Western society.

Most of sub-Saharan Africa did not face, throughout the twentieth century, the kinds of pressure for land redistribution that deeply affected Latin America and parts of Asia. White minorities opened large estates in East and South Africa; many of these remained, after independence, in white or African hands, although some African governments were able to introduce limited land reform. In more populous West Africa, peasant small-holding remained the norm, except for the cash-crop estates that relied on low-wage labor.

Nevertheless, the persistence of village-based agriculture raised issues of its own. During the colonial decades, Western governments pressured African peasants to convert to cash crops like peanuts or cotton. Some farmers made profits on such crops, but others had to minimize the production of basic foods for subsistence in favor of meeting commercial quotas. When, in addition, many village men were forced or induced to labor in distant mines, the result could be massive economic and social disruption. Portuguese Mozambique, for example, compelled women farmers to grow cotton on lands ill-suited to that purpose. Food production faltered, leading to malnutrition. And although a few village headmen made money on cotton sales and then bought bigger homes, bicycles, and even art reproductions, the bulk of the population suffered.

Commercial pressures often continued after independence in Africa, although some areas reverted to more localized agriculture. Major gains in agricultural production came slowly, as peasants lacked both the capital and education to undertake new methods. Many governments were more concerned with creating public works and factories than with modernizing agriculture. Despite the clearance of new lands for farming, agricultural production lagged in many parts of Africa. Dependence on root crops in the drier lands meant that the gains of the Green Revolution were irrelevant. Agricultural stagnation plus population growth made key regions vulnerable to disasters of climate. In the early 1970s and again in the early 1980s and 1990s, drought conditions on the Sahara's southern rim and down the east coast caused widespread famine. More generally, agricultural lag promoted inadequate nutrition and helped explain widespread poverty, even when severe weather problems did not add to the burdens. Finally, reliance on cash crops like cocoa, cotton, or peanuts for export, while it brought profits to some African landowners and merchants, continued to distract from well-balanced agricultural production, leaving many nations divided between export farmers and a subsistence-minded peasantry wedded to largely traditional methods.

Development of the cash-crop system continued to tie many African countries closely to the Western-dominated world economy. This dependence did not disappear with decolonization. Despite their nationalism, many African countries remained firmly linked to the markets, shipping, and commercial know-how of their erstwhile European rulers. Despite a brief flurry of radical rebellion against Belgian business in Zaïre, for example, Belgian capital and expertise remained fundamental to the nation's economy, as the mineral wealth of the mines continued to be directed toward Western markets almost exclusively. No African country aside from South Africa created a large industrial base of its own. Government encouragement promoted factories for local food processing and clothing and tool production, in countries like Kenya. By the late 1990s, a few countries, including Botswana and Uganda, reported rapid manufacturing growth, leading some observers to wonder if Africa might finally begin to participate in the kind of industrial evolution that had taken root in Latin America and parts of the Middle East some decades before. Everywhere, however, reliance on the technologies and manufactured imports of the West remained significant. Many African nations ran up huge debts because of the gap between export earnings and import needs.

Despite the limits of economic change, a new class of wealthy, urban Africans took shape both under colonialism and with independence. Merchants, the cash-crop landlords, and top government officials stood apart from the African masses in their luxurious life style, as Africa joined other agricultural societies in a radical division between the wealthy and the masses. In Swahili-speaking East Africa, common people called the new elite *"wa Benzi,"* meaning "those who ride in a Mercedes-Benz." In stark contrast, per capita annual income for the general population often stagnated; in mineral-rich Zaïre, for example, average income stood at $137 in 1976 and $160 in 1985.

Furthermore, substantial population growth hit sub-Saharan Africa during the twentieth century. Medical and public-health measures promoted by colonial regimes and extended by independent African governments accounted for some of the gain. So did disruption of village community controls as a result of new market earnings from commercial agriculture or labor in the mines and cities. Population increase occurred despite the absence of a real agricultural revolution and the severe limits of climate and soil fertility in many regions. Indeed, population growth helped worsen agriculture in some cases, as land was overfarmed, its fertility declined—hence, there were recurrent famines in key regions that, ironically, did not halt population growth.

From the 1970s onward, the spread of AIDS in East Africa added to economic woes, as many children and young adults became afflicted—over 25 percent in some regions—thus curtailing the available active labor force. Rapid population growth continued, however, as Africa remained one of the regions in which new forms of birth control spread most slowly. This growth, new transportation facilities, and more modern forms of government, along with some growth in commerce, spurred the rapid expansion of African cities, particularly after World War II. Only 8 percent of the population throughout the entire African continent was concentrated in cities in 1925 and only 13 percent in 1950, but by 1973, the percentage had soared to 23 and this trend gained momentum. Most urbanization did not depend on the expansion of factories; it was based on trade, political concentration, and, above all, the absence of alternatives in the countryside, as population growth and cash-crop estates increased the number of property-less poor. As in Latin America, urban populations crowded into hastily built slums, hoping for survival by means of occasional unskilled jobs, begging, or prostitution, or peddling in the omnipresent open markets of the African city.

African urbanization, unlike that in Latin America, involved considerable family disruption. Because far more men than women moved to the cities, a significant number of families, particularly in the countryside, were headed by women. Indeed, Africa resembled the West, by the 1970s, in the dissociation of a growing minority of men from their families and the problems, economic and psychological, that occurred when women had to raise children on their own. The African tradition of an extended family modified these pressures to some extent, as relatives provided moral support and more tangible assistance to female-headed households. And, while their husbands toiled in urban centers or mining villages, some women found their new independence challenging and exciting, as the traditions of male domination faded. Nevertheless, issues of family disruption in Africa—a civilization proud of its close and supportive family ties—seemed inescapable as part of social change in the later twentieth century. Changes in social structures and personal values stood in stark contrast to more traditional expectations, in one of the several urgent dramas of twentieth-century Africa.

A weekly newspaper in Zambia featured a "Dear Josephine" column that mirrored the process of change, as urban Africans developed new and more individualized patterns in a society long characterized by strong family traditions and tightly knit communities. Africans wrote to ask if they could marry despite the fact that older brothers in their families remained unwed; tradition held that the eldest should marry first, but what should the middle son do when he found the right girl? Or, how was a city dweller to pay a bridal dowry in cattle, which his intended's family, back in the village, insisted on? Or, how might the tribal traditions of mutual support be continued? For example,

> I am well-known, with a big family to feed. My house is by the bus-stop and every day I receive visitors from the home village. It is my duty to give my tribesfolk food and money for their journey needs. But my family suffer from hunger and I go without the decent clothes my position calls for. Though I have a good job I am kept poor by home-people. I do not dislike them, but what can I do to be saved from them?

Women's role also began to shift. The impact of larger changes—social, economic, and political—on African women provoked important debate. On the one hand, women gained new roles as men's ties to their families loosened. On the other hand, women were typically concentrated in more traditional economic sectors, including agricultural areas, in order to protect their economic status. As governments became more effective, first under colonial rule and then with independence, the informal local power of women often declined. Some observers argued that women were net losers in this process, despite certain new freedoms. In addition in some areas, such as the Muslim northeast, traditional limitations on women persisted, including practices of circumcision that were designed to limit a woman's sexual pleasure and consequently promote fidelity. Nonetheless, growing educational opportunities and even some of the social disruptions promoted new ideas among women, including a growing belief that women should stick together; here, traditional ideas of family unity combined with a desire for education and birth control to create a novel outlook. Upper-class urban women also managed to pressure some governments to improve legal rights for all women. But, battles over outside influences often complicated this process. Many women won rights to property by appealing to U.N. declarations on women's rights. By 2000, some courts overturned these rulings in the name of African tradition.

CONCLUSION: DEFINING THE NEW AFRICA

Disruptive transformation was no African monopoly in the twentieth century. Most civilizations faced challenges to established institutions and values. And, Africans in various ways remained able to rely on traditions; their life styles were not totally disturbed or undone by surrounding change. Nonetheless, the upheaval brought about by colonial impositions, population growth, and new urban and commercial institutions was considerable, particularly when it was not matched by significant improvements in the standard of living. At the same time, change brought new hopes to many Africans. Intellectuals proud of their culture and politicians enthusiastic about national independence were joined by more humble people, like the young woman in Kenya who noted the opportunities available for the self-sufficient and the resourceful. Describing her mother's large family and hard physical labor on a subsistence farm, she discussed how her own views had been shaped by the experience of school:

> My life is very different from my mother's. . . . Women have to get an education. Then if you get a large family and don't know how to feed it, you can find work and get some cash. That's what I will teach my children: "Get an education first."

Africa remained the poorest of the world's civilizations by the late 1980s, as its vulnerability to famine starkly attested. Modernization, including political independence, had not reaped all the benefits that many had hoped for and may have jeopardized some sources of cultural strength. However, change continued to generate aspirations for the future, in a culture still defining its relationship to the contemporary world.

SUGGESTED WEBSITES

For a website on apartheid, see *www-cs-students.stanford.edu/~cale/cs201/apartheid.hist.html;* on decolonization in Africa and the role of African writers, on the African National Congress, see *http://www.anc.org.za/.*

SUGGESTED READINGS

Various source materials have contributed to research in recent African history. W. E. B. Du Bois, *The World and Africa* (1974), presents an American black nationalist perspective. Works by nationalist leaders include J. Kenyatta, *Facing Mount Kenya* (1953), and, from South Africa, A. Luthuli, *Let My People Go* (1962). F. Fanon, *Wretched of the Earth* (1965), is a stinging indictment of Western colonialism. Novels by C. Achebe, particularly *Things Fall Apart* (1978), deal with changes in African society and culture. See also B. Fetter, *Colonial Rule in Africa: Readings from Primary Sources* (1979). The colonial period is covered by R. O. Collins, *Problems in the History of Colonial Africa, 1860–1960* (1970). See also Ali Mazrui and

Michael Tidy, *Nationalism and New States in Africa* (1984); Martin Meredith, *The First Dance of Freedom: Black Africa in the Post-War Era* (1984); and S. A. Akintoye, *Emergent African States* (1976). On more recent developments, consult P. C. Lloyd, *Africa and Social Change* (1972); A. Hopkins, *An Economic History of West Africa* (1973); and C. Legum, *Congo Disaster* (1961). Competent works on South Africa include R. W. Johnson, *How Long Will South Africa Survive?* (1977), and Gail Gerhart, *Black Power in South Africa* (1978). On an important social topic, see N. H. Afkin and E. Bay, eds., *Women in Africa* (1977).

Toward the Future: World History Yet to Come

What are the connections between the past, present, and future? How does world history help us understand the surrounding world and the world that is likely to emerge in the future? This chapter focuses on several different approaches to using world history for an ongoing understanding. Issues of continuity and change make for one approach. The historical basis for prediction provides another, along with an assessment of leading twentieth-century trends. Finally, the legacy of the twentieth century as a new period of time, and some specific questions about civilizations and global forces, connect to analytical themes that have long been part of the study of world history.

CHANGE AND CONTINUITY

At any stage in world history, some balance between change and continuity has described the world as a whole and major civilizations within it. This remains true. Recent developments remind us of the importance of continuity. Various Asian leaders urge values of collective loyalty and obedience, or an adaptation of Confucian heritage, against what they see as excessive Western individualism. Islam has changed, but its ongoing vitality is obvious. In the cultural arena, particularly, legacies from deep in the past often continue or reassert their sway. The collapse of communism in Russia has led to a reassertion of beliefs in Orthodox Christianity and Russian spirituality; decades of repression had not crushed cultural influences that date back to the postclassical period and were redefined by conservative nationalism in the nineteenth century. A whole set of questions about the present and future involves asking about what will happen to beliefs and institutions that are at least partly traditional, whose force can be understood only through the perspective of a long span in world history.

However, key questions also emerge from change. We know that the twentieth century introduced novel technologies, a redefined world economy, and important new cultural values. We know also that developments in the late twentieth century, including the spread of democracy and new levels of industrial growth, raise additional issues. Over the past decade, industrial giants like Western Europe, Japan, and the United States have faced new competiton from other areas: How will they adjust? Will powerful multinational companies, developing for at least a hundred years, make nation–states increasingly irrelevant? Have some of the important political responses that punctuated the earlier part of the century, like fascism and communism, run their course, or might they reemerge? Change leaves its mark in two ways: We know what some of the shifts have been and we wonder if they will continue, and if they will further erode some of the persistent earlier legacies. We know that some changes are still open-ended—the world future of democracy, for example—and we wonder when and how their impact will be clarified.

World history does not provide definitive answers, so much as shaping the right questions to ask. Nevertheless, the attempt to formulate a historical perspective is inescapable: We can only surmise and judge the future by juxtaposing it against what we know of the past.

FORECASTS AND PERSPECTIVES

Since the formation of civilizations, the history of the world has involved relatively rapid change—sometimes in directions already set, but sometimes in new trajectories. People in various civilizations have attempted to devise schemes to look beyond the present. From the ancient river valley civilizations to the twentieth century, some have used astrology or other divinations to predict the future. More systematically, some scholars have assumed that time moves in cycles, so that one can count on repetition of basic patterns. Others, as in Christian belief or in more secular faiths such as Marxism, have looked toward some great change in the future: the Last Judgment, the classless society, toward which history is steadily working. The idea of some master plan guiding history, so that it moves in a steady direction and toward some purpose, runs deep in the thought of several cultures, including our own. Whatever the approach, the human impulse to know what we cannot definitely know seems unavoidable.

Nonetheless, all the evidence suggests that our vision of the future remains cloudy at best. It has been calculated that well over 60 percent of all predictions or forecasts offered by serious social scientists in the United States since 1945—called upon to predict future business cycles, for instance, or family trends, or political currents—have been wrong. How many observers, just 50 years ago, could have predicted such basic transformations as the end of the cold war, the invention of computer and genetic engineering technologies, the industrial breakthroughs of many Pacific coast regions of Asia? How many observers just 25 years ago could have foreseen the Iranian revolution or the collapse of the Soviet empire? A few of these events might have been discerned by some in advance, to be sure, but many were great surprises. And, other developments, confidently predicted, have not come to pass: Americans are not riding about in helicopters rather than automobiles (a common anticipation in the 1940s), nor have families been replaced by communes (a forecast of the 1960s).

Even if we cannot know the future, we can use history to develop a framework for evaluating it, even partially anticipating it as it unfolds: We know what factors to monitor. Recent patterns, and their relationship to older themes in world history,

Global Relationships at the Beginning of the Twenty-first Century: Change and Diversity in the Contemporary World

ALASKA

CANADA

UNITED STATES

GREENLAND (Denmark)

ICELAND
UNITED KINGDOM
IRELAND

ATLANTIC OCEAN

PACIFIC OCEAN

CUBA
BAHAMAS
JAMAICA
DOMINICA
ST. LUCIA
BARBADOS
GRENADA
TRINIDAD & TOBAGO
SURINAME
GUYANA

SOUTH AMERICA

C. VERDE IS.
GAMBIA
SIERRA LEONE
GHANA
NIGERIA
SÃO TOME & PRINCIPE

ATLANTIC OCEAN

RUSSIAN FEDERATION

MONGOLIA
CHINA
KAZAKHSTAN

BELARUS
UKRAINE
CYPRUS

ERITREA
S. YEMEN
UGANDA
RWANDA
BURUNDI
KENYA
TANZANIA
MALAWI
MOZAMBIQUE
SWAZILAND
LESOTHO
ANGOLA
NAMIBIA
BOTSWANA
ZIMBABWE

N. KOREA
JAPAN
TAIWAN
VIETNAM
BANGLADESH
INDIA
SRI LANKA
MALDIVE IS.

MALAYSIA
PHILIPPINES
INDONESIA
PAPUA NEW GUINEA

MICRONESIA
SOLOMON IS.
VANUATU
AUSTRALIA

INDIAN OCEAN

PACIFIC OCEAN

KIRIBATI
TUVALU
FIJI
TONGA
NEW ZEALAND

Area of inset

RUSSIA
KAZAKHSTAN
UZBEKISTAN
TURKMENISTAN
KRYGYZSTAN
TAJIKISTAN
CHINA

Independence gain since WWII
Communist countries
Former Soviet Union

2000 Miles
2000 Kilometers
0

671

allow us to make generalizations about what is to come. There are several possible relationships from past to present to future, but no assessment or prediction can take place without some examination of history.

THE WORLD'S FUTURE AS PROMISE OR THREAT

One tempting way to end historical surveys is to offer glowing words of hope about the achievements and bright prospects of humankind. Contemporary Western culture continues to value optimism and to believe that students especially should be inspired to think well of the society around them, not discouraged as they face their own future. However, the message of history, including contemporary history, is decidedly ambiguous on the question of hopefulness.

World history is without question a record of impressive, even inspiring, human achievement. The twentieth century contributed at least its fair share to the record of progress. Advances in industry and agriculture have permitted the birth and survival of more people in our century than in all previous centuries combined. Life expectancy has risen notably in almost all societies and not just in those with sophisticated industry. Scientific discoveries add greatly to our knowledge as well as to our technology, although some civilizations continue to prefer alternate ways of viewing the world. Our capacity to organize large groups of people has also improved, at least in certain respects. Most societies today can operate larger businesses or school systems or census-taking operations than ever before. The spread of education, another general development of the previous twentieth century, also provides a basis for claiming a genuine increase in human knowledge, not just at the level of advanced research but also among ordinary peasants and workers. Many of these developments provide additional hope for the future as well.

Nonetheless, history is also, unquestionably, the record of humankind's inhumanity toward its own. The twentieth century generated particularly troubling questions about human impulses once united with awesome technologies and involving wider contacts among peoples. The century has produced the bloodiest wars on record; 60 million people were killed in World War II alone. The introduction of sophisticated weaponry, combined with ongoing political tensions, has resulted in massive slaughter even aside from formal wars: the deaths of hundreds of thousands as part of the revolution in Russia and China; Hitler's insane efforts to exterminate the Jews; the execution of additional hundreds of thousands stemming from racial or religious conflict in Uganda, Cambodia, Bosnia, and on the Indian subcontinent. The twentieth century was a violent period, taking its rank among centuries marked by nomadic invasions and surpassing these in the sheer volume of slaughter, if only because of the availability of technologies for mass killing.

There is even more to contemplate. The technologies that allow more people to survive in our world have also generated frightening levels of pollution and created potential imbalances in the natural environment. The daily elimination of acres of natural vegetation, in expanding societies like those of Latin America and Africa, hinders the natural production of oxygen through photosynthesis, while in other regions industrial plants lower air and water quality—the United States and China are

The beginnings of the new warfare: U.S. atomic testing, Nevada, 1952.

now world leaders in the emission of pollution, but other centers, new and old, add to the problem. Our ability to sustain growing populations, although unquestionable in recent history despite warfare, may be jeopardized in the future, or at least the amenities to which many people have become accustomed may be reduced.

The twentieth century also stands open to some attack for its relative neglect of spiritual and aesthetic expressions, although here, of course, evaluation is more subjective. Crowding, war, and the sheer concentration on economic development may have tended to shunt artistic and religious creativity to the side, reducing the beauty humankind then finds in their lives and the surrounding world. Critics who worry about the undermining of African cultural traditions and those who bemoan the mindless mass entertainments of the contemporary West may be identifying an important common problem in our own time and in our future.

The point here is not to argue that the world's prospects are glorious or they are unrelievedly dismal, although a review of both optimistic and pessimistic examples provides useful ways of summing up historical patterns and deciding what one's own standards of evaluation are. Some of humankind's most hopeful recent endeavors have not had particularly good results: The U.N. organization, for example, founded after World War II to provide a forum for the preservation of world peace, has not produced serious mechanisms for conflict resolution, although its efforts to reconcile disputes are not altogether useless. Some of humankind's direst recent fears have not come to pass either: Population has not yet overwhelmed available food supply, the United States and the Soviet Union did not yield to some inevitable dynamic that forced the world rivals to resort to an all-out war.

HANDLES ON THE FUTURE

ANALOGY

Besides philosophizing about human prospects on the basis of history, several kinds of forecasts attempt to use history to make educated guesses about what is yet to come—to speculate intelligently about what is inherently unknowable. One technique involves using historical analogies. Many people who predict that new technologies like computers will revolutionize education or the economy compare the future with the known example of the industrial revolution. "The computer will do for education what the steam engine did for manufacturing," is an example of an analogy. The result does not provide details about the future and, of course, the whole example may simply be wrong. But, many people use analogies routinely, always drawing on history to provide guidelines for the future.

Western thinkers in the twentieth century recurrently used analogies drawn from the fall of the Roman Empire, contending that the West is about to decline the way Rome did 1500 years ago, and for similar reasons of moral decay and inept leadership. Some analysts similarly compare prospects for the United States to the decline of Britain at the end of the nineteenth century: Here, say the analogists, are two cases of societies that overextended themselves in military commitments, lost the internal drive that had made their economies powerful, and inevitably slipped in world power or stature. Of course, what actually happened to Britain has not yet fully happened to the United States; even beguiling analogies may be wrong.

Some Latin Americans like to compare their civilization to that of the West at the end of the Middle Ages—still behind in world affairs but gaining new vigor and about to surge ahead. Similar analogies, we have seen, apply to contemporary Africa. Again, analogies can be spun out endlessly, and the results may both confirm a particular view of history and raise at least some intelligent questions about the shape of the world in the future.

PROJECTION

The second most common form of forecasting on the basis of history involves using current trends and projecting them into the future. We "know," for example, that populations in the United States and Japan will increasingly include more aged, for the birthrate is already low and life expectancy is gaining. Therefore, the average age in both countries, already unusually high by historical standards, will go up further by the year 2010, bringing new problems of pensions and medical care. This forecast assumes, of course, that present trends will not be disrupted by some new surge in the birthrate, a higher death rate among adults in late middle age, or new patterns of immigration that alter the demographic structure. Trend projections are always vulnerable to new, unforeseen factors.

By the twenty-first century, trend projections were also complicated by the sheer novelty of developments in many parts of the world. Questions, rather than projections, seem to be the current order of the day. What kind of durable political and diplomatic structures will emerge in central Asia or Eastern Europe, now that the Soviet Union has collapsed? Will China manage to continue its combination of economic liberalization and authoritarian politics? Will Western Europe make good on its halting march toward greater unity? Events since the late 1980s have been unusually significant, producing all sorts of interesting developments but suggesting an unclear future.

Nevertheless, even amid more than the usual pattern of changes, several trends developed in the twentieth century, or in its final decades, that pose more precise questions about the future than simply, "What do you think will happen next?" One trend is demographic. Although huge population gains continued in the 1990s, the world growth rate is slowing down. China and many parts of Latin America, although in quite different ways, achieved lower birthrates; other parts of the world followed suit more gradually. Will this trend continue? Will it stabilize the population in time to prevent catastrophic pressures on resources and the environment? Will most of the world, in the rest of the twenty-first century, become similar in demographic structure to the model established earlier by the West, Russia, and Japan?

Political trends provided another set of coherent questions. Except for China and the Middle East, democratic forms were spreading widely by the 1990s. One of the key twentieth-century themes—what political structures will work best, given the decline of traditional forms like monarchy?—seemed to be receiving a clear answer. Other twentieth-century options, such as communism and authoritarianism, persist, but with decreasing importance in most regions. Will the democratic surge continue? What caused it, and were the causes clear-cut? Can fledgling democracies in Eastern Europe and Latin America survive almost certain problems of economic adjustment and growth? The democratic current resulted, in part, from a belief that political change would generate economic vitality. Was this assumption correct? And, if democracy fails, what will replace it?

Two kinds of questions are used to explore world economic trends. The first, standard since World War II, involves the ongoing gaps between industrialized and "underdeveloped" areas. Can new areas make the turn to full industrialization, as South Korea and Taiwan have done since the 1960s, and begin to catch up with the industrial giants? Or, will a have–have not division continue to impact world politics and the living standards of the majority of people around the globe? Actual twentieth-century history reminds us that the two-fold division around industrialization has become vastly oversimple, which is where a second set of questions comes into play. A number of societies have expanded their modern manufacturing sector without undergoing a full process of industrial revolution. Mexico, Turkey, Brazil, China, and, to an extent, India have all developed a significant economic dynamism, along with countries like Malaysia and Indonesia on the fringe of the Pacific Rim. A few African countries may be joining this contingent. Where will such an evolution lead? How will the advanced industrial economies adjust to ongoing competition in metallurgy and textiles produced successfully outside their borders? How will the world economy, and the many kinds of participants in it, continue to develop, and how will its growing complexity be managed?

Cultural issues also loom large. Many regions worry about their cultural identity in an age of growing international contact and standardized mass offerings in sports, television, and films. Most attempts at cultural isolation had failed by the 1990s. A growing division emerged between groups and societies whose cultural definitions remain strongly religious, and those that have moved to a more secular orientation. New militance and intolerance among some religious groups within regions like the Middle East and India, directed against both foreign influences and secular elements in their own societies, highlight this division. Where will the future balance lie?

A variety of social issues also cut across the boundaries of civilization. Most societies face new questions about the role of women. Feminism influences international bodies like the United Nations, and the power of Western public opinion in this area is considerable. However, feminism is not a uniform international force. Some regions resist it in the name of tradition; furthermore, in India, the Middle East, and Africa, some women's voices seek a different kind of feminism, less influenced by the individualism of the West. Concrete questions vary: Western women focus strongly on their new economic roles, but in other parts of the world, women worry more about the erosion of traditional production-related jobs because of new commercial forms. Are there some common issues and probable trends for women worldwide, or do regional differences in traditions and current economic and political status predominate? Trend projection—including current patterns of declining birthrates—suggests flux in gender relations, but it does not necessarily establish clear trajectories for an international future.

DISRUPTIVE FORECASTS

Predicting future trends, or at least asking questions about them, on the basis of major recent developments risks the failure to identify major changes in direction. By definition, forces that might introduce vital new themes cannot be easily anticipated; however, these can readily change the shape of the relationship between the future and the past. The ending of the cold war left a considerable vacuum in the world's diplomatic framework. Many observers predict that regional tensions will increasingly define the horizons of international relations. Certainly, potential trouble spots are numerous. The Middle East is an obvious candidate; so potentially is divided Korea, the divided Indian subcontinent, divided central Asia, and the disputed states of east-central Europe—and all contain nations capable of nuclear development. But, will some larger diplomatic alignment, currently unforeseen, supersede these regional conflicts, as the cold war once had done?

Forecasters frequently project other dramatic factors that might change the face of world history to come. In the 1960s, "population bomb" predictions argued that the current rate of global population growth promised increasing misery, environmental strain, and have–have not warfare. This gloom was less fashionable by the 1990s, as population growth had not led to a global worsening of living standards. Here was a disruptive forecast that had not generated the proclaimed results. However, predictions of environmental catastrophe, as a result of growing industrialization, wastefulness, and population growth, sent a somewhat similar message. Many

UNDERSTANDING CULTURES

Homogeneity and Diversity

The 20th century offered more chances for cultural sharing than ever before in human history. Many people believed that the various parts of the world were becoming more similar culturally. Scientists or athletes shared cultural values across civilization boundaries, and met regularly in international settings. Consumer culture, exported particularly from the West and Japan, spread widely. Almost every region highlighted soccer matches and knew about Mickey Mouse. Some critics worried that the values of cultural diversity, including even diverse languages, might be lost.

But against this vision, many regions asserted a more vigorous, and sometimes newly intolerant, version of distinctive cultural identities. This was part of ongoing nationalism, and also the revival of fundamentalist religions. More subtly, even people who accepted some aspects of international culture, shaped it to their own values. Thus the Japanese copied American-style TV quiz shows, but used the shows to heap shame on failing contestants, reinforcing this Japanese value in ways Westerners would not easily recognize. As more regions gained political and some economic strength, independent from Western dominance, cultural diversity might actually increase. So what was the most accurate scenario, in looking at the future of culture from a world history perspective? What blend of contact and separation would ultimately prevail?

of the current issues in world history might be overtaken by the radical deterioration of the environment.

Another viewpoint expressed by pundits in the postindustrial age was that new technologies, led by the computer, might create unprecedented vistas for information exchange and economic growth. Societies might be able to bypass the industrial revolution and directly engage in postindustrial, computer-driven production. Cities will go from being manufacturing centers to serving as meeting places and entertainment meccas. Social structures will be based on not property, but educational levels and control of information.

Forecasts of a radical break—and these predictions are quite varied—assume the importance of a single major factor: diplomacy, population, or technology. They argue that other facets of world history will come to reflect this basic determinant. Other world historians argue that not only have many dramatic forecasts not come to pass, world history has been shaped more commonly by a combination of factors rather than a sole dominant cause. But by definition, predictions of a major change in direction cannot be disproved—or proved. They can only be discussed on the basis of prior analogies and an understanding of other significant trends.

Revisiting a New World History Period

Modern people encounter both major types of forecasts. Pundits bombard us with projections of current trends—about aging, for example, or about the movement toward democracy. Others make a dramatic case for some major new factor that will move society away from its recent past—toward a technology-dominated postindustrial future, for example. What the actual mixture will be, in moving the world from the past to the future, cannot be determined until we get there.

One forecasting complexity seems obvious when the past century is interpreted in terms of world history. Insofar as a major new period has begun, we can assume that many past patterns will progressively weaken, but because the period is still emerging, we cannot possibly say what durable patterns will take their place. Political structure offers an obvious example: It would be startling if the monarchy revived as a form of government, for it has been declining worldwide for at least a hundred years. But, confidence that democracy will become the international norm is harder to come by. Assessing the twentieth century as a new period of world history fairly readily demonstrates that the relative power of the West has diminished (although some Westerners dispute even this). Nonetheless, will a new world-dominant civilization come into view (as the West did, after a period of transition following Arab decline), or will world power be more evenly distributed (as it was during the classical period)? Growing international contacts suggest an increasingly common international culture, but the growing strength of key regions may support the reassertion of more particular identities. Is increasing homogeneity or diversity, and possibly friction, the most likely future path? It is just as difficult to define the full dimensions of the emerging period of world history as it would have been in the fifteenth century, beyond considerable assurance that most trends of the previous period—in our case, the nineteenth century—have either declined in importance or, as in the case of Western power, shifted direction.

The Role of Civilizations

A final question related to the process of prediction requires comment on the perspective of world history: Will civilizations continue to be as important as they have been during the past 3000 years? Will major international contacts and trends continue to be mediated by the distinctive traditions and institutions of the world's key regions? Or, will one of the features of the new period in world history see the gradual decline of this familiar framework, thanks to accelerating global contacts?

Not surprisingly, there are voices on both sides. Regions continue to differ greatly. Although all areas participated in expanding education in the twentieth century, literacy rates in the 1990s range from 30 to 40 percent of the adult population, in Africa and India, to 80 percent in Latin America, to 95 percent in Western Europe, Japan, and Russia. Annual population growth is well under 1 percent in the West and Russia, almost 3 percent in sub-Saharan Africa. There are 700 television sets per 1000 people in North America, 50 in Asia. Some of these distinctions may decline with more general economic development, but they added up to very different lives as we opened the twenty-first century.

Different cultures matter too. One forecaster in 1993 argued that, given the end of the cold war, the next set of conflicts in the world will follow lines of civilization, as zones of Muslim, Confucian, and Western tradition clash on the basis of their widely different values. Such a forecast is uncertain, partly because several key regions like Africa are not clearly aligned, but it has called attention to the continued relevance of often long-standing cultural boundaries. Persistent tensions divide people of Christian background and the new Muslim minorities in Europe. The Common Market remains hesitant to admit Muslim Turkey despite the latter's urgent plea. These patterns, along with Islamic fundamentalism, bring home the force of traditional values. So do recurrent disputes about individual rights and social authority between Western commentators and their counterparts in China and Singapore.

Cultures, clearly, have taken on new functions in the contemporary world. Since the classical period and before, beliefs and styles have been used to integrate peoples

TABLE 33.1 ✦ ANNUAL RATES OF POPULATION GROWTH, 1975–1980

World	1.7%
Africa (entire)	2.9%
North America (includes Mexico)	1.0%
Latin America	2.5%
East Asia	1.4%
Southeast Asia	2.1%
Indian subcontinent	2.2%
Western Europe	0.3%
USSR	0.9%

TV sets per 1000 people

	1975	1982
World	98	121
Africa	6	17
North America	564	618
South America	84	111
Asia	25	38
Europe	232	309
USSR	Data not available	

Commercial energy consumption per capita, 1982 (equivalent kilograms of coal)

World	1900
Africa	300
North America	6700
South America	900
Asia	400
Europe	4200
USSR	6000

Source: U.N. statistics.

into common political and even economic systems. The same process has provided identity when a society encountered cultural forces from the outside. In recent decades, assertions of separate identities, often partly traditional, partly imagined, have assumed greater force, precisely because so many pressures threaten to submerge the ways people distinguish themselves from others. Understanding this dynamic becomes part of understanding cultures and their deep roots.

Nonetheless, the world is drawing closer together. This trite generalization draws meaning from the increasing cultural as well as commercial contacts around the globe, and from the operations of giant multinational corporations that spread specialized manufacturing and distribution activities literally worldwide. But, common cultural interests—for example, in seeking new consumer goods—affect traditional identities as well. By the 1990s, many international groupings existed that defy the boundaries of civilization. Scientists and social scientists accept many assumptions that allow them to perform common work whether they are in China or Chile, Boston or Bombay. International sports figures make the same easy transition from one competition to another regardless of locale. Businessmen share key values across national lines, particularly with the increased popularity of capitalism in the final decades of the twentieth century. One of the leading questions for the future, in fact, involves the still unpredictable balance between homogenizing and differentiating cultural characteristics.

World history has long consisted of new contacts and parallels, juxtaposed with the ongoing divisions among cultural and institutional traditions. The first year of the twenty-first century has, in one sense, merely repeated this long-lived tension. However, the force of contacts attained new levels during the twentieth century, based on new methods of communication and exchange. Many of the leading issues in predicting the future—how much democracy, how much industrialization—really center on whether the world is likely to follow some roughly common political and economic patterns. No sensible observer claims that homogeneity is right around the corner. The example of Japan's success reminds any Westerner of how different a fully industrial society can be from the Western model of modernization. No matter, the sharp edges of individual civilizations might blur further, making world history in the future more a matter of shared developments and less a catalogue of separate dynamics than had been true for the 5000 years since distinct civilizations began to be defined.

Even at the start of a new millennium, the hand of tradition does not rest lightly on the contemporary world. The key task of the historian is to convey how this force plays against the pressure to change. Revolutions never prove to be fully revolutionary, as they build within certain traditions while attacking others. Even the undermining of agricultural society—a fundamental drama of twentieth-century world history—did not destroy all traces of the past. Traditions, themselves evolving, give an identity to key civilizations and shape responses to international markets and technological exchange, world diplomacy, and international fads and styles. Changes within specific civilizations alter traditions and, often, contribute new ingredients to worldwide patterns—as witness Japan's industrial surge. The revival of religion at the end of the twentieth century demonstrated a need for traditional beliefs and particular identities—in part because homogenizing forces generate their own resistance. We can assume that the interplay between tradition and change will continue, but our uncertainty about the future lies in the inability to know precisely what balance will result.

We cannot assume the directions of world history as it further unfolds. Informed by knowledge of trends and examples from the past, we must instead examine them as they occur. Here is a source of understanding and also of pleasure, for world history has never lacked for drama, or analytical challenge, or even humor. The human species, along with its capacities to destroy, to create, and to master, also has the precious power of contemplation, and the traditions of many cultures would argue that this remains one of the surest sources of satisfaction. We can count on the emerging future to challenge our understanding, even as we learn to use our grasp of the past as a partial guide.

SUGGESTED READINGS

Several serious books (as well as many more dubious popular efforts) attempt to define the world's or the West's future. On the postindustrial society concept, see Daniel Bell, *The Coming of Post-Industrial Society* (1974). For other projections, consult R. L. Heilbroner, *An Inquiry into the Human Prospect* (1974), and L. Stavrianos, *The Promise of the Coming Dark Age* (1976). See also Ronald Inglehart, *Modernization and Post-modernization: Cultural, Economic, and Political Change in 43 Societies* (1997), and Harold Perkin, *The Third Revolution: Professional Elites in the Modern World* (1996). On environment and resource issues, D. H. Meadows and D. L. Meadows, *The Limits of Growth* (1974), and L. Herbert, *Our Synthetic Environment* (1962), are worthwhile. M. ul Haq, *The Poverty Curtain: Choices for the Third World* (1976), and L. Solomon, *Multinational Corporations and the Emerging World Order* (1978), cover economic issues, in part from a non-Western perspective. On military and diplomatic issues, A. Sakharov, *Progress, Coexistence and Intellectual Freedom,* rev. ed. (1970), is an important statement by a Russian dissident; other useful texts include S. Hoffmann, *Primacy or World Order: American Foreign Policy Since the Cold War* (1978), and W. Epstein, *The Last Chance: Nuclear Proliferation and Arms Control* (1976). On women, see P. Hudson, *Third World Women Speak Out* (1979). A major interpretation of the twentieth century is T. von Laue, *The World Revolution of Westernization* (1989). For a recent forecast based on the cold war's demise, see F. Fukizawa, *The End of History* (1991). Samuel Huntington, *The Third Wave: Democratization in the Late Twentieth Century* (1993) predicts new cultural conflicts. See also Richard Bulliet, *The Columbia History of the 20th Century* (1998).

CREDITS

Page 14: AP/Wide World Photos; page 19: Courtesy Phoebe Apperson Hearst Museum of Anthropology and Regents of the University of California; page 24: Borromeo/Art Resource, NY; page 25: Courtesy of the Freer Gallery of Art, Smithsonian Institution, Washington, D.C. (F1939.42); page 42: Courtesy Department of Library Services, American Museum of Natural History, Neg. #219658; page 48: The Field Museum #CSA35933; page 51: Courtesy of the Freer Gallery of Art, Smithsonian Institution, Washington, D.C. (F1915.103); page 52: AP/Wide World Photos; page 54: Ets. J.E. Bulloz; page 55: Wan-go Weng Inc. Archives; page 64: Borromeo/Art Resource, NY; page 71: Punjab Government Museum, Simla/Werner Forman Archive, London; page 73: AP/Wide World Photos; page 75: Giraudon/Art Resource, NY; page 90: Alinari/Art Resource, NY; page 93: Alison Frantz/American School of Classical Studies, Agora; page 95: Giraudon/Art Resource, NY; page 96: AP/Wide World Photos; page 99: Fritz Henle/Monkmeyer Press; page 114: Scala/Art Resource, NY; page 121: The Granger Collection, New York; page 124: Alinari/Art Resource, NY; page 139: New York Public Library, Spencer Collection, Astor, Lenox and Tilden Foundations; page 147: Israel Department of Antiquities and Museums; page 149: Gerd Ludwig/Woodfin Camp & Associates; page 151: Courtesy of the Freer Gallery of Art, Smithsonian Institution, Washington, D.C. (F1930.60); page 152: © Bettmann/Corbis; page 165: Government of India Information Services, Washington, DC; page 167: Indian Museum, Calcutta; page 170: Corbis; page 178: Bibliothèque Nationale de France, Paris; page 179: Courtesy of the Fogg Art Museum, Harvard University Art Museum. Gift of Mrs. John D. Rockefeller, Jr. (Abby Aldrich-Rockefeller). (1937.38); page 186: Alinari/Art Resource, NY; page 189: The Granger Collection, New York; page 190: GEKS; page 193: Sovfoto/Eastfoto; page 195: Hirmer Fotoarchiv, Munich; page 209: The Granger Collection, New York; page 210: Giraudon/Art Resource, NY; page 212: Giraudon/Art Resource, NY; page 222: Collection, National Palace Museum, Taipei; page 225: The Metropolitan Museum of Art, Gift of John M. Crawford, Jr., in honor of Douglas Dillon, 1981. (1981.276); page 227: Courtesy of the Freer Gallery of Art, Smithsonian Institution, Washington, D.C. (F1935.10); page 229: Werner Forman Archive/Art Resource, NY ; page 239: Peter Menzel; page 242: National Museum of Anthropology, Mexico City/Lee Boltin Picture Library; page 250: The Granger Collection, New York; page 269: The Metropolitan Museum of Art, Bequest of Benjamin Altman, 1913. (14.40.627); page 270: Alinari/Art Resource, NY; page 272: The Metropolitan Museum of Art, Fletcher Fund, 1919. (19.73.85); page 278: Grant V. Faint/Image Bank; page 282: Art Resource, NY; page 283: Alinari/Art Resource, NY; page 298: The Granger Collection, New York; page 305: Courtesy of the Lyndon Baines Johnson Library and Museum; page 311: Hulton/Archive; page 312: Max Simon/AP/Wide World Photos; page 313: © Bettmann/Corbis; page 318: Institut Amatiler d'Art Hispanic, Barcelona, Spain. Archivo Mas; page 326: Novosti/Sovfoto; page 331: Sovfoto; page 332: Beniaminson/Art Resource, NY; page 333: The Granger Collection, New York; page 343: The Granger Collection, New York; page 347: The Granger Collection, New York; page 360: Giraudon/Art Resource, NY;

INDEX